D1356480

THE GAME
OF
THE FOXES

British and German intelligence operations and personalities which changed the course of the Second World War

by
Ladislas Farago

HODDER AND STOUGHTON
London Sydney Auckland Toronto

A fox went out in a hungry plight
And he begged of the moon to give him light . . .

  —From an old folk fable

Contents

Introduction: How the Abwehr Papers Were Lost and Found   xi

Epitaph for a Secret Service   xvii

PART I
THE HALCYON DAYS

1. The "Kieker" at the Helm   3
2. Operation Sex   14
3. Windfalls in America   27
4. The Bombsight Fixation   38
5. Project 14—How to Cripple the Panama Canal   51
6. Operation Crown: The First Debacle   55

PART II
BRITAIN IN FOCUS

7. Journey to Brixton Gaol   71
8. Double Agent at the Top   77
9. Mission to Fort Belvedere   87
10. Uncle Richard vs. Uncle Claude   100
11. The Battle of the Trojan Horses   108
12. A Frontier Incident   121
13. Perfidies in Albion   130

PART III
THE FOXES GO TO WAR

14. Johnny Calling from Golf Course   149
15. Intermezzo on Tirpitz Quay   164
16. The Master Spy   169
17. The Phantom of Scapa Flow   185
18. The Lion Plays the Fox   192
19. Canaris vs. Churchill: The Race for Norway   200
20. The Trawler *Treff*   211
21. Operation Mainau and Other Capers in Eire   220
22. The Doomsday Spies   229
23. Countess Vera, Lady May, and the Duchess of
    Château-Thierry   243
24. The Round of the Hound   256
25. Detour to Germany: Johnny's Last *Treff*   267
26. The Double Life of Mutt and Jeff   281

PART IV
THE FOXES IN AMERICA

27. Silhouettes in Black on Gray   293
28. The Mexican Cockpit   305
29. The Communicators   312
30. "We'll Call Him Tramp"   322
31. Target: F.D.R.   330
32. The Strange Case of John L. Lewis   351
33. The Big Deal   366
34. The Thomsen Formula   376
35. Edge of Treason   390

PART V
THE SPIES ON EMBASSY ROW

36. . . . Some of Man's Best Friends are Spies   399
37. The Purloined Pell Papers   414
38. "Fetch the Devil From Hell"   427
39. Tramp in a Trap   448
40. The House on Massachusetts Avenue   467

41. After the Fall   492

PART VI
"THIS IS A NEW WAR"

42. The Iberian Black Market   511
43. The Swedish Cockpit   521
44. The "Baron" Goes North   532
45. The Affairs of Josephine   538
46. The Road to Casablanca   557
47. The President's Agent   570
48. Tapping the Roosevelt-Churchill Hot Line   582

PART VII
TWILIGHT OF THE FOXES

49. The Riddles of Overlord   595
50. Pawns of Fortitude   609
51. Mr. Churchill's Spy in the Family   630
52. Operation Heinrich and Josephine's Last Report   640
53. The Spy Who Fooled J. Edgar Hoover   645

BIBLIOGRAPHY   661

INDEX   681

Introduction

How the Abwehr Papers
Were Lost and Found

*F*OR over ten years I had been gathering material for a book about the Abwehr, the German secret service under Admiral Wilhelm Canaris. But the problem of unravelling the super-secret activities of this organization, whose records presumably had been destroyed at the end of the war and were forever lost to history, seemed well-nigh insurmountable. Then in 1967, in a dark loft of the National Archives in Washington, D.C., I stumbled over a metal footlocker, the kind American naval officers used in World War II. It held hundreds of little yellow boxes containing rolls of microfilm, and it turned out to be part of the litter of recent German history the Allies had captured in 1945.

It was obvious from the dust on the boxes and the seals on the old metal rolls that they had never been opened for inspection, not even by the remarkable team of researchers of the American Historical Association who had catalogued literally millions of other captured enemy papers. The collection was as raw as it must have been when originally found in Bremen by American intelligence officers headed, as the name on the footlocker indicated, by Captain L. S. Vickers, USN.

Guided by Dr. Robert Wolfe and Richard Bauer, the dedicated custodians of the captured German records, I made a sampling of the films and realized immediately that I had come upon an extraordinary find. Dozens of the rolls, with about a thousand frames in each, contained the papers of the Hamburg and Bremen outposts of the Abwehr, the two branches of the German senior military intelligence agency that specialized in the clandestine coverage of Britain and the United States.

For years I had tried to uncover primary documentation of the Abwehr's personnel and activities, but was told categorically and honestly by the authorities in Washington and London that the vast bulk of the Abwehr papers had been destroyed by their original custodians to save them from capture by the Allies. Yet now I had before me a very substantial part of those very records.

For the first time the Abwehr was bared as it really was, not as its apologists and detractors offered it for public view. From these films emerged the accounts of some operations already known, but in an entirely new light. Innumerable secret transactions that might have been buried forever were now revealed, involving well-known American and British personalities.

The profiles of Germany's espionage executives now suddenly appeared in sharp focus, together with detailed biographies and photographs of long-forgotten agents. There were the voluminous fiscal records with all the painstaking bookkeeping insisted upon by Herr Toepken, the Abwehr's meticulous and tight-fisted paymaster.

In all the vast literature of espionage never before was the secret service of a major power presented as comprehensively and authoritatively, certainly not from the firsthand evidence of its own records.

For obvious reasons the massive records of a big power's secret service remain locked up in inaccessible vaults, supposedly forever. Although the Bolsheviks, in the first flush of their victory in 1917–18, permitted the examination of the papers of the Okhrana, the Tsarist secret police, the Soviet government never allowed the publication— or even an objective scholarly study—of the archives of the Tsarist General Staff's intelligence bureau. The archives of the veteran British Secret Intelligence Service are closed and impregnable, including some papers going back to Sir Francis Walsingham and Sir William Eden in the sixteenth and eighteenth centuries.

Now, practically the entire files of one of the world's greatest secret services became available to shed light on every aspect of its operation.

The German secret service operated in two separate and more or less autonomous compartments. One covered the East, mainly the Soviet Union. The other was engaged in operations against the West, primarily France, Britain, and America.

This book concentrates on the German espionage offensive against the United Kingdom and the United States.

It covers the period between 1920, when the German military intelligence service was revived in defiance of the Versailles Treaty, and 1945, when the defeat of the Third Reich resulted in the apparent demise of the German secret service.

The hoard of Abwehr papers comprised a relatively small part of the enormous mass of documents found, practically all the paperwork of German bureaucracy. This unique collection is preserved for posterity on 17,478 rolls of microfilm containing almost eighteen-million pages of documents. By comparison, the entire United States

War Department collection of Civil War records is available on 2185 rolls.

The German secret archives fell into Allied hands partly as a result of shrewd planning, partly by accident, but chiefly because for some reason—bureaucratic or sentimental—the pedantic custodians of the confidential files failed to destroy them. The dispersal of classified records began in 1943, when the bombing of Berlin became more intense. Various records were shipped to a number of secret places, then shipped again to what the masters of the Third Reich regarded as safe redoubts—to bomb-proof shelters in the Giant and Harz mountains, to hideouts in Thuringia, and even to locations as far from Berlin as Berchtesgaden and Lake Constance.

During the final weeks of the war in 1945, the badly mauled German roads were cluttered with convoys of trucks carrying the archives of the Foreign Ministry, the Wehrmacht High Command, Himmler's organizations and other key agencies, in a race to outdistance the rapidly advancing Anglo-American forces. It was a futile attempt. On April 19, units of the First U.S. Army discovered more than 300 tons of Foreign Ministry documents with innumerable copies of Abwehr papers among them. Shortly afterward, other archives were found in Bavaria, all intact. Still in April, at Tammbach, advance elements of General Patton's Third Army captured a convoy carrying the entire historical record of the German Admiralty, including the original of its super-secret war diaries and the logs of U-boats.

Orders to destroy the secret archives had been issued on April 10, and among the papers then burned were those of the *Wehrmacht-Fuehrungs-Stab* of General Jodl, the Gestapo archives of the Prinz Albrecht Strasse, and the files of the Abwehr in Zossen. But in most cases, the orders were either disregarded or carried out so slowly that when the American, British, and French units arrived at the Nazi hideouts, they found that only a fraction of the files had been destroyed.

Although many key documents were missing in one or another place, they were not obliterated altogether. In the familiar bureaucratic process, several copies of even the most secret documents had been made. These showed up in other collections, enabling the diligent researcher to reconstruct the activities of important agencies even when the originals had been burned. Many of the Abwehr documents could thus be recovered from the other archives.

Most important, by my fortuitous discovery in our own National Archives, the complete records of the Abwehr's Bremen branch included innumerable copies which originated at its Berlin headquarters and other outposts in Germany and abroad.

Over a thousand of these rolls of microfilm with more than a million pages of documents have been examined and used in the preparation of this book. In addition, thirty-four "uncatalogued" films have also been inspected, yielding vast source material never before used in research.

The historic significance of this find cannot be overstated. If the records prove anything, it is that no secret service, however big, efficient or industrious, is capable of forecasting the course of events on their relentless march. The Abwehr had hundreds of spies in the area of the Western Mediterranean, yet it could not alert its clients to "Torch," the Allied invasion of North Africa in the fall of 1942. For all its massive efforts, the German intelligence establishment could not tell Hitler when and where the Allied invasion of 1944 would strike.

Secret services have exerted far greater influence on history than on the historians. Behind every great event, and behind the statesmen who shaped them, stood the spies. Yet they rarely show up in the scholarly annals that haughtily or squeamishly ignore their contributions. Politicians, diplomats, and generals who have benefited most from the aid of their secret agents invariably have ignored them in their memoirs.

By tapping archives not easily accessible, which only a world war made available for scrutiny, this book attempts to compensate for this omission.

What do the documents of the Abwehr of Canaris demonstrate?

By the incontravertible evidence of its own papers, it was an odd bird in the huge aviary of the secret services. It had none of the pitiless, vulgar methods of the Russians' Okhrana, Cheka, and RU; none of the cynicism and hypocrisy of Their Majesties' Secret Intelligence Services; none of the mindless curiosity of the Japanese; none of the intrigue-mongering of the Italian agencies under Mussolini; none of the conspiratorial trait of the *Deuxième Bureau*. Despite its unsavory reputation, caused mainly by confusing it with the Gestapo and the *Sicherheitsdienst* of the Nazis, the Abwehr was, in fact, a plodding, utilitarian and rather mild-mannered organization whose plots and strategems seemed—and often were—naïve and diffident.

As General George C. Marshall once succinctly expressed it, a secret service must be secret. Real names are changed to whimsical pseudonyms, even at the administrative level. Agents are referred to by numbers. Meetings—which the Germans called *Treffs*—are held in circumspect secrecy. Business is conducted in so-called "safe houses." The whole life of a secret service is a romantic masquerade, a grandiose pageantry that often seems anachronistic and even childish.

It was, therefore, no small task to penetrate behind the mask of the Abwehr, despite the superabundance of documents. A signal reading "Will meet A.3504 in Country 18" was meaningless by itself until I could decipher it and find that "A.3504" was a notorious double agent named Arthur George Owens and "Country 18" was Portugal, one of the spies' favorite hunting grounds in World War II. Numbers and code names popped up as tantalizing teasers, blacking out the individuals and operations they were designed to conceal. It took me two years, for example, to uncover the identity of a remarkable secret agent stationed in the United States and conjure him up as he really was, in order to place him in this narrative.

In the end, the huge system of the Abwehr emerged from its paraphernalia of concealment, together with the organizations and personnel of its adversaries, locked in a lethal battle. The documents on which this book is based then revealed more than just the inside story of the Canaris organization. By holding up the mirror to the Abwehr, one can see every big intelligence agency that has existed in the past or that functions in the present.

LADISLAS FARAGO

Church Hill
New Milford, Connecticut

Epitaph for a Secret Service

A return to the scene of a crime or an old love affair—or for that matter any passing strange episode in one's past—is always a harrowing experience. So it was in the summer of 1970, when I traveled to Berlin to revisit the old seat of the Abwehr or whatever I could find still standing of it. I remembered it only vaguely from my days as a correspondent in Germany. Although it was a landmark of sorts, it was certainly not one of those—like the Brandenburg Gate or the Pergamon altar—that would be pointed out to tourists passing by in sightseeing buses.

As I recalled it through the haze of fading memories, it used to stand in gray anonymity on the Tirpitz Ufer, a stone quay along the Landwehrkanal on which fronted the enormous block that housed Germany's vast military bureaucracy. At the corner of the quay and Bendler Strasse (the street whose name became the synonym of German militarism) once sprawled the main Defense Ministry building with its tall columnar front and broad steps. Headquarters of the Army General Staff was further down the street, its huge fieldstone complex stretching almost to the Tiergarten Park's manicured meadows, pampered trees, little swan lake, rose gardens, and meandering bridle path.

Along the torpid black waters of a narrow side canal stood a row of elegant town houses. At 72–76 Tirpitz Ufer, five stories high, rose the graystone edifice of the Abwehr.[1]

Because of the menacing ways of German militarism even before Hitler, this was an ominous block with built-in melodrama previous to its sinister growth and bustle in the Third Reich. During my tenure in Berlin as a journalist, the "Bendler Block" was my special beat beginning in the early Thirties. It was no simple matter to cover this labyrinthine den of conspiracies, the nerve center of German defiance of the Versailles Treaty. But I had contacts inside, including a handful of well-placed, well-informed younger officers—like Eugene Ott, Erich Marcks, Ferdinand von Bredow, Erwin Planck and Walter Jost—who were destined to rise to fame.[2]

My beat had its puzzling incongruities. Behind closed doors in spartan offices highbrow members of the General Staff were busy, even then, drawing up the blueprints of war.

I would see them all, coming or going, climbing out of their big limousines, vanishing through the discreet side gate further down the street—khaki-celebrities of the swagger set, the proud, pompous dreamers of vast martial schemes, the great captains of battles yet to be fought. General Werner von Blomberg, General Hans von Fritsch, Admiral Erich Raeder, Colonel Wilhelm Keitel contrasted with a gray-haired, sallow-skinned little man in ill-fitting mufti, his face obscured by a battered felt hat he wore pulled down on his head. He was Captain Wilhelm Franz Canaris, master of the Abwehr.

Surrounding the block on all sides were spies of other nations. The boldest among them came brazenly close. They could be seen sauntering up and down the Bendler Strasse like so many streetwalkers, trailing General Staff officers with cocked ears, hoping to catch fragments of their shoptalk. Their brash enterprise in alfresco eavesdropping became so apparent that Section III of the Abwehr, whose responsibilities included plugging up leaks, issued a formal memorandum warning German officers not to talk about anything confidential in the street.

"There is reason to believe," the quaint memo read, "that the British and French secret services are planting agents in the vicinity of Bendler Strasse to listen in on the conversations of officers, who are easy to identify when in uniform. According to reliable information, several of these agents have been trained and are skilled in lip reading. Men suspected as spies have been seen loitering at the bus stop on the Bendler Bridge daily around 6 P.M. when the offices close and officers stand in groups while waiting for transportation. An agent working for the French *Deuxième Bureau* confessed when apprehended that he had come into the possession of valuable intelligence both at the bus stop and on the buses in which he had followed certain officers riding home in pairs."

The British Secret Intelligence Service had one of its listening posts in a corner house on nearby Luetzow Platz, over a store that displayed enormous Maybach automobiles. Behind the chromium-plated façade of the Frigidaire showroom across the square, the Berlin representative of the American Office of Naval Intelligence hid out.

Around the corner, in a sumptuous flat that occupied an entire floor in Berlin's most luxurious apartment house, a handsome sybaritic Pole named Juri de Sosnowski was getting copies of the Germans' super-classified operations plans as soon as they were drawn up and typed. They were delivered directly to his mirrored bedchamber by a couple of confidential secretaries employed by the General Staff whom he had seduced in the familiar ploy that mixes pleasure with business.

Now I was back in Berlin to visit my old beat, after an absence of thirty-three years, for it was in the summer of 1937 that I had last called on Major Jost to coax from him some information that was becoming increasingly hard to get in these parts. I wondered what had happened to the old "Bendler Block." The young cabdriver I hired to take me there had never heard of it. Eager for a fare he consulted his street guide—obviously in vain—for he turned to me with a vacant look and said: "I'm afraid, sir, there is no *Bendler* Strasse in Berlin nor any quay called *Tirpitz* Ufer."

When I described the place as it used to stretch between the canal and the Tiergarten, his face lit up. "Ach," he said, "you must mean the Stauffenbergstrasse and the Reichpietsch Ufer. I think I know the place you're looking for."

Between a half-filled parking lot and a neglected patch of grassland a massive gray building appeared before my eyes. It was the granite edifice the Abwehr had occupied during its halcyon days, intact and virtually unmarked by all the savage bombardments.

This, then, was the *Fuchsbau* or "Fox Lair," as it was called by the men and women who worked in it—the official mischief-makers of the Third Reich's military establishment.

Entering through a low portico off the quay, and passing a number of somber-faced, shabbily clad men and women shuffling in and out, I mounted the few steps to the dimly lit entrance hall, moving hesitantly, for I did not know what to expect in this mausoleum of a dead era. Suddenly, in a flash of *déja vu*, I remembered the place from my visits in the early Thirties.

Still there, on each side of the hall, were the tiny old-fashioned elevators that were usually out of order. Facing me was the split staircase leading to a landing on the mezzanine where tall windows let in the modicum of light that illuminated the hall below. At my left was the guard's cubbyhole at which, more than three decades before, I had to get my visitor's pass from a stern corporal.

The military guard was gone, his place taken by a slim youngster, gazing with bored eyes at visitors who needed no badges or passes. But nothing had changed in this historic building except the tenants.

The old Abwehr headquarters is now occupied by a branch of the Prussian State Library and the Berlin division of the Federal Insurance Bureau. It also houses a number of other offices that pay rent to an absentee landlord, a management firm on distant Fasanen Street.

I walked up the staircase to the left, then sauntered along the dark corridors of the second and third floors. With a yellowed once-secret directory of the Abwehr guiding me, I stopped at doors behind which once sat the great spymasters of the Third Reich: Colonel Hans Piekenbrock, chief of the secret intelligence and espionage section; Colonel Erwin von Lahousen, a tall Austrian who headed the sabotage group; and Colonel Joachim Rohleder, the taciturn, introverted manager of Branch IIIF, the mystery-shrouded department in charge of counterespionage.

It was an eerie passage, and I conjured up shadows of the old occupants in offices where now only clerks and auditors sat poring over ledgers or foolscap, like characters from a Gustav Freytag novel, scribbling, typing, lighting cigarettes, sipping stale coffee from paper cups.

I reached the high-ceilinged top floor of the building where, until a grim February morning in 1944, Wilhelm Canaris, chief of the Abwehr, had his office. There it was, at the center of the front corridor, its tall doors left wide open to create a cooling draft on this hot summer morning.

Where Canaris once had his big desk, its top cluttered with a whimsical collection of bric-à-brac; where his black leather sofa used to afford him brief siestas during his long office hours; under the wall that was once covered with an oversized map of the world, there now stood scarred desks behind which sat six rather prim women in cotton dresses, manipulating a battery of adding machines.

I halted on the threshold, surveying every square inch of what once was the sanctum sanctorum of a great secret service. The women gazed at the stranger in obvious bewilderment. "Pardon me, ladies," I said. "This was the office of Admiral Canaris during the Second World War, wasn't it?"

The women looked at each other, evidently checking which one of them had the answer to my query. An elderly lady spoke up.

"What did you say the gentleman's name was?" she asked.

"Canaris," I said, and added with a bit of emphasis, "*Admiral* Canaris."

The old lady in the cotton dress seemed to be thinking back, her eyes and brow showing the effort. But then she just shrugged and shook her head.

"I've been here since 1958," she said quietly with a touch of apology in her voice, "but no, sir . . . I don't think I've ever heard the name."

NOTES

1 Although the central military intelligence service had a more elaborate official designation in the table of organization (that periodically changed as it grew), we will use the abbreviated name "Abwehr" throughout this book. It was generally so called and still is. Members of its own staff went even further in shortening the name and called it "Abw," pronouncing each letter separately, in their intimate references to it.

2 General Ott became Military Attaché and then Ambassador to Japan, and survived the war. Marcks, a full general commanding an army corps in Normandy, was killed in action near St. Lo in 1944. Bredow was assassinated by the Nazis in the Blood Purge of 1934. Jost, commanding the 42 Chasseur Division, was the last of three German generals killed during the campaign in Italy.

Part I

THE HALCYON DAYS

Chapter 1

The "Kieker" at the Helm

ON September 24, 1934, Rear Admiral Bastian, commander-in-chief of the ships-of-the-line, sat down at his desk aboard the old battleship *Schlesien* to prepare the latest fitness report on his flagship's skipper, a captain named Wilhelm Franz Canaris. As a rule, flag officers with a heart dislike the business of rating the officers who serve under them, for only too often too many warts show up on closer scrutiny. But in this particular case Bastian cherished the chore.

Canaris was leaving the *Schlesien* for an unspecified assignment on shore and this was the final act of service Bastian could perform for his old friend. Then too, Canaris was a paragon of virtue—a model officer, a congenial shipmate, a *Kamerad* whose burning patriotism and broad vision was sorely needed by the new navy.

Admiral Bastian quickly filled in the spaces provided on the printed form for vital statistics and the officer's service record:

Appearance and conduct: Medium height, striking appearance, excellent military bearing, splendid social manners.

Foreign languages: English, French, Spanish, Italian, Portuguese, Russian.[1]

Finances: In good order.

Then Bastian pulled out all stops. Under *"General Opinion,"* he gave a glowing report on Canaris's sterling character and special virtues as a naval officer: "Captain Canaris," he wrote, "handled his command with admirable firmness and consummate professional skill. He maintained strict discipline and good spirit on his ship, and worked tirelessly to train and indoctrinate his crew in seamanship to assure the combat readiness of his vessel. He promoted the physical fitness of his officers and men through wholesome sporting exercises."

3

He also spoke of his "talent as a keen observer" . . . of "his diplomatic skill" . . . and of his "great intellectual gifts."

In answer to the final question—*"For what special positions would this officer qualify?"*—Bastian listed a whole string of posts and commands: "Naval Attaché; commandant of the Hamburg Naval District; Inspector General of the Navy; Deputy Admiral at a Naval Station; commanding admiral, ships-of-the-line" and, last but not least, "chief, Abwehr Department in the Reichswehr Ministry."

After a brief tour of duty at a Baltic port, Canaris's appointment came a few days before Christmas. As if taking his cue from Bastian, Admiral Erich Raeder, commander-in-chief of the Navy, named him to replace Captain Konrad Patzig as chief of the Abwehr.[2]

Captain Canaris's orders came up from Berlin as a Christmas gift. He was to report for his new duties on January 1, 1935.

When at 8:00 A.M. New Year's Day he arrived at Abwehr headquarters as the new director of Germany's senior secret service, fresh snow covered the Berlin streets. So early was the hour on this silent holiday morning, and so deserted the city after the revelries of St. Sylvester's Night, that Canaris was the first to disturb the virgin white blanket with his footsteps as he walked with birdlike steps down Bendler Strasse and turned right into the Tirpitz Ufer. Except for the guard at the door and a few young officers standing watch, the offices were empty. Nobody expected him to take his orders so literally and show up on New Year's Day.

"I'm Captain Canaris," he introduced himself to a startled duty officer. "Please call Captain Patzig on the telephone and tell him that I am in the office, and would like to see him here at his convenience."

Patzig arrived shortly before ten o'clock and found Canaris waiting like a petitioner in his anteroom. A genial man who made friends easily, Patzig took his successor by the arm and escorted him into his office, ready to hand over the Abwehr then and there. "To be completely frank," he said, "I didn't expect you this morning. But I *am* glad you came."

Then the outgoing and incoming Abwehr chiefs settled down to a chatty conference. Patzig made no secret of his glee at leaving for greener pastures as skipper of the *Admiral Scheer*. He spoke feelingly about his problems and aggravations, embroiled as he was in a bitter feud with Heinrich Himmler's internal security agency, the powerful *Reichssicherheitshauptamt* (RSHA). He regaled his successor with embarrassing and painful incidents in Himmler's design on the Abwehr, and described the subtle but determined rivalry of young Nazi Reinhard Heydrich, chief of the *Sicherheitsdienst* or security service charged with political espionage.[3]

Patzig now told Canaris bluntly: "I am sorry for you, Captain, because you don't seem to realize what a mess you're getting into."

"Please don't worry about me, Captain Patzig," Canaris said with a faint smile. "I'm an incurable optimist. And as far as those fellows are concerned, I think I know how to get along with them."

Patzig stiffened, then said quietly: "If that is what you think, Captain Canaris, then I am sorry to say that this day is the beginning of your end."

Who was this man Canaris?

And why was he picked to direct the Abwehr just when it was to become one of the most important cogs in the new German war machine?

While he lived, Wilhelm Canaris attracted public attention only once. In 1928, Socialist parliamentary investigators stumbled upon him squatting in the background of several insidious plots to overthrow the Weimar Republic, and the newspapers featured him as a Machiavellian schemer. At the end of World War II, I could not find a single line published about him either before or after that brief appearance in the limelight; and came upon only one article printed abroad, in an English periodical in 1939, that identified him as the spymaster of the Third Reich.

He seemed to enjoy his anonymity.[4] He was an unassuming, self-effacing man who was secretive even with members of his immediate family. But after the war he suddenly emerged into public view as an authentic mystery man. He became the subject of innumerable articles, several books, and even was portrayed as the hero of a rather mushy motion picture. Some authors eulogized him as a spiritual leader of the pathetic anti-Nazi movement, who died a martyr for his courage and convictions.

Much that has been said and written about Canaris has merely obscured his biography, falsified his record, and especially deepened the mystery that goes naturally with any chief of a secret service and was, in this case, assiduously cultivated by himself. He succeeded admirably in his own camouflage. Seldom has a figure of historical importance been judged with so many contradictory verdicts, even by those who professed to have known him well.

Even so astute a biographer as Ian Colvin subtitled his *Master Spy* as "the incredible story of Admiral Wihelm Canaris, who, while Hitler's chief of intelligence, was a secret ally of the British," although, in fact, no such alliance ever existed.

His vital statistics and the milestones of his career are on record in his personnel file and in twenty-eight *Qualifikations-Berichte* (fitness reports) his commanding officers prepared. I found them intact in the German archives captured in Berlin, although one would expect that such an important secret record would have been destroyed.

Wilhelm Franz Canaris was born on New Year's Day in 1887, in Aplerbeck near Dortmund in the heart of the Ruhr, the youngest of three children of a well-to-do engineer who managed an ironworks. Although undersized and frail he was a healthy and lively boy enjoying a normal childhood, brought up by doting Lutheran parents.

He was called Willy at home. In his youth he acquired the nickname "Kieker" which in English would mean either "Peeper" or "Snooper." In 1917 he met Erika Waag, the sister of a naval officer, and married her on November 22, 1919. She was the only woman ever known to figure romantically in his life.

He was supposed to be a descendant of Admiral Constantine Kanaris, the nineteenth-century Greek statesman and partisan fighter.[5]

Young Wilhelm entered the Imperial Naval Academy in Kiel on April 1, 1905. His first tour of sea duty was terminated abruptly in December 1914, when the cruiser *Dresden* on which he served, was caught in the Battle of the Falkland Islands. Pursued into Chilean waters she was thrown upon a reef and scuttled, the only ship of Admiral Graf Spee's hapless squadron not sunk by British gunfire. Young Lieutenant Canaris was interned on Quiriquina Island off Valparaiso, and there embarked on the "Homeric" part of his life's adventures.

He vanished from the Chilean camp by rowing to the mainland, then going crosscountry on horseback to Argentina over the Andes. In Buenos Aires, in the guise of a young Chilean named Reed Rosas, he took passage on the Dutch Line steamer *Frisia*, going to Rotterdam in neutral Holland to "look after an inheritance left to him by the relations of his mother."

He was passed by every British control on the way and wound up briefly in Hamburg. Then still using the name of Reed Rosas and his Chilean passport, he went to Madrid on his first full-time assignment in intelligence.

In February 1916, while attempting to return to Germany to be trained for command in U-boats, Canaris was arrested by the Italians at Domodossola, not far from the Swiss border, and was held as a suspected spy (his cover as "Reed Rosas" was wearing thin) in a prison in Genoa. Canaris escaped again. He made his way out of the jail by killing the prison padre (whom he had coaxed into his cell), donned his garb and walked out before the body of the murdered priest could be discovered. He returned to Madrid, was given command of a U-boat, then held a variety of other naval appointments during the rest of the war.

In the wake of World War I, under the impact of defeat, he reached his full maturity as a conspirator. In November 1918, he was one of the first professional officers to volunteer his services to the Weimar Republic, and also embarked on a career of disloyalty to those in power. He joined the staff of the new Reichswehr Minister, the old Socialist Gustav Noske, and, for a few weeks, served as his junior aide-de-camp. By January 1919, he was a clandestine member of the notorious naval brigade of reactionary officer-adventurers who occupied the Eden Hotel in Berlin under Lieutenant Commander Georg von Pflugk-Hartung. When the Eden desperadoes were charged with the murder of Karl Liebknecht and Rosa Luxemburg, the Spartacist leaders, Canaris took over the unit and set himself up as a protector of its arrested members. One of the chief defendants at their trial was a brother officer named Vogel who allegedly dumped the body of Rosa Luxemburg into the Spree canal. Canaris procured money, a false passport, and managed Vogel's escape to Holland.

In February 1920, Canaris was raised in rank and made executive officer of the cruiser *Berlin* stationed in Kiel. It was a blind. In actual fact he functioned as the aide-de-camp of Rear Admiral Baron von Gagern, commandant of the Baltic Naval Station, one of the Navy's fronts for political conspiracies and secret rearmament. In March 1920, Canaris opted without hesitation to restore the Kaiser. He provided money and arms for the rebels from the secret funds and stores of the naval station.

In 1922 he appeared in still another secret role, becoming one of the chief manipulators of the Navy's unauthorized rearmament program. In collaboration with two others, he organized clandestine shipyards and torpedo factories in foreign countries and juggled considerable slush funds to pay for these hidden projects.[6]

Canaris was "a restless spirit," as one of his superiors characterized him in a secret report, "provoked to great performance by extraordinary and difficult challenges in the handling of confidential military-political assignments on his frequent missions abroad." During these days Canaris was always on the road, traveling under false names and in a variety of disguises, going about the Navy's surreptitious building program.

So it went during most of the turbulent Twenties. Others appeared and vanished from the scene but Canaris remained the permanent fixture in the conspiratorial consortium centered in the arch-conservative Navy—the idea man, chief wirepuller, workhorse and troubleshooter, trustee of the admirals' clique. Though he missed none of the plots he became the target of Socialist suspicions and attacks. He managed to remain in active service, collecting in his secret file one glowing fitness report after another from his admiring superiors. He rose steadily in rank. His power and influence grew even faster. As one of his commanding officers put it in his evaluation of this unorthodox officer, Canaris had become an indispensable factotum in the mushrooming conspiracies undermining the Weimar Republic.

In 1933, he welcomed the advent of Hitler.

In his late forties, Canaris seemed much older. He was small-boned. His sallow skin was furrowed with wrinkles. His subordinates called him *der Alte*—"the Old Man."

Nothing he did during his first weeks in the Abwehr alleviated the misgivings or justified his selection for the job. He holed up in the office from which Patzig had removed all the personal furnishings that made the room seem warm and cozy. Now it was barren of all but a few office furnishings that had no style or taste. Canaris, it seemed, had few personal souvenirs. His inner sanctum reflected an unsentimental, impersonal character. On his desk stood a little piece of bric-à-brac that Canaris had chosen to be the symbol of the Abwehr: the familiar little statue of three monkeys who hear, see, and speak no evil. One wall was covered with a big map. On the other wall hung three pictures: an etching of Admiral Kanaris, a Japanese painting of the devil, and a picture of his favorite dachshund, Seppl.[7]

He could be seen slinking along the dimly lit corridors, keeping close to the walls, nodding with a faint, almost obsequious smile to anyone who happened to pass by, senior officers and secretaries alike. He gave the impression that he felt like a stranger among strangers.

I met Canaris in January 1935, a few weeks after his arrival on the Tirpitz Ufer, at a private lunch at the restaurant of the Aero Club near his office. It was arranged by a mutual acquaintance, the publisher of a weekly magazine who was scouting for the Abwehr. Probably misled by my frequent travels as the roving correspondent of an American newspaper in Germany, he might have thought that I would make a good R-agent, an *ad hoc* informant whose job was to collect "useful information" on legitimate trips. I had recently visited and photographed (in proper journalistic pursuit but without authorization) the Westerplatte, a closely guarded, fortified Polish ammunition dump in the Neufahrwasser, commanding the approaches to the Free City of Danzig. This seemed to justify an introduction to Canaris.

I was unimpressed by this wispy man. Looking back on our brief encounter I realize he must have hurt my vanity. It was obvious from his flaccid handshake and the distrait greeting that he had a distaste for this meeting. I later found out he was opposed in principle to employing journalists, even as *ad hoc* informants. He hardly spoke during the lunch and, most of the time, looked not at but through me, with his characteristic glance beyond.

I could not believe that this rumpled, tongue-tied, absent-minded little man was the new chief of the Abwehr. It was not the E. Philips Oppenheim-type of flamboyance or captious cynicism I was looking for in Canaris. I had anticipated the eager curiosity that sparkled in the eyes of Captain Reginald Hall, the legendary chief of British Naval Intelligence in World War I, or the quiet competency of the Frenchman called "General Dupont" of the *Deuxième Bureau*, two of the great intelligence chiefs I had known. Nothing of their flair, their sophistication, their quixotic quality and sure-fire grasp of the craft was apparent in the German. He impressed me as an honest dullard who had been given the job to assure the Abwehr's impotence in the competition with the up-and-coming Himmler-Heydrich organization. Only much later did I become aware that Canaris had sized me up right at the outset, decided that I was not a promising candidate for his organization, and regarded the lunch as a waste of time.

When Captain Canaris appeared on the scene, all of a sudden the moribund Abwehr came to life. He went to work with an energy and brisk spirit nobody suspected in "the Old Man." He made the Abwehr palatable to the Nazis. When he told Patzig that he knew how to get along with Himmler and Heydrich, he expressed, not a hope, but a determination.

He struck up a close and seemingly genuine friendship with Heydrich, in whom he recognized his potentially most dangerous adversary. The young Nazi was flattered by the attention of this high-ranking naval officer, if only because he had been thrown out of the Navy a few years before in an amorous escapade involving the daughter of a naval architect. Canaris bought a house next to the Heydrichs' in a Berlin suburb, and the two families became good neighbors, Canaris treating the Heydrich boys to candy and Frau Canaris fawning on the pretty blonde wife.

Canaris brought in a major named Rudolf Bamler and made him chief of the counterespionage section that worked most closely with the Gestapo, because Bamler was one of the few General Staff officers who flaunted Nazi sympathies and had a number of Party bigwigs among his friends.[8] Canaris, not normally a party-giver, organized convivial dinners for the entertainment of Heydrich and his staff in what he called *Kameradschaftsabende*, evenings of comradeship. They were held regularly in a private room of the restaurant in the House of Flyers on Prinz Albrecht Strasse, next door to the grim Gestapo building where Heydrich had his office.

This seemingly one-sided accommodation with Heydrich was of shrewd design and not necessarily a reflection of Canaris's true sentiments. While he was mending his fences, he placated the Nazis mainly in order to develop the Abwehr according to his own ambitious plans: to make it the biggest and best secret service in the world!

The organization was restructured to operate in three major functional groups. The old *Geheimer Meldedienst* (secret service gathering intelligence and conducting espionage) was considerably enlarged and became Group I. A new Group II was built from scratch to conduct sabotage operations, foment insurrections and sedition, and organize "black" propaganda. A training camp for saboteurs was set up at Quenzsee in Bavaria. Laboratories were equipped in Berlin and Tegel to develop the paraphernalia the saboteurs (as well as Group I spies) needed, from secret ink that looked like mouthwash to explosives that smelled and felt like flour. Counterespionage was established as an autonomous activity in Group III.

Personnel was recruited by the hundreds and senior officers were brought over from the General Staff to serve as executives. The chief appointed a shrewdly balanced trio to head up the new groups— the genial, apolitical, independently wealthy Rhinelander Hans Piekenbrock to manage "secret intelligence" (euphemism for espionage); a sensitive, deeply religious, fanatical anti-Nazi named Helmuth Groscurth in charge of the sabotage section; and the rabid pro-Nazi Bamler for the delicate counterespionage group.

This was to be a global organization and it needed efficient lines of communication. Canaris gave highest priority to the development of courier systems and electronic links to be used by the agents he was about to plant abroad.

Canaris invited the Telefunken Company to develop for the Abwehr a special "spy radio"—called Afu (for *Agenten-Funk-Geraet*)—small enough to conceal yet powerful enough to permit long-distance operations. This remarkable foresight on his part became both a boon and a bane when Telefunken managed to construct such a set, and its exceptional quality enticed the Abwehr into too much dependence on it.

On May 1, 1935, in another move to improve communications and firm up the base of operations overseas, Canaris coaxed the Foreign Ministry into collaboration with the Abwehr. Through this arrangement, diplomatic missions in different parts of the world would function as regional bases for local espionage. Members of the Foreign Service—usually younger attachés—were enlisted to serve as so-called resident representatives *(Abwehrbeauftragte)*, to administer the Abwehr's clandestine business in their areas.

As one of his first acts, Canaris assembled kits—called *Geheimausruestungen fuer Vertrauensleute* (secret equipment for confidential agents), and arranged with the Foreign Ministry to ship them as privileged courier mail under diplomatic immunity to the various diplomatic missions, to be on tap for later use by his spies. Cryptographic material, developed by Kurt Selchon of the Foreign Ministry's code bureau, went out in locked boxes. Their keys were sent separately in sealed envelopes addressed to the chiefs of missions personally, with instructions to open the steel cassettes only in the event of war or during so-called *Spannungszeiten* (periods of crisis) when specifically so ordered in a signal bearing one of ten different passwords. The password for England was *"Nautilus,"* for Canada *"Jimmy,"* and *"Robert"* for the United States.

In another sealed envelope, Canaris sent to the envoys the rosters of agents who were already active in their respective territories. He forwarded to each chief of mission a check drawn by the Deutsche Bank on Barclay's Bank in London, in the sum of £406, 2d, to be used as a revolving fund from which the agents could be compensated or reimbursed, or helped out in emergencies. The envoys were instructed to turn the checks into cash in local currencies and keep the money in their personal safes until needed.

The shipment to the missions in the United States was sent aboard the freighter *Schwaben* of the North German Lloyd in custody of its skipper. He personally delivered the crates and envelopes into the hands of the Ambassador in Washington and the Consul General in New York, the first two diplomats Canaris had chosen as silent partners in this country. A few months later, similar kits were also sent to the Consul Generals at New Orleans and Seattle, the Minister in Mexico City, and the Charge d'affaires in Panama.[9]

In April 1935, when he had been in office a little over three months, Canaris sent out a number of special emissaries to establish bases of operations at key spots. The man sent to North and Central America traveled on a diplomatic passport made out to "E. Derp," who was Commander Hermann Menzel, a career officer soon to become head of Abw/IM, the naval intelligence division in Group I.

Incredibly, all of this was accomplished during the first eight months of the Canaris regime. Suddenly, German mischief-making flared up throughout the world, demonstrating to all security services that the Abwehr was under new management.

German agents abruptly appeared in Austria, Czechoslovakia, Yugoslavia, and Switzerland, in the Balkan countries, Finland, and even in Ethiopia and Japan. They were especially active in Poland, France, and the Low Countries, and everywhere showed signs of having been hastily assembled, perfunctorily trained, and sent on their missions posthaste.

During these labor pangs of the new Abwehr, the Canaris agents were inexperienced and quite vulnerable. In Belgium ten German spies were caught between April 7, 1935, and the end of the year. The first major German agent since World War I was arrested in England.

France, which was swarming with German spies, caught twenty-one of them within the first ten months of the new era, one red-handed in the act of removing air defense plans from a safe at the Bron airfield near Lyons. Another was photographing fortifications at Metz, a couple scavenged for discarded documents at an army camp, a barmaid in Strasbourg was pumping soldiers for defense information, and two men at Verdun were sending coded messages one night to someone with the flickering beam of a flashlight.

In early September, Canaris (who had by this time been made an admiral) went south on an errand of considerable urgency and importance. In Munich he met General Mario Roatta, chief of the Italian Military Intelligence Service, to arrange closer collaboration in their coverage of common adversaries.[10]

Although Italy was at the height of the Abyssinian crisis, and in the last stage of preparations for the imminent invasion of Ethiopia, Roatta proved most obliging. He agreed to everything Canaris proposed. An alliance between Germany and Italy was sealed and signed by their respective secret services, long before Hitler and Mussolini joined their countries in the Axis.

From Munich Canaris motored to Berchtesgaden for the most important meeting of his new job. He had an appointment with Hitler to report on his accomplishments and to receive instructions for the future.

NOTES

1 Bastian grossly exaggerated his friend's linguistic acumen. Actually, Canaris was fluent only in Spanish. While his English was adequate, he had only a smattering of knowledge of the other tongues.

2 Raeder actually disliked and distrusted Canaris, and was personally opposed to the appointment, but acquiesced under "pressure from higher-ups."

At this time, the Abwehr (properly called *Abwehrabteilung*) was still but a subordinate branch of the Reichswehr Ministry.

3 Under the roof of the RSHA functioned the various branches of Nazi Germany's state security. The Gestapo, or Ast IV, (secret police), headed by Heinrich Mueller, was a domestic agency, while the SD of Heydrich had both domestic and foreign responsibilities, and was the de facto political intelligence service of the Nazis.

4 He himself allowed his name to be used in print only once, in 1936, when he agreed to write a signed essay for a book called *Wehrmacht and Party*. Edited by the army's propaganda chief, the book was supposed to promote the rapprochement between the armed forces and the Nazis. It was un-avoidable to be positive on this touchy theme, but Canaris overdid his panegyric. His tribute to Hitler was so excessively fulsome that the devoutly anti-Nazi, Colonel Hans Oster, his protégé and chief of staff, was heard to remark after reading the article: "A fool always finds a bigger fool to admire."

5 Canaris never bothered to set the record straight. Instead of refuting his Greek ancestry and alleged descent from Admiral Kanaris, he encouraged the legend, even when he was called "the Little Greek" behind his back.

6 Under the strict provisions of the Versailles Treaty of June 28, 1919, Germany was allowed to maintain only a minuscule military organization.

7 Later he added the autographed picture of Generalissimo Francisco Franco of Spain to this modest gallery of favorites.

8 When Bamler left the Abwehr to return to the General Staff, he was sent to the Eastern Front in command of a division. Captured by the Red Army, he became an ardent Communist in captivity. After the war, he went to live in East Germany where he attained a high position in the security services.

9 Other such shipments consigned to the Western Hemisphere went to Brazil (Rio de Janeiro and Porto Alegre), Argentina (Buenos Aires), Uraguay (Montevideo), Chile (Valparaiso), Colombia (Bogota) and Peru (Lima) and in 1938 to Abwehr representatives in Portland, Oregon, and Colon, in the Canal Zone.

10 The secret aftermath of the meeting with Roatta was somehow character-istic of the way Canaris liked to do business. Back in Berlin a few days later, he spoke enthusiastically about the agreement with the Italians and praised Roatta for his all-out cooperation. But then he told Colonel Pieken-brock: "Incidentally, I want you to set up an outpost in Rome right away. Staff it with some of the best men you've got, and start recruiting agents. We must do our utmost to bring the Italians under our closest surveillance." A second such alliance was concluded at about the same time with the Hungarians; in October, Canaris made a similar covenant with the Japanese, five years before Premier Prince Konoye agreed formally to join the Axis.

Chapter **2**

Operation Sex

SEPTEMBER 8, 1935, was a serene Sunday in the Bavarian Alps, when Canaris sat down with Hitler in the big living room of Hitler's chalet for his first real tête-à-tête with the Fuehrer.

Unlike Winston Churchill, who had the born buccaneer's keen interest in the spy game and frankly voiced his all-out support of His Majesty's Secret Intelligence Service, Hitler professed to be no espionage buff. He was, of course, a native conspirator and a consummate practitioner of the most intricate schemes. He repeatedly told his associates that he had nothing but contempt for secret intelligence and would never stoop so low as to shake the hand of a spy.

In one of his endless lectures to his cronies at his famous after-dinner talks, that produced some of his most startling statements seasoned with contrived anecdotes, he cited with approval the story about Frederick the Great who, he claimed, had once censured his intelligence chief for getting some valuable piece of information, simply because it had been procured by a spy.

But his squeamish attitude was not evident now, when listening to Admiral Canaris. He had never granted an audience to Captain Patzig, but this was not his first private session with the Abwehr's new chief, and Hitler had already given every indication that he liked him. Canaris understood how to ingratiate himself with the Fuehrer by telling him only what he knew Hitler liked to hear and seasoning his reports with the trash—called "incidental intelligence"—that secret services pick up in the course of their snoopings.

At this early stage of their relationship, Hitler already preferred Canaris's reports from abroad to those of his diplomats, because they were more interesting and titillating. It was the practice of German envoys to report only what they believed to be fully confirmed and

14

felt ready to stand by. Canaris was not bound by such traditions and limitations. As a result his stories were more gaudy, abounding in fascinating gossip and dealing with the private lives of interesting people than the staid analyses of dull events in stilted diplomatese.

Canaris also kowtowed to Hitler. He told him: "I have asked for this meeting, my Fuehrer, to give you my first full progress report, and especially to ask you to brief me about your plans for which you may need the Abwehr's loyal assistance."

Hitler spoke of *Anschluss* with Austria and Canaris assured him that the Abwehr was on top of this situation. An officer of the Austrian secret service, Major Erwin von Lahousen, had been "won over" and was working for him behind the back of and, indeed, against his own government. The Fuehrer mentioned the Free City of Danzig and the Polish Corridor, an "intolerable anomaly." Canaris replied that he was working on these questions, as he was on the Sudetenland in Czechoslovakia. In fact, he said, he had just recruited Konrad Henlein, the Sudeten-German leader, as an Abwehr agent.

The Soviet Union? A very difficult target. But Poland and France were under control.

England? No, Hitler said, he did not want any spies in England. His policy of *rapprochement* was paying dividends. In June, the Anglo-German naval agreement had been signed with the Baldwin government. Other "accommodations" were in the offing. There was no need for spies in England! They would only jeopardize the success of his diplomacy.

The United States? Hitler shrugged. It was too remote and too little involved in the affairs of Europe. He did not care, he said, what happened in America. Canaris was visibly relieved that Hitler was not extending the ban on espionage to the "Anglo-Saxons" on the far side of the Atlantic. For strange as it was, for a country so remote and neutral, the United States loomed enormously in the affairs of the Abwehr.

Canaris was an unusual chief of intelligence—he had been implicitly incurious about foreign countries. The only one that really warmed his heart was Spain, where he had spent the best years of his life and which he had come to regard as his second country.[1] France and Poland interested him professionally, but England only mildly, and the United States not at all.

When he took over on the Tirpitz Ufer, he made an astounding discovery. While he was pushing for an expansion of the existing web of agents in Poland and the establishment of networks in France, Denmark, the Low Countries and Czechoslovakia, he was told that the Abwehr already had a full-blown espionage outpost in a country for which he was making no plans at all—the United States.

At this time all the problems confronting the United States appeared to be domestic, yet the Abwehr had a dozen agents in this country, including several rated high-grade. Even more remarkable, this deep penetration of a distant and complex land was not the result of any deliberate effort on the Abwehr's part. It was the work of an exceptional man, going by the cover-name of "Sex," who had carried the secret war to those far shores virtually on his own initiative. He would, in the course of time, make the United States the most lucrative target in the history of German espionage, especially in the field of all-important aviation.

Toward the end of the Twenties interest in the United States was revived, mainly because the Reichswehr, the minimal army left to Germany, had decided in 1926 to add an illegal air force—the so-called "Black Luftwaffe"—to the Wehrmacht, which German militarists were secretly assembling. A start was made with the establishment of a special bureau of military aviation, the *Fliegerzentrale* under Major (later Field Marshal) Hugo Sperrle, a World War I ace, that had a few squadrons equipped with antiquated planes.

Badly shackled as it was, the German aviation industry could not supply even this embryo of an air force. Scouts were sent abroad to buy whatever was for sale. The United States in particular attracted these German explorers—for revolutionary aircraft designs; gyroscopes and automatic bombsights; landing gear that could be retracted in flight; and other new inventions such as flight indicators, four-bladed propellers, and better fuels.

A few of the devices were bought, but then the Germans ran into two snags. They exhausted their funds and they discovered that some of the most desirable items—especially those produced for the U. S. Navy—had classified tags on them and were not for sale.

The plotters of the *Fliegerzentrale* hit upon the idea of getting under the counter what they were prevented from buying in the open market, and to steal what they could not afford to purchase. The job of surreptitious procurement was handed to the Abwehr, and Colonel Fritz Gempp, its diminutive chief, was asked to send a man to New York to establish a ring of spies specializing mostly in aviation.

The agent Gempp picked for the mission arrived in the United States on March 27, 1927, landing at Hoboken from the North German Lloyd liner *Berlin*. A plain, pale, placid man, he became a face in the crowd. Though his nose was a bit too long, his mouth a little too tight, and his ears too big, his face was not especially memorable in its commonplace homeliness. Quietly groomed and simply clad, of medium height and weight, he was average in every respect.

His German passport identified him as Wilhelm Schneider, born

1893 in Wetzlar-on-the-Lahn, married, a piano tuner by profession. He was coming to the United States, as were thousands during those peak years of immigration, to seek a better life in the New World. Cleared quickly by Immigration and Customs he walked down the gangplank at the pier and faded into the big city on the other side of the Hudson River.

Like a bee that dies when expending its sting, "Wilhelm Schneider" expired the moment he passed the Immigration inspector—only to be reincarnated in an elaborate and ingenious masquerade. This man luxuriated in a long string of aliases. He was called Willie Meller, William Sexton, Bill Lonkis, to mention only a few he used during the next eight years. He is best remembered as William Lonkowski in an initiated circle of certain connoisseurs.

Schneider was not his real name. Nor was he born in Wetzlar. And though he carried the kit of the craft in his battered suitcase, he was no piano tuner.

He was a Silesian by birth, an aviation mechanic in World War I, twenty-five years old when it ended. After a few false starts toward new careers (including a brief spell at studying medicine), he returned to his first love and tried to carve out a future in aviation. He was a competent designer, but he couldn't land a job with any of the few plane manufacturers of Germany. He drifted back into the Reichswehr, where he found his niche in the Abwehr.

Lonkowski was not taken fully into the fold. In the summer of 1922 he was sent to France to review the state of French aviation. His report gained for him such high marks that, although he failed to pass his physical examination which showed him to be suffering from a chronic gastric ulcer, he was kept in reserve as a promising "sleeper," to be saved for a mission big enough for his obviously exceptional talents. His opportunity came in September 1926. Gempp invited him to take on the job in the United States and Lonkowski accepted eagerly.

Prior to his departure Lonkowski was assigned a cipher by which he would be carried on the books and his mission was given a corresponding symbol. The code names chosen seemed quaintly offbeat. This man, who possessed no carnal thoughts or traits, was henceforth to be called "Sex," and his venture was to be referred to as "Operation Sex." Actually, the cover-name did not have the obvious connotation. It was the abbreviation of "Sexton," the original alias— "William Sexton"—which the Abwehr had coined for him but later dropped.

Lonkowski was allotted a monthly stipend of $500 from Abwehr funds. It was not a miserly sum during those days, yet it was astonishingly small for a spy with the scope of Lonkowski's assignment. It was all the Abwehr could afford from its small stock of foreign currencies.

Lonkowski was given his "shopping list" which the *Fliegerzentrale* had compiled from items found in American aviation magazines and engineering journals. He was expected to get data about a new motor E. G. Smith was developing, which supposedly "doubled the horse power of existing engines"; the Caminez air-cooled engine undergoing tests at the Fairchild Aviation Corporation on Long Island; and the Micarta propeller with which Westinghouse Electric was reported to be experimenting.

When candidates are "assessed" (as the scientific process of selection is called) as to whether they would make good spies, they must prove that they possess a high quotient of emotional stability and a low degree of nervous tension. Lonkowski was a congenital worrier. His sensitive nerves could make him taut and edgy, and he had ulcers to prove it. Yet he came closer to being the perfect spy than any of the cool operators and imperturbable dandies of the British.

A first-rate aero-engineer, sophisticated at his specialty, Lonkowski was otherwise an uncomplicated man. His bland diet of milk and toast, coupled with his other spartan habits and taciturnity, caused some of his associates to regard him as a kind of Caspar Milquetoast. He was nothing of the sort. He had no pretenses, no fancy personal ambitions, no exaggerated regard for his own importance. He was contemptuous of the hoary melodrama of espionage and its bizarre rituals. He was indeed the perfect spy.

The idea of covering the entire American aviation industry, especially through a single man, was staggering in its very concept. Lonkowski was neither baffled nor discouraged. By early 1928 he felt comfortable in his new environment and had completely worked out his mode of operations. It was quite safe for him to give up piano tuning and revert to his true profession as an aviation specialist. Accordingly, he looked around for employment with one of the aircraft factories on the Atlantic seaboard, where he could gain the prestige and connections he needed to build up his network. He chose the Ireland Aircraft Corporation on Long Island as his first base, using it also as a springboard for other agents he was to plant elsewhere.

Starting out modestly as an aviation construction mechanic, Lonkowski became an instant success at the Ireland plant, rising quickly until he wielded considerable influence in the hiring and firing of personnel. He was soon ready to give up spying by himself and turn into the resident director of espionage in keeping with his original intentions. As a first step he acquired a new cover to justify his curiosity in matters that did not concern a piano tuner. He was made the American correspondent of a German air magazine called *Luft-reise*, and henceforth carried his credentials as an aviation writer with business cards that continued to label him a piano tuner.

He proceeded promptly to set up a couple of his own countrymen whose reliability and loyalty he could trust implicitly; and then scout for and "develop" other agents from among his new crop of contacts in the United States.

Before his departure from Germany, he had selected two ac-quaintances to assist him in the United States. One was a youngster named Werner Georg Gudenberg, a native of Hamburg, an engineer-ing draftsman with a smattering of electronics. The other was also a Hamburger, Otto Herman Voss, a 29-year-old graduate of his city's Technical Trade School and a better-than-average aviation me-chanic.

In the fall of 1928 Lonkowski sent for Gudenberg and Voss, start-ing them off in Ireland Aircraft. Thus began the coldly calculated preparations for the penetration of the American aviation industry and other sensitive areas of the nation's military machine. By 1932 Lonkowski was running a substantial private espionage business. Voss and Gudenberg (by then so safely entrenched and comfortably settled that they were preparing to become American citizens) were still his senior agents. They had left the Ireland plant for greener pastures. Voss went to Baltimore to work for a company that was developing propellers for the United States Navy. Gudenberg moved to an aircraft factory in Bristol, Pennsylvania, that had attracted Lonkowski's attention because it was experimenting with novel ap-plications of aluminum in the manufacture of airplane frames. Lonkowski sent Berlin an astounding assortment of reports and blueprints including the design of a "fireproof plane," and what he de-scribed as "the world's most powerful air-cooled motor," which the Wright Aeronautical Corporation was building for the United States Army. He procured the plans of a pursuit plane said to be capable of "landing either on a ship or on water," straight from the drawing boards of the Curtiss Aeroplane and Motor Company. The response was not what he anticipated. He continued to receive his monthly salary but that was practically his only link with the Abwehr.

Colonel Gempp was gone and his successors had lost interest in "Operation Sex." The *Fliegerzentrale* had its own contacts and was no longer dependent on an outsider working through the Abwehr.

"Operation Sex" was allowed to wither. Lonkowski was hardly discernible even among the scattered "sleepers" of the Abwehr. But we shall hear of him later.

It was now 1934, Hitler's second year in power.

The United States had become a major target for Nazi propaganda. It was assumed that the millions of German-Americans could be organized into a potent political force that might influence the new Roosevelt administration. The part that Americans of German descent had played in the miraculous progress of the New World was a matter of great pride to their compatriots at home. It was also looked upon with chauvinistic conceit by the Nazis. Hitler once claimed that two-thirds of the American engineers were Germans. "The people," he said, "who were originally responsible for the development [of the United States] were nearly all of German stock."

Taking their cue from the Fuehrer, the Nazis reached out for the fellowship of German-Americans and succeeded in befuddling thousands of them with their shrill propaganda. Their disciples under the swastika swaggered, demonstrated, and made trouble. Efforts to recruit spies, especially among those "engineers" of whom Hitler spoke, remained disappointing. To begin with, the sum total of such efforts was the discovery of a single candidate—a New York physician named Ignatz Theodor Griebl.

Born in Wuerzburg, the beautiful baroque city in Bavaria, in 1899, Dr. Griebl served as an artillery officer in World War I and was wounded on the Italian front, where he met his future wife, Maria Ganz, an Austrian army nurse. After the war, supported by Maria, he studied medicine in Munich until 1922, when Miss Ganz left for the United States promising that she would send for Griebl as soon as she had money for his passage. Early in 1925 she was able to finance the trip, then helped Griebl through studies at Long Island Medical College and Fordham University, and gave him the money he needed to buy a practice in Bangor, Maine.

They made a few lasting friendships among the Germans in Maine. But they did not feel comfortable among the Down Easters. The ambitious young doctor yearned for the cosmopolitan atmosphere of New York, with its greater opportunities for his talents. They moved down in 1928, and Griebl established himself in Yorkville, the heart of Manhattan's German colony, specializing in obstetrics and the surgery of varicose veins. He became popular in the neighborhood, was chosen official physician by a number of German societies, and waxed prosperous. He and his wife took out American citizenship, and Griebl joined the United States Army as an officer in the Reserve.

Griebl was an intensely political man to whom Nazism had become the patent of nobility—copestone of his innate prejudices, panacea for all of his craving for status. Even before Hitler's seizure of power, this pudgy, dimple-cheeked, bespectacled man had been active as a Nazi propagandist. In 1933 he decided to add a new dimension to his subversive activities. He had several well-placed friends at various sensitive American defense installations and thought he could persuade some of them to join him in forming an espionage ring for the new Germany.

On March 3, 1934, he volunteered his services in a letter to Dr. Joseph Paul Goebbels because, as he pointed out, the Propaganda Minister knew his brother Karl, a veteran Nazi, who could vouch for him. He was not a total stranger to spying, he wrote to Goebbels. Back in 1922, when he was a medical student in Munich, he had undertaken a secret mission for the fledgling Abwehr during a summer vacation in France, and returned with information that Colonel Gempp described as "interesting and useful."

Goebbels forwarded the letter, but not to the still-hibernating Abwehr, which showed no sign of interest in developing secret agents in America or, for that matter, anywhere else except in Poland. He sent it on to the Gestapo because he knew that it was building up an international network of police spies and confidential informants. Gestapo headquarters in Berlin then turned over Griebl's application to one of its branches called the Maritime Bureau in the Stella Building, the great clearing house of seafaring men in Hamburg, where an official named Paul Kraus was engaged in organizing Nazi cells in ships on transatlantic routes.

Kraus thought merely of utilizing members of his floating nuclei as couriers. "From Hamburg," Kraus had written in his original recommendation to establish such a global net, "an average of a thousand ships each month sail to all ports of the world, so communications with foreign countries could be maintained by using agents recruited from among members of their crews." Work on this network had already begun in 1930, illegally, of course, for the Nazis were not yet in power. By 1934, a year before Canaris took over, Kraus had hundreds of candidates neatly indexed on white, yellow, and light blue cards, to be called up when needed. Most important among them, as far as the United States was concerned, were crew members of the *Europa*, the *Bremen*, the *New York*, and the *Hamburg*, the fastest ocean liners the North German Lloyd and the Hamburg-America Line had in their transatlantic service.

On the *Europa,* an engineer, an officer, and Steward Karl Schlueter were carried as prospective agents; in the *Bremen*, Karl Eitel and another steward were available. Theo Schuetz was among the candidates on the *New York*, and another was an officer on the *Hamburg*. Although they were expected to supply intelligence, they were to act mainly as couriers as soon as rings of producing spies could be organized in the United States.

Griebl's application afforded Kraus an opportunity to develop such a ring and he invited the doctor to visit him at his headquarters in Stella House in Hamburg, to explore the possibilities of a collaboration.

Paying the expenses of the trip out of his own pocket, Dr. Griebl journeyed to Hamburg and eagerly accepted Kraus's invitation to work for the Maritime Bureau as a scout, recruiting men and women in the United States who could be "developed" as producing agents. On his return to New York, Griebl became active in an organization called "Friends of the New Germany," with the idea of making it the base of and front for his espionage activities. He hoped to create a number of cells within it, but at first succeeded in putting together only one, consisting of himself and three "friends"—Axel Wheeler-Hill, Oskar Karl Pfaus, and another young man.

The cell was not as inconspicuous as a spy ring should have been. The little band of would-be agents was widely known among the "friends" and joked about as "Dr. Griebl's undercover boys." As it turned out, Griebl's moonlighting was no laughing matter. Wheeler-Hill and Pfaus were to become important cogs in the German spy machine. In 1934, however, these ardent Nazis had little going for them to qualify as secret agents. They had no access to secret information and knew nobody who had. When they failed to produce anything he could send to Hamburg, Griebl looked around among his own acquaintances for more promising candidates.

He remembered an old friend, an elderly-looking man he had known in Maine, who seemed to be ideally placed for the spy game. Griebl's file in the Abwehr later referred to him as "Daneberg," and listed him as an H-man (for *Hintermann*) or sub-agent of "F.2307/ Dr. G.," which was Griebl's number in the central registry.[2]

I discovered "Daneberg's" dossier among the overlooked Abwehr files, and can now reveal that he was a 51-year-old, one-armed German-American engineer, Christian F. Danielsen by his real name. What made him so attractive to Griebl was the fact that he was employed in the Bath Iron Works in Maine as a designer of destroyers for the United States Navy. Griebl invited Danielsen to New York for a reunion, sending him seventy-five dollars to pay for his fare.

It proved a lucrative visit. Danielsen had come to the United States almost forty years before and was a naturalized citizen. He had three daughters living in Germany, some real estate holdings, and a more than nostalgic attachment to the old country. He agreed avidly to work for Griebl, and thus became, not only the first, but one of the most valuable members of the budding ring. Even after the first visit, Griebl accompanied Danielsen back to Bangor, checked into a hotel and waited there while the designer motored to his office in the Bath Iron Works and copied the blueprints of the warship on which he was working. He then returned to the doctor with what became the first major item in Griebl's loot of American defense secrets.

Then, suddenly and unsolicited, a real professional joined the Griebl ring. One October afternoon in 1934, a new patient showed up in the doctor's office in Yorkville, telling the nurse that he was seeking treatment for a bothersome duodenal ulcer. Later in the privacy of the consultation room, the man said to Griebl: "Don't you remember me, Ignatz? We met in 1922 on that mission to France for old Colonel Gempp."

"But of course," Griebl exclaimed. "You're Willy Lonkowski! Man alive, what are you doing here in America?"

Lonkowski told him everything—how he had been sent to the United States six years before, how he had succeeded in constructing a ring of his own virtually without any help from Germany, how he was inexplicably forsaken by the Abwehr. "I read about you in the papers," he told Griebl, "how eagerly you are aiding the cause of our new Germany. And then I heard that you're looking for people in my business. I'm here to offer you my services."

This became the most bizarre consultation in Griebl's whole practice both as a physician and as an espionage scout. While the "patient" was stretched out on the examining table, Lonkowski agreed to merge whatever he had left of his organization with Griebl's new spy ring.

"Agent Sex" returned to action with renewed vigor. He had sat out 1933 and most of 1934, puzzled that the Abwehr apparently had no more use for him. But he had by no means been idle. He was spinning his web ever wider, improving his own little network, and making sure he would be "getting the stuff that really mattered" as soon as Berlin gave the word.

His old colleagues, Otto Voss and Werner Gudenberg, were standing by to begin "deliveries." He had others waiting, too. After Griebl and Lonkowski pooled their resources, they eventually had in their net a Swiss-born captain in the United States Army who supplied details of new infantry weapons; a draftsman in a firm of naval architects in New York; a designer of guns in Montreal; an engineer in the metallurgical laboratory of the Federal Shipbuilding and Drydock Company at Kearny, New Jersey; contacts in the Navy Yards in Boston and Newport News, Virginia, and in a number of scattered aircraft factories; all in addition to Danielsen in Maine.

It was a phenomenal ring, with a high espionage quotient and considerable potential. But it was running in a vacuum. The Abwehr was still aloof, Canaris not yet in the scene. Kraus in Stella Haus did not know what to do with the material the Griebl-Lonkowski ring was ready to supply. His own branch in the Gestapo was neither interested in nor equipped for the handling of defense intelligence. His courier organization had grown tremendously, ready to begin operation at a moment's notice. For the time being, however, Kraus still had far more couriers than reports to carry.

This anomalous situation ended abruptly. In late 1934, the Abwehr branch at Wilhelmshaven, which handled naval intelligence, acquired a new chief, a man referred to variously as "Herr Doctor" or "Dr. Erdhoff" or "N. Spielman." Actually he was a career naval officer, Erich Pheiffer, with a doctorate in political economy. Pheiffer, in his forties, had returned to the Abwehr with the modest rank of *Kapitaenleutnant* (lieutenant senior grade) after fifteen restive years as a businessman, to tide himself over until the *Reichsmarine* would again have a slot for his special talents. He was made second in command at the Wilhelmshaven branch, with the title *V-Mann Leiter,* "leader of agents," at a time when he had practically no agents to lead.

Tall, lean, bespectacled Dr. Pheiffer was destined to become the elusive Pimpernel of German espionage in the United States during this hectic decade. His name kept cropping up in every espionage operation the FBI managed to crack, and Pheiffer was indicted by several grand juries in New York as one of the major conspirators in those plots. But he had to be watched from a distance and indicted *in absentia.* In the best tradition of the great spymasters, Pheiffer remained a faceless, shadowy figure, pulling the strings but never exposing himself.

Judging him only by the failure of some of his operations and by the apparently low quality of his fallen agents, American counterspies were quick to dismiss him as an industrious but incompetent buff whose wholesale attack on American secrets was as ruthless and reckless as it was foolish and ineffectual. His successes far outweighed his failures, and on balance, he endures as one of the outstanding espionage executives of this period of Sturm und Drang.

This was still the pre-Canaris era when contacts with Nazi organizations were tenuous and rare. Pheiffer, a pragmatic spymaster, did not share Captain Patzig's aversion to them. As soon as he arrived in Wilhelmshaven, he established working relations with the Gestapo offices in Bremen and Hamburg. He was amply rewarded for his friendly approach.

On January 2, 1935, when he had been at Wilhelmshaven only a few months and had not even begun the organization of an apparatus in the field, an unexpected telephone call from Hamburg put him into business. It was Kraus calling from Stella Haus, asking whether Pheiffer could see a couple of "friends" who had brought "a present" for him from America. "I can vouch for them," Kraus said. "They have some very big fish to fry."

They were the steward from the *Bremen* and the engineer of the *Europa*, the latter coming along to volunteer his services to the Abwehr and also to act as a character witness for the steward. Their "present" filled the phlegmatic and skeptical Pheiffer with flaming excitement.

The *Europa* engineer still naïve at espionage, produced an issue of a trade journal called *Marine News* and a few back issues of the *National Geographic*. But the steward had a "present" of considerably more value. He was bringing the first shipment from Griebl and Lonkowski.

He turned over a classified United States Navy manual used at shipyards for guidance in testing metals in the construction of warships, that Griebl had procured from an engineer in Kearny, New Jersey. He produced a confidential report from Lonkowski with gossip about the private life of Frederick T. Birchall, then chief European correspondent of *The New York Times*, who was making a nuisance of himself in Berlin with his strongly worded, brilliantly documented anti-Nazi dispatches. He brought along a sample of tellurium, used apparently in some anti-corrosion experiments by the Navy. And he handed over film negatives of the drawings of an experimental plane under development at the Sikorsky plant at Farmingdale, Long Island.

The steward told Dr. Pheiffer that there was much more where these samples had come from. Griebl and Lonkowski, he said, were ready to start full-scale operations, waiting only for word from the Abwehr.

The steward also outlined Lonkowski's ideas about future cooperation: he would return to work at once, tapping his old sources and developing new ones in close association with Dr. Griebl. They planned to send everything to Dr. Pheiffer at Wilhelmshaven, using the ship-couriers. Shipments would go out each time the *Europa* or the *Bremen* sailed for Bremerhaven. All shipments would move on 35 mm. film, Lonkowski to do the reducing in a laboratory he had installed in his house on Long Island.

As Pheiffer later put it, the timely arrival of Eitel bearing these gifts radically changed the whole complexion and orientation of the Wilhelmshaven branch. The United States was moved to the top in a list of targets, and arrangements were made on a substantial scale to broaden the operation. The cast of characters was entered on the Abwehr's roster. Karl Eitel, who was to act as senior agent and chief courier, was entered as number R. 2307.[3] Griebl was given the cover-name "Ilberg" and a new number, A.2339. The engineer on the *Europa* was also accepted into the fold, as a *Forscher,* or scout, with the number F.2313. The entire "2300" serial in the roster of Pheiffer's agents was set aside for members of "Operation Sex."

On January 5, the *Bremen* steward sailed back to America with detailed instructions for Griebl and Lonkowski. From then on, under Pheiffer's brilliant direction, everything progressed according to the strict protocol of espionage. On January 12, 1935, agent "Sex" was at the Hofbrauhaus, a German restaurant on East 86th Street, for his *Treff* (as these meetings were called even in America) with Agent R. 2307.

The new phase of Operation Sex was off to a most promising start.

NOTES

1 Within ten months, he used the full resources of the Abwehr to aid the army revolt of General Emilio Mola that unleashed Francisco Franco's rebellion and ushered in the Spanish Civil War on July 18, 1936. He then became instrumental in gaining German and Italian support for Franco, assuring his eventual victory in the civil war.

2 Actually "F.2307" was Karl Eitel's registry number, the "F" indicating that he was a scout and courier. At this time, Griebl was carried in the registry merely as Eitel's sub-agent. But when the doctor himself blossomed out as a spymaster, far surpassing Eitel's importance, he was given his own registry number, A. 2339, the "A" indicating that he was a producing agent.

3 The change of letters in Eitel's designation from "F" to "R" showed that he, too, had been promoted—from scout to traveling agent.

Chapter 3

Windfalls in America

ON February 2, 1935—exactly a month after Eitel had first called on him in Wilhelmshaven—Dr. Erich Pheiffer was summoned to Abwehr headquarters in Berlin to report on his windfall in America. He described details of the operation to Commander Udo von Bonin, deputy chief of the naval intelligence section who superintended espionage in the United States, and also to Colonel Hans Piekenbrock, who had just arrived on the Tirpitz Ufer to take over the secret intelligence group, known as *Amstgruppe* I at the headquarters of the Abwehr.

Six days later, accompanied by Piekenbrock, Admiral Wilhelm Canaris went to Wilhelmshaven to inspect the little subbranch of Ast X that had suddenly become the most active and important of all Abwehr outposts.

A second shipment had come in from Lonkowski, brought by the *Europa*'s steward Karl Schlueter. Now there could be no doubt that their free-lancing agents in the United States were the best and most productive of any the Abwehr had anywhere in the world. It was up to Pheiffer and his colleagues at home to make the most of this unexpected bonanza.

Dr. Pheiffer's excitement rubbed off on the blasé little Abwehr chief, who was not easy to set on fire. Gone was his lukewarm attitude toward North America. In an impromptu lecture to the staff he described the United States as "one of the key targets" in all Abwehr efforts. "The U.S.A. must be regarded," he said, "as the decisive factor in any future war. The capacity of its industrial power is such as to assure victory, not merely for the United States itself, but for any country with which it may be associated."

He ordered Pheiffer to enlarge his branch and move it closer to his

27

couriers arriving at Bremerhaven. The move was made on October 1, 1935, as shown in the entries in the Branch's ledger. During this period of change, payments to agents were interspersed in its columns with disbursements for such mundane items as electric light bulbs (8.10 marks), a petty cash box (19 marks), and stationery (24.65 marks). Pheiffer rented an office suite in the Federal Building in downtown Bremen (at 165 marks per month), and equipped a photographic laboratory (at a cost of 237.86 marks), needed because much of the material from America was arriving on films. He also leased two post office boxes (No. 161 in Wilhelmshaven and No. 210 in Bremen), and arranged for a number of mail drops in the city to which the clandestine correspondence from America was henceforth addressed.

The two master spies in the United States kept the office on its collective toes. Each time the *Europa* or the *Bremen* docked at Bremerhaven, Pheiffer was there for *Treffs* with Eitel, Schlueter, or other couriers to pick up their shipments. These were also great days for Lonkowski for he had come into his own at last. He had moved to a house in Hempstead, Long Island, to be closer to his contacts at the aircraft plants on Long Island and the installations of the United States Army Air Corps at Mitchell Field and Roosevelt Field.

"Operation Sex" moved with precision, producing such diverse items as the design of an automatic sight for machine guns which one of Lonkowski's "friends," the Swiss-born infantry officer in the United States Army, had procured; and the blueprints of a new water tank at Langley Field, Virginia. The speed of deliveries enormously enhanced the value of his service. On July 18, for example, the new Luftwaffe's Ordnance Department asked Dr. Pheiffer to obtain the specifications of a pontoon the Sikorsky plant in Farmingdale, Long Island, had perfected for an experimental seaplane. Otto Voss, who was now employed there, supplied the data overnight, and Lonkowski's report was in Berlin on August 8.

Between January, when the new operation started, and the end of July, when it was operating at its peak, Lonkowski's deliveries included:

- specifications of every plane being built at the Sikorsky plant at Farmingdale;
- blueprints of FLG-2 planes, and of the SBU-1 carrier-based scout bomber Vought Aviation was making for the United States Navy;
- specifications of a Boeing bomber and of a plane Douglas had on the drawing board;
- classified maps of the United States Army;

- details of an anodizing process and certain experiments with chromium;
    - blueprints of the destroyers DD-397, DD-398, and DD-399;
    - drawings of several devices the Lear Radio Corporation was manufacturing for the War and Navy Departments;
    - a report on tactical air exercises at Mitchell Field, on Long Island.

At the request of Dr. Pheiffer, Griebl and Lonkowski toured the Canadian border to "survey possible points of entry of large groups from Canada to the United States." They went to Montreal for a *Treff* with a designer employed by a Canadian firm working for the United States Navy, and collected from him the drawings of "a new type of AA gun utilizing an electro-magnetic device that will increase the number of shells the gun is capable of firing per minute." Lonkowski was given a draft of the gun right off the drawing board, and Pheiffer had its photographic copy in Bremen even before the United States Navy received it.

In early September Lonkowski was ready for his greatest coup. He had his friend Gudenberg at the Curtiss Aircraft plant in Buffalo, New York. A clean-cut, handsome, open-faced man of thirty-six, apparently devoted to his adopted country and comfortably settled in a pleasant home with his pretty American wife, Gudenberg seemed to be an unlikely accomplice of a German master spy. Yet he was one of Lonkowski's prime suppliers of secret intelligence. On two previous trips to Buffalo, "Sex" had received from him the drawings of an experimental Army plane for night bombing, and of another experimental aircraft, the XO3C, its prototype already in construction.

Later in the month Lonkowski returned to Buffalo for the plans of a super-secret light bomber, called SB-C2. What Gudenberg gave him became the crowning achievement of Lonkowski's career as a spy. It also turned out to be his swan song.

On September 25, 1935, the *Europa* was about to sail for Bremerhaven. Pier 86 on the Hudson River in New York was crowded with passengers, relatives and friends, officials and Customs guards. Flowers were delivered to the staterooms, parcels were arriving for departing passengers, farewell parties were in full swing in the cabins, and acquaintances were boarding the ship to bid bon voyage. Among the visitors, talking to one of the stewards, was a lean, bespectacled man carrying a violin case. Morris Josephs, a Customs guard, stopped him alongside the ship.

"What kind of violin have you in that case?" Josephs asked.

"Oh, just an ordinary fiddle," the little man said in a casual tone.

"Is that so?" the guard said. "I'm greatly interested in violins. Would you mind letting me see it?"

Nervously the gaunt little man opened the violin case to reveal his violin. As Josephs lifted it from its velvet-lined container, he saw beneath it a collection of pictures showing the drawings of planes. The Customs guard grew grim. He replaced the violin, closed the lid, and beckoned the man to accompany him to the Customs office at the head of the pier. The guard called his superior, John W. Roberts, supervising Customs agent for the area, and together they searched the man. In his pockets they found a film strip and several letters written in German.

The negatives showed details of airplanes, and the letters, signed "Sex," contained such phrases as "of interest are the single strut, fully streamlined gear, etc." Josephs turned the man over to Roberts, who put in a call to Major Stanley Grogan, the G-2 (Intelligence) on Governors Island. Grogan was out, but a subordinate immediately came to the pier to inspect the spy and the non-musical contents of the violin case. He was a private, a clerk in Major Grogan's office. But private or not he was so impressed with what he saw that he telephoned another officer, Major Joseph N. Dalton, for instructions. The situation became tense, the dejection of the man grew deeper. Dalton asked the soldier to describe the pictures, films and letters found on the man, then he said: "I don't see anything wrong with these pictures. Anybody might have them. Let him go for now, but tell him to come back tomorrow when Major Grogan will talk to him. Incidentally, what did he say his name was?"

Until this moment nobody had thought of asking the man for his name. Roberts turned to him and asked, "What's your name?"

The man hesitated briefly, evidently considering the advantage of giving an alias. Realizing that the game was over, he decided to be cooperative.

"William Lonkowski, sir."

"Well, Mr. Lonkowski," Roberts said. "You may go now, but be back in this office tomorrow morning at ten. We'll have a few more questions to ask."

"I never set eyes on him again," Roberts later said.

What happened?

As soon as Lonkowski left the pier he called his wife in Hempstead, Long Island, instructed her to draw their money out of the bank and bring it to Dr. Griebl's office. He then took a cab to the office on 86th Street where he told Griebl what had happened and asked the doctor to get him out of the country as quickly as possible.

Canada was the nearest exit. They had no time to lose. Griebl called a young friend, Ulrich Hausmann, another Abwehr agent who was in the United States posing as the correspondent of German aviation magazines. Griebl invited Hausmann to accompany him and Lonkowski to his country house in suburban Peekskill, New York, then drive Lonkowski on to Canada.

There seemed to be no sequel to the incident as far as the American authorities were concerned. Nothing indicated that Lonkowski had been trailed to Griebl's office. Nobody had inquired about him at his house on Long Island. The coast was clear.

Hausmann got Griebl's automobile, Lonkowski climbed in, and they were off. From Peekskill they drove to the border and crossed into Canada at Rock Island, Vermont. Hausmann promptly phoned Griebl, who had meanwhile been in touch with Pheiffer by cable. Lonkowski was directed to Rivière-de-Loup, where a German freighter was unloading.

They drove to the port city on the St. Lawrence River and Lonkowski boarded the ship. The skipper had already received instructions to put to sea as soon as his passenger was on board. Lonkowski sailed for Germany on the afternoon of September 28, and Hausmann enjoyed an uneventful drive back to New York. It was as simple as that.

In the end the entire incident was reduced to a brief entry on Dr. Griebl's bio-sheet in the Abwehr. "Performed invaluable service in connection with 'Operation Sex' by acting promptly and decisively in the 1935 emergency." As far as Lonkowski's sudden journey was concerned, its details showed up in Dr. Pheiffer's ledger. On September 30, it carried a 100-mark item, cabled to Lonkowski aboard the freighter. On October 10, a 6-mark item was entered, reimbursing Pheiffer for the cab in which he picked up Lonkowski in Bremerhaven. On October 12, voucher No. 25 was attached to the ledger, with the notation, "Expenses of Frau Sex for trip New York-Berlin."

Even Frau Lonkowski—or whoever the woman was who traveled as "Frau Sex"—managed to leave New York undetected and reach Germany safely, simply by boarding a Bremen-bound ship at a Hudson River pier.

That was a 150-mark item, followed by an 8.20-mark entry Dr. Pheiffer had spent on accompanying Lonkowski by cab to the pier in Bremerhaven to welcome "Frau Sex" to the Fatherland.

But Operation Sex was by no means over.

When he recalled the Lonkowski incident in his memoirs, Rear Admiral Ellis M. Zacharias, former Deputy Director of the U. S. Office of Naval Intelligence, wrote confidently: "Even before we learned that Lonkowski had been able to warn Griebl, it was fully expected that the original detention and subsequent release would cause the whole group to become inactive for an indefinite period, which is what happened."

It was not what happened.

The incredible naïveté of the American security agents became quickly apparent to Ignatz Griebl and Karl Eitel. Instead of becoming inactive, they became more active than ever. Actually, Lonkowski's mishap, for it was hardly more than that, ushered in what could be called the heyday of German espionage in the United States. It lasted almost uninterruptedly for five years until the summer of 1941, barely five months before Pearl Harbor.

In Griebl and Eitel, Admiral Canaris had two skilled zealots in the United States; and in Dr. Erich Pheiffer he had a seasoned spymaster who could not be easily discouraged. It seemed almost as if Lonkowski's accident had been the catalyzing agent in the clandestine careers of these men. Suddenly the eager amateurs became seasoned professionals. The organization was tightened and improved until it became a model of every large-scale spy conspiracy.

Various methods were used in recruiting. Particular attention was paid to persons of German birth who were naturalized American citizens. Once established in the United States, agents received instructions to "acquire whatever information they could." They were told to refrain from any public pro-Nazi activities and to secure, if possible, established and respectable positions in their communities. Their spy work was closely kept in secrecy. In many instances, agents were unknown to each other, although they used the same contacts for transmitting their information to Germany.

Transmission of the information was relatively simple. The couriers were supplied with passwords. If an agent had some family connection with Dresden, the courier would say, "Greetings from Dresden." If the agent was well known to someone in Germany by the name of Schmidt, the courier's approach would be "Greetings from Schmidt."

At the other end of the line, the Abwehr had agents stationed at all the principal seaports in Europe, not only in Germany but also in Lisbon and Genoa, in Rotterdam and Cherbourg. So-called letterboxes (mail drops) were maintained in Holland, Italy, a busy one in Scotland, three in Brazil, and one in China. For quick service, the *Bremen* and the *Europa* were used most frequently as courier ships. When a flight steward of the Pan American Airlines agreed to serve as a courier the Clipper to Lisbon became the fastest route, but only when the weather was favorable.

Agents were trained in the use of the Leica and the making of microphotographic copies of documents and blueprints. A document written on ordinary letter paper could be reduced to a film frame of about one-inch by three-quarters of an inch. Thus the courier going one way could carry hidden on his person detailed instructions for many agents and dozens of photographic copies of documents going the other way.

Several relatively simple codes were constructed, most of them based on the pages of best-selling novels, the keys written in invisible ink on the inside cover of matchbooks of the North German Lloyd line. Later more complicated crypto-systems were developed for rapid-transit messages sent by the three radio stations the Abwehr eventually operated in North America.

As soon as a courier arrived at his destination, he would, by previous arrangement, contact his *Umleitungsstelle* (transfer agent). Usually the U-agents in these ports were ship chandlers or persons whose regular business took them to the waterfront.

The compensation of agents was handled in several ways. In some instances money was transferred from banks in South America, Mexico, and Holland and credited to the account of the agent at various New York banks, usually Chase National and the National City Bank. More often American currency was given to the couriers, who passed it on to local agents.

As shown by the fiscal records, fees were modest. A Swiss engineer in Montreal was paid fifty dollars for each piece of information he delivered. His courier received thirty dollars for taking the shipment to Germany. On one occasion, a courier carried four hundred dollars to New York, to pay off five agents. Over a five-month period in 1937, a total of fourteen hundred dollars was sent to New York to take care of as many as twenty agents.

The highest price on record paid to an agent at this time was fifteen hundred dollars in one lump sum.

By the end of 1935, "Operation Sex," now renamed "Operation Ilberg," resumed its activities with its old personnel and new recruits.[1]

In April the ring was further enlarged by the addition of a group Dr. Pheiffer developed by remote control—by correspondence and an ad in *The New York Times*. Going by the cover-name of "Crown," it consisted of Guenther Gustav Rumrich, a 37-year-old naturalized American of Sudeten-German birth who had recently served as a sergeant in the U.S. Army, and his friend, Erich Glaser, a soldier on active duty. As their special courier, Pheiffer (who went by the nickname of "N. Spielman" in this particular operation) appointed Karl Schlueter and Johanna (Jennie) Hofmann, a sedate young woman who worked as a hairdresser on the *Europa*.

The star performer of "Ilberg" was Gustav Guellich, the mystery man of the ring, for no record of his activities seems to be extant anywhere outside the Abwehr's own secret papers where I discovered their details. The astounding scope of this obscure agent's activities was as remarkable as was his ability to remain anonymous.

Guellich was a 34-year-old native of Munich who had come to the United States in 1932 with the intention of becoming a citizen, and had taken out his first papers. A competent metallurgist, he found a berth in the laboratories of a Kearny, New Jersey, shipyard, a division of U.S. Steel. Here he worked quietly (or so it seemed) minding his own business, meeting the demands of his job but attracting no special attention. A pinch-faced, emaciated bachelor, he lived modestly in Room 1150 of the Hotel Martinique on New York's West 32nd Street, near Macy's. A loner who suffered periodic spells of depression, he found it difficult to make friends until he met Griebl. He accepted Dr. Griebl's proffered friendship avidly and seized upon his invitation to join the ring, for spying provided an escape hatch from the frustrations and monotony of his life. Guellich plunged into espionage and quickly became the group's most diligent and valuable member.

He produced high-grade data about the United States Navy, gaining access from his vantage point in the sensitive laboratory. His dossiers in the Abwehr bulged with descriptive reports, formulae, and drawings.

He delivered the blueprints of several destroyers under construction and those of the gunboat *Erie*; description of a teargas shell; the drawings of a new Smith & Wesson handgun; drawings of the Boeing P-26; specifications of an underwater sound apparatus and of various deck guns and their shells; samples of cables; and considerable metallurgical information, including a secret polarizing foil.

His *pièce de résistance* was handed to Griebl on January 7, 1936, in a four-page memorandum, entitled *"Experiments with High-Altitude Rockets in the United States."* It contained a full account of the work being done by Professor Robert H. Goddard of Clark University at Worcester, Massachusetts, who had just scored what Guellich described as "a breakthrough representing substantial progress in the development of rocket-propelled missiles."

Guellich's first report was a rehash of newspaper articles about Goddard, most of which ridiculed the great physicist as a mad scientist planning to go to the moon. In Germany, however, Goddard's experiments were followed with keen interest, and Guellich's report created a considerable stir in the Abwehr. The agent was instructed to concentrate on this topic. A number of lists of pointed questions were forwarded to him and he spent much time during the year answering them. Once he went to New Mexico where Dr. Goddard was conducting his field experiments and observed the firing of one of the first practicable rockets ever launched. Guellich's dossier contains seven different reports on this subject alone. The last, dated December 7, 1936, was considered so important that its forwarding slip was signed by Admiral Canaris himself.

In it Guellich clarified questions about the cooling system of the firing chamber; gave the dates of experimental launchings scheduled for the rest of the year; and provided the formula of the liquid propellant Goddard was using. Questioned about the most likely immediate application of the project, Guellich reported that experiments were underway "to employ rockets instead of sound control in the guidance system of torpedoes."

Guellich's work as a spy illustrates how simple the business of espionage can be. There is little in his activities, even his circumspect secrecy, that lends an aura of melodrama to spying. Guellich went about his clandestine pastime quietly copying confidential papers that crossed his desk first in Kearny, and then on West 12th Street in New York City. He kept his eyes and ears open for other classified matters handled by his colleagues at the research laboratories of U.S. Steel.

Even his supposedly secret *Treffs* with Griebl or his courier were ordinary rendezvous at public places. They set the time and the locale of their meetings, at which Guellich handed over whatever he had, sometimes concealed in that day's issue of *The New York Times*, but more often over a restaurant table. He was paid in cash by his courier, with no more embarrassment or secrecy than for routine business transactions.

It took some time for Bremen to recognize the extraordinary merits of Guellich. In September 1937 Dr. Pheiffer elevated him one notch in the hierarchy. Until then Guellich had been carried simply as a sub-agent with the number F. 2307-Gue. Now he was to be recognized with a number of his own, the next one available in the 2300 series. Without any sign of gratitude or emotion the quiet Bavarian acknowledged the accolade when Eitel told him that henceforth he would be called "Agent 2338."

Things were going so smoothly that in June 1937 Dr. Griebl took his mistress, a statuesque young woman, on a holiday to Germany. It developed into the triumphal journey of a homecoming conqueror. Dr. Pheiffer welcomed them at the pier, put them up in style in the Hotel Columbus in Bremen, showed Griebl around in the *Nebenstelle*, then took him to Berlin for a meeting with Captain Hermann Menzel and Commander Udo von Bonin, chiefs of the Abwehr's M-branch, under whose auspices "Ilberg" operated. He was introduced to Admiral Canaris and to Colonel Piekenbrock. As a parting present Canaris gave him title to an estate in Giessen that had been confiscated from its Jewish owner.

Back in Bremen, on the eve of Griebl's departure for New York, Pheiffer entertained him and his girl friend at the Café Astoria and in the mellow atmosphere of the posh nightclub reviewed with them his branch's coverage of the United States. "You must realize, Herr Doktor," he told the visitor, "that it is more vast and elaborate than anyone besides us comprehends." As Griebl revealed later, they talked of "the base in Montreal, headquarters for Canada and part of New England," and discussed "outlets at Newport News, Boston, Buffalo, Bristol, Philadelphia, as far west as San Diego and Seattle, and in Bath, Maine."

His tongue loosened by the schnapps, Pheiffer confided that, independent of "Ilberg," he had other agents at large in America, including "two splendid boys in the Canal Zone." A new agent of his, who had free entry to all installations of the United States Army in the East, had recently visited the chemical warfare center at Bel Air, Maryland. In Washington he had an informant on the staff of a United States Senator and another in President Roosevelt's inner circle. Pheiffer described how the latter had procured details of a confidential conference in the White House at which deficiencies of American warships and drastic changes in their design were discussed. An agent working at the Army Signal Laboratories at Fort Monmouth, New Jersey, had produced plans of a brand-new anti-aircraft gun "even before they reached Washington."

"At every strategic point in the United States," Dr. Griebl later said Pheiffer had boasted, "we have at least one of our operatives. In every armament factory, in every shipyard in America we have a spy, several of them in key positions. The United States cannot plan a warship, design an airplane, develop a new device that we do not know of at once."

With the Japanese intensifying their own espionage efforts, in collaboration with the Abwehr in America under an alliance Admiral Canaris had concluded with Colonel Oshima in Berlin, the United States was, indeed, "in a pincer of spies." It was, as Pheiffer told Griebl in the Astoria, "the most elaborate and effective penetration of a major power in the whole history of espionage."[2]

NOTE

1 Eitel's own days in the ring were numbered. Since it was feared that Lonkowski had compromised him, a stand-in as chief of couriers was appointed to take over on a moment's notice.

2 This was no empty boast. The Germans' ability to cover the United States aviation industry had a well-nigh historic significance. The fact that they could procure practically all that they needed for the development of the Luftwaffe made it possible to have it combat-ready by 1939. Without this aid from the United States, it would have taken considerably longer, and the Germans could not have gone to war as soon as they did.

Chapter 4

The Bombsight Fixation

*T*HERE was one major item missing from the Abwehr's collection of Americana—an item regarded as so critically important that its absence almost invalidated all the other acquisitions. It was the highly secret American device which was supposed to enable a bombardier to determine the split second at which a bomb must be released in space to hit a target. It was no secret that different versions of such a bombsight had been developed in the United States by Carl T. Norden in association with Theodore H. Barth, and, separately, by Elmer Sperry. The design of the device itself was carefully guarded.

The fascination it held for all air forces (and, to be sure, for all spies) accrued from the fact that it promised to be the definitive solution to the basic problem of air power. There was much loose talk about "pinpoint" and "pickle barrel" bombing, and the layman was left with the impression that such accuracy was actually possible. But the pin in "pinpoint" was very big and the "pickle barrel" was far too broad. Those who were aware of this sought to find means "to control a bomb in flight and steer it to its target."

The idea of the bombsight was not new. Several of America's most imaginative inventors—Charles F. Kettering, John Hays Hammond, Jr., and Sperry among them—had solved the fundamental principles of the problem, and their solutions were available to anyone at the U.S. Patent Office. Yet newspapers referred to it as "this country's most jealously guarded air defense weapon" and credited it with "giving the United States a headstart in precision bombing."

As most of the publicity centered on the *Norden* bombsight, the secret services naturally had their eyes on it, even as early as 1921, when Carl Norden began experimenting with his first crude model.

38

By 1928 his Mark II series held such promise that the Navy placed an order for forty of them. The Navy also assigned Captain Frederick I. Entwistle to work with Norden on the sight's refinement.

In 1931 the first patents were secretly granted in the name of Norden and Entwistle (a public patent was granted only in 1947). Shortly afterward, the Japanese sought to buy the plans, but Mr. Norden turned them down.[1]

The United States Navy, instrumental in its development, and the Army Air Corps, which would benefit most from it, made a fetish of the secret instrument. It was so closely guarded that it took the British, hard-pressed as they were, until 1940 to coax it from President Roosevelt.

The Germans already had it in 1937, and this is the first full revelation of how they got it.

In 1936 rumors were abroad that Norden had a near-perfect bombsight in the assembly stage. According to reports the new device enabled the bombardier at a given speed to make only two basic calculations, direction and altitude, and then, at the right moment the sight automatically released the bomb load over the target.

Thanks to its splendid crew in the United States specializing in aviation secrets, the Abwehr had become a shortcut to the solution of many problems plaguing the Luftwaffe's ordnance department. Whenever it hit a snag in its own researches, an order was placed for the elusive article with Major Hans Jochin Groskopf, chief of the technical branch of I/Luft, the Abwehr's air intelligence section. Dr. Pheiffer, by now a lieutenant commander, forwarded it to Griebl on the next westbound ship. Whether it was the design of an improved propeller cuff needed to increase the airfoil area or an aneroid altimeter (to cite only two of the items actually ordered) the agents in the United States supplied practically everything the Luftwaffe asked for.

In June 1937, and again in August, General Ernst Udet, chief of Air Ordnance, personally asked Canaris whether he could get the design of the Norden and Sperry bombsights. Groskopf sent a query to New York, but nobody in the Griebl ring had access to either. In early September, a routine shipment of documents arrived at the Abwehr branch in Hamburg from a new contact in Brooklyn who had previously supplied a few stray items. One set of papers baffled Udet's aides. It consisted of two sheets of drawings showing a number of squares and circles connected by dotted lines, but without an explanation they made no sense. A brief note accompanying the sketches alerted Groskopf. The man in Brooklyn advised the Abwehr that the person with whom the drawings had originated worked at the Norden plant on Lafayette Street in New York and was eager to establish contact provided a special envoy would be sent to New York to meet him.²

Up to this time, espionage in the United States was the nearly exclusive domain of Dr. Pheiffer at the Bremen outpost, a *Nebenstelle* or "Nest," the subbranch of the Hamburg office. The designation Ast X was attached to the Tenth Military District, its headquarters on Sophien Terrace, occupying a row of sparsely furnished rooms in a huge three-story graystone building near the Inner Alster on a pleasant residential street in Hamburg.

Managed by an acting chief, Captain Joachim Burghardt of the Navy, (whose guiding principle was to let sleeping dogs lie) Ast X had none of the bustle of its subbranch. Burghardt had neither the compulsive zeal and energy of Pheiffer, nor his subordinate's ambition to operate so far out in the field. Under his management, the branch, whose territory included Britain and the whole of North America, had only a "sleeper" in the United States, an engineer named Everett Minster Roeder, who had volunteered his services to Burghardt some time before.

Although Roeder was employed at the strategic Sperry plant on Long Island and with access to critical information, Burghardt preferred to "keep him on ice"—to save him for later employment rather than risk him on premature operations. Aside from Roeder, Ast X had only a couple of free-lancing stringers in America, one of whom had tipped them off to the employee at the Norden plant.

A few months before conditions at the somnolent Hamburg branch had undergone a change for the better with the arrival of a new man to organize an air intelligence section at Ast X. He was a Rhinelander named Nikolaus Ritter, a 40-year-old ex-officer, son of a college president, and a textile manufacturer in New York. Ritter had been pulled indiscriminately from the familiar army duffel bag for his new job. He had no previous experience either as an aviator or as an intelligence specialist. His qualifications were rather peripheral. As he had lived and worked in the United States for over ten years, he spoke English fluently and had a number of well-placed friends in America. And he needed a job—his textile business had collapsed during the 1937 recession.

Ritter had been approached by Lieutenant General Friedrich von Boetticher, the German Military Attaché in Washington, with the suggestion that he return to Germany and rejoin the army. When he heeded the invitation, for lack of anything better to do, nobody was more surprised than Ritter to be assigned to the Abwehr and made chief of the air intelligence section in Hamburg.

His astonishment was compounded when, in July 1937, he received a signal from Berlin signed by Canaris himself. It ordered him to extend "intelligence work . . . immediately to cover the air force and aviation industry of the United States."

"I leaned back in my chair and stared for a long time at those cold lines," Ritter told me after the war, when he revealed his story to me. "Their implications took my breath. All I could think or feel was that they meant for me a new and grave responsibility. For the moment I forgot my surroundings and my new work. My life in the United States, with all its ups and downs, passed in review before my eyes. It was difficult to reconcile myself to the idea of working against the country which I loved best next to my own native land."

Once he became accustomed to the idea of spying on what, until a few months before, had been his adopted country (he took out his citizenship papers and traveled to Germany on a re-entry permit), Ritter made a bold decision. He would go himself to organize the collection of intelligence in the United States.

Ritter went to Berlin to secure the big brass' approval for his trip to America only to find that Canaris was vehemently opposed to it. "My message to you," he told Ritter, "to expand our coverage of the United States stemmed from a request of the Luftwaffe to procure for them the design of the Norden bombsight. This is a very important assignment and the mission is fraught with considerable risk. We should not unnecessarily jeopardize it by exposing you in the process and show our hand at its barest."

"Herr Admiral," Ritter said, "I realize that this is a most delicate mission. This is exactly why I beg to propose that I go on it myself. I know the country. I speak 'American' English. I have not been working at intelligence long enough for the Americans to be aware of it. None of the agents I work with know my real name nor where my office is located. The chance that I might be exposed cannot be ruled out, I admit. But I know how to conduct myself and am confident that I would carry off the mission without a mishap."

Canaris finally gave his consent.

"You obviously have the best credentials for the job," he said to Ritter. "All I can tell you in parting is this—stay clear of all *official* Germans, especially your friend, the Military Attaché. General von Boetticher has no understanding of our work. He thinks he could do it better than we can. Under no circumstances go near him, or any other German official stationed over there."

Ritter planned to make the trip as casually as possible, using as cover his civilian profession of textile manufacturer. He arranged for bona fide business assignments in the States from firms in Hamburg. This would also be his cover for the substantial sum of money he would need. He had it transferred in the form of a letter of credit on which he could draw openly at a branch of the National City Bank at 93rd Street in New York.

He still had his re-entry permit, but thought it advisable to make the trip on his German passport under his real name. He would travel lightly, carrying all he needed in two battered old leather bags, taking along a briefcase (without which a German businessman would never appear genuine). He concocted no special story for himself and the only unusual item he took was an umbrella in a thin wooden sheath that made it look like a cane. It was his good luck charm, but he thought it might be put to some other uses as well.

Ritter was wise to go as himself for his appearance and surface personality was his best disguise, he was such an innocuous-looking person, a middle-class businessman. He wore a gray suit and a light blue shirt, and walked with officious, rapid steps as if he had something specific and urgent on his mind even when he was just killing time by taking in the sights. Beneath this ordinary exterior, which fitted him like a uniform, he was an intelligent, shrewd, and discriminating man, with a drive to do things well. He was respected for his brains and industry, and his air of purpose in all his pursuits. If one was looking for the prototype of the spymaster it was futile to look at Ritter. But he was the spymaster as spymasters ought to be.

At six o'clock in the morning of October 11 his driver picked him up at his house and drove him to Bremerhaven where he boarded the *Bremen* for the trip to America. Captain Burghardt bid him bon voyage. Six days later Ritter was in New York Harbor.

His visit was a combination sentimental journey and business trip. He was as eager as any native to have a glimpse of the Statue of Liberty and enjoyed the freely flowing American idiom with which the Immigration and Customs officials, the porters and the cabbies greeted him. He felt at home, easing himself into the familiar environment, bantering with waiters, exchanging quips with bootblacks, even as he was getting ready to penetrate this country's secret of secrets as best he could.

How does a spymaster go about his business? Ritter had ample time during the crossing to plot his sojourn, with a scheme ready for his schedules and procedures. Much was not essentially different from a traveling salesman's tour of his territory.

Ritter began with two close shaves even before he set foot on American soil. Aboard the *Bremen* he bumped into a reporter of the *Staatszeitung*, a widely read German-language daily in New York, and his old acquaintance insisted on celebrating the unexpected reunion somewhat too loudly. "Man, Ritter!" he exclaimed, "What in the name of God are you doing here?" Ritter expected that he might meet old friends accidentally, but this was too much especially since he suspected the reporter had an inkling of his true vocation. "I thought," the man said at the top of his voice, "you were in the Luftwaffe."

"Only in the Reserve," Ritter said just as loudly, "or else I wouldn't be here, would I?" They laughed—the reporter, Ritter felt, somewhat knowingly.

The Customs inspector showed only perfunctory interest in his battered suitcases but examined the contents of his briefcase sheet by sheet, and was intrigued by his cane umbrella. He asked Ritter to demonstrate how it worked. "A pretty slick gadget for a spy," the inspector said, and Ritter laughed with the man, who obviously enjoyed his little joke.

Ritter checked into the Taft Hotel north of Times Square, and spent the next four days running down his business contacts.[3] He conducted himself ostentatiously to establish his identity, asking the hotel desk clerk to receive his messages from various firms, giving addresses in a loud voice to cab drivers for the doorman to hear, sending out his shirts to be washed and pressed to get the Taft's laundry mark on them.[4]

Ritter gradually established his second identity. From a phone booth he called the Irving Arms, a small hotel on Riverside Drive, and made a reservation in the name of "Alfred Landing." He wrote a letter on the Taft's stationery and a postcard, both addressed to Landing, mailed the letter to General Delivery at the main post office and the postcard to the Irving Arms, to have them in his pocket with Landing's name in case he needed identification.

He bought a secondhand typewriter for twenty dollars in a Bowery pawnshop, then went uptown and cashed his letter of credit at the National City Bank, identifying himself with his genuine passport. He rented a safe deposit box for all of his papers including his passport. He would have no use for it during the next few weeks. When he left the bank, Nikolaus Ritter, the textile manufacturer, ceased to exist. He was now Captain Ritter, alias Landing, the German spy, ready to collect what he had come for.

It was Friday, October 19, shortly after two o'clock in the afternoon. He still had a little time before his first appointment in his new business, so he sauntered over to Fifth Avenue to spend a couple of hours at the Metropolitan Museum of Art, as any tourist would. Shortly before five he flagged a cab and told the driver: "248 Monitor Street in Brooklyn. Do you know how to get there?"

"We'll find it, Mac."

When they arrived in front of the drab tenement, Ritter asked the cabbie to wait while he checked the address. Then he returned to the street, paid off the taxi, went back into the vestibule, and waited for the cab to disappear. He came out again, certain now that he was not being followed, and walked quickly up the street to No. 262 and rang the bell under a card that identified the tenant as Heinrich Sohn. Upstairs, a squat middle-aged man in his shirtsleeves waited for him at the open door.

"Yes?" the man asked.

"Herr Sohn?"

"I am Sohn," the man said.

"Well, pleased to meet you, *Pops*. I bring greetings from *Roland*."

"Roland" was Ritter's pre-arranged cover-name for this *Treff*, and Sohn signed his mail to Hamburg with "Pops."

"So you have come at last," he said. "We already thought you'd never show up because maybe we're not good enough for you gentlemen."

He led Ritter down a long corridor to an overstuffed den in the back, and went for a pot of coffee and a couple of cups. Then they sat down to talk business.

"I've received your shipments, Pops," Ritter said, "and I'm here to thank you for the excellent material." Sohn did not really know what those "shipments" were all about. He was merely one of the letter-boxes that Ritter had arranged in New York, to forward the mail of producing spies. He was pleased that Ritter was pleased. In this case he suspected that he had become privy to something big. Those sketches had come from a man in Glendale in Queens—identified only as "Paul"—who seemed to be eager to get them into Ritter's hands.

Ritter was not interested in Sohn. He had come to see Paul. Could Pops set up a date with him?

"Of course," the little man said. "But Paul can make it only on Sundays. If you tell me what time you can be back, I'll see to it that he'll be here to meet you."

At 3:00 P.M. on Ritter's second Sunday in the States, Paul was waiting for him when he arrived in the apartment on Monitor Street. He was, as Ritter remembers from his first impression, "a slight man in his mid-thirties, with dark blond hair and an open face that made one like and trust him at first blush."

"Paul" was Hermann Lang, a machinist and draftsman, a naturalized American who had taken the oath of allegiance to the United States during his citizenship ceremony without concern. An unsophisticated working man who had come to his moment of truth, he was elbowing his way into the most complex of games like a tinhorn who begins his gambling career by breaking the bank in Monte Carlo. He was the commonest of common men, competent at his job but otherwise almost inert in his thoughts and feelings, a walking cipher, a nonentity. He lived the regimented life of the typical lower middle-class, with a wife and daughter on Sixty-fourth Place in Glendale. Lang was a good husband, a doting father, and a fair provider. His wife and daughter would have been mortified had they known what he was up to. While they were asleep, he would sneak from his warm marital bed to the table in the cold kitchen to perform the manual labor of his spy job.

How does such a man become a spy? And why? Lang had a simple answer. He was not a Nazi, he was hazy about Hitler, and he had nothing against America. But he considered himself "a good German." Yet it was not his ardent patriotism that propelled him into espionage. It was the opportunity that had come his way when he suddenly found himself alone with those super-secret drawings of the instrument that publicity had made into a sacred cow.

"I'm an assembly inspector at the Norden plant, Herr Landing," Lang told Ritter. "The little sketches Herr Sohn here sent you were meant merely as samples. They didn't convey even an idea of the whole device. Today I have a larger sample with me."

"Is it really the Norden bombsight?" Ritter asked, barely able to conceal his excitement.

"Only a section of it," Lang said. "I don't have the prints of the whole sight, and I don't think I'll ever be able to get them for you. Some section prints I cannot keep, and I don't have anything to do with some other parts. The Americans are so secretive about this device that they have it assembled at different plants, like the Mergenthaler Linotype Company on Ryerson Street in Brooklyn. But I have no doubt that your engineers will be able to reconstruct the missing sections from the prints I'm able to give you."

How had he come across it? It was quite simple. Because of the secrecy in which the device was wrapped, separate teams handled different parts of the assembly, working from blueprints which Lang, as assembly inspector, had in his care. Each morning when he received them from the plant manager, he handed out the various drawings to the different teams. He collected them in the evening and if the teams finished their tasks the same day, the prints would no longer be needed, and he had to return them to the manager. Often the detailed work continued for several days, and then Lang could keep the prints in his custody as long as the work on one or another section went on.

Whenever he had prints overnight he took them home and copied them on tracing paper. It was such a section drawing he had sent to Germany via Pops, as an opener. Now he gave Ritter the drawing of another section of the bombsight, and promised to hand over a third next Sunday when they agreed to meet again.

This presented a problem. The drawing was too big for Ritter to carry back to Germany in his own briefcase. But he had someone to take it home for him. He had been told in Bremen that one of the First Class ship stewards was the Abwehr's chief courier on the trans-atlantic route, a regular agent referred to as "F.2341" by his registry number. He was Herbert Jaenichen, a blond, blue-eyed, fair-skinned, rotund Berliner, who had taken over when the indomitable Karl Eitel was "blown" in the wake of Lonkowski's downfall.

Ritter had identified himself to Jaenichen during the voyage, and the steward agreed to be of service if needed. The *Bremen* was due next Tuesday, and a meeting scheduled with Jaenichen for that afternoon, October 30, at the drugstore in the *Times* Building.

Ritter went to the *Treff* with Lang's drawing wrapped in his cane-umbrella and asked Jaenichen to smuggle it into Germany. The steward objected. He had left the boat without an umbrella. He could not very well return carrying one without producing it for the customs guard. Jaenichen proposed that they meet again. He would come to the *Treff* with an umbrella of his own that he would check out on his departure for shore leave and therefore would not have to check in on his return.

The next day Jaenichen showed up in Ritter's room at the Irving Arms leaning heavily on a battered old umbrella. "I had to have a reason for carrying this damned thing on such a beautiful sunny day," he explained, "so I told them that I had sprained my ankle and had only this umbrella to help me in walking."

It was in this fashion, then, that the drawing of a second section of the Norden bombsight limped out of this country aboard the *Bremen* on October 31, 1937.

Ritter had a week to kill before he would see Lang again, and he was putting it to excellent use. He had a number of superb prospects on his "sleeper list"—the best agent material the Abwehr had on tap—and was determined to develop them one by one into producing spies. On October 29, the Monday morning after his profitable *Treff* with Lang, he called Trafalgar 4-9867, the number he had memorized where he could contact Frederick Joubert Duquesne, the top man on his list.

He had known Duquesne during his years in the States when the distinguished-looking man in his sedate fifties regaled him with stories of his fantastic exploits in World War I, performing, as he put it, "invaluable services for Germany." Duquesne was a professional spy, motivated by what he called his "insatiable hatred of the British." A native of Cape Colony, South Africa, he allegedly saw his mother tortured and killed in the Boer War, and had sworn to avenge "the dastardly deed of the English *soldateska*." He moved to England when the First World War broke out, volunteered his services to Germany as a secret agent, and embarked on his career in espionage. Some of his exploits—such as his claim that he had guided the U-boat to the cruiser that was taking Lord Kitchener to Russia in 1917 and was thus responsible for Kitchener's death in the sinking—were pure imagination. But he had done some genuine spying for the Germans both in England and the United States, where he played a part in sabotaging ships and installations the British used in 1916–17.

After the war he took out American citizenship and established himself as a writer and lecturer with good connections. Ritter thought that the old pro might be interested in an invitation to return to his game. He was not disappointed. They met in an apartment at 24 West 78th Street in Manhattan.

A deal was made, and Duquesne immediately went to work for the Abwehr.

Ritter then met Captain Burghardt's "sleeper," Everett Minster Roeder, in Merrick on Long Island where the man had his staid home on Smith Street. The 44-year-old engineer turned out to be almost as great a catch as Lang. He was employed in the Sperry plant on Flatbush Avenue Extension in Brooklyn, and had access to the Sperry bombsight and the firm's famed gyroscope.

During this trip Ritter also enlisted Lilly Barbara Carola Stein, a German-born model living in style on the fashionable East Side of Manhattan. She was popular with the jet set of those days and had many influential gentlemen friends in New York and Washington. As his special mail drop, Ritter set up another young lady who was a legal secretary for the attorneys of the German Consulate in New York. Her apartment on West 81st Street became for a time the main transfer station for some of the material Duquesne, Roeder, and the beautiful Lilly collected for the Abwehr.

As Ritter's chief pipeline to Washington insiders (including a strategically placed American Foreign Service officer), and to the rumormongers of New York's café society, Lilly produced reams of useful intelligence.

Admiral Canaris later recorded that within a year Roeder procured "the blueprints of the complete radio instrumentation of the new Glen Martin bomber" and, among other devices made at Sperry's, "classified drawings of range finders, blind-flying instruments, a bank-and-turn indicator, and a navigator compass."

Before long, Ritter's third and most important member of the new ring, Duquesne, would send to Germany "the design of a classified storage battery (separator), a propeller-driven mechanism, and the drawings of numerous other secret devices." The old pro found the going easy.

Ritter returned to Monitor Street for his second *Treff* with Hermann Lang and on Sunday, November 3, received the drawing of another section of the Norden bombsight's secret design. He was so overwhelmed by what Lang had turned over that he gave the man fifteen-hundred dollars in crisp new bills, the highest remuneration ever paid by the Abwehr in a lump sum to any of its agents in America.

On November 11 Ritter sailed for Hamburg, satisfied that his trip had been phenomenally successful. If he had expected to be received like a conquering hero, he was sorely disappointed. The drawings he had received from Lang failed to give General Udet's engineers a complete enough design of the whole device. When they could not make head or tail of them, Luftwaffe experts voiced doubt that they were the drawings of a bombsight at all.

Ritter had to enlist experts to convince Udet and his associates that he had essential sections of the *Nordensches Zielgeraet* (as the Germans called the bombsight) down on those papers. Only when two outstanding scientists, Professor Eisenlohr of Frankfurt and Professor Fuchs of Goettingen, attested that the drawings indeed showed important parts of the bombsight did Udet agree to have a model built from the drawings. Still Ritter could not celebrate his triumph. The first model did not work, simply because Udet's designers could not "think up" the missing parts.

As a last resort Ritter contacted Lang in the States and asked him to come to Germany to aid in the laborious assembly of a finished product. As an inducement he promised to deposit ten-thousand marks to Lang's account in a German bank and pay all expenses of the journey. Lang accepted the invitation. Pretending that he was visiting relatives, he went to Germany in the spring of 1938 to collaborate in the final assembly of a reasonable facsimile of the American bombsight.

By then, however, he was no longer needed, as he himself conceded in some consternation upon his arrival in Berlin. Ritter was no longer around. He had to give up his agent "Paul" to Major Groskopf of I/Luft. It was Groskopf who now welcomed Lang to Berlin in style and took him to a suite reserved for him at the elegant Esplanade Hotel.

When entering the suite, Lang saw on the sitting-room table a completely assembled bombsight with all the features of the Norden instrument. "My God," he exclaimed. "You already had it! All my work was unnecessary, then!"

Groskopf reassured him that it was not. "That model," he said with a genial smile, "would not be on that table without your valuable contribution, Herr Lang." From the blueprints Lang had stolen, Groskopf explained, Professor Fuchs had developed a bombsight called *Adler-Geraet*, supposedly an improved version of the Norden. It was a model of Fuchs's reconstruction of the American bombsight that Groskopf had set up in Lang's hotel room as a welcoming gift.

Lang spent a wonderful week in Berlin, fêted by Groskopf and his associates in the Berlin Abwehr, and was even received by Hermann Goering to accept the thanks of the Luftwaffe from its highest chief. Ritter was conspicuous by his absence at the festivities to which he had paved the way. Aside from a brief letter of commendation by Canaris he went unrewarded for his efforts, the astounding end product of which had become a feather in Major Groskopf's cap.

The odyssey of the Norden device that began in 1937 in Brooklyn ended in the spring of 1945 in an obscure village in Austria. A unit of General George S. Patton, Jr.'s rampaging Third Army stumbled upon a factory the Germans tried to hide in the Tyrolean Alps, and captured its super-secret product, called *Luftwaffenzielgeraet EZ 42*.

It was thought to be one of those ingenious electronic gadgets in whose invention the Germans supposedly excelled and its captors rushed it in triumph to the technical intelligence team that followed the Third Army.

It turned out to be the Norden bombsight.

NOTES

1 Norden had arranged with the Navy to turn over to the American government all plans for the bombsight and his other military inventions, including a catapult and arresting gear for launching and landing aircraft on carriers.

2 Actually the sketches showed only a small section of the Norden bombsight, one of its rotors and stabilization screw.

3 With astounding disregard for elementary security, secret services have favorite hotels in alien cities to which they direct their espionage executives. The Taft was "the Abwehr hotel" in New York; it also sheltered other prominent members of the fraternity, including Major Ulrich von der Osten, who arrived in the United States in 1941 on a mission similar to Ritter's. The Soviet secret service sent its agents to the Hotel Manhattan, also in the Times Square area. Richard Sorge stayed there when in New York en route to a *Treff* with his employers in Moscow.

4 When he was unpacking in New York, Ritter discovered to his horror that he had neglected to remove evidence that could have given away his real purpose. One of his shirts had the label *Luftwaffe Post Exchange* on the inside of the collar. He quickly cut it out with a razor blade and burned it.

Chapter 5

Project 14—How to Cripple the Panama Canal

*P*ROMISING as Major Ritter's new network was, its agents were only getting set for the great accomplishments of their later operations. Now, in late 1937 and early 1938, a tight little ring stationed far to the south was of more immediate importance. Led by trained professionals, it worked under the personal direction of Commander Hermann Menzel, head of the naval intelligence division at Abwehr headquarters in Berlin.

It had a top-priority mission, called "Project 14," code name for the secret reconnaissance of the Panama Canal.

During the Thirties the canal drew magnetic interest. All antagonistic secret services regarded it as the critical area of our national security—our only truly sensitive strategic spot, except for Pearl Harbor. The area swarmed with Japanese and Italian spies, and had its quota of Soviet agents as well.

In 1935 when Commander Menzel visited Panama he appointed Kurt Lindberg, manager of the Hamburg-America Line's local agency and German consul in Colon, as the Abwehr's resident director. In March 1938, the importance of the outpost caused Admiral Canaris to send one of his spy kits in the care of the captain of the ship *Schwaben*, especially rerouted to make the delivery.

At a time when overseas espionage was still haphazard, the Abwehr went out of its way to assure comprehensive coverage of the canal. The effort was inspired by a special request from Naval Operations, later seconded by the Luftwaffe General Staff, to obtain a complete topographical and technical report of the canal, the ships moving through it, and surveillance of the American garrison and military installations there.

In answer to this assignment a veteran Abwehr operative named

51

Wolfgang Blaum was sent to Panama to manage the agents. A civilian specialist at this time, he was bright and imaginative, skilled in the technical aspects of the game and an inspiring leader of men. Drawing on the German colony in the area, he assured coverage by assembling two separate rings. One was a widely spread net of occasional informants planted at every key spot. The other was a hard core of regular V-men consisting of eleven operatives.

This inner group was led by two professional spies—Hans Heinrich Schackow, an honor graduate of the Abwehr school in Hamburg with a cover job at the Hapag-Lloyd Steamship Company in Balboa, and 29-year-old Ernst Robert Kuhrig, another Hamburg alumnus who masked his espionage activities by working as a typewriter repairman.

The Schackow ring was a typical team under a resident director and managed by a couple of trained pros. It had in its membership an inevitable local Nazi Party functionary named Gisbert Gross, and its Mata Hari, the 19-year-old secretary of the German consul at Colon, Ingeborg Waltraut Gutmann. She handled the clerical chores of the ring, doubling occasionally as a collector of information from transient ship officers who were attracted to the vivacious, pretty young woman.

Seven other members of the ring were simple working men of modest circumstances—machinists, mechanics, a mason, a locksmith, a crane operator, and a stevedore. They were useful and important because they held jobs connected with the canal's maintenance and operations. All were long-time residents of the area, respected at their places of work, trusted by their superiors, and well-liked in their neighborhoods. They knew their way in the labyrinth of the Canal Zone, had a wide circle of friends and, thanks to their sensitive jobs, free access to even the most closely guarded installations.

The case of Ernst Kuhrig in particular showed how boldly the German spies operated in the area, and demonstrated graphically how lax security was at the Canal Zone's restricted military reservations. Originally an apprentice seaman, he first arrived in Panama in 1931, when he was only nineteen. He had deserted ship and stayed in Panama illegally, shielded by his Chinese landlord until 1936, when he was arrested, sent to jail for twenty-six days, and deported.

A year after his ouster, Kuhrig was back in Panama. As a typewriter repairman, he gained access to Fort Randolph (U.S.) where he was well known to the sentries passing him in and out without challenge. He took Schackow and Gross, with Miss Gutmann as a decoy, on visits to the Fort, telling the sentries that he was planning to entertain them at the restaurant of the Post Exchange and swearing, as the formality required, that they had no cameras with them. Instead of going to the restaurant, they would walk casually like tourists on a sightseeing trip to gun emplacements on Caleta Point and the other restricted installations at Fort Randolph, photographing them with the Leica Kuhrig hid in his repair kit, the familiar trademark by which he was known to the guards.

From Schackow and his V-men flowed a steady stream of intelligence to Blaum who used the facilities of the German Legation in Panama to transmit their reports to the Abwehr. A few random samples illustrate how detailed and timely the coverage was:

"Owing to shortages of construction materials, the building of a third lock near Pedro Miguel had to be discontinued in favor of other defense installations. Similar cutbacks affect the development of additional locks at Miraflores and Gatun."

"A new trans-isthmian highway is to be built between Colon and Panama City. Two lanes between Panama City and Medden Dam have already been completed. A one-lane road is under construction between the Dam and France Field."

"The electric power station at Gatun Dam is located west of the lock, covered with straw for camouflage purposes. Fort Randolph, Fort Sherman, Fort Kobbe and Fort Amador are equipped with long-barreled coast artillery pieces up to 14-inch caliber."

"The garrisons at Fort Davis and Fort Clayton consist mostly of infantry units equipped with light weapons. The great number of mules at these forts indicates that the troops are slated for duty in the jungle."

"The United States Navy's submarine base at Coco Solo was recently reinforced through the addition of a flotilla of motor torpedo boats."

Their remarkable collective reports, although halted in 1941, survived in one of the captured Abwehr archives. There I found the whole "Project No. 14" in dossiers bulging with detailed maps of the Canal, including close-ups of the dams at Lake Gatun and Pedro Miguel that supplied the water for all the locks, power stations, and military installations, leaving little if anything to the imagination.

Inspired by the remarkable data that Canaris's spies had managed to produce from this Achilles heel of American defenses, Marshal Goering once indulged in a bit of daydreaming about the long-range opportunities of his Luftwaffe. In April 1939 he declared publicly that the Panama Canal was not as invulnerable as the Americans thought. "Two of my bombs," he said, "dropped on the Culbra Cut would render the entire waterway unusable in ten minutes."

Goering presumably meant the Culebra Pass in the Sierra de Panama, a mountain bordering on the Canal, a spot Wolfgang Blaum, chief of spies in the Canal Zone, pointed out as one of the strategic region's most critically vulnerable points. When Goering made his statement in 1939, he still hoped that his Luftwaffe might develop long-range bombers of the Condor-type with which he could stage raids against key targets in the Western Hemisphere. Manufactured by Focke-Wulf (which called it FW 200), it was a four-engine, low-wing monoplane, with a cockpit crew of three. Cruising at about 200 mph, its service ceiling was approximately 20,000 feet. Originally intended as a transport to carry twenty-six passengers, the dreamers of the Luftwaffe hoped that it could be converted into a long-range reconnaissance plane to aid the U-boats in the Atlantic and could also be used as a bomber in nuisance raids against the United States.

The spies did an admirable job.

Goering, nevertheless, found no chance to drop those two bombs.

Chapter 6

Operation Crown: The First Debacle

BY 1938, the Germans had dozens of spies in the United States—more, in fact, than in any other country except Poland and France. Neither Hitler nor the Wehrmacht High Command had any but secondary interest in this country. Yet their spies rubbed shoulders in the cheap eateries of the Times Square area, close to the Hudson River piers through which the secret traffic passed. They tripped over one another in the cafés and beerhalls of East 86th Street, the mainstream of Germandom in New York. Many paraded their supposedly secret errands with carefree indiscretion.

One night at Maxl's, the most popular of the Yorkville rathskellers, a man who called himself Karl Wiegand (in reality, the steward Theodor Schuetz) got tipsy. When he reached into his pocket for money to pay the check he pulled two crisp new one-thousand dollar bills from his wallet, then handed them around the table for his companions to admire.

On another occasion at the Café Hindenburg, a man known as "Herr Schmidt" (actually Karl Schlueter) dropped a pistol out of his pocket while putting on his coat. His companions pretended not to notice as the agent picked it up with a grin, and showed the gun to his friends.

If any innocent bystanders witnessed the scene it seemed to pass unnoticed. A gun in the crowded café would have been considered nothing more than a trick-toy displayed for a prank.

The night of St. Sylvester that ushered in the year 1938 was wild with celebrations in Yorkville, paper streamers and confetti flowing, toy horns blowing, rattlers going full blast, in an admixture of German *Kitsch* and American corn. Every café, beerhall and rathskeller on 86th Street was crowded and each had its quota of German spies in attendance, conspicuous as usual by being the drunkest and loudest, and the biggest spenders.

Dr. Griebl was at the Café Hindenburg, in the company of a good-looking statuesque brunette who had been his traveling companion on his triumphal journey to Germany in 1936. At Maxl's, Karl Schlueter had a tableful of guests, among them two young ladies he was romancing simultaneously—his regular girl friend, the frizzy-haired redhead named Johanna Hofmann, the hairdresser on the *Europa,* and a tall blonde in her early twenties, the only one at the table who spoke English without an accent. She was an American girl from Queens. Schlueter had befriended her a few months before on the *Europa,* when she was sailing to Germany for a course at the University of Berlin after her graduation from Hunter College.

There was another guest at the table, a funereal-looking man in his thirties with deep-set sad eyes and black hair, which he wore brushed back from his high forehead. He seemed to take the revelry in his stride, courting the blonde in a low, sepulchral voice. His bemused detachment almost spoiled the fun.

Schlueter was toasting in the New Year with bottle after bottle of Mosel *Bluemchen.* It promised to be a very good year, thanks especially to the man at his table whom he was addressing as "Theo" and was slapping on the back from time to time.

Theo was the star runner in his stable, who had volunteered his services nearly two years before in the hoary manner in which espionage thrillers describe the first contact of a would-be agent with a secret service. While browsing in the New York Public Library through books on espionage, the man had come upon one by Colonel Walter Nicolai, chief of German Military Intelligence in World War I. It gave him the idea of making his fortune by spying for the Germans.

In early January 1936, he wrote to Nicolai in care of the *Voelkischer Beobachter,* the Nazis' big daily newspaper in Berlin, describing himself as "a high official in the United States Army" and asking the old-timer to forward the letter to "the proper authorities." If they were interested in his services, he wrote, they should insert an advertisement in the "Public Notices" column of *The New York Times,* to read: "Theodor Koerner—Letter received, please send reply and address to Sanders, Hamburg 1, Postbox 629, Germany."

This was an old-fashioned method of correspondence, long discredited in real-life espionage, for an ad like this would be certain to alert the counter-spies. But U.S. authorities seemed so complacent that the Germans had no qualms about going along with the suggestion, in a procedure evenly mixed with horseplay and bureaucracy.

Nicolai forwarded the letter to Colonel Piekenbrock in Berlin who sent it to the Hamburg branch for action. There the case was assigned to Captain Ernst Mueller, former Hapag skipper; Mueller, in turn, instructed the courier officer on the *SS Hamburg* which was about to sail for New York, to insert the ad in *The Times*. Mueller gave him a ten-dollar bill to pay for it, together with a duly executed permit from the Reichsbank that he was authorized to take the cash through Germany's strict currency control.

In New York the officer passed his errand on to Captain Emil Maurer, assistant superintendent of the Hapag-Lloyd agency, and Maurer sent the ad to *The Times* with a covering letter, enclosing the ten-dollar bill.

The procedure interested Charles W. Hoyt, an investigator of *The Times*. He found it strange that Maurer sent cash instead of charging the ad to the Hapag-Lloyd account. And why should a reputable firm like Hapag have to use *The Times* instead of the regular mail for getting in touch with "Koerner." His suspicion was fully justified, of course, for "Sanders" was Mueller, now serving as an officer in naval intelligence at Ast X, and the ad was the first move to contact a would-be spy. Hoyt passed the copy when Maurer assured him that it was a bona fide business communication.

All of this took time. It was only on April 6, 1936, that the message appeared in *The Times*. The man calling himself "Theodor Koerner" (after a noted German poet of the nineteenth century) sat down at once, and composed a long letter to "Sanders," describing his qualifications. Although, he wrote, he was holding "an important post in the [United States] Army," he was eager to serve Germany "in any way possible." He had many "excellent connections," and was close to "an officer in the Signal Corps at Mitchell Field" who handled confidential codes.

Money was no object, he told Sanders, but he would need some funds "for expenses, to pay bribes and buy information."

He signed the letter with his real name—Guenther Gustav Rumrich—and gave as a return address the "Denver Chemical Manufacturing Company on Varick Street" in New York.[1]

Sanders then faded out of the picture. Hamburg was not yet ready for operations in the United States, but Bremen was already in business. Captain Burghardt forwarded Rumrich's letter to Commander Pheiffer at the subbranch, and Karl Schlueter was assigned to make the contact in New York to size up the man.

A *Treff* was arranged for 8:00 P.M. on May 3, at the Café Hindenburg, and the scout returned to Bremen with a glowing report, recommending strongly that the Abwehr hire the man.

Rumrich was not the paragon Schlueter depicted to Commander

Pheiffer. At thirty-seven, he was a dissipated bounder, a borderline alcoholic, forever high on marijuana and even harder drugs, a philanderer, a thief, a liar, and a dud at every civilian job he ever had, even as a cafeteria dishwasher. It was only in the United States Army that he had endured for seven years and was finally made sergeant, despite two desertions, the embezzlement of mess funds at Fort Missoula in Montana, and a six-month stretch in the brig. He was again AWOL when he offered his services to the Germans.

It would matter little to describe such milestones in this life of unbroken disasters. If a social psychologist ever wanted to find out why men who never succeed at anything else make out well as spies, Rumrich's experience would supply an illuminating case history. For this notorious quack and bungler made a splendid spy. He worked as one of Commander Pheiffer's best agents in America for twenty months between May 1936 and February 1938, running his own network that went by the cover-name of "Crown." He produced some information on his own initiative, but mostly answered—and usually correctly—Pheiffer's increasingly complex and searching queries about the "strength and disposition of the regular army of the United States stationed on the Eastern Seaboard."

Whether it was the directness of his methods or the laxity of American security that made him so successful, he produced promptly whatever was demanded of him. When Pheiffer asked for information about the rate of venereal diseases in the United States Army, Rumrich procured it straight from the confidential files of Fort Hamilton, one of the army installations guarding the entrance to New York Harbor in the Narrows. On January 11, 1936, he phoned the Fort, telling the corporal who answered the call:

"This is Major Milton of the Medical Corps speaking from the corner of Fourth Avenue and 86th Street in Brooklyn. I'm in New York to deliver a classified lecture on VD in the army, but unfortunately I left my notes in Washington. Would you be so kind to get me the data—you know what I mean—the number of officers and men at Hamilton, how many of them contract venereal diseases, of what kind, and so on."

The corporal referred the request to the clerk who quickly assembled the data and gave it to a private to take it by taxi to "Major Milton" waiting at a street corner in Brooklyn. Rumrich handed the soldier a dollar bill to pay his taxi fare of thirty cents, then told him magnanimously, "Keep the change."

The ease with which Rumrich was collecting such data whetted Commander Pheiffer's appetite. His orders became increasingly ambitious and sophisticated, but nothing fazed "Crown." In November

1937, Bremen asked for cryptographic information, the Army's most closely guarded secret, "the signal code of the United States Army currently used for communications between the fleet and shore batteries."

Rumrich got it for thirty dollars from a soldier he had befriended during his service in the Canal Zone. His old buddy was twenty-eight-year-old Private Erich Glaser, a native of Leipzig then serving with the Eighteenth Reconnaissance Squadron of the Army Air Corps at Mitchell Field. Glaser brought to a *Treff* the book of the Army's confidential "Z-code" which was being used in ship-to-shore communications, and Rumrich copied it for Pheiffer while the band at the Hindenburg played snappy German songs.

During Rumrich's career as a spy he supplied information about the coast artillery regiments stationed in the Canal Zone; data concerning the Atlantic Fleet; a number of confidential army manuals; plans of anti-aircraft guns being installed in the Metropolitan area, and many more "things secret and confidential."

The latest of Dr. Pheiffer's shopping lists was brought by Schlueter on this New Year's eve of 1938, and was slipped to Rumrich—Theo—at the party in the Hindenburg. "Please," it read in the commander's usual courteous style, "obtain copies of construction drawings of aircraft carriers *Yorktown* and *Enterprise*; and information about experiments at the Signal Corps Laboratories in Fort Monmouth, New Jersey, involving the detection of approaching aircraft."

"Incidentally," Schlueter told Rumrich, "we would need a number of American passports for agents we're sending into Russia. Do you think you could get about fifty blanks? Herr Spielman [the cover name Commander Pheiffer was using in this operation] has a special price tag on this item. He's prepared to pay one thousand dollars for the batch."

One thousand dollars! It was the biggest lump sum ever offered him by the Germans. The prospect alone drove away his gloom at the silly party. Schlueter had even more to offer. "Herr Spielman is also interested in the mobilization plans of the army for the Eastern Seaboard. You could get another thousand for them."

Then and there Rumrich made a New Year's resolution. He would get the mobilization plans and obtain the "passport blanks" by any means, fair or foul.

But Rumrich was spying on borrowed time.

On February 27, 1938, a quiet Saturday morning, during his daily briefing on the dispatches that had come in the previous night, Joachim von Ribbentrop was told that Rumrich had been arrested in

New York on charges of espionage. He did not exactly know what to make of the news. This was the beginning of his third week as Foreign Minister, occupying at last the center of German diplomacy after having spent four or five restless years on its outskirts. When his personal press officer showed him the dispatch about Rumrich's arrest, Ribbentrop was already every bit the proper foreign minister. He was outraged, as secretaries of state usually are, when the conduct of foreign relations is suddenly shown up as a dirty business.

Something else had aroused him, too. He was especially irked when he learned that his Foreign Ministry rated rather low in Hitler's estimation. "The Fuehrer," he said, "had various sources of information of his own so far as the United States and England were concerned, which I was not aware of. . . . He also saw them [his informants] without my knowing or hearing about it."

Among these trespassers, he quickly found out, Admiral Canaris was the most prominent.

Here was his opportunity to strike at him. The exposure of the Rumrich spy ring produced what Ribbentrop considered conclusive evidence that the Abwehr was nothing but a cabal of blockheads whose operations in foreign lands muddied international waters and caused Germany irreparable damage.

Thus began a feud that endured to the bitter end. Exactly six years later it resulted in the downfall of Canaris and the eclipse of the Abwehr. Now, in 1938, Ribbentrop was prepared to deliver the first blow by warning Hitler about Canaris's mismanagement. He was rebuffed. Canaris glibly talked himself out of this confrontation by assuring the Fuehrer that the men and women caught in America— the exposure of Rumrich had resulted in a dozen arrests—had no links with the Abwehr. "They were, my Fuehrer," he said, "patriotic Germans and devout National Socialists whose only motivation was to serve you and your new Germany."

Canaris was not satisfied with his own explanation. Returning to his office he called in Colonel Piekenbrock and ordered him to conduct a "merciless investigation" of the "accident."

The probe proved embarrassing for it showed up a number of chinks in the Abwehr's armor. Moreover, it was the first indication that the Germans were no longer alone in the game. Aside from the FBI, British counterintelligence had also returned to the hunt, and this Anglo-American combine of spybusters boded ill for future operations in the United States.

Guenther Rumrich's nemesis was a Scotswoman named Jennie Wallace Jordan, the 51-year-old operator of a beauty parlor on Kinlock Street in Dundee. She would undoubtedly have gone unnoticed in the spy game except for the heavy mail she was receiving. Toward the end of 1937 it aroused the suspicion of the mailman on her route, who reported his misgivings to the authorities in London. The information wound up on the desk of Major W. E. Hinchley Cooke in Room 505 of the War Office in Whitehall, where MI.5, Britain's counterespionage agency, was headquartered.

Major Cooke placed Mrs. Jordan under surveillance, and soon detected that though she herself was British, she was the widow of a German who had died in World War I fighting for the Kaiser. Then it was learned that several times in 1937 she had gone to Germany on trips for which there was no reasonable explanation. Although she said that all her relatives lived in the British Isles, she was receiving letters from the United States, France, Holland, and South America, and posting bulging envelopes to all sorts of faraway places.

Mrs. Jordan's mail was opened, and what Cooke read in her letters convinced him that the trim widow was the mail drop of a broad German espionage network. A number of the letters she received and passed on originated in New York. Signed "Crown," they contained unmistakable evidence that the correspondent was not only a spy, but a superlative operator. He appeared to be doing a land-office business in the United States, heading up a widespread ring whose tentacles reached from Buffalo to Newport News, Virginia.

It was decided in Whitehall to acquaint the Americans with this discovery. Captain Guy Liddell, deputy chief of MI.5 (Britain's least known but most formidable counterespionage agent) was sent to Washington where he presented the incriminating material to Director J. Edgar Hoover of the FBI.

On January 28, 1938, the FBI picked up the chase. But it needed the active cooperation of its quarry to track down Crown and establish that he was, in fact, Guenther Gustav Rumrich.

Ever since Karl Schlueter had baited the hook with the two one-thousand dollar rewards he could get for the mobilization plans of the Eastern Seaboard and "blank passports," Rumrich worked frantically on schemes that would gain him the loot. Recalling the ideas that Rumrich eventually had come up with, Dr. Pheiffer told me after the war: "Unfortunately Schlueter, an otherwise sensible man and reliable agent, had come under the spell of this fantasist. He was so dazzled by the weird schemes and giddy plots produced by the man's feverish imagination that he agreed on his own initiative to undertake certain operations of which we in Germany knew nothing."

In actual fact, Pheiffer had known of at least one of these plots but found it to be so "giddy," that he himself aborted it. It involved the mobilization plans. Rumrich had found out that one of the Army officers who had access to them was Colonel Henry W. T. Elgin, commander of the Sixty-Second Coast Artillery, an anti-aircraft unit at Fort Totten, Long Island. He concocted a bizarre abduction plot to get hold of the plans, by luring Colonel Elgin to a room in the old McAlpin Hotel in midtown New York with forged orders from Major General Malin Craig, the Army's chief of staff, directing the colonel to take to a "staff meeting" in the hotel all the "mobilization and coast defense plans in [his] possession, also maps and charts."

Once in the room, Rumrich schemed, Elgin would be rendered unconscious by a chloroform bomb and then Glaser, who was to rent the room and handle the colonel, would seize his briefcase with the plans and take it to Rumrich waiting in the lobby. Schlueter also was given a part in the melodrama. He was to be on hand with the chloroform, disguised as a window cleaner.

When Rumrich presented the idea to him the courier recoiled. "This is too big and too risky an operation," he protested, but Rumrich reassured his friend with a ghoulish smile:

"Our little coup," he said, "might stir up some dirt. But it is perfectly safe."

"I think," Schlueter said, "we better clear it with Herr Spielman."

He suggested that Rumrich outline the weird plan in a letter to Dr. Pheiffer and send it to Bremen via the mail drop in Dundee. This letter was one of the intercepts signed "Crown" which Major Liddell had taken to Washington. Colonel Elgin was told of the plot and primed to play the dupe's part. Army gumshoes and FBI agents were alerted to spring the trap when Colonel Elgin, summoned by his forged instructions, would show up at the McAlpin. The call never came. When Pheiffer received Crown's letter with the details of the scheme (forwarded by MI.5 after it had been copied), he exclaimed in consternation: "Is this man out of his mind?"

He promptly cabled Schlueter in New York forbidding the inane plot and, in fact, ordered the steward to return to Bremen at once "for urgent consultation." The utter monstrosity of Rumrich's plan set him on his toes. He now sought to curb him altogether, before it would be too late.

It was during Schlueter's absence that Rumrich, crazed by his need of money and the prospect of getting one thousand dollars from "Herr Spielman," decided to carry out his other big scheme that might enable him to obtain the fifty passports. He was under a misapprehension. What Commander Pheiffer wanted were blank *passports*, not passport *blanks*, as Schlueter apparently had conveyed the order to him. Passports are difficult to get. The blanks were merely forms which had to be filled out when applying for passports, available to anyone just by asking for them.

Rumrich did not know the difference. He was determined to get the blanks one way or another. Finally he decided to call for them at the New York branch of the State Department's Passport Division in the Sub-Treasury Building.

This was now February 14, six weeks after Schlueter had asked Rumrich to get them. In the morning, he called his office from a candy store near his home in the Bronx saying he was too sick to go to work. Then he went all the way downtown to the corner of Wall and Pine Streets, with the intention of picking up the blanks in person. In front of the Sub-Treasury Building he got cold feet. Instead of going in, he took the subway to Grand Central Station where he put in a phone call to Ira F. Hoyt, the New York chief of the Passport Division. Identifying himself as "Edward Weston, Under-Secretary of State," he demanded in an imperious voice that Hoyt send thirty-five "passport blanks" to the Hotel Taft where, he said, he would be waiting for them in the lobby.

The call puzzled Hoyt. He did not know any Under-Secretary of State by the name of Weston. Then, too, he understood that the caller had asked for application blanks, the form which may be had by anyone. Why a telephone call for them in such a circumspect manner?

He notified the Alien Squad of the New York Police and alerted T. C. Fitch, a security officer of the State Department. Together they prepared a dummy package for Mr. Edward Weston and had it delivered by messenger, shadowed by Fitch and a couple of city detectives, going along to clear up the mystery.

But Rumrich was nowhere to be found in the hotel. He had become uneasy by Hoyt's voice that "sounded suspicious," and decided that it would be better to send somebody else to pick up the package the messenger was supposed to leave at the desk in the hotel.

Now began a chase that, one would have thought, went out of fashion with the Keystone Kops. Rumrich first phoned the Western Union office in Grand Central Station and ordered the clerk to send a messenger to the Taft for the package. An hour later he called again, this time from the Bronx, to inquire whether they had "a package from the Taft Hotel for Mr. Weston." The answer was no.

He waited until noon the next day, then called Western Union again. This time a girl's voice told him, "Yes, Mr. Weston, we're holding the package for you."

"Fine," Rumrich said. "Send it to your office on Varick Street. I'll call for it in half an hour."

With that he took up a vigil outside the Varick Street office, waiting for a messenger from Grand Central to arrive with a package that looked like the one he was expecting. None came.

Rumrich still refused to give up. At 3:00 P.M. he phoned a nearby tavern on Hudson Street and asked a woman who answered the call to accept a package for Edward Weston. At 4:00 P.M. he phoned Western Union on Varick Street, and was told the package had arrived at last. He ordered the clerk to forward it to the tavern.

Within fifteen minutes, while he was having a beer at the bar, he saw a uniformed messenger come in with the package. He had second thoughts. Instead of claiming the package from the woman who had signed and paid for it, he walked out of the bar to the corner of Houston Street, where he stopped a neighborhood boy bouncing a ball. "Look, sonny," he told him, "there's a package for me over there at the Kings Castle Tavern, but I owe the bartender money. Here's two bucks. Get it for me and keep the change."

He watched the boy come out of the bar with the package, and took it from him. At that instant, two detectives from the Alien Squad closed in and asked him to go with them to Police headquarters on Lafayette Street. They were somewhat uneasy about holding him—after all, what was so wrong about picking up three dozen empty passport application blanks? The detectives asked him only routine questions, and it seemed that Rumrich would be able to lie himself out of his predicament. But then, the detectives called for Fitch who rushed over with L. Clifford Tubbs, another State Department security officer.

They questioned him at the offices of the Passport Division February 16, 17, and 18, putting him up in the Hotel New Yorker the nights of the 16th and 17th. Friday evening, on the 18th, the police escorted him home for a visit with his wife and baby. They did not know how they should treat him. So far they had nothing on him.

It was only on the morning of February 17, that the people who had the keenest interest in Rumrich learned he had been arrested two days before. They found it out from the *Daily News* which carried a garbled item, describing the arrested man who had tried to get passport blanks as an obvious nut. It took two more days to get Rumrich over to the FBI on Foley Square.

On Saturday, February 19, at 3:00 P.M., the case broke wide open. Confronting him with copies of some of the "Crown" letters, Special Agent Leon G. Turrou suddenly yelled at Rumrich, "Stop trying to paint a picture of yourself as a fool. I'll tell you what you are—you're a damned important German spy, *Mr. Crown!*"

When Rumrich heard himself called by his cover-name, he jumped, his eyes widening with shock. "All right, Mr. Turrou," he said, "you win. Let me see my wife so that I can arrange for her to go home to her folks—and I will talk."

Back in Bremen, Pheiffer first heard of Rumrich's downfall on February 27, the morning after the FBI had made public his arrest.

But he did not know what made him fall. Even when I discussed the case with him more than fifteen years later, he thought Rumrich had been tripped up when he tried to kidnap Colonel Elgin. "He hit upon the idiotic idea," Pheiffer told me, "of luring a senior officer of the United States Army to a fictitious meeting to obtain from him the mobilization plans of his unit as well as the layout of his fort. The officer showed up at the rendezvous, but so did the FBI." Up to this point, of course, Pheiffer was wrong. He was right when he added: "When Rumrich was arrested he promptly revealed the names and addresses of all his fellow agents in Karl Schlueter's ring."

Rumrich's arrest it seemed, had enormous ramifications. Wilhelm Lonkowski's existence was also discovered in the process, even if only three years after he had escaped. Two of his major aides, Otto Hermann Voss and Werner Georg Gudenberg, who continued in harness under the supervision of Dr. Ignatz T. Griebl, were exposed, as was Griebl himself. The Abwehr's phenomenal courier system, which Commander Pheiffer had set up in 1935, was badly dented with the exposure of Schlueter and the arrest of Johanna Hofmann, his girl friend, who was carrying the messages in his absence.

Admiral Canaris summoned Dr. Pheiffer to Berlin to account for the mishap, but the commander made light of it. "Actually," he told his chief, "I'm almost relieved that this Rumrich has fallen by the wayside. I always regarded him as nothing but a windbag and never really trusted him."

Canaris was not convinced. For the time being, he left Pheiffer in his job as manager of agents in America at the Bremen subbranch. Then, however, two events persuaded him that the officer—who was now called "the Pied Piper" by his admiring associates—had outlived his usefulness.

In October, the Rumrich case was being thrashed out during a trial in New York, when some of the ramifications of his exposure became known to the Abwehr, showing that Pheiffer had gone stale and negligent at his job, compromising the operations in the United States with his carelessness. Though he had assured Canaris that Rumrich had known him only by his cover-name of N. Spielman and was unfamiliar with his position in the German secret service, it came out that others in his ring knew him as Lieutenant Commander Erich Pheiffer, the general manager of German agents in America. The Grand Jury that indicted the arrested members of the Rumrich and Griebl networks produced enough evidence against Pheiffer to warrant his indictment *in absentia*.

Then, while the Rumrich trial was still in progress, the Abwehr was shaken by what Admiral Canaris preferred to call "another accident." Four members of the phenomenal ring of Wolfgang Blaum—

Schackow, Kuhrig, Gross, and Miss Gutmann—were arrested in the Canal Zone in the act of photographing some gun emplacements at Fort Randolph. Although the rest of the ring managed to escape exposure and continued in harness until December 7, 1941, a deep dent was made in the operation. Blaum himself was exposed and escaped arrest only by leaving Panama posthaste.

Canaris now ordered an immediate shake-up at the top of the two sections which were responsible for the coverage of the United States. Commander Pheiffer was transferred out of the subbranch, henceforth to be given only assignments at which, Canaris said, he would be unlikely to do any more harm.

Erich Pheiffer took the blow hard. Even fifteen years later when I saw him, he refused to agree with Canaris that the demolition of the Rumrich and Griebl rings had damaged the Abwehr in America. In the meantime, Leon Turrou had published a somewhat euphoric book about the case (for which he was promptly dismissed by Director Hoover). But Pheiffer was unimpressed by his revelations.

"Although it was quite a thriller," he told me, "the book merely demonstrated how little the FBI had learned about our operations. As a matter of fact, they succeeded in uncovering only the fringe activities of certain dilettantes among our agents who produced intelligence of little or no value."

Judging by the trial record and especially by Mr. Turrou's "revelations," the FBI gained little real insight into the nerve center. The Abwehr (which Turrou consistently confused with the Gestapo) was presented vaguely as something called *"the Nationale Geheim Abwehr."* It was supposedly headed by "the august Colonel Busch," whoever he was. Admiral Canaris managed to preserve his anonymity.

More important was the inability of the FBI at this stage to penetrate to the hard core of the Abwehr rings in the United States. As Pheiffer later boasted, his "real organization was totally undamaged." And so, for that matter, was Major Ritter's. If anything, the Rumrich debacle merely induced them to tighten their security. They did it with such excellent results that, as we shall see, they continued to operate with impunity for three more years, and in some instances even longer.

For the time being, though, the Abwehr lost interest in the United States. This was a period of *Spannungszeit.* There was so much to do closer to home.

Even as the Rumrich case broke in America, the Abwehr was preoccupied with preparations for Hitler's imminent annexation of Austria next door.

At the same time, it was preparing for the impending crisis over the Sudetenland.

In the West the emphasis was shifting to France, for it had to be anticipated that the French would not stand idly by while Hitler was demolishing Czechoslovakia, their chief ally in Central Europe.

Then, all of a sudden, England appeared on the horizon as a legitimate target at last. By 1936, Hitler had already partially lifted the ban on espionage against the British on their homeground. Then, in 1937, he told Canaris that despite Chamberlain's appeasement policy he was henceforth free to do as he pleased concerning the British Empire.

The blurred picture of England now moved into sharp focus, for the first time on a full scale since the end of World War I.

NOTE

1 Actually Rumrich lived in the Bronx. He was reluctant to give his home address, apprehensive as he was that "the Nazis might be suspicious of a man who lived in a Jewish neighborhood."

Part **II**

BRITAIN IN
FOCUS

Chapter 7

Journey to Brixton Gaol

A few years before World War I, when Sir Augustus Francis Andrew Thorne was a mere lieutenant in the Grenadier Guards, someone in the War Office gave him a bicycle and sent him to East Anglia to "inspect local obstacles that might impede a German expeditionary force." The possibility of a Teutonic invasion was far fetched, of course, and young Thorne's mission was merely a routine exercise. But wherever he rode on the dusty roads of Norfolk and Suffolk, he saw tourists flitting past him in big, powerful automobiles. They were officers of the German General Staff in mufti, engaged in a study that was strikingly similar to Lieutenant Thorne's own.

During those carefree years, the big powers of Europe extended hospitality to officers of each others' General Staffs, bent on collecting information for the contingency plans they were busily concocting for a possible war against the very countries they visited on *pro forma* vacations. These were swift and superficial trips, covered by unwritten gentleman agreements. They produced only covert intelligence from which the tourists had to conjecture whatever secrets their hosts tried to hide.

Did this mean that the Germans, insatiable in their curiosity elsewhere, thought they could get along without spies stationed in Britain? Not quite. The Germans' clandestine interest in England began at the turn of the century, when the Kaiser's aggressive imperialism and ambitious naval policies ushered in an era of active snooping by German agents throughout the world.

Britain's coverage was assigned to the German Admiralty's intelligence department under a captain named Joachim Tapken. From his headquarters in Wilhelmshaven, he manipulated twenty-six resident agents at fixed posts from Scapa Flow to Land's End. This was "the dreary procession of spies" of which Sir Basil Thomson of Scotland Yard spoke so contemptuously in his memoirs.

They had the misfortune of having been forced to operate against the two most formidable spybusters of all time—Sir Basil, whose Criminal Investigation Division in Scotland Yard was the executive organ of British security, and Major Vernon Kell, founder and chief of MI.5, the bureau His Majesty's Government had set up in 1909 within the intelligence directorate of the War Office to "frustrate the attempts of foreign powers to obtain British secrets."

As a result, Captain Tapken's spies became so well known to the British that only five of the original contingent managed to escape on August 5, 1914, the day after the outbreak of World War I. During the war itself, only a single German agent succeeded in escaping the irresistible scrutiny of Thomson and Kell—Jules Silber, a quiet South African of Austrian ancestry who worked as a censor in Britain.

After the war, England was practically immune from German snooping—until the summer of 1932, when Norman Baillie-Stewart, a foolish young lieutenant of the Seaforth Highlanders, sold himself to the Germans as a spy. His career in espionage lasted only five months and seventeen days. But it yielded some of the most jealously guarded secrets of Britain's new mechanized force concerning tanks and armored cars, tactics, and organization. Baillie-Stewart's inane treachery was an unexpected windfall. When he was unmasked by MI.5, the Abwehr under Captain Konrad Patzig's indolent regime made no attempt to solicit others like him or develop any replacements for the fallen agent from its own resources. To the day he died he denied everything, even in the light of evidence from the captured Abwehr files.

Then Hitler issued his categorical injunction in the summer of 1935, forbidding the Abwehr to employ agents in England while he was trying to work out some sort of an alliance with them. The ban came too late. By then, the first major V-man recruited under the new Canaris regime was already there.

Anyone who was ever subjected to the ritual of being checked in or out by British immigration inspectors knows how spies must feel when crossing frontiers on secret missions. The officers are agents of the security services. Their much-used black books bulge with the names of "undesirables" who are either "wanted" by Scotland Yard for one felonious reason or another or "unwanted" by MI.5. Since the black books are exasperatingly comprehensive, spies assigned to Britain go to extraordinary lengths to conceal their identity.

The German who, on August 29, 1935, presented his travel documents to the immigration officer at Harwich was composed and calm, convinced that his name was in no confidential roster of international rogues. He traveled on his own real name as Hermann Goertz from Hamburg. Everything his passport listed about him, and what he now told the inspector, was true—except his declaration of the purpose of his trip.

"I am an international lawyer," he said, "going to Cambridge to study English export laws. I also have another reason for this particular visit. I am taking a sabbatical to write a book. It is about a Hanseatic family like the Buddenbrooks whose roots were both in Germany and England." Goertz pulled a half-finished manuscript from his briefcase and showed it to the inspector. "Now that I've finished the German part of the family history," he said, "I feel that I'll do much better if I write the English part in the natural setting of my story."

The rubber stamp that went into his passport checked in the first full-time major secret agent the Germans had decided to station in Britain since the end of World War I. He was sent at the demand of Hermann Goering, who wanted Dr. Goertz to go to England so that he might resolve, through personal observation, a controversy over an estimate of the Royal Air Force his intelligence staff had prepared. A World War I aviator who had secretly joined the Reichswehr's "Black Luftwaffe" in 1928, Dr. Goertz believed that the RAF was offensively oriented strategically and that England was forming "a large bomber force aimed against Germany." Others argued that the RAF was being developed mostly along defensive lines, with fighter bombers predominating.

When Goertz offered to go to England to collect the data he needed to prove his contention, several senior officers among the Luftwaffe's top planners asked Admiral Canaris to take Goertz into the Abwehr and arrange his journey. Canaris welcomed the assignment. This was his purple period in the Abwehr. He was still carried away by his patriotic zeal and eager interest in the new job. Under different circumstances he would not have dared to circumvent Hitler, and would have rejected Dr. Goertz. Now he could justify the violation with the pressure from the Luftwaffe, and shift the blame to Goering if anything went wrong and the mission became known to the Fuehrer.

The quality of the man chosen for the mission reassured Canaris. Dr. Goertz was a versatile, highly gifted person. Scion of a distinguished Hanseatic family of Luebeck, into which he was born in 1890, he was reared by an English governess in an atmosphere of culture and affluence. After his World War I service, which included a tour of duty as an interrogator of British and American pilots shot down on the Western front, Goertz married an admiral's daughter. He became a lawyer in Hamburg and also represented the huge Siemens electronics company in Great Britain, where he had traveled extensively.

With abundant elegance and masculine charm, he was an early version of James Bond. He missed no opportunity to keep himself physically fit, and was especially good at swimming, riding and box- ing. He was musical, he sketched, painted, and carved and wrote essays, short stories and plays. In addition, he had an exceptional gift for mathematics. His Abwehr dossier described him as a man with a high agent-potential. He possessed an unusually developed sense of topography. "A quick glance at the map," his assessment read, "en- ables him to find his way in the country with the certainty of a sleepwalker. His sincerity and high sense of honor make him well- qualified to work as a V-man abroad."

Even so, Admiral Canaris's enthusiasm was not shared by the men who were responsible for the success of his mission or accountable for its failure. For all his glittering background and apparent qualifi- cations, Goertz was a "restless and romantic spirit" who had been "unable to settle down to the quiet routine of a successful civilian life." He was a failure in everything he undertook—from his business ventures to his professional practice, from his marriage to his favorite pastime as a writer. As a matter of fact, he had decided to go to Britain as a spy mainly to escape from the troubles of his private life, which now threatened to wreck his brittle marriage and bankrupt him in business.

But Canaris prevailed, and so this dubious 45-year-old adventurer embarked on his mission. It was to last exactly seventy-one days, of which he would spend only forty in actual spying.

Having survived the scrutiny of the immigration inspector, Goertz headed for Mildenhall in Kent, the spot chosen because it was the hub of a cluster of RAF installations. He rented "Havelock," a bungalow on Stanley Road in Broadstairs, from Mrs. Florence E. Johnson, and on September 14th, moved in "to begin work on his book." He was accompanied by Marianne Emig, a pretty 19-year-old blonde glider enthusiast. She shocked Mrs. Johnson by her presence alone in the house with a married man. Dr. Goertz suavely reassured her that Marianne's functions were solely those of a secretary-typist.

The morning after his arrival in Mildenhall on a brand-new mo- torcycle, with Miss Emig seated behind him, Dr. Goertz began his "research." His first excursion took him to nearby Manston, where Marianne promptly began her brief career as a *femme fatale* by strik- ing up a frivolous friendship with a young aircraftman named Kenneth Lewis. While Goertz was busy sketching the airfield, Marianne was squeezing information from Kenneth. Each day they would ride to different localities that had some RAF installation. When Marianne was not acting as bait, she served as a lookout for Goertz while he was sketching airfields at Lee-on-the-Solent, Hunstanton, Feltwell, Cardington, Martlesham, and elsewhere. Goertz was buoyed by his easy access to the secrets he sought, and confident that all was going well. Marianne was not so sure.

Young and inexperienced as she was, her instinct had begun to warn her that things were not as smooth as her companion believed. They were no longer alone on their outings. Aircraftman Lewis had grown more interested in Marianne's curiosity than bewitched by her seductive beauty, and decided to report the over-friendly couple he visited for cozy evening drinks at "Havelock," to his superior officer. Colonel Hinchley Cooke of MI.5 was called into the case, and he sent a detachment of inspectors to keep the pair under surveillance. Three detectives from the Kent County Constabulary followed them everywhere, to airfields in East Anglia, Norfolk, Suffolk, and Lincoln. They duly observed Goertz sketching or photographing them.

On October 23rd, after a return visit to Manston, Goertz and Marianne sensed that they were being followed. One of the detectives, John Fredrick Smith, was watching them from behind a bush. Back in the bungalow, Marianne broke down. She insisted on leaving at once in such threatening terms that Goertz thought it best to escort her back to Hamburg. Anyway, his forty days of spying in England had yielded so much that he decided to make a full report to the Abwehr.

Thanks to the gifts he was now bearing, Goertz was received with open arms in Berlin. He was praised too soon. Back in England his landlady, who had been uneasy about the Germans and was now holding Goertz's locked suitcase pending his return, called in the police. Colonel Cooke himself went to the bungalow and had the suitcase opened. In it he found all the evidence needed to convict Goertz as a spy—a special camera, a diary in which he had recorded his surveys of the airfields, voluminous notes of a military nature, and many sketches of various RAF installations.

Goertz returned to England on November 8th, embarking from the channel steamer again in Harwich. By then his name was in the black books of the immigration inspectors.

Colonel Cooke was notified and he, in turn, alerted Superintendent Webb of the Special Branch of Scotland Yard. Goertz was taken into custody and tried before Mr. Justice Greaves-Lord at Margate, on charges under the Official Secrets Act.

At first the English seemed to regard the case as the clumsy trial run of an over-eager free lance and were inclined to make light of the matter. But then two things happened. In the bungalow Goertz had so abruptly vacated Mrs. Johnson discovered a couple of stray papers —a copy of Goertz's application to the Abwehr and his cipher.

The other was an event of far greater significance whose repercussions were felt far beyond the musty courtroom in Old Bailey where Dr. Goertz was in the dock. Two days before his trial ended, on March 7, 1936, Hitler began his demolition of the Versailles Treaty by marching into the Rhineland which the Germans had agreed to keep demilitarized.

The British had intended to deport Goertz with a suspended sentence. Now, compromised by copies of his Abwehr papers, and under the impact of the Rhineland march, he was sentenced to four years in jail.

The British were more amused than annoyed by the gauche adventure. But it made Hitler furious, and not merely for its lack of finesse. It was a crass violation of his explicit orders. He reiterated the ban on September 8, in their long session on the Obersalzberg. The morning after Goertz's arrest in November, he summoned Canaris to the Wilhelmstrasse and made the embargo absolute.

Canaris was not convinced of the wisdom of the ban. Pressured by the Luftwaffe and the Kriegsmarine, which clamored for secret intelligence from Britain, he pleaded with Hitler to let him plant at least a few agents in the British Isles. Hitler was adamant.

"I'm going to hold you responsible," he said, "for the strictest observance of my instructions. I don't want any wretched spies creeping about in England and jeopardizing my plans."

Canaris, who blamed the Luftwaffe for the ill-fated Goertz mission, now told Hitler: "As far as the Abwehr is concerned, my Fuehrer, it does not have a single V-man anywhere on British soil. I will see to it that none will be sent as long as your edict remains in force."

Chapter 8

Double Agent at the Top

BRITAIN was not quite as unmolested as Hitler's interdiction and Admiral Canaris's assurance might have made it seem. From 1933 on, several Nazi bureaus competing with the Foreign Ministry and the Abwehr inundated London with their special envoys whose avowed aim was to woo the British to Hitler's side. While most of these emissaries worked overtly as propagandists, many of them also operated covertly as collectors of confidential political and military information.

Alfred Rosenberg, the effeminate-looking, sleepy-eyed mythologist of Nazism who dabbled in diplomacy through his own Foreign Political Office, was working on England with the help of a retired naval lieutenant named A. D. Obermueller and a Baron William de Ropp, a debonair political adventurer.

Through these eager envoys the Germans gained scores if not hundreds of enthusiastic adherents in the British Isles, many of them highly placed people turned Nazi sympathizers by their rancorous suspicion of Jews and fear of Communists. They were gathered together in several seemingly respectable organizations, like the Anglo-German Fellowship and The Link, or they met at such stately homes as Lady Astor's magnificent Cliveden. Mushrooming Fascist parties and "clubs" of right-wing extremists, basking in the reflected glory of Mussolini and Hitler, attracted the political scum, but also, amazingly, many distinguished men and women.

The Nazis infiltrated the Fellowship and The Link with secret agents who tried to turn them into conduits of propaganda and intelligence. Rosenberg claimed that his organization had contacts with key figures of the establishment, including a Captain Fyans, identified in his papers as "aide-de-camp of the Duke of Connaught"; a Colonel MacCaw, whom he described as "apparently a private individual but actually a confidential consultant at the War Office"; a man named Badlow, presented as "the private secretary of former Prime Minister Ramsay MacDonald"; and somebody he, with his characteristic ignorance of British protocol, called "Sir Cunningham."

Rosenberg, of Baltic gentry, who thought he looked like an Englishman and tried to enhance the appearance by wearing Savile Row suits and a perennial umbrella tightly rolled up, fancied himself a special expert on the British. But he was completely dependent on de Ropp's counsel, and the Baron, who was making a good living in the job, would pull his leg as often as he fed him straight material.

Baron William S. ("Bill") de Ropp was one of the most mysterious and influential clandestine operators of an era in whose political undertow secret agents of his kind thrived. A tall, slim, blond, blue-eyed "Aryan type," he was born in Lithuania in 1877, the son of an impoverished Baltic landowner and his aristocratic Russian wife. Educated in Germany, he moved to England in 1910. Upon his naturalization five years later, he took a commission in the Wiltshire Regiment, then transferred to the Royal Flying Corps in which he served as a balloon observer and the interrogator of German prisoners of war.

He reached Rosenberg through a chain of old acquaintances in Germany. Among his friends was the prominent Nazi journalist Arno Schickedanz, a Balt like himself, who worked for the *Voelkischer Beobachter* of which Rosenberg was editor-in-chief. For Bill de Ropp, Schickedanz made the initial contact with Rosenberg very much on the run—in the restaurant of the Anhalter railroad station while Rosenberg was waiting for the train to Munich. It was from such a seemingly perfunctory beginning that de Ropp's astounding penetration of the Nazis' highest echelons developed.

The Baron and his delightful English wife Jimmy moved to Berlin, into an elegant flat on the Kurfuerstendamm where they became famed for their hospitality, thanks to de Ropp's ingratiating charm and Jimmy's culinary art. It did not take long to establish himself at the top of Nazi society. Rosenberg introduced him to Adolf Hitler, who took an instant liking to the engaging, well-informed Balt from London. A close personal relationship developed between the Fuehrer and de Ropp. Hitler, using him as his confidential consultant about British affairs, outlined to him frankly his grandiose plans and even confided to him some of his intentions, a trust no other foreigner enjoyed to this extent.

Baron de Ropp reciprocated by becoming his chief agent of Anglo-German *rapprochement*. He acted as Hitler's mouthpiece with influential Britishers the Fuehrer was anxious to reach and sway. He brought to Germany many of his highly-placed British friends—"several peers," as he himself boasted, "two generals, an admiral, a number of journalists, and a 'sporting' parson"—and was able to assure Hitler that they were all "extremely impressed" with what they saw in the Third Reich.

Before long, Bill de Ropp was firmly entrenched as Rosenberg's "English agent," with "a direct pipeline" to Whitehall and Buckingham Palace at one end, and Hitler on the other. Was he a double agent? The only person in the Wilhelm Strasse who ever suspected him of such duplicity and cautioned the Fuehrer about him was the erratic Putzi Hanfstengel, the Harvard-educated chief of Hitler's office dealing with the foreign press. When Bill was told by Rosenberg about Putzi's intrigue, he dismissed Hanfstengel contemptuously as "that well-known nut," and survived in Hitler's confidence.

During these years, when many Britons who should have known better hunted with the Nazis, it was not especially difficult for de Ropp to tap his friends and acquaintances in England for privileged information, and obtain favors from them to the advantage of his German employers. He could dazzle both Rosenberg and Hitler—truthfully at times—with the exceptional quality of his contacts.

This extraordinary relationship endured even after the outbreak of the war, when Baron de Ropp moved to Switzerland, to continue his "operations" from neutral soil. Several times during the war he was summoned to Berlin by Hitler for consultations.

I found in Alfred Rosenberg's secret papers the intriguing pastiche of his most ambitious operation—an attempt by this layman to arrange behind the back of the Foreign Office close cooperation between the Royal Air Force and the still illicit Luftwaffe. The plot was launched by Baron de Ropp, but soon developed beyond him, and was eventually managed by Rosenberg.

Looking for an outlet on which he could practice his skill at skullduggery, Lieutenant Obermueller had discovered that the Luftwaffe's clandestine General Staff was the keenest customer in the mushrooming military establishment for classified information from England. He instructed de Ropp to plug himself into this circuit and collect the information the Luftwaffe wanted but apparently could not obtain from any of the regular intelligence services.

When Under Secretary Erhard Milch of the German Air Ministry, the organizing genius of the secret Luftwaffe, expressed interest in the project, de Ropp established contact with an acquaintance of his, a retired RAF officer he called "Major W" who still seemed to have some connection with the Air Staff. The friend was Squadron Leader Frederick William Winterbotham, a somewhat mysterious fixture in the clubs around St. James's Street.

Born in 1897, Freddy Winterbotham, a likable character out of P. G. Wodehouse, had what he called "a normal upbringing . . . in a lovely part of Cottswolds" where he "learnt to ride and hunt, to shoot and fish, play cricket and golf." At the age of seventeen, after a trip around the world (on which he became a fan of the Chicago White Sox) he joined the Royal Gloucestershire Hussars Yeomanry, then moved over to the Royal Flying Corps. His career as an aviator in World War I came to an abrupt end on Friday, July 13, 1917, when he was shot down over the German lines and had to spend the next eighteen months in a prisoner-of-war camp.

After the war, with a law degree from Oxford, he went into farming and was raising pigs until 1929 when the depression forced him to look for some other work. He found it in the RAF where he became "specially employed" in the Air Staff working for Group Captain K. C. Buss. Since Buss was the chief of intelligence, Bill de Ropp assumed that his friend Freddy was engaged in some secret activity.

Indeed he was. He had been hired by Admiral Hugh Sinclair as chief of air intelligence of the Secret Intelligence Service, also to act as liaison with the Air Staff's intelligence department. "It was a splendid cover," Winterbotham told me when I saw him on his farm in Devonshire in the summer of 1971. "I was listed in the Air Force list as a member of the Air Staff. I had a small office in the Air Ministry at Adastral House, mostly full of other people's filing cabinets, and I was seen there often."

In a real sense the Winterbotham-de Ropp axis that ensued was not accidental. The squadron leader welcomed his friend's approach, hoping for a chance to ingratiate himself to the Germans in order to gain as much information as possible about the mysteries of the new Luftwaffe.

Under such circumstances de Ropp found the going easy. Winterbotham went out of his way to sympathize with the aspirations of the Third Reich. He expressed himself in favor of its rearmament in the air as a balancing factor in European airpower dominated by the French and Soviet air forces. So promising was this contact from the outset that Lieutenant Obermueller rushed to London to meet de Ropp's interesting friend and also Squadron Leader Archibald R. Boyle of Air Intelligence to whom he was introduced by Winterbotham.

Shortly afterward Winterbotham's annual leave became due and he accepted Obermueller's invitation to spend his holiday in Germany. He arrived in Berlin on February 27, 1934, and was taken in tow by Rosenberg, who introduced him triumphantly to Milch and a couple of Luftwaffe generals, Major General von Reichenau, the Reichswehr's Nazi-minded top planner, and Bruno Loerzer, a World War I ace who now headed the German Air-Sport Federation, one of the fronts of the still "Black Luftwaffe." He also met Rudolf Hess and as the *pièce de résistance* of his holiday—Hitler himself. Winterbotham conveyed to the Fuehrer, as Rosenberg noted in his diary, "the greetings of British aviators."

This was not a feigned gesture, for the Air Ministry under both Lord Londonderry and Lord Swinton had for some time spearheaded the growing forces of appeasement in Britain. The aviator-politicians favored an "understanding" with the Nazi government, already bursting at the seams, even as Hitler was banking on it.

The British sought the "understanding" at the price of acquiescing in what they recognized was the irreversible growth of German air power. They were alarmed and hoped some kind of arrangement with the Germans would divert the sharp edge of this development from Britain.

On March 6, after "a very satisfactory sojourn," Winterbotham returned to London, accompanied by Loerzer, whom he was supposed to introduce to British aviation circles both in the Air Ministry and in the industry. Upon his return to Berlin, Loerzer advised Rosenberg that Winterbotham had submitted "a glowing report" to the Air Staff about his observations in Germany. He had introduced Loerzer to a certain Captain Kenneth Bartlett, chief of the overseas sales branch of the Bristol Aircraft Company, who expressed interest in doing business with the illicit Luftwaffe under the counter.[1]

Baron de Ropp continued to cultivate Squadron Leader Winterbotham in order to "deepen the penetration" of the Air Ministry. "The struggle for England continues," Rosenberg wrote in his diary on July 11, recording that his man Obermueller had been in London again, chaperoned by Winterbotham, and had had "very productive discussions" with Lord Londonderry, the Air Minister, and Major Boyle of the Intelligence staff.

Lieutenant Obermueller returned from this trip with an attractive suggestion. Pro-German circles in the Air Ministry, he told Rosenberg, were trying to arrange for Winterbotham to be stationed in Berlin as the Air Attaché. He would replace the incumbent Group Captain Francis Percival Don, who, Obermueller said, "did not have the faintest idea of what was going on" and, besides, was sending to the British Air Staff "very antagonistic reports."

Winterbotham's appointment was sidetracked in London. He was able to assure his German friends that a new man would be sent to Berlin nevertheless, "a regular chap" the Germans could trust and show around safely, in exchange for which, the squadron leader promised, he would arrange "similar tours [in Britain] for the [German] Air Attaché." Group Captain Don was duly recalled and Flight Lieutenant William Edwin Coope, a very junior officer for such a big job, was sent as acting Air Attaché.[2]

The Luftwaffe, keenly interested in an "understanding with the RAF," went along with the Winterbotham deal. In order to avoid anything that might jeopardize or compromise this invaluable connection, and to keep this effort secret even from Major General Wenninger, the German Air Attaché in London, another officer was "built into" the Embassy in London in a civilian capacity with a diplomatic cover. He was to act as a direct link between Winterbotham on the one side and Major Josef ("Beppo") Schmid, the chief of intelligence in the German Air Staff, on the other. Rosenberg was told that such a direct connection was desirable to shorten the line of communications. Actually the officer was sent to London to bypass Rosenberg's amateurs who tended to overdramatize the Winterbotham maneuver.

In September Captain Bartlett of the Bristol Aircraft Company arrived in Berlin with a letter of introduction from Winterbotham, to explore the possibilities of sales to the Luftwaffe as proposed by the squadron leader a few months before. Bartlett brought with him some good news. He told Rosenberg that "the [Royal] Air Force [was] prepared to lend all-out aid to the Luftwaffe without letting the Foreign Office know anything about it."

Rosenberg hastened to Under Secretary Milch with the message but found that he had cooled on the project. Encouraged by Winterbotham's visit to Germany in March, Milch had asked Rosenberg to prepare a trip to London for him, and Rosenberg called on Baron de Ropp to make the arrangements. But de Ropp failed to generate any enthusiasm for Milch's visit. He notified Berlin that such a courtesy call was considered "inopportune" at this time, and that neither the Secretary for Air nor the Assistant Secretary would receive Milch if he came.

The rebuff had made Milch suspicious of the whole Rosenberg-de Ropp affair. He expressed his skepticism frankly when Rosenberg breathlessly conveyed to him the stunning message Bartlett had brought, and questioned the authority and sincerity of Winterbotham.

"How can you have any doubts on this score," Rosenberg said indignantly. "Captain Bartlett came to me with a letter of introduction from Herr Winterbotham *written on the official stationery of the Air Ministry*."

"Well," Milch said, "I'll believe it when you produce written confirmation of the RAF's willingness to cooperate with us behind the back of the Foreign office, *also on the official stationery of the Air Ministry.*"

"How naïve can you be?" Rosenberg gasped. He showed Milch the letter of introduction Winterbotham had given Bartlett. He could not, of course, produce the "confirmation" Milch demanded.

After that, Winterbotham became a bone of contention between the Bureau Rosenberg and the Milch cabal. The friction over the Englishman became so bad that, on December 18, Rosenberg complained to Hitler that the "bureaucrats" of the Luftwaffe were "botching up" his invaluable secret line to the British Air Ministry.

Hitler asked Goering to look into the matter, and was told that, far from "botching up" the connection, Milch and his associates were trying to save it from miscarriage. What in the hands of Rosenberg and his charlatans was but a meddler's caper was developing into a momentous enterprise which promised to bring about the "understanding" both parties were seeking, each for its own special reasons, but mostly to spy on each other by mutual consent in a unique arrangement between two rival air forces.

It was obvious that outsiders like Rosenberg and de Ropp had outlived their usefulness. The contact they initiated in their own amateurish ways was taken over by professionals, Squadron Leader Winterbotham staying in the plot until the end of 1937.

In late 1936, the Air Ministry formally proposed and the Luftwaffe agreed to "exchanges of information on [their] respective establishments." A British delegation consisting of two air vice marshals and two intelligence officers was allowed to inspect "every Luftwaffe establishment of importance." In January 1937, General Wenninger, the German Military Attaché in London, was briefed in the Air Ministry on the RAF's build-up, followed by the visit of a German delegation headed by General Milch for additional briefings and a tour of RAF installations. As it turned out, it was a lopsided barter. While the Germans concealed little if anything from their guests, they were given mere morsels of information by comparison, leaving their knowledge of the RAF as fragmentary as before, and their "cooperation" with the Air Ministry ("behind the back of the Foreign Office") a disappointing experience. General Albert Kesselring was so put out by the lopsidedness of this exchange that he denounced Milch to Goering for high treason. Years later, recalling the exchange, Hitler charged that Milch had "betrayed the secret of radar to the British."

This unprecedented two-way snooping continued until 1937, two years after that March day in 1935, when Hitler announced the official constitution of the Luftwaffe, a formal affront to Article 198 of the Versailles Treaty, which outlawed the maintenance of "either a land-based or a naval air force."[3]

By the end of 1934, in the immediate wake of his complaints to Hitler, Rosenberg was out of this particular game (and Winterbotham receded into the background to do his snooping on the Luftwaffe by more indirect means).[4] But there were other worlds to conquer, to compensate him for the loss of his plum. He reverted to his favorite pastime of secret diplomacy, concentrating on political intrigues behind the scenes in England.

In January 1935, when the Nazi cauldron began to boil over, de Ropp reached to the top of British society to impress his starry-eyed sponsor Rosenberg with another triumph. He informed him from London in the strictest confidence that he had succeeded in enlisting a man he called "the political adviser of King George V" as a confidential broker of Hitler's cause, establishing what Rosenberg described as "a direct pipeline to Buckingham Palace."

So delicate and secret was this contact that its details could not be entrusted to the mail. On February 2, the Baron journeyed to Berlin to report to Rosenberg in person, revealing that the new recruit was none other than the Duke of Kent, the King's youngest son. He claimed he had had several secret sessions with the Duke, one of which, he said, had lasted through the greater part of a night. Rosenberg was so elated that he rushed to the Chancellery to tell Hitler about his latest *coup*.

Because of the special nature of this incident, I made an extra effort to check out Baron de Ropp's version of this contact, and what I found bore out only part of his claims. The Duke did meet de Ropp by pre-arrangement, knowing that he was a German agent. But they met on a single occasion, January 23, when the Duke kept the Baron up until dawn.

It was the Duke who pumped de Ropp for information and not the other way around. England was reconciled to Hitler's determination to rearm Germany, he told the Baron, but what after that? What was the real "mentality" of Germany's new masters? Were they aggressive, congenital troublemakers or could they be tamed to work in traditional political and diplomatic grooves? What made Hitler tick? Hess? Goering? Goebbels?

What Baron de Ropp told the Duke and how he characterized the Nazi bigwigs can well be imagined without recourse to a transcript of this nocturnal conversation. As Rosenberg recorded in his diary, "R[opp] gave the Duke the benefit of his knowledge based on his personal experience of many years."

The captured records do not show whether this contact was developed any further. The Duke, somewhat of a playboy, was far more

interested in astrology and phrenology and other sciences more occult than Nazism. He neither sought nor had any access to the corridors of power, and was not an ideal partner for such a game.

What the Nazis mistook for pro-Nazi sympathies on the Duke's
part was merely the reflection of his brother's sentiments who, both as
Prince of Wales and King Edward VIII, sometimes seemed to have
had undue admiration for Hitler and his apparent accomplishments
in building up Germany as a bulwark against the Bolsheviks. As far
as could be ascertained, no privileged information ever flowed directly from the Duke of Kent to any of Rosenberg's or Ribbentrop's
agents, even though several of them attributed "intelligence" they
submitted to him as a source. His reputation as a "pro-Nazi" lingered
on in Berlin even after the outbreak of the war. When in 1940 he
died in an airplane crash en route to America, Rudolf Likus, chief of
Ribbentrop's intelligence bureau in the Foreign Ministry, prepared
an obituary about the Duke in which he offered the preposterous suggestion that the "accident" had been "engineered by the
nefarious British Intelligence Service to get him out of the way before
he would embarrass the Royal family still further with his outspoken
sympathies for the German cause."

Although the Duke may have been only an exhibit in Baron de
Ropp's glittering collection, others proved more accommodating and
illuminating. Considerable political and some military intelligence
flowed from them, as we shall see, to German listening posts in Berlin
and London during the days of the crisis when Hitler needed such
critical information to shape his plots with knowledge of his adversaries' intentions and capabilities.

Putzi Hanfstengel was, of course, right. Bill de Ropp was playing
the game in both camps—a double agent at the very top. He was
handpicked by both the Germans and Freddy Winterbotham on behalf of the British Secret Service for the part which the gregarious de
Ropp then played with such consummate skill. Winterbotham had
known him from World War I. "He was a close friend of mine," he
said, "and a lively companion. In one way he was true to type of
many of the more intelligent exiles from Russia [sic]; he delighted in
exercising his mind with politics and had a superb nose for intrigue."
He appeared to be the ideal man to reach into Hitler's inner sanctum
and became the only British agent who managed to penetrate so high
and so deep.

De Ropp was a remarkable double agent in that he served both
his masters with equal zeal and loyalty. A rabid foe of the Bolsheviks,
as were Rosenberg and Winterbotham, he saw in an alliance between
Germany and Britain against the Soviet Union the salvation of Europe. Up to the outbreak of the war he worked assiduously to keep
Britain neutral, to save it up "for the inevitable war with Russia."

He proved useful to both sides as a conveyor belt of top-level information, keeping Hitler posted about developments in Britain and the
British about some of the Fuehrer's weird plans and innermost
thoughts.   ·

The miserable Goertz mission in 1935 demonstrated for all to see
how primitive German military intelligence still was in its efforts to
probe the secrets of British airpower. By contrast, the political coverage of England was remarkable for its depth and astuteness, thanks
to a large extent to the aid and comfort German emissaries were
receiving from high-grade British contacts.

Their gratuitous contributions produced a fantastic dividend in
1936 when Hitler, as Churchill phrased it, terminated "the years of
underground burrowings, of secret or disguised preparations," and
"felt himself strong enough" or his adversaries too weak and soft, "to
make his first open challenges."

NOTES

1 This was not as extraordinary as it may seem. Even while the disarmament
clauses of the Versailles Treaty were fully in force, British armament manufacturers defiantly advertised their wares for sale to the Reich, including
weapons which the peace pact had explicitly outlawed.

2 In 1939, the job was upgraded again with the appointment of Group Captain John Lyne Vachel, an astute aviation expert and keen observer.

3 In 1936, another party appeared in the game, an American Military and
Air Attaché, Colonel Truman Smith, who revived the "Winterbotham ploy"
by persuading Colonel Charles A. Lindbergh to exploit his enormous popu-
larity in Germany to obtain a firsthand insight into the Luftwaffe. By then
the British had no illusions on this score. They had more reliable information
about the German air force, and a far less emotionally charged estimate of
its strength and capabilities, than Lindbergh was to produce after four controversial visits to the Third Reich.

4 Recalling his association with Rosenberg and de Ropp, Winterbotham
later wrote: "As a result of the success of Rosenberg's visit to London [in
the late autumn of 1931], I decided to assume the character of one who was
both interested in and even mildly enthusiastic about the 'new Germany.' It
would be easy to be interested, not so easy to be enthusiastic." It seemed,
however, that he had become more than just mildly enthusiastic. The Foreign Office, behind whose back this contact was maintained, found out
about it in 1937 and, as Winterbotham put it, "was not pleased either with
my visit or with the information I had obtained." He was reprimanded by
the Foreign Secretary and ordered to discontinue his flirtation with the
Nazis, no matter how ulterior his motives might have been.

Chapter 9

Mission to Fort Belvedere

*I*T was March again, the alluvial month of Neptune and Mars, whose raw air, for some reason, always filled Hitler with mercurial agitation.[1] He was seeing Wilhelm Canaris more often than at any time during the admiral's tenure in the Abwehr. Hitler's appointment book listed seventeen sessions between December 1935 and March 1936, all of them "private meetings" of just the two behind closed doors.

The sudden frequency of their duologues was introduced by certain urgent developments in Europe that produced considerable *secret* fallout behind the explosive headlines. Canaris was there to brief the Fuehrer about them.

The year, 1935, had brought a string of phenomenal moves, to be sure. On March 7, a plebiscite returned the Saar to Germany. On June 18, a naval agreement with England authorized Germany to build up its skeleton fleet to one-third of the Royal Navy's tonnage. And the old enmity with Poland was buried when Hitler opened negotiations with Marshall Joseph Pilsudski and startled the world by signing a treaty of Friendship with the opportunistic Poles. But Hitler upset the delicate balance. His repudiation of the disarmament clauses of the Versailles Treaty provoked a series of angry countermeasures. On May 2, 1935, France and the Soviet Union signed a treaty of mutual assistance. It was followed within a fortnight by the signing of a similar pact between the Soviet Union and Czechoslovakia.

Hitler's reaction to what he called "provocations" was prompt and violent. Far from retreating in the face of these concerted countermoves, he resolved on the boldest aggressive stroke of his regime so far. On the very day in May when France and the U.S.S.R. initialed their mutual assistance pact, he had decided to send the Reichswehr into the demilitarized zone of the Rhineland, and ordered General Werner von Blomberg to begin staff work on the plans for the march.[2]

Called *Schulung* (or "Exercise") by its code name, the plan was quickly drawn up by a staff of handpicked officers sworn to secrecy. On June 16, *Schulung* was presented to the Reichs Defense Council by Colonel Alfred Jodl who had just been named chief of a super-staff of planners. These preparations were so secret that Blomberg who wrote out Hitler's original order in his own hand, did not reveal the true purpose of the plan even to General Ludwig Beck, chief of the General Staff, and General Werner von Fritsch, commander-in-chief of the army.

Schulung was then held in abeyance, for Hitler did not dare risk such a bold move without the acute provocation that would presumably justify it. Again and again Blomberg conveyed to him the misgivings of his generals—the Reichswehr was still too weak and ill-equipped for the adventure they suspected Hitler was hatching in his mind.

Then a series of developments induced Hitler to unwrap *Schulung*.

On December 26, in the first of their series of briefing sessions, Canaris told Hitler that the French and the British military staffs had begun talks to coordinate plans for an emergency in the Rhineland.

On February 11, 1936, the French cabinet placed the still unratified treaty with the Soviet Union on the agenda of the Assembly.

On the same day Admiral Canaris requested an immediate audience with the Fuehrer. When he saw Hitler, again alone, at eight o'clock in the evening, he submitted a top-secret paper which, he said, his chief V-man in Paris had just succeeded in procuring. It was a stunning document—the verbatim transcript of the secret *military* clauses of the Franco-Russian pact, placed in German hands by a high official of the Quai d'Orsay who was violently opposed to *rapproachement* with the U.S.S.R.

The key clause provided, in so many words, for an *invasion* of Germany in collaboration with the Czechs to short-circuit Hitler's policy of aggrandizement.

Canaris was barely out of his office when Hitler sent for General von Blomberg and instructed him to prepare the *Schulung* plan for execution at the earliest possible date.

Blomberg was back in Hitler's study on February 27, the day the French assembly ratified the treaty with Russia, to advise Hitler that preliminary preparations had been completed and to receive his marching orders from him with X-day firmly set for March 7, only a little over a week later.

Up to this point, *Schulung* was treated as nothing more than what its name implied—a training exercise supposedly designed to give the planning staffs something to do and afford the troops a realistic drill. This was the impression Blomberg assiduously cultivated even in the circle of his closest associates. On March 2 he called in Generals Beck and Fritsch to tell them that *Schulung* was not a contingency plan after all, and conveyed the Fuehrer's order to be ready for the march within five days.

A storm of protest broke loose. Fritsch remonstrated that all he had for such an adventurous operation was a force of 35,000 men of which only a single division could be formed for combat. Beck argued that the French could quickly mobilize at least twenty superbly equipped divisions to pit against Fritsch's little expeditionary force and, as he put it, "make mincemeat of it."

"The atmosphere," as Jodl later described it, "was very like that of the roulette table when a player stakes his fortune on a single number." Blomberg, whose sole argument was Hitler's peremptory order, took Beck and Fritsch to the Fuehrer for the peptalk he thought they obviously needed. The generals confronted Hitler with their misgivings. "What are we going to do," Beck asked, "if the French march?"

Hitler was adamant.

"I know better!" he said. "I have *absolutely reliable* information that the French will not move a single *poilu*. You will see that, and more than that! The world will accept the liberation of the Rhineland from the Versailles yoke as an accomplished fact, and leave it at that."

Then, betraying that he himself harbored at least some apprehension, he solemnly told his startled audience: "As for myself, I am willing to stake everything I have and cherish on this bid. I am firmly convinced that it will succeed. But should it fail, and should French intervention force us to withdraw, I will accept the consequences as my own defeat and submit my resignation as Fuehrer and Chancellor."

The generals acquiesced. Beck, who loathed Hitler and was so opposed to the Nazis that he eventually gave his life in the struggle against them, actually hoped in his secret heart that the venture would fail and Germany would rid itself of Hitler in the aftermath. Now he had no choice. The deployment of the forces began at once, in such secrecy that only units of battalion strength were moved to the jumping-off points—"to use as weak a force as possible at the spearhead so as to cut losses to a minimum in case of French countermeasures." The commanding officers of the spearhead had sealed orders to withdraw at once if they encountered even advance patrols of an incoming Franco-British expeditionary force.

The intelligence picture they had was by no means reassuring. The Abwehr, which was undergoing its first acid test under the Canaris regime, was already firmly entrenched in the Rhineland, a few giant steps ahead of the armies as usual. Camouflaged as a commercial enterprise, an extensive branch operated in Muenster against France. The day-by-day management of the spies was the responsibility of the subbranch at Trier in the Rhineland-Palatinate, where Major Hans Stephan, the Abwehr's foremost expert on the Maginot Line, acted as spymaster, shortly to be joined by Captain Oscar Reile, a former police inspector in Danzig, as the new *V-Mann-Fuehrer*, the comptroller of agents in the field.

Canaris now was able to present to the Fuehrer the copy of the actual order the French had drawn up for the mobilization of thirteen divisions in the emergency. Spies of the Trier branch reported that the fortifications were in the process of being manned all along the German border, with reinforcements moving from as far away as Marseilles and Lyons to Metz, Nancy, and the other key forts of the Line.

At the same time, the *Forschungsamt*, the Luftwaffe's code-cracking establishment that monitored and read diplomatic traffic, produced intercepts of the decoded dispatches of André François-Poncet, the brilliant French Ambassador in Berlin. Since November 1935, François-Poncet had been warning Paris that the Fuehrer "intended to use" the Franco-Soviet pact "as a pretext to occupy the demilitarized zone of the Rhineland"; that "his sole hesitancy [was] concerned with the appropriate moment of the act"; and that, as the ambassador phrased it in a telegram dated February 13, Hitler was "preparing the ground for the march into the Rhineland."

From London the dispatches of the three service attachés—Colonel Gayr of the army, Captain Wassner of the navy, and Major General Wenninger of the air force—were heavy with forebodings and warnings. The Military Attaché in particular sounded most pessimistic. His friends in the War Office, he wrote, were strongly admonishing him that England would definitely march at France's side if Hitler dared to make as much as a move in the general direction of the demilitarized zone.

What in the face of all these alarming reports made Hitler so sure that he had nothing to fear from the French? What, in fact, was that "absolutely reliable information" he had mentioned to the generals that made him so confident?

At this same time, the Fuehrer was receiving other sets of intelligence from Paris and London and he preferred to trust them more than his Military Attaché's defeatist dispatches to the Reichswehr Ministry.

In the flood of reports Admiral Canaris was submitting there was one in particular that impressed Hitler. According to the highly-placed Abwehr agent who was covering the Quai d'Orsay in the crisis, British cooperation was regarded as a *conditio sine qua non* in French military planning. "[Foreign Minister Pierre] Flandin," the agent wrote, "has been told by General Maurice Gamelin, chief of the army, that he would not be able (or, for that matter, willing) to send any forces into the Rhineland unless the British were marching at their side."

At the same time, Foreign Minister Baron von Neurath was assuring Hitler *in no uncertain terms* that the British had no intention to give the French the support Gamelin was demanding. The unequivocal advice of the Foreign Minister, not a diplomat willing to go out on a limb, was inspired by a stream of telegrams he was receiving from Dr. Leopold Gustav Alexander von Hoesch, the German Ambassador to the Court of St. James's since 1932. *"The West will not march"* was the unequivocal refrain of Ambassador von Hoesch's dispatches, as Baron von Neurath phrased it in one of his presentations to the Fuehrer.

A 55-year-old impeccable bachelor celebrating the thirtieth year of a brilliant career in the Foreign Service, Leopold von Hoesch was playing an ambiguous part in the crisis, typical of the pathetic personal conflict of many German diplomats during these years. He had spent the best years of his official life in Paris and London, and was imbued, not merely with the form, but with the substance of Western democracy.

Alienated in all his personal convictions and inclinations from Hitler's vulgar regime, Hoesch was nevertheless serving it faithfully and well to the bitter end.

The ambassador had superb sources to gauge the trend of British policies and intentions, and was tapping them on both sides of the fence. Enormously popular in the best English society, he was well-liked in the Foreign Office and trusted implicitly by Sir Robert Vansittart, the Permanent Under Secretary, and Ralph Wigram, its rising star at the head of the Central Department.

He was on intimate terms with a growing number of pro-Germans in Mayfair and Belgravia, but also with such ardent and outspoken anti-Nazis as Winston Churchill, Sir Archibald Sinclair, the Earl of Salisbury, and even Ernest Bevin. He had especially close ties with the Royal family. Queen Mary referred to him as "my favorite foreigner," and had him as her regular luncheon guest at Ascot, a signal honor she bestowed only upon a privileged few in her small coterie of personal friends.

In this galaxy of influential confidants, he was closest to the Prince of Wales whom he addressed as "David" and who called him "Leo." At this time the bond between the two popular bachelors was especially strong. The prince was going through the violent crisis caused by his delicate friendship with Mrs. Ernest Simpson, the American divorcée, buffeted by his family's and the Baldwin government's opposition to this relationship. In his grave personal plight, the Prince sought out Ambassador von Hoesch as one of his personal counselors —"the best friend I have," as he once chose to describe his relationship with the distinguished German diplomat.

From Hoesch's point of view the Prince was considerably more than just a personal friend and frequent partner at tennis and golf. He was his best source of information and in a real sense, his guarantee that he would be left at his post despite his known liberal sentiments. Certain derogatory information was reaching Berlin, objecting to the Ambassador's lukewarm attitude toward the Nazis, and the Foreign Ministry was seriously contemplating a change at the top of the Embassy in London. His position seemed firm, not the least because of his close friendship with the Prince of Wales. It became decisive when his friend was slated by destiny to become the King of England during the Rhineland crisis.

It was on January 20, 1936, on the death of George V, that the Prince acceded to the throne as King Edward VIII. The morning after, Ambassador von Hoesch sent a long telegram to von Buelow, the Under Secretary of State, in which he outlined the significance of the change with all of the eloquence of his deeply felt emotions. "George V," he wrote, "will live in the memory of the British people, in the first place as the King who stood at the head of the Empire during the World War, and beyond this as a wise and kindly ruler who was in close sympathy with his people.

"King Edward VIII," he went on, "resembles his father in some respects, but differs greatly from him in others." Perhaps the most significant difference, he ventured to say, was in their attitudes toward the Third Reich. While, Hoesch wrote, the late King was "certainly critical of Germany . . . King Edward, quite generally, feels warm sympathy for Germany. I have become convinced during frequent, often lengthy, talks with him that these sympathies are deep-rooted and strong enough to withstand the contrary influences to which they are not seldom exposed."

As recently as January 15, "the day before [the Prince] was

summoned to his dying father," von Hoesch was given "some further evidence of this sympathy." The Prince, as he then was, informed the Ambassador that it was "his firm intention" to go to Berlin in the summer for the Olympic Games. He asked Dr. von Hoesch to see to it that the delegation of German ex-servicemen, expected to arrive in London on the 19th, would have at least a couple of hours in their crowded schedule for a private audience with him, for he "wished to talk to each of the delegates personally."

"At any rate," the ambassador concluded his telegram, "we should be able to rely upon having on the British Throne a ruler who is not lacking in understanding for Germany and in the desire to see good relations established between Germany and Britain."

There seemed to be considerably more to this assessment of the new King's attitude to Nazi Germany than Hoesch cared to spell out in his tactful diplomatese. The man who is now the Duke of Windsor, while no all-out admirer of Hitler during those days, or a convinced pro-Nazi, saw in an accommodation with Hitler's Germany the best safeguard of the peace of Europe he so ardently sought to preserve. But the secret German papers demonstrate that, in confidential conversations with influential Germans he was meeting privately, he deliberately and assiduously cultivated the impression that he saw much justification for their more moderate asperations.

On April 11, 1935, for example, in one of his talks with him, Ambassador von Hoesch reported that he went out of his way to leave no doubt about his sympathies. He strongly criticized his own Foreign Office for their "lack of understanding of Germany's position and aspirations," and confided to the ambassador that, unlike the people in Downing Street, he fully approved the introduction of conscription which Hitler had proclaimed unilaterally a few weeks before. The Prince's own views, according to von Hoesch, "corresponded word for word" with those of the Fuehrer and the Ambassador reported that he closed the conversation by assuring von Hoesch that he was not only reconciled to "Germany's resurgence" but determined to "further" it.

The Duke of Coburg, a close relative of the Royal family known as "the Nazi Duke" for his intimate friendship with Hitler, recorded that Edward was outspoken in protesting his sympathies for the Third Reich in three talks he had with him. Held between official functions in January, 1936, the day after his father's funeral, the interviews were sought by the Duke upon secret instructions from Hitler to sound out the new King. What the Duke told of the views of Edward VIII had the Tudor touch of royal conspiracy.[3]

When Coburg brought up the desirability of a meeting between

Hitler and Prime Minister Stanley Baldwin to promote closer Anglo-German relations, in the face of Mr. Baldwin's known opposition to such a confrontation, the Duke wrote that Edward VIII exclaimed: "I myself wish to talk to Herr Hitler, and will do so here or in Germany. Tell him that please."

The King realized, according to the Nazi Duke, that this would not be easy under the British system. The Duke reported that he was cautioned by the new King to treat his remarks confidentially because his "resolve to bring Germany and England together would be made more difficult if it were made public too early."

At noon on March 7, even as Hitler was telling the Reichstag that "we have no territorial demands in Europe," the 35,000-man expeditionary force of the Reichswehr was entering what the Fuehrer called "their future peace garrisons in the Reich's western provinces."

It was a Saturday, the first of many weekends Hitler was to spoil with his recurrent coups.

In France, there was "a hideous shock." But exactly as Canaris had told Hitler, the French generalissimo would not move an inch toward the Rhineland without the concurrence of Britain. At this most critical moment of the crisis, however, there was not a sign of encouragement from London. On Monday, Eden rushed to Paris, but only to counsel his French friends to place the issue before the League of Nations instead of precipitating action.

Two days later, on the 11th, Flandin journeyed to London where the League was to meet in an extraordinary session in the musty, chilly confines and medieval air of Henry VIII's St. James's Palace. Mr. Churchill's criticism of this shadowboxing was devastating in retrospect. Yet what he placed on record in *The Gathering Storm* was not the whole story of these hectic and fateful days.

As the troops marched, Berlin, too, was in a turmoil. All the antennae of the Foreign Ministry and the Abwehr were out to pick up every fragment of foreign reactions. The service attachés and Canaris's agents were at their battle stations in Paris and London to monitor the French and British countermeasures and report them to Berlin in frantic cables and telephone calls. In the Wilhelmstrasse, Hitler was sweating it out with Blomberg and von Neurath.

The news from Paris was grave but not necessarily hopeless for the Reichswehr. The intelligence pouring in from London was portentous and threatening. The two service attachés were sending erratic warnings that joint intervention by an Anglo-French force was but a matter of days, if not hours.

There was, indeed, a crisis within the British government, caused by frictions between the political and military leaders of the two countries.

In England, the War Office and the Admiralty were for drastic and immediate military action, but the politicians under Baldwin procrastinated, seized as they were by a panicky fear of war.

The determination of the British generals and admirals was evident to the German service attachés in London. Captain Wassner and Colonel Gayr commuted between their offices and Whitehall, trying desperately to ascertain how the crisis was shaping up in the Admiralty and the War Office.

Monday morning Captain Wassner went to the Admiralty hoping to see Admiral William James, deputy chief of the Naval Staff, to find out whether the fleet would be mobilized and naval reserves called up. Made to cool his heels in the admiral's anteroom, he was eventually told that Sir William was too busy elsewhere to receive him. He was referred to Rear Admiral J. A. G. Troupe, the Director of Naval Intelligence, whom he found grim and cold, and exasperatingly elusive.

The inconclusive *pourparler* produced a gloomy telegram by Wassner to his Admiralty Staff, voicing his belief that the British were preparing the mobilization of the fleet, presumably to back up an expeditionary force Britain seemed determined to send to France for joint action against the Germans in the Rhineland.

While Wassner was on his fishing expedition in the Admiralty, Baron Gayr was in the War Office listening to General Pownall, the director of Operations and Intelligence, reproaching him angrily that he had "deliberately misled the British Government about German intentions and German rearmament."

To his stunned astonishment he was invited into the office of the German Intelligence Section, an inner sanctum he had never before been permitted to enter. There he was received with more harsh words, but endured them quietly, preoccupied as he was with stealthily examining an illuminating display on the walls—*all the Section's top secret operational maps showing both French and British troop dispositions* for what he assumed was imminent intervention in the Rhineland.

Actually Britain had no intention to move those troops and was, in fact, restraining France from moving any of its forces. Colonel Gayr's "indoctrination" was designed as a deterrent. This was as far as the War Office could go in light of the decision in Downing Street to do next to nothing. Pownall and his associates hoped that the German colonel would be sufficiently awed by what he saw on the wall with his own eyes, and convey his alarm to Berlin.

Today we know that Colonel Gayr was duly impressed, and made his fears known to Berlin. He rushed back to his office and sent a top-priority telegram to the Reichswehr Ministry, that read: "Situation grave. Fifty-fifty war or peace."

It was but one in a series of frantic signals all of which voiced his apprehensions (or misapprehensions, as the case turned out to be).[4]

By this time nerves in Berlin were on edge. As viewed from the Bendler Strasse, there was something unreal, something tentative about this blasted *Winteruebung* (as *Schulung* was now called by its operational code name). In the light of Wassner's and Gayr's cables, the whole "Winter-Exercise" seemed to be hanging in the balance.

The generals huddled glumly in the map room of the Reichswehr Ministry, with orders ready to be flashed to the troops in the Rhineland, to recall them on a moment's notice if need be. General von Blomberg was as dismayed and apprehensive as the rest. When Gayr's telegram arrived in the early afternoon of Monday, with its warning that there was a fifty percent chance of war, he rushed to the Chancellery with it and demanded that Hitler order the immediate evacuation of Aachen, Trier, and Saarbruecken.

Hitler reprimanded his Reichswehr Minister for losing his head, but Hitler was putting up a show. He was unnerved, as he later conceded to one of his top aides among the planners. "This," he told Colonel Bernhard von Lossberg, "was the greatest risk I ever took in all the conduct of my foreign policies. During that hectic week in March 1936 I really hoped I would not have to go through another such ordeal for at least another ten years."

Wednesday morning, upon their return from another round in Whitehall, Colonel Gayr and Captain Wassner called upon Ambassador von Hoesch to acquaint him with their estimate of the situation. They urged him to formally advise Berlin that war had become a distinct possibility, unless the Reichswehr voluntarily withdrew.

Present at this confrontation was Dr. Fritz Hesse, correspondent of the official German news agency in London, who doubled as the Embassy's press attaché, and who recorded the impact of the service attachés' *démarche* in his diary. "We were aware . . . the danger of war was very near and that France, in the end, would succeed in persuading Great Britain to take military action on her behalf."

Reports flooded the Embassy and Hesse's office at Reuters from English and French contacts, all of them indicating the rapid deterioration of the situation. Hoesch hesitated to send the strongly-worded warning Colonel Gayr and Wassner had practically demanded that he cable. He put in a telephone call to von Neurath instead, and when he was unable to reach the Foreign Minister, he talked to his deputy, Dr. Bernhard von Buelow, to inquire about the mood and outlook in Berlin. Buelow told him that both were grim. Hoesch decided to play his trump card, according to Dr. Hesse: "I will go to the King in person and beg him to intervene before the die is cast."

It was not, Hesse mused, to the monarch's sympathy for Germany that the Ambassador would appeal, but to his love of peace. In his original assessment of the new King's political philosophy, von Hoesch had written on January 21:

"In foreign affairs, Edward VIII shares his father's conviction of the absolute necessity of preserving peace for his people. King Edward is not a pacifist; on the contrary, he desires a Great Britain that is strong, armed and endowed with a sense of honor, ready, if need be, to defend her honor and her possessions.

"He is most profoundly convinced, however, that in modern times war no longer affords a means for settling international disputes; he is, moreover, convinced that a fresh European war must result in the ruin of Europe, its submergence in Bolshevism and thus in the destruction of civilization. Although firmly attached to the old British parliamentary traditions, Edward VIII nevertheless shows far-reaching understanding towards the course followed by other States, and especially by Germany."

It was the King's special "understanding" of the course followed "especially by Germany," that now persuaded the Ambassador to act on his own by making a secret trip to Fort Belvedere, where the King was staying in semi-seclusion to sustain the privacy he craved in his relationship with Mrs. Simpson.

Hoesch prepared his case with meticulous care, in consultation with his closest associates. "I mean to convince His Majesty," he told Prince Otto von Bismarck, his counselor at the Embassy, "that war would be a European as well as a national calamity. I will readily admit that Hitler is formally wrong. But I think I will be able to present his actions as being at least understandable."

That Monday night, on March 9, even as Foreign Minister Flandin was arriving in London for the most critical conferences over the crisis, Hoesch motored to Fort Belvedere. He embarked upon his mission in the utmost secrecy, even using a private car for the trip.

He was back at the Embassy shortly after 9:00 P.M. and called Bismarck and Hesse into his office to describe what had transpired at his audience with the King.

"My argument," he said, "had two main points—one, the military clauses of the Franco-Soviet pact contradicted both the spirit and the text of the Locarno pact; and two, the permanent unilateral demilitarization of the left bank of the Rhine represented an intolerable

humiliation for Germany. I told His Majesty that, after all, the reoc-
cupation of the left bank involved only Germany's own territory, and
assured him that our Fuehrer was now ready to replace the Locarno
pact by a new treaty."

He told Bismarck and Hesse that his argumentation could not have
failed to make "a most favorable impression on a man of good will as
the King undoubtedly was," and that he had succeeded in persuading
Edward VIII to "intercede for peace" with Mr. Baldwin.

The three Germans waited in great excitement in the Ambassador's office for word from the King. It was a long vigil and Bismarck
got tired of waiting, but Dr. Hesse was still with von Hoesch when the
telephone rang.

"The King!" Hoesch told Hesse and beckoned him to take the
other receiver so that he could eavesdrop on the conversation.

"Hello," they heard the familiar voice. "Is that you, Leo? Do you
know who's speaking?"

"Of course, sir," von Hoesch said.

Hesse reported the King as saying: "Listen carefully, I've just seen
the Prime Minister." The King concluded with the fateful words:
"There won't be war!"

As Hesse later described the scene, Hoesch replaced the receiver,
jumped up and danced around the room. "I've done it!" he cried.
"I've outwitted them all! Herr Hesse, we've accomplished the impossible! There won't be war! I must inform Berlin immediately."

Hitler later gave full credit to Edward VIII for preserving the peace
in 1936 (and saving his neck in the process), ascribing the British
decision that the demilitarized zone was not worth fighting about to
the King's intervention at the critical moment. Walter Goerlitz, historian of the German General Staff, later called this "a triumph of
misinterpretation." The morning after, Mr. Baldwin received
M. Flandin at 10 Downing Street, and told him: "You may be right,
but if there is even one chance in a hundred that war would follow
from your police operation, I have not the right to commit England,"
adding after a pause, "England is not in a state to go to war."

The crisis petered out. Hitler was left not merely in the Rhineland,
but in the full possession of his powers.

Actually, as Ralph Wigram of the Foreign Office mused when he
watched the departure of the French delegation with empty hands,
"War is now inevitable, and it will be the most terrible war there has
ever been."

The excitement of these March days proved too much for Dr. von
Hoesch. On April 16 he was struck by a massive heart attack which
killed him, a little over a month after the climactic triumph of his
distinguished service.

NOTES

1 Between 1935 and 1939, he repudiated the disarmament clauses of the Versailles Treaty, moved into the Rhineland, annexed Austria, occupied Bohemia and Moravia, took Memel from Lithuania, and denounced the friendship pact with Poland, all in March.

2 Articles 42–44 of the Versailles Treaty prohibited either the maintenance or the new construction of fortifications of any kind west of the Rhine and within 50 kilometers east of its right bank, and the garrisoning of any part of German armed forces in this demilitarized zone. The ban was reinforced in the Locarno Pact to which Germany was also a signatory.

3 His Grace Karl Eduard, the 45-year-old Duke of Saxe, Coburg, and Gotha, was a double agent of sorts. So close to the Royal family that he was lodged at Kensington Palace (where his sister lived) on his frequent visits to England, the former general in both the Prussian infantry and Saxon cavalry was an ardent admirer of Hitler who made him a senior officer in the brown-shirted Storm Troops and president of the German Red Cross. On this particular occasion in 1936, he arrived in London when King George V was still alive, and planned to visit him at Sandringham because, as he reported to Hitler, his cousin was anxious to discuss with him "certain events in Germany." But before he could make the trip, the King died. The Duke immediately called on Edward VIII and was his sole companion when the new King first motored to Buckingham Palace to take over the rein.

4 When it was all over, poor Colonel Gayr was made the scapegoat of the crisis. Hitler ordered Blomberg to fire him as Military Attaché and even suggested that he be retired altogether. But in this one instance the "Rubber Lion," as the Reichswehr Minister was called for his subservience, dared to defy the Fuehrer. He did recall Gayr from London but allowed him to remain in the army where he rose to the rank of full general in command of a Panzer Army during the Normandy invasion. Captain Wassner was also replaced as Naval Attaché.

Chapter 10

Uncle Richard vs.
Uncle Claude

*W*HEN the mission of Hermann Goertz collapsed in November 1935, its failure was regarded in the Abwehr as the unavoidable misfortune of a brave man tripped up by the hazards of the profession. Dr. Goertz himself contributed to the legend that was developing around him. While he was in Brixton Prison, he managed to smuggle out a letter in which he professed to be indignant about his light sentence. "I did very much more," he wrote to a friend in Germany, "and [the English] knew much more which they could have charged me with than they cared to publicize."

Admiral Canaris considered Goertz's "mishap" a personal blow, and went out of his way to ease the fallen agent's plight. He arranged for the best possible legal defense and paid for it from Abwehr funds via the man's family. He also approved a monthly stipend for Frau Goertz, and even a subsidy for Goertz's girl friend throughout the spy's imprisonment.

Canaris would neither blame Goertz for his downfall nor credit the British for catching him. He was somehow convinced that the man had been betrayed by someone inside the Abwehr and that the internal security of his organization was badly in need of tightening.

He sent for "Uncle Richard."

Commander Traugott Andreas Richard Protze had been a troubleshooter in the old *Marinenachrichtendienst*, Naval Intelligence Office, then continued as the ace spybuster of the Abwehr. A fox among the foxes and a cynic with a strong stomach, he was an odious old pro who regarded every man as guilty even when proven innocent. He could be affable and charming. His personal diplomacy consisted in doing and saying the nastiest things in the nicest way. He could operate with dazzling brilliance, but only in matters that were inherently crooked. Totally dedicated to secret service work, he was probably the only executive of the Abwehr to whom nothing was sacred.

A one-man operator, Protze was incapable of sharing responsibility or delegating work. He remained a loner throughout his years in the Abwehr—dedicated, diligent, and self-effacing on the one hand but eccentric, iconoclastic, and rather sinister on the other. If one doesn't crave credit for things well done, he liked to say, he is not likely to be blamed for mistakes. This principle enabled him to survive a series of crises so that his mistakes were forgotten and only his accomplishments were remembered.

Canaris and Protze were bound to each other by old ties and a new triumph. From his first plunge into clandestine activities in Chile throughout the Twenties, when he was the permanent fixture of every reactionary plot, Canaris considered Protze his mentor and aide. It was whispered in the Abwehr that Protze was privy to Canaris's darkest secret, the killing of the priest in Italy, and that he knew more about the enigmatic little man than anyone else. Whatever it was, Canaris seemed to have ample reason to cultivate his friendship.

At the time of the Goertz crisis, Protze was riding especially high. In the mid-Twenties, an elegant, apparently rich, young ex-captain of the Polish army, Juri de Sosnovsky-Naletz, showed up in Berlin and immediately became the darling of the capital's top society. He was a spy whose lavishness was financed by both the Polish and French secret services. In an intricate plot that included the seduction of two confidential secretaries of the Reichswehr Ministry's Operation Division, Sosnovsky came into possession of some of the most highly classified German military secrets, including the essential parts of the mobilization and deployment plans.

Late in 1933, on a tip from a Countess Bocholtz, a society lady who viewed Sosnovsky's escapades with the jaundiced eyes of a woman who had never been invited into his bed, Commander Protze went after the Pole with an intricate plot of his own. His secretary, Helena O. C. Skrodzki (his closest collaborator and, incidentally, his mistress) gained the confidence of a key figure in the plot—a Hungarian dancer who had been jilted by the Polish captain. With her help, Aunt Lena, as Miss Skrodzki was called in the Abwehr, unraveled the mystery, step by step, until in 1934 the entire Sosnovsky operation could be exposed.[1]

Though the Gestapo was given credit for the coup, Canaris knew that it was the Abwehr's operatives who really deserved the laurels. Protze's investigation went much deeper than the Gestapo was allowed to learn. Aside from the amorous ladies of the Reichswehr Ministry, Canaris also discovered that a socially prominent member of the Abwehr itself was Sosnovsky's chief source of information.[2]

The discovery of an Abwehr officer among the accomplices of a Polish-French master spy gave Protze the idea of setting up a little secret service of his own within the organization to spy on members of the Abwehr. He called it *Hauskapelle*, after the private orchestras the princes of Germany had maintained in their palaces in the eighteenth century.

The thought of such a junta within his agency was repugnant to Captain Patzig. But when Canaris was told about the *Hauskapelle*, he hailed it as a brilliant idea and approved it enthusiastically. The rapid spread of foreign espionage in Germany naturally disturbed him, and he was also concerned that this proliferation of spying on Germany's secrets might bring the Nazis into the Abwehr.

Since the Abwehr had no law enforcement powers, it had to call in the Gestapo to make an arrest whenever it turned up a suspect. Canaris feared that if he proved incapable of stemming the tide of foreign espionage in Germany, Himmler would seize upon this failure as a pretext to seize control of the Abwehr's counterespionage group as the first move toward taking over the whole organization.

Canaris was convinced that only his old friend could solve his problem. "Well," Protze said, "I believe the *Hauskapelle* will uncover any traitors we may harbor in the Abwehr. But the only foolproof way to stop this influx of spies is to penetrate the enemy secret services and deal with the problem at its source."

Every secret service has a branch specializing in the penetration of rival espionage agencies.[3] But without one at that time Protze had to wait idly by until the spies were at their stations inside Germany, and even in the Abwehr, before he could go after them.

Now was born a super-secret activity deep under cover in the Abwehr, mentioned as "GV" in hushed tones even by the few who knew what the letters concealed. They stood for *Geheim-Verbindungen*, or "secret connections," but it was never revealed what those "connections" really were.

Protze was made head of a subbranch in Abwehr III called Section IIIF. His new mission was spelled out in a special directive:

1. To recruit persons for employment in special activities abroad, for the surveillance of espionage suspects, and of the outposts and personnel of enemy secret services.
2. To find ways and means for the clandestine penetration of enemy organizations, to gain insight into their methods, and to ascertain their plans and intentions.
3. To develop confidential contacts with whose help misleading intelligence can be syphoned into enemy organizations.

Penetration is the most difficult and perilous part of the espionage effort. It was an assignment that presupposed the special talents Uncle Richard possessed in abundance.

Protze moved quickly and efficiently to organize Branch IIIF. Captain Adolf von Feldmann of Ast Hamburg, an architect by profession but a passionate hunter of spies in Protze's own mold, was given what, at this stage, appeared to be the most difficult part of the venture—penetration of the British secret service.

Around 1934, after years of stagnation caused by a combination of troubles at home and embarrassing mishaps in the field, the British Secret Intelligence Service appeared to be making a remarkable recovery. Ironically, the promising comeback of the venerable institution originated in a bitter feud that had threatened to wreck the only agency of His Majesty's Government that was "authorized to collect secret information from foreign countries by illegal means."

At this time, S.I.S. was run by an asymmetric triumvirate. It was composed of Admiral Hugh Sinclair, the CSS (Chief of Secret Service), and two colonels, Valentine Vivian, a former high official of the Indian Police, and Claude Dansey, a Territorial officer who made secret intelligence his career after World War I. Admiral Sinclair reigned serenely and supreme but ruled as little as possible, abhorring, as he would say, "the melodramatic chaos" that ensues from too much wheeling and dealing, even in the best-run secret service. He abandoned the day-by-day management of S.I.S. to Vivian and Dansey, though he knew that his two deputies had a passionate distaste for each other and were locked in a feud that virtually paralyzed the service.

It was difficult for anyone to get along with Dansey. Even today, many years after his death, his memory lingers on in an aura of disrepute. A rugged, bearlike man with a purely pragmatic and somewhat lowbrow approach to all his pursuits in life, Dansey was an opinionated, irascible bore. He preferred, as Kim Philby phrased it, to "scatter his venom at long-range" in barbed little memos "which create a maximum of resentment to no obvious purpose."

At close range, Colonel Vivian, lean and elegant, a sensitive person who was easily intimidated, was Dansey's favorite target. Relations between the two became so intolerable even under Sinclair's tolerant rule that the normally imperturbable admiral had to intervene. He turned against Dansey with something akin to the latter's own venom. In the end, he ordered him off the premises, allowing him to show up in the office once a day, and then only to pick up his mail. Dansey, who was becoming superannuated and had no place to go except into oblivion, sought desperately to find a post that would permit him to remain in S.I.S. without occupying space at its main office. He persuaded Admiral Sinclair to let him move to Italy and establish an organization for the purpose of penetrating Germany from bases on the Continent.

Life in Rome without Vivian was comfortable and pleasant, but Italy was not the right place for the operation he had in mind. Dansey moved on to Switzerland and, within a year, built up an organization which he, with the melodrama he liked, called "Z."

Dansey's venture split the continental secret service in two. The old system, managed by Vivian, continued unchanged. It consisted of a string of "stations" called, for the sake of camouflage, Passport Control Offices, attached to the various embassies and legations in the key capitals of Europe. They were headed by S.I.S. career officers, who posed as Passport Control Officers. Their immunity was assured through accreditation at the missions behind whose façade they worked.

The "Z" organizations were set up as separate entities, with their own agents, their own codes and ciphers, couriers, and communications facilities. They were separated from the stations in their own quarters, usually in the guise of commercial enterprises. So complete was Dansey's autonomy, and so tight his security, that some station heads were totally unaware that a parallel branch of the S.I.S. was functioning in their bailiwicks.

By 1935 the boisterous new Germany was ringed by two British espionage organizations, practically encircling her from Vienna via Zurich to Brussels, the Hague and Copenhagen. "Z" made itself felt almost overnight. The annual Abwehr summary reported that about ten percent of all foreign agents caught in Germany that year belonged to a mysterious new outfit, the identity of which even Commander Protze could not establish.

When "Z" was only two years old, two of its outposts became paramount. The one in Copenhagen operated two enormous rings that reached deep into Germany—the "Jens Dons" ring whose members engaged mostly in the collection of intelligence, though one specialized in sabotage.

In the Hague outpost, Dansey's man was Payton Sigismund Best, an ex-captain of the British Army who had spent all his adult life in the secret service. Best had gone to Holland in World War I and remained afterward as a kind of caretaker for S.I.S. He went into the export-import business with two Dutch partners, married Maria Margareta van Rees, the daughter of a retired admiral, and prospered. He lived a life of cultured elegance accepted in Holland's high society, keeping an open house that was famous for its exquisite meals and delightful musicales.

He was a conspicuous figure—the Savile Row type complete with monocle and spats, bowler hat and rolled-up umbrella. He knew how to conceal his association with "Z" and keep his spies under cover, even though his outpost was by far the biggest, most efficient, and most active of all of Dansey's branches.

Best operated several rings, each unaware of the existence of the others, their agents never permitted to know or meet each other.[4] Captain Best's house at 19 Nieuwe Uitweg (adjacent to the brownstone that Mata Hari had occupied during her days as a German spy in World War I) was nominally the head office of his lucrative Continental Trading Company. Actually, it was a teeming center of espionage. But it was not the only one at The Hague.

Another busy outpost was at 57 Nieuwe Parklaan, a quiet residential street on one of the canals, identified as "His Majesty's Passport Control Office" by the shining copper plaque at its main entrance. Here Colonel Vivian had a parallel conglomeration of high-grade agents under his brilliant station head, Captain Hugh Reginald Dalton, who, like Best, was a career S.I.S. officer of World War I. Entirely by his own efforts and from his meager resources, this imaginative spymaster assembled a staff of eleven aides, a miniature secret service by itself.

His second in command was a shadowy character remembered by his nickname, "John," and variously as Augustus de Fremery and Captain Jan Hendricks. The station had its own wireless attended by two radiomen on the staff, Inman and Walsh, who were to gain some prominence during the climactic and tragic days of the outpost in the fall of 1939.[5]

Dalton's phenomenal success in the assembly of a crew of crack spies was due to the efforts of two members of his staff, known to different people by different names at different times. One, called by such names are Zwart, Emmering, Dalmeyer, and Frinten, was Adrianus Johannes Josephus Vrinten, a 42-year-old retired Dutch investigator formerly employed by the Ministry of Justice, who still had exceptional connections in places where they mattered. In the employ of the British since 1919, he was now running an *Informatiebureau*, a combination private detective agency and credit bureau, but only as a blind to conceal his association with Dalton's station as his "recruiter and chief of agents, and liaison to the Dutch police authorities."

The other man was Dalton's indispensable personal factotum, 30-year-old John William (Jack) Hooper, a naturalized British subject of Dutch birth. So completely was he trusted by Dalton that he was given charge of the secret roster of agents and entrusted with the filing of their reports.

Thanks to Vrinten and Hooper, the station boasted the largest number and some of the best agents the British had in the field. According to the roster kept by Vrinten, the station employed fifty-two spies of the first rank. It also had innumerable sub-agents, mostly inside Germany, managed by ring leaders.[6]

Dalton's station had so close a working relationship with the Dutch military intelligence service that the latter's chief, Colonel Willem van Orschoot, was carried on the station's roster as "Agent No. 945." Members of Orschoot's staff thus worked for two masters—for their own colonel, a remarkable spymaster in his own right—and for Major Dalton.

Although The Hague network was a British espionage organization in name, it was a part of Germany's anti-Nazi underground, and deserves to be remembered as such.

NOTES

1 Among the documents Sosnovsky had procured were certain plans for Russo-German military cooperation in the event of a Polish attack.

2 The Abwehr officer's participation in the Sosnovsky plot was covered up for years. When the Germans captured the files of the Polish secret service in 1939 and found documentary evidence of his guilt that could no longer be suppressed, the case was quickly closed by persuading him to commit suicide.

3 Protze had adamantly demanded that he be allowed to organize an Abwehr branch called *Gegenspionage,* literally counterespionage, but in Protze's interpretation it stood for "countering the espionage of others inside Germany."

4 One was called "Brijnen," after its organizer and field manager whose true identity is still unknown. Another was called "Pfaffhausen" and a third was "Willem II," named for Gerhard Hubert Willems, a 27-year-old German socialist, mechanic and six-day bicycle racer. Still another ring was composed of members of the German aristocracy such as Felix Count von Spiegel-Siesenberg and Baron von Gerlach, and managed by an agent in the German Legation in the Hague, the violently anti-Nazi Wolfgang Ganz Edler Herr zu Putlitz.

5 Military intelligence was the province of Captain Lionel Loewe, who was also the station liaison with the Dutch army's intelligence service. Air intelligence was in charge of Squadron Leader, J. B. Newhouse. Others in the office were young Christopher Rhodes, Gustaf Steetman, a Dutchman who once served as a ship's radioman, and another Dutchman, 35-year-old Karl Brewer.

Captain Rodney Dennys (who doubled as the security officer of the station and so had a technical connection with S.I.S.) and a Dutchman named Posthuma, actually handled passports and visas.

6 Theo Hespers, for example, was a 27-year-old native of Muenchen-Gladbach, who had been an eloquent leader of anti-Nazi Catholic youth groups.

Chapter 11

The Battle of the
Trojan Horses

*I*N 1936 the British colony in Holland was badly shaken by a scandal. On September 4 Major Dalton was found shot dead in his quarters. Those who knew what he was doing in The Hague suspected foul play, but it was a plain case of suicide. A team of S.I.S. investigators was not long in discovering why the major had taken his life. An audit of his books revealed a substantial shortage in a special slush fund entrusted to his care.

Earlier in the year the British had abruptly begun to block the migration of Europe's frantic Jews to Palestine and the Zionists responded to the ban by organizing an underground railroad on which able-bodied young Jews were smuggled into the Holy Land from Germany and Poland via Hungary, Rumania, and Turkey. S.I.S. was assigned the task of combatting this illegal immigration and a special "Palestine Fund" was appropriated for the Secret Service by the Foreign Office to finance the operation.

Dalton was given £60,000 from this fund, an enormous sum by the fiscal standards of the chronically stingy S.I.S. and far in excess of the total budget of the station in The Hague. Although he had a salary of 12,000 guilders a year with an expense account, Dalton dipped into the Palestine till to defray a costly love affair that was overtaxing his own means. When an audit discovered that the sum of £2000 was missing from the Palestine Fund and Dalton could not raise the money to make up the shortage, he killed himself.[1]

Dalton's abrupt departure created an awkward situation for S.I.S. It had to find a successor for a dedicated, experienced, and effective station chief in the midst of the build-up of its most ambitious and promising network of spies.

The "Passport Control Officer" sent to take his place was Major

M. R. Chidson. Although an old S.I.S. hand, his main qualifications for the job were that he was married to a Dutch lady and could speak the language fluently. It did not take long for Colonel Vivian to realize that Chidson was "completely unsuited for the secret service." He produced very little of any value, and even that so clumsily that his indiscreet management of the key station threatened to compromise it. "He wanted everything one hundred percent," Sergeant Vrinten later complained, "when in this business forty percent is considered good enough."

Major Chidson lasted for only a few months. In early 1937 the harassed Passport Control Office in The Hague was assigned its third chief in a little over one year, Major Richard Henry Stevens.

A former India hand, as was Vivian himself, Stevens was no newcomer to intelligence work. But though he spoke fluent German, French, and Russian, he was new to service on the Continent. When Vivian asked him to take on a "special job" in The Hague, "to run a bunch of spies in Holland and Germany," Stevens was not apprised of the true circumstances of Dalton's departure. He was told that his predecessor could not get along with Commandant Trutat, his French colleague, and that the station needed somebody like Stevens, an affable and gentle man, who would reestablish cordial relations.

"There won't be anything hazardous about your assignment," Vivian told him. "But, of course, you don't have to accept it if you don't want to. Why, old chap," he added pointedly, "I'm sure your superiors will be glad to ship you back to India."

At first Stevens was inclined to turn down the job. "I had never before been a spy," he later said, "much less a spymaster. My intelligence work, mainly the evaluation of military reports on the deployment of armed native tribesmen, was done solely on the Northwest Frontier." Stevens was a singularly decent and honest man, and he wondered how he would fit into a world in which nothing was ever straightforward. "But I felt challenged," he said, "and so I agreed to go to The Hague as long as my superiors realized that I thought myself to be lacking in experience and training for the assignment and was, in my own eyes, altogether the wrong sort of man for such work."

While still in London Stevens was told nothing about the satellite network Captain Best was running for Dansey. He was briefed only superficially about the organization he was to manage. In The Hague he found a well-oiled machine functioning with clocklike precision and yielding gratifying results—and rapidly growing as more and more anti-Nazis were recruited by Sergeant Vrinten to serve as watchmen in Germany.

Nobody who casually follows the spy game as fragments of it appear in the newspapers can visualize fully—it is difficult even for its students to imagine—the extent of the espionage offensive that was now raging in Europe.

As the crisis deepened with the *Anschluss* in Austria and the noises Hitler was beginning to make about Czechoslovakia, more and more agents working for the British appeared in Germany. They came to represent a distinct majority both among those caught and those still at large. Of the six spies beheaded in 1936, four had worked for the British. Scores of those the Germans had in custody had come via Holland and Denmark, the staging points of British agents enroute to Germany. Their interrogation had supplied the contours of the mysterious network. But no matter how Commander Protze and Captain von Feldmann tried, they could not clear a passage to the employers of the fallen spies.

The first break came in the summer of 1936.

A man named Gustav Hoffmann was arrested for taking some forbidden pictures near Magdeburg. When questioned by Feldmann, he confessed that he was, indeed, a spy, and had been recruited by a Dutchman who, in turn, was working for a British outfit in Holland. Thus the German got his first lead to the S.I.S. station in The Hague.

With half a foot in the door, von Feldmann strove hard to open it a little wider. His opportunity came later in the year with the arrest of another agent, Richard Lange. He, too, had been recruited in Holland, by the same Pied Piper who had lured Hoffmann into espionage. A civil engineer who had agreed to spy on his own country because of his distaste for the Nazis, Lange developed into one of the station's best operatives. But his success turned him into a mercenary professional who became Dalton's most expensive agent. Before long, several hundred pounds were due him, and though he kept dunning his go-between, none of the money was forthcoming. At last, when he threatened to tell the Germans in Holland about his operation, Vrinten agreed to arrange a meeting with the "big boss" himself. Lange thus became the only operative of the Dalton network to learn who the head of The Hague station was.

At the rendezvous Dalton paid part of the debt, promising the balance upon his return to his post in Germany. The agent went back to Hamburg with another shopping list. When the money failed to arrive, Lange with an acute grudge disclosed everything he knew, including the story of his financial difficulties with Major Dalton and Sergeant Vrinten.

Dalton now materialized like a spirit summoned by a medium, and became the prime quarry in the chase. Captain von Feldmann went to The Hague to check him out, but Dalton was dead by then. However, he learned enough about the S.I.S. station to persuade Commander Protze that a frontal attack on the British in Holland would have a good chance of success. Protze, who had the top job in Section IIIF in Berlin, was busy with a number of other promising leads and wanted von Feldmann to go to The Hague and organize the penetration. Admiral Canaris demurred.

"This is too big a job, Uncle Richard," he said. "I think you better go yourself."

Protze, now in his sixties and due for retirement, left the Navy, resigned from the Abwehr *pro forma* (where his place as chief of section IIIF was taken by Colonel Joachim Rohleder), and moved to Holland. Accompanied by Aunt Lena (who was now calling herself Fräulein Schneider), he arrived in The Hague in the fall of 1937, rented a villa at 36 Bloemcamplaan in nearby Wassenaar, a tree-shaded town in the heart of the tulip region, and girded for the battle between the German and British secret services.

As it turned out, it was not as simple as Captain von Feldmann had thought. For all his cunning and ruthless determination, Protze had to bide his time for six months, and then he stumbled on an opening to his coveted target only by an astounding *faux pas* of the opposition.

It was on a warm July evening in 1938, when he was returning with Aunt Lena from shopping in The Hague, that Protze first noticed a short, thickset, young man riding with him in the train, saw him alight at their destination, follow them slowly to their street, stop briefly in front of his villa, then walk on quickly and vanish around the corner. Protze had the feeling that the man was there to shadow him, but he could not be sure.

The man was back the next day. He came on a bicycle and rode around the block several times. "Then," Protze later told me, "he stumped out of the shadows, and strolled up and down in our street, stopping from time to time to glance at my house. He hardly took the precaution to conceal himself. He could be a police investigator, I thought. I suspected that the Dutch did not quite believe me."

"Or," Protze continued, "he could have been sent by the competition. But which one? I knew, of course, that the Big Three had major outposts in The Hague, the British at Nieuwe Parklaan, the French at their Legation, and the Russkies on Celebesstraat. It was the best and most insidious of the three, actually the center of the Red Army's military intelligence in Western Europe, headed by the notorious Walter Krivitsky. He used the name of Dr. Martin Lessner and posed as a rare-book dealer from Austria. At first I was convinced that Krivitsky had sent the man after me, because it was usually his agents who behaved so conspicuously. Anyone of the three had a legitimate right to be curious about me. I resolved that I would find out which one of them this vagabond was working for."

On the third day the man showed up shortly before sunrise, when the people of Wassenaar were still sound asleep. But Protze was awake and up. When he looked out of his bedroom window and saw the familiar figure skulking below, he decided it would be a good time to challenge his shadow. He dressed quickly and started on a long hike, drawing the man toward the deserted beach. With only the two of them strolling on the white sand, Protze stopped abruptly in his tracks and turned around, almost bumping into the man.

"Don't you meddle with me," Protze told him sternly, "it won't do you any good. I have in mind to call the police and charge you with molesting me."

The man was undaunted. He was back the next day and now Protze decided to act, by calling the police as he had warned him. The policeman he sent after the loiterer was not a real cop. He was the field manager of his own agents, a Dutch Nazi named Hooge-veen, whom he had inherited from the Gestapo for which the man had been spying on German refugees in Holland.

The bogus policeman accosted the young fellow and was about to "arrest" him when Protze appeared to take over. He knew who he was, he yelled at the startled man, and what he was up to—a spy sent to shadow him! As the man stared at him in sullen silence, Protze asked sharply how much he was being paid to keep an eye on him. Well, the man said, it was all part of his job. What job? Protze shot back, and the man blurted out that he was working for the British Passport Office at Parklaan.

Protze suddenly realized that the big break he was so impatiently hoping for had come. He commanded the man to follow him into the villa, and then, in the privacy of his parlour, he made his first deal. The man said his name was Van Koutrik, and was actually employed by the firm of Mueller & Company, but was performing occasional jobs like this, doing a bit of sleuthing on the side. His assignment was to keep tabs on "Mr. Roberts," as he called Protze, and also to jot down the numbers on the license plates of cars that were bringing visitors to the villa.

When Protze asked him how much the British were paying him for this moonlighting, Van Koutrik said that he was supposed to be getting 200 guilders a month plus expenses, but he had to fight for every heller as far as his expenses were concerned.

All right, Protze said, offering him a chance, as he put it, of making some real money. If he agreed to work for him, too, he would pay him another 200 guilders a month, and he could be sure that he would get it without a hassle. Van Koutrik accepted the offer avidly. He would be glad to work for Protze, because, he told the old fox, he liked the Germans. He'd report everything he could find out about the passport office.

It was a rare case of penetration, even if it took Protze a little time to realize how fantastic this windfall really was.

Folkert Arie Van Koutrik had made his way to the shadow world of the secret service through a man named Zaal, Sergeant Vrinten's genuine partner in the Information Bureau. Zaal was still another veteran of the S.I.S. in World War I. In 1937, when his workload was increasing by leaps and bounds, Vrinten invited his associate to rejoin S.I.S., but Zaal turned him down.

Instead, he recommended the 24-year-old son of an old friend of his, a former detective. He then introduced young Van Koutrik to Vrinten; the sergeant, in turn, arranged a rendezvous for the promising candidate with Dalton's replacement, Major Chidson, in a café in Rotterdam. The eager, intelligent Dutchman so impressed the major at first sight that Chidson hired him for such odd jobs as trailing and cut-outing (acting as a go-between agent or courier), despite the potential security risk in his background, Van Koutrik's comely German wife.

Given the cover-name of "Oliver Kendall" on the station's roster of go-betweens, and an advance of 500 guilders, Van Koutrik received his first assignment then and there. He was to shadow Herr zu Putlitz, the German diplomat in The Hague who was making his first overture to the British and had to be checked out before being accepted into the fold.

Herr zu Putlitz became the first British agent whom Van Koutrik betrayed to Commander Protze. When, however, Protze informed zu Putlitz's superior in The Hague that "one of his aides" was suspected of being a British spy, the startled envoy, to whom the identity of the suspect was not yet revealed, chose to discuss the embarrassing scandal with none other than Herr zu Putlitz himself. Thus warned, the diplomat escaped to London where he became an important link in the chain of anti-Nazis who worked for the British.

It was in the course of this string of events that Van Koutrik became a double agent, working for the British as before while telling all he knew about them to the tall, stocky old German with the icy blue eyes. Since Van Koutrik was a fair and a basically honest man, he worked for both with equal diligence.

Protze moved quickly to make the most of his opportunity.

As a first step, he summoned Captain von Feldmann to The Hague to assist him in this intricate operation.

The two of them bought one of the flat-bottomed barges that cruise indolently up and down the gray canals of The Hague, put a movie camera on it, and anchored it on the *gracht* on which the passport office fronted, barely thirty yards from its entrance. Everyone who entered or left the building was filmed, and then, in nocturnal *Treffs*, the pictures were shown to Van Koutrik to identify the subjects for Protze. Before long, the Germans had a well-nigh complete list, not only of the personnel employed at the British station, but also of its callers, as well as of some of the agents who worked in the field.

The tide had turned. The British had lost the first round of the battle. It was only a matter of time before they would lose this whole secret war.

Now Protze was getting his breaks wholesale. He had a foothold inside the S.I.S. station in The Hague. He was becoming increasingly confident that sooner or later he would be able to destroy the entire S.I.S. operation on the Continent.

First to go, oddly enough, was not The Hague network. By one of the game's strange coincidences, it was Colonel Dansey's Danish outpost in Copenhagen that was initially smashed.

In November 1938 the Danes, disturbed by the increased espionage activities of foreigners on their soil, instituted an elaborate spy hunt, and one of the "Z" saboteurs, a man named Waldemar Poetsch, and an associate named Knueffken were caught. At that time all espionage agents were presumed to be in German service, but Knueffken's interrogation developed the startling fact that he was working for the British. The Danes were most reluctant to interfere with the operations of British agents, but, since the arrests had already been mentioned in the newspapers, they had to go through with prosecuting them. Although their trial was held *in camera*, the Germans managed to procure Knueffken's confession, and so learned a lot about the management and the operations of the British secret service on the Continent.

Additional damaging information reached the Germans from another Danish source. One of Protze's aides, Lieutenant Meyer of the IIIF branch at Wilhelmshaven, managed to infiltrate the Copenhagen police department and enlist the confidential assistant of the chief of police. From this source, the Germans obtained additional information about the activities of the Continental secret service, not only in Denmark, but in all of Scandinavia.

Captain Protze (Canaris had promoted him) went after Poetsch with a vengeance. He became obsessed with the idea of abducting him because he was certain that the agent could be "persuaded," in German hands, to crack open the British secret underground.

He first planned to kidnap Poetsch from his Danish jail. When the Danes stumbled upon the plot and allowed Dansey to smuggle the man out of Copenhagen aboard a freighter, Protze went so far as to arrange for an act of piracy on the high seas. A speedboat of the German Navy was to intercept the freighter and hijack it to a Baltic port where Poetsch could be removed. Admiral Canaris vetoed the raid, and Poetsch reached Belgium safely, where Colonel Dansey was trying desperately to salvage what he could of his badly shattered Danish ring.

After the debacle in Denmark, all subversive activities shifted back to The Hague, with Vivian and Dansey unwittingly playing into Captain Protze's hands. For one thing, Major Stevens was not quite the right substitute for Dalton any more than Chidson. For another, Protze now had Van Koutrik.

The German, whose greatest asset was his skepticism, had no illusions about Van Koutrik, at least not in the beginning when it was obvious that the young Dutchman was playing the game slyly. The situation gradually changed as Van Koutrik changed. Step by step he drifted away from the British, and closer to the Germans. His association with Protze became more intimate and increasingly profitable, even as his relations with Stevens and Vrinten cooled.

His old ties loosened; his loyalty weakened. He was thinking more of himself and less of the station. The British, always so stiff and never too generous either with praise or financial rewards, had become, after the slipshod management of the station's finances, outright stingy. Van Koutrik was still getting only 200 guilders a month, and Stevens never thought of slipping him bonuses as Chidson had done.

Slowly Protze was replacing Stevens in Van Koutrik's secret life. The German had none of the condescension with which Stevens treated him. Where Stevens was becoming more and more tight-fisted, Protze was becoming increasingly liberal with his money. Van Koutrik cleverly concealed his change of heart, never giving Stevens reason to suspect that he was shifting his allegiance. He was no longer a British agent; now he worked for the Germans.

He was tipping Protze off to nearly every spy ready to go on a mission, betraying his assignment, cover, and itinerary, actually ensuring that the man would be dead on arrival.

Suddenly Stevens found the going hard. Although he could not help noticing that something must have gone wrong, he still suspected no treachery within his own organization.

In early 1939, Van Koutrik led Protze to the crowning coup of this hectic period—to an agent whose discovery in itself made this entire project worth all the effort and money Uncle Richard had spent on it. The postmortem of the Dalton suicide had also exposed another culprit, a blackmailer *pro domo* rather than an embezzler *per se*. He was John ("Jack") Hooper, Major Dalton's trusted assistant. When Hooper discovered that his chief was dipping into the slush fund, he threatened to denounce him unless Dalton cut him in. From then on the two men shared the loot, as Hooper, who did not choose to follow Dalton into death, confessed to the investigators.

It would have been the smart and proper thing, as propriety goes in such instances, to arrange for Hooper's body to be found floating in one of the *grachts*, and Colonel Dansey was tempted to give the man his just deserts. Colonel Vivian vetoed such drastic retribution. Hooper was dismissed; all that could be done as an alternative, for it would have been impossible to turn him over to the police.

The man vanished into limbo, trying to eke out a living as a salesman in Rotterdam of aircraft parts, unaware that two people were eagerly looking for him. One was Colonel Dansey, who had concluded in the meantime that Jack Hooper was too valuable a secret servant to be dumped over such trivia as blackmailing and embezzling.

The other was Commander Protze. He had been trying to find Hooper, on the assumption that the thief the British had permitted to disappear could still be helpful. But he could not track him down. Then he casually asked Van Koutrik whether he knew what had become of the missing man.

Jack Hooper had kept in tenuous touch with Nieuwe Parklaan during his blue period, and so Van Koutrik had learned where he could be found in Rotterdam. A meeting with Hooper was arranged, and Protze made contact.

By this time the German contingent of counter-spies in Holland had also been reshuffled. Protze was left in Wassenaar, but he had been compromised by Sergeant Vrinten and presumably also by Van Koutrik.

The ambitious counterespionage operation against the British in The Hague was entrusted to the care of Section IIIF at the Hamburg outpost where, almost three years before, Captain von Feldmann had started the ball rolling. Now in 1938, when the penetration attained its full momentum, von Feldmann was given an assistant, a stocky, rosy-cheeked middle-aged captain with sparkling blue eyes and a perennially sardonic smile on his thin lips. He was Hermann J. Giskes.

The new man at Section IIIF had come from the vast reservoir of former army officers whom the Versailles Treaty had unfrocked and who sat out the interval making a living in whatever civilian occupations they could find. Giskes went into the wine business in the

Rhineland but rejoined the army in 1937, and was detailed to the Abwehr, because he was considered "a sly fox" with the ingenuity and taciturnity the job required. In Section IIIF he served as von Feldmann's deputy. When, in the spring of 1939, his superior received an assignment to go to Portugal for three months, to lay the foundations for a penetration-bureau there in anticipation of the impending war, Captain Giskes was put in charge of the unfinished business at The Hague with the British.

Captain Protze had turned his contact with Hooper over to von Feldmann, and Giskes inherited him. Now he was to become the Abwehr's most precious possession in Holland, and Giskes made a special trip to Rotterdam to see him. The meeting was to become one of the most lucrative *Treffs* in his remarkable career as a counterespionage executive.

Bitter about his former employers, and well paid by the Germans, Hooper betrayed the British to Giskes with unbounded glee, proving, if nothing else, how right Colonel Dansey's first impulse was to dispose of him once and for all. Hooper's close relations with the station in The Hague had ended, of course, a few years before. But he had its secrets stored away in his head, and many of them still proved of great interest to Giskes.

The day came, eventually, when it seemed that Hooper had nothing more to give away. Naturally anxious to keep the lucrative connection going, he continued to regale the German with revelations, embellishing old tales and inventing new ones. Catching him in one of his fantasies, Giskes, who could be very tough behind his genial exterior, became stern. He was convinced that Hooper still had a few stray secrets that, for some inscrutable reason, he was keeping to himself.

The showdown came in April 1939 during a stormy session when Giskes told Hooper to go to hell, that he would not get another red *heller* from him. Fearful that he was through, Hooper played his trump card. He gave away the ace among the agents the British had in Germany, the one spy so big and so important that he alone was worth more than all the small fry Van Koutrik had betrayed.

Back in 1919 the British secret service in Hamburg had come upon an engineer in the flotsam of German naval officers that the war had made unemployed and restive. They offered him a job as a spy and the man signed up. He went into private practice as a consulting naval engineer in Kiel and prospered, doing nearly all of his business with the Reichsmarine. He knew all of its secrets, many of which he himself had produced with his inventions. From this unique vantage point, he developed into a one-man secret service, covering the entire German Navy by his own efforts.

The British referred to him as "Dr. K" and built a wall of seemingly ironclad security around him. Hooper knew who he was and how he operated. Now he asked Giskes how much "Dr. K" would be worth to him. Giskes, sensing the importance of the man, agreed to pay him the unheard of sum of 10,000 guilders in pounds sterling, half when Hooper revealed the man's real name, the remainder when he was caught.

"His real name is Otto Krueger," Hooper said after pocketing the front money. "They call him Doktor Krueger. He lives in Godesberg near Bonn, but comes to Holland for his meetings with the station head, and stays in the Amstel in Amsterdam or in the Hotel des Indes when he is in The Hague."

When Giskes discussed the case with Protze, the old pro was stunned. He knew Krueger from his old days in the Navy when the man had served as an engineering commander at the Northern Naval Station. For twenty years, then, this former officer had lived a double life. He flourished in business and grew steadily in affluence and respectability. In the Thirties, he had reached the pinnacle of his postwar profession. He was elected to the board of directors of the Federation of German Industries, and was so highly regarded that one of the German institutes of technology had awarded him the honorary degree of the Doctor of Engineering.

Yet all the time he was a British spy!

His relation with S.I.S. was perfectly camouflaged. Krueger was a gifted engineer who had several valuable naval inventions protected by patents he franchised to English and Dutch firms. The substantial sums the British were paying him reached Krueger camouflaged as payments for the manufacturing licenses he had sold abroad. It was a legitimate income, it seemed. All he had to do to conceal this added revenue was to pad his bills, including in his accounts receivable the fees the British were paying him for his profitable sideline in espionage.

Dr. Krueger was placed under surveillance. He was shadowed, his offices and home in Godesberg were bugged, his telephone was tapped, and his mail was intercepted and read. His private life was closely scrutinized. But the comprehensive investigation produced no evidence, furnished no clues. His life was exactly what it was supposed to be—affluent, dignified, completely above board, without blemish. He had no vices, kept no mistress, did not drink or gamble, was no drug addict. His bank accounts showed no extra income. He seemed to have no hidden assets.

Late in June, after a visit to the teeming Blohm & Voss shipyards in Hamburg and calls at the Naval Station, Dr. Krueger left for Holland on one of his regular business trips. The moment of truth was at hand, for Hooper had told Giskes that it was on these trips that this distinguished gentleman became a spy. Giskes planted his agents at both the Amstel and the Hotel des Indes, and arranged for the discreet surveillance of Dr. Krueger during his stay in Holland. This time his quarry went straight to The Hague and checked into his hotel, then remained in his room. All day he could be heard typing furiously. The waiter on his floor, who was one of Giskes's agents, brought in his meals and saw a score of typed sheets strewn on the floor, but no notes at the typewriter. Kreuger carried everything in his head, all the innermost secrets of the German navy, which he was now committing to paper for his employers.

At seven o'clock in the evening, dressed in a tuxedo, he left the hotel in a car that had come to pick him up, and then dined with an elegant elderly couple at a Javanese restaurant famed for its rice table. At half-past nine, he was driven to a villa at the seaside resort of Scheveningen.

A search of his room in his absence produced no incriminating evidence. The man he dined with was known as a business associate. Nothing was observed during the dinner to arouse the suspicion of the man Giskes had sent to keep watch on Krueger. When his car was trailed to the villa in Scheveningen he was seen entering the house, then leaving it at shortly after midnight. He was driven straight to his hotel.

Except for the few hours he had spent in the villa, his conduct was above suspicion. Inquiries about the house at Scheveningen failed to reveal anything to indict him as a spy. Was Hooper telling the truth when he fingered Krueger? Captain Giskes was beginning to fear for his 5,000 guilders.

There was still the unexplained trip to Scheveningen. The villa was owned by August de Fremery, a Belgian of apparently independent means. He proved an authentic mystery man. No amount of probing produced any hard information about him, until Captain Protze asked Van Koutrik at their next meeting:

"Does the name August de Fremery mean anything to you?"

"Why, of course," the Dutchman said. "It's the real name of 'Jan,' our Captain Hendricks."

Hendricks was the British deputy station head on Nieuwe Park-laan.

On July 8, Hooper was paid the other 5,000 guilders. Dr. *honoris causa* Otto Krueger alias "Dr. K" had been taken into custody the day before in Hamburg and confessed everything during the night.

The first phase of the Protze operation was over. The amazing network Major Dalton had built had been smashed. All S.I.S. agents in Germany were either dead or awaiting execution or at large on borrowed time. Britain's one and only superspy was in prison.[2]

NOTES

1 The grapevine in The Hague was buzzing also with a different version. According to Lieutenant Colonel Tiete Solke Roosebloom of the Netherlands Secret Service, no embezzlement of the Palestine money was involved in the tragedy. Dalton committed suicide when it was discovered that he had set himself up in the business of selling pre-dated British passports and visas to the Holy Land to rich German Jews who were only too glad to pay any price to escape from the Nazis.

2 On September 4, 1939, the morning after the outbreak of the Anglo-German war, Dr. Krueger committed suicide in his cell.

Chapter 12

A Frontier Incident

*T*HE great battle of the Trojan horses now moved rapidly toward its ending.

On September 3, 1939, Britain declared war on Germany, and on the same day Colonel Claude Dansey instructed Captain Best to take his "Z" organization into Major Stevens's station in The Hague. The move was made mandatory by the conditions created by the war. The ring that Best was managing had no line of communication except the link with Dansey, who had his headquarters in Brussels. The day war broke out Dansey returned to London and, after that, he had to use the facilities of The Hague station to maintain contact with his "Z" men on the Continent.

This was the fatal move. Van Koutrik needed only two or three weeks to find out as much about its operations as he had already known about those of Major Stevens. In a last fling of treachery he betrayed them all to Captain Protze. Within a month the Germans had completely smashed the remarkable network Dansey had put together in six long years.

The roundup of the "Z" men was done so quietly in Germany that Stevens and Best still had no inkling of the demise of their network. They themselves were operating on borrowed time. Plans were being made in Berlin, in a rare collaboration between the Abwehr and the SD, to close down the British station in The Hague and, for all practical purposes, liquidate the S.I.S. on the Continent.

This was the worst debacle the British suffered in the history of their secret intelligence—and all through the failure of a small cog in their machine.

Although the Germans had every reason to believe that they had a devastating Trojan horse inside the S.I.S., there were also such beasts

121

within their own camp. Folkert Arie Van Koutrik continued to live a double life. He went on working for the Germans, still via Captain Protze, while serving the British to their complete satisfaction.[1]

But Jack Hooper had had a change of heart.

During the tense days before the outbreak of the war, he made a pilgrimage to Major Stevens, and confessed that he had "played a little ball" with the Germans, without disclosing, of course, his betrayal of Dr. Krueger. He was forgiven and allowed to return to British service.

Major Stevens now thought that Hooper's straying from the fold could be exploited by using him to penetrate the German outposts in Holland and to compromise Captain Giskes with whom he remained in touch. A bizarre project then developed from this game—a plot to eliminate Giskes from the bout.

Hooper was to notify Giskes in Hamburg that he had "something so big" that he could give it to him only in person in Rotterdam, and a *Treff* was set up. The plan was to kidnap Giskes in Holland, get whatever information could be squeezed from him, then surrender him to the Dutch authorities (who would have had enough on this meddler in their affairs, especially with Hooper as a star witness) to lock him up for the duration.

At this point, in early October 1939, Captain Protze suddenly reentered the game. He had just been told by Van Koutrik that Hooper had returned to the British side, and Protze flashed a warning to Hamburg. By then Giskes was on his way to the *Treff* with Hooper. His office sent out frantic calls all along his route, and reached him at last when his train stopped at Enschede on the German-Dutch border, with a message to contact his headquarters. When Giskes put in the call, Captain Wichmann of Ast X ordered him to return to Hamburg, where he then learned that Hooper had become a double agent again, this time loyally working for the British.

Although this kidnapping was thwarted, it inspired another of far greater consequence. While the Germans had infiltrated the supposedly impregnable Secret Intelligence Service, the British were able to tap an even richer lode by reaching into the highest councils of the Third Reich in a plot so big and bizarre that it seemed beyond belief.

Shortly before the outbreak of the war the British found out, through the courageous action of two young anti-Nazis, Ewald von Kleist-Schmenzin and Ferdinand von Schlabrendorff, that a conspiracy was brewing in Germany to overthrow the Nazis. They had come to London to establish contact with the British Government and enlist its support. The members of the group formed a heterogeneous group of professional men, clergymen, high officials in the government, and officers in the Wehrmacht, scions of the upper classes largely, but also containing a sprinkling of Social Democrats the Gestapo had somehow overlooked. They were bound in a common purpose by their irrevocable opposition to Hitler and their generally pro-Western orientation.

Their effectiveness depended on support from abroad, and they solicited it avidly, at considerable peril. But it was not a simple matter during the heedless years of appeasement to kindle the imagination of the British and to attract their attention to this potential gold mine.

Now that the war had broken out, Whitehall at long last bestirred itself to exploit the unprecedented opportunities it had so long neglected. Stevens and Best were instructed to establish contact with the German anti-Nazi underground.

The conspirators were to go into action early in November, assassinate Hitler, overthrow his regime and make peace with the West. Several plans were drafted to ambush the Fuehrer, and it looked as if the war would be over before Christmas.

Unfortunately, Britain and the German plotters were no longer alone in the conspiracy. Just when the British decided to deal directly with the plotters, there appeared in the background the ubiquitous Uncle Richard and a new intruder, Reinhard Heydrich.

At Canaris's instructions, Protze took a back seat in the counterplot and let Heydrich attack the conspiracy indirectly, by hitting the British secret service, which maintained contact with the anti-Nazis via The Hague.

As usual, the admiral kept a watchful eye on the venture by delegating his officer Lieutenant Commander Johannes Travaglio to cooperate with Heydrich in the development of the plot.

Contact was made with Captain Best through a mousy little German who called himself Dr. Franz and posed as a Catholic refugee from the Reich. Actually he was a Gestapo informer, Agent F.479, who had been sent to Holland in 1938 to infiltrate circles of German refugees as well as Commandant Trutat's branch of the *Deuxième Bureau* in The Hague. He succeeded admirably in both endeavors, and was sending reports about German refugees to Heydrich while, at the same time, feeding doctored "intelligence" to the Frenchman.

In 1939, when Protze found out about Stevens and Best, Dr. Franz was instructed to establish relations with them as well. He managed to get to Best through a Dutchman named Vrooburgh, who was to the "Z" organization what Vrinten was to Stevens, and kept the British supplied with information about the Luftwaffe that the

Germans had concocted for him. Best had no reason to trust him unreservedly, if only because Dr. Franz was extremely loquacious and far too prolific for his own good. But he was tolerated in the fold. At least once in a while some of the intelligence he was submitting turned out to be accurate.

Early in September, Franz, who until then had dealt with Best through Vrooburgh, demanded to see his chief in person. He had some momentous information that he would entrust only to the chief himself. Contrary to his normal practice and against his better judg-ment, Best agreed to meet Franz. The phony refugee revealed that the information he had been funneling to the Secret Service origi-nated with a Luftwaffe major named Solms, who was a member of the anti-Nazi underground. Solms now had information about certain events that could lead to the downfall of Hitler, but he refused to entrust them to Franz. He had instructed the doctor to arrange a meeting with Captain Best.

Best agreed and suggested that the major come to Amsterdam or The Hague. Solms replied through Franz that he could not come so far. Best then agreed to meet him at Venlo, a village on the Dutch-German frontier.

Solms turned out to be a bluff, self-confident, excitable Bavarian who talked as big as he looked. It soon became evident that he was only an errand boy for more important people. A second meeting was arranged for the following week, again at Venlo. This time the major was calmer and less boastful. He talked coherently of his mis-sion, which was to get British support for an ambitious plot, headed by an anonymous general, to overthrow Hitler. Best made a mini-mum effort to check up on the man's *bona fides*. He asked him a few technical questions; and, when Solms answered them precisely, Best was satisfied that his man was on the level. No other efforts were made to check up on Solms or, for that matter, on Dr. Franz. Both men were accepted at face value.

During the second meeting a code was devised in which Solms would communicate with Best, via Franz and a mail drop in the Netherlands. A few days later Franz told Best that he had received a call from another officer in Germany, who informed him in the code that a letter had been sent to the drop for Best's eyes only. The letter arrived, and in it the anonymous correspondent advised Best that the mysterious leader of the plot, "the General," was prepared to meet him in person, provided Best could convince him that he was a top-ranking British agent. Attached to the letter was an ingeniously worded news item which Best was to have broadcast by the BBC on its German beam. The item was broadcast twice on October 11.

Solms had faded out of the picture with the explanation that the

Gestapo had him under surveillance. The General was to handle things in person. As the plot moved to higher echelons Best thought it advisable to draw Major Stevens into the maneuver. The developing drama was also revealed to General J.W. van Oorschot, director of Dutch military intelligence, who assigned a young Dutch intelligence officer, Lieutenant Dirk Klop, to act as his liaison.

At last, Franz told Best that the General was ready to meet him. A rendezvous was arranged for 10:00 A.M. on October 19, this time at the small frontier village of Dinxperlo.

The Germans arrived at noon, two hours late. There was no general in the group, only two officers, both in their early thirties, who introduced themselves as Lieutenants Seydlitz and Grosch. Franz vouched for them. Best drove the party to an isolated roadside café, and there treated them to lunch. An undefinable tension arose during lunch, and Franz in particular seemed to become very excited.

The party attracted attention, the worst thing that could have happened during a clandestine meeting. Best thought it advisable to remove to safer surroundings, called a friend in nearby Arnheim, and continued the conference in the friend's dining room.

The party had attracted the attention of a Dutch soldier, who called the police and told them that "a bunch of German spies" was having a meeting, first at the café and then in the Arnheim house to which he had tracked the party. The police surrounded the house, broke in, and demanded an explanation. Lieutenant Klop explained things to the officers and they withdrew, but the basic security of the enterprise had been breached. During this episode the two Germans were thrown into a panic and tried to escape through the windows. Little Dr. Franz nearly passed out. Still, nothing kindled Best's suspicions.

To a great extent, all the excitement was in vain. The two Germans had brought no information. They were simply authorized to arrange another meeting, holding out the phantom general as bait. Best agreed, and the next meeting was planned for October 25, then postponed to the 30th. On that day, Klop alone went to Dinxperlo with instructions to bring the Germans to The Hague.

The General was still not in the group, but this time there were three officers instead of two. Seydlitz was missing, but Grosch was present, with a man who identified himself as Colonel Martini, and a Major Schemmel, who was apparently the leader of the group. He was a stocky young man in his late twenties, his baby face furrowed with dueling scars, making him far too conspicuous for such a secret mission. Although he looked like a dullard, he turned out to be exceptionally well-informed; he had a decisive manner and a firm control over the situation.

Schemmel gave a clear and concise exposition of the internal situation of Germany and told Best that, on behalf of the General, he could guarantee an end to the war provided the British were willing to give Germany an honorable peace. Stevens and Best gave Schemmel a noncommittal answer, pending instructions from London.

Best had given the Germans a wireless set to facilitate communication. The Germans radioed their messages to the communications center of British Intelligence in The Hague. The messages were relayed to the S.I.S. in London and were then forwarded to Mr. Chamberlain and Foreign Secretary Lord Halifax.

Best and Stevens were instructed by London to "pursue the matter with energy" and to deal with the Germans sympathetically, but cautiously, to save His Majesty's Government embarrassment in the event of failure. Another inconclusive meeting was held at Venlo on November 7 (there was still no general) and still another was arranged for November 9. This one was to be decisive.

The morning was dull and cold; rain hung in the autumn air. The weather dampened Best's enthusiasm and he was also disturbed by the fact that for the last few days he had been trailed by an unpleasant looking stout man, though he did not connect this shadow with the plot.

At ten o'clock he went to Stevens's house on Nieuwe Parklaan, and found that his colleague was also uneasy. The major went to a drawer, took out two Browning automatics, loaded them, gave one to Best and slipped the other into his pocket. While they waited for Lieutenant Klop, the Germans came in on the radio, on a direct beam. Best expected another cancellation, but this turned out to be a routine request for a change in the hours of transmission. Best concluded that everything was going well.

Klop arrived and, with Best's driver, a Dutchman named Jan Lemmens, at the wheel, the party proceeded to Venlo at a leisurely pace. As they drove, their conversation drifted to the possibility of invasion, and Stevens did a most unusual thing, especially on a mission of this kind. He took a pencil and a piece of paper and jotted down a list of the contacts he would have to get out of Holland if the Germans invaded. Whether the list was still on him at the climax of this adventure only Stevens knew. Best thinks Stevens succeeded in destroying it.

It was shortly after four when the party arrived at the rendezvous, the red-brick Café Backus, just two hundred yards from the frontier and popular with smugglers. Nobody was in sight in the street, but Best noticed that, for the first time in his experience, the frontier barrier on the German side had been lifted, though the Dutch was not.

Best spotted Major Schemmel on the second-floor veranda of the Backus and saw him give a signal with a sweeping move of his right arm.

He thought the major was beckoning him to drive up to the café but, just as his car was coming to a stop, he heard an outburst of shouting and shooting. A large green car sped up from the German side of the border past the unguarded Dutch barrier and stopped as it hit the bumper of Best's automobile. It was filled with men, two of whom sat on the hood firing submachine guns.

Stevens leaned over and said, "I am afraid our number is up, Best!" The next moment both Britons were subdued and handcuffs snapped on their wrists. With little courtesy, they were marched into Germany as the frontier barrier slowly came down behind them.

The driver, Lemmens, brought up the rear, but there was no sign of Klop. In the commotion the young officer tried to escape, but just as he was vanishing under a bush a German spotted him. A machine gun opened up and "Cloppens" was mortally wounded.

What Best and Stevens should have suspected long before, since the Germans had managed their end with remarkable clumsiness, was now made abundantly evident: their fabulous plot was a German trap. The idea had originated in Heydrich's active brain. Its execution was assigned to a rising young star in the *Sicherheitsdienst*, Walter Schellenberg, only twenty-eight years old, a cold and calculating intellectual with consummate talent for secret service work.

Schellenberg was "Major Schemmel." "I admit," Best later wrote, "that he had completely taken Stevens and me in when we met him in Holland, but this was not really surprising since he was exceptionally well-informed and had been well-briefed for the occasion. Besides, the man was a natural conspirator, who, as events showed, kept faith with no one."

"Colonel Martini," introduced as "the General's" personal aide and confidant, was Professor de Crisis, an Austrian psychiatrist who had risen to the top of his profession in the Third Reich solely because he was Heydrich's friend. "Lieutenant Grosch" was Lieutenant Commander Johannes Travaglio, representing the Abwehr. Though never actually produced as promised, a "General" was in readiness should he be needed. He was an industrialist and a high-ranking SS officer whom Heydrich had picked for the cast of the hoax.

Heydrich had scored a stunning victory, although he failed to reach the German opposition. Stevens and Best were merely at the fringes of the greater plot. They knew none of its real leaders and few of its details, so they could reveal nothing about it during their intensive interrogation by Schellenberg. They were at the very heart of conventional espionage efforts aimed at Germany, the *spiritus rector* of the British spy network operating inside the Reich.

Even as Stevens and Best were being incarcerated in the Gestapo dungeons in the Prinz Albrecht Strasse in Berlin, Schellenberg used the wireless link to The Hague to continue the game. Seven days after the incident, Captain Jan Hendricks, Stevens's deputy, was still so ignorant of what had really happened at Venlo that he responded eagerly to Major Schemmel's suggestion that they play a little longer.

At 12:30 P.M. on November 16, he gave radioman Walsh a signal for Major Schemmel that read: "We are prepared now as before to continue negotiations along lines previously agreed upon. Next meeting must await results of consultation with Premier Daladier of France. In view of what happened, must proceed henceforth with utmost caution." The British were still convinced that this was a genuine operation, and naïvely assumed that somehow the Gestapo had cracked its security. Although the Germans had kidnapped the participants of the Venlo conference, the British clung to their belief that the Nazis were incapable of smashing the conspiracy. They were disabused by "Schemmel's" next signal, which contained a venomous little touch added by the malignant Schellenberg. It read: "Negotiations for any length of time with conceited and silly people are tedious. You will understand, therefore, that we are giving them up. You are hereby bidden a hearty farewell by your affectionate German Opposition."

It was signed "The Gestapo."

On Nieuwe Parklaan in The Hague, the message was routinely intercepted and transcribed by the British radio operator, who acknowledged it with a polite "Thank you." As was his custom, he added his name—"Walsh."[2]

NOTES

1 So completely was Van Koutrik trusted by the British that, on the day of the German invasion of Holland in 1940, he was evacuated in one of His Majesty's warships with the rest of the staff of S.I.S. Accompanied by his German wife, he landed in Folkstone on May 10, and was then given the sensitive job of screening Dutch refugees in the so-called Patriotic School, who were volunteering their services for the underground in Holland. The British became somewhat wary of this man, but not on security grounds. He was dismissed from the School on August 5, 1943, on charges of misusing some of the official funds he handled. Van Koutrik still managed to hide his secret, because now he was hired by the Dutch Naval Intelligence Service in London. He was repatriated after the war, but was never tried

in Holland, for, after all, he was a double agent in the service of two *foreign* powers and never worked as a spy against his native land. When I saw him in Amsterdam in the summer of 1970, he appeared to be thoroughly penitent, regretting his cooperation with the Germans which he described as "the tragic indiscretion of foolish youth."

2 Major Stevens and Captain Best spent the war years in Gestapo prisons, but both survived. Despite their incredible blunders, the British Secret Service thought they had been punished enough by their Gestapo confinement and allowed them to retire without disciplining. After the war Best wrote a cautious book about his experience, blaming Stevens for the Venlo disaster. Stevens resigned from S.I.S. after the war to eke out a living as a translator of books until his death a few years ago.

Chapter 13

Perfidies in Albion

*T*HE Continental Secret Service—the once formidable
"Z" organization of Colonel Claude Dansey—was a shambles. Schellenberg's savage blow had a frightful impact on MI.6's approach to
the secret war—it discouraged the embittered British from dealing
with even the most deserving Germans who came bearing such gifts.
At the same time, however, it also had a salutary effect. In a relatively slow and soul-searching evolution it led to the long overdue
reorganization of the British intelligence establishment.

The Germans experienced no such hiatus after 1933. Their espionage against England never ceased completely during this period of
trials and errors. If anything, it grew in scope until it reached its peak
at the critical moment, on the eve of the war, in accordance with
Colonel Nicolai's old dictum that "preparations for war must always
go hand in hand with an intensification of espionage against one's
future enemies."

Even while Hitler's ban on spying in England was in effect, the
Abwehr and the SD were engaged in the "development" of secret
agents on a long-range basis. Several of their *Forschers*, or scouts,
were in Britain, searching for men and women who could be enticed
into espionage or sabotage. Just as they recognized a source of support in the fears and prejudices of the upper-classes, they sought to
draw allies into their grip from the basin of discontent and uncertainty of the lower- and middle-classes. Some of the latter were easily
accessible, as in American fascist organizations, through Sir Oswald
Mosley's British Union of Fascists, William Joyce's National Socialist
League, and the mushrooming anti-Semitic right-wing "clubs," and
through groups of Irish extremists and Welsh and Scottish nationalists.

There was a spirited scramble as representatives of the Abwehr and SD competed for their affections. The manager of a German engineering firm in South Wales was one of the most diligent *Forschers*. A visiting lecturer doubled as recruiter from his base at Cardiff University. The Abwehr worked through the manager of an enamel factory at Barry and a mysterious woman who claimed to be a nurse from the Channel Islands. She did her scouting in Pembrokeshire, a maritime province of South Wales washed by the sea on all sides except the northeast, until she was found dead in 1943, the victim of some still unexplained foul play.

The scouts returned empty-handed from their raids on the splintered Fascists groups. Deplorable as were the aid and comfort which members of these organizations gave the Nazis with their strident propaganda and shrill demonstrations, none of them had any actual or direct connection either with the Abwehr or the *Sicherheitsdienst*.

Mosley frowned upon such drastic subversion and admonished his Blackshirts to remain steadfastly loyal to their native land.

"We give ourselves to England," he said with unaccustomed flourish on the eve of the war, "across the ages that divide us, across the glories that unite us, we gaze into your eyes and we give to you this holy vow: we shall be true today, tomorrow and forever—England lives!" And when the war came he told his followers: "I ask you to do nothing to injure our country, or to help any other power."

Not even William Joyce, the Nazi's most effective propagandist of the airwaves, stooped to espionage in his otherwise unbounded pro-Nazi fervor. Aside from a single Mosley aide, a naturalized British subject of Balkan origin named Dr. A. A. Tester, the copious record of pro-Nazism in pre-war Britain exposed no espionage agent or saboteur in the ranks of this particular group of people.

Contact was made with irredentist dissenters in Scotland, like Angus Baxter, a boisterous but rootless agitator, W.E.A. Chambers-Hunter, a one-armed former planter in Ceylon, and William Weir Gilmour, founder of the Scottish Fascist Democratic Party, but they were rebuffed by them. It was a different story with a handful of Irishmen and Welshmen. They agreed to organize rings of spies and saboteurs to be ready for action when the Germans would need them.

In early 1937, when Canaris got the green light, every Abwehr outpost facing west hastened to get into the act. Not only the branches in Hamburg, Bremen and Wilhelmshaven, but also those in Muenster, Hanover, and Kassel, and even as far away as Dresden, Stuttgart, and Kiel, developed agents and sent them to Britain, without the slightest coordination of their efforts, without any firm operations plans, without regard for their spies' hazardous welfare. The proliferation produced some quantitative results in the number of agents set at large and the mass of material that flowed in from them. But the quality of both was low.

As a result, the coverage of Britain was chaotic to begin with, as was demonstrated by the apparently high rate of what Admiral Canaris called "accidents."

In the late fall of 1938, a tall, heavy-set, darkish man named Joseph Kelly wangled an audience with Dr. Walther Reinhardt, the German Consul General in Liverpool and offered his services as an espionage agent. Although Reinhardt had tacit instructions to be on the lookout for prospective spies, he disliked this sideline of his consular duties. An old-fashioned diplomat somewhat contaminated with liberal ideas in a brief brush with Western democracy during his tour of duty in Seattle (where he wrote a lively biography of George Washington), he tried to discourage Kelly, as he had nine other similar unsolicited applicants before.

Kelly in particular did not impress him as promising. A 30-year-old former boxer who was now making a living as a bricklayer in nearby Euxton, he was, as Reinhardt described him, rough-hewn and uneducated. The Consul threatened to call the police, but Kelly told him: "I'm sure you're a gentleman, sir, and wouldn't do any such thing as that."

"Exactly because I am a gentleman," Reinhardt shot back, "I don't want to have anything to do with traitors."

But Kelly was persistent and persuasive. "I am no traitor, sir," he said. "I'm an Irish patriot, anti-English to the marrow of my poor bones. Besides, I've a family to support. I am working at the Chorley munitions works and could get hold of the site plans of the factory. After that, I'd be willing to carry out whatever assignments your secret service might have for me."

Dr. Reinhardt jotted down his name and address in Euxton in Lancashire, and told the man that he would see what he could do. The next time he was in London, he gave the slip of paper to the Military Attaché, and washed his hands of the affair. Nothing happened until February 27, 1939, when Kelly received a letter from the Netherlands signed "Pete," instructing him to go to Cook's travel bureau in Liverpool where he would find a holiday trip all arranged for him. Waiting for Kelly at Cook's was a round-trip ticket to Osnabrueck, a grim, sooty steel and iron city in Western Germany, not exactly an enticing holiday resort. On March 8 Kelly went as told, taking along two secret plans of the great shell factory. He was met in Osnabrueck by a cut-out who took him to the branch at Muenster where he was formally checked into the Abwehr.

The information he brought was rated "valuable," even though Kelly was paid only £30 for his loot. The factory, which already had 14,000 employees, was one of the largest and most secret of the Royal ordnance plants. Familiarity with its layout, as a security officer at Chorley put it, "would prove of the greatest assistance to an enemy who might desire to bomb the great factory from the air."

When a search for the missing plans revealed that Kelly had gone on "an unauthorized holiday" to Germany, his name went into the black books of the Immigration officers at all British ports of entry. He was promptly detained in Dover upon his return and was found to have ten £1 bills and a crisp new £20 Bank of England note in his pocket.

He insisted that he had won the money in a poker game on the Channel steamer "from a bloke with an awful duelling scar on his bloody cheek," and protested that he knew nothing of "the mislaid plans." But he was seen chewing hard while protesting his innocence, and the detectives quickly prevented him from swallowing a small piece of paper on which the Germans had written out a simple code for him.

Kelly was given seven years for his brief escapade. Dr. Reinhardt was expelled in June and left Liverpool vigorously protesting his innocence, on explicit instructions from Berlin "to deny categorically any involvement on [his] part in the Kelly espionage case." I found this quaint correspondence between the Consul General and the Foreign Ministry in the top-secret part of the German papers. On April 24 Reinhardt wrote a rueful letter to his superior in the Foreign Ministry, insisting that he was "merely the hapless victim of a traitor," expressing the hope that the "regrettable incident [would] do no damage to [his] career."

For the British, the upshot of this incident did more harm than Kelly's theft of the classified plans. The Germans seized upon Consul Reinhardt's expulsion to arrest, in the guise of retaliation, Captain Thomas J. Kendrick, the Passport Control Officer at the British Consulate in Vienna. Kendrick was, of course, chief of the S.I.S. station, and up to his neck in espionage against the Nazis, who were in the process of developing the defunct Austrian secret service into the major branch of the Abwehr for the coverage of Eastern Europe. Kendrick was making a nuisance of himself with his efficient management of compact networks in what had been Austria and Czechoslovakia, and also in Poland and Hungary. At this moment before the war the Germans had far too many secrets and were naturally most determined to conceal them.

Captain Kendrick's departure in August resulted not only in closing down the key station in Vienna, but in the disintegration of his groups, at a time when the destruction of Colonel Dansey's and

Major Stevens's organizations terminated such British activities in the West as well.

At about the time of Kelly's arrest, MI.5 also unmasked another German agent, a 56-year-old seedy racing journalist named Donald Owen Reginald Adams, who had sold details of the British 4.5-inch anti-aircraft gun and other military information; and further exposed a quartet of Russian agents at the great Woolwich arsenal.

The unmasking of these agents was hailed in England as proof of the superiority of Britain's much-vaunted security organs over whatever agents foreign espionage establishment dared to pit against them. The impression these much publicized successes created was deceptive.

In actual fact, MI.5, the once great agency of the world's best counter-spies, was in bad repair. Colonel Vernon Kell, the prodigious spybuster of World War I, had grown old beyond his 67 years and was ill. The organization, which he had created and headed for thirty years, had become stale, and its methods antiquated.

When Admiral Canaris ordered a postmortem on the three cases, the probe demonstrated that the downfall of those six spies was due, not so much to MI.5's undimmed intrepidity and infallability, as to their mismanagement by their German controllers. Kelly had been the ward of the Muenster branch; Adams and the four men at Woolwich had been managed by Hanover.

Canaris ordered a tightening of the home organization and a thorough overhaul of the operation. Muenster, Hanover and other peripheral branches were taken off the British beat. The coverage of the United Kingdom was assigned to the Hamburg and Bremen outposts whose secret emissaries had successfully evaded MI.5's noose.

When MI.5 unmasked the handful of Abwehr spies the Germans had, by my count of active agents listed in their register, 253 operatives at large in the British Isles. The scope and quality of their output was so excellent that in a letter to the Luftwaffe on August 25, 1938, Canaris could legitimately notify his clients that "most of the British airfields [have] been mapped," and that the Abwehr had collected reliable data, including maps and aerial and ground photographs of "the harbours, docks, major warehouses and oil tanks in the whole area between London and Hull." On October 10 he was able to advise the air staff that "the reconnaissance of the London and Hull districts [have] also been completed."

This was an unbeatable feat by any standard of modern intelligence collection, this coverage of a country in less than two years of clandestine sightseeing. It was the collective accomplishment of spies whom MI.5 did not catch.

The long-range implication of this surveillance was apocalyptic. It produced the raw material that went into the uncannily accurate selection of strategic targets the Luftwaffe attacked during the air blitz of 1940–41. It was the data from which its aerial maps were drawn up; it supplied the myriad fragments the Germans needed to complete the mosaic of their air force's strategy and tactics in its struggle with the RAF.

It was largely the work of one man, a seemingly indolent, super-annuated career veteran of the Abwehr. He was Captain Joachim Burghardt, the acting chief of Ast X in Hamburg. He is another one of the Abwehr's unsung leaders. I do not think that even his name has ever appeared in all the millions of words written about the Abwehr. A long-nosed, ruddy-faced, gravel-voiced, bearish, unkempt-looking old sailor with a real passion for the blessings of anonymity, and a penchant for the leisurely way of doing things, Burghardt was nearing retirement age and did not really care how he wound up his long and seemingly humdrum service. He organized the coverage of England exactly the way in which he had performed all of his chores —in a manner that appeared to be routine and even bureaucratic, but with unmistakable, superb competence.

Burghardt's real strength was not in imaginative planning but in the assembly and management of able associates to whom he dele-gated full authority while retaining responsibility for what they were doing. He thus relied on his four deputies for what was called "I-activity," or the collection of secret intelligence. Captain Wolfgang Lips was a career officer in charge of military intelligence. Cap-tain Hilmar Gustav Johannes (Hans) Dierks, a swarthy, almost sinister-looking former insurance broker in his forties, had free-lanced for the Abwehr in Brussels (and had his nose broken in close combat with a British agent) long before joining the Hamburg branch full time, working in naval intelligence, headed by Burghardt and later by Captain Herbert Wichmann who also became chief of the Abwehrstelle during the war. Major Karl Praetorius, an expert in national economy, supervised the collection of economic and techni-cal information and doubled as the branch's chief recruiter of agents. Captain Nikolaus Ritter, the air intelligence specialist, we have already met on his profitable journey in the United States. He was aided by Dr. Nautsch, collecting technical aviation data, and Captain Hermann Sandel alias "Heinrich Sorau."

At the Bremen subbranch of Ast X, the elusive Pimpernel of German espionage in America, Commander Dr. Erich Pheiffer, now plunged into new activity with the benefit of his longer experience. He was aided by two civilians who had free-lanced for the Abwehr before signing in as regular members of Pheiffer's staff. One was S.2115, a big, dark-blond, blue-eyed cotton broker, 40-year-old Johannes Bischoff, whose old established family firm, Bischoff & Company, had allowed its branches in England and America to serve as fronts for espionage in World War I. Wilhelm Schierenbeck, partner in the Bremen firm of Lampe & Schierenbeck, exporters and importers, had already worked in 1934 under the Patzig regime as F.2346. We will meet both of them later as managers of a global network that went by the code name of "CHB" and endured longest of all the independent operations of the subbranch.[1]

These men were seasoned espionage executives who had devised the prototype of a self-contained espionage organization. It consisted of two sets of networks, each assigned to a different type of effort—one made up of producing spies, the other of auxiliary agents.

In the former group, spies were organized in two chains, one for immediate employment, the other to be kept available until emergencies required their activation. The first, called the "R-chain," was composed of *Reiseagenten*, or traveling agents, who would move in and out of Britain, collecting secret intelligence on apparently legitimate business or vacation trips. The other, called the "S-chain," was made up of *Schweigeagenten*, "silent agents," or sleepers. These were mostly Germans, but also Britons and nationals of countries who would be expected to remain neutral in the event of an Anglo-German war.

The backup organization consisted of a "U-chain" of cut-outs and mail drops, and of an "S-chain" of scouts, recruiters, and couriers. In addition, Captain Dierks, who had a masculine way with women despite his unseemly and somewhat ravaged exterior, in his mid-thirties, organized his own network of lesser agents that had a ladies' auxiliary.

Much was made in the postwar literature of German espionage in England of this latter group of women, both to illustrate the insidiousness and the indifferent quality of the effort. Women by the hundreds allegedly had been planted in the homes of important Britons —buxom matrons as cooks and bright blonde maidens as chambermaids, supposedly trained at the Abwehr school in Hamburg for such diverse chores as preparing good English roast beef and operating shortwave radios.

Although hundreds of German women flocked to Britain during these years in search of employment as servants, the vast majority of them were genuine housekeepers, cooks, and ladies' maids, and had nothing to do with spying. I found in the Abwehr registry only a handful of such women formally listed as agents—six working for

Bischoff and four for Dierks and Ritter. The latter group included two middle-aged ladies serving as housekeepers in the homes of naval officers near London. One cooked for a family in Manchester, spending all of her free time in recruiting candidates for espionage in the Midlands (and was, in fact, the scout who originally found Joseph Kelly). The other was the best of the group, if only because she had found employment in the home of the First Lord of the Admiralty.

The construction of such a huge spy complex was a difficult and tedious task involving considerable risks. The hour was late; arrangements had to be made in a hurry. But the framework of the network was completed before the year 1937 was out. Mail drops were ready to handle the agents' correspondence in Holland and Belgium. The Neptune Line steamer *Finkenau* was pressed into service as a courier ship, with its skipper, Captain Honorious Henning, acting as the chief of couriers. Scouts and recruiters were planted both in Britain and on the Continent—a veteran seaman named Charles Diggins scouting among British sailors from ships calling at Hamburg and Bremen and a Sicilian adventurer named Calogero Combatti looking for candidates in Belgium and Holland, to mention but two of scores.

A few "silent agents" had been recruited and held in escrow. Two of them attained prominence in this twilight world—Arthur George Owens, an excitable little Welshman destined to become one of the authentic master spies of World War II; and a 22-year-old East Prussian named Kaspar Haslinger who operated in the heart of the great shipbuilding center on the Tyne in Northumberland. The real hard core of this remarkable pre-war organization consisted of the itinerant R-men.

Captain Burghardt[2] had begun to forge this chain by calling up a handful of promising prospects whom he had in reserve. Two years before, an eccentric Londoner in his mid-thirties, who called himself Captain Fox Newman-Hall in his correspondence with the Abwehr, had volunteered his services as a spy and had sent to Bremen five reports until he was told to stop and wait for the ban to be lifted. Commander Pheiffer now tried to reactivate him, but Newman-Hall must have undergone a change of heart, for he failed to answer repeated invitations to resume work.

However, another prospect responded eagerly. He was R. L. Brandy of Dublin, a heavyset, apoplectic, naturalized Irishman in his sixties, who had worked for the Germans in World War I, "conducting," as his *Personalbogen* in the Abwehr files stated, "certain sabotage operations in enemy countries." A great admirer of the Fuehrer, Brandy had gone to Hamburg in March 1935, approached the Foreign Trade Bureau and volunteered for whatever duty the Third Reich would assign to him. He was referred to the Abwehr where he was received warmly.

A respected member of his community and a friend of the Irish Minister of Defense, Brandy was a consulting engineer with clients in England, necessitating frequent trips across the Irish Sea to Liverpool, Manchester, and London. It was obvious that he would have ample opportunities to collect intelligence of high quality, and was enlisted promptly to specialize in technological developments in Britain. Pheiffer also asked him to organize a ring of his own, with himself as *Hauptagent* or chief agent. Brandy was instructed to remain dormant for the time being, until the ban on espionage would be lifted.

In 1937 he was summoned to Bremen and was activated by Dr. Pheiffer to run his independent operation with its own agents, couriers, and mail drops. Unfortunately, Brandy dropped dead shortly after his return to Dublin, and the ambitious project had to be abandoned. His widow, Gertrud, volunteered to take over the management of the orphaned ring, but she proved capable of acting only as a conveyor belt. Other arrangements had to be made, and quickly, to replace the Brandy chain with a ring of live R-men.

Several were developed in short order. One of the first R-men sent to Britain in 1937, was a professional photographer named Hans Tschirra, traveling as a ship's photographer on vessels of the North German Lloyd that put into British ports. Tschirra returned from two such voyages with excellent pictures of warships and harbor installations. On a third trip in the summer of 1937, he was equipped with a special telephoto lens for his Leica, and the NGL ship *Anconia* was rerouted to take him to Spithead to photograph the assembled ships of the Royal Navy during Fleet Week. We will meet some of the others working in Britain later in this narrative.

The search for agents who could broaden this base of espionage never ceased. Eventually it yielded two men whose accomplishments were so satisfactory and contributed so much to the Germans' knowledge of their future enemy that the Abwehr, that had no medals of its own to hand out, awarded them the coveted rank of *Haupt-V-Mann* or "Chief Agent."

One of them was treated as so secret that he was given neither a registry number nor a cover-name. Listed merely as *"Ungenannt"* (Unnamed), his dossier was kept in Commander Pheiffer's personal safe in Bremen, to preserve this man's anonymity even from the confidential clerks.

He was a mild-mannered, self-effacing, 39-year-old Pomeranian engineer named Fritz Block. After a humdrum career in Germany in the employ of large engineering firms, he moved to Holland in February 1934 and started in the garment industry with the modest capital of 10,000 guilders. His company, N. V. Sablofa at 168 Heerengracht in Amsterdam, manufactured ladies' dresses for export, mostly to England. Block was married to an American woman whose parents lived in London, an ideal cover to justify frequent trips to England.

The record begins with his acceptance into the fold in Bremen on November 8, 1937. It took only a few weeks to check him out, and two months later, on February 15, 1938, he was sent to London. It was the mandatory field test of new agents, and Block was required to "undertake," as Commander Pheiffer wrote in his orders, "a photographic reconnaissance of certain sensitive installations."

Block easily passed the test. For one who had never done any spying before, he returned from his maiden voyage with a collection of photographs, sketches, maps, and descriptive material that far surpassed Dr. Pheiffer's expectations. Block brought back pictures of the water storage reservoirs of King George and Queen Mary, and pumping stations at Staines, Surbiton, Hampton, Hanworth, New River Head and Leyton, eight of the thirteen main sources of London's water supply; relay stations of the Metropolitan Electricity Board, and a report on fire-fighting. This information was later incorporated into the special target maps, Nos. 53 and 54, provided for the Luftwaffe raiders during the Battle of Britain.

During the remainder of 1938 Block returned to England on an average of twice a month, his visits to his in-laws yielding the incredible total of 130 separate reports with over 400 photographs, sketches, and maps. They ranged far, and included snapshots of such strategic targets as airfields in London, near Sunderland and Walford; shipyards at Newcastle-upon-Tyne; and gun emplacements around Dover. His reports included information about breakdowns in the aviation industry and delays in the deliveries of aircraft from the United States, as well as details of newly introduced air raid precaution measures.

Block was drawing upon contacts he had saved from his engineering years with such mammoth companies as AEG, Siemens, Lorenz, and Heliawatt, and had made while serving as chief engineer on the *Florenz* and *Irmgard*, which used to call regularly in British ports.

One of his ingenious methods of procuring intelligence deserves particular mention. At this time, the British government was issuing confidential "D" notices to editors, listing certain defense installations, including fortifications and ammunition depots, which the papers were requested never to mention in their columns. Through a reporter friend in Fleet Street, Block gained access to these notices, and from them obtained not only the listing of these installations, but also data about their locations and purposes. He also managed to photograph several of them. Such elaborate spying was not without risk. It was not so much the vigilance of the authorities as the suspicions of people themselves, who, alerted by sensationalized stories of widespread "Nazi espionage" elsewhere, viewed every German as a potential spy.[3]

Block intuitively knew how to evade the tightening noose of suspicion. An unpretentious little man, he pursued his perilous pastime with the same equanimity and plodding that characterized the performance of his engineering chores and his administration of his garment factory. "His firm is well managed," the German consul in Amsterdam reported when the Abwehr had originally inquired about him. "Block is respected as a good businessman who earns his living, and though he has no substantial means, he meets his financial obligations promptly."

Like so many of the best spies, Fritz Block was a Walter Mitty type, who took up spying to compensate for the frustrations of his philistine life. He did not do it in any excess zeal of patriotism, for he was no flag-waving German or rabid Nazi. Nor did he do it for the money. Throughout his career as an agent, the Abwehr paid him a regular salary of only 300 marks a month.

The other top agent, R.2220, was made of similar stuff.

Friedrich Wilhelm Kaulen was born on November 29, 1915, in the comfortable family of a businessman in Muenchen-Gladbach, and grew into a slim, thin-boned, bespectacled young man, intelligent, quizzical, and somewhat emotional—hardly the ingredients to make a first-rate spy. Working as a clerk in his father's prosperous business he could well afford such expensive hobbies as photography and shortwave radio, and spending his vacations abroad. In the summer of 1937 he visited England, hiking in Lancashire from the lowlands north to the Lake District, then west to the Irish Sea, taking snapshots with his Rolleiflex all the way.

On his return to Germany he showed his photographs to a friend, who suggested that he might be able to sell them to someone interested in pictures of the English countryside. Before long, Freddy Kaulen was in one of the Abwehr hideouts in Bremen, displaying his wares to Pheiffer who was impressed, especially since some of the photographs showed airfields at Heywood and Burry near Manchester that had been unknown to the Germans.

Pheiffer invited Freddy to work for him, but then a hitch developed. A few years before, the Gestapo had tracked down an illicit radio transmitter in Muenchen-Gladbach to 10 Albertus Street, Freddy's home. Though the investigation proved that the boy was a harmless amateur operator, the Gestapo was not amused and refused to clear young Kaulen for a regular job with the Abwehr.

Dr. Pheiffer kept in touch with him nevertheless and sent him back to England several times. Freddy was too good to lose. He seemed to have the uncanny knack of spotting obscure airfields, the brazen courage to photograph them, and the luck to evade detection. Moreover, he was covering the west of England, while Block was working in the east.

In July 1938, Freddy Kaulen's case was reopened at the request of Commander Pheiffer. After a long and thorough investigation he was cleared, the Gestapo conceding that his "operation of the black transmitter was merely the childish prank of an over-enthusiastic, irresponsible radio ham."

Kaulen joined the Abwehr formally on January 9, 1939. A few weeks later there began an ominous period that Canaris called *Spannungszeit*. Hitler was moving rapidly toward a showdown with Poland over Danzig and the Corridor. The Abwehr went on a war footing, well ahead of the Wehrmacht, to collect the latest data the army and the Luftwaffe needed for completing their war plans. While hundreds of agents were being smuggled into Poland and France, Captain Herbert Wichmann, who had become chief at Ast X for the duration, also mobilized his handful of R-men to move into England, no longer to procure intelligence haphazardly, but to collect precise, up-to-the-minute information.

During this period of simmering tension which lasted until August 2, Kaulen made three trips, each meticulously plotted in advance. On his first trip he went back to the Liverpool area. His second one took him to Pembrokeshire. On his third trip he started out in Blackpool, moved east to Barton, then south to cover the area around Manchester.

On August 3 Admiral Canaris placed his organization in condition red. For all practical purposes the Abwehr was already at war, almost a month before the actual beginning of hostilities. Code words were flashed to the "silent agents," alerting them to stand by. Other agents still held in reserve were deployed to their battle stations. The R-men, the workhorses, were dispatched on what was to be their last missions before the war to gather together the loose ends and collect the latest data about enemy defenses.

In Britain the Abwehr focused on air defense installations to pave the way for the Luftwaffe's bombers. Was the mysterious radar in operation? How were the anti-aircraft batteries deployed? Where were the balloon barrages? The agents were now ordered to conduct pinpoint *target intelligence*, singling out conspicuous landmarks, waterworks, dams, airfields—anything that might be of value to the air force.

During the month that was left, Block and Kaulen had to review every key item on their previous itineraries, like tourists returning to sights they had enjoyed on former sojourns. Block was to comb the vast strip of land between London and Newcastle. His young colleague was to go west. Still traveling under their own names and genuine passports, they arrived in England on August 5, Block coming from Holland via Harwich, Kaulen by way of Ireland on the steamer from Dun Laoghaire, landing at Holyhead. He started out on his final reconnaissance the next day by surveying the Birkenhead docks at Liverpool.

On August 26 he was back in Liverpool, spending his leisure time on the Mersey waterfront and in the pubs, listening to what the people were talking about, trying to monitor their mood.

That night in his room at a hotel on Formby Street, he wrote a "Dear Aunt" letter to a woman named Hanna von Balluseck in Bremen, apparently an ordinary note summing up his impressions as any tourist would during these breathless, uncertain days. Actually, it was what the Abwehr called a *Stimmungsbericht*, a morale report meant for Commander Pheiffer, for whom Frau von Balluseck served as a mail drop. While even Hitler still hoped that Britain would stay out of the war, young Kaulen had no illusions. "My trip is finished," he wrote to *Liebe Tante Hanna*. "I hope to see you soon."

Fritz Block left England on August 28 on an A.B.A. plane to Copenhagen, then went home to Amsterdam for a *Treff* with Pheiffer to submit his final report and snapshots. Kaulen stayed until September 2, to the last minute, taking the 8:30 P.M. steamer out of Holyhead. In Ireland he quickly crossed to the west coast, where a German ship, the *Theseus*, was waiting for him with a special Afu transmitter. He never had a chance to use it. The *Theseus* left at dawn and was barely six hours out of Galway Bay when Kaulen heard on the radio that Britain was at war with Germany. His ship was now running the blockade, with orders to keep radio silence.

A week later in a *Treff* with Dr. Pheiffer in Norway, Kaulen submitted his final report. It was a masterpiece of secret reconnaissance —his ninety-eighth report in a year during which he had spent ninety-eight days in England.

"Between February 5 and September 2, 1939," Pheiffer later wrote when recommending Freddy for the Iron Cross, "R-man Kaulen carried out his mission tenaciously and successfully, reconnoitering and photographing strategic targets without regard for his personal safety. Thanks to his efforts, several hitherto unrecognized airfields of the RAF became known. It was possible, on the basis of his detailed reports, to reconstruct British air defenses, pinpointing the locations of AA batteries, balloon barrages, and searchlight emplacements in the western part of Central England between Linney Head in Pembrokeshire and the north of Lancashire."

But the recommendation was of no avail. Freddy Kaulen was a mere secret agent, and only soldiers and sailors on the battlefronts were eligible for the coveted Iron Cross.[4]

It was Canaris's nature to be involved only in matters that personally interested him. During the swift evolution of the Abwehr between 1935 and 1939, he went all out to promote those branches of the espionage section that "procured" for the Army and the Luftwaffe. In the process Canaris became extremely close to the colonels in espionage and sabotage, and gave them all the encouragement and help they needed.

There was no such intimacy with the captains and commanders of the "M" branch of I, the Abwehr's naval intelligence service. They worked in such obscurity, and produced their output so quietly, that they survive only in the shadow of such well-known Canaris confidants as Piekenbrock, Lahousen, Groscurth, and Hansen, all army officers on the staff of an apostate admiral.

Fortunately for Canaris he had as naval intelligence chiefs a pair of career officers who were as competent and conscientious as they were self-effacing. Chief of the M-branch since 1935 was Captain Hermann Menzel, a rawboned, round-faced, baldish man in his early fifties. His deputy was Commander Udo von Bonin, a debonair officer, unlike Menzel who appeared "civilian" even in the elegant blue uniform of the navy.

Since the Fuehrer's naval policies had none of the firm foundation and purposeful orientation that characterized his other military projects, and since no secret service can effectively operate in a vacuum, the absence of definitive plans precluded any effective pursuit of naval intelligence.

Even so the M-branch managed by its own means and with its own limited resources to spin a spy web, especially by organizing officers of the German merchant ships into an auxiliary group of naval observers. It was done quietly and piecemeal, but eventually on such a scale that it seemed to turn the entire German merchant marine into a subsidized secret arm of the Abwehr.

This was the so-called DK-group (the letters standing for *Dampfer-Kapitaen*, or merchant marine master). It consisted of the skippers or first or second officers or radiomen serving aboard ships of the Hamburg-America Line, the North German Lloyd, the Neptune,

Hansa, Argo, and Levant lines, and other, smaller operators of merchant vessels. They were formally inducted into the Abwehr and were carried in the roster of V-men with cover-names and code numbers assigned to each, as already described on the transatlantic voyages to the United States.

Most significant, and of immediate importance, was the operation Captain Menzel designed to fill the gaps in his branch's coverage of the British waterfront. By mid-1939 it had become too late (and too precarious in the face of considerably tightened British security arrangements) to plant agents in British ports or at bases to undertake last-minute surveillance of harbor facilities. It fell to the DK-group to collect this information about ports and ships and installations that, within a few weeks, were to be targets of Luftwaffe raids and sneak attacks by U-boats.

Three DK-men in particular distinguished themselves in this phase of the venture. From several trips to British ports during the first eight months of 1939, Captain Kirschenlohr and Captain Schmidt returned with charts of the ports of Greenwich, Dagenham, Gravesend, Purfleet, Plymouth, Swansea, Barry, and all the busy harbors of the Thames Estuary. Their reports included the latest topographical and hydrographic information; detailed descriptions of the port installations and what they called "Harbor fortifications"; and a complete accounting of the ships in port. Kirschenlohr, an intelligent and eager man with previous experience in "observing," even went beyond the collection of purely naval intelligence. On each trip he would spend time in the pubs listening to small talk, engaging friends and strangers in ingeniously loaded conversations. He then submitted a series of so-called *Stimmungsberichte* of his findings, shrewd observations about the mood and morale of the English common man during the weeks of mounting tension that preceded the outbreak of the war.

Captain Franz was the third member of this elite group. Since he operated in the Mediterranean out of Trieste in Italy, the Abwehr saw to it that he was given cargo consigned to such key targets as Alexandria in Egypt and Valetta in Malta, major bases of the British Mediterranean Fleet. He was instructed to stay close to units of the fleet at sea to observe their drills and tactical exercises and to eavesdrop on their wireless traffic.

DK-men thus covered the entire immense British waterfront, from Kirkwall in the Orkney Islands to Penzance in Wales near Land's End, and followed the fleet in the Mediterranean.

The initiative to report on what they saw was not left to them. The M-branch maintained an elaborate *Befragungsdienst* (interrogation service), in which specially trained officers debriefed the DK-men in searching interviews.

Centers with Abwehr-trained interrogators were set up in German ports on the North Sea and in the Baltic, and also abroad. In Antwerp a large network of interrogators was maintained under Captain Carl Mohr, a veteran merchant marine skipper who served as one of the senior agents in Belgium. Holland swarmed with people who worked for the Abwehr, all but one of them native Dutchmen.[5]

Aside from the DK-men, Captain Menzel planted some of his full-time, trained and experienced agents on merchantmen skippered by DK-masters, with specific assignments. When Naval Operations expressed interest in the Isle of Wight, he put one of his regular V-men, a middle-aged photographer, aboard the steamer *Scharnhorst,* who returned with a long written report of his observations, and photographs of what he described as "coastal fortifications" at Cowes, the famous yachting resort, and Ryde. He added snapshots he took at Portsmouth on the return voyage.

Two agents were sent to the Firth of Clyde. A radio operator was insinuated into the chief naval base at Portsmouth harbor aboard a DK-ship to monitor the wireless traffic of the Royal Navy. His efforts produced an excellent plot of the fleet's communication pattern, when its mobilization was already underway.

Another agent, aboard a cargo ship on an especially arranged trip to England, returned with a report about the flying-boat base at Harwich. One of the most productive of such trips was undertaken by a secret agent on a ship of the Argo Line. He charted the anti-submarine defenses of the Firth of Forth, and produced detailed reports on the ports of Leven, Buckhaven, Dunfermline, and Musselburgh, and a "special study" of the Inverkeithing fortifications.

After the war Grand Admiral Doenitz dismissed all of these efforts by claiming in his memoirs that "the intelligence apparatus of Admiral Canaris . . . never provided the U-boat command with even a single usable bit of intelligence." This was a sweeping charge, patently untrue. It stemmed from their enmity that dated back to the early Thirties when Doenitz served unhappily under Canaris.

The DK-group was, of course, neither the only nor an enduring source of intelligence to the German Navy. But contrary to Doenitz's all-too-categorical disclaimer, many if not most of its reports went into the enormous portfolio that the Admiralty used in general. The U-boat Command in particular was soon using this in planning their operations in the struggle soon to come.

It came to England at 11:00 A.M. on a bright and clear Sunday,

September 3, 1939, as London's church bells ceased ringing. Prime Minister Neville Chamberlain went on the air to say in a slow and steady voice: "I am speaking to you from the Cabinet Room at No. 10 Downing Street. This country is at war with Germany."

NOTES

1 They were set up in Bremen behind the cover of a dummy firm called Seevag whence they conducted the operations of seven specially numbered agents (CHB-1 to 7) at large in Britain and the United States. They were H. Cyriacks, Hermann Lemermann, Carl Hansen, Herbert Osmers, Margarete Sohr, Friedrich Kutschau, Margarete Sietz, a potent ring of high-grade spies, rated as "among the best the Abwehr had in the field."

2 Despite his remarkable accomplishments in Britain, Captain Burghardt was fired in the wake of the exposure of the Rumrich and Schackow rings in the United States in 1938. His place was taken by the quiet, conscientious, erudite naval officer, Captain Herbert Wichmann, who remained at this major outpost throughout the war.

3 An incident demonstrating this growing popular preoccupation with German spies occurred just when Block was embarking on his new career. On February 24, 1938, an experimental Vickers-Wellesley (later Wellington) two-engine low-wing monoplane featuring a novel-type wing, piloted by Flight Lieutenant F. S. Gardiner, took off at 9:15 A.M. from Farnborough and vanished. When no trace could be found of the "mystery plane," one of three RAF bombers designed for a world's non-stop record attempt, rumors spread that it had been shot down by the Germans, off the Scottish coast, salvaged, and the wreckage carted off to Germany by a U-boat. They supposedly had been alerted to the flight and given the plane's routing by a spy at Farnborough. Although there is some reason to believe that the rumors had some foundation (the Germans did have an agent covering Farnborough and apparently had been tipped off to the flight) insufficient documentation was found in Abwehr papers to warrant the crediting of this spectacular success, if it really was that, to the Germans.

4 Kaulen remained in the Abwehr during the war and eventually received the decoration, for serving as a radio operator on one of the German spy ships on the eve of the invasion of Denmark and Norway in the spring of 1940.

5 The exception was a German who nominally clerked for the local office of Krupp in the Netherlands. In Rotterdam alone, there were seven interrogators specializing in England. One man hired eight interrogators on his own, working for the Abwehr as a contractor.

Part III

THE FOXES GO TO WAR

Chapter 14

Johnny Calling from Golf Course

ON the night of August 27/28, 1939—a few days before war broke out, a boyish-faced, blue-eyed, towheaded radioman named Heinz Valenti sat at his shortwave set in the Europa Saal, a hall in a concrete dugout with twenty listening posts in separate soundproof booths. Each was tuned to a different frequency, monitoring the incoming messages of secret agents the Abwehr had on scattered stations in Western Europe.

On the grounds of what looked like an estate in Wohldorf, a tree-shaded town just outside the city limits of North Hamburg, was the nerve center. It had been built by Major Werner Trautmann, an electronics wizard, to keep in touch with the Afu-spies who had been equipped with the *Klamotten* (junk), as the Abwehr jargon called the handy little suitcase-transceiver Telefunken had developed for Admiral Canaris. Until a fortnight before, the operators idled aboveground in the mansion the Abwehr had bought for its communications center when it became evident that atmospheric conditions around Berlin were not conducive to good reception. Two huge shelters had been prepared to accommodate the operators in acute war emergencies or, indeed, in war. When Canaris placed the Abwehr on war footing earlier in the month, the radiomen moved to their sets underground, to stay there like moles until a bitter spring day in 1945 when the British captured Wohldorf and flushed them out.

Radioman Valenti was one of the ace operators in a crack crew of sparks Major Trautmann had handpicked because they had a sixth sense in addition to their technical skill at the shortwave set. They uncannily recognized the "fingerprints"—the uniquely characteristic touch of the Morse key that distinguished the agents from one another as clearly as fingerprints—no two of them were ever identical. This

149

was indispensable to alert them to messages put on the air by some-body other than the agent who was supposedly sending them.

Valenti had been told to stand by and watch for "A.3504." He had been glued to his set since midnight, waiting for the dots and dashes of the man's call letters to resound in his earphones.

The night air—dry, clean, coolish, and summer-breezy—was full of crackling sounds, some almost showily mysterious. The Germans were broadcasting peremptory orders, issuing emergency rules, or chitchatting with shadowy partners identified only by their call signs or quaint nicknames like "Job" or "Peacock." This was the first time that the wireless was used in such profusion for the transmission of secret intelligence. The air was crowded with the sounds of impend-ing war, filling those of us who eavesdropped on them with awe and foreboding.[1]

Somewhere someone was tapping out a signal in Morse code. The dots and dashes of another transmission were barely audible as, ap-parently, a fishing boat on a secret mission was trying to contact DAN, the big German radio station at Nordeich. It was an uproari-ous international concert that seemed badly orchestrated. Signals ov-erlapped and interlocked. One message intruded on another.

At exactly 4:30 A.M. on the 28th, Radioman Valenti suddenly recognized the familiar fingerprint of an agent he had trained in long and exasperating sessions (because the man was an impatient, irasci-ble pupil). It was a short signal repeated again and again as the agent tried to contact Wohldorf: his call sign and a couple of three-letter groups—*ALB . . . SSD . . . QRV*—meaning that the agent whose call letters were "ALB" had a "most urgent" message he was "ready to send."

The coded message itself could be heard in a string of five letter groups that read: CCHRI JAZTP GHIJN APXZF TSOEN MOPRN AHFTZ XZGNL EOSPR UNKPS XZYWN. Then came a brief postscript in plain English: "I am standing by. Will be sending more tomorrow."

Valenti tore the transcript of the intercept from his pad, rushed to one of the booths with a direct line to Abwehr headquarters on Sophein Terrace in Hamburg, and told a man who answered the call: "Your boy has come in, sir. I have his signal."

"How is it?" the man was Captain Ritter, waiting for word from A.3504.

"I don't know, sir, I haven't decrypted it yet."

"Call me as soon as you have."

The transmitter on which this message had originated was the least conspicuous but the most baffling in the chattering chain. It was the only one broadcast in English.

Kingston, near Richmond Park, a staid residential district eleven miles southwest of the heart of London, would seem the most unlikely locale for any such mischief. The house in which the sender was located stood silent and dark, as were all the other identical dwellings under the belfry of All Saints parish church, where once the Saxon kings were crowned. Alert to the crisis and naturally tense, people slept through it all with helpless equanimity, abandoning the management of their fate to the troubled men in Whitehall.

Behind drawn curtains in a room facing the backyard, by the dim light of a hand-torch that illuminated a wireless set packed in a suitcase, a dark little man with a hawklike face hammered away at the Morse key. He was a "*V-Mann*" in "*Golf Course*"—a German agent in England—making his first report by radio.

As every spy could tell you, there is occult exhilaration in this moment for which secret agents were meticulously groomed. Spies are the loneliest of creatures, like small ships at sea moving on their solitary courses. Once they go on the air, the oppressive spell of their loneliness is broken. They know that they are needed and wanted at last; that people at the far end of the line are eager to hear what they have to say.

A few days before, when Admiral Canaris had put his agency on war footing, Captain Ritter had instructed the little man in Kingston to start a series of brief test transmissions. A timetable Ritter had given him set the first test for the half-hour period between 4:00 and 4:30 A.M. on this August 28th.

Now it was 5:10 A.M. and Valenti was on the phone again, reading to Ritter the deciphered transcript, garbles and all: "*Something* navy reserve convoy leaving Portsm . . . for Gibraltar *something* seven-thirty."

It was not much. And whatever sense it made when it was put on the air, static had knocked it out of the message. But Ritter was elated.

The little man was his baby. He called him "Johnny" and carried him as "Agent No. A.3504" on his roster of extra-special spies.

Johnny had found his way to the Abwehr in 1936 with credentials that seemed too good to be true.

He was Arthur George Owens who drifted into the spy game to satisfy his political fantasies and personal needs. Born in Wales in 1899, he went to live in Canada then returned to England in 1933, when G. C. Hans Hamilton, a director of Expanded Metal Company, had become interested in Owens's inventions of improved accumulators which the Royal Navy could use.

Upon his return Expanded Metal hired him as a consulting electrical engineer, and then Hamilton set him up in his own business, the Owens Battery Equipment Company, to merchandise some of his inventions. He could have lived comfortably on his income with his wife and child at their home in Hampstead. But Owens was not made for domestic bliss, and although he was Welsh in speech and his way of life, he was a non-conformist in creed. Charming, mercurial, irresponsible and corrupt, living beyond his means, always in need of money to finance his affairs with the sleazy mistresses he kept and the Scotch whisky of which he was inordinately fond. He enjoyed his job as a traveling salesman, and was always on the road, going regularly to Holland (where he had close business relations with the mammoth Phillips electronics concern), to Belgium, but also occasionally to Germany.

He returned from these trips with technical information which he passed on to the Admiralty in London, until early 1936 when he thought of making some money on the side by selling the intelligence instead of giving it away gratis. The Naval Intelligence Division expressed interest in taking him in on a regular basis, and Owens was introduced to Colonel Peel of the Secret Intelligence Service, who employed him as an agent.

Before long he began to strain on the S.I.S. leash, resenting the condescending manner in which Colonel Peel seemed to be treating him. Even more, he was dissatisfied with the pittance S.I.S. was willing to dole out. The resentment ignited in his volatile soul a rampant feeling of Welsh nationalism with an irrational hatred of the English. By the end of 1936, fanned by his attitude toward Peel, his nationalism grew into a foaming, malignant passion and his resentment of S.I.S. into a craving for revenge.

As a spy he had quite a bit to offer the Germans. His firm held a number of contracts with the Admiralty where he could come and go practically as he pleased; he was a regular visitor at such sensitive RAF installations as the Farnborough and Hendon experimental stations. He was already privy to some of Britain's supposedly best guarded naval and aviation secrets.

He thought surely he could ingratiate himself to the Germans further: he had among his friends a number of like-minded Welsh extremists, several holding key jobs in factories like Short Brothers in Rochester and the Rolls Royce plant in Coventry. He could organize them into a spy ring with himself as their boss—if only he could get to the Germans safely without betraying his new orientation to his suspicious contacts in S.I.S.

One short-cut to the Abwehr was an establishment in Bayswater, maintained by the German Labor Front as a social club for German servants employed in British homes. He began to frequent it on weekends, ostensibly to pick up pretty German maidens while hoping that someone would pave his way into the German secret service.

The club on Cleveland Terrace proved to be a lucky choice. Its manager, a young blond German, Peter Ferdinard Brunner, was London representative of Captain Dierks, the Abwehr officer in Hamburg who tried to exploit these girls as sources of information.

Owens confided to Brunner his fondness for Germany, and talked about his frequent visits to Hamburg and Cologne. "I wonder," he said, "if you could get me in touch with some of your friends I could meet when I'm over there. It's awfully lonesome for a stranger on those long evenings when I'm cooped up in a bloody hotel room."

A few weekends later, when Owens was back in the club, Brunner accosted him. "You asked me," he said, "to find friends for you in Germany. Well, here's one. He's an engineer like you and travels a lot. Next time you're in Brussels let me know, and I'll arrange a meeting for you two lonely birds. His name is Pieper, Herr Engineer Konrad Pieper."

Owens had no doubt that Pieper was a scout for the Abwehr. He quickly set up a business trip to Brussels and, on the theory that a prospective spy must bargain from a position of strength, checked into the elegant Metropole Hotel on Place de Brouckere, the best in the city. He called the telephone number Brunner had given him and was told that Herr Pieper was expected the next day and would, by sheer coincidence, also be staying at the Metropole.

Pieper showed up but all he brought was a message. "I am not authorized by my firm," he told Owens, "to make any business details. I suggest that you go to Hamburg and contact my firm, A. G. Hillermann, Ltd. We deal in electrical goods and such things—I'm sure we'll be interested in buying your accumulators, if they are as good as you say. Incidentally," Pieper added, "you'll be our guest in Hamburg. Just call my firm, and ask for Herr Mueller. He's our specialist in batteries, and, by the way, quite a man-about-town. He'll take good care of you."

In Hamburg (where, in turn, the Abwehr wanted to impress him) Owens was lodged in the swank and expensive Hotel Vier Jahreszeiten on the Alster, and was received by Herr Mueller upon his arrival to negotiate the deal.

He was Captain Dierks, at last; there was no beating about the bush—each man knew what the other wanted. Owens volunteered his services for the Abwehr and Dierks agreed to employ him.

After that they had *Treffs* from time to time, in Cologne, Brussels, and Antwerp, whenever Owens had to be in these cities on his legitimate business, but not yet in Hamburg. Dierks had decided to keep the man at arm's length for the time being and to avoid meeting him on his own grounds. Owens (who was now officially "Va-1002" by his listing in the roster of the Abwehr's probationary agents) had decided to stay with S.I.S. but keep his contact with Peel to an unavoidable minimum while working sincerely for the Germans to the best of his ability. He did not think it the smart thing to confide to the Germans this parallel link in his secret life.

Even so, Dierks, who had spent all his adult life in or around the secret service and trusted nobody on principle, had a gnawing suspicion in the back of his mind that the little Welshman might be a plant after all. As he came to know him better his doubts evaporated. Owens seemed so artless in everything he did, so candid in parading his few virtues and many sins, so obscene in his Anglophobia whether he was sober or drunk, that Dierks accepted him at face value without really checking him out beyond the simple traps and tricks used in the profession for catching spies in lies and contradictions.

Owens passed the elementary tests with flying colors, including the language probe that Ritter later decided to try out on him. The man insisted that he neither spoke nor understood any foreign language, least of all German, which actually stumped him when he tried to learn it to please his new clients. But Ritter remained skeptical. Once in a hideout in Hamburg when he was debriefing Owens and had his secretary with him to make notes, he suddenly told the girl in a casual voice:

"Watch out! I'm going to turn over this lamp here so that it'll fall right smack on the little fellow." He watched Owens's reaction to the sentence, but the man seemed completely unaffected by the warning. Ritter then got up and, with feigned clumsiness, bumped into the lamp and watched it falling on Owens. It was obvious that the Welshman did not know what was coming. He jumped from his seat as if bitten by a tarantula, his startled expression and indignant cussing providing the proof Ritter needed.

Dierks found his *Treffs* with Owens rewarding. The Welshman always arrived loaded with good stories, interesting gossip about key figures in the Admiralty and the Air Ministry, and abundant technical information. He proved a disappointment in the long run because he did not have exactly what Dierks needed. The captain was at the Hamburg station's *naval* intelligence branch. But the Welshman's knowledge of naval matters was slight and his connection with the Admiralty turned out to be perfunctory.

On the other hand, he was doing considerable business with the Air Ministry, had entered into some of the most closely guarded RAF installations, and seemed to know much of what was going on in the aviation industry. To one of their *Treffs* Dierks brought a man who was interested in exactly what Owens had in such abundance. He presented his friend as "Dr. Rantzau" and told Owens that he represented Reinhold & Company, an export-import firm. For all the intimacy that developed and though they had no illusions about each other, the captain still played the game by keeping up the hoary masquerade.

Dr. Rantzau was Captain Nikolaus Ritter, who had just arrived in Hamburg. From this summer day in 1937 Owens was working for Ritter, the brightest feather in the captain's cap.

He himself lived a double life—a spymaster on the third floor of Sophien Terrace, a businessman at large. On his desk in the office he had four telephones he alone was permitted to handle. Each was listed in the name of a different commercial firm which he maintained as "legal roofs" or fronts, each with a separate office in downtown Hamburg. One of them was Reinhold & Company as the representative of which Dierks had introduced him to Owens. It was to the two-room office of this dummy firm that Ritter directed Owens.

Under Ritter, Owens became an S-man or "sleeper," to be kept dormant until some real emergency or war between Germany and England would warrant his full activation. In the meantime he would meet Ritter once in a while when he would be in Holland, Belgium, or in Hamburg, for that matter, to take care of legitimate business the Abwehr solicited for him, to cover up their secret transactions. At the *Treffs* he would submit his reports orally. Otherwise he would communicate with Ritter only when he had some perishable intelligence to forward. A code was designed for such communications and Owens was to send his letters to a mail drop care of Post Office Box 629 in the Central Post Office in Hamburg.

This went on until the end of 1937, when Owens suggested that perhaps it would be best for Ritter to "put him on ice"—to deactivate him altogether and turn him into a "deep sleeper," saving him up for greater things. This sounded like a reasonable proposition. Ritter agreed that it would be a great pity if these premature efforts compromised Owens before some real emergency.

Actually Owens had a pressing personal reason for having himself deactivated. He had gone to the *Treff* with Ritter straight from the first crisis in his career as a spy, one so serious that it threatened to destroy him. For some reason Colonel Peel disliked Owens as much as the Germans liked him, and showed neither understanding for the Welshman's innate eccentricities nor compassion for his loose habits. Although he had no tangible reason to distrust him, Peel had asked the Special Branch of Scotland Yard to keep half an eye on this errant Welshman, just in case.

After that Owens was shadowed occasionally. The surveillance revealed nothing suspicious in his conduct, mainly because it was confined to England and missed his meetings with Ritter abroad. But a spot check of Owens's mail gave him away. Special Branch intercepted one of his letters addressed to Box 629 in Hamburg. Although it seemed harmless enough—containing merely an invitation to "Dr. Rantzau" to meet him in a few days hence—Box 629 was known to the security services in London as one of four cover addresses of Ast X, hinting rather strongly that Owens was in touch with the Abwehr.

He was allowed to make the trip, but this time under surveillance, and now Special Branch obtained the proof it needed. Arrangements were made for a couple of detectives to visit Owens and invite him to accompany them to Scotland Yard, as such arrests are discreetly called in the polite language of the British security organs. Owens beat them to it. The extra-sensory perception of the good spy, which Owens possessed in abundance, alerted him to his shadow on the trip. Now, to forestall disaster, he decided to expose himself.

He went to see Colonel Peel and gave him the story he had concocted for such an eventuality. As it was recorded in the minutes MI.5 later prepared of this confrontation, "Snow" (which was Owens's cover-name in S.I.S.) "said that his business had brought him into contact with a German engineer named Pieper, from whom he had attempted to obtain information. The information which Pieper had supplied had not been wholly satisfactory, and after a while Snow had found himself unable to continue to pay Pieper's expenses." At this point, Owens told Peel, Pieper had suggested that he should work as an agent for the Germans rather than the British. Owens said he had fallen in with this suggestion in order to "penetrate the German Secret Service in the British interest." Pieper had then arranged a meeting for him with the Germans and this was, Owens said, how he had become an Abwehr agent.

Colonel Peel was totally unconvinced by Owens's tale and told him that he had no choice but to advise Special Branch to arrest him as an espionage agent in the Germans' pay. But Owens told him quietly, with his eyes half-closed as was his wont: "I doubt you can do that, sir. You cannot very well put me in the dock unless you are willing to put up with my defense of having been a British agent and drag the Secret Intelligence Service into this mess."

As the minutes of MI.5 described the disposal of this incident, there were indeed "some difficulties in the way of proceeding against Snow on account of his previous connection with S.I.S." No action was, therefore, taken against him.

He was permitted to come and go as he pleased, to conduct his business both at home and abroad, and, indeed, to visit all those sensitive installations of the RAF now as before. Since he continued to work for S.I.S. as if nothing had happened, Special Branch removed him from its list of suspects.

But Owens was that strange bird in the business—the compulsive spy who could not desist even in the face of mortal danger. He no longer sent any letters to Box 629 in Hamburg, to be sure, but otherwise he kept up his increasingly friendly relations with Dr. Rantzau.

Ritter on his part took it seriously when Owens suggested that he should be kept on ice and refrained from pressing him for any information. He kept in touch with him whenever the Welshman showed up in Germany, but only to give him a good time in the lively port city where a good time was easy to have.

Owens had that sybaritic streak and Ritter quickly discovered that his friend was inordinately fond of "dames and booze." The German, anxious to keep Owens in the fold for those "greater things" at some future date, supplied both generously, and very soon this complex business relationship became a convivial affair. Ritter (accompanied by his secretary, who was called "Fräulein Busch," in these parts) and Owens (with a succession of blind dates the Abwehr hustled up for him) could be seen together painting the town red at the Muenchner Kindl or in the raucous Valhalla Klub on the Reperbahn, the mainstem of Hamburg's notorious neon-lit, noisy red-light district. They usually warmed up in the evening at the Kindl and then Owens would go off on his own to the Valhalla. He had become fascinated by the tinsel-studded club's specialty, a system of table telephones that enabled Owens to make contact with sultry young ladies sitting at nearby tables, waiting to be called or calling him unsolicited.

The evolution of this enterprising salesman of electric goods into the Abwehr's master spy in England progressed according to plan. Ritter and "Fräulein Busch" became genuinely fond of their little Welsh friend who was so easy to entertain and who, on his part, entertained them with nostalgic Welsh folk ditties which he sang in his pleasant tenor voice at parties in Ritter's home.

In January 1939, these frolics came to an abrupt end.

The Abwehr had gone into one of its periodic crisis-alerts. This time Hitler's personal instructions to Admiral Canaris geared his organization for the next item on the agenda—the final smashing of Czechoslovakia with the occupation of Bohemia and Moravia scheduled for March. Beyond that, the contours of war with Poland over Danzig and the Corridor also became visible to the insiders.

This was the busiest time of the Canaris regime so far. Every branch both in the east and the west was working overtime. The Hamburg outpost was a beehive. It was impossible to gauge exactly how England would react to the breach of Chamberlain's pact of Munich and the occupation of the country whose territorial integrity it was supposed to assure. But the worst had to be anticipated.

R-agents had been deployed in full force with orders to complete the reconnaissance of the British Isles before travel restrictions, expected to be introduced even before an outbreak of hostilities, would severely restrict their movements. Ritter on his part rushed two of his best men—the industrialist Guenther Reydt and "Simon the Hobo" —back to England, and last but not least, sent word to Johnny that the time when he would have to go into harness was not too far off.[2]

During his gambols in Hamburg the time had not been entirely wasted on "dames and booze." Johnny had been given lessons in the technical intricacies of the craft by Captain Jules Boeckel, Ritter's controller of spies in the field, and was trained by Radioman Grein to operate an Afu-apparatus. In late January, Ritter decided to smuggle to him one of the *Klamotten*. A late-model set was sent to London in the privileged diplomatic pouch, with instructions to the chief of the mailroom at the German Embassy to check "the suitcase" into the cloakroom of Victoria Station and send the ticket to Johnny at his new address. He was no longer living with his family at Hampstead. He had deserted his wife and child for an Englishwoman of German extraction, and was living with her in a house in Kingston which he had chosen as a locale for his clandestine activities.

Owens received the ticket in the mail and redeemed the "suitcase" on February 7. Though he had no explicit instructions from Ritter beyond the basic alert, he unilaterally reactivated himself and plunged into the most feverish activity in all the secret part of his life.

The Snow File, as the record of the Owens case is called in MI.5, is rather vague about this period of Johnny's career. "Substantially," the pertinent passage reads, "from the end of 1936 until the outbreak of the war, Snow worked as a straightforward German agent, whose activities, although known to the authorities, were not interfered with in any important respect. . . . During the three years between 1936 and 1939 he was in reality acting in England as a kind of one-man *Stelle*. Although we cannot be certain on this point, it seems from his own account that Snow successfully represented to the Germans that he possessed a number of sub-agents in England, amounting perhaps to a dozen or fifteen men. It is probable, though not certain, that all these persons existed only in Snow's imagination."

But Johnny *was* busy developing single-handed a phenomenal espionage organization under the noses of S.I.S., MI.5 and the Special Branch. Today we know this from the documents in Johnny's original dossier in the Abwehr and from Colonel Ritter's account of the case he gave to me in 1969–70, when I revealed to him in Hamburg the photostatic copies of the original "correspondence" that passed between him and his star agent in England.

Not everything he tried during this period of tension yielded dividends. He thus made contact with certain friends at the Duckett Street headquarters of the British Union of Fascists, not to recruit them for espionage, but to set them up as propagandists. The scheme was to establish with German help four secret wireless transmitters on the British Isles, and use them, after the outbreak of hostilities, for broadcasting so-called "black propaganda" to British listeners.

This plan was aborted by the categorical refusal of his Blackshirt friends to participate in anything injurious to Britain in time of war. Far from merely imagining it, Owens had succeeded in spinning a web of sub-agents, consisting of congenial Welsh nationalists, until he had confidential informants planted in thirty-five strategic localities.[3]

In early August, accompanied by his mistress and a friend named Alexander Myner, a candidate he wanted to present to Ritter, Owens went to the continent on a combination holiday-and-business trip. It was designed to mask the real purpose of the excursion, a detour to Hamburg where Johnny had his last pre-war conference with his German employers.

He himself had sought the meeting, for he was anxious to clear with Ritter an extraordinary scheme he had conceived. It involved a hoax perpetrated on the British security organs, behind which Owens hoped to operate with impunity, and then actually managed to operate for almost two years after the outbreak of the war. It even made MI.5 an accomplice in Johnny's amazing efforts to service his German clients with intelligence over the barriers of war.

The "plan" became operational immediately upon his return to Kingston. He had received his instructions from Ritter—to use his Afu-apparatus to test transmissions on a pre-arranged schedule immediately after he had heard his own favorite song, *"Du, Du liegst mir im Herzen,"* played *twice* in succession on the midnight program of popular music the Germans were beaming to England.

The song was played twice as arranged shortly after midnight on August 28. At four-thirty that same morning, Johnny went on with his first transmission.

He returned at four-fifteen the next morning sending meteorological information. It was the one thing he had learned to do best on the Afu-apparatus. Now he produced in precise detail the kind of data the Luftwaffe and the Kriegsmarine would soon need in earnest— the weather in England with temperature, barometric pressure, ceiling and visibility, precipitation, wind direction and velocity.

Reception in Wohldorf was still bad. The air was crowding up. Atmospheric disturbances obliterated or blurred the signals. Valenti managed to get down the weather report and teletyped it to Sophien Terrace with a little note of triumph to Ritter: "In spite of heavy static reception was adequate to enable deciphering of the signal. Contact with 3504 definitively established. Ast Hamburg can now assure continuous satisfactory traffic."

Johnny kept sending on schedule. He radioed weather reports twice daily. On September 2, when the Wehrmacht had already attacked Poland but Hitler still hoped that England and France would leave him alone, Johnny went on the air with two SSD—most urgent —messages. On his regular schedule at 4:30 A.M. he radioed: "Situation now extremely grave. Declaration of war expected momentarily. More to come at twelve-hundred." He was back at high noon with a signal of sixteen five-letter groups, his first piece of hard intelligence. Its plain text read: "Planes loading at Bigginhill, Hornchurch, Blenheim. Starting regular transmissions, stand by day and night."

Captain Ritter, normally a placid, businesslike man, could barely control his excitement. His risky investment was yielding fantastic dividends. He took the transcripts to Captain Wichmann, his chief at Ast X. "Johnny is coming through perfectly, Herr Captain. Look," he said, "he covered Portsmouth on the 28th, and now these three airfields of the RAF! It's obvious that he has his Welshmen already working for him."

Johnny was now transmitting as often as he had a chance, frequently with reckless disregard for his security. Aside from the weather reports he was pouring in tactical information, mostly about the deployment of the RAF, he himself covering airfields around London. And he was forwarding tidbits of intelligence from his sub-agents at thirty-five different places throughout the United Kingdom.

Then, less than three weeks after Ritter had activated him, he showed that he could do much better than just reporting the number of Hurricanes at Croydon or the appearance of a barbed wire fence near Dover. To evade detection by the English who were monitoring this kind of radio traffic and had means to track down the clandestine transmitters, Johnny had strict instructions to limit his messages to not more than four-hundred letters each. But he had such important news, and was so eager to share it with Ritter, that he boldly disregarded the rule. On September 18, he put on the air his longest report to date. It read in full: "Personal observations and from Dutch War Ministry engineer with Phillips in England:

"Installation of net of UHF [ultra-high-frequency] stations to monitor approaching enemy aircraft in progress all along coast from

Isle of Wight to Orkneys. Said to be capable of detecting airborne planes by using beamed and reflected radio-waves or by picking up UHF produced when sparks of plugs jump to magnets of engines. Device enables with fair accuracy to determine distance of aircraft and makes possible to estimate number of engines. Network supposedly operates in three stages called Advance, Intermediate, and Final. Already operational are stations in Suffolk, Essex, and Kent, with easily identifiable 350 and 240-foot steel or wooden aerial masts. More in process of construction.

"Only possibility to eliminate penetration of these electro-magnetic waves or forestall their reception is believed to be through application of so-called suppressors. Will try to procure details."

This was a crucial bit of high-grade intelligence. It had a direct bearing on one of the greatest mysteries that heretofore had stumped both the Abwehr and the Luftwaffe's intelligence department.

Since 1938 the British had been working frantically on the perfection of radar as a foolproof instrument of their air defenses. The Germans were trying, just as desperately, to find out whether any part of the new radar net was already operational. Those installations Johnny referred to in his report had not escaped their attention. Since early 1939 they had kept England under surveillance, using He-111C high-flying aircraft of a super-secret aerial spy circus under Colonel Guenther Rohwel, and two specially rigged Zeppelins in what was the first electronic reconnaissance in history.

When their photographs of the towers were produced and the pictures showed high steel masts with crossed lattice aerials, General Wolfgang Martini, head of the Luftwaffe Signal Establishment, concluded that they seemed to be unsuited to the wavelengths which his own experts regarded as best for radar. Martini decided that, unusual as they were, they must have been the towers of ordinary radio stations.

When the war broke out, General Martini still did not know with any certainty whether those masts had anything to do with a fixed functioning radar system to detect approaching aircraft.

It was into this darkness that Johnny's message of the 18th seemed to be shedding at least a ray of light. He had identified the odd towers as definitely belonging to radar stations and not as Martini guessed, to ordinary radio transmitters. He stated well-nigh categorically that at least those in Suffolk (at Orfordness), Kent (at Dunkirk and Dover) and Essex (at Canewdon) were already operational. Suddenly the heavy pall of uncertainty was lifted. The Germans had the evidence General Martini's electronic snooping had failed so dismally to produce.

Johnny's report hit Sophien Terrace like a bombshell. This was the kind of spy scoop secret services scarcely dare even to hope for. Johnny's report seemed far too important to be simply put on the teletype and sent to Berlin for an uncertain fate. With Captain Wichmann's permission, Ritter took it personally to Abwehr headquarters. He wanted to make sure that it would be forwarded to General Martini, but was also eager to demonstrate to the Doubting Thomases in Group I that the time and money he had spent on Johnny during his costly sleeper days had not gone down the drain.

He found Major Brasser, chief of air intelligence in the Abwehr and usually the friendly suporter of even his most extravagant projects, skeptical for a change. "It's an interesting item," he told Ritter. "But really, it doesn't say too much. Query your Johnny for more specific data. Only if he can spell out this mysterious thing in more exact detail will I agree to send the report to the Luftwaffe."

Ritter thought the report was far too important even so far as it went to let it vanish in one of Berlin's pigeonholes. "Herr Major," he told Brasser. "I think this report is so good that it warrants immediate forwarding to Luftwaffe Ic. As you know, sir, they could not resolve whether or not the British have a working aircraft detection system. They could not figure out for sure what those steel towers are for. This report may not be the whole solution of the riddle. But I believe it contains certain major clues that will help them in making up their minds."

Major Brasser took him as far as Colonel Piekenbrock, the next link in this chain of command. "Come with me," the then colonel told them. "I was about to go to the Chief when you burst in. We may as well let the Admiral decide this particular match."

This was one of Piekenbrock's regular morning sessions when he briefed Canaris and presented to him a selection of the juiciest intelligence reports that had come in the night before. In the Chief's inner sanctum he laid the folder on the desk before Canaris, but handed him Johnny's signal separately. He waited until he read it through, then said:

"There is some disagreement over this, Excellency. Ritter wants us to send it over to Major Schmid immediately. But Brasser thinks it's too vague to warrant submission and that we would make a laughing stock of ourselves if we submitted it in its present raw form."

Canaris bristled, but only for a moment. "Never mind," he said in a deceptively calm tone. "Send it on to Beppo. Let's see what he'll make of it."[4] Turning to Ritter with a thin, weary smile, he said warmly: "Good for old Johnny! Send him a well-done for me, Ritter."

He opened the folder and began to peruse Piekenbrock's selection of incoming dispatches. At the top of the pile was a brief report from the Breslau branch, a flippant and nasty little item. Piekenbrock, a waggish Rhinelander sought forever to lighten his chief's perennial gloom with a gag here or some Nazi drollery there, and had included it in the batch merely for "comic" relief. "According to reliable V-man from Tauentzien," it read, "the alleged wife of Signor Renzetti, secretary of the Italian Embassy, is actually a German Jewess originally from Breslau whose maiden name is Blaustein. V-man says that Signora Renzetti recently had her prominent semitic nose bobbed in Rome."

Canaris shook his white-maned head with laughter. "I'll keep these two reports," he said with an impish grin, "Johnny's and the one from Breslau for the Fuehrer. Perhaps it will convince him that we miss nothing."

He again picked up Johnny's dispatch, re-read it, and said, "You know, gentlemen, this may yet turn out to be one of the most important pieces of intelligence we'll ever get in this rat race. Thank you for bringing it to me. It's the nicest birthday present I dared to expect."

The date was September 21, 1939. It was not Canaris's birthday.

Exactly twenty years before on this day the Abwehr was born.

NOTES

1 In New York, radio station WOR recorded this ominous traffic and rebroadcast it during these days of crisis.

2 Walter Simon, or "Simon the Hobo", an adventure-bent man already in his fifties, was Ritter's "ace" in England. He was later to come a cropper on a return appearance.

3 All of them disgruntled Welshmen, they were located at Swansea, Southampton, Bournmouth, Odiham, Worcester, Brixham, Padstow, Ilfracombe, Exeter, Youghol, Warminster, Bristol, Gloucester, Bicester, Rochester and Oxford, Avonmouth, the Catterick Camp at Aldershot, Southend, Dover, Harwich, Folkstone, Portsmouth, Caddington, Northholt, Hendon, Pembroke Docks, Chatham, Putney Hill (where the RAF had its big communications center), Kenley, Farnborough, Liverpool, West Hartlepool, and in the London suburbs of Ilford and Richmond.

4 "Beppo" was Major Josef Schmid, intelligence chief of the Luftwaffe General Staff, the proper channel through which Johnny's report should have reached General Martini.

Chapter 15

Intermezzo on the
Tirpitz Quay

*W*HAT does a chief of intelligence do on the day the war breaks out?

To Admiral Canaris, ensconced in his plainly furnished office in the main Abwehr building, the actual outbreak of the war was anticlimactic. He felt good. Gone were his restive, frustration-filled days in the Navy when he always craved to be out of a service in which he never felt completely comfortable. He was satisfied that he had done well during the past five years.

Since 1935, when he was named chief of the Abwehr, he had built it into an enormous intelligence machine. Whatever it was now in qualitative terms (and the admiral was satisfied that it was the best), it was certainly the biggest secret service, probably of all times.

He now had thousands of men and women on his staff and in the field operating as V-men, all over the world from Aden to Zanzibar. In the United States several rings were operational even though it was not a priority target. A couple of his agents had been planted in the uncharted Boias region of Brazil, and a two-man team was standing by high up in the Khyber Pass to go on a mission to the Fakir of Ipi, Britain's relentless enemy in India's wild Northwest Frontier.

There was no formal declaration in this war.

A "frontier incident" had been staged at Gleiwitz, on German soil near the Polish border. A hundred odd Germans wearing Polish uniforms "attacked" the radio station, read an inflammatory "proclamation" into a live microphone, then fled posthaste, leaving behind the still warm body of an inmate shipped up from a concentration camp and killed on the spot to make the show look more realistic.

Admiral Canaris was in on the plot to stage this macabre prologue.

Major General Erich von Manstein, the chief of staff of Army Group South who had supervised the planning of the Polish campaign, had thought up the idea of starting the war with a fake provocation and proposed that the sham attack be staged by the Abwehr with three storm battalions clad in Polish uniforms. The bogus Poles would "break into Germany," do some shooting in the countryside around Gleiwitz, and vanish, permitting Hitler to describe the premeditated invasion of Poland as a "counter-attack with pursuit."

The Abwehr had spent much time on preparing the operation. Lieutenant von Frankenberg had picked 364 men from the Abwehr's own storm troops, a unit called the Brandenburg Training Company; and Master Sergeant Kutschke assembled the uniforms and equipment they would need.

But at 3:00 P.M. on August 17, Hitler took .the *coup de main* away from the Abwehr and gave it to Heinrich Himmler's SS. When Canaris asked why, the Fuehrer told him: "I am resolved once and for all to exclude the Wehrmacht under all circumstances from any enterprise that even remotely has a provocative character."

The Abwehr still had to furnish the props. Shortly after midnight on August 19, coming with two trucks from the Abwehr warehouses at Breslau, Sergeant Kutschke delivered the shipment into the hands of an SS bully named Ratz, at Oppeln near Gleiwitz where the operation was staging. Colonel von Frankenburg gave Ratz the list of the Abwehr-men he had chosen for the enterprise, but was told they were no longer needed. Reichsfuehrer Himmler was using his own SS men.

Early in the morning of September 1, Admiral Canaris heard on the radio that his uniforms had been put to excellent use between 8:00 and 8:07 o'clock the night before. Since 4:45 A.M. the counter-attack with pursuit had been on.

Even if the Abwehr had lost this particular "special enterprise," it was still left with plenty of others. The plans of the Polish campaign envisaged a lightninglike, unimpeded advance into the heart of Poland to decide the issues before the Poles could begin their own mobilization. The Abwehr was given a critical part to play in the execution of these plans. Among other intricate tasks it had to preserve intact the bridges and roads the Wehrmacht needed, and destroy those the Poles would use.

Already in April, Canaris was given special instructions by General Wilhelm Keitel to begin laying the groundwork for its pre-invasion mission, and was told to be ready with his arrangements by August 25. From the rabble of Nazi fanatics, mostly shiftless *Volksdeutsche* adrift in Germany, Colonel Erwin von Lahousen-Virremont, chief of Abwehr II put together sixteen separate *Kampfgruppen* (combat teams) to pave the armies' way into Poland.

This army of hooligans included a group of "miners" he was to infiltrate into Poland just a step ahead of the German troops, on the pretext of seizing and holding precious mines, and prevent their destruction by the retreating Poles. The "Goergey" and "Bisok" teams smuggled arms and explosives to saboteurs at key spots inside Poland, to destroy on the ground what the Luftwaffe could not hit from the air. There were other teams, identified by various letters of the alphabet, whose mission was to destroy airstrips, blow up bridges and electricity pylons, cut telephone and telegraph wires, or conversely, to keep certain bridges and roads intact for the German troops.

They were ready on schedule. On August 15 the Wehrmacht High Command, in an operations order for their employment at preselected spots, specifically authorized Admiral Canaris to engage them in offensive operations up to twelve hours prior to the commencement of hostilities, against a country with which the Germans would still be at peace.

At 12:30 P.M. on Thursday, August 24, Lieutenant Colonel Adolph Heusinger, operations officer of the Chief of Staff, informed Canaris that the Fuehrer had set 4:15 A.M. on Saturday the 26th as the time for the invasion.

At 8:30 P.M. on the same day, Captain Gaedke, one of Heusinger's aides, telephoned the orders to send the men into action beginning at 8:00 P.M. on the next day.

The orders were flashed to the scattered combat teams, only to be canceled on the evening of the 25th, when most of the teams were already at their jumping-off stations. Gaedke called the Abwehr to say that the Fuehrer, on political grounds, had called off the invasion. "You must do everything humanly possible to halt your combat teams," Gaedke said.

The hour was late, but the Abwehr still managed to stop all its K-groups—except one. The team sent to secure the Jablunkov Pass in the Beskids, through which a railroad meandered from Slovakia to the station of Mosty and points beyond in Polish Silesia, could not be reached. Holding to its original orders and unaware of any change in the plans, the "lost" combat team opened fire at 0001 on August 26, defeated a superior Polish force in Mosty, captured the pass and the railroad station, then waited for the division it had hacked the way for to arrive. But, of course, it did not come. Baffled by its absence Lieutenant Albrecht Herzner, commandant of the combat team, asked the Polish colonel he had taken prisoner of war: "What's the matter? Aren't Germany and Poland at war?"

"I told you they aren't," the Pole replied. "You can find it out for yourself if you don't believe me."

"How?" Herzner asked.

"By calling your base on the telephone."

And sure enough, the phone in the station worked. Herzner got Zilina in Slovakia, where his base command was, long-distance, and was told by his frantic division intelligence officer to drop everything —prisoners and booty—and come back to Zilina, please, as quickly as he could.

It was too late. Herzner had already won his war.

This incident was minor in the enormous conflict that soon followed, but it has a historic significance. *It was the Abwehr of Canaris whose forces actually fired the first shot in World War II, six full days, four hours and forty-four minutes before its outbreak at 4:45 A.M. on September 1.*

At first, when it seemed that the precipitate action of this wayward team would alert the Poles and cause them to accelerate their mobilization, Admiral Canaris was worried that Hitler would punish him for the mishap. When the incident passed virtually unnoticed and the Poles did nothing in its wake, he expressed his pride in this Abwehr gang and sent congratulations to Lieutenant Herzner.[1]

In Poland the war was to last just twenty-seven days.

How was it possible, military experts asked, for a nation of thirty-two million people to melt away before the German onslaught?

Within twenty-four hours after Hitler launched his Blitzkrieg, seventy-five percent of the Polish planes were destroyed, most of them in their hangars. The Germans forestalled aid from Britain and France by destroying every Polish airfield capable of receiving military craft. In the first few days of the campaign the Wehrmacht smashed communication lines and railroad bridges behind the Polish lines.

Army transports operating on secret schedules were located by the Luftwaffe planes and bombed out of existence at their terminals. Mobilization centers and staging stations, presumably known only to the planning staff of the Polish High Command, were found by German planes and smashed. Munitions dumps and oil stores, to the last isolated depot at Leczyca, were blasted. Nothing of military significance escaped.

Never before had a major military power been subdued so rapidly and with such finality. What extra special ingredient in the German war machine made this stupendous victory possible so fast?

The answer was given by inference a few days after the conclusion of the campaign. A group of foreign correspondents were taken on a conducted tour to the ruins of Warsaw, and Colonel von Wedel, their guide from the High Command's propaganda section, was asked to explain the secret of this amazing success. The colonel answered with unusual candor:

"Victory was due to our irresistible arms and to our superior intelligence service."

Probably never before had the debt the warlords owed their intelligence service been so publicly acknowledged.

On this Friday everything was speeding ahead. The invasion was on. Those who saw Canaris during these hours recall vividly how elated he was.

He had spent the night in his office sleeping fitfully on a cot. He was up at dawn, fresh and full of vim. His office resembled a command post, as signals were brought in and Lahousen appeared again and again to report on the progress of the special Abwehr enterprises. News from the combat teams kept coming in and all of it was favorable.

For 9:15 A.M. Canaris had ordered an assembly of the officers on the Abwehr staff, and buoyed by the good news, he was ready to go over to the auditorium to give the peptalk the historic occasion warranted. He spoke to them briefly, in his low voice, of the great significance of the hour, admonished them to remember that they were "members of the silent service," and concluded with a slight flourish in his best pro-Nazi vein: "Gentlemen," he said, "I demand unquestioning and unconditionally positive loyalty to the Fuehrer. Heil Hitler!"

On his way back to his office, in one of the dark corridors of the Abwehr building, he bumped into Dr. Hans Bernd Gisevius, the young lawyer-politician who later gained both fame and notoriety as one of the most flamboyant and prolix of the anti-Nazi rebels.

Gisevius looked glum. "Herr Admiral," he said. "This has just come in. England has ordered total mobilization."

The smile vanished from Canaris's face. "My God," he said in a hushed tone. "If England comes into this, it will be the end of our poor Germany."

NOTE

1 The chronic political schizophrenia of Abwehr-men was well illustrated in the case of young Herzner. Only a few months before he was working underground with a group of anti-Nazis plotting the assassination of Hitler. Now he was paving the way, with conspicuous heroism and unquestioning determination, for Hitler's war, which he fervently opposed. Herzner died during the war, nobody knows how.

Chapter **16**

The Master Spy

CAPTAIN Willy Janke, a Luftwaffe officer who was his principal aide, was at Admiral Canaris's side both in the auditorium and at the encounter with young Gisevius, and was baffled by the abrupt change in his chief's mood. These hectic days had challenged his virtuoso talent to walk the tightrope in the big three-ring circus of Nazidom. He appeared to have two different solutions for every problem that confronted him, two different ways to deal with every demand he had to meet.

As a result, even men closest to him could not resolve in their own minds whether Canaris was now for or against the war, or for or against the Nazis. In conversations with strangers he would accentuate the positive, but stress the negative when reviewing the mad rush of events with men he was sure were anti-Nazis.

Canaris began to have doubts about the regime he was serving in 1938, when the Nazis drummed General Werner von Fritsch out of his command of the army on spurious charges of "unnatural vice." He swallowed this insult that was so plainly calculated to discredit the uniform he wore, as did all the other generals and admirals, and continued to support the regime as loyally as before.

Then, within the first fortnight of the war, something snapped in Canaris's inscrutable soul. His equivocations continued. But his doubts were resolved. Very deep within himself he broke with Adolf Hitler.

On September 10 Canaris had gone into the field to watch the Wehrmacht in action, and what he found in Poland turned his stomach.

At different stops, several of his Abwehr officers, who were accompanying the troops deep into Poland, reported to him in great consternation that special SS and Gestapo murder squads that traveled behind the army, had embarked on an orgy of massacre. Polish civilians were lined up at open mass graves which these unfortunates themselves had to dig, then were cut down with machine-gun salvos. Major Helmuth Groscurth, who had been in charge of Abwehr II but was now on a mysterious assignment for General Franz Halder, chief of the General Staff, showed Canaris a secret directive signed by Himmler. Citing a *Fuehrerbefehl,* an order issued by Hitler himself, it explicitly called for the systematic extermination of Poles, especially, as the directive stated, members of the aristocracy and of the Roman Catholic clergy.

Admiral Canaris refused to believe that Hitler had anything to do with such a monstrosity or even that he was familiar with Himmler's directive. He went looking for the Fuehrer to take the matter up with him and found him on September 12, in his special train at a railroad siding in Ilnau. Although Hitler was on the train the admiral was advised to see General Wilhelm Keitel, chief of the Wehrmacht Staff, before he approached the Fuehrer.

He found Keitel in his office in one of the railroad cars, and told him in obvious excitement: "I have information, Herr Colonel General, that mass executions are being planned in Poland, and that members of the Polish nobility and the Roman Catholic bishops and priests have been singled out for extermination. I feel obliged to give you a word of warning. For such outrages," he said, "the world will eventually blame the Wehrmacht, if only because it acquiesced in these unheard-of atrocities."

"If I were you, Herr Canaris," Keitel said coldly, "I would not get mixed up in this business. This 'thing' has been decided upon by the Fuehrer himself. He has told General von Brauchitsch that since the Wehrmacht does not want to have anything to do with this 'thing,' it will have to let the SS and Gestapo do it. As a matter of fact," he added, "every military command in Poland will from now on have a civilian chief besides its military head, the former to be in charge of the 'racial extermination' [*Volkstuemliche Ausrottung*] program."

Canaris did not think he had heard right. He was stunned, mortified, scandalized, and was about to upbraid Keitel—but just then Hitler entered the car, and the general signaled him to keep quiet by sealing his lips with an index finger. Hitler greeted the admiral amiably, then asked him what information he had about alleged French intentions to mount a major offensive in the direction of Saarbruecken.

Canaris was barely coherent and it seemed that Hitler noticed that something was bothering him. Actually the admiral was thinking how he could raise the atrocity issue with Hitler despite Keitel's warning, but he could not summon the courage. The confrontation passed without Canaris bringing up the heinous question that was foremost in his mind and which he had come to raise.

He was emotionally convulsed and physically sick when he got back to Berlin on the 14th. It was not his habit to put down on paper anything unpleasant or controversial for fear that such a record might come back to haunt him. But this time he sat down immediately upon his return and prepared the minutes of the conference. He gave it to Groscurth to preserve for posterity in the file of documents the major was collecting as evidence of the Nazis' ghastly crimes to be used against them on their day of retribution.

Canaris never recovered from the shock of this experience. He asked himself, could he, in good conscience, remain faithful to a master like Hitler? It took him some time to answer this question conclusively. But the mere fact that he raised it so bluntly for himself loosened his allegiance.

There was something else. For the first time he found himself fundamentally critical of the Fuehrer—over the issue of England. Already in 1935 in his peptalk to the little band of officers in Wilhelmshaven, Canaris warned that any country that enjoyed the support of the United States would inevitably win in a war. He had no doubt that England would receive such aid, and was, therefore, reassured by Hitler's efforts to placate the British. Several times in their private meetings he had heard the Fuehrer say resolutely that he would do anything to avoid a war with Britain.

Even on August 23, 1939, when Prime Minister Chamberlain had warned Hitler that England would stand by Poland and on the 25th, when the Anglo-Polish treaty of mutual assistance was signed in London, Hitler told him not to worry—the British were merely bluffing. "They have enough trouble in their empire," the Fuehrer said, "and know full well what a disaster another European war would be for them. They will make noises, they will rattle their sabres, but war? No! When the chips are down, the lion will pull in its tail."

Canaris left the meeting forcing himself to believe that the Fuehrer would be proven right as usual. This time Hitler was proven wrong. England and Germany were at war.

Canaris feared no other country, not Poland, not France, not even the Soviet Union. But this war with England frightened him.

He did not know it yet but he had some reasons of his own to be apprehensive. The Abwehr seemed to be in trouble in England.

Relying on Hitler's repeated assurances, no special arrangements had been made to adjust its network in the British Isles to wartime exigencies. Only in the eleventh hour, in utter haste and with improvised measures, was an effort made to convert the relatively easy peacetime coverage to the much more difficult wartime surveillance. R-men like Block, Kaulen, and Simon were ordered home. They, and a few other agents, left on the last ships that sailed on their final peacetime schedules.

Even without waiting for word from Hamburg, S.3503—the seemingly impeccable industrialist Guenther Reydt who served as Ast X's chief V-man in England—boarded a Danish plane for Copenhagen on August 26, the morning after the signing of the Anglo-Polish pact. He was in one of the Abwehr's dummy downtown offices in Hamburg the next day, giving Wichmann and Ritter a detailed account of what he had seen of England's war preparations.

"Bluffing?" Reydt shook his head. "Maybe last year, during the Sudeten crisis. Then they put up a few AA batteries in the parks, but if you looked a little closer you could see that they were rather antiquated and had no ammunition supplied to them. Now the parks are bristling with brand new guns, and there are huge piles of shells all around them.

"And not only in the parks. I saw emplacements with new batteries all along the London-Ramsgate road, plenty of them east of Rainham and Chislehurst, more between Longfield and Newstead, west of Rochester and on the islands in the Medway river, all around the Eastchurch airfield on the Isle of Sheppey.

"All the warships are assembled at their bases, except perhaps the three destroyers I saw in the Thames near Gravesend. Buses have been requisitioned to transport the troops and evacuate women and children. Merchant ships have been impounded to be converted to war service.

"Bluffing? Not this time!"

Reydt urged Wichmann and Ritter to accept war with Britain as a foregone conclusion, and make their arrangements accordingly and promptly.

Then history repeated itself and the roof fell in.

On September 4 all enemy aliens in Britain were ordered to report to the police to have their cases individually investigated by 120 special tribunals. When they finished their work, close to 74,000 men and women had been processed, among whom 600 persons were found "unreliable," aside from 6800 whose "reliability" was considered "uncertain." The "unreliables" were then interned, while the "uncertains" were subjected to certain restrictions.

The big roundup had none of the precision and severity of 1914, directed as it was then by the incomparable Sir Basil Thomson and a much younger Vernon Kell. MI.5 and the Special Branch did have a "Class A" list of espionage suspects with 350 names on it. However, unlike their predecessors of twenty-five years before, who had pinpointed the German spies in advance and picked them out one by one, now they had only vague or circumstantial evidence against those suspected of being enemy agents.

It was assumed nevertheless that whatever operatives the Germans had had at large in Britain, had been caught in the dragnet. General Kell, for one, regarded this "initial coup as a success comparable with the breaking of the [Karl Gustav] Ernst ring at the beginning of the first war." He was satisfied, as it was put, that "by this action Germany would go into the war 'blind,' without any effective network in England."

To begin with, the Abwehr people probably would have been inclined to go along with Kell's assessment of the situation if they had known about it. When within ten days they learned about the measures, which, at first blush, appeared to be reminiscent of those of 1914, they assumed that their networks had been smashed. Frantic discussions were held in Berlin, Hamburg, and Bremen. The situation seemed bleak.

But then, scattered bright spots appeared in the darkness. "A.3529," a woman agent, reported from Bournemouth that she had been missed by the dragnet and was in harness. Word came from "U.3527," a young Anglo-German working for Captain Dierks, that he, too, was safe, as was his brother, "A.3528." One agent after another checked in, communicating with their Abwehr contacts via mail drops in neutral countries.

And, last but not least, "Johnny" Owens was, of course, also in business.

Incredibly, Ritter received word from him on September 23, suggesting that they meet in Rotterdam on the 28th.

At dawn on September 4 Johnny put his last signal on the air, then returned his Afu-set to its suitcase, and waited.

Shortly after eight o'clock in the morning he put in a call to Scotland Yard, asked for Inspector Gagen of Special Branch, and when Gagen answered the call, made an appointment to see him at Waterloo Station.

The inspector went to the meeting with a detention order and served it on Owens, who was then taken to Wandsworth Prison. No sooner was he ensconced there than he sent for Colonel Peel of S.I.S. He also asked to be put in touch with MI.5, because he had a present to give them. When they came he revealed to them the place where he had hidden his Afu set in his house at Kingston. The gift so pleased its recipients that Owens was freed with the best wishes of MI.5, but only after he had demonstrated how the set worked, by establishing contact with Wohldorf—from his cell.

Phase One of his master plan had now become operational.

Even the bravest and boldest spy is filled with anxiety about the security of his mission and his personal safety, and sees in his clandestine wireless a prime vulnerability factor. He knows that each time he goes on the air from his hideout, he runs the risk of giving away his anonymity and security.

Owens, who was as brave and smart as the best of them, did not think much of this Afu business. He knew all about the electronic surveillance the British authorities had prepared for the emergency. Occasionally he thought he recognized monitoring and direction-finding vans of the General Post Office, which was in charge of this effort, already cruising the streets, searching with their sensitive instruments for unauthorized transmitters.

Moreover, the Special Branch and S.I.S. knew that he had an Afu apparatus simply because he himself had told them about it. Back in January when "the suitcase" arrived and he checked it out of the cloakroom in Victoria Station, he took it straight to Inspector Gagen in Scotland Yard. The inspector looked over the magic box, showed it to the people in S.I.S., and together they praised the workmanship that produced such a powerful yet compact transceiver. But that was all. To Owens's amazement the set was returned to him to do with it as he pleased.[1]

Owens could not make sense of this. Was this sheer laxity? Or was it the gumshoes' usual stupidity? He assumed, for what else could one think, that Special Branch was preparing a trap and had let him keep the set so that he would fall into it so much harder.

When he received Ritter's instruction to go on the air he had used the set, not so much to try it out, but to probe the proficiency of the British surveillance system. Nothing happened. If the British monitored his transmissions (and today we know that they missed them) they, he thought, did not interefere in order to give him more rope. He was stretching his luck. He put on the air some vital information to provoke the monitors. Still nothing happened. The absence of any reaction was not making him over-confident. He was convinced that sooner or later, as security improved, the British would stumble on his transmissions.

He was determined to act before they would. He made up his mind to surrender "the suitcase" in a gamble that he was not absolutely sure might succeed. By giving up his Afu, he hoped, he would buy his freedom of movement and could stay in harness, collecting information, managing his ring, then getting the intelligence produced to the Germans in some safer way than broadcasting it for the whole world to hear.

The idea behind all this was daring yet plausible. Owens took into consideration the manner in which he found the British were handling such questions. They would regard the surrender of the set as proof positive that he had definitely discontinued his relations with the Germans. Or perhaps they would set him up in the business as a double agent working loyally for Britain to feed misleading information to the Abwehr.

It happened exactly as he anticipated.

The British not only appreciated his gesture but rejoiced in getting hold of the first of several agent-radios they suspected the Germans had smuggled into England before the war. The people in MI.5 went so far as to call this an historic occasion.

Being a double-edged weapon, such clandestine radios are used by the secret services for the emission of both genuine and bogus intelligence. Whenever a radio spy is caught, and it is assumed that his employers remain unaware of his fate, the agent may be salted away or hanged or shot—or he may be "turned 'round" to cooperate with his captors against his former customers. Whatever happens to such fallen spies, determined efforts are made to keep their radios alive, to be operated by men with the special aptitude of imitating somebody else's Morse touch.

The most brittle part of the secret agent's natural equipment is his allegiance. Once set adrift on missions to swim or sink by their own wits, they are subjected to enormous challenges, temptations, and threats, with life itself as the stake in an uneven gamble. Although spies have certain characteristics in common, there are many different types and they react differently to stress and strain.

John Cecil Masterman, the official historian of this intricate operation, and himself an outstanding member of the "Double-Cross" team, told me that most spies would prove willing to commit treachery under duress if it meant survival. Those likely to break under pressure—for which the spybusters have devised a sinister, ingenious physical and psychological repertory—can be bent by degrees.

The British, to whom intelligence was traditionally a game, were not unmindful of the potentialities of double-agentry. Plans had been made by both MI.6 and MI.5 before the war to utilize fallen agents in a systematic deception campaign aimed at their original employers. The first impetus to institutionalize the system in the coming war was given in a lecture by a member of the *Deuxième Bureau* delivered on

May 5, 1939, to an audience of officers from the secret services. He pointed out the value of double-crossing agents and gave some rudimentary advice for the management of controlled spies.

The idea was hatching in the mind of a young major formerly with the Seaforth Highlanders (where he served as a contemporary of Norman Baillie-Stewart), now with MI.5 under such deep cover that his name had been erased from the British Army List. He was Thomas Andrew Robertson, a remarkably brainy Scot in his twenties, strikingly handsome with devastating charm, imaginative and enterprising. He contemplated a deception system, but had to bide his time. During the hectic months after the outbreak of war Britain was swept by a spy hysteria, automatically dooming every German spy who fell into British hands. They were disposed of in short order, some without the benefit of due judicial process.

After seven German agents had been executed in 1940, Major Robertson decided to gain acceptance for his double-cross plan. He took up the idea with Colonel Dick White, the most erudite and energetic innovator among the younger executives of MI.5. He lobbied for it in the Naval Intelligence Division and the Air Staff, where Admiral John Godfrey, the DNI, and Wing Commander "Archie" Boyle, the leading air intelligence expert, expressed interest in the project. Robertson then sold it to John Bevins who headed a super-secret central deception bureau in the Cabinet Office under Prime Minister Churchill's chief military aid, General "Pug" Ismay.

Robertson, using his native eloquence at its most persuasive, convinced them that it was a senseless waste to hang or shoot every captured German spy. A place could be found for some of them in the war effort by utilizing the cream of the crop in a game the British would play with the unsuspecting enemy.

This was the origin of the Double-Cross System within MI.5. It was established formally in Colonel White's B-Division, where Robertson and his closely-knit group of associates built the finely tuned instrument which MI.5's faceless double-crossers played with such virtuosity throughout the war.

The Germans, with unaccustomed but apt flippancy, called this *Funkspiel,* or "radio game." The British coined a somewhat ruder but franker term, calling it "XX" for "Double-Cross."

Robertson was looking forward to the day when he could double-X the Germans, and now the opportunity had come much sooner than anybody dared to expect. Masterman, even long after the war, said that Snow's first message from Wandsworth Prison was one of the most dramatic incidents in the XX system.

His *bona fides* established to the satisfaction of MI.6 (as S.I.S. had come to be called) and with MI.5 that managed the "XX" operation, Owens was returned to the fold, now as a trusted double agent. Great plans were made for him on the pattern of his previous experience.

His radio would be kept hot, beaming intelligence to the Germans so concocted as to contain some factual information to sustain its apparent reliability, most of it plausible but fictitious. Owens himself was excluded from this part of the enterprise. A so-called VI.-man—a Voluntary Interceptor, one of the radio hams who had been drawn into the service mainly to monitor the enemy's wireless traffic —was assigned to operate his Afu-set, after the volunteer had studied Owens's characteristic fingerprint and succeeded in acquiring considerable deftness in simulating it.

Then in an astounding display of trust in a spy who had operated in so devious a fashion before, his British masters went considerably further.

For his signal transmitted from the cell in Wandsworth Prison Owens had chosen what struck his British friends as a cryptic text. *"Must meet you Holland at once,"* it read. *"Bring weather code. Radio town and hotel. Wales ready."* The British passed it when Owens explained that Ritter was expecting him to send weather reports, and also to establish contact with trustworthy members of the Welsh Nationalist Party who could be engaged in some "special" work.

But how about that urgent meeting in Holland?

Owens used his considerable powers of persuasion to explain what he meant by this. Why, of course, he would have to keep up the old system of meeting Dr. Rantzau at least from time to time, the only way to sustain the impression that all was well. Belgium and Holland were still neutral. He had to take care of his business in Rotterdam and Antwerp. Why not let him meet Dr. Rantzau on these trips and enable him to palm off more phoney intelligence on the naïve Germans.

It sounded like a reasonable proposition. MI.5 not only consented to the resumption of Owens's old mixed bag of business outings, but, satisfied that his loyalty was beyond doubt, actually arranged his package tours and paid his expenses.

Captain Ritter acknowledged the signal Johnny had sent from the cell, and invited him to a *Treff* in Antwerp on September 28, in the apartment of a German shipping broker living in Belgium.

Now began a period in Johnny's secret life that taxes one's imagination and belief even if hardened on the best spy stories, true or fictitious. Here was a spy in a truly extraordinary mold. Although he worked for both the British and the Germans, neither of them really knew what he was doing when he was on the other side of the hill. All they knew was what he was telling them, and believed more or less uncritically well-nigh everything he said.

He slipped up once in a while for it was a backbreaking job to take care of his bustling legitimate business and also cater to two sets of secret customers; to keep apart and remember all his different cover stories and contrived subterfuges; to be "Snow" to the British and "Johnny" to the Germans; to live three distinct lives. He managed to slip out of his *faux pas* as quickly as he slipped into them—to keep all concerned (or unconcerned, for that matter) satisfied and happy, and blissfully ignorant of the full scope of his activities.

Nikolaus Ritter, by then a lieutenant colonel, was captured by MI.5 after the war and quizzed relentlessly in a succession of P/W cages for well over a year. But he never divulged to his British interrogators all the details he knew of the Johnny operation. And, of course, the British never confided to him their side of the story. This is the whole account of this impossible mission, coordinated and synchronized, and told for the first time in its entirety, to take its place in the anthology of history's great espionage exploits.

Snow vanished from London on the morning of September 28, and materialized as Johnny a few hours later in the living room of the broker, at his first wartime *Treff* with Dr. Rantzau. Ritter was accompanied by a new assistant of his, a young lawyer-diplomat named Karl-Heinz Kraemer, because the broker was his friend and it was he who had arranged the use of the flat as a safe house.

On the way across, Owens contemplated just what and how much he should tell the Germans, and then decided to play it by ear, telling them as little as possible. When Ritter asked him pointedly how it was possible that he was permitted to leave England, Owens replied that his business contacts in Belgium and Holland were considered essential for the British war effort, and that his sales were to be kept up since every transaction in hard foreign currencies helped, as the British would soon need them desperately.

Ritter swallowed the explanation, and also accepted Johnny's assurance that his signals were on the level. That was how far Owens had decided to go in fooling the Germans. He was determined to protect them because he liked them genuinely, and to compromise the British, whom he loathed.

Without confiding to Ritter in so many words that his messages were mere concoctions of MI.5, he proceeded at the *Treff* to revise them, eliminating the chaff and the lies, pointing up the true parts of their contents. This way, from now on, he would minimize the damage while letting the Germans benefit after all from this source, in effect trapping MI.5 into providing the enemy with quite a bit of straight information.

He did have a piece of great news, though. When he had signaled from London that "Wales [was] ready," he meant to say that he had succeeded in enlisting, not just any ordinary Welshman, but none other than Gwyllem Williams himself, a retired police inspector from Swansea who headed the Welsh Nationalist Party. More than that, he would bring him along to their next *Treff* so that Dr. Rantzau could make his arrangements directly with Williams.

In this part of the game, for a change, it was MI.5 that held a trump card. Johnny's relations with Williams seemed to be genuine enough, as far as he could tell. They met under impeccable circumstances, in the circle of the Welsh dissidents in whose ranks Johnny was searching for recruits for Ritter. But—the ex-inspector had been set up by MI.5 when it was discovered that Owens was scouting for those Welshmen.

The *Treff* was held a few weeks later, on October 21 and 22, the first part of it in Antwerp, where Ritter received Johnny in a suite in the Hotel London (which he thought was a good joke to select under the circumstances). This time the German was accompanied by two friends, a middle-aged man with the bearing and mannerisms of the professional officer, and a handsome, suave, younger man whom he called "the Commander."

The older man was Major Brasser, chief of the air intelligence branch at Abwehr headquarters, who had come along to share in the unusual thrill of such a meeting. The other was Kapitaenleutnant Witzke, holding a rank whose British equivalent was only that of lieutenant but whom Ritter had promoted for the occasion to impress Williams.

Witzke headed Section II at the Hamburg branch, in charge of the sabotage operations in England for which he hoped to obtain William's help. Vouched for by Johnny, the ex-inspector was quickly initiated into the Abwehr with the registration number "A.3551." He was later described on his bio-sheet as "sub-agent of A.3504," and was credited with being "absolutely reliable and very valuable"—a fair characterization so far as the Abwehr was concerned. Williams had agreed at the *Treff*, as well as at subsequent encounters with Witzke, to recruit willing Welshmen for the outrages the Germans hoped to stage with his help. He had but one objection. He told "the Commander" that under no circumstances would he procure the paraphernalia the saboteurs would need, such as containers, explosives and fuses, in the United Kingdom.

"You need not worry, sir, on this score," Witzke assured him.

"We're working hand in hand with a band of Belgian smugglers who operate from Ostende across the English Channel, and know how to elude the British coastal patrols. We'll send whatever your friends will need via them, properly camouflaged as their usual contraband, like canned goods, cartons of cigarettes, tins of coffee, and other such things."

On October 22 Ritter and Johnny moved to Brussels for a session that lasted practically the whole day, attended by just the two. There was so much to tell and listen to, so much to give and take. As it turned out this was a phenomenally productive *Treff*. It yielded enormous dividends to both investors—to the Abwehr, to be sure, but also to MI.5.

He again discarded the bogus material MI.5 had prepared for this *Treff*, but gave Ritter the genuine intelligence he himself had collected since their last meeting only a little over three weeks before. It was a stupendous collection. Although a mere listing of such data may be lacking in entertainment, I will nevertheless give briefs of the eighteen different items Johnny delivered to Ritter in this one *Treff*, to illustrate the scope and importance of his gleanings. He was able to accomplish this, not only behind the back, but literally with the assistance and under the protection of MI.5.

Behind the locked doors of Ritter's room in the Metropole, Johnny supplied information later found in his Abwehr file, on the following topics:

1. Identified RAF headquarters in France in the vicinity of Strasbourg.
2. Described the balloon barrages that had been set up to protect communication centers of the RAF and the Royal Navy in the vicinity of Portsmouth.
3. Reported his personal surveillance of Croydon Airport on October 10.
4. Gave an exact description of the camouflage of the administration building at Croydon.
5. Briefed Ritter about surveying work going on at Llan Stephan in Wales preparatory to the construction of new airfields.
6. Supplied "general information" about conditions in Wales.
7. Informed Ritter that no more RAF raids would be mounted in the immediate future against naval bases in West Germany, because certain instrumentation of the planes reserved for these raids had been found to be defective.
8. Described the addition of new batteries of searchlights to improve coastal defenses at West Hartlepool.
9. Reported that ten RAF planes had been shot down at Southampton, Portsmouth, and Ilford by the accidental fire of their own anti-aircraft guns.

10. Gave his personal observations on a trip he had made on October 4, in a train transporting 600 RAF officers to St. Athens, and related their conversations on which he had eavesdropped.

11. Accounted his personal observations on a trip to Pembroke, and reported that he had seen en route an assembly of merchant ships at Gravesend.

12. Reported on a visit to Neath and Moriston in Glamorgan, north of Swansea.

13. Sketched out an oil refinery of the Royal Navy at Skewen, its tanks being filled with crude oil, arriving from overseas via the Swansea docks.

14. Noted that the oil tanks in Swansea still had their peacetime silver-gray paint, and could be identified easily from the air.

15. Revealed that RAF warehouses at Didcot were storing up to 3000 Rolls-Royce engines, and suggested that they would make profitable targets for the Luftwaffe.

16. Described certain operational methods of the Royal Navy's destroyers in anti-submarine warfare and gave details of their tactics when releasing depth charges.

17. Gave details of the air raid warning system, adding that there was usually considerable confusion and disorganization after the all-clear, especially in the Ilford-Degenham area.

18. Informed Ritter that "most of the synthetic fuel used by the RAF" was supplied by a plant of Powell Dyffrin Steel and Iron Company "at Merthyr, on the road to Treharris."

Johnny was not traveling on a one-lane road. Consequently, not everything that this *Treff* produced redounded solely to the advantage of the Germans. The British, too, reaped important benefits from this strange journey.

Being a counterespionage agency pure and simple (although, at this early stage, it was more simple than pure), MI.5 was not involved in the collection of positive intelligence. Indeed, it did not require or expect Snow to obtain such data, especially not from an officer in Ritter's position.

It was using Owens to spy on his spies. The "penetrators" or "E-men," as these specialists were called, had the most delicate and potentially perilous job in the hierarchy. It required more than just a thespian talent to dissemble and to survive in this most intricate of all confidence games. Aside from iron nerves and a cold heart, it needed a very strong stomach. It was an unsavory, callous, mean task, snooping and squealing on colleagues and comrades, to open their way to the gallows or the firing squad. Johnny Owens was totally unscrupulous, unsqueamish, selfish and ruthless. He was cheating so many people as it was, that he did not care how many more he betrayed.

I do not presume to know just what streak caused these supposedly sophisticated people to have such implicit faith in him, both the British and the Germans believing that he was playing one side alone. To deserve and sustain the confidence of each, he catered to both.

Ritter had no doubts—and he recently told me that at this stage Johnny had given him no reason to harbor any—that A.3504 was "genuine" and loyal to the Abwehr without any qualifications.

By this time, Owens was recognized in the Abwehr as their ace operative in England. Since he could come and go with apparent impunity, it was decided to use him also as a courier to keep in touch with other agents in Britain. This was exactly what MI.5 hoped would happen, and Owens, on his part, had no qualms when Ritter proposed this addition to his regular chores. He was staying alive even if it meant that others would die in the process.

Just before their meeting broke up in Brussels, Ritter gave him a number of film clips about the size of postage stamps. They were the microphotographed instructions Captain Dierks had prepared for delivery to A.3527, one of his agents in England who could be serviced by Johnny. Ritter revealed to him the spy's address in London and asked Johnny to see to it that A.3527 would promptly receive the films. Then he told him: "We have a splendid mail drop in Bournemouth. We are in touch with her via Spain and Switzerland. It will be quite safe to use her if we want to contact you between *Treffs*, and also to send her money for you on urgent occasions."

Back in London, Johnny went through his usual metamorphosis and turned into Snow again. When he reported to MI.5, he proved his worth—and his loyalty and credibility—by delivering the films meant for A.3725 straight into the hands of the men in "XX" who handled him. He gave them the address where the spy lived, and also tipped them off to U.3529, the Bournemouth woman (whom we shall call Margarde Kraus, although this was not her real name), the first agent to report to Hamburg after the outbreak of the war that she had escaped the dragnet of the Special Branch and was ready to function as a mail drop.

This was a day of triumph in MI.5. The gamble was paying off. Both of the German agents Snow now denounced had been missed in the first roundup. The finding of Margarde was a masterpiece of criminal investigation to which Owens's contribution was indirect. Her identity was never revealed to him explicitly and they never met in person—the Abwehr money she dispensed reached Johnny by mail. It came in crisp new five pounds notes, and when Owens surrendered them to MI.5, it was found that they had been marked with the letter "S" indicating that they originated at Selfridge's department store on Oxford Street. Detectives from Special Branch

visited the store and located the cashier who had handled these particular bills. She recalled that she had given them out in exchange for
a number of one pound notes as a favor to a customer whose name
and address she had jotted down.

Mrs. Kraus was given the familiar rope—left at large for a time but
placed under surveillance and her mail watched. She was "subsequently lodged in Holloway Prison," as the case history in MI.5 concluded the abbreviated saga of her brief career in espionage. Her
downfall did not redound entirely to Owens's advantage, for some of
the tainted money she was doling out had been intended for Johnny
(who was allowed to keep part of the subsidies the Abwehr was
paying him).[2]

Then A.3527 was also pulled in.

He turned out to be the older member of the brothers whom
Captain Dierks had developed the year before in Cologne. Naturalized
as a British subject in the meantime, this man gave the Germans as
little intelligence as he could, not because he was getting cold feet,
but because he had grown genuinely devoted to his adopted country
and was loath to hurt it.

Now he avidly agreed to join "XX" as the second member of the
"Double-Cross" stable of double agents, to be known henceforth as
"Charlie" by his new cover-name in MI.5.

The younger brother of the team, A.3528, presented a problem.
Although he was still a German national and was, like Charlie, a
registered operative of Ast X supplying more intelligence than his
brother to Dierks, he had also been overlooked by the Special
Branch. When his employment in "XX" was ruled out, he was put
into the "Class A" category of "unreliables" and ordered to be interned.[3]

Just when the intricate apparatus of "XX" was becoming a fixture
for the duration, promising to be the best mousetrap ever set up by
any counter-spies, MI.5 itself was shaken in its very foundations by a
major crisis in British security.

On October 14 a German submarine commanded by Lieutenant
Günther Prien penetrated Scapa Flow, the great Scottish base of the
Home Fleet, sank the old battleship *Royal Oak* and damaged the
target ship *Iron Duke*, then left as it came, undetected and unscathed. Since its passage through any of the Flow's entrances was
believed to be impossible without navigational aids and up-to-the-
minute charts, it was assumed that the U-boat had been guided to
its targets by a spy in the Orkneys, presumably yet another one MI.5
knew nothing about and the Special Branch had overlooked.

The mere assumption hardened into practical certainty, and the
Admiralty, deeply embarrassed and humiliated by the blow, blamed

MI.5 for the mishap by its failure to flush out this German watchman at Scapa Flow.

NOTES

1 This was what Owens told Ritter. In actual fact, MI.5 found out about his radio the moment it arrived in London. It was MI.5 that loaned it to S.I.S. where it was nearly ruined by its communication experts who took it apart, then did not know how to put it together again. It was left to the skill of MI.5's radio chief to repair the set for further use.

2 The name of U.3529 has been changed in this narrative because although the evidence incriminating her as an Abwehr paymaster is conclusive, she was never charged with violation of the espionage statutes.

3 His inconclusive career as a German agent then came to an untimely and tragically ironical end. He was unwittingly killed by his own compatriots when the ship *Arandora Star* which was taking him to a camp in Canada was torpedoed and sunk by a German submarine.

Chapter **17**

The Phantom of
Scapa Flow

*I*N October 1939, in the wake of Lieutenant Prien's daring and brilliant coup, all the organs of the British security services "were sent into action," as the historian of MI.5 put it, "to find the man who had made the German exploit possible." They all failed.

As the spy scare mounted and the crisis deepened, the phantom agent gradually emerged from his incognito. At first, as in the incarnation of H. G. Wells's invisible man, only his contours became visible. Then he gained flesh and blood. He appeared in the full splendor of his colossal deed, complete with a name, a pseudonym and vital statistics, until his whole story took root.

He was presented full-blown in an article by Curt Riess, the well-known author-journalist and espionage expert, in the *Saturday Evening Post*, in the spring of 1942. According to Riess, the spy of Scapa Flow was Captain Alfred Wehring, a former officer of the German Imperial Navy, who had been chosen in 1927 by the Abwehr to cover Scapa Flow. He changed his name, his nationality, and vocation for the mission—becoming Albert Oertel, a Swiss watchmaker. He then settled at Kirkwall in the Orkneys, "whence from time to time," wrote Walter Schellenberg, the SD director who later succeeded Admiral Canaris as chief of intelligence, "he sent us reports on the movements of the British Home Fleet."

After twelve years on station, Wehring-alias-Oertel came out of his masquerade in October 1939, and signaled to Captain Karl Doenitz of the U-Boat Command detailed information about the dismal state of the Flow's defenses. Doenitz thereupon sent the U-47 under Lieutenant Prien to break through to the Main Anchorage by way of the undefended Kirk Sound entrance, guided by Wehring who was to

board the boat, act as a pilot-navigator, and return home in triumph from his long exile, provided the attempt succeeded.

With this description of the man and his mission, the phantom of
Scapa Flow entered the lore of espionage. He became so real that
Schellenberg included this incident in his postwar memoirs, to demonstrate "how important intelligently planned long-range preparatory work can be—and how rewarding in the end."

That the spy of Scapa Flow was not the mere product of journalistic daydreaming, but a phantom accepted for real on the highest
levels of the British government, was attested to in 1963 by John
Bulloch in his book about "the origin and history of the British counterespionage service." It contained an authorized biography of Major
General Sir Vernon George Waldegrave Kell, the MI.5 chief.

"It was obvious," Bulloch wrote in his account of the Scapa Flow
incident, "that the Germans had been supplied with up-to-date information by a spy. And as there had been no aerial reconnaissance
before the submarine got in, it was equally obvious that the spy had
been able to send to Germany the message that the *Royal Oak* was in
the anchorage within a day of her arrival. . . . This was a serious
defeat for British security."

On station in Kirkwall, Wehring had broken completely with the
past. In 1932 he became naturalized under the name of Oertel and a
more loyal subject His Majesty never had. He was industrious,
thrifty, honest, a pillar of the community, and skilled at his craft. It
was no wonder that he prospered. When he established himself in his
own business as a jeweller-watchmaker, his store was frequented by
the sailors of the Home Fleet on shore liberty because his work was
good, his prices were reasonable, and because he was always ready
with a good seaman's yarn. His customers repaid him in kind by
regaling him with their stories and tidbits of information about their
ships.

"It was in the beginning of October 1939," Schellenberg wrote,
"that he sent us the important information that the eastern approach
to Scapa Flow through the Kierkesund [sic] was not closed off by
anti-submarine nets but only by hulks lying relatively far apart. On
receipt of this information Admiral Doenitz ordered Captain Prien to
attack any British warships in Scapa Flow."

A rendezvous was arranged; Wehring was to wait for the arrival of
U-47 at the easternmost tip of Kirk Sound and identify himself to
Prien with light signals from the mainland. He was then to transfer to
a rubber dinghy to reach the submarine and pilot it on the basis of
the charts he had prepared from the telltale data he had collected
from his friends, the talkative sailors.

At 11:07 P.M. on October 13, U-47 arrived at Rose Ness and

made it into Holm Sound. Just twenty-four minutes later Kirk Sound itself became visible. "It is a very eerie sight," Prien wrote in his log. "On land everything is dark, high in the sky are the flickering Northern Lights, so that the bay, surrounded by highish mountains, is directly lit up from above. The blockships lie in the sound, ghostly as the wings of an empty theater."

Just then he noticed the headlights of a car turned on and off, and recognized it as Wehring's contact signal in the pre-arranged code. The dinghy was sent to pick him up, and a few minutes later the great spy was welcomed aboard. He took up position at the side of the helmsman. Although the boat had been turned by the strong current, he promptly showed that he had forgotten nothing of his nautical skill by bringing it back onto course with rapid maneuvering.

It was twenty-seven minutes past midnight. U-47 was in Scapa Flow.

The Home Fleet was gone, the Main Anchorage yawned deserted. There were two battleships at anchor north by the coast, and a row of destroyers further inshore. At 1:16 A.M. on the 14th, the fireworks began. Twelve minutes later, at full speed both engines, U-47 began its retreat march. It was low tide, and the currents were against her. Wehring piloted the ship in a masterly fashion until, at 2:15 A.M., she was out again in the open sea, safe.

In the morning the Oertel shop did not open up for business, and his house was found to have been deserted. His abandoned car was later discovered on the road that skirted Kirk Sound along the southern brim of the mainland.

In point of fact, Oertel no longer existed. Captain Wehring was on his way home to Germany.

It was a corking good story, with a single fault.

Captain Wehring never existed in fact. The watchmaker who was supposed to have helped Lieutenant Prien to his victory in the Flow came from somebody's imagination.

It was not especially difficult to establish that even Schellenberg's tale, cited with a straight face as one of the great feats of the German secret service, was nothing but a hoax, perpetrated on the British to add insult to their injury and to compound their confusion.

I found no "Alfred Wehring," captain or otherwise, in any of the registers of either the Imperial Navy, the postwar navy, or the Abwehr.

No reference could be found anywhere to "Albert Oertel" in all the documents of the naval intelligence divisions of either World Wars or of the Abwehr.

Nowhere in the voluminous records did I come upon even the

most tenuous evidence that either the Abwehr or any other German intelligence agency ever had an operative stationed in Kirkwall or the Orkneys for any such length of time as twelve years.

Interviews with surviving Abwehr executives drew complete blanks.

A visit to Kirkwall produced no sign of an "Albert Oertel" ever having lived there or that anybody by that name ever owned a jewelry-watch repair shop anywhere in or near the town.

Satisfied that the phantom spy of Scapa Flow was nothing but a spectre, I had to answer three questions for the sake of history.

How and where did the Wehring canard originate?

What was the source of the information on the basis of which Doenitz decided upon the attack and prepared his operations plan?

Why did the British accept such a patent humbug and persist even as late as 1963 in claiming that the Orkney spy version of the incident corresponded to fact?

It took me years to run down the story, following leads in Germany and Britain, interviewing scores of people-in-the-know, and benefiting from an independent, but inconclusive, investigation the eminent author-historian Juergen Thorwald had conducted.

Today I am satisfied that the mystery of the Scapa Flow spy can be cleared up conclusively, once and for all.

The first question can be answered quickly even though, alas, a bit sadly, if only because the solution of this part of the riddle casts some reflection on my own profession as a journalist.

Wehring-Oertel was dreamed up and the entire story of his exploit fabricated by a Central European newspaperman living as a refugee in New York. He had been prominent in his profession in Europe, but had fallen on hard times in the United States where he tried to establish himself as a writer in a language with which he was not yet familiar.

He was respected and trusted as a reputable journalist on the strength of his past record. He found it relatively easy, therefore, to merchandise his sensationalistic confections to American news associations, magazines, and fellow writers, including Riess, who were looking for dramatic material about the European scene for articles which were then in great demand in the literary market.

This was how Riess got the story, how Wehring-Oertel was born, how his alleged feat got into circulation, how the story made it into the *Saturday Evening Post*. And it was on this grapevine that the British authorities picked it up. They checked it out by the simple process of an MI.5 agent in New York interviewing the inventor, and accepting his veracity at face value.

A thorough official investigation tended to bear out the fable. The probe revealed that certain "accidents" did indeed contribute to the unpreparedness of Scapa Flow and made the penetration possible.

It had been decided in the Admiralty to make all entrances to the Flow as secure as humanly possible. This took time, partly by the nature of the task, and partly because of red tape. The old anti-submarine net which normally closed the entrance through Kirk Sound had eroded so badly that it had been removed pending re-placement. A blockship "destined to be sunk in the entrance actually used by U-47" was en route but was delayed and "arrived in Scapa on the day after the *Royal Oak* was sunk." The Home Fleet had left the harbor, to be sure, but the *Royal Oak* and its screen of two destroyers had returned, on October 11, from a sortie to the west of the Fair Isle Channel, from a futile fleet operation to intercept a German task force consisting of the battle cruiser *Gneisenau*, the cruiser *Koeln*, and nine destroyers.

All this was classified information that, it was assumed, could have been known to the enemy only through aerial reconnaissance and/or espionage. Contrary to the exaggerated prognostication of the British Naval Intelligence Division, Scapa had been subjected to only two aerial surveillance flights by the Luftwaffe, the second one on September 26, three weeks before the Prien venture. It was, therefore, further assumed that such precise information must have come from a spy in Scapa who had become privy to all this more timely critical intelligence and forwarded it to Doenitz.

Although we now know that no such spy existed, the question still remains wide open as to how Doenitz was able to plot Prien's mission with such pinpoint knowledge of conditions at Scapa. This mystery was partly cleared up by Admiral Doenitz himself in his memoirs.

"From the very outset [of the war]," he wrote, "I had always had in mind the idea of an operation against Scapa Flow"—especially because, in a fashion characteristic of this inordinately ambitious officer, he was always straining to succeed where others failed, and two such attempts had come to naught in World War I.

It was on September 6, when the war with England was only three days on, that Doenitz began to collect the data he needed for the planning of the operation, by asking SKL-III, the intelligence depart-ment of his High Command, for "a copy of their report on Scapa Flow which they had drawn up on the information available." It arrived on the 9th, six days after war was declared, but proved dis-couraging. It listed formidable obstacles which SKL-III *assumed* had been placed across the entrances.

Undaunted, Doenitz then asked the Second Air Fleet of the Luftwaffe to fly a special reconnaissance mission to Scapa for him. It was mounted on the 10th. The planes brought back only a single usable photograph showing heavy and light ships at anchor in the Flow but little if anything of its underwater defenses.

All this failed to dampen Doenitz's enthusiasm, and he was justified in his optimism, for very soon more encouraging data started pouring in. Later in September, Lieutenant Commander Wellner returned in U-16 from a war cruise in the Orkneys. Since this was still Hitler's deceptive era of good will, when he hoped to restore peace with England and, therefore, had banned all offensive U-boat operations against the British, Wellner spent his time on the cruise in reconnoitering the waters around the Orkneys and observing enemy activities in them. He ventured quite close to Hoxa and Switha Sounds in the south, which he found more or less blocked, and to Holm Sound where he found conditions somewhat different. He discovered the hulks of three merchant ships in the Kirk Sound, but also spotted a narrow channel about 50 feet wide running as far as Lamb Holm, which appeared to be comparatively open, except for a few stray sunken ships.

Upon his return to his base in Wilhelmshaven, Commander Wellner gave Doenitz a "very valuable report," not only of these findings, but also "on the patrols, the lighting and the prevalent currents in the area."

At this point, and totally unmentioned by Doenitz, the Abwehr also entered the picture with a very valuable report of its own. It had been pieced together from information on file from the kind of overt sources that every intelligence service collects in the open market. It also contained an agent's report that had come in during the last week of August. It was, of course, not from "Captain Wehring" (who, at this time, was not yet conceived in anybody's imagination), but from a real-life spy working for Commander Menzel of the naval intelligence division at Abwehr headquarters.

Interested in Scapa Flow but finding that the information he had in his files was sketchy and old, Menzel arranged a trip to the Orkneys for one of his most astute DK-men, a merchant master who doubled as an Abwehr spy. He was DK.3508 or Captain Horst Kahle, skipper of the Neptune freighter *Theseus*. From a trip to Kirkwall in late August, just before the war, Kahle returned with a fairly complete account, describing the shore on both sides of Lamb Holm as "practically uninhabited." He also reported that no anti-aircraft batteries had been placed anywhere along the southern coast as far as the western shore of the mainland where, however, he had spotted three sets of heavy AA guns.

Moreover, he informed Menzel that the neglected state of Scapa's defenses was the talk of the town in Kirkwall. He mentioned specifically that, according to gossip he had picked up, the boom and anti-torpedo defences, guard and mine loops, indicator loops and anti-boat nets were either in very bad repair or non-existent in the eastern approaches.

On September 25, Doenitz asked Air Fleet II to fly another reconnaissance mission for him, to obtain "as precise and detailed aerial photographs as possible of all the obstacles guarding the various entrances to Scapa Flow." When two days later he received "a set of excellent photographs," he asked the Luftwaffe to suspend all further activities at Scapa, in order to refrain from attracting the attention of the British to what they could construe as too keen a German interest in the Flow.

This was the sum total of the intelligence which Doenitz had available when he concluded that "here [through Kirk Sound] . . . it would certainly be possible to penetrate—by night, on the surface at slack water." He then prepared his operations plan for the attack, and handed it to Prien to execute it.

From a professional point of view, this painstaking montage of scattered data into one complete, accurate and up-to-the-minute intelligence picture was a far more respectable and fascinating feat, and a far more realistic piece of work, than the single-handed, unverified, flash-in-the-pan contribution of the best secret agent, even if such an agent had really existed at all.

Chapter 18

The Lion Plays the Fox

*T*HE case of the Scapa Flow spy was still not completely cleared up. Even today it is puzzling why British authorities accepted the story of the phantom agent. It is possible that the story was believed (if it was ever *really* believed) because the Admiralty investigators were told that some unidentified person in a car with its headlights blazing had driven along the southern mainland road in an east-west direction when the U-boat was approaching the Flow, giving some substance to the theory that Prien had a guide on the shore.[1]

Whatever the reason behind such apparent gullibility, the incident was destined to have an influence on the personal fortunes of Major General Vernon Kell and the future of MI.5. It was seized upon as one of the excuses to get rid of Kell.

"Five" was getting deeper into trouble, and not only because of imaginary spies.

A little over two months after the sinking of the *Royal Oak*, MI.5 received a tip that the Royal Gunpowder factory at Waltham Abbey had been singled out as a target by unknown terrorists. Kell assigned the case to Chief Inspector William Salisbury, a police officer who had just come into MI.5 on a wartime assignment from Scotland Yard's famed murder squad. On January 18, 1940, before Salisbury could do anything to act on the information, three violent explosions in widely separated parts of the factory killed five persons, injured thirty, and almost totally wrecked the strategic plant.

The British government steadfastly and somewhat indignantly denied that these explosions, and a number of similar bombings which had occurred since September, had been caused "by enemy action."

This was technically correct, for none of the perpetrators were *enemy* nationals. But the record of Abwehr II, the department responsible for sabotage and sedition, listed this outrage among its victories in England, attributing it to "a group of Irish patriots with whom we are in contact."

The idea of using Irish agents against Britain (and in the United States, if needed) first occurred to Dr. Jupp Hoven and Howard Clissman, two German intellectuals living in Eire, in January 1939, when I.R.A. terrorists blew up power stations and business premises in London, Birmingham, Manchester, and Almwick, and damaged the cable that ran over the Grand Union Canal near Willesden.

In March, a bomb on Hammersmith Bridge snapped the suspension chains, made the support-girder sag, and dropped the whole span almost a foot. In August, an infernal machine planted in London's crowded King's Cross Station destroyed the checkroom, killed a young Edinburgh University lecturer, wounded his wife and fourteen other persons.

Duly impressed, Hoven and Clissman established contact with the leftover leadership of the Irish Republican Army. In September they joined the Abwehr and recommended to Colonel Erwin von Lahousen, chief of its division of sabotage and insurrections, that he plug Abwehr II into this live socket and tap the 15,000-member I.R.A. for a large-scale sabotage campaign in England.

Although the English were wont to pooh-pooh these boisterous, unforgiving Irish terrorists as "men of no account" (*The Times* of London editorialized at the time of their rampage in January that the I.R.A. was dead), the Germans took them very seriously. Their bombings ingratiated them to Lahousen who agreed that the I.R.A. was very much alive and could do for Germany what they were doing in their own behalf.

He created a special Irish desk in Abwehr II and named a man called "Dr. Pfalzgraf" to establish contact with the Terrorists. "Pfalzgraf" was Captain Friedrich Karl Marwede, a beefy, rather pompous career intelligence officer specializing in "dirty tricks," with the help of a civilian expert named Kurt Haller. They approached the I.R.A. leaders Hoven and Clissman had solicited and found that they already had an elaborate "S-Plan" which had as its object "the paralysis of all official activity in England and the greatest possible destruction of British defense installations."

The Irish responded avidly but on a rather mercenary ground. They regarded the Germans' interest in them as manna from heaven and proceeded to shake them down. In the end they bilked the Abwehr out of very substantial endowments, in exchange for which they delivered only relatively few genuine outrages, while shrewdly claiming credit for all sorts of industrial, marine, and railroad accidents with which they had nothing to do.[2]

Even so, in the early winter of 1940, the specter of sabotage became reality, with costly and painful damage to the war effort. Not only was MI.5 unable to forestall this fury, but, in the case of the Royal Gunpowder plant, it proved incapable of finding the perpetrators, despite advance warning and the most energetic investigation.

Attention in Whitehall focused on General Kell as the man basically responsible for this failure. His beginnings in the intelligence game went back to the Boxer Rebellion of 1899–1900 and service along the turbulent Sino-Russian border. He had just celebrated his sixty-sixth birthday, was past retirement age and the peak of his powers. He belonged to a generation of spy catchers who either passed into limbo or became fossilized in their jobs. Their methods had been effective in the past, but seemed woefully outdated and inadequate in a highly mechanized new war in which espionage and sabotage were playing an unprecedented part.

Kell was also quite ill and the day-to-day management of MI.5 had slipped into the hands of other old-timers, like Holt Wilson, his deputy since 1913, and a group of hunting and fishing types of Kell's vintage. The leadership crisis in MI.5 reached 10 Downing Street. Although the Prime Minister had been persuaded that Kell would have to be replaced, (especially by the controversial Sir Joseph Ball who coveted the job) he preferred to wait a little longer, for another acute crisis that would justify a blunt request for his resignation.

Then quite abruptly Kell's entire career went up in the smoke left in the wake of a Luftwaffe raid. By this time the rapidly expanding agency was lodged in Wormwood Scrubs Prison, with its sacrosanct files and records and its enormous index system of names of supposedly dubious people. This vast hoard of largely derogatory information was hit by an incendiary bomb and burned to ashes. Although this was the backbone of "Five," the damage was not considered irreparable, as photocopies were stored in fireproof vaults—precisely to save them from such an auto-da-fé.

But when the copies were brought out it was found that most of the negatives had been over- or under-exposed and could not be printed. So many other mistakes had also been made in reproducing the files that the whole collection proved useless.

Kell was summoned to 10 Downing Street and asked to resign. He went reluctantly but unbowed. On his return to headquarters he assembled his staff and bade them a seemingly unemotional farewell, then left immediately never to be seen again in "Five." He died "unknown to the public and forgotten by authority," as Bullock lamented two years later.

Kell was succeeded briefly by one veteran spybuster, and then by Sir David Petrie, a Scot who had a long and distinguished record of service in the Indian Police. Petrie remained for the duration, brilliantly aided by two top lieutenants, Dick Goldsmith White, a graduate of English and American universities who had chosen the secret service as his career, and Guy Liddell, a cellist in his youth, in MI.5 since 1919.

Even before Kell's departure new men were flocking into "Five," mostly from the services and Scotland Yard. Then others arrived; bright, shrewd, erudite, eager people from the universities and the professions, with an adventurous, imaginative turn of mind and a hankering for melodrama. They had the predilection of zesty newcomers to out-gumshoe the professionals by applying the methods of spy thrillers to the catching of real-life secret agents.

One of these mavericks was Kim Philby, making his first penetration in Britain's secret cloud-and-cuckoo land. He would not stay long. His assignment from his Soviet masters was to infiltrate the Secret Intelligence Service and he soon transferred to MI.6.

Most of the others remained for the duration, better men than Philby. Among the first such gifted amateurs to arrive in this inner sanctum was the distinguished jurist Herbert Lionel Adolphus Hart, then practicing at the Chancery Bar; the art historian Anthony Frederick Blunt; Kenneth Gilmour Young, a barrister of the Inner Temple (later a Labor minister); and John Cecil Masterman, Provost of Worcester College of Oxford University and avid cricketer, the author of a historical drama about Napoleon's Marshal Ney. At 49, the oldest among the newcomers, Masterman became an outstanding senior member of the Double-Cross team.

Although it was keenly curious about MI.5 and, as we shall see, had a spy of its own among the British counter-spies, the Abwehr knew nothing of this change of the guard. To begin with, no sudden improvement of the competition was evident. As far as Hamburg knew only one of their operatives had fallen by the wayside. Canaris felt so proud of his network that he boasted to Count Galeazzo Ciano of Italy that he had better than a score of producing spies in England, including one who was sending up to twenty-five signals each day.[3]

Soon enough, the Abwehr was made aware of a change for the better in British security by an abrupt deterioration of its own fortunes in England. One after another, agents who had so fortuitously escaped the first dragnet vanished from contact. Margarde Kraus and one of Captain Dierks's two spies, betrayed by Owens already in October, were the first to fall.[4]

They merely spearheaded the demise of others.

In the registry of the Hamburg office, series 3500, 3600, and 3700 had been reserved for its agents in Britain. By the time the war broke out, the outposts had almost used up the available numbers for the seriatim listing of these spies. Each number cloaked a real-live operative, actively engaged in espionage at his station, in more or less regular contact with a *V-Mann-Fuehrer*.

Now more and more of them were falling silent. Some had retired from the business by their own decision (without even bothering to send to Hamburg or Bremen formal letters of resignation). Others were stymied in their clandestine efforts by insurmountable obstacles of war. Still others had been interned, rendering them harmless without passing through the formal prosecution under the Official Secrets Act.

In the early winter and spring of this 1940, England slipped out of focus. The Abwehr was busier than ever working on a number of crash programs for the invasion of Denmark, Norway, and the Low Countries, and for the showdown Battle of France. It became instrumental, through cunningly nurtured Fifth Columns, in the bloodless occupation of Denmark and the rapid conquest of Norway. The Blitzkrieg in the West was aided materially with a number of stunts, such as taking over intact several key bridges in the Netherlands needed for the unimpeded advance of the Wehrmacht, which were captured by Abwehr-soldiers in uniforms stolen from depôts of the Dutch army for these *coups de mains*, before the invasion.

In England the table was initially turned, not by Sir David's bright dons and barristers, but shortly after the outbreak of the war by a prodigiously gifted young research fellow of Merton College in Oxford who joined the Military Intelligence Directorate and was assigned to MI.8-C, a super-secret branch involved in the surveillance of German wireless traffic.

He was Hugh Redwald Trevor-Roper, the fastest rising star among a new generation of British historians, all of 25 years old at this time.

MI.5, usually thought to be Britain's senior or sole counterespionage agency, was that only within the British Isles. In an admirable division of labors and responsibilities, all secret work in foreign countries, whether involving positive or negative espionage, was reserved exclusively for the Secret Intelligence Service, or MI.6 by its wartime name. Within MI.6, counterespionage abroad was the function of Section V, headed by Major Felix Henry Cowgill, known from Kim Philby's barbed memoirs as the butt of his most condescending sarcasm and the victim of his most inspired stab-in-the-back.

MI.8 (called Signals Intelligence Service by its formal designation) was another area of counterespionage. Its Section C had a direct share in the Germans' coverage by recording their wireless transmissions and collecting a mass of raw intercepts, depending on other agencies to bring the information they contained out of their cryptographic cloak.

Trevor-Roper went for these mumbo-jumbo texts with the curiosity and zest of Champollion attacking the hieroglyphs of the Rosetta stone. Not being a cryptographer, he could not crack any of the German codes and ciphers in which these intercepts had been sent. But he noted that many of them did not fit into any of the familiar slots of ordinary military and naval signals or diplomatic or commercial telegrams.

As a very junior member of the staff at MI.8-C, he could not on his own authority get these oddities out of Section C and into expert hands. He was, however, fortunate in having Major Gill, an enterprising, unconventional officer, as his superior. Gill agreed to forward a sample of the intercepts to Commander Alastair Denniston, an alumnus of Captain Hull's famed 40 O.B. of World War I, at the Government Code & Cypher School, then still at Berkeley Street, the nerve center of code cracking in Britain, rather than a mere school as its name seemed to indicate.

At G.C. & C.S. the intercepts wound up with Oliver Strachey, brother of the iconoclastic literateur Lytton Strachey. With the late Dillwyn "Dilly" Knox, brother of the great Monsignor Knox, they formed the incomparable team of cryptanalysts to whom the British people owe so much and about whom they know so little.

In this case, however, Strachey slipped up. The intercepts which so puzzled Gill and Trevor-Roper were left untouched in his in-basket. Only when prodded did Strachey bestir himself to examine them, concluding that most probably they were Russian signals emanating from Shanghai. "It is *not* thought," Strachey wrote to Major Gill in his covering letter returning the samples, "that they are German."

It so happened that Gill had some experience in cryptanalysis during World War I. And fortunately, he and Trevor-Roper were sharing a flat in Ealing. Thoroughly fascinated by these odd signals, they took them home and spent practically all of their free evenings in an effort to decrypt them.

They first succeeded in breaking into the cipher around Christmastime in 1939, and solved it altogether in early 1940. Trevor-Roper

then examined the transcripts of these decrypted messages and discovered that they were the top-secret communications of the Abwehr
with some of its outposts abroad and most of its agents in the field.

During the war, the Abwehr relied on three different cryptographic means for radio transmissions:

1. To addressees in countries under firm German security control
   and within the confines of their diplomatic missions, they employed their own modified version of "Enigma," a commercially
   available cipher machine.
2. To agents at large or their outposts in countries where the security of cipher equipment could not be guaranteed, they used
   variations of so-called paper-and-pencil ciphers, keyed to all sorts
   of published books, a different one of which was issued to each
   agent.
3. In certain individual and relatively rare cases, they used *Satz-
   buecher*, or specially constructed codebooks.

Because of this diversity in the Abwehr's cryptosystem, the important discovery of Gill and Trevor-Roper was only a beginning. There
was much more to come. An Enigma was recovered intact from a
captured U-boat in May 1941; another was brought back from a
Marine Commando raid on the Lofoten Island; and a third had been
secured by Commander Denniston in Poland shortly before the outbreak of the war. By early 1942, "Dilly" Knox had compromised all
Abwehr codes and ciphers, including the machine-based system.

Gill and Trevor-Roper made only a first step toward the total
compromising of the Abwehr's communications security. It was a
giant step nevertheless. Since agents on sneaky missions could not
very well lug around an Enigma device without running the risk of
attracting attention, all communications with spies—including those
stationed in England—had to be encrypted in the paper-and-pencil
cipher, the basic cryptographic elements of which Gill and Trevor-
Roper had cracked. This enabled the British to share in the secrets of
the Abwehr traffic moving by wireless, and also to recover en-
ciphered messages sent by mail or other earthly means (and concealed by secret ink, microphotography and microdotting), provided
they could get hold of them through censorship or rifling.

As it was, in contrast to World War I when personal contacts via
cut-outs and go-betweens and written communications in secret ink
predominated, the Abwehr now relied on its Afu gadgetry, on an
unprecedented scale. It seemed preferable, because of its speed and
presumed security, in the belief, endemic to the Germans, that their
codes and ciphers were unbreakable.

NOTES

1 Lieutenant Prien himself noted in his log at 1:20 A.M. on October 14, 1939: "I must assume that I was observed by the driver of a car which stopped opposite us, and drove off towards Scapa at top speed." Obviously, the driver was not the spy.

2 As it turned out, even if they had engaged in these activities on the scale they promised the Germans, their sabotage would have produced mere pinpricks compared with the havoc the Luftwaffe was soon raising during the air blitz of 1940–41.

3 Ciano recorded Canaris's remarks in his diary with evident envy, but the Abwehr's own records fail to bear out the Admiral's silly boast. Actually, very few Afu-reports were sent during this period of wait-and-see. Moreover, agents had their schedules calling for only one or two transmissions a day, each limited to 400 letters. Even the still embryonic electronic detection apparatus of British security would have had an easy job to find and silence a spy foolish enough to go on the air twenty-five times a day.

4 Dierks's other V-man continued to report but now—unknown to his old employers, of course—under the auspices of Double-Cross.

Chapter 19

Canaris vs. Churchill:
The Race for Norway

THIS was "the Twilight War," as Neville Chamberlain called it with a subtle Freudian touch, so much more germane a phrase than Senator William Borah's callous and ignorant reference to it as "the Phoney War." Aside from scraps at sea which a dozen U-boats of the ambitious and impatient Doenitz unleashed the moment hostilities commenced, the declaration of war was followed by that prolonged and oppressive pause that puzzled the world.

No massive armies clashed on land as in 1914, no air fleets collided on the awesome pattern of H.G. Wells's shape of things to come. There was utter sullen quiet on the Western front along the Westwall and the Maginot Line. The Anglo-German "war" was confined to sporadic reconnaissance flights of the Luftwaffe over scattered British targets and to "raids" of the RAF against Hamburg, Bremen, and the Ruhr cities, dropping leaflets "to rouse the Germans," as Churchill wryly remarked, "to higher morality."

The spies in England were also idle; little happened that was worth the risk of sending clandestine reports. The one big newsworthy move, the crossing of two entire army corps of the British Expeditionary Force from Southampton to Cherbourg, passed almost unnoticed in the commotion created by the outbreak of the war, when German agents thought it advisable to lie low.

This stillness at Armageddon cloaked the confusion rampant in both camps.

Standing on the ruins of Warsaw on September 29, 1939, Hitler appeared to be satisfied with the carnage he had wrought. But he seemed perplexed, toying with both peace and war. On October 6, he made a clumsy attempt in a speech to induce Britain and France to talk peace, but he was rebuffed. Groping for something else, he considered half a dozen ideas, for each of which they had to design separate operation plans and code names. "Sunflower" was a possible campaign in North Africa. An operation called "Alp Violet" had Albania for its goal. "Felix" contemplated crossing Spain to seize Gibraltar. "Operation Yellow" was to conquer the Low Countries as the opening move in the showdown in the West.

Traveling salesmen were flocking to Berlin to peddle their countries to the Fuehrer. From Holland came a fluffy, shifty-eyed philistine named Anton Mussert, a puppet dangling from strings held by the Abwehr. From Belgium came a scheming, pampered dandy, Leon Degrelle. From Norway arrived the man whose name stands for all traitors in the book, Major Vidkun Quisling.

On October 9, Hitler issued top-secret order No. 4402/39, instructing his generals to make preparations for the campaign in the West, to begin with the violation of Dutch and Belgian neutrality, all dispositions to be completed by November 5. The pending onslaught was consistently compromised by delays and leaks. The invasion was postponed twenty-nine times before it was eventually mounted in the spring of 1940.

Trying desperately to gain time to make up for the neglect of complacent years, the British reverted to the Baden-Powell streak in their national character, attempting to secure advantages by some gallant tomfoolery on secret fronts. Inspired by Winston Churchill, sabotage teams of gentleman adventurers and proletarian daredevils had been assembled on a shoestring, some as early as March 1938— by both S.I.S. (called the "D" organization and headed by Lieutenant Colonel Laurence Grand of the Royal Sappers) and the Military Intelligence Directorate of the War Office (called by a succession of cover-names around the word "Research" and commanded by two very proper lieutenant colonels, John Holland and Colin Gubbins).

In the fall of 1939 and early 1940, pioneering saboteurs went into action to destroy strategic spots in Europe. Prominent among their targets were installations at Oxelösund in the Baltic where Swedish iron ore was processed for shipment to the Reich; the Iron Gate, a narrow rocky gorge of the Danube through which flowed oil and wheat from Rumania and Yugoslavia; and the Ploesti oil region in Rumania.

The efforts proved too little and far too early. The "special operators" of this era were exceptionally brave men. But they lacked the skill and finesse in the art of destruction that later made British and American sabotage experts the scourge of the transient Nazi landlords of occupied Europe. The Abwehr, led personally by Admiral

Canaris in this brief but bitter initial bout, was on its toes. The bold gambit produced nothing but headaches that were to plague the British for the rest of the war.

Two distinguished amateurs in sabotage work sent to Sweden to blow up the facilities at Oxelösund from which flowed indispensable high-grade iron ore to the munitions factories in Germany were caught practically *in flagranti*. The scandal whipped up by his exposure made similar British efforts on or from Swedish soil much more difficult later on in the war.

The plot against the Iron Gate was discovered by Major Stransky von Greifenfels and Commander Weisz, two anti-sabotage experts Admiral Canaris had stationed in Bucharest in anticipation of Allied efforts to sabotage the oil fields. The operation at the Danubian bottleneck was thwarted by a detachment of Abwehr soldiers ambushing the saboteurs as they arrived in two cement-laden barges which they were supposed to scuttle in the Gate.

The scheme, aimed at Ploesti, was the most ambitious but proved the most counter-productive. Conceived as a joint Franco-British project, it was approved by the Supreme War Council in one of its first sessions. On September 16, the French oil engineer Leon Wenger and Captain Pierre Angot, a sabotage specialist of the *Deuxième Bureau*, arrived in Bucharest, where they were joined by a British engineer of Ploesti trained by the "D" organization of S.I.S. to blow up the oil fields, the refining facilities, and their railroad feeders.

Through a leak in the French Legation, the project became known to Colonel Moruzov, head of the *Siguranza*, the Rumanian secret police. A venal Balkan bully who pretended to be pro-Allied, he was working for the Abwehr under a well-subsidized arrangement Canaris had made with him personally shortly before the war at a *Treff* in Venice. Summoned by his friend, the Admiral rushed to Bucharest and, using Moruzov's tip-off as evidence blackmailed permission from the pro-Allied King Carol II to station Abwehr soldiers, disguised as watchmen and supervisory personnel, not only in the oil regions but throughout Rumania. He thus gained a major foothold in the country months before its formal occupation by Wehrmacht regulars.

The secret war of this ambiguous period was remarkable for the energetic part Admiral Canaris was playing *personally* in its conduct against the British on a number of invisible fronts. For all of his qualms and doubts and fears, these were his balmiest days. Between September 1939 and November 1940, he, who had viewed Britain's entry into the war with such misgivings and anxiety, fought England with the best he had, on secret battlefields ranging from northern Norway to Gibraltar. Sensing the contradiction in the man's double image as the leader of the anti-Nazi opposition and as Hitler's dedicated accomplice in some of his weirdest schemes, Colonel Oscar Reile, an articulate and sensitive Abwehr officer who became one of its most prolific postwar historians, wrote of the eager, hard-working, hard-plotting Canaris of this period:

"His membership in the resistance movement was one thing, premeditated treason was another—the fight against Hitler on the homefront had nothing to do with the struggle against the enemy secret services."

It was at the far northern end of the long secret front where Canaris's initiative and personal involvement produced an actual extension of the war, leading to the occupation of Denmark and Norway.

Looking back on his activities in this endeavor, and viewing all of his erratic moves in an orderly, purposeful array, one realizes that this, too, was a game. It was on a truly historic scale, the greatest he would ever play, with two masterly gamblers pitted against one another—Winston Churchill and Wilhelm Canaris.

The first move was made by Churchill almost immediately after he had joined the War Cabinet on September 4, 1939. He arrived in his old room in the Admiralty, which he had "quitted in pain and sorrow" almost exactly a quarter of a century before, burdened by a host of misgivings and apprehensions—he felt fearful that the U-boats might be refueled in the unattended coves and inlets of western Ireland by secret agents; he was worried about the inadequate defenses of Scapa Flow and troubled by the shortage of destroyers. But nothing weighed heavier on his mind than the problem of Norway as an escape hatch through which units of the German fleet "could communicate," as he phrased it, "with the outer sea to the grievous injury of our blockade . . . under the shield of neutrality."

Placing this problem at the top of his agenda, he sought to solve it boldly and ruthlessly, citing the precedent of World War I when, he claimed, "the British and American Governments had no scruples about mining the 'Leads,' as these sheltered [Norwegian] waters were called."

Although his recollection was faulty, for neither of the Allied fleets had laid any minefields in Norwegian territorial waters during World War I, Churchill proceeded to push the issue vigorously and relentlessly both in the Cabinet (which he found quite lukewarm about the proposition) and in the Admiralty (whose Naval Staff enthusiastically welcomed the First Lord's bold initiative). He first raised the issue during a cabinet session, then presented it formally in a paper on September 29th, irrespective of the risks and international complications such "drastic action" might entail.

Within a day or two of the delivery of Churchill's memorandum to the War Cabinet, Admiral Canaris apparently learned of what he called "British intentions to violate the territorial integrity of Norway." At face value this would seem to have been one of the outstanding scoops of the Abwehr. It indicated that somehow it had succeeded in penetrating to the highest echelons of His Majesty's Government and gaining access to matters discussed in the strictest confidence only in the Cabinet Room or Churchill's own inner sanctum in the Admiralty.

Did such a link really exist? Was Canaris's information based on solid intelligence? Or did he divine Churchill's preoccupation with Norway?

Whether his source had actual knowledge of Churchill's efforts, it provided Canaris with solid intelligence of the exact moment the delicate issue was ignited by the new First Lord. The information reached Canaris from a man he regarded as well-informed and reliable—Hermann Kempf, the senior Abwehr agent in Oslo in the guise of a shipping executive, who had exceptional contacts in Norwegian military and naval circles.

It seems that between September 19 and 29, the problem of the "Leads" had been taken up with Eric Andreas Colban, the Norwegian envoy in London implicitly trusted in Whitehall as a friend of Britain. It was from the dispatch the attaché sent to Oslo reporting the informal inquiry that Kempf's friends learned of British preoccupation with the "Leads."

Nothing at Kempf's end indicates that he regarded this intelligence as anything exceptionally important or urgent. But a report came from Stockholm, quoting a member of the Admiralty staff that Britain would "sooner or later insist" on certain concessions granting "permission to lay mines in territorial waters north of Bergen" and to use "certain harbors in southern Norway as auxiliary bases."

Whatever the sources and the scope of his enlightenment, Canaris was propelled into a flurry of his most feverish activities during the whole war. He regarded the information as sufficient and resolved at once that something had to be done to forestall this British encroachment.

Overcoming his intense distaste of the man, he called on Grand Admiral Erich Raeder, commander in chief of the navy, and told him that "certain irrefutable evidence" was on hand "strongly indicating" that "the British intended to gain a foothold in Norway." Raeder was startled by Canaris's visit, and not merely because of the tidings he brought. "The report of the Abwehr chief," he wrote in his memoirs, "assumed greater significance by virtue of the fact that he deemed it necessary to present it in person, something he would do only on exceptional occasions."

Raeder was so impressed with the information, and so pleased with Canaris's idea of stealing a march on the British in the race for Norway, that twice he carried the matter to Hitler, on October 3 and 10, only to find that the Fuehrer was not interested.

Churchill continued "to press [his] point by every means and all occasions," while Canaris pursued his line just as relentlessly on two different tangents. Shrewdly leaving the political and strategic implications of a Norwegian venture in Admiral Raeder's care, he mobilized the Abwehr in a crash program to reconnoiter the country to the last little fjord and remote ski trail.

It was an elaborate project involving the establishment of vast espionage networks virtually overnight. The Hamburg branch, placed in charge of the technical arrangements, set up a subbranch at Flensburg close to the Danish border, and an outpost under diplomatic cover in the German Legation at Oslo. Two of the Abwehr's foremost Scandinavian specialists, Major E. Pruck and Major Bennecke, were sent to Norway to work in close collaboration with Hermann Kempf whose original report had started the entire commotion.[1]

For the time being it was the Abwehr alone that took seriously an invasion of Denmark and Norway and worked earnestly on preparing it. October and November came and went but Hitler still showed no interest in this detour, despite Admiral Raeder's protestations that the possession of Norway would give Germany decisive strategic advantages in the war against Britain.

His attitude changed somewhat in December when Major Quisling was brought to Berlin to sway Hitler. In three lengthy confrontations, the Norwegian conspirator submitted to the Fuehrer "conclusive evidence" that *de facto* arrangements already existed between the British and the Norwegians, the latter agreeing "under pressure" to acquiesce in "the occupation" of the country to plug this loophole in the British blockade.

Quisling's "evidence" (obtained, as he told Hitler, from secret supporters in high places, including "an officer in the King's closest entourage") visibly shook the Fuehrer. Yet he refused to commit himself. When in parting Quisling asked him with some flourish, "Are we to understand that you will help us to save our country from the British and the Jews?" Hitler replied vaguely, "I will help you, Major Quisling, but in a manner that will preserve Norway's neutrality."[2]

The situation changed radically within the next fortnight in the light of a number of Abwehr reports that seemed to underscore the seriousness of the situation. On January 4, 1940, an agent stationed at Metz in France discovered that the *Chasseurs Alpins*, a division of crack mountain troops, had been withdrawn from the Maginot Line and shipped to England on the first leg of a trip to someplace in Northern Europe—either to aid the Finns who had been invaded by the Russians on November 30, or to Norway to seize Narvik.

The agent's report was immediately submitted to Raeder who took it to Hitler and then fed him additional dispatches as soon as Canaris received them from Pruck in Norway. In one of them Pruck reported that British soldiers had secretly arrived in Norway, some in uniform. Although they were supposed to be medical corpsmen allegedly en route to Finland, Pruck insisted that they were sappers sent to Norway to prepare the landings of British forces.

These alarming dispatches may well have sealed the fate of Norway.

On January 16, Hitler postponed the West offensive *sine die* and issued orders to begin staff work immediately on the Scandinavian enterprise, henceforth to be referred to as the "Weser Exercise." The Jodl office assembled a special task force of its super-planners, camouflaged as "Commando for Special Employment No. 31," and work started on the operations plan on the 27th. It was completed in only two weeks.

From January on, the two competing designs moved at breakneck speed on parallel tracks toward their identical destination, the British and the Germans plotting "with precision," as Mr. Churchill later put it, "along the same lines in correct strategy." However, the advantage was clearly with the Germans. They apparently knew what the British were up to, while the British remained in the dark about the simultaneous German plans.

The two separate schemes produced some uncanny coincidences and concurrences, demonstrating the basic identity of the plots.

Battered by Churchill's increasingly impassioned papers, the War Cabinet finally consented *in principle* to his plan. A joint Anglo-French war council was held in Paris to discuss details of the Norwegian venture in the guise of aid to the Finns. It met on February 5. On the same day Hitler held a war council of his own to review details of Weser Exercise with his top commanders.

On March 28, the British War Cabinet resolved definitively to mine Nowegian territorial waters and to occupy several ports in Norway. On the same day Hitler directed Admiral Raeder to put the finishing touches to the German plan. On April 4 the date of the operations were set—both in England and Germany—for the 8th.

Then on the 7th, even as British and French troops were embarking at Rosyth in Scotland for the expedition and the fleet was deploying at sea, the German expeditionary force consisting of parts of three divisions sneaked out of Hamburg, Swinemuende, and Stettin, escorted by practically the entire German navy.

At dawn on April 9, the two projects finally collided—at 5:00 A.M.—just half an hour after British destroyers completed the mining of the waters off Bodoe, Stadtlandet, and the West Fjord at Arendal, Kristiansand, Bergen, Trondheim, and, finally, in Narvik.

By this time, Canaris's involvement in the gamble had become murky.

According to the postwar legend, Canaris who had conceived the plot and nurtured it so cunningly, soured on it the moment it received Hitler's approval. Walter Goerlitz, the historian of the German General Staff, went so far as to say that Canaris, "in his fanatical determination to cut across every plan of Hitler's," actually warned the Danish and Norwegian Military Attachés in Berlin of what was coming, only to encounter "crude incredulity" because the attachés assumed that the warning was a feint.

To be sure, there was a great deal of Aladdin and Hamlet in the inner Canaris. With unbounded faith in his magic power he would conjure up vast and bold plans, but then, brooding and soul-searching, he would shy away from their implementation, projecting the subconscious abhorrence of his own instability and vacillation to loathing those who acted. It is true that Canaris was gradually lost in the Norwegian shuffle, as was usually the case in projects which had their beginnings in the Abwehr but shifted to the operational arms of the Wehrmacht when they ripened for execution. It is not true that his own interest ever slackened in the venture. It can be stated categorically that he never betrayed the impending invasion either to the Danes or the Norwegians. He was, for all the infirmities of his character and the erosion of his loyalties, no simplistic traitor.

Another postwar legend, propounded chiefly by General Bernhard von Lossberg, the most enthusiastic planner of "Weser Exercise" in General Jodl's bureau, begrudged Canaris any share in the success of the enterprise. According to Lossberg, the Abwehr failed dismally in supplying even a minimum of the advance information the planners needed. The necessary maps and charts had to be purchased at Berlin bookshops, "a very tricky business considering the secrecy that had to be preserved."

General Nikolaus von Falkenhorst—pulled by Hitler from some duffle bag to command the invasion—was forced to buy a Baedecker guide of Norway to familiarize himself with the topography and the landmarks of the country he was about to conquer, in the absence of intelligence the Abwehr was supposed to provide.

It is possible that in the maze of the German military bureaucracy, the Jodl office—which was in the habit of dismissing contemptuously any help it got from the Abwehr—did not know or care about Canaris's crash program and failed to make use of the mass of information Pruck, Bennecke, Kempf, and their helpers had assembled.

In actual fact, from beginning to end, the Abwehr was an important and, as it turned out in a moment of crisis, indispensable cog of the operation.

Shortly after 4:00 A.M. on the 9th, Pruck, Bennecke, and Kempf underwent a pre-arranged metamorphosis. They ceased to be secret agents and became officers of the Wehrmacht (including Kempf who was made a lieutenant of the reserve for the occasion) to act as a reception committee for the invaders, expected to arrive off Oslo within the hour.

Commander Hasso Schreiber, the German Naval Attaché who had plotted on his own as Admiral Raeder's representative in Oslo, also donned his uniform and went down to the harbor to welcome the incoming German warships led by the heavy cruiser *Bluecher*. "Everything that I could do here," he wrote in his log before he left, "has been considered and prepared down to the smallest detail." On his drive to the harbor, Schreiber passed the British Legation and saw a thin ribbon of smoke rising from the garden. "They are burning their papers," he thought to himself with a smug smile.

He waited in vain. Even as the German armada with the landing troops aboard passed the narrows of Droebak in Oslo Fjord, the Norwegian coastal batteries opened up, sank the *Bluecher* with a direct hit, damaged the cruiser *Emden*, and forced the other ships, including the cruiser *Luetzow*, to withdraw. The soldiers, on their way to conquer the land, reached Norway as miserable shipwrecks. It seemed that Oslo had saved itself.

At 9:30 A.M. Commander Schreiber rushed back to his office in despair and tried to raise Berlin by telephone and radio, but he could not establish contact. In the expectation that the police would break into the house momentarily, he, too, issued orders to burn his papers.

The invasion had been mounted blindly—the Wehrmacht, supposedly so meticulous in its preparation, had failed to arrange adequate lines of communication. As a result, the high command in Berlin did not know how the operation was progressing. As usual when he was left in the dark, Hitler staged one of his temper tantrums. "Excitement terrible, chaos of command," read the laconic entry in Jodl's diary, describing the atmosphere in the special war room he had prepared in the Chancellery to enable Hitler to follow events.

News from Oslo was a mere trickle and all bad. It reached the war room in a roundabout way, on a single wire that connected Oslo with a forlorn telephone in Jodl's bureau. From time to time Keitel would call it from the Wilhelmstrasse, relaying Hitler's impatient questions, then attempts would be made to phone Oslo on this one line to get the questions answered. Most of the time nobody picked up the phone at the Oslo end. This is how historic operations frequently bog down in a primitive bottleneck, simply because some prop man forgot or neglected to arrange all the materiel needed in an invasion.

In the absence of good news, Hitler assumed the worst. Jodl needed all his persuasive powers to keep the Fuehrer from calling off the whole venture and ordering the immediate evacuation of whatever footholds his troops had gained in Norway.

In this supreme moment of crisis, help came from the Abwehr.

Among the gimmicks Canaris had prepared for the invasion was a special arrangement to assure a line of communication with Major Pruck and his associates. Two seemingly ordinary freighters of the Neptune Line, the *Widar* and the *Adar*, were sent into Oslo harbor on apparently routine calls a few days before X-day. They had been furnished with the most sophisticated communication equipment (including a couple of handy Afu sets) and had aboard detachments of Abwehr radiomen (among them young Kalau whom we have met before on his missions to England), with orders to open up two-way traffic the moment the first German warship came into sight.

While Hitler and his staff, as well as the entire Wehrmacht High Command—army, navy, and Luftwaffe—were dependent *exclusively* on that single telephone in Jodl's bureau, Canaris had this perfect connection with Oslo, receiving a blow-by-blow account of the invasion from his far-ranging teams of intelligence operatives.

At 8:10 A.M. the *Widar* made its decisive contribution to the astounding success of the blitz invasion. By then the ships which Commander Schreiber had gone to greet were at the bottom of the fjord or stopped cold with mortal wounds. Just when it seemed that the attempt to take Oslo from the sea would have to be abandoned and, perhaps the whole campaign given up because of the failure to capture the capital, Lieutenant Kempf rushed to the ship to transmit one of the truly historic signals of World War II.

In a message to Canaris he reported that there was, after all, one bright spot in the dismal picture. The airfield of Fornebu was firmly held by a small detachment of German soldiers who had been flown in at dawn and seized it in a *coup de main*.

Kempf's signal, picked up at Wohldorf, was teletyped to Canaris in Berlin who immediately telephoned it to General Keitel at the teeming headquarters of the Wehrmacht High Command. In all haste, the better part of an airborne division was flown to Fornebu. In a frontal

assault it captured the city which had just defied the mighty amphibious armada. By 5 P.M. Oslo was in German hands, with Kempf
guiding the conquerors to the strategic targets.

To the British the invasion came like "a cataract of violent sur-
prises." To Canaris it was something of an anti-climax.

He had once again won one of his private wars—as in Austria and
the Sudetenland in 1938, and in the Jablunkov Pass on August 26,
1939.

This time he scored in the Abwehr's running bout with the British
Secret Service—in a well-nigh personal clash with Winston Churchill
himself.

Looking back on his own investment in this new triumph of Adolf
Hitler, the admiral was not quite sure that it was worth his sweat and
toil.

NOTES

1 The Danish part of the operation was assigned to Franz Liedig, a naval
officer on the retired list who was one of Canaris's old friends, and to
Major Klug, an expert in communications intelligence.

2 Behind Hitler's guardedness was both ignorance and ruse. He knew little
about this fellow Quisling and had not thought seriously of an extension of
the war to Norway. He did not want to show his hand to this foreigner about
whom he knew nothing except what Raeder had told him. Quisling might
be a double agent, an Allied tool to obtain information about his plans
straight from the horse's mouth.

Chapter 20

The Trawler Treff

ON the evening of February 5, 1940, German diplomatic missions in every neutral country played host to coteries of distinguished guests, screening a documentary film of the campaign in Poland. In Rome, Foreign Minister Count Ciano sat in the audience which was composed, as he afterward noted in his diary, "partly of pro-German functionaries and partly of self-appointed pro-German pimps."

"It is a good film," he wrote in his brief review, "if the Germans wish merely to portray the brute force, but it is bestial for purposes of propaganda."

In Oslo the propaganda was unmistakable. The film culminated in a crescendo of horror scenes showing the bombing of Warsaw with a caption that read: "For this they could thank their English and French friends."

At the same time, the intelligence services of countries in Eastern Europe observed German troop concentrations in Slovakia. General Cuno Heribert Fuetterer, the German Air Attaché in Hungary, bluntly told Colonel István de Ujszászy, chief of the secret service, that the Wehrmacht was planning to move into Rumania "to keep the Ploesti oil fields out of the hands of the British."

The hint was promptly conveyed to all interested parties, including the British via their envoy in Budapest. Attention was clearly focused on the south as the next objective of German aggression.

"They did not march in the direction of Rumania," Count Ciano wryly noted only four days later.

The showing of the Poland film and the threat about the march to the south were but samples of a German *tour de force*. They formed part of the shrewdly designed deception campaign to assure the element of surprise which the Jodl plan specified as imperative for the success of the Scandinavian venture.

It worked almost miraculously. The Weser Exercise thus became a landmark in the history of intelligence operations, the high point in the trial of strength between the German and British secret services. In the same measure as it was a triumph for the Germans, it was a painful and humiliating defeat for the British, comparable to the debacle American intelligence would suffer at Pearl Harbor nineteen months later.

It was obvious, Churchill told Admiral Dudley Pound, the First Sea Lord, on April 10 in their dreary postmortem, that Britain had been "forestalled, surprised and outwitted."

How was it possible for the Germans to elude British vigilance with an expeditionary force of seven army divisions, some eleven-hundred aircraft and an armada of seventy-four warships?

It was, of course, not possible. Captain Henry Mangles Denham, the astute British Naval Attaché in Copenhagen, had informed the Admiralty of the German build-up that, he surmised, was "meant to seize Narvik." On the 6th, a German troop transport had been spotted by RAF planes moving across the mouth of the Skaggerak in the direction of Norway. The next day, RAF reconnaissance planes observed a German fleet on the northward dash toward "the Naze," the Lindesnes Cape of the extreme southern tip of Norway. And in the afternoon of the 8th, still twelve hours before H-hour, a report reached the Admiralty that the German troopship *Rio de Janeiro* had been torpedoed off Norway by the Polish submarine *Orzel*, and that soldiers rescued by Norwegian fishermen had admitted that they were bound for Bergen.

There were still other straws in the wind to alert the British—two in particular which are pertinent to this narrative, for both involved Johnny Owens. When we left him in October 1939, he had just returned from his *Treff* with Captain Ritter in Brussels and Antwerp, with some sabotage detonators concealed in wooden blocks and information about the three Abwehr agents left at large by Scotland Yard's roundup. He also met Ritter, who was again accompanied by Major Brasser, on December 18 and 19 in Antwerp. He took along the "game material" which his masters in MI.5 had prepared, with eighteen other pieces of genuine information ranging from such vital target intelligence as the location of an RAF depôt at Beeston-Bromwich (where it was rumored twenty million gallons of high-octane gasoline and lubricating oil was stored) to "incidental intelligence" about rumors that a U-boat had been captured intact in the English Channel.

For MI.5, the game with Snow continued without progressing noticeably. According to Ritter, on the other hand, this was Johnny's most productive period. He continued to send radio reports almost daily, though of course this part of his activities was run by Double-Cross." However, he had gone back to the Continent on a five-day sojourn between February 6 and 11, 1940, this time to tell Ritter about a scoop he had scored under the noses of his British controllers within their own super-secret domain.

He had succeeded in suborning W. N. Rolph, a businessman working for MI.5. From Rolph he was getting hard intelligence, the first the Germans would receive from inside the British security system, identifying, for example, certain Dutchmen and Belgians (including employees of KLM and Sabena airlines) who, according to Rolph, were working as British agents on the Continent.

In late March and early April, as the situation edged toward some sort of a showdown, Snow was scheduled to go on another fishing expedition for Britain; and Ritter was invited in a signal to meet him in Brussels on April 5. But the German was working overtime on the Weser Exercise and also on a crash program involving the Netherlands, which was to be next on Hitler's timetable. He signaled back that he would not be able to see Johnny any time in April and advised him not to undertake any trips to the Continent, because, as he bluntly put it, *"major offensive operations are expected to take place between April 1 and the end of the month."*

Major Ritter's not-too-cryptic statement whetted the curiosity of Johnny's handlers, so they made him go anyway. Ritter rushed to Brussels to meet him.

It was April 6, three days before the landings in Norway, five weeks to the day before the invasion of the Low Countries. The meeting produced startling information.

Ritter told Johnny point-blank that this could very well be their last meeting for some time unless they could think of some safe perch untouched by the war. The big offensive in the West would begin momentarily, he said, and engulf all the cities where they usually met.

Johnny asked: "You mean Brussels and Rotterdam? Are you planning . . ."

Ritter interrupted him.

"Well," he said, "very soon the only place we might be able to see each other will be on some pirate ship in the middle of the English Channel." It sounded like a joke. But Ritter was not the joking type.

More important, and far more specific for Norway, was the other clue. The Voluntary Interceptor, who was operating Johnny's Afu set, had considerably broadened his activities within the framework of this delicate maneuver. Since he was in touch with the Abwehr-station in Wohldorf in his capacity as Johnny's radio-double and was able to recognize by now the "note" of the station and the "style" of its various radio operators, he undertook to monitor Wohldorf regularly and record its transmissions, not only with Snow but with other agents as well.

In early April, the sharp-eared V.I. stumbled upon a traffic that interested him by its direction and volume. What he discovered was the Abwehr circuit with the *Widar*, one of the two spy-ships moving up and down the Norwegian coast in preparation for the impending Weser Exercise.

The clue was striking; yet it was ignored. No deductions were made from the *Widar*'s mysterious presence off Norway, nor were any conclusions drawn from its lively traffic with the Abwehr, even when it increased by leaps and bounds as the hour of the invasion drew closer.

So, even though Johnny unwittingly became an opening through which flagrant hints leaked to British intelligence, the opportunity was completely missed. Nothing was undertaken either to widen the breach, or to utilize Snow as a baited hook to gain more specific information.

Then all hell broke loose. Exactly a month after Norway, at 5:35 A.M. on May 10, the great offensive began in the West, on a front stretching from the North Sea to the southern borders of Luxembourg. During its first week all of Johnny's continental bases were wiped out—Rotterdam was destroyed on the 14th in the first deliberate terror raid of the war; Antwerp and Brussels were captured by the Germans on the 17th.

No more *Treffs* with Dr. Rantzau!

Under the frightful impact of the offensive, when Britain first began to strain all of its intelligence resources to gauge the mad rush of events, Snow became a very important pawn in this British effort. He could be used positively to procure intelligence from his German friends. He was needed negatively for an even deeper penetration of the German secret service. It was rightly assumed that the Abwehr would try to enlarge its base in England in the light of the Wehrmacht's triumph in the West.

At this stage, when the war was only eight months old, Double-Cross was barely off the ground. Aside from Snow, it had but a single active double agent, the fallen spy of Captain Dierks's stable, now a trusted tool of "XX," called "Rainbow" by his new cover-name. He was trying to fool Dierks with a string of judiciously concocted reports about Britain's air defenses and was sending some industrial and economic intelligence (culled from the daily press and paraphrased in signalese). His reports were so soft and his coverage so feeble that Dierks expressed little if any interest in him.

That left Johnny all by himself in the maneuver. Arrangements were made to salvage his relations with Ritter despite the loss of their former points-of-contact.

Their liaison was continued, but only by radio. On April 11, Ritter was advised that Johnny was going on a tour touching Southampton, Bournemouth, Odiham, Worcester, Brixham, Padstow, Ilfracombe, Exeter, Yeovil, Warminster, Bristol, Gloucester, Bicester, and Oxford, and asked whether he had any special orders for him from these places. Ritter immediately queried his clients, then radioed Johnny their shopping lists.

On the 16th Ritter was informed of the departure of French and Canadian troops for Norway. On the 18th he was sent a summary of what purported to be British plans for Norway, Holland, and Belgium.

But the opportunity for personal meetings seemed to have passed.

Then Johnny recommended Lisbon as an alternative, because, he said, Ritter could go anywhere in Europe to keep up the periodic *Treffs*. He suggested that he meet Ritter there, on the plausible pretext that he needed new outlets for his business overseas and was planning to replace his lost customers in Holland and Belgium with new clients in Portugal. The proposition was accepted and, on May 9, a signal was sent to Ritter:

"Have secret papers which must deliver in person," it read. "Applied for exit permit for *Treff* preferably Lisbon."

Major Ritter was thinking along the same lines. He would have hated to see Johnny drown in the backwash of the victory in the West. Interest in Britain was reviving in direct ratio to the speed with which the Panzers were approaching the English Channel.

It does not happen often that spy facts measure up to spy fiction. But what then occurred in the crowning adventure of this espionage tangle surpassed anything the most imaginative mystery writer could invent. The maneuver was so complex, and had so many plots and subplots in its contrived melodrama, it is not easy to make proper sense of what actually happened in one of the zaniest true-life spy thrillers that only a mercurial Welsh madcap could have inspired.

A *Treff* was arranged for somewhere in the North Sea instead of in Lisbon—Johnny to come by trawler and Ritter to arrive either by submarine or seaplane.

The travel plan was nothing short of fantastic.

This was one of the hottest periods of the whole war, German armor racing toward the French coast, the North Sea between Britain and occupied Denmark patrolled by the Royal Navy and the RAF, trying desperately to control the sea and the air in the face of the Luftwaffe's and the U-boats' challenge.

It required mindless courage to venture into this no-man's-sea, and matchless navigation to hit the pinpoint of the *Treff*. Yet this was how they arranged it, an indication by itself of how urgently and eagerly both parties sought the rendezvous.

The *Treff* on the trawler was Ritter's idea, one he had been hatching ever since he had known that places like Rotterdam and Brussels would go up in the smoke of the campaign. He had been impressed by the ease with which Belgian and Norwegian smugglers crossed back and forth, and he knew that Abwehr II had made a deal with them to carry sabotage material to Williams's Welshman along with their regular contraband. Also, Ritter was smarting at his desk in Hamburg while the Wehrmacht was rampaging on its triumphant warpath, and he sought an outlet for his pent-up martial yearnings in a bang-bang sortie into enemy territory under wartime conditions.

When Ritter radioed the plan to Johnny, London was stunned, not so much by the daring of the proposed venture, as by its complexity and inanity. But a *Treff* even in the foggy, stormy North Sea was better than no *Treff* at all, and the invitation was accepted. Ritter was advised that Johnny would try to borrow a trawler "from a reliable Welshman who's sailing a fishing boat out of Grimsby." A couple of days later Ritter was told that the arrangement with the congenial skipper had been made. He was asked to set the place and the time for the rendezvous at sea.

Ritter went to Commodore Doenitz to borrow a U-boat for the mission but was scornfully rebuffed—Doenitz would not think of risking a rowboat on the hairbrained antics of those Canaris goldbrickers. But Ritter found Admiral Cyliax, commandant of the North Sea, sympathetic, and secured from him a Do-18 twin-engine seaplane with a handpicked crew of three, including the best navigator at List, where the naval reconnaissance squadron had its base.

Ritter signaled Johnny on May 16: "Meet me fifty-three deg forty min north three deg ten min east, twenty-six fathoms, midnight Tuesday twenty-first or Wednesday twenty-ninth May." The position was south of the deserted fishery grounds of the Dogger Bank.

The trawler *Barbados* was borrowed for Johnny officially from the Fisheries Board. But there was still something that had to be arranged. At their last meeting in April, Johnny had promised Ritter that he would produce one of his sub-agents, and Ritter now asked him to bring the man with him so that he could be taken to Hamburg to be trained as a saboteur. MI.5 was thus faced with the problem of providing a trustworthy companion for the trip without Johnny knowing that he was an employee of the agency. A man called "Biscuit" by his cover-name, a reformed petty criminal who was now working as a stool pigeon for Scotland Yard, was insinuated into Johnny's circle of Welsh nationalists. Calling himself Sam McCarthy, Biscuit avidly agreed to accompany Johnny and hence on to Germany by his perilous route to undergo the training Ritter had in mind.

On May 19, Johnny and McCarthy left for the great fishing port of Grimsby at the mouth of the Humber river in Lincolnshire, boarded the trawler, and set out on the voyage. They were giving themselves plenty of time to make the contact on the dot of Ritter's meticulously plotted timetable.

Biscuit was, of course, familiar with the setup. Not only was he himself a bona fide British agent, but assumed, from what he had been told in his briefings, that Johnny also worked faithfully for MI.5 while servicing the Germans with bogus intelligence.

On the trip, Johnny—who was consuming larger than usual quantities of Scotch whisky to make himself seaworthy—confided to McCarthy that he was only pretending to be a double agent for MI.5, and was in reality a dedicated German spy. This confession at sea scared the daylights out of Biscuit. He began to fear for his life, even assuming that Johnny might know he was really an MI.5 stooge and would deliver him to the Germans at the *Treff* as his prize.

On the evening of the 20th, Biscuit decided to stage a mini-mutiny and cut short this dubious journey. While Johnny was sleeping below after a prolonged communion with the bottle, Biscuit locked him up in the cabin and took command of the trawler. He ordered it blacked out and to return to Grimsby at once.

In the afternoon of May 21, Ritter motored to List, boarded the Do-18 waiting for him and flew to the pinpoint at the Dogger Bank. The weather was turning bad and the sea was becoming heavy in spots, an insipid fog reducing visibility. Aided by the crack navigator Admiral Cyliax had chosen for the mission, they reached the pinpoint, on the nose, where the trawler was supposed to be. There was no sign of it. The plane circled the spot, looking for Johnny, until the pilot told Ritter that he had only enough fuel to take him home.

Ritter had no choice. He had to abandon the mission, wondering what had kept Johnny, usually the most punctual of spies, from showing up. Perhaps, he mused, the trawler he had borrowed did not have good enough navigational instruments to make it to the pinpoint. Or perhaps something had gone wrong with the arrangements he made to get the boat.

Back in Hamburg he was handed a signal that had been received earlier in the evening. It was from Johnny and it cleared up the mystery to Ritter's satisfaction. "Had to lay low," the message read. "Captain under surveillance. Report follows."

Actually Johnny was in serious trouble.

When he went ashore back in Grimsby, he was promptly detained by detectives from the Special Branch. Alerted by the signal from Biscuit that Johnny, according to his own admission while in his alcoholic haze, was a *genuine* German agent, they had been sent by MI.5 to ask a few searching questions. It was a turn that caught Johnny completely unprepared. The detectives found on him a number of classified documents he was hoping to take to Ritter in the course of his bona fide service to the Germans. In addition, he was carrying several reports Rolph had produced about the MI.5.

It seemed Johnny was really dead this time and Snow had been definitely exposed as a triple-cross agent in the game. In addition, Rolph was accidentally unmasked as a German spy (I found him duly listed a A.3554 in the Abwehr registry).

Poor Rolph got out of his predicament by committing suicide.

Johnny—brash and brazen as ever—decided to face the music.

Turning the tables on the not-too-bright and, by now, thoroughly bewildered Biscuit, he insisted that he had taken the papers along as a safeguard against some treacherous mischief on McCarthy's part. He did not like the man's eager enthusiasm for the sabotage job, he said, and suspected that he was a Gestapo agent planted on his neck to set this elaborate watery trap for him. He feared that McCarthy, who seemed to know more than was good for both of them would undoubtedly reveal to Ritter his ambiguous position, whereupon the Germans would capture him and either throw him overboard "like some garbage" or take him to Germany to give him his just deserts.

He needed those papers to prove to Ritter that he was on the level—an explanation which, strange as it may seem, MI.5 swallowed.

In the NKVD doubts like these would have been resolved by firing a bullet into the base of the man's brain. Such solutions of tricky problems involving double agents were still repugnant to the western intelligence services (which, however, became quite adept in them during the Cold War). Snow's employment was continued as before, except for a brief cooling-off period to see what would happen.

Even without the mishap of the trawler incident, the day did not seem too far off when this particular double-cross would come to its natural end and Snow would melt away. They were ready to give him up—provided they could gain control over the replacement Ritter would send.

At an earlier *Treff*, the German had told Johnny that he was grooming a South African in Belgium, just in case it became necessary to take over if things got rough for him. Now "Double-Cross" went into action in the hope that they could lure the man to England with Johnny's help.

A number of increasingly frantic signals were sent in his name to Ritter, variations on the theme of the one radioed on May 31, that stated without any prevarication, "Getting scared. When is South African coming to help?" But MI.5 was caught in its own game. Although Snow had been put on ice, they continued to use his line to Ritter to arrange a meeting—in Lisbon after all. They decided, however, to send the hardy and completely trustworthy Biscuit in his place, in the guise of a wine merchant, this time with nothing but fake intelligence.

Biscuit-McCarthy—the professional confidence man—now joined the growing "XX" menagerie of double agents, getting ready for the trip to Lisbon to meet Ritter at last. Johnny was about to make an astounding recovery from what had threatened to become a fatal crisis. He was back in harness by the summer of 1940, when Britain went on Hitler's timetable as the next country to be conquered.

Chapter 21

Operation Mainau and
Other Capers in Eire

*T*HE "invasion" of the British Isles, began auspiciously even before the war broke out. The Abwehr was confident that it had a ready-made expeditionary force for the secret war against England in the Irish Republican Army. It was in action, turning one English city after another into bloody battlefields.

Only five days before the invasion of Poland, Coventry was hit in an especially savage attack. A time bomb hidden in the basket of a bicycle left at a store during the rush hour on Broadgate killed five persons and injured fifty. When two of the "I.R.A. soldiers" were sentenced to hang for the outrage, the whole wide volatile Irish world exploded in righteous indignation and the I.R.A. went on war footing.

Late at night on December 23, a task force of the I.R.A. broke into the Magazine Fort, an army depôt in Phoenix Park in Dublin, disarmed the guards, emptied the stores of all weapons, and got away with more than a million rounds of ammunition.

The Abwehr was following these developments with great expectations.

Even though an official account of the incident was published only five months later, the Abwehr learned the exact details of the coup within forty-eight hours from Dr. Carlheinz Petersen, its correspondent in Dublin. Petersen theorized that the raid had to be staged because the British blockade had cut the I.R.A. off from its sources of supply in the United States. He suggested that Germany could gain decisive influence with the Irish terrorists by replacing America as the supplier of arms.

By this time Colonel Erwin von Lahousen, whose responsibilities included sabotage and insurrections as head of Abwehr II, had ac-

220

quired something he rarely had in any of his schemes—a sense of perspective. His old euphoria about the I.R.A. had dimmed. He no longer considered the Irish an effective and dependable ally against the British. The most diligent and costly efforts of his "Bureau Pfalzgraf," the Irish section under Major Marwede and Kurt Haller, to conclude a working alliance with the I.R.A. had bogged down in acrimonious, mercenary squabbles. The Irish were willing to cooperate, but strictly on their own terms. They would accept money, arms, explosives, radio sets—especially money—as much as they could get from the Germans. They made it absolutely clear that they intended to remain the masters in their own rebellion, and would not abjectly carry out any orders from the Abwehr, nor take any advice on how to conduct their operations and what targets to hit.[1]

Lahousen reviewed the situation with his aides and decided on a radically changed new policy. Instead of supporting the I.R.A. and getting little if anything in return, Abwehr II would set up its own bases in Ireland, man them with its own agents, and sustain them with its own lines of communication and supplies. He would then mount the attack on Britain, in collaboration with the I.R.A. if possible, preferably without it, and even against it if necessary.

This new era of independence began on January 28, 1940, modestly enough, with the dispatch of a single agent to Ireland. His mission, however, was not so modest. The man was to reconnoiter the situation on the spot, dangle the prospect of substantial financial support before greedy I.R.A. eyes, and arrange a trip to Germany for "a top-ranking Irish revolutionary" with whom details of a "mutually advantageous" collaboration could be ironed out at long last.

The man chosen for the trip was a 61-year-old Austrian ex-acrobat named Ernst Weber-Drohl, remembered by older vaudeville buffs as "Atlas the Iron Giant" or "Dr. Drohl, the World's Strongest Man," as he was variously billed during his heyday when his bulging biceps and fierce flexors used to be the talk of the town wherever he performed.

His qualification for the mission to Ireland? Well, he had appeared in music halls in Dublin, Galway, Limerick, and Cork, and at county fairs as a wrestler and weight lifter—thirty-three years before.

His own reason for accepting the assignment? He was broke but was itching to go back to Ireland, where he once had had a self-supporting comely mistress with whom he had had two illegitimate sons. He hoped his "relatives," as he called them, would remember him and set him up in practice as a chiropractor.

The Abwehr took him to Ireland by U-boat, then left him to his own resources which were quickly revealed as totally inadequate for anything except tracking down his old mistress. He was picked up by the police on a charge of illegal entry a few weeks after his arrival, and fined three pounds by a kind judge to whom he promised that he would not engage in any activities inimical to Ireland.

Left high and dry, he went looking for the forsaken Irish lass, found her in fairly prosperous circumstances, but unwilling to take him in. His two sons had grown into respectable manhood and had left Ireland to make their fortunes in England. He located one of them, a minor official of London Transit, and wrote to him for help. The son journeyed to Dublin, spent four days with this prodigal father, gave him a little money and some sound advice, and then returned to London.

Today we know that the "sound advice" was the most critical aspect of the visit. His son, who seemed to be rather well informed about "Dr. Drohl's" reasons for being in Ireland, suggested that he turn his back on the Germans and work for the British instead. The first agent the Abwehr managed to plant in Ireland thus became the first Irish double agent. Through him the British security organs got a grip on the Abwehr in "Mackerel" (as Ireland was called in the Abwehr's secret nomenclature) never to let it go.

In the meantime, two seemingly bona fide Irish revolutionaries reached Berlin to make their own deals with the Abwehr. One of them was Francis Stuart, a reputable scholar and noted author, who used to lecture at Berlin University on Irish literature before the war. The other was a certain "Held," his cover-name in the Abwehr's Central Registry, which described him, somewhat grandiosely and prematurely, as "our chief V-man in the Republic of Ireland." He was Jim O'Donovan, an elderly adventurer free-lancing on the periphery of rebellion. He had nothing to do with the I.R.A. except to use it as bait to ingratiate himself with the Abwehr and shake it down.

Stuart and Held told Lahousen that Ireland was in a state of undeclared war with Britain and was, therefore, the ideal spot from which to mount sneak attacks across St. George's Channel and the Irish Sea. They found their hosts interested in a deal, hoping that respectable revolutionaries like Stuart and O'Donovan might bring the I.R.A. around to more reasonable cooperation.

Lahousen decided to send to Eire his own personal envoy "to initiate on his own," as his orders stipulated, "espionage and sabotage actions against England, and to establish contact with prominent Irish personalities who [were] sincerely interested in and capable of promoting the cause of Germany."

The ambassador-at-large was a most unlikely choice—a veteran spy who had already fallen hard once before. He was none other than the hapless Hermann Goertz, the Hamburg lawyer who had drifted into espionage in 1935 because he had been a failure in everything else he tried. His main qualification for the new mission was that while sitting out his four year sentence at Maidstone Prison, he had befriended a Dubliner, serving a life sentence for a crime of passion. "He," Goertz later wrote, "was very well informed about Irish affairs and had given me considerable enlightenment about Ireland."

Goertz rates a special page in any book about espionage if only because he was undoubtedly the most inept and, even worse, the unluckiest of all spies in history.

He started on the mission on the night of May 5, 1940, (on his third try, for he had failed to make it to Ireland twice before because of bad weather conditions) in a stripped He-111 bomber piloted by Lieutenant Gartenfeld, the young Luftwaffe ace who ferried most of the Abwehr spies to Britain. Goertz parachuted down to the wrong place—in County Tyrone in *Northern* Ireland, wearing the heavy flight overall of a Luftwaffe officer and carrying a mixed bag of forged military identity papers, some made out to a "Lieutenant Gilke," others to a "Lieutenant Kruse."

The mission began rather unpropitiously in other respects as well. He failed to find a second parachute that brought down the container with his kit, including a radio and a spade. He could not bury his parachute as instructed, because the spade was in the lost container.

When he discovered that he was in the wrong spot, he hiked on foot for four days the seventy miles to Laragh in County Wicklow in Eire, where he knew he would be welcome in the "safe house" of Professor Stuart's wife, Iseult, an active member of the I.R.A. On the way he had to swim the Boyne river (because he found that the bridge was guarded by soldiers) with, as he later wrote, "great difficulty since the weight of my fur combination exhausted me." The swim also cost him the loss of his secret ink. It had been sewn into the shoulder padding of his overall, in the form of yellow cotton impregnated with the solution which was washed out by the waters of the Boyne.

Goertz was hungry and tired, and hot under the May sun in the fur-lined uniform. He took it off, along with his tunic, and hid them by the wayside near Newbridge in County Kildare, hoping to return later and pick them up. At night he repeatedly lost his way because the batteries in his flashlight had run out. "I was now in high boots," he wrote, "in breeches and jumper, with a little black beret on my head. I kept my military cap as a vessel for drinks and my medals [from World War I] for sentimental reasons."

Although he was carrying a substantial sum in English and American currencies, he had no Irish money, and was so unfamiliar with conditions in Ireland that he did not know that he could use English money freely. He marched twenty hours a day and ate absolutely nothing until he reached Mrs. Stuart's house on the fourth day of his wandering.

Goertz was the living symbol of the whole Irish project—a lonely, baffled figure trudging across the empty countryside in jackboots, with a little black beret on his head and a pocketful of old medals.

Eventually he found an uncertain haven in a villa called "Konstanz" on Templeogue Street in Dublin, the home of another Held— a 38-year-old wealthy factory owner named Stephen Carroll Held, a shadowy figure suspected of being an *agent provocateur* in British service. There he met Stephen Hayes, the legendary chief of staff of the I.R.A., who looked and acted, as Goertz ruefully noted in his diary, "like a superannuated soccer player, his dignity sadly impaired by alcohol and anxiety."

Goertz still had his money, and soon after Hayes's visit it became obvious that the I.R.A. was interested merely to relieve him of these funds. A few days after Hayes's call, the Held villa was invaded by four young "I.R.A. messengers" who took away the money in a coup that reminded Goertz of "a holdup by gangsters in America."

On May 22, his sixteenth day in Ireland, the police raided the villa for a change, and arrested Held in a specious maneuver that smacked of having been staged. Goertz escaped by scaling the wall of the garden in the rear, and submerged himself in the big city, leaving behind all that remained of his espionage paraphernalia.

Without any money, cut off from his home office, abandoned by his friends and hunted by the police with a £3000 price on his head, Goertz was through. "Operation Mainau," as his mission had been dubbed, had come to an end even before it could begin.

He was almost relieved when he was finally found and arrested in November 1941. After a few months in an Irish internment camp he was scheduled to be repatriated. Goertz had given up hope that anything good could still happen to him. He was convinced that instead of letting him go home, the Irish were planning to hand him over to the British who knew him so well from their previous encounter. The night before his release he committed suicide by biting into a capsule of cyanide coaxed from Admiral Canaris as a parting gift eighteen months before.

The I.R.A.? "It is rotten," he wrote in his testament, "to its very core."

But Captain Goertz was not the only Irish card in the Abwehr's hands. In this same spring of 1940, a celebrated I.R.A. exile, Sean Russel, Hayes's predecessor as chief of staff, was brought from the United States to Germany where Lahousen was training a handful of

Irish terrorists in the Abwehr's camp for saboteurs at Quenzee. Since the Germans had the notion that a full-scale insurrection was feasible in Ireland, provided the I.R.A. had a selfless, energetic, and effective leader, Lahousen decided to send Russel home, accompanied by a former Communist named Frank Ryan, to lead the uprising. A submarine commanded by Lieutenant von Stockhousen was requisitioned for the journey, but by the time Russel arrived at the French port of Lorient to embark, he was a very sick man with an old ulcer flaring up. Lahousen sent orders to ship him out anyway, but Russel had a hemorrhage and died, only a hundred miles from his destination. He was buried at sea.[2]

The Abwehr had still another Irish link, at this time, in London. He was a prominent and wealthy Irish businessman who claimed to have some tenuous association with the I.R.A. although he himself was not a member. He had been sought out before the war to serve as liaison between his friends in Ireland and the Abwehr. When the war broke out, it had become extremely difficult to keep in touch with him.

Now that the Irish project was progressing, Lahousen thought of re-activating him in his lair. An agent was developed in Spain to establish contact. She was a brave little angry Irish lady, a Mrs. Daly working in Madrid as a governess, better remembered by her Abwehr alias of "Margarethe." She volunteered to go to London to take instructions and even an Afu set to the businessman, then go on to Ireland with a letter, a new code, and some money for poor Goertz.

She reached London safely on a Japanese ship sailing from Lisbon, but when she called on the businessman, she so frightened him that he refused to go through with the deal he had made with the Abwehr. Using the usually effective argument of blackmail, Margarethe threatened the reluctant spymaster with denunciation to the British authorities if he persisted in his refusal to cooperate.

This gave the man an idea. He went to the authorities and denounced himself, then accepted the radio Margarethe had brought him, with the code and the query list, and functioned thereafter as a charter member of the "XX" fraternity.

More of the same followed, in what was undoubtedly the Abwehr's most bird-witted project throughout the war.

It was at this time that Johnny Owens, in the wake of the near-disaster of his ill-starred fishing expedition in the North Sea, became restive and asked Major Ritter to send the South African the Abwehr was grooming in Belgium as a possible replacement for him. Actually Ritter had the choice of *two* South Africans—the students Herbert Tributh and Dieter Gaertner, starry-eyed enthusiasts slowly grinding in the Abwehr's erratic spy mill.

When Ritter received Johnny's frenzied signals, Hamburg alerted the two students to stand by for transfer to England—but how to get them there?

Just then, Ast X learned that a nautical expedition was in the making to run the British blockade with a veteran V-man of Abwehr II whose expert touch was sorely needed to bring some order into the snafu-ridden Irish project. The man survives in the annals as one of the few authentically melodramatic figures in this gallery of pathetic rogues. He was a 38-year-old brown-skinned Hindu, Henry Obéd, the name under which he lived in Brussels as a trader in Oriental spices and the owner of a pet shop.

The impending journey of Obéd offered a good opportunity to get Tributh to England to join Johnny and Gaertner to Ireland to assist Obéd, until all three of them could be reunited in Britain. But then the project began to grow. Before long it produced an ambitious plan to merge the apparently flourishing Welsh network, managed by Johnny and Gwyllem Williams by way of Hamburg, with the floundering Irish operation which Lahousen was running personally from Berlin.

A Falangist with the cover-name of "Pike" was found in Spain to go to England with a message to Gwyllem Williams, advising him of the projected merger. Williams gave Pike a glowing report about the activities of his Welsh network, but complained that its work was badly hampered by the Abwehr's failure to finance it adequately and to smuggle funds into England.

Some £4000 were promptly appropriated, and sent to Williams through another Falangist via Spain.

Gwyllem Williams was the former Swansea police inspector who supervised the MI.5 penetration of the Welsh nationalists. The missions of the two Spaniards became promptly and directly known to the British authorities. However, they let the couriers return to Spain unmolested, because their arrest would have killed the promising venture in the bud.

So far as the Germans knew, the multiple project was progressing without a hitch: a path had been cleared for master saboteur Obéd to England via Ireland; Ritter could send the promised South African to relieve Johnny; and everything was ready for the fusion of the Welsh nationalists and the Irish extremists in a viable conglomerate.

Since the air route was proving unreliable, and Canaris was experiencing increasing difficulties in getting planes from the Luftwaffe for drops, Christian Nissen was summoned to the Abwehr and asked to take these people to Ireland by boat. Popular in the international yachting community by his salty nickname of "Hein Mueck," Nissen was a blithe old pirate straight out of *Moby Dick*, who savored "the delight and deliciousness of the wide-rolling watery prairies."

An experienced old sporting seaman, he was given the freedom of the French coast to requisition any boat that seemed suitable to him, train his crew, organize the voyage, do anything at all, but please do it quickly. Hein Mueck found what he needed at Camaret-sur-Mer, a tiny fishing village on the Brittany coast—a 35-foot sleek luxury yacht, the *Soizic*, owned by a French colonel. Since he decided to make the journey by sail, he rigged her over as a yawl, but kept her luxuries, including the well-stocked bar, intact.

He knew from happier days where he was going. As a competitor in the Cowes races, he was familiar with every square inch of the waters between the Isle of Wight and the frill-fringed southern coast of Ireland, from Toe Head to Cape Clear.

Hein Mueck threw a party the night before their departure on bottle after bottle of Clos de Bèze, his favorite vintage from Côte de Nuit. At 11:00 P.M. on July 3, they boarded the *Soizic* which was then towed into the open Atlantic. A fresh ocean breeze grabbed her sails and they were outward bound.

The voyage to Ireland was a resounding success. "After three days sailing," Hein Mueck reported later, "I landed my passengers by dinghy under cover of darkness in the gulf of Baltimore, near the Fastner Rock in the southwestern extremity of Ireland."

By the time he got back to Brest and checked in with the Abwehr officer, his three voyagers were behind bars. Did the Irish know they were coming? Since Williams was considered the key man in the project in his capacity as the Abwehr's sabotage superintendent in England, he was kept posted of these pilgrims' progress. It was reasonable to believe that he shared his information with his friends in MI.5 and that the British authorities alerted the Irish who, by this time, did not cherish this kind of tourism.

Undaunted by so many mishaps, the Abwehr still regarded Ireland as a convenient lock through which agents could be sluiced into England. In June, Hamburg chose two of its veteran V-men for missions on its British beat via the Irish by-pass.

Steward Willy Preetz of North German Lloyd had worked for Commander Pheiffer at the Bremen subbranch as a courier before the war. His value to the Abwehr had increased lately. He had married an Irish girl and somehow managed to come by a *genuine* Irish passport, made out to one Paddy Mitchell. It seemed a cinch to get him to Eire and then on to England with such a traveler's aid. The plan was to set him up somewhere on the coast between Southampton and Liverpool, to keep an eye on the convoys coming and going.

The other man was Major Ritter's old protégé, the venerable Walter Simon of Elberfeld, who just could not desist from spying. Like Hermann Goertz, Simon was well-known to British security from his days in Wandsworth Prison in the early winter of 1939, when they could not prove that he was a spy but took it for granted nevertheless.

It was unconscionable and foolish to return fallen spies to their old beats, but Hamburg had exhausted its pool of agents, and was now scraping the bottom of the barrel. It had to cover England as best it could, and sending men like Willy and Walter was obviously the best they could do.

Simon was hastily trained at Wohldorf in the operation of an Afu set, then sent on the mission just as hastily. He was calling himself Karl Anderson on this journey, and traveled as a seaman on a Norwegian passport.

He waded ashore at dawn on June 13, in Dingle Bay in southwest Ireland, then walked to a nearby railroad station where he bumped into three men, apparently waiting for the train.

"When," he asked them, "is the next train due for Dublin?"

The strangers stared at him, then one of them said:

"The last train left here, mate, fourteen years ago. I reckon it might be another fourteen years before the *next* train will leave."

Two hours later, Walter Simon was in the cell of the police station at Tralee in County Kerry, through with spying for the rest of the war. Willy, too, was caught on the day of his arrival, despite his genuine Irish passport.

The whole Irish project was in shambles. The back door to England had been slammed tight. The Abwehr diary acknowledged this tersely on July 18, with a laconic entry. "Orders of the Chief," it read: "No more sabotage missions to be staged via Ireland. In the future, all operations of this kind will be arranged on direct route to England."

NOTES

1 In actual fact, much of the I.R.A.'s mordancy was sheer bluff to mask its inner weaknesses. Its leadership was torn between competing factions, and was quite venal besides, bent on pocketing much of the money pouring in from the United States in an Irish sweepstakes that had no winners. And though the I.R.A. professed to have "an invasion plan," no less, to "destroy England's capability to wage war," the scattered terror acts were staged to keep the illusion alive.

2 Ryan returned from this macabre journey without touching Irish soil. He cut a strange and lonely figure in this inane conspiracy, a convinced Communist who aligned himself with the Nazis, to speed "the liberation" of his country which he passionately loved. He never again played a significant role in any of the Abwehr's Irish plots.

Chapter 22

The Doomsday Spies

ON June 26, 1940, Adolf Hitler ventured the closest to Britain that he would ever go in this war—he drove to Dunkirk, whence the British Expeditionary Force had fled only three weeks before. It was an impromptu stop on a sentimental journey. The triumphant war lord now stood in front of the gutted houses on the promenade, looking out to the macabre mass of wreckage in the sands and the twisted skeletons of abandoned vehicles half-sunk in the water. He was neither interested in nor impressed by the grim mementoes of the campaign he had just won. His mind still fondled memories of the old war in which he had fought as a corporal.

Accompanied by Max Asmann, his sergeant in World War I, and another old friend named Ernst Schmidt, he was on a leisurely sightseeing tour to such famed battlefields as Messines and Fromelles, Ypres and Langemarck. He had decided on this detour only when they had passed through Peperinge and Asmann told him that Dunkirk, a new sight worth seeing, was only a few miles away.

This was, throughout all of World War II, the only spot at the water's edge Hitler would visit. Only thirty miles from where he now stood, on the far side of the Strait of Dover, was the English coast. Hitler looked out toward the horizon with quizzical eyes as if trying to see land in the distance.

The idea of crossing over to England had not occurred to the Fuehrer when he was drawing up his plans for the campaign in the West. Now, in the light of his enemies' proven weakness and the demonstrated power of his own arms, he was toying with the idea. Twice during the past thirty days, the subject of invading the British Isles had come up in conversations with Grand Admiral Erich Raeder. On May 21, the day after the Panzers had reached Abbéville

229

and the Somme estuary, Raeder, who was observing the campaign as an interested bystander, visited the Fuehrer in his sumptuous command post near Muenstereifel and asked him, almost casually, whether he would consider an invasion of England. Hitler's answer was noncommittal. Raeder returned to the project on June 20, three days after France had sued for a truce.

Now, on second thought, Hitler seemed inclined to consider the venture. "I'll let you know in a few days," he told Raeder. He had more important business to attend to in the meantime. On the 21st, at Compiégne, he accepted the surrender of the French. Then he went on what Peter Fleming called a honeymoon with victory—his tour to the old battlefields and a carefree holiday in the Black Forest.

He was still vacationing at the Knibis, a mountain resort in the Black Forest, on July 2, when he made up his mind. He told his military staff to begin preparations at once for the invasion of England, to be mounted, "if necessary," by the middle of September. The drafters of the plan coined the code name "Lion" for the operation. When Hitler proofread it, he changed it to "*Sea* Lion," for whenever he thought of England, the sea weighed heavily on his mind.

Admiral Raeder did not wait for Hitler's final decision to begin his preparations. As soon as he arrived in Berlin, on June 21, he called in Admiral Canaris and asked him to concentrate on intelligence about England. Next morning, Canaris conveyed the order to his associates at the Tirpitz Ufer. As the Abwehr diary recorded the event, "Upon orders of the Chief, operations of the Abwehr will henceforth be concentrated on the war with England." The enterprise was given a cover-name, "Hummer," with variations according to the chronological order and the destination of the missions. The first party going to England was called "Hummer I-South"; the one sent to Scotland, "Hummer I-North." As it turned out, very few numbers were needed for these undertakings.

At the session, the admiral asked Piekenbrock and Lahousen how they stood with agents in "Golf Course."

Piekenbrock replied that the coverage was better than adequate, and mentioned Johnny by name as an example. "We check this agent daily," he said, "his Morse style, his facts, all the usual safeguards of his security. Wohldorf assures me that he's still genuine."

Though British security seemed to be getting better with each passing day, the Abwehr was apparently not doing too badly in England. Piekenbrock was wrong as far as Johnny was concerned. Whatever "genuine" there used to be in him had been knocked out by that fateful outing halfway to the Dogger Bank.

At this time, the Abwehr had a handful of uncompromised spies whose existence was (and until now probably still is) totally unknown to the British authorities.

For three long years at this critical period, its real ace in the hole was not Johnny but an officer of the Iraqi Army. The work of this man demonstrated graphically how invaluable a single expert agent could be when stationed at the fountainhead of crucial military secrets.

Captain Mohamed Salman, in England since March 1938, was on leave from the Iraqi Armored Force to study tank warfare at Aldershot, Sandhurst, and Woolwich. Like many Arabs of his generation, he was in his secret heart as hostile to the British as he was infatuated with the Nazis. He had agreed, before his departure on this tour of duty, to act as an Abwehr operative at the heart of Britain's secrecy-shrouded Mechanized Warfare Experimental Establishment.

Salman's own division at home was a satellite of the British Army during these years of close association with Iraq under the pro-British regime of Nuri Pasha. He, therefore, had unrestricted access to some of the most sensitive installations, and was able to keep the Germans posted about the development of British armor and tank tactics.

Equally important in this order of things, he could send his material out of England easily and regularly without ever jeopardizing the security of his secret mission. His brother, Major General Ahmed Salman, was commander in chief of the Iraqi Air Force, and, like Mohamed, a secret foe of the British. Captain Salman mailed his reports to Baghdad in the pouch of the Iraqi diplomatic mission in London, in the form of personal letters to his brother. The General then gave the letters to Colonel Werner Jung, the Abwehr representative in Baghdad, who radioed their contents to Berlin.

This phenomenal link lasted until early May 1941, when Captain Salman terminated his tour of duty in England and returned home to participate in the pro-Nazi coup of Rashid Ali el Ghailani in which his brother had a key role. Arriving in Lisbon on the 8th en route to Baghdad, he contacted the Abwehr mission in Portugal. On a Bulgarian passport made out to an engineer named Magid Sirhan, the Iraqi officer was flown to Berlin for debriefing on his mission to England, and also to be briefed for his new mission in Iraq as one of the leaders of the short-lived rebellion.

Collaboration with the Abwehr by a supposedly neutral diplomatic mission in London or in a British Embassy abroad was by no means unprecedented or unique. The Italians served as the conduit for the avalanche of top-secret documents, including the Roosevelt-Churchill correspondence, stolen from the code room of the American Embassy in 1939–40. The Japanese acted as paymasters on the Abwehr's behalf when larger sums had to be smuggled to spendthrift agents. From time to time, the Portuguese and Swiss missions would serve as unwitting "roofs" for agents the Abwehr managed to insinuate into Britain. The Swedish Legation was exploited in a different manner, and the Spanish Embassy became on and off a hothouse of espionage. But no other diplomatic mission harbored a bona fide espionage agent of such position, importance, industry, and perception as the Hungarian Legation.

Headed by Dr. Gyoergy Barcza de Nagylásony, an able and correct career diplomat, and a devout Catholic who made no secret of his pro-British sympathies, the Hungarian mission was considered safe by British security despite Hungary's shotgun alliance with the Germans.[1] Dr. de Barcza himself was trusted and used by the Foreign Office in a *quid pro quo*. The Legation was allowed considerable latitude despite the war and Hungary's ambiguous position in it.

The confidence was misplaced. The Legation harbored two Abwehr agents who abused the supposedly sacrosanct diplomatic pouch of the mission to get their reports out of England. One of them was an attaché whom I shall call André, a suave, smooth, bridge-playing type, who specialized in political intelligence and society trivia. Far more important and productive was the representative in London of VK-VI, the ubiquitous and obnoxious secret service of the Hungarian General Staff. Here was a den of spies out of all proportion to the size and importance of this little country that loomed so prominently in practically every intrigue of Europe between the two world wars.

Its dean was Major Lóránd Utassy de Ujlak, a career intelligence officer well-versed in all the tricks of the game, in London since 1937 as the Military Attaché.

Major de Utassy's sideline as a German spy originated in Canaris's old alliance with the Hungarians, harking back to April 1935. He made a special trip to Budapest then to reaffirm the standing arrangement Colonel von Bredow had made six years before for "the exchange of information," with Colonel Sándor Homlok, then head of VK-VI, a rabidly pro-Nazi officer.

Shortly before the outbreak of the war, Canaris and Homlok drew the wide-ranging Hungarian secret service closer into the German orbit. The idea was to exploit Hungarian neutrality for the collection of military information at places from which the war would evict the Germans. To this effect Homlok was moved to Berlin as Military Attaché, to work closely with Colonel Piekenbrock, organizing the network of Hungarian service attachés as observers for the Abwehr.[2]

Colonel Homlok was not successful everywhere, for not all these officers were as pro-German as he was, and several of them categorically refused to moonlight as Abwehr agents. Moreover, Homlok's successor at the head of VK-VI, Colonel Istvan de Ujszaszy, viewed this hazardous collaboration with increasingly jaundiced eyes.

But Homlok succeeded in assuring the cooperation of the Military Attaché in London where such an arrangement mattered most.

Working directly for Piekenbrock in Berlin, Utassy covered the British Army through this critical period of its wartime evolution. He rendered his most valuable service during the crisis in the summer of 1940, and throughout the air blitz between September 1940, and March 1941. His damage reports after raids on London, Portsmouth, Birmingham, Liverpool, Glasgow-Clydeside, and Bristol, pleased Goering no end. They characterized the raids as cataclysmic, described the damage as conclusive, and the morale of the people as irreparably broken.

Had Utassy confined himself to written reports sent via the pouch of his Legation, probably he would have been found out only after the war. But his sanguine dispatches made him so popular in the Luftwaffe that the Abwehr was asked to equip Utassy with an Afu set to expedite his reportage. A radio was smuggled to him, and the major set it up in a flat on Grosvenor Square (not far from the house where Eisenhower was to have his headquarters in 1944 while preparing the Normandy invasion).

Instead of speeding up his communications, however, the radio cut short this contact. The story (probably apocryphal in part) was that the G.O.P. monitors had picked up a new signal in April, traced it to the heart of Mayfair, then pinpointed it as emanating from a clandestine radio operated by the Hungarian Military Attaché. Although his diplomatic privileges did not extend to such blatant espionage for a third party, the most the British could have done was to declare Utassy *persona non grata* and demand that the Hungarians recall him.

This, however, would have certainly resulted in the reciprocal expulsion of the British Military Attaché in Budapest, who was also up to his neck in activities bordering on espionage. Instead of moving against Utassy through Foreign Office channels, MI.5 decided to handle the case with the methods of its cruder diplomacy. Security agents burglarized the hideout, removed the radio but left a note telling Utassy where he could pick it up. The colonel got the message. He went to the address given in the note, which turned out to be an apartment MI.5 used as one of its secret quarters, and made a deal. According to this version, he joined the still small fraternity of the "XX" operation, henceforth radioing specially concocted target intelligence designed to divert attention of the Luftwaffe from truly sensitive to certain sacrificial targets.

Even after the fall of France, when the coast of Western Europe was sealed off, there still remained an opening through which travelers could get to England. Ships sailed regularly from Spain and Portugal, Liverpool, and Glasgow. Planes from Lisbon continued to fly on regular schedules twice a week, seaplanes landing at Poole near Bournemouth and land planes at Whitechurch near Bristol.

These routes were utilized as much as possible by the Abwehr, to get its Spanish and Portuguese agents into England, and also several of its R-agents, apparently reputable businessmen and professionals on legitimate errands. Two Americans in particular were frequent travelers on this route—William R. Davis, an independent oil speculator doing considerable business with the German Navy even after the outbreak of the war, and a man named Hermann B. Kolmar, described as "vice president of the Chemical Bank of New York" in the Abwehr's roster of these itinerant agents.

Davis abused his American citizenship and exploited his connections with influential British businessmen and financiers to collect intelligence for the Germans, and then delivered it outward bound to Abwehr contacts in Lisbon and Madrid.

Kolmar on his part journeyed to London, where he claimed to have entry even into 10 Downing Street while Neville Chamberlain was Prime Minister. His mission accomplished, he would go to Holland whence he made a beeline for Germany for *Treffs* with his secret friends, on special travel permits issued to him clandestinely by the Foreign Ministry at the Abwehr's request, to make it unnecessary to use his American passport on these detours.

Debriefed in Berlin, he would be taken back to Rotterdam whence he then returned to the United States. While the Davis contact lasted well into the war, the Kolmar link endured only shortly after the fall of France, when he vanished from the scene, probably because the British became wise to him and barred his return.

The motley assortment of traveling agents was extremely useful, but only for the collection of strategic information—imperishable political, economic, and social intelligence from which the mosaic of conditions in England could be assembled. These were rather independent agents over whom the Abwehr exercised only limited and tenuous control. Even Salman and Utassy enjoyed a certain autonomy. They could not be harnessed to supply pinpoint information on a day-to-day basis—the kind of *tactical* intelligence the Abwehr now needed to backstop the "Sea Lion" planners.

When Colonels Piekenbrock and Lahousen told Canaris candidly that with the collapse of the Irish venture they had practically no tactical spies in Britain, the admiral was shocked. The Abwehr was at the peak of its prestige, he himself at the pinnacle of his career.

A visit to General Franz Halder, Chief of Staff of the Wehrmacht, reassured him. At Halder's headquarters every member of the staff was busy with Sea Lion. Halder now told Canaris that he did not think his planners needed the Abwehr. They agreed that it would be impossible to do now what the Abwehr had done on the eve of the invasion of the Lowlands when it procured masses of tactical intelligence at the last minute. It was already late in June. The planning of Sea Lion had to be completed in about forty-five days. Halder was looking to his own intelligence department, the *Fremde Heere West*, for the data he needed. Its chief, Colonel Ulrich Liss, had assured him that all the necessary information was in hand.

Until only a few months before, *Fremde Heere West* had compiled only the rudimentary intelligence manuals about the British Army: its order of battle, combat tactics, equipment, signal apparatus—all that is usually included in such surveys every intelligence service routinely prepares about every other country. But most of Liss's information had been gained from the enormous mass of loot the Germans had recently captured after the British flight from Dunkirk. It was a windfall of historic proportions. Millions of classified British army and navy papers had been found abandoned in France.

Not the least miraculous, in General Halder's words, were the rapid accomplishments in Colonel Liss's office of a handful of topographic specialists under Major Soltmann in Group III of *Fremde Heere West*. Within a few days map information for the German combat forces began to pour forth in printed or mimeographed publications. On July 18, only twelve days after he had been given the assignment, Major Heidemann presented his volume *The Coastal Defenses of Great Britain*, complete with maps ranging in scale from 1:25,000 to 1:1,000,000, based on the latest aerial reconnaissance. It also contained a number of recent aerial photographs, as well as many pictures clipped from current newspapers and magazines, one showing King George VI and Queen Elizabeth inspecting a camouflaged 12.7-cm. battery; another of Winston Churchill in front of a bunker; still another of Anthony Eden at a barbed-wire entanglement in Dover. The mass of data grew to such proportions that when the collection was issued to the troops on the eve of the invasion, Colonel Liss asked each division intelligence officer to send a pickup truck for the material.

Momentarily Admiral Canaris was relieved that not more was expected of him.

This detachment was to end abruptly. On July 16, he was called to General Alfred Jodl, the chief planner of Sea Lion at the Wehrmacht High Command, and was asked point-blank: "Do you have any agents in England?"

"Yes," Canaris said, somewhat uncertainly. He was thinking of Johnny and his ring of Welsh rebels but knew full well that Jodl was not interested in their kind of spying. Even so, he told Jodl about Johnny, praising the Welshman in glowing terms. Canaris also spoke of other efforts that Ast X of Hamburg and Nest Bremen had underway, building a new network of agents sent to Britain via Spain, Portugal, and Switzerland.

Jodl was not satisfied. That was not what he had in mind, he told Canaris. A brand-new network was needed, or perhaps even several networks, to execute special missions before and during the invasion. The invaders needed spies to guide them in, supply them with hot intelligence on the spot, and act as the eyes and ears of the forces in a hostile country. Canaris had to admit that he had no such people in England.

"Well," Jodl ordered, "get them at once and send them into England as quickly as possible. The landings may take place as early as September 5," Jodl said, "but not later than the 15th. We need these wretched people in England well before then. Your target date is August 15. You must have your spies at their stations by then. Do you think you can do that?"

"Undoubtedly," Canaris replied firmly. But he had his doubts.

The admiral rushed to Hamburg to see what could be done, and found Captain Herbert Wichmann far from encouraging. The outpost did have a small reservoir of S-men who could be mobilized. Unhappily they were newcomers, staid, middle-aged men, most of whom had never seriously expected to be called.

There was still one hope—Lieutenant Johannes Bischoff's group. By then it had three fully developed S-men in England. Bischoff insisted that they were potentially fine, but he begged Canaris not to waste them on missions for which they were not qualified. "We will need them later," he said, "when they will certainly come through with what they can do best. It would be suicidal to employ them on these low-level tactical jobs whose technique is totally alien to them."

This was one of the few occasions when Canaris completely lost his temper. He ordered Wichmann to find a platoon of candidates at once, train them, equip them, and get them into England—*by September 7 at the latest.*

"But that's impossible, Herr Admiral," Wichmann moaned.

"This is one time," Canaris insisted, "when the impossible must be possible."

The moment he left Sophien Terrace to drive back to Berlin, he lost interest in this particular crisis.

In the capital, Canaris saw Goering, who told him casually that he did not think Sea Lion would ever come off, and then went to see Hitler, who, strangely, did not stress it at all. The Fuehrer was absorbed in another operation, called "Felix," the frontal attack on Gibraltar by German troops from Spanish soil. "If," Hitler told Canaris, "for any reason 'Sea Lion' would have to be postponed, I want to seize Gibraltar."

He gave Canaris what amounted to *carte blanche* for Felix, making him practically the supreme commander of the offensive to capture the Rock. Canaris was to gain General Franco's consent for the deployment of German troops, reconnoiter the area in front of Gibraltar, draw up the plans, and lead the attack.

While everybody was busy with Sea Lion, Canaris left for Spain to talk to Franco and survey the approaches to the British bastion.

He returned to Berlin on August 2, and spent the next few days seeing Hitler, Keitel, and Jodl about Felix. His report was so enthusiastically positive that on August 7, General Walter Warlimont, Jodl's top aide, set aside all other work to concentrate on drafting the Felix operations plan.

During these weeks, Canaris busied himself with everything except Sea Lion. He tackled some problems the Abwehr outpost was facing in Afghanistan, difficulties of the Italians in Albania, a plot to overthrow King Carol in Rumania, some clandestine stirrings in North Africa—anything but Sea Lion. Goering was pressing him for more material he needed to prepare his own air blitz that, he assured Canaris, would make Sea Lion superfluous.

In Hamburg, Wichmann was doing what he could to find the men for a mission that came to be called *Himmelfahrt* by the skeptics—a "journey to heaven." Wichmann had assigned the project to Major Hans Dierks and Major Ritter, and two junior members of his staff. Captain Jules Boeckel, a personable blond giant who looked like the idealized skier on the travel posters, was a hospital supplies salesman and had come back from South America to join the Abwehr. Special Officer (*Sonderfuehrer*) Karl-Heinz Kraemer, a very smart, 28-year-old lawyer, had been with the German Embassy in London just before the war. All of them were reserve officers and, except for Dierks, relatively new to the game, inexperienced in its new exigencies, baffled by its imponderables. It was one thing to mastermind espionage in peace, when frontiers were wide open and security was lax, and another thing to manage such operations over the barriers of war.

The special mission of Sea Lion spies was given the cover-name of "Operation Lena," after Colonel Piekenbrock's wife, the popular daughter of a general. Ritter recorded the gist of its mission in his diary:

"Lena agents are not to engage in any routine daily tasks except the transmission of weather reports. They concentrate on topographical reconnaissance in specified areas; on locating beaches suitable for landings and fields where airborne troops and troop and supply carrying gliders can land. They are required to map out such obstacles as road blocks, tank traps, booby traps, barbed wire and other barriers, etc. After the landing, they will act as guides for the troops in coastal areas, since it must be assumed that all waymarks, fingerposts, milestones, etc. will be removed or replaced by misleading signposts."

The big problem was to find in double-quick time as many sturdy, intelligent, brave young men as possible for "Lena," and scatter them all over Britain—those assigned to the south crossing over in boats, those going to the north to be dropped from planes.

Hamburg itself had only two such men on tap, both from Dierks's stable—34-year-old Theodore Druecke, an old friend who had worked for him in Belgium and France and seemed to be ready for greater things, and a dim-witted Swiss named Werner Heinrich Waelti, who had worked for the French consul in Hamburg as a chauffeur and spied on him for the Abwehr.

The branch at Wiesbaden contributed an agent rated high-grade, Jose Rudolf Waldberg, a bilingual Franco-German who had never had a regular job until he signed up with the Abwehr in March 1938. He then distinguished himself, if that is the word, in the crash programs in Belgium and France on the eve of that decisive campaign.

The others had to be located in the flotsam and jetsam where prospective spies supposedly breed. Captain Wichmann detached Lieutenant Colonel Dr. Praetorius, chief of his economic section, to find them. The jovial Praetorius had the innate qualities of a talent scout and was called "the Pied Piper" for his proven ability of luring people into the espionage game. He hit upon the idea of recruiting men in recently occupied countries on the theory that they could easily pass as refugees. He went to Holland and Belgium, then on to camps in Schleswig-Holstein that held Nazi refugees from Scandinavia, young storm troopers who had made themselves unwanted in their own countries. Though most of the fugitives from Denmark had been repatriated, a few were still lingering in the camp together with a handful of Norwegian and Swedish Nazis.

Within a couple of weeks, Dr. Praetorius had lined up scores of candidates, leaving it to Dierks and Ritter to pick the men they wanted. Aside from Druecke, Waelti, and Waldberg, they chose twelve men for what became known as the "Lena Team":

Carl Heinrich Meier, a 24-year-old Dutchman of German birth who had worked in Mussert's Nazi underground in The Hague; a 26-year-old Eurasian-Dutchman named Charles Albert van den Kieboom, a former receptionist and bookkeeper at the YMCA in

Amsterdam; 28-year-old Sjord Pons, Kieboom's friend, recently demobbed as an ambulance driver in the defunct Dutch Army; a Dane and a Swede, industrial draftsmen; five other men who failed so fast and so humiliatingly that their records were expunged in embarrassment; and the mystery man of the team, called "Jan Villen Ter Braak," remembered merely by a name on the death certificate issued by a coroner's jury in Cambridge with the verdict of "apparent suicide."

There was a fifteenth person added to the team in Hamburg, an enigmatic woman in her late twenties, the kind of apparition the young Garbo could have done much more convincingly than her portrayal of the aging, flabby Mata Hari. She was a bewitching Nordic blonde, athletic yet graceful, very feminine, with a brash seductive air about her. She was chic and bright, and had nerves of steel. What was such a woman doing in this random company of vagrants? It was no secret that she was Dierks's mistress. Nor was it a secret that she was being added to the team because Dierks had tired of the affair and was trying to get rid of her. She was called "Vera Erikson," a cover-name devised for her in anticipation of an ambitious espionage project she was to carry out in England, as we shall see.

The team was assembled in two separate groups—Meier, van den Kieboom, Pons, and Waldberg in Brussels, where they were put up in style at two hotels, the Metropole and Les Ambassadeurs. The others were bunched together in Hamburg in the Abwehr's supposedly safe boarding house, the "Klopstock."

Time was of the essence, and the Abwehr could not waste it giving these people the thorough training such a hazardous mission required. After a pleasant week of sightseeing and merrymaking the four men at Brussels were shown how to operate the Afu set, given a cram course in elementary cryptography (their code was based on a simple form of the one-time pad system), and taught "recognition" —how to identify guns, planes, weapons, and army units from the telltale symbols of their insignia.

Only Meier's training went a bit deeper. "They gave me lessons," he later said, "in the structure of the English Army—division and brigades, what they are formed of, what were important things to tell; for instance, where battalions were situated and how we could recognize them. Go to the café and listen, for soldiers always talk. Make friends. There were more things like that; if you see tanks pass, give their exact number if possible; also about troops marching through towns, remember their direction and destination."

Even so, they were not ready on General Jodl's deadline of August 15. It did not matter. Sea Lion had ben postponed. There were even rumors that it might be canceled altogether. But nobody thought it necessary to inform Hamburg.

Late in August, the "Brussels Four" were driven to Boulogne-sur-Mer in the Pas de Calais, and put up in a deserted house near the beach. Then on September 2, zero hour was upon them. They were picked up by Captain Jules Boeckel, who acted as the dispatcher of the Lena spies with the breezy good humour and unctuous servility of a high-class headwaiter, and were taken to the best restaurant in nearby Le Touquet, the elegant seaside resort, for a farewell lunch. There was the usual light-hearted banter that characterized these occasions, and the men were given their final instructions.

Waldberg was "to find out what divisions and brigades were on the south coast, what were the nature óf fortifications, and what were the type of guns, both coast-artillery and anti-aircraft artillery." Meier was to collect information about the economic situation in general and the morale of the people, but also some intelligence, mainly about the RAF. Kieboom and Pons were told to snoop in a more general way: "How the people is living," as Pons put it in his high-school English, "how many soldiers there are, and all the things."

They were to report their observations by wireless between five and eight in the morning, and eight and two at night. These men were as different as their assignments, except for one thing they all had in common—their trouble with the language of the country for which they were heading. Kieboom and Pons spoke very little English and understood it only if it was spoken very slowly. Waldberg, bilingual in German and French, did not know a word of English.

In the late afternoon, they were driven back to Boulogne and boarded a trawler that was to take them on the 35-mile voyage across the Channel. Their luggage was carried aboard for them, as it would have been on an ordinary holiday outing. Their suitcases contained some English-made clothing of which the Abwehr had a wide assortment in its warehouses, a waterproof sack with food and cigarettes, and the bags with the Afu sets, one for Kieboom and Pons, the other for Waldberg and Meier.

Out of Boulogne they waited near Cap d'Albrecht for nightfall. Then they were picked up by a couple of minesweepers that escorted their vessel across the narrow channel, seven miles from the Kent coast. They transferred to dinghies and rowed the last part of the way to their destinations. Kieboom and Pons were heading for the area of Romney Marsh, not far from the grand redoubt, West Hythe, one of the Cinque Ports where the British Army had a School of Small Arms. Waldberg and Meier were going for Dungeness, just fifteen miles to the south, near Lydd. This had been in the path of the Romans going to conquer Britain in A.D. 43.

By four in the morning they were all ashore, and Waldberg, who was the eager beaver of the expedition, rigged up an aerial between a tree and a bush. He got out his wireless set, made contact with Wohldorf, and signaled:

"Arrived safely, document destroyed. English patrol two hundred meters from coast. Beach with brown nets and railway sleepers at a distance of fifty meters. No mines. Few soldiers. Unfinished blockhouse. New road." He signed it, "Waldberg," his real name.

A few hours later, he sent another message, but it was no longer triumphant. It read: "Meier prisoner, English police searching for me, am cornered, situation difficult." And, with a premonition of the inevitable, he concluded with "Long live Germany."

Waldberg had started the sequence of mishaps that led to their doom by becoming thirsty. Since he could not speak English, Meier was to try to fetch him a drink—cider, if possible. Meier made his way to nearby Lydd, found a pub and asked the proprietress for some cider and cigarettes. She immediately recognized Meier as a foreigner, for no Englishman would dare ask for service at nine o'clock in the morning, well before the legal opening hours.

Meier was told to come back later, and when he returned at ten, he found an official waiting for him. At the Lydd police station he conceded that he had just landed from a boat, but insisted that he was a Dutch subject and had come from France to join the new Dutch resistance organization. He said nothing about Waldberg, and the British had to find his partner through their own efforts. It did not take long. Early the next morning, September 4, Waldberg's thirst forced him out of his hideout and straight into the arms of the police.

The downfall of Kieboom and Pons was even more abrupt. They landed near Hythe shortly before 5:00 A.M. on September 3, unaware that a unit of the Somerset Light Infantry was stationed nearby. At five o'clock sharp, Private Tollervey saw the silhouette of a man on the far side of a road. He challenged the figure, and that ended the brief career of another spy. Kieboom came forward and surrendered.

The infantry instantly alerted, at 5:15, Private Chappell discovered the sack with the sausage and chocolate, and a suitcase. Ten minutes later, Lance Corporal Goody caught Pons, quite literally with his pants down, in the act of changing his wet trousers for a dry pair. The Dutchman surrendered before he could finish buttoning up. It was not until the afternoon that the case containing their Afu set was discovered. It was lying on the ground with grass bent over it.

Waldberg and Meier died on the scaffold at Pentonville on December 10, 1940. They were followed by van den Kieboom a week later.

They were not too bright and turned out to be miserable spies. But they were resolute young men with the abundant courage of their hazy political convictions, and went to their deaths bravely. Only Sjord Pons was (or pretended to be) an opportunist. He persuaded the merciful (and gullible) jury that he was really a Dutch patriot and had joined the expedition merely to get out of Holland. He escaped with his life without giving the British anything in exchange for it.[3]

NOTES

1 The Hungarian Legation in Britain endured in the full possession of all the usual diplomatic privileges until December 6, 1941, when at last Britain broke off relations, partly because of reasonable suspicion that the Legation in London was used as a German espionage link.

2 Although a minor power perennially plagued by a shortage of foreign currencies, Hungary could afford nevertheless to station service attachés in the United States, Austria, Bulgaria, Czechoslovakia, Poland, Finland and the Baltic states, in France, Greece, Yugoslavia, Germany, Great Britain, Italy, Rumania, Switzerland, Sweden (from 1938 on), the U.S.S.R., and Turkey—thanks to a special subsidy the Hungarians received from the Germans via the Abwehr.

3 A more dramatic version of the capture of these four men was given by Lieutenant Colonel Oreste Pinto, wartime chief of Dutch counter-espionage in exile, in his book, *Spy-catcher,* claiming that it was he who captured them, practically single-handed.

Chapter 23

Countess Vera, Lady May, and the Duchess of Château-Thierry

*I*N the other splinter group of the Lena Team, Theo Druecke, its oldest member at thirty-four, was regarded as the only agent on this task force who had the experience to make a mission like this succeed.

Son of a distinguished international lawyer of a patrician Hanseatic family, he was a well-educated, sophisticated, attractive large man who had seen quite a bit of the world. He had first met Dierks in Brussels during the mid-Thirties; they had become close friends and then colleagues in espionage. Druecke performed admirably in Belgium. His wide circle of posh friends produced a number of useful contacts for Dierks, including an agent who spied on King Leopold and the royal family.

A habitué of the hottest night spots of Europe, where anybody who would buy him a drink immediately became his boon companion, Druecke once fell in with an international gang counterfeiting American one-hundred dollar bills. He put them in touch with Ritter and Dierks and they bought a supply of the excellent forgeries to finance several of their operations.

It was Druecke, too, who had found Vera, called "the Countess" during one of his missions to France. He bumped into her in a sleazy nightclub near Place Pigalle in time to rescue her from a dreadful liaison when her lover, a South American gigolo, stabbed her in the chest in true Apache fashion. He took her to Brussels and promptly lost her to Dierks who had an irresistible appeal to women despite his coarse exterior and maimed face. But Druecke persisted in his blighted love, following her to Hamburg when Dierks was transferred to Ast X, and took her along.

The triangle flourished with the consent of all concerned, until

243

Dierks, who never could stay with any of his mistresses very long, felt a discomfort in an affair that was assuming the kind of wedded bliss he so loathed. To break it up, he asked to be sent on a mission on which the woman could not accompany him, but the girl, who spoke English quite well, disconsolate at losing Dierks, volunteered as one of the Sea Lion spies. It was then, in order to stay with her, that Druecke also asked to be sent on Sea Lion, along with a fellow named Waelti.

During their working hours while preparing for the mission, Captain Jules Boeckel explained to his wards the fine points of the profession (of which he himself did not know too much) in informal lectures at the Klopstock boarding house. He took them singly or in pairs on field trips in his car, to teach them such technical details as map reading, visual observation, measurement of distances, recognition of targets. In the brief time available before their departure they were also taught the art of a new coding system, and whatever they could learn about operating a wireless set.

Otherwise their period of incubation was little more than a big binge. It almost seemed as if Hamburg had realized that Druecke and his colleagues were doomed and was trying to make amends by giving them one last good time on the town. Their evenings were spent in excursions to nightclubs, beerhalls, and the bordellos of the Reperbahn. At these carousings, the secret agents appeared in full view, chaperoned by companions easily identifiable as officers of the Abwehr.

The Druecke group was scheduled to leave Hamburg on September 3. Major Dierks arranged a farewell party that promised to be especially gay. He took his beautiful mistress and her two companions to the restaurant of the Hotel Reichshof for dinner, and then, for more drinks, to Jacobs, an elegant wine restaurant that was one of the favorite hangouts of the Abwehr crowd. The party became a wild shindig.

Plans called for the team to go to the airport straight from the restaurant to catch a plane to Stavanger in Norway where, at dawn, they were to board a seaplane of the X Luftwaffe Corps to fly to their point of landing off Banff in Scotland. Shortly after midnight they staggered to the BMW convertible that was parked in front of the bar. Dierks drove, with uncertain hands and leaden eyes.

It was a dark night with heavy clouds, the streets slippery from a steady drizzle. Dierks was taking the car down the broad Elbchaussee when Druecke cried out: "Left, Hans, we've got to turn left here!" Dierks tore the wheel to the left, the car jerked sideways on two wheels, plunged against the curb, bounced back and, careening out of control for some twenty yards, turned over with a crash of metal and the sound of tearing from the fabric top.

Druecke was the first to climb out of the wreckage. He crawled to a phone booth and called the police. When the squad cars and the ambulance arrived, they found Druecke and Waelti sitting numbly by the wrecked little car. The woman was weeping uncontrollably as she bent over her lover, stretched out in the gutter, his blood mingling with the rainwater. Dierks was dead. The party was over.

The mission was not canceled. It could not be. These spies were needed in England, and orders came from Berlin that the show must go on with Druecke to take over as leader. He assumed his new responsibilities with a weird exhiliration. His rival was no longer obstructing his path to Vera. Druecke was now looking forward to the perilous journey with the bloodshot eyes of a desperate lover, hoping to gain the girl at last, even if it had to be on a secret mission.

He spent his days in a trance, as if waiting for a tryst, while Vera sank ever deeper in her gloom of mourning, determined more than ever, she assured Captain Boeckel, to go on the ill-starred mission— to avenge, as she put it, the death of her hero.

Colonel Lahousen now ordered the team to leave Hamburg on September 21 on the changed timetable. Accompanied by Boeckel in a Luftwaffe transport, they flew to Norway and were turned over to a Norwegian Nazi named Andersen, an Abwehr dispatcher. Only now, on the very eve of their departure, were they given their equipment. "I have orders from Berlin," Andersen told them, "that under no circumstances must you travel by train. You must move on bicycles."

This was a strange second thought on Berlin's part, not a simple one to act upon. Lahousen feared that the broken English of these men would arouse suspicion if they traveled by train. He ordered Andersen to procure three British bicycles for the mission. This seemed an impossible assignment, but Andersen had the bright idea of visiting the deserted British Consulate at Stavanger, and, sure enough, found three bicycles in the cellar of the deserted building. As luck willed it, they were of the collapsible kind, ideal for the mission.

At dawn on September 30, the trio boarded a seaplane and flew to a point in the North Sea off the rolling fertile Banffshire coast, the scene of many battles between the Scots and the much earlier Norse invaders. When they transferred to a rubber dinghy in which they had to row ashore, they dropped their precious bikes irretrievably into the water. There were other problems. They had to wade ashore because the water proved too shallow even for their rubber boat. The fact that they had to set wet feet on Scottish soil was to hasten their downfall.

On land they did not have the faintest idea where they were. Since they were to operate independently, they decided to split up and grope their separate ways to some inhabited places. Following his luminous compass, Waelti walked to a nearby whistle-stop, then waited for a train that took him to Edinburgh.

Druecke and the Countess made their way to another small station and sat down in the waiting room. When the ticket booth opened at 7:30 A.M., Vera stepped up to the window and asked the clerk: "What's the name of this station?"

"Port Gordon, madam," the man said. Druecke then went to a timetable posted on the wall, ran his finger down the column of stations, and told Vera to buy two tickets to Forres (the legendary place in Morayshire where Macbeth was supposed to have murdered Duncan).

It was a very odd show—a couple of strangers who obviously did not know where they were and did not care where they were going. The stationmaster noticed that though this was a dry morning, the man's trousers and the woman's stockings were wet. And though the woman's English sounded faultless, the few words the man had spoken were heavily accented.

The clerk put in a call and soon an officer arrived, Constable Grieve from the Port Gordon constabulary. "Could I see your national registration identity cards?" he asked them, and Druecke produced his, made out in the name of "François de Deeker," as was his passport.

"He's Belgian," the woman intervened. "I'm Danish."

But the number "1" in the year "1940" on the British ID card was written with a long tail, the way no Englishman would write it. Constable Grieve had enough. He asked them to go with him to the police station where he was sure, he told them, Inspector Simpson, his superior, would like to ask a few questions.

Simpson did more. He searched Druecke and found in his overcoat pocket nineteen rounds of revolver ammunition, a torch marked "Made in Bohemia," £327 in English notes, a piece of German sausage, and the third-class ticket he had just bought for Forres. He then asked him to open his suitcase. Druecke refused. Simpson told Grieve to force it open, and there he found a Mauser pistol with six rounds in its magazine, two cardboard discs (which was the new coding device), a list of bomber and fighter stations in the Eastern Counties, a sheet of graph paper, and a complete Afu set.

"I'm sorry," the Inspector said quite formally and politely, "but I have to take you into custody."

In the meantime, Waelti finally managed to reach Edinburgh. He arrived at five o'clock in the afternoon, checked his baggage, and went to get a haircut and see a movie. He had time on his hands. He was to meet his contact—a man in a gray flannel suit with a scar on his forehead—the following morning at Victoria Station in London.

While Waelti was at the cinema, Inspector Sutherland of the Edinburgh Special Branch picked up his trail. He opened the suitcase left by the young Swiss in the baggage room and found in them a complete espionage laboratory. When Waelti returned to pick up the suitcase, he suddenly felt a big man on either side of him; one of them caught his hand as it was moving quickly toward his hip pocket. It was evident that Waelti would have been willing to fight for his life. As it was, he had to wait for the end of the venture until August 1941, when he was walked to the scaffold in Wandsworth Prison, accompanied by his partner in misfortune, Theodore Druecke.

After Captain Boeckel had returned from Stavanger with the good news that the seaplane had landed the trio safely off the Banffshire coast, Hamburg sat out the customary eight-day waiting period for word from Druecke and Waelti, hoping that all was well. Nothing was heard from them for several weeks, when a brief item in a Zurich newspaper cleared up part of the mystery. According to a dispatch from London, a Swiss citizen had been arrested in Scotland and confessed that he was a German spy. Poor Waelti could not make it! But how about Druecke and the Countess?

Exceptional efforts were undertaken to track them down in the enemy country. Hamburg went so far as to parachute a special agent to look for them. From his report, virtually the only one he would ever send, Ritter then learned what he still believes to be the true account of Theo Druecke's odyssey to the scaffold.

As Ritter recorded the story in his diary, Theo had succeeded in reaching Birmingham. There as he was boarding a train for London, he was challenged by security agents. Crying, "They'll never get me alive!" Druecke drew his Mauser, killed one of the agents, wounded the other, then tried to commit suicide with the last bullet in the magazine. But he merely wounded himself.

Nursed back to health in a prison hospital, he was tried, sentenced to death, and hanged. "He was a brave man," Ritter quoted a British intelligence officer who had told him after the war: "We had to execute him. After all, he had killed one of our chaps."

And the Countess?

"She vanished without a trace," Ritter wrote tersely in his diary.

The mystery of Vera's fate was compounded by a cryptic remark of Sir William (later Lord) Jowitt, the Solicitor-General in the Churchill government who prosecuted the Druecke-Waelti case. "It was decided," he wrote after the war, "to take no proceedings against Madame Erikson. I have no doubt that she was detained here during the war, and it may be that she was able to be of some use to our authorities."

Who was this strange woman? Why was she never tried?

What happened to her after the incident in the Port Gordon police station?

Beyond doubt, she was the most shadowy figure of her sex in a war that produced such towering female agents as Violet Szabo, Odette Sansom, Christine Granville, Hannah Szenes, Noor Inayat Khan, and the slippery "Cat," Mathilde Carré.

When her name came up in talks with my new friends of the old Abwehr in Hamburg, invariably a lot of rolling of the eyes accompanied the conversation. She was obviously far more celebrated in these circles for her exquisite good looks and sex appeal than for her prowess in espionage. I could detect a lingering envy of Dierks for having had her as a bonus, and a nostalgia for one's younger days when such an apparition would bring a touch of romance into the humdrum life of the spymasters. Her youth and beauty retained in their collective memory nothing but pleasant reminiscences.

They knew her or called her by different names—"Vera" and "Viola" and "the Countess." Although neither Ritter nor Boeckel knew her real family name, they professed to be quite familiar with her past, extremely hectic and dramatic as it was, even for a woman who seemed to forever commute between the world's oldest and second oldest professions.

Although romantically she was Dierks's woman, professionally she belonged to Major Ritter. She was slated to play a prominent role in his schemes until her trail suddenly disappeared at the little Scottish railroad station.

In actual fact, she was Vera de Witte, the daughter of a Baltic aristocrat and Tsarist naval officer, who died in action with the White Russian forces while fighting the Bolsheviks.[1] Vera was six years old at the time of her father's death. Her mother managed to escape to Latvia with her little daughter and son, and then to Copenhagen, where she made her new home, eking out a living as a language teacher and interpreter.

She gave her children the best education. The son became a Danish subject, chose the navy as a career, rising to the rank of lieutenant commander, and was assigned to the Court as a *Kammerjunker*, a member of the King's bodyguard.

But he also had a secret career. His unquenchable hatred of the Bolsheviks who murdered his father drove him to the far right in his politics. He joined the underground of Fritz Clausen's notorious Danish Nazi Party and eventually became a leader of its clandestine storm troops.

Vera moved in the opposite direction.

While she was still in finishing school she became infatuated with a much older Frenchman, and when her mother refused to permit her to marry him, they eloped. Her family heard nothing from her for years afterward, until she was living in Paris. Abandoned by her French lover, she was left to the not inconsiderable resources of a beautiful and charming young woman with a seductive air. But somehow Vera felt more comfortable in the gutter than in the drawing rooms. She drifted from bed to bed, danced in shabby cabarets, and lived with a succession of squalid swains in the wretched poverty of the Montparnasse slums.

One of the men she had picked up on this sordid merry-go-round made a living as an Apache dancer in a basement café on rue de Champollion, but was in fact a political agent of the Soviet secret police, spying on White Russians in France. Vera, who was as undiscerning in her politics as she was in her liaisons, became a GPU agent under her friend's tutelage. It was this double-barrelled pimp who tried to kill her during one of their quarrels when Theo Druecke found Vera and took her to Brussels.

In the spring of 1938 she was twenty-six years old, and Dierks was in his forties, but she always had a weakness for big, strong, homely older men. Life now confronted him with a strange dilemma. He was devoted to her with perhaps more sincere passion than he had ever felt before, and it was obvious that this real-life *femme fatale*, who had a special knack for ensnaring men and drawing their innermost secrets from them, was too good to be wasted on a selfish love affair.

He arranged for her to move to England where she obtained a job as a lady's companion in the household of a prominent politician, a vantage point from which she could procure information of interest to Dierks.

At this time her brother discovered not only that she was in England, but that she was there as a German spy. On May 8, 1939, he put on his dress uniform and made a call at the German Legation in Copenhagen, demanding to be taken to the Minister, Herr von Renthe-Fink. Alone with the envoy, he revealed that he was a leader of the Danish Nazis' paramilitary formations, and asked the

Minister to intervene in a delicate family matter of grave political implications.

"My sister," he said, "was once a GPU agent, but she reformed and had been won over to work for the anti-Komintern. Now, however, it seems that the German secret service is using her, not merely in the struggle against the Communists, but also as a secret agent against England."

If this were to become known, he said, his sister would be in danger for her life from her former Bolshevik comrades, and he himself would forfeit his honor and reputation in Denmark. This would do irreparable damage to the Danish Nazi party.

"I implore your Excellency," he said solemnly to the startled envoy, "to use your influence to effect the immediate release of my sister from the German secret service."

"What you're telling me," Herr von Renthe-Fink told him, "sounds rather like the trite plot of some mystery thriller. If your sister really worked for the anti-Komintern, I cannot see how the German secret service could have had anything to do with her activities. I doubt very much that the Legation will be able to intervene in this muddy matter."

No sooner had the distraught officer left his office than the Minister wrote to the Foreign Ministry which in turn promptly queried the Abwehr. In an answer dated May 16, Herr von Renthe-Fink was advised that it was true that Vera had "certain connections with our friends" (the Foreign Ministry's euphemism for the Abwehr). "Arrangements are being made to discontinue them in view of the embarrassment they might cause her brother."

Dierks was instructed to recall Vera from London. In Hamburg she became his pampered mistress, refusing to take any of the "civilian" jobs Dierks was lining up for her to keep her occupied and also to lighten the financial burden she was becoming to him. He put her up in a flat on Papenhuder Street in the posh Alster district of the city, where she entertained Dierks's friends and acted once in a while as a decoy for strangers in whom her lover had a professional interest. Otherwise she was kept out of the secret service. The beautiful young woman was immensely popular on Sophien Terrace, a sort of mascot of the Hamburg branch, privy to many of its secrets freely discussed in her presence.

Occasionally her eager interest in their business alarmed Ritter. He would warn Dierks that, who knows, the Countess might be an *agent provocateur* after all, planted on his neck by the British secret service. Dierks dismissed the suspicion indignantly. "It's her love for me," he said, "that makes her so wrapped up in our affairs, because she knows that the Abwehr means so much to me."

When the war broke out in September 1939, a niche was found at last for the Countess in one of the Abwehr's meandering projects, the origins of which harked back to 1937.

Shortly after Ritter had returned from his successful sojourn in the United States, a businessman friend who acted as one of his scouts introduced him to an interesting prospect. She was a gay divorcée in her mid-forties, May Erikson by name, a handsome, voluptuous woman with dark hair and sparkling brown eyes, obviously fond of a good time.

There were several qualifications in her background that recommended her instantly to Ritter. A German by birth, she had been married to a Swede and still had a foothold in Stockholm where her two children lived and where she maintained a circle of friends, including a retired colonel of the Swedish army. More important, she was now housekeeper for a British captain of the Naval Air Arm, living in his house at Grimsby.

After their first meeting in the friend's house, Ritter invited Madame Erikson to an afternoon of coffee and cakes at the Café Huebner, a famed haven on Post Street of single women in search of a date. Learning that her feelings for her native land were still as strong as ever and sensing that she would be willing to aid the cause of the Fatherland, as it was usually put on such occasions, Ritter popped the question—would she be interested in working for the Abwehr?

She seemed to be thrilled and Ritter made plans for her. She could, at the house of her British employer, at least come by some intelligence. But he was loath to jeopardize her with further active involvement in direct espionage. He would rather use her as a mail drop for his producing agents in England (Johnny had just joined his stable). They could send their letters meant for Ritter to her in Grimsby, a truly safe and innocuous address. She would then forward them to her Stockholm address whence they would be sent on to one or another of Ritter's cover-boxes in Hamburg.

Major Ritter accompanied her to Stockholm, to explore the setup there, and was delighted to find that her friend, the Swedish colonel, was also willing to act as a relay station for this stealthy correspondence. He also arranged for the legal secretary in New York he had just recruited as a go-between, to send her mail to the colonel in Sweden, as safe a mail drop as he could wish.

Entered in Ritter's roster as "Lady May," Mrs. Erikson returned to Grimsby, now a German spy, another fixture in Ritter's growing network in England.

She would, from time to time, send him information she could safely pick up in the captain's household, but she functioned mostly as a conveyor belt for others.

In 1938, Ritter met Lady May twice in Stockholm for debriefing *Treffs*, and then she came to Hamburg, accompanied by a little old lady she introduced to Ritter as one of her best friends in England who needed help. She was called Duchess Montabelli di Condo[2] whose noble Italian husband had died long before, leaving her nothing but his formidable name and some badly encumbered real estate in Bavaria. The Duchess had confided to Mrs. Erikson that she was in danger of losing the property because she could not keep up the mortgage payments on it, and Lady May suggested that a friend she had in Germany could probably help her in her plight. Mrs. Erikson told Ritter that the Duchess—a Scotch-loving merry old widow with ideas and manners much younger than her years—was a popular figure in the best English society, with many interesting and influential friends. When Ritter went with her to Munich to straighten out her real estate, the Duchess bluntly confirmed what Lady May had merely hinted.

"If you help me here," she told Ritter with a suggestive twinkle in her eyes, "I'll help you over there."

Convinced by so blunt an approach that the Duchess was a plant, Ritter decided to test her before he would take her into the fold. Yet the most superficial screening apparently convinced him of her *bona fides*. "I let her have," Ritter said later, "some information that could have been useful to our competitor. But it was conspicuously doctored material, all bad stuff. The fact that she never asked me for anything better persuaded me that she was no double agent."

Now the Duchess, too, was entered on the roster, under the cover-name of "Duchess of Château-Thierry," after the focal point in the second Marne battle in which Ritter had had his baptism of fire in 1918.

For some time, Ritter used the Duchess perfunctorily. In 1939, he hit upon a scheme in which, he thought, the vivacious little dowager could play an interesting part. The idea had been floating about in the German secret service ever since the formidable Wilhelm Stieber, Bismarck's secret police chief, had first thought of it. In Berlin Stieber maintained a place called the "Green House," a glorified bordello where any imaginable vice and perversion could be arranged for special guests. In this way Stieber could acquire secret information by blackmail.

Nikolaus Ritter was no Stieber. He was a prudish man with Victorian morals, always correct and decorous even in the conduct of intelligence gathering. He would have been congenitally incapable of even thinking of "green houses" on the old pattern. What he had in mind was "a salon" or "a teahouse," as he called them, which the Duchess could open in London with funds supplied by the Abwehr, to entertain her fine-feathered friends. At such a listening post, stray information could be picked up through the small talk of people "in the know."

He sent word to the Duchess via Lady May that he would like to see her "with a proposition," and they met in The Hague, in a café in Korte Vorhout near the Hotel des Indes. The Duchess seemed enchanted by the idea. She told Ritter that she would explore the project and report back to him as soon as she made the arrangements.

She returned to the café in The Hague a few months later, to let Ritter know that all had been arranged. She was opening "a tea salon" in Mayfair "for our better type people," she said, "politicians, scientists, writers, actors," then, with that suggestive twinkle in her eyes, "especially senior officers of the RAF."

But, she said, she would need someone—"a beautiful young girl" —to act as her hostess. "You know what I have in mind," she said, "somebody gay and spicy who would charm the pants off those bloody old buzzards, even willing to sleep with some of them once in a while, if the occasion warranted it."

It sounded terrific! A beautiful girl? How about the Countess?

The Duchess now met Vera.

It was strange that she should have been permitted to meet her, for they were both in the agent category, both assigned to England, and, according to the rules of the game, should have been kept apart. Each secret service has its own methods for arranging meetings with its classified personnel. The GRU and NKVD prefer to have it *al-fresco*, meeting on secluded benches in deserted parks. The Americans set up seemingly chance encounters in crowded public places like railroad stations and museums during their busiest hours. The British hire little flats for their rendezvous.

The Germans, too, held their *Treffs* on dummy business premises maintained for this purpose. But they had a custom quite bizarre in this shadowy world. Whenever the hush-hush part of such *Treffs* was over at these safe havens, Ritter and his colleagues would violate the cardinal rule in the good book of espionage. Animated by a hospitable streak in the German character, they would take their supposedly furtive friends to restaurants, cafés or nightclubs, where they would be joined by other members of the Abwehr to make their entertainment so much merrier.

It was on such an indiscreet divertissement that the Duchess and

Lady May met the Countess—and privately, too, on the usual departures of ladies to the powder room where Ritter could neither follow them nor eavesdrop on their conversations.

Like everybody else, the Duchess was captivated by the Countess.

"She would be ideal, of course," she now told Ritter. "But do you think she would be willing to leave Dieter," the name by which she knew Dierks, "for a little old thing like me?"

"I think I might be able to persuade her," Ritter said.

Shortly after, the war broke out and it seemed that the "tea salon" would be one of its first victims. Ritter not only refused to abandon it, but mused that it would be more important than ever. In a coded exchange of letters via the Swedish colonel, he ascertained from Lady May that the Duchess was willing—but could the Countess still come to London? Obviously they needed somebody who was already privy to the arrangements because they could not hire just any girl from the nearest employment bureau for such a delicate job.

This was when Vera was brought back into the Abwehr, but not as simply as Ritter thought. Her break with Dierks hit her harder than it seemed at first. After their stormiest sessions at which their separation was made final, she tried to commit suicide by taking barbiturates.

When she recovered from the attempt, she seemed a quite different person, or rather the old Vera again—light-hearted, prankish, skittish, flirtatious and irascible, apparently raring to return to her old life of whimsey and fun.

It was all arranged. Vera "Erikson" posing as a niece of Lady May Erikson was to reach Britain from Norway, escaping from the Nazis as so many other young people were after the occupation.

A special task force was assembled for the venture. Druecke was to be in charge, to pick up whatever intelligence she collected and relay it to Hamburg on his Afu set, and also to forward to her Ritter's queries and instructions.

This was how, on the morning of September 30, 1940, she happened to be at the police station at Port Gordon, watching impassively as her traveling companion was taken into custody. Even before Druecke was out of the room and her turn would come, she suddenly asked the Inspector: "Could I have a word with you privately?"

When they were alone, she showed Simpson a scrap of paper on which was written Lady May's address. "Your authorities know all about this," she said. "Please see to it that I am taken to Grimsby as quickly as possible. That is all I can tell you."

Inspector Simpson called Special Branch in Scotland Yard, and they came for her and took her with them, so that she might be able, as Lord Jowitt put it later, "to be of some use to our authorities."

Major Ritter's three ladies figured admirably in a masterpiece of what is called "penetration" in the lingo of secret services. Soon after Lady May had agreed to work for the Abwehr, another neatly laid espionage project left its single track and became a game which moved on parallel lines.

On her return from the Continent in December 1937, Mrs. Erikson, as "Lady May" was really called, confided her experience in Hamburg to her employers and the authorities were notified. It was really as simple as that.

Mrs. Erikson was asked to accept Ritter's invitation and keep the line open for somebody who could widen the breach. The "Duchess" was chosen. She was one of the veteran executives of British security whose connection with this secret world was known only to a handful of insiders. A legend was concocted for her—the long-dead Italian nobleman and that over-mortaged Bavarian real estate.

Afterward everything proceeded—according to *both* plans.

Vera, too, was playing the game.

When she was in London in 1938–39 working for Dierks, she had been reached by British authorities and agreed almost avidly to work against them from behind her anti-Komintern cover.

However, her overriding infatuation with Hans Dierks seemed to change everything. She remained steadfastly loyal to him, both in their personal and professional relations—until that big scene in her apartment in Hamburg, when Dierks told her that he had made his choice between her and the Abwehr, and was resolved to terminate their affair.

Her attempted suicide was the big crisis of this conflict. But by the time she returned from the nursing home, she had her mind made up.

So when the Countess went to Scotland, Vera was returning home.

NOTES

1 Although Vera was later identified by her family name in the Abwehr papers, I prefer to refer to her as "Vera de Witte," the pseudonym by which she became known after the war when the mystery of her life and of her wartime adventure first began to intrigue her devotees.

2 This was not the name she used, but I do not feel at liberty to disclose the one by which she went in this encounter.

Chapter 24

The Round of the Hound

*H*ANS Hansen never went to college and though he wanted to become an engineer, he had to be satisfied as an industrial draftsman. He had plenty of native intelligence, was bright and well-read, and had the integrity and courage of his convictions.

In Denmark, Hans was a Nazi where such an affiliation was considered an aberration. He was a storm trooper in his native Jutland, performing all sorts of illegal acts for the Party, for which he was persecuted until he had to flee to Germany.

Now that Denmark had been occupied, he could have gone home to his hometown of Skaerbaek to strut and gloat with the rest of the Danish Nazis. But the big battles of the war were still to come and the issue would be decided by the conquest of England; he decided to stay in the fight by becoming a German spy and going to Britain ahead of the Wehrmacht.

"Hans Hansen" may or may not have been his real name. I saw him called "Schmidt-Hansen" and "Schmidt" in the documents of his case, but they could also have been nothing but cover-names. In this game, such things as genuine or forged passports with real or phony names hardly matter. He is remembered best by two unorthodox designations—one a mere number, "3725," by which he was carried in the Abwehr's register; the other was "Tate," as he was known to the British.

He was found by Dr. Praetorius when the Abwehr's crack talent scout combed the camps of displaced Scandinavian Nazis in Schleswig-Holstein for grist for the German spy mill. Another young man the "Pied Piper" brought back to Hamburg was variously called Jorgen "Bjoernson" and Axel "Hilberg," described as either a Swede or a

Finn. To the Abwehr he was "3719." The British called him "Summer." He was, in fact, Goesta Caroli, a Swede.

Hansen's father and Caroli's mother were Germans by birth. Their sons opted for Germany when the Nazis took over and such allegiances became a matter of emotional decision rather than national reality.

We do not know much about their vital statistics. Hansen was twenty-six years old, slim and dark blond with a sturdy frame, his face, as his Abwehr sheet put it, "fine and energetic, all his features and manners testifying to a good upbringing." Caroli, a mechanic by trade, was a year older and a little taller, with a coarser face marred by a long, broad nose. He had a pair of "clear, laughing eyes," as his Abwehr biographer noted, "that inspired confidence in him."

Praetorius did not bother to probe further. He was satisfied that they were trustworthy and healthy and apparently brave young men. It came as a surprise when it came out that both spoke English well. They had a taciturn streak and did not like to discuss their past, for fear, perhaps, of embarrassing parents who did not share their unquestioning allegiance to Hitler.

By the time we meet them in the Abwehr papers, they were already in Hamburg, living in Fräulein Friede's Klopstock boarding house, and undergoing their training under the genial Captain Boeckel. There were others at the Klopstock, but somehow Hansen and Caroli enjoyed special treatment. By their appearance, diligence, enthusiasm, and patience, they were the best men caught in Dr. Praetorius's baited trap.

They belonged to that segment of the Lena Team consigned to the big triangle between Birmingham, London, and Bristol. They would be dropped to a pinpoint chosen by Major Ritter, who was in command of the airborne spies. Although agents were supposed to "go in" singly, Ritter decided to pair the Dane and the Swede, and drop them together to work as a team within the Lena Team. They became inseparable. It was obvious that Hansen had the brain and Caroli had the brawn, an ideal combination.

It was now late July. Sea Lion was scheduled to jump off on September 5. Word had just been received from Admiral Canaris that Ritter was chosen to be chief of the soon-to-be-established Abwehr branch in England, both during the invasion and after the occupation. He was scheduled to "go in" with the second wave on September 6, to take over on the spot the management of all Abwehr operations, including the command and control of men like Hansen and Caroli.

Their hasty training completed, their farewell entertainment was quite a bit more joyous than the others. When Captain Boeckel was through with their technical initiation, Ritter took them personally on the grand tour. Its high point was in Paris where he lodged them in the Hotel Lutaetia, the Abwehr's brand-new headquarters at the corner of Raspail and Rue de Sevres, a big baroque, balconied building on the Left Bank.

In the morning, he escorted them to the roof, where they tried out their Afu sets by contacting Wohldorf. At night he let them roam as they pleased—at the "Sphinx," the city's plushest bordello that was doing land-office business with the conquerors, and with *"les poules"* on the Rue Blondel. Then on to Brussels, staying in style at the Metropole, for final briefings with Colonel Dischler and Major Lebewohl, and finally to the airfield at Rennes, where Captain Gartenfeld was waiting for them with his black-coated Heinkel. Then they were off.

It was September 3, 1940. The Abwehr's most successful mission, which was to endure for almost five years, was on.

Hansen and Caroli came down in a grove near Salisbury, the old county town of Wiltshire, whose thirteenth-century cathedral with its high spire served as a landmark for Captain Gartenfeld. Their arrival was marred by a mishap. Hansen broke his ankle on the landing, but the resourceful Caroli managed to get him to a doctor who put him in a cast, delaying the start of the mission only slightly.

Hansen was soon on his way, broken ankle notwithstanding. Three days after landfall, even while he was still making his way to London, he put on the air his first business signal. "Roads blocked with refugees. Most of them look Jewish."

The story of his mission was then written in more than a thousand messages he sent to the Abwehr during the war. They also formed his memoirs of these years, his confessions—salty, no-nonsense messages of nothing but hard facts when reporting intelligence, mixed with topical biographical notes from time to time, occasional chitchat, and angry reproaches abounding in the German versions of the English four-letter words (*Scheisse* being one of Hansen's favorite expletives) when the Abwehr was not reciprocating his efficiency in kind, was tardy in meeting his demands for money, or was giving him "inane tasks."

Businesslike: "Personal observation: new barrage balloons between Newport and Cardiff, and at Peterborough to protect Whitehead Torpedo factory making Diesel engines for submarines."

Petulant: "You never let me know what you think of my work. An occasional pat on the back would be welcome. After all I am only human."

Domesticated: "I have just become father of a seven-pound son."

Indignant (when he was once asked to radio to the Abwehr the quality and price of a loaf of bread, and how it tasted): "Don't you have anything more important to ask? It tastes all right."

Furious: "What is delaying the man with the promised money? I am beginning to think that you are full of shit."

On his regular transmission of September 21, 1944, which was a kind of personal millennium for him, this brash young man was uncharacteristically sentimental and solemn. "On the occasion of this," he signaled, "my one-thousandth message, I beg to ask you to convey to our Fuehrer my humble greetings and ardent wishes for a speedy victorious termination of the war."

Shortly afterward he was his old frivolous self. He had struck up an apparently intimate friendship with a girl named Mary who happened to be one of the secretaries at invasion headquarters in Norfolk House, and was feeding him inside information about preparations for D-Day. "Well," he signaled in between, "what do you think of Mary? Isn't she quite a gal?"

And he was vulgar again, when asked to investigate the quality of clothing the British people could buy on their meager ration cards. "You can kiss my arse," he radioed, using up twenty precious letters, thus quoting, in the original German, of course, Goethe's famed oath from *Goetz von Berlichingen.*

He was "the rare bird," wrote Gilles Perrault, "that evaded the snares of the counterespionage for four years, as the spy who had carried the policy of integration to the point of marrying an English-woman and becoming the father of a British subject."

He figures prominently in all informed annals of espionage in World War II, as the super-spy who accomplished the impossible— the perfect, ideal, incomparable, unsurpassable secret agent. He was the prototype of the dream-spy "who spent five happy and, to himself profitable years in Britain from 1940 to 1945," and could truthfully write the still-to-be-published book, *The Years I Spent Spying in England.*

In his excellent anthology *The Great Spies*, Charles Franklin described him as the outstanding German spy in England "throughout" the Second World War. "He got a cover job on a farm," Franklin wrote, "where he fell in love with the farmer's daughter and married her. In between his busy domestic and agricultural life he made valuable investigations into the military preparations for the Canadian Dieppe raid and D-Day, details of which he reported accurately to Hamburg . . . faithful to his own side right to the bitterness of defeat."

As far as the Abwehr was concerned, he was their pet, their pride, their miracle man. Ritter wrote of him in his notes: "Soon after his arrival, Hansen was on the job and henceforth worked exceptionally well. Aside from regularly sending us weather reports, he radioed his observations of airfields and other strategic targets, all of which was rated 'extremely valuable' by the competent authorities in Berlin."

In the sixth week of the mission, Ritter recommended him for the Iron Cross First Class, and Hansen became the first spy in the field to be awarded the coveted decoration comparable to our Distinguished Service Medal. Poor Caroli was filed and forgotten by the Abwehr when he had to check out in December, 1940. But Hansen continued to prosper and flourish.

On the occasion of that one-thousandth signal, in which he sent the Fuehrer his best wishes, the astounded Abwehr went to exceptional lengths to establish his *bona fides*. A special committee was formed under the chairmanship of a colonel named Maurer, regarded as the most scrupulous and skeptical judge of these cases, composed of the most hard-boiled intelligence specialists, communications experts, even a psychiatrist. Their verdict was that the man sending those incredible signals was, indeed, Hans Hansen, and that he was doing fine. Captain Wichmann, head of the Hamburg branch, then submitted his case to Admiral Canaris and recommended him for the German Cross in Gold.

Hansen brought a lot of satisfaction and pleasure, but not only to the Abwehr.

He was also the pride and joy of MI.5, the star performer of its Double-Cross game—practically from the day of his arrival in England.

The morning after the drop, Captain Gartenfeld reported to Major Ritter that, so far as he was able to observe it, all went well. They flew low over the English Channel to evade the radar, then climbed to an altitude of 20,000 feet. The night was perfect for such a mission. Near the target they came down to 3,000 feet, throttled the engines, then descended to 450 feet for the drop.

Caroli was the first to go. Hansen seemed to be hesitant at the last moment, but only briefly. Gartenfeld was in a hurry. "What are you waiting for, man?" he yelled to him. "Let's go!" By then Hansen, too, was gone, floating down through the darkness. "I saw both parachutes open," Gartenfeld told Ritter. "I am sure they've made it."

Caroli landed in a small clearing just outside the grove. But Hansen fell into a tree, and when he cut himself off the parachute, dropped to the ground.

"Are you all right?" Caroli asked him.

"I don't think so," Hansen growled. *"Schoene Scheisse.* I think I've broken my ankle."

Caroli was stunned. This was something *they* had not prepared them for. "What are we supposed to do now?"

"You go on, Goesta, and leave me here," his companion said. "Somebody will find me and perhaps I'll be able to work things out. I don't think they hang spies with broken ankles."

"That's out of the question," Caroli said. "We'll get out of it together or drown together."

He asked his friend to leave it to him. He had an idea. "Look," he said. "We aren't as cut off as you think. We have the *Klamotten*," he pointed to their radios which had reached the ground with their equipment by another parachute. "They're keeping the circuit open at Wohldorf, standing by day and night, waiting to hear from us. Well, they are going to hear from us sooner than expected. I'll get in touch with the major. He has that Welshman of his. Maybe he can raise him to help us."

He had no difficulty contacting Wohldorf, and a call was put in to Ritter at around five o'clock in the morning. "Trouble with 3725," he was told. "Just signaled he must talk to you! Please come at once!"

Now began a sequence of events without parallel in the spy game.

Ritter motored to Wohldorf, "talked" to Caroli, then contacted Johnny and asked him to go to his boys' aid at Salisbury. Johnny radioed back, "It's too dangerous." But Ritter signaled, "You must go! They're our best men. They need help. You're the only one who can save them."

But of course Ritter was not exchanging signals with Johnny.

Johnny had no access to his radio.

Ritter was talking directly to MI.5.

He was betraying his own men, unwittingly and unknowingly, to be sure, but carelessly and foolishly nevertheless.

From here on the whole mission was controlled by the British. Owens was summoned and sent to the aid of Hansen and Caroli, as instructed by Ritter on an elaborate and complicated plan he arranged with Caroli.

The young Swede was to hide his Danish partner in the grove, make him as comfortable as circumstances permitted, then go to the Salisbury railroad station and wait for Johnny. In frantic dispatches that went to-and-fro Ritter described Caroli to Johnny and Johnny to Caroli. Identification would be by password. Johnny was then to accompany Caroli back to Hansen who was waiting at the grove and take the injured man to a reliable physician.

After that Caroli was to go on his way, while Hansen would have to make his own comeback as best he could—after all, he was self-sufficient with his own Afu set.

Johnny carried out this fantastic assignment. At their last *Treff* in Lisbon a few months later, he related to Ritter how it went.

"Believe me, Doctor," he said, "it was a nerve-racking experience. I arrived at the station at the time you set for the meeting, but let the fellow wait while I was observing him. I had to be sure that he was alone. There weren't many people in the lobby. Your man was standing there alone, apparently studying a timetable, busily making notes of train connections. A stranger wouldn't have noticed anything unusual in the way he acted.

"When I eventually stepped up to him and pretended to look for a train for myself while giving him the password, he asked curtly, 'Where shall I take my friend?' I gave him the address of a doctor I knew, a trustworthy Welshman like the rest of us, and the time of the day when the doctor was expecting him.

"They showed up on the dot, the taller one carrying the shorter chap. I took an instant liking to this Danish bloke, and while the doctor was fixing his ankle, I told him he could contact me any time he wanted to, maybe we could work together. He said nothing, didn't even nod. He's a loner, I guess, a stand-offish bloke. The doctor said he'd keep the fellow at his home, but that was the last I saw or heard of him."

This was, of course, not what exactly happened.

Accompanied by a doctor in an ambulance, and a retinue of security agents and officers from the Special Branch, Johnny was followed to the *Treff* and fingered the two men. Also in the party were a couple of rather exhilarated men, observing the proceedings from the sideline.

They were from Double-X.

Things were not progressing too well. For all practical purposes, Johnny was still their only prize. But now they hoped things might get off the ground with these two men in their lap.

The young Dane Ritter had thought to be rocklike in his devotion to Germany, the fanatical Nazi, was the first to cave in. After a long and friendly discussion of the great issues of those times with the sincere intellectuals of "XX," Hansen appeared to view things in a different light—even a little in the British light—and agreed rather quickly to become a double agent.

Major Robertson, the keen-witted, wise and genial headmaster of "Twenty" (as "XX" was usually referred to by its practitioners) picked the cover-name "Tate" for him after the popular comedian Harry Tate whom he was supposed to resemble. He was assigned Russell Leigh as a case officer, and was also given a radio operator, although Hansen was expected to operate his own Afu set. After a brief period with his ankle in a cast, "Harry" (as Tate was called by his new intimates) was lodged in one of MI.5's hideouts on the outskirts of Watford, eighteen miles from Double-Cross headquarters in London.

He was looked after by Robertson's young wife, Joan, a delightful, outgoing, very pretty lady in her late twenties who shared in her husband's adventure by becoming a kind of den mother of "XX" and the special hostess-guardian of Tate. The shelter was humming with the activities of "Twenty," with wireless sets on which the double-agents there communicated with the Abwehr, and case officers and radio operators coming and going.

Hansen enjoyed a pleasant domesticity and comfort, staying with Mrs. Robertson, her little daughter, and the infant's nanny, more as a guest than as a prisoner. He reciprocated the hospitality by helping out with the household chores and taking superb pictures of the Robertson's baby daughter. The controlled agents were all housed in such comfort at various shelters around London, and even in flats in London itself. It was correctly assumed that the men and women performing this intricate task would cooperate more willingly when treated so generously.

But the brash, ribald, strong-willed young Dane was not always easy to handle, and his perceptive hostess needed both her charm and pluck to keep him in line. Yet Hansen could be ingratiating and fun. Shortly after his arrival in the house in Watford, when Britain waited tensely for the overdue German invasion, he gave his first exhibition of his coarse sense of humor. Seated at the dinner table with Mrs. Robertson and the nanny, he heard the two ladies discussing the German's coming.

"I wonder," the nanny mused in some apprehension, "what would happen if a German spy suddenly dropped out of the sky and showed up here." It was a cue for Hansen. He got up and, playing the imaginary German agent, demonstrated how the intruder would behave, ending the grisly show with a feigned attack on the nanny. The horseplay of this German spy, acting the part, did not amuse Mrs. Robertson. But it broke up the nanny, who was unaware of Harry's background.

Caroli proved far more difficult to handle than Hansen. Given the choice between detention at Ham Common, MI.5's harsh cage for German spies on the snakepit-like premises of an old lunatic asylum in West Surrey, and the relative comforts of "XX" work, he chose the latter. Assigned the cover-name of "Summer," "XX" used him to give the Germans "general information on the area around Birmingham," the place for which Ritter had slated him. But he remained recalcitrant and troublesome. In December 1940, when he was at "Double-X" less than four months, he made an attempt to escape from the shelter where MI.5 was keeping him under guard, and had to be imprisoned for the duration. He would have been tried and hanged but his life was saved through his familiarity with "XX" which he so valiantly tried to double-cross.

When Caroli tried to defect in December, he had to be written off. "XX" used Hansen to let the Germans know that his friend and partner had fallen by the wayside. " '3727,' " he signalled, "compelled to suspend operations for pressing security reasons. His radio safe with '3504.' "

"3504" was Johnny and Johnny was MI.5.

Hans Hansen never gave any such trouble, despite the unusual freedom he enjoyed in a land which he had come to harm.

Actually, he was allowed access to the genuine secrets he had been sent to spy out, for it was one of the basic principles of the "XX" system to let double agents "live the life and go through all the motions of a genuine agent." When Hamburg once asked "3725" to inspect and report on factories at Wolverhampton, a visit was arranged for him to the place before he replied. It was shrewdly assumed that the agent on such an excursion would seek information exactly as a spy would and secure the sort of intelligence which a real spy would get. As a result, Tate's messages always appeared to be true, and he never tripped up over details of topographical or local observation.

He was a lot of fun in his official work, too, and was praised for his terse and virile telegraphese. For Russell Leigh, who handled his dispatches, this was a cherished and fascinating chore, using Hansen's free-flowing cuss words in profusion and reflecting his temper tantrums in the messages.

Hansen had two personal foibles in his character.

He was extremely close to his family and was forever trying to find out how they were doing. He was permitted to intersperse his straight signals with inquiries about his relatives. This way he was able to attend, so to speak, the wedding of a sister, by getting from Wohldorf a blow-by-blow account of her wedding.

His erratic, free-wheeling way of life was fully and enchantingly reflected in his correspondence with the Abwehr. A message from him might abruptly inform Hamburg that he was taking off on a holiday he thought he amply deserved. Or he would let his German friends know that he would suspend operations for a week or so, because he just did not feel like doing any spying for a while.

Far more lucrative from MI.5's point of view was a stingy, mercenary streak in his personality. He would never do anything for nothing, not even on a secret mission which he originally undertook on ideological grounds. He filled his dispatches to the Abwehr with demands for money and then always for more money, caring little how Hamburg would arrange to get it to him.

In the beginning it was found relatively simple to send him funds on lines the Abwehr thought it still had to England for the care and feeding of its agents. But they dried up, one after another, even as Hansen's greed was increasing by leaps and bounds. It was realized how highly this purported super-agent was regarded by his home office, and indeed, how indispensable he had become to the Germans. This whetted the appetite of his handlers.

One day in September 1941, he shocked Hamburg with an ultimatum. Unless they paid him the unheard-of sum of £4000, they could go fuck themselves, he signaled. Appalling though the message was, Ritter was reassured and relieved by it. "It was so typical of him," he later said. "The message by itself was positive proof that '3725' was still as genuine as ever."

The money was eventually appropriated, but then no means could be found to smuggle it to Hansen. His dunning was becoming more and more urgent and arrogant, and Ritter was reconciling himself to the loss of his indispensable man. Just when what appeared to be Hansen's final message arrived—sent *en clair* for the whole world to read, *"I shit on Germany and its whole fucking secret service"*—Ritter, amused rather than annoyed by "another characteristic Hansen outburst"—found the way to get the money to him.

The money was given to the Japanese intelligence chief in Berlin who then instructed Captain Viscount Kano, the Naval Attaché in London, to get it into Hansen's hands. In a series of signals, Ritter advised Hansen to be at a bus stop on Edgeware Road near George Street at exactly 10:00 P.M. one evening, wait for the next No. 9 bus going in the direction of Marble Arch, and look for a Japanese in the bus reading *The Times* of that morning. He was to board the bus, seat himself next to the Japanese, and ask him after a while: "Anything interesting in the paper today?"

The Japanese would look at him briefly and give him the paper with the words: "You may have it. I'm getting off at the next stop."

This was exactly what happened at 10:11 P.M. on October 26. Concealed in *The Times* were no fewer than eighty £50 Bank of England notes pasted on the inside pages.

Next morning Major Ritter was handed a signal from Hansen.

"Won't be reporting for a couple of days," it read. "I'm getting drunk tonight."[1]

There were thirteen of them when it all began.

Now Hansen and Johnny were the only ones left, as far as Hamburg knew.

Waldberg, Pons, van den Kieboom, Meier, Druecke, and Waelti were in prison.

Vera was missing.

What happened to the others?

Three of the anonymous members of the Lena Team managed to drop to their pinpoints, bury their parachutes, and make their separate ways undetected almost to their destinations.

One of them reached London but was caught the day he got there after his first dinner in a Soho restaurant; he handed the waitress some food coupons for his meal. The Abwehr did not know that none was required in British restaurants.

The other came a cropper when buying a railroad ticket for Bristol, the city to which he had been assigned. The clerk told him that the price was "ten and six," and the police were called when the man handed over ten pounds and six shillings.

The mystery man of the team—the "Dutch refugee" called "Jan Villen Ter Braak" in his phony papers—was found shot dead in a deserted air-raid shelter in Cambridge. He must have been killed or committed suicide shortly after his arrival, for he still had the familiar suitcase with his belongings and his Afu set.

That left only one man unaccounted for.

If ever an eccentric philanthropist decides to erect memorials to Hitler's follies, the odd man of the Lena Team would qualify as the unknown soldier of Sea Lion.

He was sent to Lancashire, and came down in the Manchester Ship Canal near the Mersey estuary above Birkenhead. He drowned, helpless and alone, on the night of September 7, 1940.

He was never missed. His loss was never felt.

Hitler had given up the whole idea of going to England.

Caroli was kept at Ham Common until 1946, and was then deported to his native Sweden where he now lives, a victim of amnesia.

Hansen was permitted to remain in Britain after the war.

NOTE

1 MI.5 collected the astounding sum of £85,000 from the German secret service in this manner. It was almost sufficient to pay for the total operating costs of "XX" throughout the war.

Chapter 25

Detour to Germany:
Johnny's Last Treff

*T*HE fateful summer of 1940 was destined to become the most perplexing, paradoxical period in Johnny Owens's hectic career as a triple agent. For a while, it seemed, his very usefulness to either side was hanging in the balance. In MI.5 it was feared that his failure to show up at the misbegotten trawler *Treff* off the Dogger Bank would shake Major Ritter's confidence in his favorite spy, and the priceless connection might be broken off by the Germans.

The "North Sea episode," as Johnny's handlers called the aborted rendezvous, raised some questions as to the little man's *bona fides*. But the doubts were resolved in his favor. They concluded—by some rather tortuous reasoning in which all benefits of the doubt were given him—that "a great part of the trouble had had its origin in a genuine misunderstanding between 'Snow' and 'Biscuit' of each other's motives and methods of work." They kept up the game, especially when the wireless signals Johnny was continuing to receive from Hamburg clearly indicated that Ritter had not lost faith in his man and was continuing the contact.

The Wehrmacht was in feverish turmoil. Preparations for Sea Lion were reaching the terminal stage. The Luftwaffe was getting ready for "Eagle Day," the unleashing of its apocalyptic air blitz. Early in August, as the Abwehr prepared for the impending double blow, Owens was alerted to stand by, and was then given specific instructions for the role he was to play in the historic events. He was to radio weather reports daily between midnight and 2:30 A.M., and send signals as often as possible about the damage the raids would be leaving in their wake. Although he could not be told explicitly about Sea Lion without risking a breach of its security, he was asked to

267

have the coastal area between Dover and Plymouth reconnoitered by his Welshmen and report on its defenses.

Johnny rose to the occasion—so well, indeed, that whatever bad feelings remained in the aftermath of the North Sea mishap completely evaporated as far as Major Ritter was concerned.

Owens tapped out his first weather report of the new cycle on August 8: "Wind direction south, velocity 1 . . . Temperature 73 degrees Fahrenheit . . . Visibility 4500 yards . . . Ceiling 2500 yards."

Otherwise his reports on the eve of the storm were erratic and contradictory, as if the uncertainties and indecisions which held both camps in their grip during these febrile days had cramped his style. In one report he complained that butter, rationed at two ounces per person, was hard to come by and that the government was trying to force the population on a potato diet relieved only by powdered eggs. In his next signal he advised Ritter that "the food situation" was "normal." He sent a businesslike message about coastal fortifications and obstacles at Dover, Folkestone, Hythe, Farnborough, Portsmouth, and Reading, but followed it up with a silly signal about the doubling of shoe prices and the disappearance of silk stockings from the stores on Oxford Street.

It seemed that his warped pride in Britain rose up in him now that his native soil was threatened, for the first time in five centuries, by foreign invasion. His signals sounded a bit too confident when touching on this topic. Their boastful undertone, subtly designed to discourage the onslaught, should have tipped off Ritter to the true authorship of these reports.

Those coastal defenses around Dover were described in terms that sounded a trifle too glowing. A message described how the Home Guards were issued thousands of tommy guns and automatics. On August 14 his ghostwriters almost showed their hand when they put on the air a message in Johnny's name the purpose of which was unmistakable.

"Home Defense Staff anxious for invasion," it read. "Defense measures terrific. Large forces ready to attack you if invaded here."

Even on the 15th, the bravado was clumsily apparent in his signal of the day. "Air Ministry friend informs," he wrote, "plane production above expectation. Supply dumps full [of] spares. British and American confidence [in] RAF personnel greatly increased. New machines give good results."

Then all hell broke loose, and the bluff and bluster of his puffed-up messages vanished in the smoke of the Battle of Britain. The invaders failed to show, but the Luftwaffe came, and Johnny gave a grim blow-by-blow account of the savage pounding.

His first damage report was put on the air on August 18, about the raid on Croydon that, he wrote, "Hit oil tank, components factory and landing ground." Then followed in rapid succession a series of gloomy signals: "Wimbledon hit" . . . "hundreds of houses, railroad station and factories destroyed at Morton-Malden" . . . "many private dwellings damaged at Kenley and Mitcham" . . . "the airport at Biggin Hill hit."

"Informed," he radioed on the 18th, "Air Ministry moving soon to Harrogate."

"Sewage works Perryonk West Drayton direct hit on the 29th," he wrote on September 1. "HMW plant in Hayes hit same day. Barracks hit Feltham 30th."

"In raid on Vickers in Weybridge," he radioed on September 5th, "seventy persons killed, the assembly plant hit."

"The Albert Docks at Silvertown," he signaled the next day, "as well as warehouses and oil tanks on fire."

He was off the air on the 9th and the 10th, then apologized for his silence in a message on the 11th. "I was unable to transmit," he informed Ritter, "because my garden in Richmond was hit by a bomb with delayed action fuse." He made up for his brief absence with a new string of damage reports: "Southern Railway blocked" . . . "the hangars at Croydon are totally destroyed" . . . "seventy-five transport planes smashed at the aircraft factory of Short Brothers in Rochester" . . . "the Kingston Boat Yards are in flames."

On the 19th, he began to transmit a series of reports recommending targets for the raiders. The first one directed them to a munitions plant and an aircraft factory at Seighton.

None of these messages was, of course, written by Owens. He had no part in collecting the information they contained. All of them were concocted in MI.5 where the Double-Cross organization was beginning to gain its stride under the management of John Cecil Masterman, now a major "specially employed." But if the British themselves produced Johnny's reports, what was to be gained from giving the enemy such detailed, pinpointed intelligence about his handiwork?

This was the first attempt—feeble as yet—to gain a measure of control over the Luftwaffe's selection of targets by manipulating damage reports beamed to the Germans by double agents, planted reports in neutral newspapers, and such other channels as foreign correspondents and neutral diplomats, whose reportage was likely to reach the Luftwaffe. It was to become highly effective and was used broadly with a degree of ruthlessness under Mr. Churchill's personal supervision.[1]

Aside from this strategic role assigned to the Double-Cross organization, the sending of this grim and generally accurate information had a tactical reason. It was designed to establish Owens's reputation more firmly and enhance his credibility with his friends in the Abwehr. Major Masterman and his associates in Double-X realized that the Germans' cataclysmic onslaught was also a supreme test of their intelligence services. Destruction from the air could be gauged from the air. But aerial reconnaissance in the wake of the raids did not completely meet the Luftwaffe's needs.

Goering, fretting in Berlin to find out the full extent and exact nature of the devastation he was wreaking, became so nervous groping in the dark that he once personally led a much publicized reconnaissance mission and flew over the ruins to see for himself.

It was imperative that the Germans obtain conclusive evidence for their success or failure from astute observers on the ground. Much more was involved in the battle than the physical destruction of factories and bridges, docks and homes. The vicious campaign was designed to knock the RAF out of the skies and cripple British productivity, but also to destroy the morale of the people and their will to fight. Goering sought to force Britain to surrender, without the need of landings. Information about the intangible elements of the raids' effectiveness could not be obtained from aerial photographs. It could be procured only from agents who mingled with the people, observed them in the streets, at their places of work, in their pubs and homes, holding their fingers on the pulse of the nation and counting its beat.

There could be no tricks played upon the German spymasters, no trifling with the work of the spies, no blatant fooling of the men in high command for whom the agents were supposedly risking their lives. The material the Masterman group had to provide for its own controlled agents had to be concocted with supreme ingenuity—to give comfort to the enemy without giving him too much aid. Information sent in the name of the double agents had to be more than plausible, give more than just the appearance of truth. It had to be *true*, to sustain the credibility of the spies and convince their employers of the accuracy of their output. The intelligence transmitted on Owens's Afu set would be checked against data from a variety of other sources. It could be easily exposed as fakery if it failed to tally with the intelligence picture they presented.

It was a cruel responsibility, this submission of accurate and timely intelligence directly to the enemy. It had to be drawn up with the utmost caution and greatest finesse. To carry this burden, a special collegium was officially created within MI.5 in January 1941. Called the Double-Cross Committee and headed by Masterman, its task was to devise the intelligence the British were contributing gratuitously to the German war effort. Exceptional care and ingenuity was used by the Committee in the selection of the items and in their exact formulation in the outgoing reports. Chances had to be taken. The risks had to be calculated. Obviously, an agent was expected by his employers to supply only authentic information; a controlled agent had to communicate a great deal of true information if he was to survive in the trust of the men for whom he professed to work.

It became one of the cardinal principles within the Double-Cross System that no message should ever go to the enemy which had not been approved by the competent authority through the medium of the Double-Cross Committee. Major Masterman later avowed that the transmittal of such material could never have occurred without higher authorities assuming the final responsibility.

Controlled agents must be "built up"—as keen observers, accurate appraisers, good reporters, and, above all else, as reliable purveyors of accurate information. As early as September 1940, the Double-X group was especially anxious to "build up" Owens. It was working on another mission for him—so bold, bizarre, and pretentious that it staggered even its authors' lively imagination.

Owens was to be used to palm off another agent on Ritter, to penetrate the Abwehr on its home ground, and return with firsthand information about the inner workings of the competition. The question was, could Owens be trusted?

The stakes were enormous. Failure of the mission would give the Germans all the advantages. The life of a man depended on Johnny's discretion. If he betrayed the scheme to Ritter, the infiltrator would certainly be dead on arrival in Germany. Colonel Robertson and Russell Leigh, who was Johnny's case officer, were convinced that Owens would cooperate faithfully. A change had come over the man after the trip on the trawler, and especially since the beginning of the blitz. All of a sudden, he began to regard the Germans as *the* enemy. After years in the game he was overcome by fatigue, both physical and mental. He no longer enjoyed working at the difficult job of fooling both friend and foe, and was tired of scavenging for secret information. He was planning to quit, move to Canada and go straight. He was willing to take on this one last assignment, the most intricate and sophisticated he ever tackled, then retire in a blaze of glory.[2]

The plan of the mission was perfected shortly after the stillborn trawler *Treff* in May. Johnny Owens's companion on the *Barbados*, the con-man "Biscuit" whom he knew as Sam McCarthy, was dusted off for another voyage. Now going by the name of "Jack Brown," he was groomed to play the part of a deserter from the Royal Air Force, and insinuate himself into the Germans' confidence.

The maneuver was to be mounted in two stages. First, Owens would contact Ritter, arrange a meeting in Portugal, and offer him the RAF deserter on a silver platter, as the supreme loot of all he had produced. Then, he would bring Brown along to a second *Treff*, letting the man do his own bidding.

On June 6, 1940, the following cryptic message was appended to one of Owens's daily weather reports: "Applied for exit permit. Have secret documents, order of battle of RAF. When can I meet you?"

Ritter promptly replied, arranging to see him in Lisbon during the period between June 26 and 30, 1940. Johnny left a fortnight later, going by boat from Liverpool, arriving on the 30th in Lisbon where Ritter was waiting, holed up in the Hotel Duas Nocas under the name of Dr. Rankin. The occasion was not entirely auspicious. Ritter, who was always meticulous in observing the outward forms of espionage, had instructed Johnny to be at a certain café in Lisbon at 11 A.M. sharp, where he would be taken in tow by a go-between, a German-Brazilian called Carlos, who was doing such odd jobs for the Abwehr in Portugal.

To identify himself, the Welshman was to seat himself at a corner table, order a *large* glass of *lemon* drink and sip it while apparently absorbed in the reading of the London *Times*. He was to repeat the procedure until he would be picked up.

Johnny did as he was told, except for one slight deviation from Ritter's instructions. Popular with Germans, a lemon drink was a somewhat repulsive beverage for a Welshman. Although he abhorred any drink that had no alcoholic content, he compromised by ordering a large glass of *orange* juice. But he could not make himself stoop so low as to actually drink it.

Carlos recognized him promptly on his first appearance from the photograph Ritter had shown him, but he did not dare to accost him because of the wrong drink. The next day Johnny was back at the café and again ordered orange juice. This time Carlos decided to make contact. "Pardon me," he said, "it's none of my business. But why do you order this *orange* juice when you don't touch it?"

Johnny took in the situation. "I'll be a monkey's uncle!" he exclaimed. Then he yelled out: "Waiter, bring me a large glass of *lemon* drink, goddammit!"

Carlos took him to Ritter at a safe house on the outskirts of Lisbon. This was their first encounter in months, during which so much had happened. But there seemed to be a strain on their reunion. Ritter had developed some gnawing doubts about his little spy. It was not the painful memory of the missed rendezvous that irked him or made him suspicious. He was puzzled by Johnny's ability to obtain the exit permit, book passage on a ship, and make it to Lisbon, apparently without any difficulty at all.

Johnny sensed what Ritter had in the back of his mind. Probably because he was planning to retire and no longer cared about the future of his relations with "the Doctor," he revealed to Ritter that he had become a double agent.

"I couldn't help it any more," he said. "At first I thought I could come as a stowaway with one of the skippers I know, but that proved impossible. They wouldn't let me go near the docks without a permit. So I decided to offer myself to the secret service, pretending, nothing more, that I would be working for them, simply in order to make this bloody trip possible.

"They were suspicious at first. I can't blame them. I tried the patriotic line, saying that since I was too old to be a soldier, I hoped to be able to do something for the war effort by working for them. As a matter of fact, I didn't have to tell them too much about myself. The captain who took my case told me to my face that I had worked for the Nazis. But then he said, 'Well, all right, if you tell me everything I might help you.' "

He went on to relate how he exposed himself to the captain, revealing his relationship with Ritter. "That did it," he said. "The captain asked me point-blank, 'Do you think you could meet him somewhere, maybe in Casablanca?' I suggested that Madrid or Lisbon would be simpler to get to, and he fell for it. This is how I made it."

"A fine story," Ritter said with a sardonic grin.

"Doctor," Johnny shot back, "you got to believe me! Don't I deserve that, after we've known each other for such a long time? Did I ever let you down or fool you?"

He unloaded the material he had brought along—first what he described as "the rubbish" the secret service had given him for the trip (the outline of a new airport somewhere on the Kentish coast and the description of some instrument using ultraviolet rays for detecting planes at night), and then "the real stuff," the sample of a new alloy for the manufacture of shells and the casing of the shell itself.

"This is nothing, though," Johnny said. "I have something for you so big that it'll take your breath away. I can bring you a cashiered pilot-officer who could tell you all about the RAF."

The bait was out. And Ritter swallowed it.

It took time to arrange the next *Treff*, with the RAF-man in tow. It was already September when Johnny signaled Ritter that he was ready to produce the man, and Hamburg could inform Abwehr headquarters in a cryptic message that the keenly awaited meeting was about to take place. "3504 reports 20.7, 2330 o'clock" Ritter's telegram to Berlin read, "his emissary will go 24 or 26 to capital of country 18." The emissary was "Biscuit" alias "McCarthy" now called "Jack Brown," whom Johnny characterized in another signal to Ritter as "a 100 percent friend." "Country 18" was Portugal.

Ritter arrived in Lisbon on September 24, then Johnny came in on the 26th, pale, trembling and weak from seasickness after a stormy voyage.

"Where is your friend?" Ritter asked.

"We couldn't possibly come on the same boat," Owens said, "without attracting attention. Don't worry, Doctor. I'm a man of my word. Jack will be here tomorrow."

Two days later there still was no sign of the flyer. The storm grew to hurricane force in the Atlantic in which the U-boats roamed, taking their toll virtually at will. Carlos kept vigil at the piers checking out all incoming ships. Two Portuguese vessels and a Spanish ship came in from England, and then an American freighter, but the man he was expecting was on none of them.

Late in the afternoon on the 29th an English ship arrived, and from a snapshot Johnny had given him, Carlos spotted his man coming down the gangplank. Passwords were exchanged, a car drove up, and Jack was whisked away to the safe house where Ritter was waiting.

"He was a fairly tall, good-looking chap in his thirties," Ritter later told me, "with even features. There was something unusual only about his eyes. They were brownish-green and slightly bulging, and absolutely cold, without a glint of expression, like a blind man's eyes."

From the moment Carlos brought in the man, there was a noticeable tension in the room. "Well, Doctor," Johnny said exuberantly, making the introduction formal, "this is Jack—Mr. Brown, that is—the RAF bloke I promised you."

"How do you do," the newcomer said in a soft voice with a faint smile, staring at Ritter blandly with his icy look.

"Well," the major began, "Johnny told me all about you—you have been kicked out of the RAF—am I correct?—for some malfeasance or indiscretion. Do you really think that you want to work with us and that you've something in which we might be interested?"

"I've no doubt about that," the man said in a monotone that went well with the unfeeling glance of his eyes.

"Then we don't have to beat about the bush," Ritter said, "and can come down to brass tacks."

Jack pulled his British passport from his pocket and handed it to the German who shrugged it off. "There is no need for such formalities," he said. "Your pass may be just as counterfeit as mine. After all, we're in the same business."

The man took the rebuff unruffled. "As far as we're concerned," Ritter continued, "we're interested solely in your performance. Let's see what you've got to offer."

"Johnny told me," the man said, "that you are an aviation expert. Well, so am I. What with my experience, knowledge and connections, I think I may be able to give you quite a bit of what you want."

"For how much?"

"Two hundred pounds sterling a month," the man said.

"That's reasonable," Ritter said, and the deal was made.

For several hours afterward, Jack Brown gave the major a sampling of the wares he brought along. "The RAF has on order in America," he said, "forty Flying Fortresses—the B/17BB/299/Y, and they are nearing completion. Two of these planes, the pilot models, are in service already, on experimental flights with a new type of oversized bombs."

"What are the specifications of the plane," Ritter asked.

The man rattled off the statistics, and went on to the next item. "This may not be too important," he said, "but the leader of the American squadron is Bob Sweeney, an American who lived in England for some time."

He talked on. "The three Clippers," he said, "the RAF has purchased from Boeing are used to take the American ferry pilots back to the United States as quickly as possible. Until recently, they were returning home by sea in slow convoys. On their eastward flight, the Clippers land in Northern Ireland, with Canadian pilots who come to join the RCAF in England. Incidentally, the Flying Fortresses won't be flown over but shipped by boat."

There was more. "The Bristol engine assembly plant," he said, "was recently moved to Patchway on the Great Western Railway line north of Bristol."

And still more. "The 3, 4.5 and 7 inch AA guns are getting their mobility improved. The wheels had been shifted to the side and the guns are placed on a four-legged platform, making it possible to make them ready for use in less than ten minutes. The tractors that move the guns are made by Dennis on Portsmouth Road in Guilford at the foot of a hill that can be easily identified by a half-finished church. The fuselage is manufactured by Scannel near Chelmsford and by Vickers."

After Ritter had listened for a while, he told the man, addressing him as Mr. Brown for the first time: "I can see that we'll need some time to cover everything, and I cannot remain here in Lisbon any longer. Moreover," he added, "I am not sufficiently versed in technical things to get the most out of your information." He then popped the question that was so cunningly anticipated in MI.5.

"Would you be willing," he asked, "to come to Germany for a few days for conferences with our experts. I give you my word as an officer that I will arrange your safe return to Lisbon."

The man seemed stunned, but Johnny exclaimed: "That sounds wonderful, Doctor, when are we leaving?"

"Wait a minute, Johnny," Ritter said sternly. "The invitation does not extend to you. I am sorry but I cannot take you both."

He turned to the man. "What do you say, Mr. Brown?"

"What assurance do I have," Jack said, "that I will be able to get out of Germany?"

"I gave you my word of honor," Ritter said.

"Go on, Jack," Johnny piped in, "you can trust the Doctor."

Brown seemed to be weighing the offer. Then he said, without any sign of emotion: "All right, sir. I'll go."

Ritter left ahead of Brown, whose passage was arranged by Carlos with the help of the local Abwehr outpost. Traveling on a Norwegian passport made out to Knut Carlsen, he was escorted by a young officer of the Hamburg branch on a Lufthansa plane, stopping in Madrid and Lyons. On February 18 he was in Hamburg, the enemy's land, put up in style at the Vier Jahreszeiten the city's best hotel. Considering the nature of the venture, Brown's sojourn in Hamburg went off uneventfully. A group of technical experts of the Air Intelligence Section headed by Major Groskopf and three officers from Luftwaffe Ordnance flew to Hamburg for conferences with the man, pumping him for information, the range of which seemed endless. Brown gave a good account of himself, and convinced his interrogators that he was honestly trying to help. The experts' final verdict was that he did not know much of real value, either about aviation technology or about the RAF organization, and no wonder—Biscuit was no aviator. What he knew about the RAF was learned in a cram course he was given for the mission. They thanked him and went back to Berlin.

There was a moment of crisis on the last day of the visit that could have ended unpleasantly for Biscuit.

Major Ritter had arranged with the Gestapo to keep the man under surveillance. Two rooms adjoining his in the hotel were occupied by the detectives. Others trailed him on the brief tours of the city he was allowed to make apparently unattended. His shadows reported no untoward incident, nothing suspicious in the man's conduct. He talked to nobody on his excursions, received no visitors in his room, made no telephone calls. He asked no questions. If he came, as Ritter never ceased to suspect, as a double agent, either to make contact with a resident British spy or to obtain some intelligence on his own, he apparently failed to accomplish his mission. He saw little in the city and found nothing of value to a secret agent— beyond the Abwehr set-up with which he was in touch.

It never occurred to Ritter, and is still doubted by him, that this was exactly the purpose of his mission—to discover as much as he could about the Abwehr, find out who its key officers were, how they were organized, how much they knew—and especially to learn what interested them about England and the RAF.

Ritter was called to Berlin to report to Canaris, who had taken a personal interest in the quaint enterprise. "Well," the admiral asked, "how did it go, Ritter?"

"Splendidly, sir," the major said. "The man is ready to leave."

"Why do you let him go?" Carnaris asked. "He may be a British agent after all. Don't you think it might be better to keep him here?"

"I gave him my word, Herr Admiral," Ritter said, "that he will be allowed to leave. Otherwise he would not have come."

"That settles it," the admiral said. "Wish him bon voyage from me."

This was to be Brown's last night in Hamburg and it called for a celebration. Accompanied by his wife and Captain Boeckel, one of his assistants, Ritter took Jack to Jacobs, the elegant wine restaurant frequented by the Abwehr brass.

It was a jovial party and Brown seemed to loosen up, laughing occasionally at Boeckel's jokes, treating Frau Ritter with exquisite courtesy, praising the food and imbibing the wine. He did not notice or could not understand when Frau Ritter whispered to her husband in German. "Look at his signet ring! It's the kind you can open. Don't you think you ought to examine it a bit closer?"

That ring became an obsession with Ritter for the rest of the meal.

He could hardly take his eyes from it, trying to fathom the secret it concealed. "Your ring . . ." he said at last when he could no longer control his curiosity. He thought Brown recoiled slightly.

"It's a beautiful ring," Frau Ritter now chimed in.

Brown regained his poise. "Oh," he said, "it's a family heirloom, I got it from my father who got it from his." With that he snapped it open and removed the tinted miniature photograph of a beautiful young woman from the tiny round receptacle.

"Your wife?" Frau Ritter asked.

"Not yet," Brown answered and he seemed to be blushing faintly. He then replaced the picture, snapped the ring closed, and the subject was changed.

Ritter was convinced that it contained some greater secret than just the mysterious object of unrequited love. The meal was over, the bill was paid, then Ritter excused himself. He went to the telephone in the rear and called the Abwehr office, arranging for one of the technicians of the G-branch to meet him at a nearby bar. Returning to the table, he turned to Brown.

"It's time for our nightcap before we turn in," he said.

"I'm afraid I had a bit too much to drink," Brown said. "Your wine is excellent but too heady."

"It's your party, old man," Ritter said with contrived joviality. "I insist on a round of farewell drinks. I know a delightful bar not too far from here with a splendid gypsy violinist. I am told he's one of the best in captivity."

Settled at their table in the bar, Ritter ordered double brandies, and toasted Brown: "Here is to your safe return to Lisbon!" He emptied the glass bottom up. Brown had to follow suit. Two minutes later Brown was sleeping soundly. The technician Ritter had summoned was on the job. A potent barbiturate had been slipped into Brown's brandy to put him to sleep. Leaving him in his chair, apparently sleeping off his fuddle, the ring was removed from his finger, opened, the photograph removed and rushed to Abwehr headquarters for closer scrutiny. Within the hour, the technician was back with it. "Nothing on the picture side," he reported to Ritter, "but it had a kind of code on the other side written in invisible ink. There isn't anything more I can do, Herr Major. This is a job for our cipher bureau."

"How long will they take to break the code?" Ritter asked.

"It's difficult to say," the technician said. "Perhaps a week. Maybe longer."

Ritter decided to keep Brown in Hamburg until the finding of the cryptanalysts was in. They arrived in four days, but proved inconclusive. The secret writing consisted of a set of unconnected letters and numbers, a street address apparently somewhere in Spain, and what could have been a telephone number.

Ritter was inclined to cancel Brown's return trip. In the end he decided that the strange clue was not sufficiently incriminating to justify the breaking of his word. Brown was allowed to leave, escorted to Lisbon again on a Lufthansa plane by the same young officer who had brought him in. After a brief stopover in Lyons, they had to change planes in Madrid, and while they waited at the airport, Brown excused himself to go to the bathroom.

He was never seen again.

It was as simple as that. His mission was over. He had accomplished the impossible—penetrating the enemy's secret service in wartime and getting away with it. From the airport he called the number the Abwehr cryptanalysts could not figure out—it was the telephone number of Kenneth Benton, Madrid representative of MI.6—and reported back. He left the men's room unobserved and took a taxi to the address written on the picture in the signet ring in invisible ink. That same night he was taken to Gibraltar and flown to England by one of the courier planes of the RAF.

In the meantime, Johnny had returned to London and reported on the mission up to the day of Brown's departure for Hamburg. Jack himself supplied the details of the sequel. After having successfully palmed off "the RAF-man Jack Brown" on his old friend the Doctor, both Major Ritter and Johnny Owens faded out of the picture. The major was transferred to other, less strenuous duties in the Luftwaffe in which he rose to the rank of full colonel by the end of the war.

Owens's last message was put on the air at 11:30 A.M. on April 13, 1941. It was a report about the weather on a gloomy day, all he was transmitting by this time: "Wind, direction southwest, velocity five MPH . . . Sky, completely beclouded . . . Temperature, 50 degrees Fahrenheit . . . Visibility, 4 miles . . . Ceiling, 3200 feet."

It was the pitiful swan song of the master spy who had outfoxed himself in the game of foxes. Owens was taken into custody by the British. When he was finally freed in 1945, Owens vanished from sight. He is said to be living somewhere in Ireland on an assumed name.

But Jack Brown's venture was an extraordinary one, unprecedented in espionage. It enabled MI.5 to size up the enemy so much better, to acquaint itself with some of its key personnel snooping on the Royal Air Force, and to find out something about their methods. Security of the RAF could be considerably tightened, in the intimate knowledge of what the Germans were eager the learn.

There was something else. The Jack Brown mission revealed that the competition, for all the Abwehr's reputation, was not too smart. It was the first major scoop scored by the Masterman team, still struggling to prove itself. The Double-Cross System had come of age.

NOTES

1 Mr. Churchill's somewhat fiendish scheme was to divert the Luftwaffe from strategic areas by giving them bogus intelligence that built up expend-

able areas as desirable targets. He could be quite callous in selecting the latter. They included certain residential districts and most of the time the diversionary targets he picked happened to be working class districts. This led to a violent clash between the Prime Minister and Herbert Morrison, the Cockney statesman, in a heated cabinet meeting. The Home Secretary, a leader of the Labour Party, protested bitterly and vehemently against Churchill's choice of targets, exclaiming, "Who are we to play God?"

2 Since Owens never could do anything straight, he also nurtured another plan for his retirement. He would not betray his companion, he would allow the mission to succeed. He would go along on the perilous journey to Germany, but then remain there for the duration, letting the other man return to London alone.

Chapter **26**

The Double Life of
Mutt and Jeff

*I*N the small world of espionage connoisseurs, two young Norwegians are considered to have been the best and most durable agents the Abwehr had in Britain during World War II. They went by a string of pseudonyms and registry numbers, but today we know that their real names were Olaf Klausen and Jack Berg.

Olaf was tall and lean, a handsome Viking. Jack was squat and fleshy, and half British. Both were ardent members of Major Vidkun Quisling's Nazi party. Recruited in Oslo by Commander Mueller, the Abwehr talent scout in Norway, they were trained as saboteurs, and taken by seaplane to a spot a few hundred yards off the Scottish coast, the point of arrival of actual refugees from Scandinavia, which they posed as. They paddled ashore in their rubber dinghy, made their way to London on bicycles, and went to work immediately.

That was in March 1941, when Britain was still shaken by Goering's relentless air offensive. Even at the time of their arrival in Scotland, the Clydeside region was being pounded by the Luftwaffe. The week they reached London they could see by just looking around that they were working for the winning side.

Shortly after getting settled in their new job, several reports about sabotage in southern England appeared in the newspapers, and they promptly claimed credit for them in brash reports to Mueller. With skill and luck they managed to stay at large and carry on, getting the money, equipment, and the explosives they needed from Germany in a succession of air drops. In early 1943, they moved back to Scotland, which was filling up with Allied troops, had a number of attractive targets they could ferret out, and offered better security than the heavily guarded regions in the south.

On February 20 and on June 18, their stores and funds were

281

replenished for a new series of sabotage operations, the Luftwaffe flying two logistic missions especially for them. The February drop was quite elaborate. To distract attention from the actual purpose of the intrusion, the Germans staged a real raid in the vicinity of the drop, causing heavy casualties among the civilian population of two Scottish communities.

It seems incredible that Klausen and Berg could endure so actively for so long with such impunity. But they were not the only ones so lucky on similar assignments. Just before Christmas in 1942 an agent called Fritz was dropped in Cambridgeshire on the war's most daring errand. His mission was to blow up the de Havilland aircraft works at Hatfield just north of London (less than ten miles from St. Albans where MI.6 had one of its bases), then return to his headquarters in Paris either under cover by U-boat or by a neutral ship via Portugal.

It became the most ambitious and, by all appearances, most successful of all such enterprises staged by the Abwehr. Carrying his sabotage formulae, radio code and cover address in his head, his Afu set, and some £7000 in a waterproof bag, Fritz landed safely at 2 A.M. on December 20 in a ploughfield at Wisbech near Littleport. Burying his parachute and erasing all traces of his arrival, he hid in the countryside until daybreak, then caught a train to London.

He made his first radio contact on the 23rd, reporting to Captain Stephan von Grunen, his Abwehr contact in Paris, then continued to send him increasingly optimistic progress reports. He had gone to Hatfield several times, creeping around at night casing the plant. He also had made a trip to a quarry at nearby Sevenoaks where the explosives he needed for the operation could be had. Finally, on January 27, he signaled von Grunen: "Will attempt sabotage this evening at six o'clock."

Later that same night he sent the triumphant message: "Mission successfully accomplished." He had blown up the powerhouse with two time explosive packages, using an ordinary wristwatch timer in each.

It could be confirmed. The Luftwaffe sent a couple of Ju-11 reconnaissance planes to verify Fritz's report. What they brought back satisfied the worst skeptics in the Abwehr. The photographs showed gaping holes in the roof of the powerhouse through which could be seen pieces of generators strewn around. The damage seemed extensive.

A week later, Fritz asked von Grunen to send a U-boat for him. When no submarine could be obtained for the voyage back home, he made his own arrangements to leave by boat from Liverpool. It took time, but Fritz was not idle in the meantime.

Paris was in regular touch with him on *Dauerempfang,* monitoring his radio day and night, and he rewarded the vigil of Maurice, the French collaborator who served as his radioman, with a description of American divisional insi; nia which he observed on his wanderings in London. When on the night of January 17–18 the Luftwaffe bombers raided London, Fritz told his home office that it was not much of a success. All they hit, he chided von Grunen, was the residential area around St. John's Wood, near Lord's Cricket Grounds.

In mid-February he put his final message on the air. "Closing transmission," he signaled. "Too dangerous to work. Am returning via Lisbon." He boarded a Portugal-bound freighter and arrived in Lisbon on March 12. A week later he was in Paris again, regaling his admiring friends with lurid details of his exploits over champagne at a celebration in Maxim's.[1]

If Fritz could drop in almost casually, put de Havilland out of business, send more than a score reports on his clandestine radio, and get out unharmed, why could not Klausen and Berg endure similarly unmolested? Even so, their feat seemed a little bit too good to be true. "Considering the rate at which our agents are caught and hanged in Britain," the skeptics argued in Berlin, "it is astounding that they manage to remain at large." Fritz's story was accepted on his word. But the Klausen-Berg team was subjected to an investigation. A special committee was appointed to scrutinize this remarkable duo. Its members examined every message from the two Norsemen since April 1941, then concluded that "nothing indicated that Klausen and Berg were under duress or forced to send false information."

Despite a handful of skeptics, the Abwehr was satisfied with the work of their agents in the United Kingdom. As far as the Germans could tell, even the year 1940 was not a total loss. The Sea Lion spies, sent hurriedly to southern England to spearhead the invasion that never came, had fallen by the wayside. Nobody had expected them to succeed. The loss of Theo Druecke was a blow, and Vera's disappearance without a trace was mystifying. But other efforts of the year were not all. futile. The Swede Caroli, sent in with young Hansen, had suspended operations on January 27, 1941, under mysterious circumstances. But his Danish buddy was performing phenomenally. Owens, too, continued to function, though a little more erratically than usual. Of the members of the Lena team, Ter Braak was operational in the Cambridge area; another Lena spy was active in northwest England; a Czech was working inside the RAF; a debonair Yugoslav was running a ring of his own; and a British seaman named George Armstrong, who had been recruited in the United States, was supplying invaluable convoy information via Lisbon.

All this added up to an at least adequate coverage of Britain under excruciatingly difficult circumstances. Encouraged by the results thus far, the Abwehr decided to enlarge its crew of agents in Britain in the face of all odds. So, in 1941, seventeen men and women were sent on missions to England, five more than the year before. Klausen and Berg were among them.

Their success story intrigued Giles Perrault, the French historian of espionage. When during his research for a book about the German D-Day spies he found that they were still on the job in the spring of 1944, three years later, he made a special effort to find out what made them tick. But his probe was inconclusive. "Were they single or double agents?" Perrault posed the rhetorical question. "Nobody knew . . . it is still a mystery."

It need not remain a mystery any longer. The fate of the German spies active in England during World War II can be cleared up conclusively once and for all.

They were either caught, interned and executed, or they were turned into double agents, *all of them.*

After Major Gill and Professor Trevor-Roper had pried open the Abwehr's cipher in December 1939, MI.5 monitored the traffic and obtained a mass of information about the movement of the German spies. In 1941, a major breakthrough enabled MI.5 to gain direct access to all Abwehr messages that went on the air. The brilliant cryptologist Dillwyn Knox, working at the Government Code & Cypher School at the Bletchley center of British code-cracking, solved the keying of the Abwehr's Enigma machine.

After that, little could be concealed from the British. Advance warning was obtained whenever German agents were heading for Britain. MI.5 was usually ready with a reception committee to welcome them. Agents caught *in flagranti* or spotted by alert civilians and uninitiated members of the constabulary—all went the way of fallen spies in wartime—execution. Two of the seventeen spies sent to Britain in 1941 were tried *in camera* and paid the supreme forfeit. One was Josef Jakobs, a 43-year-old meteorologist from Luxembourg; the other was Karl Richard Richter, a 29-year-old marine engineer from the Sudetenland, a foolhardy man who had volunteered for espionage and was sent to Britain though he could barely speak English.

The fallen spies' *via dolorosa* had its stations and ritual. They were first subjected to shock interrogations, designed to produce critical information while the agents were still badly shaken by the unnerving experience of their capture. British and American spies of World War II were indoctrinated for the eventuality of such "stress and strain" being drilled on how to conduct themselves during their interrogation and endure a degree of torture without breaking. No such training was given the Abwehr agents, probably on the theory that this motley crowd of spies would have recoiled from going on with their missions if hazards had been pointed out to them realistically and dramatically. Quite the contrary, the dispatchers who saw them off tended to minimize the risks they were taking. This explains why the German spies caved in so quickly.

Shock interrogations usually brought out the quality of the captured agent and also his potentialities as a double agent. Those who passed this test were taken to Ham Common, the detention and interrogation center named after the bucolic Green of the old parish in Surrey. This was actually Latchmere House, set back from a narrow country road behind a wall. The manor itself, a rambling three-story building painted light green, was an architectural hodgepodge without style or taste, unlike the other old houses of Ham.

After World War I, the British Army had bought Latchmere House for use as a "home" for "shell-shocked" officers. It was, in fact, a mental hospital under a Major Oliver of the Army's Medical Corps. When MI.5 needed a detention center off the beaten path, it borrowed the old mental institution, so well hidden from curious eyes and easy to guard. The hush-hush place was tolerated, or ignored by the good people of Ham. No questions were asked, not even when it was rumored in the village that Rudolf Hess had arrived at the House.

The drive to this way-station on a fallen spy's odyssey was reassuring. It meandered through the lovely countryside, passing St. Andrew's Church, the only other edifice on the road. But what awaited the prisoners at the heavily guarded compound quickly shattered all illusions. An enclosure had been added on the grounds (it is still there). The spies, housed in makeshift frame barracks behind tall barbed wire, were taken for interrogation to the spacious rooms of the big house. Ham Common was managed by its own warden, a bemonocled colonel from Rhodesia called "Tin-eye" Stephens, assisted by "Stimmy" Stimson, his deputy.

The inmates had few options. Doughty romantics imbued with the dreadless knightly spirit of the game, who refused outright to "cooperate," were secretly tried and either hanged or shot. Those who heeded the invitation to membership in the Double-X fraternity and agreed *pro forma* to become controlled agents, but then attempted to double-cross the double-crossers, were either imprisoned for the duration (as was Caroli) or were quietly liquidated.

Most of the guests lodged here realized sooner or later what was the best for them, yet turning a spy into a controlled agent was a delicate and intricate process. For all their callousness, Abwehr agents planted in Britain were by and large sensitive people, rather fragile when cornered. Most of them had a predilection to live in a world of deceit; many were capable of attaching themselves with equal facility to one side or the other. They had a code of warped honor and professed to be appalled by the very idea of becoming double agents.

The procedure of doing so required considerable skill beyond giving them the basic choice between life and death. Tact was not always exercised at its best by the Pied Pipers of MI.5.

In her new London flat in November 1943, shortly after she checked into Double-X, Lily Sergueiev, the great lady of double-agentry who later distinguished herself in the Normandy deception campaign, was quickly put at ease. In the spring of 1944, however, when she was sent back to Lisbon to pick up a late model Afu set from her contact in the Abwehr, Lily returned with a new "security check," the danger signal which she was to insert in her messages when and if she would be broadcasting under duress.

By then she was so exasperated by the condescending manner with which her hosts treated her that she refused to divulge this critical secret. She had to be "put on ice" on June 14, 1944, only six days after the Normandy landings, when her services were sorely needed for the second phase of the deception campaign.

Fortunately for Double-X, it had on its staff men and women who possessed the proper understanding of the personal idiosyncrasies of their charges. One of the best in this group was a woman known as Mrs. Maud at Ham, a sweet-voiced, kind lady with gray hair and twinkling eyes, who could put the tense "girls" of Double-X at ease. There were as many as a dozen of them which the Abwehr had managed to get into Britain by the end of 1943, such as "Francine," a little Belgian, "Nelly," an aristocratic French lady, a simple girl from Brittany, and a Czech redhead.

On the male side, the most effective persuader was probably the late Thomas Harris, remembered as the ace practitioner of the tricky art of turning German spies from the Iberian Peninsula into double agents. A handsome dark man of considerable wealth, Harris was an artist in everything he did, and a gifted painter as well. A Britisher with roots in Spain, a collector of and dealer in fine antiques, Tommy was a *bon vivant* and a gourmet who could charm his victims into unconditional surrender even when he needed less polite means to gain his ends.

After initiation, controlled agents were assigned quarters in "safe houses" near London, where they lived in comfort under guard, each with his case officer directing operations and catering to his whims. Most of them served faithfully as double agents as long as they were considered useful. Well over a hundred German spies became thus controlled, including two (called "Edda" and "Ilse" by the Abwehr, "Cobweb" and "Battle" in Double-X) in Iceland, and one in Canada with two cover-names, "Bobbi" and "Moonbeam."

Some did not develop satisfactorily. Others proved of no great importance and were discarded. But forty of them made major contributions to the British war effort while pretending to be serving the German cause.

Olaf Klausen and Jack Berg were in the last category which explains their longevity and apparent success. Shortly after their arrival in Scotland in March 1941, they endured in Double-X until February 1944. Klausen went by the code name of "Mutt," and Berg was called "Jeff."

Their case illustrated both the usefulness and the hazards of the Double-X game. Berg cooperated satisfactorily throughout his long tenure, and enjoyed the privileges and comforts of a trusted double agent. Klausen went along at first, then balked, and became so recalcitrant that he had to be separated from his buddy and imprisoned for the duration. However, his radio was used as if he were still at large. A string of messages sent in his name broadcast his sanguine claims of sabotage.

Such acts had been staged for them, usually by giving them credit for ordinary industrial, railroad, marine, and other accidents. They drew considerable quantities of sabotage materiel from Germany as well as substantial funds in pound sterling, and the Abwehr did not deem it necessary to send in other saboteurs so long as Klausen and Berg appeared to perform satisfactorily.

The double agent Fritz, called "Zigzag" in Double-X, was actually Eddie Chapman, the notorious British criminal whose specialty was safecracking. Wanted several times over by Scotland Yard, he hoped to escape by moving to the Channel Islands, where he was arrested nevertheless. When the Germans occupied Jersey in the summer of 1940, they found Chapman languishing in jail whence he promptly volunteered his services for espionage. He was accepted by the Abwehr which was satisfied that Eddie, who had ample reasons to loath his native land, would make a reliable spy.

Actually Chapman never intended to become a traitor. He reached Double-X in due course, traveling his own route. As soon as he arrived at Welbech in December 1942, he checked in with the police in Littleport. The people at XX welcomed Eddie into the fold. Coming as he did for a specific assignment—to blow up the de Havilland plant at Hatfield—it became mandatory to carry it out, if Chapman was to return to the Germans as originally planned, where he could function as a British agent.

Eddie was left to his own devices to arrange the outrage. This was done in accordance with one of the cardinal principles of the organization that "a double agent should, as far as possible, actually live the life and go through all the motions of a genuine agent."

Chapman, or Zigzag, was allowed to visit the plant in Hatfield and steal explosives at Sevenoaks. He was physically on the spot in the dusk of a foggy winter evening, at 6 P.M. on January 27, 1943, when the powerhouse of the de Havilland factory was to be blown to bits.

It took him so long to "accomplish the mission successfully," as he reported afterward to his case officer in Paris, because MI.5 needed time to make the wanton act appear as realistic as possible. Robertson and his colleagues took it for granted that the Germans would seek confirmation for Eddie's claim by reconnoitering from the air the damaged plant. An elaborate scheme was devised to show the Germans exactly what they expected to see.

The British had serving in the Camouflage Experimental Station of the Royal Engineers a major named Jasper Maskelyne, the scion of a famous dynasty of magicians and himself an accomplished make-believe artist. His job was to adapt on a huge scale the conjurer's tricks to the fields of battle. He invented dummy guns, dummy shell barrages, dummy tanks and even dummy men; hid naval harbors; launched a fleet of dummy submarines each 258 feet long; built a dummy battleship. Once, with the help of mirrors, he conjured up thirty-six tanks in the desert where in fact there was only one; and concealed the Suez Canal for part of its length.

Major Maskelyne and his "Magic Gang" also invented all sorts of paraphernalia for secret agents. He was now called in by MI.5 to devise the damage Eddie would be doing at the doomed plant so as to look real on the photographs of the German reconnaissance planes.

Maskelyne used a big relief canvas to cover the entire roof of the powerhouse. Painted on it in technicolor was the damage that supposedly had been wrought below. In one of his magic factories (of which he had three), he built papier-mâché dummies that resembled the broken pieces of the generator. He strew them, as well as chipped bricks, battered blocks of concrete, smashed furniture and other such props all around the place, until it looked thoroughly wrecked to observers from the air.

It was Maskelyne's masterpiece rather than Eddie's handiwork which the German reconnaissance planes photographed. Chapman was allowed to go back in triumph, and was received like a conquering hero in Paris. The Germans were so impressed with his feat that they sent him to England again in June 1944, this time on a straight intelligence mission. At MI.5 he participated in the massive deception campaign that upset German dispositions at the time of the Normandy landings. This time, too, he was permitted to return to his German friends, but by then the Abwehr had been smashed and the Nazis who were now running the intelligence establishment put him on ice. In November 1944, he was abruptly dropped by Double-X on grounds of what was cryptically noted as "lack of security on the part of the agent."

The System that began in 1939 with a single double agent had grown enormously by the end of 1941. It had nineteen major stooges, lulling the Abwehr into the belief that all was well with its network on the British Isles.

· Aside from such fixtures as Tate (Hans Hansen), and Mutt and Jeff, the show consisted of the following featured players:

• Balloon, an Englishman, specializing in intelligence about arms and armament;

• Careless, a Pole, reporting on the production of anti-aircraft defenses and the delivery of American aircraft;

• Celery, another British subject, dealing with air force developments;

• Sweet William, also a Britisher, sending reports on morale and the food situation via the Spanish diplomatic pouch;

• Tricycle, a Yugoslav playboy, who pretended to have a whole ring of spies working for him, collecting military and economic data;

• Mullet, an Englishman, whose specialty was economic and industrial espionage;

• Peppermint, a member of the Spanish Legation in London, covering a broad range of military and economic subjects;

• Rainbow, a Portuguese of German parentage, reporting on aviation, air defense, industrial, and economic matters;

• The Snark, a Yugoslav woman, keeping the Abwehr posted on food prices and living conditions;

• Dragonfly, a British subject of German parentage, sending daily weather reports, military and general information, especially about aerodromes and troop movements;

• Father, a Belgian, supplying technical information about the Royal Air Force, whose original instructions called for his return to Germany on a plane he was supposed to steal;

•Gander, a German, reporting on morale, road obstacles and the defenses of northwest England;

• Gelatine, an Austrian woman married to a distinguished Briton (whose circle of friends included Major General J.F.C. Fuller, the noted tank pioneer and military analyst), sending political information supposedly straight from Whitehall;

• Giraffe, a Czech aviator, reporting on the RAF purportedly from inside it;

• G. W., the Welsh police inspector from Swansea, sending intelligence reports also in the Spanish pouch and running a sabotage organization of rebellious Welshmen.

NOTE

1 Captain von Grunen was not at the party, nor was he with the Abwehr any longer. He had been transferred peremptorily to the Eastern Front after a quarrel with Colonel Waag, chief of the Paris Abwehr branch in the Hotel Lutetia, the latter a nephew of Admiral Canaris's wife.

Part IV

THE FOXES
IN AMERICA

Chapter 27

Silhouettes in Black
on Gray

*E*VEN before the war broke out in Europe, Colonel Piekenbrock and Colonel Lahousen drafted plans for "special operations" in the United States, to interfere with the Allied war effort at long range. However, their plans ran into a couple of snags. When Hitler failed to coax peace from the Allies in the wake of the Polish campaign, his determination to keep the United States neutral became firm. He told Admiral Canaris to avoid doing anything that would stimulate American aid to Britain or bring the United States into the war.

This policy was echoed in the Foreign Ministry. Lahousen once formally queried Foreign Minister von Ribbentrop whether there were any "political objections to Abwehr II activities," meaning sabotage, "in the U.S.A." Ribbentrop wrote back, "We are opposed by such serious political disadvantages that we must voice the strongest possible objections to any such plans."

Besides this suspension of clandestine activities, the Abwehr's line of communication with the United States was tied exclusively to fast German ships in the transatlantic service. The war swept them off the ocean, and the line was cut overnight. Setting up secret radio stations in America would take time. Pending that, and the transfer of the courier system to neutral vessels going to Genoa and to the Pan-American Clipper flying to Lisbon, the agents were told to bide their time.

During this brief period of hibernation, the Abwehr's attention focused on the strangest and most mysterious operation ever mounted in the United States. It lasted eighteen months, from late summer of 1939 to February 1941. A single Abwehr special agent on American soil was directed in a maneuver that otherwise did not

affect the United States at all. The target had been the chief of the
Soviet Secret Service in Western Europe, who called himself General
Walter Gregorievitch Krivitsky.

In the fall of 1937 he had created a world-wide sensation by coming out from the shadows at The Hague, announcing that he had
"broken with Stalin," and would seek asylum in the West.

Every secret service in the world was keenly interested in this
fugitive, but none more so than the Abwehr. Commander Protze
hoped to establish contact and obtain from him, amicably with generous bribes or under duress if need be, information about the network of the Soviet Secret Service.

While Krivitsky was in Paris, Protze selected from his stable a
shabby journalist whose allegiance was usually for sale to the highest
bidder. Pretending to be a hunted renegade from the Communist apparatus and a Jewish refugee from the Nazis, the man managed to
reach Krivitsky in Paris and gained from him some clues that would
have enabled Protze and the Gestapo to hunt down a number of
Soviet spies at large in Germany. This came to an abrupt end when
Krivitsky suddenly obtained a visitor's visa for the United States and
departed.

To pick up the chase in America, Protze chose his ace operator for
the surveillance of refugees. He was Dr. Hans Wesemann, an ex-
Marxist like Schwarz, but unlike his bedraggled colleague, a clever,
charming, debonair man welcome in the best circles in all the Western European capitals. Behind his soigné and respectable exterior,
Wesemann was absolutely unscrupulous. His specialty became the
kidnapping of emigrés. In January 1935, he arranged the abduction
of the German trade union leader Balling and his wife from their
haven in Copenhagen. A few months later he engineered the kidnapping of Berthold Jacob, a famous military writer living in Strasbourg.

The Jacob case kicked up an international storm and the Swiss
authorities, on whose soil the abduction was engineered, arrested
Wesemann. During his trial he confessed his association with the
Nazis, but after a few years in prison, secretly returned to their
service, now trying to endear himself to German political refugees by
citing his confession and break with the Nazis.

At this time in early 1939, Wesemann was working on a Gestapo
plot to kidnap Willie Muenzenberg, the leading Communist propagandist living in exile in Paris. Then he was suddenly sent after
Krivitsky in America. He traveled on a fake passport listing his profession as "journalist."

He was seen in New York by several old acquaintances. One of
them was Emery Kelen, the world-famous political cartoonist, who
had been friendly with him during the late Twenties in Geneva where

Wesemann managed the news service of the Social Democratic Party. Kelen bumped into Wesemann at a bus stop on Lexington Avenue. Amazed that such a notorious Nazi agent could enter the United States, he approached Wesemann who turned on his heels and fled. Kelen called the FBI from the nearest telephone booth and notified them that Wesemann was in the United States. The Bureau was apparently not interested in following up the clue.

Seeking to hide out in America, Krivitsky was meanwhile causing one stir after another. A small thin man with craggy eyebrows that all but obscured his eyes, he was unable to conceal his fear of Soviet avengers. He published sensational articles in the *Saturday Evening Post* and then he testified before the Dies Committee on Un-American Activities; he produced a book about his life, written "in secret— working behind drawn shades." He had quickly become a conspicuous figure in New York and Washington, frequenting crowded restaurants in Times Square and making one public appearance after another on Capitol Hill in the glare of floodlights and pursued by hordes of reporters. After every excursion into the limelight, he issued frantic statements claiming that he had been shadowed by professional assassins of the GPU.

In New York, Wesemann quickly picked up Krivitsky's trail, following the Russian wherever he went. By then he was not the only foreign agent interested in Krivitsky. Another was a notorious GPU triggerman known as "Hans the Red Judas," who had arrived fresh from the liquidation of Ignace Reiss, Krivitsky's closest associate in the Soviet Secret Service, who was also a defector.

From his awareness of the persistent surveillance by this odd couple, Krivitsky knew that both were trying to corner him. The Red Judas was in the States to kill him, but knowing Wesemann's uncanny ability to get his men alive, Krivitsky feared that the German would abduct him aboard one of the German ships in New York harbor and ship him to the Third Reich, a fate the hapless man dreaded more than death.

He conveyed his apprehension to the American authorities, but nothing was done. Then, when he was coming out of a restaurant on Times Square, Krivitsky literally bumped into Hans. Desperate and exasperated, he walked up to his shadow and challenged him. "Did you come to shoot me, Hans?" he asked, but the Red Judas pretended to be shocked. "Not I," he said. "I am myself marked for the assassin." No doubt scared of being caught with his victim, Hans faded from Krivitsky's trail. But Wesemann continued to shadow him, ever more ominously and threateningly.

When the European war broke out on September 1, the FBI and the Office of Naval Intelligence entered Krivitsky's shadow on their suspect lists. Wesemann advised Commander Protze in an urgent cable that "the American authorities obviously suspect that my presence here is connected with activities for you," and asked that he be recalled. Protze responded by return cable, ordering him to stay.

His cover was wearing thin nevertheless, and a few weeks later he was permitted to depart from the United States on a Japanese ship. When he reached Tokyo, a cable was awaiting him with instructions to return to the States via Brazil. He was not able to leave Yokohama until August 13, and was required to spend time in Nicaragua before entering the United States in December.

By then Krivitsky was finding the strain of his precarious exile unbearable. Harrassed both by bogies of his imagination and actual pursuers presumably gunning for him, he left his New York sanctuary for Virginia, where he hoped to be able to borrow a gun from the only friend he knew who had one.

On Sunday, February 9, 1941, returning from his brief sojourn, he stopped in Washington at the Hotel Bellevue near Union Station where, apparently, he planned to spend the night. It was almost 6:00 P.M., a dark, wintry evening, when he registered. He was found the next morning by a maid, behind the locked door of his fifth floor room, sprawled out on the bed with the borrowed gun near his hand. He had been dead about six hours.

Bernard Thompson, chief of Washington detectives insisted that there was no foul play in his death. "All the physical evidence," he said, "points to suicide." Hans Wesemann agreed with Thompson's conclusion, but with a macabre twist. His mission washed out, he left a few days later for Venezuela, where he checked in with the Abwehr representative at the German Legation—a man who posed as the Commercial Attaché—to give him a coded cable for transmission to Berlin. It was his final report. In it he claimed that he had trailed Krivitsky all the way to Washington, and was actually in front of the Bellevue watching Krivitsky as he checked in for the night. "I am positive that he saw and recognized me," he concluded. "I think I have frightened him to death."

True or false, Wesemann's mission was completed.

On April 25, 1940, Admiral Canaris was asked to call on Foreign Minister von Ribbentrop to discuss "a rather delicate matter." German troops had reoccupied Narvik, and the Abwehr was working around the clock on last minute preparations for the imminent invasion of the Low Countries. But when he arrived in Ribbentrop's airy office in the Wilhelm Strasse, Canaris was startled to hear the Foreign Minister again revive the issue of his spies in the United States, of all things and of all places. The difficult task of assuring American neutrality had been assigned to him, said the Foreign Minister.

Canaris assured Ribbentrop that he did not have to worry, that he had no agents in America "spying on the United States Army and the United States Navy." But even as he did so, Canaris was energetically promoting his activities in the United States. "It is imperative," he wrote in a directive to his higher staff on the same day he had given his pledge to Ribbentrop, "that we collect classified information about [American] technological and economic developments . . . including those within the armed forces."

A few weeks later he issued another directive in which he spelled out the items his agents were expected to procure. They included "inventions and new constructions of all kinds," he wrote, "for the army and the navy, especially new types of aircraft, aero engines, and warships.

"Our agents are independent of one another. The exposure of one or another of these groups is, therefore, confined solely to its members, leaving the other unaffected."

As soon as the ripples of the Rumrich scandal subsided, Commander Pheiffer and Major Ritter, the two officers responsible for the American coverage, decided that it was safe to go back into business. "Operations were resumed," Pheiffer wrote, "with improved security measures, and they continued to yield gratifying dividends. A score of super-agents, now following strictly our instructions, operated brilliantly with astounding impunity."

They represented a formidable force.

Hermann Lang, the little man who stole the Norden bombsight, was still at large, as was his colleague at Sperry Gyroscope, Everett Minster Roeder. A super-agent named Simon E. Koedel was getting much of his intelligence directly from the War Department because he was on its classified mailing list. Lilly Stein, the indispensable *femme fatale*, was still Ritter's chief link to Washington insiders (including a high-ranking Foreign Service officer) and to the rumor-mongers and gossips of New York's café society. She was producing more than ever, as was the indomitable Frederick Joubert Duquesne, recognized at last as the dean of the Ritter network.

These were their halcyon days. As Admiral Canaris later recorded in a letter to General Wilhelm Keitel, it was during this period that Roeder had procured "the blueprints of the complete radio equipment of the new Glenn Martin bomber" and, among other devices manufactured by Sperry, "classified drawings of range-finders, blind-flying instruments, a bank-and-turn indicator, and a navigator compass." At this same time, Duquesne sent to Germany "the design of a classified storage battery (separator), a propeller-driving mechanism and the drawings of numerous other secret devices." The old pro found the going so easy, and was feeling so secure that he boldly went straight to the sources to obtain the secrets. When he read a brief item in *The New York Times* about a mysterious new gas mask the Chemical Warfare Service in the Army was said to be developing, he immediately recognized this as an important lead. The design of a new gas mask was of interest in itself. Moreover, it would provide clues for the nature of the new poison gases the United States Army was developing. Determined to procure details of the gas mask, he wrote a discreetly worded letter to the chief of the Chemical Warfare Service, describing himself as a "well-known, responsible and reputable writer and lecturer," and asking for information about the new mask. "Don't worry if this information is confidential," he wrote at the bottom of his letter, "because it is in the hands of a good citizen." He received the information by return mail.

Looming largest in this cavalcade of shadows was an agent going by the code name of "Dinter," yet his profile in espionage is presented here for the first time. He was accepted and fêted by high society because he was of authentic European nobility and married to a lady of German aristocracy. Count and Countess Douglas, as they called themselves, were received with cordial friendship at the most exclusive parties in Washington and New York, where they were served exquisite meals by unsuspecting hosts and high-grade intelligence by fellow guests.

Count Douglas posed as a citizen of Chile, where he said he had extensive properties. It was true that he had come from Chile to the United States, but that was not the whole story. He was Count Friedrich Sauerma, a German pilot officer of World War I, later a member of the Free Corps. He played a prominent part in the murder of Karl Liebknecht and Rosa Luxemburg, the Spartacist leaders, on January 15, 1919. When the outrage came under scrutiny, Count Sauerma was spirited to South America by his influential friends in the Reichswehr.

On the run he married Freda von Maltzahn, adopted his Scottish mother's maiden name Douglas for his own, and settled in Chile. He became a Chilean citizen and did fairly well in a variety of ventures until 1934. Then old friends in Germany suggested that he go to the United States to become a spy.

For a secret agent he acted rather openly at the outset of his American sojourn. He plunged eagerly into intrigues in New York, in association with Dr. Hubert Schnuch, a demagogue who dreamed of seizing power in the United States by force and violence. Schnuch organized his private army, called "Bunaste," and named the Count chief of its secret service. At the outset Douglas confined his activities to spying on German clubs and societies that were openly anti-Nazi, and on Nazis who set themselves up in opposition to Dr. Schnuch. Corruption became so rampant in the Nazi underground that one of Schnuch's former aides, Anton Haegele, decided to clean out "the pig pen of the leadership clique." Haegele undertook an investigation and found that Schnuch and Douglas had embezzled substantial sums from the Bunaste's secret treasury. They were thrown out of the organization, at a time when Dr. Schnuch boasted that he had "10,000 men all over the country, willing and ready to lay down their lives for a Nazi America."

Schnuch vanished and Douglas was forced to seek another job. He found it in the Abwehr. With his excellent credentials as a political assassin, he was given the cover-name "Dinter," $500 a month, and a generous expense account to enable him to move about in high society, where he was soon at home.

His major contact in Washington, he claimed, was a couple we shall call "the Whites." According to Douglas's dispatches, the Whites were popular in the capital's most exclusive and influential circles. He reported that Mrs. White had attended a dinner party at which she was seated between General George C. Marshall and an unnamed member of President Roosevelt's Cabinet. The normally taciturn Chief of Staff suffered from a momentary lapse of discretion, according to Douglas, when he told Mrs. White that "it was now definite that Greenland, Iceland, and the Azores would be used as [Allied] bases."

Cabled in Douglas's special code through the Consulate in New York, this proved a most timely bit of intelligence. Soon after it had reached Berlin, the information was partly corroborated. On July 7, United States forces landed on Iceland to relieve British troops defending the island since the spring of 1940. By September 25, plans were completed for the construction of air and naval base facilities in Greenland and Iceland, exactly as Douglas forewarned. Washington learned of the German leak and General Marshall ordered an investigation to track down the source. Several innocent officers of the War Department came under suspicion, but neither the FBI nor War Department investigators could clear up what came to be called the "Greenland leak." They never discovered that the information came from Dinter and that General Marshall himself helped Douglas to one of his greatest feats.

The Count continued his spying among high echelons, aided mostly by the hospitable Whites. Douglas once overheard "Bud," the White's son, talking on the telephone about a heavy machine gun on the assembly line at one of the General Motors plants. The Army Air Force was "planning to build it into the wings of combat planes, to be operated by a pushbutton on the elevator, sighting through a mirror on the control panel."

Count Douglas engaged the best-informed guests in conversations, dropping loaded questions, making them talk carelessly by feigning knowledge of what he was seeking. After a dinner at the house of a man he referred to as Baron, where he sat next to "an American pilot serving in the Royal Canadian Air Force," Douglas was able to describe an "improved American bombsight" in all of its intricate details. In the wake of another party he told Cologne that a new device would soon replace the cross-wires in American range finders with two colored disks positioned one above the other. "Where normally," he wrote in his report, "the cross-wires would be, the complementary colors converge, rendering the disks colorless to indicate the desired range."

At another party, Douglas met an employee of the Bendix aeronautical works and managed, as he put it, to subvert him on the spot. He trapped the engineer into discussing certain "new designs," then persuaded the man to show him the plans by criticizing the original conception. As an accomplished aeronautical engineer himself, he warranted that he could improve them in a redrafting. "Use the improved version as your own design," Douglas taunted the engineer. "That would be a feather in your cap."[1]

In New York, Dr. Herbert Gross was posing as an economist and finance writer for German trade journals. Actually a full-time Abwehr agent, he specialized in industrial and economic espionage, and the intricacies of American relations with the Soviet Union. He headed a small ring whose members were identified in his dispatches as "Prochoroff" and "Rurick." His reports so pleased his superiors in Berlin that Colonel Piekenbrock commended Gross for his "excellent work" and saw to it that he was amply rewarded.

As befitting an agent specializing in high finance, Gross was the best-paid member of the American network. While the rank and file received a mere pittance, Dr. Gross was sent $9,500 on April 18, 1941, and more than $75,000 in all. The money was funneled to him through the Consul General in New York.

The Abwehr's ranking political agent in 1939–41 was an internationally famed newspaperman and dean of German foreign correspondents—Paul Scheffer, former editor of the once distinguished *Berliner Tageblatt*.

Scheffer, a burly man who, someone once said, looked like the Abbot Superior of a monastery contemplating sin, was in the United

States as the correspondent of *Das Reich*, Dr. Goebbel's shrill propaganda weekly. He understood well how to camouflage his new Nazi association by parading his liberal past and keeping in touch with old friends who were unaware of his political metamorphosis. An immaculately groomed *boulevardier* type with exquisite manners and expensive tastes, he had a knack for disarming doubters with whispered anti-Nazi talk during meals at the Chambord on Third Avenue, New York's best and most expensive French restaurant of those days, where he always insisted on picking up the tab.

Scheffer, a professional spy of the romantic school, still practiced some of the hoary melodrama of the profession. He lived at 227 East 57th Street, but had his confidential correspondence sent to an old brownstone on East 51st Street that was apparently unoccupied, its windows boarded up. Once each day Scheffer would drive up in a cab, walk quickly to the mailbox in the doorway and pick up his letters, then drive away.

Such stealth was nothing new to Scheffer. He had represented both the *Berliner Tageblatt* and the Abwehr in Moscow, Canaris's personal liaison to the highest ranking agent the Germans ever had in the Soviet Union. Carried by the code name of "Reinhold" on the Abwehr's roster, he was Mikhail Alexandrovich Chernov, head of the Ukrainian Commissariat of Trade before becoming People's Commissar of Agriculture of the U.S.S.R.

In the late winter of 1937, when the NKVD discovered Chernov's lucrative pastime, Scheffer was expelled from the Soviet Union. His work as a go-between became fully exposed during Chernov's trial. Yet there was no objection when, after a brief tour of duty at Abwehr headquarters, he was sent to the United States as the correspondent of Dr. Goebbels's venomous weekly. His job was *political* reportage—openly for *Das Reich*, but surreptitiously for the Abwehr. His secret dispatches were so highly regarded that Colonel Piekenbrock insisted on processing them personally.

Carl Edmond Heine, resembling what the French call *preux chevalier*, was an automotive executive of Detroit, in whom the irritating edges of German mannerisms were smoothed over by long association with the motor city's affluent, hard-living country club set. A nattily dressed, glib man of forty-eight, he had worked as foreign sales manager of the Chrysler and Ford Motor Companies, until Ford sent him to Germany as general manager of its subsidiary there.

In Germany, Heine came to the attention of Dr. Ferdinand Porsche, Hitler's favorite automobile designer and the genius who developed the Volkswagen, who also acted as a scout for the Abwehr. Porsche tactfully asked Heine whether he would be interested in going back to the States, "to work in your own field but in a different capacity." Hinting that the job he had in mind would involve "certain hazards," he added persuasively that it would be "extremely useful to Germany." Heine was fond of his adopted country but he now experienced a resurgence of his old Germanic feelings and expressed interest, whereupon Porsche referred him to Dr. Wirtz, manager of the aviation department of the Volkswagen Werke, and an Abwehr executive.

Dr. Wirtz told Heine that the work would be collecting information, "not normally available" about the American automobile and aviation industries. Heine balked. He was loath to give up the high managerial post with Ford that was paying him the phenomenal salary (for those days) of $30,000 a year. Porsche and Wirtz appealed to his "patriotism" and Heine consented. He was then sent to Hamburg for the usual secret sessions with Major Ritter and Captain Hermann Sandel at Ast X, and the deal was made.

Heine was given perfunctory training in cryptography and the use of secret inks, and "indoctrinated" to bolster his "patriotism," which showed occasional signs of sagging. Just prior to his departure he was told to keep his American passport but to renounce his citizenship in secret (that is, without telling the American authorities about it), and to resume his German allegiance so that he could be commissioned a captain in the Luftwaffe Reserve. Heine was reluctant to burn all his bridges behind him and arrived in the States via Peru still an American citizen, traveling with his genuine passport to begin his new career. He returned to Detroit, settling down in suburban affluence. He reestablished his professional contacts and renewed old friendships.

Utilizing his connections he found it simple to collect automotive data, but not so easy to procure material about aeronautics. When he despaired of getting what he needed most he resorted to a rather simple method of "collection." He placed ads in *Popular Aviation* magazine stating bluntly that he was in the market for information about "developments in aeronautics." He received several answers, including one from a young man named Bob Aldrich who appeared to be excellently informed on the subject.

Heine told Aldrich that he needed the information for his business, but knew so little about aviation that he could not discuss even the simplest model airplane with his young son. Then he baffled Aldrich by asking him pointed questions about such complex devices as certain boosters used in high altitude planes and new types of condensers. He paid Aldrich and others who had answered his advertisement twenty dollars for each piece of information and forwarded it as the product of his own labors.

He also had a letter of introduction from a Luftwaffe pilot named Loehr to a "Mr. Vollmecks," who was an official at the Detroit branch of the Civil Aviation Board. Vollmecks gave him a batch of unclassified releases issued by the CAB, but when Heine asked him for details and elaborations the alert official suggested that he should obtain them officially from the proper authorities in Washington. Heine heeded the advice and, to his astonishment, received much of the presumably classified information Vollmecks had refused to give him.

Although his methods of collection were primitive the information he was accumulating became valuable intelligence in his expert hands. He improved and amplified the raw material from his own knowledge and experience, collated and focused the scattered data, and filled in whatever gaps remained with educated guesses.

There were many more—petty Peeping Toms, stringers, sleepers, straphangers, go-fors, cut-outs and go-betweens, couriers—in addition to other informers waiting for small handouts. These were the invaluable *Hintermaenner*, men and women behind certain V-men in places where the secrets were made. Some of these were willing partners in the game. Others were mere dopes or dupes, blissfully unaware that the information they dispensed to presumed friends would wind up in the Abwehr's files.

It was a motley crowd of ordinary people caught up by national interests in the *grand aventure* of their otherwise humdrum lives. They had none of the snooty elegance and cunning of the legendary British agent nor the jaded mien and cynicism of the French *espion*.

But Admiral Canaris had every reason to be satisfied. In the summer of 1940 he felt justified to boast a little by sending a memorandum about the accomplishments of his agents in the United States to General Franz Halder, the Army's Chief of Staff. After describing the scope and scale of their activities, he listed "our successes to date" as follows:

1. They assured for us a continuous flow of technical reports, mainly about the United States Navy—complete blueprints of the newest warships, aircraft carriers, and destroyers. The high costs of research and development could be saved through the acquisition of the detailed blueprints of important devices (Norden bombsight, etc.).
2. They reported continuously on Anglo-American negotiations involving the supply of arms, ammunition, and equipment (aircraft) and their delivery from America to England. Between April 1 and December 31, 1939, we received 171 such reports, exclusive of press clippings.

3. They reported continuously the departure of convoys from American ports for England and France.
4. They kept us continuously informed of the movements of all ships all along the Eastern Seaboard of the United States.

NOTE

1 Dinter endured in the United States as an Abwehr agent until the fall of 1941, when he left New York with what he claimed were the blueprints of an improved bombsight, going first to South America, then on to China, continued on the Abwehr's payroll all the time. The last time he was seen was in 1943 in a Peking hospital, suffering from the illness that caused his death shortly afterward.

Chapter 28

The Mexican Cockpit

*W*HEN Hitler himself objected to espionage in the United States in one of their private sessions on June 8, 1940, Canaris did not dare to defy him as he had Ribbentrop. He decided to leave his American organization intact beneath its double-cloak. But he would recall his resident director from the United States and move the base of his North American networks to Mexico.

The man who was nominally Canaris's super-spy in America was not as important or influential as his grandiose title of "resident director" indicated. He was a mere kibitzer on the American scene, hardly remembered by his name, much less by anything he accomplished. An impoverished, footloose Austrian baron named Meydel, he had inveigled his old friend Lahousen into giving him the job.

He had been sent to America in the first flush of excitement after the outbreak of the war when it was thought that the Abwehr needed a "chief V-man" in the United States. He turned out to be an indolent, arrogant playboy, living it up in New York and Washington on the Abwehr's slush fund. This was resented in the Embassy and drew sharp protests from the career men who complained that the indiscretions of this pompous ass threatened to expose the Abwehr and compromise the Embassy. Canaris seized upon Hitler's ban to get rid of Meydel.

But he expected great things from the move to Mexico.

The great Latin republic in North America always attracted German imagination in martial designs on the United States, probably because they believed that bitter hatred of the "gringo Americans" continued unabated south of the border. Twenty-two years before, the decisive factor in the American entry into World War I was Foreign Minister Arthur Zimmermann's foolish promise to the pro-

German President Venustiano Carranza, to restore New Mexico, Arizona, and Texas to Mexico if he declared war against the United States. Then, too, Mexico swarmed with German spies and saboteurs —among them such dangerous operatives as Walter Jahnke, Lothar Wittke (alias Pablo Waberski) and S. Anthony Delmar—using the country as a sanctuary in their sneak-attacks against the United States.

Bribery and Latin laissez-faire made it relatively easy to use facilities in Mexico for clandestine purposes. With forged passports and identity papers, the Germans could maintain secret shortwave stations in Mexico which they could not hope to sustain with impunity for any length of time in the United States.

Already in 1936, Dr. Heinrich Norte had been sent to Mexico City in the guise of Chancellor of Legation, to prepare the ground and especially to collaborate with the already widespread Japanese espionage apparatus all along the Pacific coast. Immediately after the outbreak of the war in Europe, the Germans set up a major *Aussenstelle* (outpost) in Mexico City, comparable in size and endowment to the so-called *Kriegsorganisation* (war organization) the Abwehr established in Spain.

The German Minister, Baron von Ruedt, a career diplomat of the old school, knew little of what was going on behind his back and was uneasy about even that much. From the Legation fanned the tentacles of the outpost. An agent named Hilgert, posing as a bank clerk, was sending military and naval intelligence to Hamburg whenever he was sober. Another agent, Hermkes, a businessman *pro forma*, worked for Commander Pheiffer. Major Georg Nikolaus and agent Ruege specialized in economic espionage.

Dr. Joachim A. Hertslet, a dynamic young Saxon posing as a counselor at the overcrowded Legation, was in and out of Mexico arranging the surreptitious flow of oil to Germany via Italy, Japan, and the Siberian maritime province of Primorski to circumvent the tightening British blockade. He also tried to establish secret bases in the Gulf of Mexico and the Caribbean where long-range U-boats could refuel. No newcomer to Mexico, he had concluded a barter agreement under which Germany had been exchanging industrial products for oil as early as 1938. Hertslet had a wide circle of influential friends in Mexico whom he and his pretty young wife entertained lavishly at their house on Monte Blanco, and he even knew President Cárdenas.

Karl Berthold Franz Rekowski, an Austrian businessman once employed by H. Bischoff and Company in New York in the export-import trade, was the Abwehr's sabotage expert interested solely in targets in the United States. He organized Irishmen to damage armament plants and ships.[1]

Sent to Mexico in October 1939 to preside over this motley assortment of spies, saboteurs and mischiefmakers was Lieutenant Colonel Friedrich Karl von Schleebruegge, a regimental commander at the Berlin garrison before the war and a veteran of the recent Polish campaign. A field officer of undoubted competence, he was without any previous experience in the intelligence game. Just what made Admiral Canaris pick him as head of this important outpost was neither known in Mexico City nor apparent to his associates.

A relative of Franz von Papen, Schleebruegge was a tall, stiff-necked, debonair gentleman, the Junker version of Colonel Blimp, complete with monocle and spats. He hovered over the sordid proceedings of his new job, keeping aloof most of the time, holed up in his elegant house at 142 Donata Guerra where he mingled only with his equals, never with his subordinates from the outpost for whom, it seemed, he had mild contempt. Soon even Baron von Ruedt concluded that the transplanted colonel was not the right man for such a delicate venture. "Herr von Schleebruegge," the envoy wrote to the Foreign Ministry, "inevitably attracts attention to himself with his martial bearing and military mannerisms."

It did not matter how good or bad the chief was. The other members of the outpost knew their business and did remarkably well, paying no attention either to the whims or the instructions of their boss.

In spite of its bumbling Colonel, and with only tenuous and excruciatingly slow communication 7000 miles from its home base, the Mexican outpost performed brilliantly, scoring one triumph after another. The energetic Dr. Hertslet smuggled thousands of tons of oil out of the country on Japanese and other pro-Axis ships. Dr. Norte laid the foundations for what became the fantastic "Bolivar network" of clandestine shortwave transmitters relaying to Germany such perishable intelligence as convoy routings.

Gradually the shortcomings and hardships of a major espionage operation over such a distance began to show. The enormous outpost in Mexico was among the costliest the Abwehr had anywhere outside of Germany. Its fiscal problems were aggravated by the fact that most of its operations had to be cash transactions in the specie of the lands where the deals were made. Schleebruegge needed pesos, colons, sucres, quetzals, lempiras, and cordobas to pay his agents in Colombia, Costa Rica, Ecuador, Guatemala, Honduras, and Nicaragua respectively, and thousands of dollars for the United States. Wartime restrictions everywhere made transfers increasingly complicated. They became well-nigh impossible as the British currency blockade, aided by the American government, began to take.

By the summer of 1940 the Mexican outpost ran out of money. Its poverty was manifest in many forms, and it hit the agents where it hurt them most. Rekowski was so broke at times that he could not pay his weekly bill at the Hotel Geneve, where he stayed in Mexico City. According to a telegram of Minister von Ruedt to the Abwehr in Berlin, one of the top agents did not have funds even to buy the food he needed for his survival. Schleebruegge had to make discreet touches in his circle of affluent friends to make ends meet.

Agents suspended operations throughout Central America for lack of funds. At the peak of the crisis when it seemed that the entire apparatus would go into bankruptcy, Berlin bestirred itself to help. The Italians had a special hoard of money in New York that had been sent from Rome to finance Fascist espionage and propaganda in the United States. There was not much the Italians were doing along these lines, and what little they did proved to be extremely cheap. The fund was almost intact when Canaris stumbled upon it. He rushed to Rome and persuaded Il Duce to lend the money to the Abwehr. It was, to the bitter end, probably the greatest single contribution Mussolini made to the joint war effort.

The fund, amounting to $3,850,000, was kept in a number of special accounts in various banks in the United States. It was all there, and Canaris now had it—but the question remained how to get it out of the United States and to the Abwehr people in Mexico and South America. A plan they made left the transaction to the Italians. The money was withdrawn from the banks, packed in diplomatic bags and taken by three special couriers—two consuls carrying $2,450,000 to Rio de Janeiro, and an embassy secretary lugging a single bag with $1,400,000 to Mexico City.

The three men traveled together as far as Brownsville, Texas, where they separated. The consuls went to New Orleans, boarded a ship for Brazil and reached their destination safely. The embassy secretary took the train to Mexico City, but as soon as he reached Mexican soil, a man who introduced himself as a special agent of the secret police challenged the Italian, opened the bag, then not paying the slightest attention to the protestation of the young diplomat and the sanctity of his privileged pouch, confiscated the money.

The Italian Minister in Mexico City rushed to the Foreign Ministry to protest the seizure. The Foreign Minister commiserated with the envoy and apologized profusely for what he described as "the inexcusable act of a new and inexperienced clerk." But neither the Italians nor the Germans ever saw any part of the money again. The

Mexican government placed it in a blocked account where it was held till the end of the war.

A crescendo of frantic messages from Mexico City to Berlin documented the gradual deepening of the German troubles. They spoke of sudden detention of key agents; of mysterious exposés appearing in Mexican newspapers, describing with a pinpoint accuracy not characteristic of native reporters, the operations of the network and the escapades of its personnel; of secret policemen shadowing Schleebruegge, Nikolaus, and Hermkes. An agent reported that his super-secret cipher had been cracked.

No amount of stern diplomatic notes, which Minister von Ruedt showered on the Foreign Ministry, helped to stop the harassments. Things became so intolerable that the envoy recommended to Berlin that the whole Abwehr outpost be dismantled. "I consider continued concealment of these activities no longer possible," von Ruedt cabled. "Moreover, they jeopardize my primary mission which is, of course, the protection of German nationals in Mexico."

"Let's face it," Colonel von Schleebruegge told Dr. Norte in a crisis conference on October 14, 1940. "We are through!" That same night he cabled the Abwehr in Berlin, asking that he be relieved of his post in Mexico and be permitted to leave, either for another country in South America or for home via Japan. His cable created consternation in Berlin. But with the high stake the Abwehr had in Mexico Canaris refused to throw in the sponge.

On October 7 he signaled Schleebruegge: "Your continued stay in Mexico absolutely imperative. If your expulsion is threatened take whatever countermeasures possible." When no countermeasures were available to von Ruedt, Canaris thought that he might be able to apply some in Germany, harassing the Mexicans there in exchange for every German harassed in Mexico, matching every expulsion, every arrest, every single incident.

He asked Colonel Bentivegni, chief of Abwehr III in charge of counterespionage, whether he had any Mexicans on his suspect list. Bentivegni came up with five individuals, but three of them were members of the Mexican Legation, protected by diplomatic immunity. The other two, a journalist named José Calero and the engineer Fernando Guttierez, were above suspicion. Canaris sent a similar inquiry to the Gestapo, but was told that the secret police knew of no Mexican in Germany who could be suspected of espionage or, for that matter, of any illicit activities.

Some light was shed on the source of these troubles when, on August 6, a special investigator from the Mexican Prosecutor General's office called on a German by the name of Weber and questioned him for three hours because, as the visitor put it, Weber had been denounced as an espionage agent. When the formal interrogation was over the men stayed on for some genial small talk. It turned out that the investigator had been a member of the Mexican team of gymnasts at the 1936 Olympic Games, and as he told Weber, still had nothing but pleasant memories of Nazi Germany. "As a matter of fact," he said with a suggestive smile, "personally I am not anti-German."

Weber seized upon the obvious opening. Now it became his turn to interrogate the investigator. Well, the man told him, they were getting derogatory information about Weber and his friends, and they could not very well ignore it. Where did the information come from? Weber asked. Most of it came from Washington, the man said, but some came from "other sources right here in Mexico City." What sort of information? Weber pressed the issue. All sorts of information, the man said evasively, leaving it to Weber to make the first move toward a deal.

Weber made an offer, the deal was made. A substantial sum of money changed hands. The next day the man returned with some original documents from the secret files of the Prosecutor General. One of them was a 47-page memorandum from J. Edgar Hoover of the FBI to the Prosecutor General's office, studded with facts and figures about German subversive activities in Mexico. It included, as Weber breathlessly reported to Berlin, "excerpts from intercepted and deciphered telegrams, specific data about our radio connections, addresses of mail drops, and other pinpointed data." Weber added reassuringly: "By paying additional bribes, I was able to persuade this official to keep me posted continuously."

Most of the information on which the Mexicans based their counterespionage campaign originated with another and, for the time being, far more dangerous source, of which the Germans remained blissfully unaware. In the summer of 1940 the British Secret Intelligence Service had opened a huge branch in New York, to collect "information on enemy activities [in the Western Hemisphere] aimed against the continuance of Britain's war effort" and to "plan appropriate countermeasures." Called British Security Coordination, it was headed by William Stephenson, a diminuitive Canadian millionaire, of whom Ian Fleming later wrote: "He is the man who became . . . the scourge of the enemy throughout the Americas."

Stephenson's cable address in New York was "Intrepid." The word characterized his operation. Within weeks of his arrival, in partnership with Colonel William J. Donovan, who later became head of the Office of Strategic Services, and "with Mr. J. Edgar Hoover of the FBI, as a formidable fullback," Stephenson developed a well-nigh perfect coverage of German subversive activities in the Western Hemisphere.

He was behind the seizure of the Italian money en route to the German agents in Mexico. The Italians had made the mistake of withdrawing those millions too hastily in lump sums from their bank accounts. The banks reported their withdrawals to the FBI and Mr. Hoover, in turn, tipped off his friend Stephenson. The rest was simple. Stephenson's agent in Mexico, who had great influence with the chief of police, arranged for the interception of the Italian courier as soon as his train reached Mexico. He then persuaded the Mexican government to block the money that was seized illegally.

It was the opening blow in the secret war waged with unprecedented bitterness and cunning, thousands of miles from the actual theatres of war. Not until a year later was the concentrated assault on German agents successful in completely demolishing the Abwehr's huge and once promising Mexican outpost.

NOTE

1 Other agents in Mexico included an economist; some coast watchers; and one man in Mexcio City, two in Tampico, and one in Mazatlán. There were dozens of others.

Chapter 29

The Communicators

*I*N December 1939, an American citizen named Karl Alfred Reuper completed his training in Hamburg, and arrived back in the United States in time for Christmas to embark on his new double life. Since he was a competent draftsman-mechanic, he quickly found a job with Air Associates in Bendix, New Jersey, working on classified contracts which the firm had with the government. Simultaneously he began his secret mission, by assembling a ring of sub-agents "to collect," as his directive stated, "documents, code books, sketches, photographs, and blueprints relative to the national defenses of the United States."

By 1940 Reuper was one of the busiest agents the Abwehr had in America. June 11 was just a typical day for Reuper.

He rose at 5:45 A.M. in his house on Palisades Avenue in Hudson Heights, New Jersey, and was at his place of work in Bendix when the day shift started at seven o'clock.

He spent an eight-hour day working at the plant, was home by four in the afternoon, had his meal, changed his clothes, and then took a Public Service bus to Manhattan to keep a *Treff* with one of his sub-agents at Pennsylvania Station. The man he went to meet was 33-year-old Peter Franz Erich Donay, a private in the United States Army stationed on Governors Island. Donay, had "something big" that needed "processing" before it could be sent to Germany by courier. It turned out to be a classified Army field manual which the soldier had borrowed for the day.

With the manual, Reuper took the subway to Woodhaven in Queens to see a machinist named Paul Grohse who was his go-between with Frank Grote, a commercial photographer in the Bronx. He used Grote to prepare the mail for the couriers by reducing documents and blueprints to ¼ inch by ¾ inch microphotographs.

312

He left the manual with Grohse to be taken to Grote. He himself subwayed back to Manhattan to meet Friedrich ("Fritz") Schroeter, another member of his ring, collecting waterfront information from a net of coast watchers.

Reuper and Schroeter met in the Little Casino Restaurant on East 86th Street (whose owner, Richard Eichenlaub, was another member of the ring) where Fritz told Reuper that the freighter *Indian Prince* had sailed the day before with ten twin-engine airplanes aboard.

From Yorkville Reuper went to an apartment on St. Anna Avenue in the Bronx, for a *Treff* with Felix Jahnke, operator of a clandestine radio station hidden in an apartment on Cauldwell Avenue. Reuper wrote out the message—*Indian Prince departed June 10 with ten twin-motor airplanes presumably for England*—and handed it to Jahnke to encode and put on the air on his next regularly scheduled transmission.

By the time Reuper got back to Hudson Heights it was past eleven o'clock. But the work was not yet over.

Grohse took the army manual to Grote who microphotographed it page by page in his studio on 181st Street in the Bronx. The next morning Grote delivered the filmstrip to a cut-out, one of the owners of a bookshop on East 86th Street. The cut-out slipped the strip into a book, wrapped it up and put it aside.

On June 14, a man named Carl Heinrich Eilers, library steward on the American ocean liner *Manhattan*, appeared in the bookshop, picked up the package, took it back to his ship and put the book on one of the shelves in the library.

The *Manhattan* arrived in Genoa, Italy, on the 24th. Eilers went to a *trattoria* on the waterfront to meet a man to whom he handed the book. He was an officer from Ast X who "handled" Eilers and another courier, the chief baker of the SS *America*, whenever their ships arrived in the Italian port.

The manual which Reuper received from Donay on the 11th reached Hamburg only fifteen days later, on June 26th, and this was considered a fast passage under the circumstances.

The waterfront information about the sailing of the *Indian Prince* which Reuper gave to Jahnke went out on June 11 and was picked up by Ast X on the 12th, the next day.

The Abwehr still had a well-functioning courier service through the British blockade in the Atlantic. They could count on the services of a seaman on the *President Harding*; a German working on the SS *Siboney*; and a number of stewards and seamen on ships flying Spanish, Portuguese, and Swiss flags. Another route via South Amer-

Uruguay; one on the American Export Line's *Excalibur*; another on the steamship *Argentina*; and a barber on the *Excambion*.

They took the films—tacked inside the barrel of fountain pens, stitched to the backbone of magazines, or rolled around yarn spools and covered with silk thread—to go-betweens in Brazil and Bolivia, where they put them on the planes of L.A.T.I., the Italian air line which was still flying to Naples and Genoa.

In Italy the courier service was managed by Karl Eitel, the pioneer who started it all in 1935, when he first showed up at the Bremen office of the Abwehr with the unsolicited shipment from Wilhelm Lonkowski. After the outbreak of the war, Eitel was sent to Genoa to handle the Italian terminus of the service and organize a new crop of couriers sailing in neutral ships.

Only a relatively limited number of agent reports were moved by couriers. Most of them continued to go by the regular mail and some by commercial cable. And the mail represented a real problem.

British censorship had established a huge station in Bermuda, manned by an efficient crew of cryptanalysts, chemists, handwriting experts, and security officers. Both the Clipper and the ships taking mail to Europe were required to stop in Bermuda and deliver their bags to the censorship office. The letters were examined scientifically, subjected to tests by chemicals and ultraviolet rays.

The matter of concealment became a problem of the utmost importance. The agents in the field had their paper-and-pencil codes, but the Abwehr was under no illusion that any of them was unbreakable.

There was greater confidence in the security of the so-called *G-Tinten* or secret inks, especially three brands developed for the Abwehr by the *Chemisch-Technische Reichsanstalt*, the German Bureau of Standards. One was called "Apis," the other two "Pyramidon" and "Betty." Their formulae were among the Abwehr's most closely guarded secrets. Lulled into complacency by the belief that they could not be detected, agents were encouraged to use them as much as they pleased.

Then a German agent going by the code name "Hamlet" was sent to Lourenço Marques, capital of Mozambique in Portuguese East Africa, to spy on enemy shipping and aid German raiders in the Indian Ocean. He was equipped with the usual paraphernalia, including the Apis and the Pyramidon.

As long as Hamlet was *sending* messages concealed in them, all was well. But when he began to *receive* instructions written in them, a hitch occurred. Someone forgot to send him the formulae of the reagents, and consequently he could not develop the secret writing.

Berlin was advised of the agent's plight by cable and asked that the developers be sent to Hamlet. Another agent, named Dr. Viljoen, happened to be en route to Lourenço Marques and had in his possession all the chemicals needed for both the inks and the developers. Hamlet was told by return cable to await the arrival of Viljoen who would enable him to read his instructions. But somehow Viljoen was prevented from reaching Mozambique. A frantic cable was sent to Berlin now demanding that the developers be shipped without any further delay.

In the emergency, Colonel Piekenbrock decided to send the formulae to the agent in the Foreign Minister's highest-grade cipher. Thus, on October 11, 1940, the following cable was sent to "Consugerma" (the consulate's cable address) at Lourenço Marques:

> Prescriptions for compounding developers: Developer (a): Solution of 1 percent ferrous-chloride in water to which should be added 25 percent cooking salt. Developer (b): Solution of 1 percent calcium-ferro-cyanide in water, with 25 percent cooking salt added.
>
> Imperative you procure chemicals there since no means to ship them from here.
>
> Tell Hamlet to proceed as follows when developing: Equal parts of both solutions (a teaspoon of each, for example) should be mixed shortly before use. The letter should then be rubbed over with the solution, using a small cotton tuft around a toothpick.

Piekenbrock's cable was intercepted by the British and this critical German secret became known to them. The amazing ability of British censors in World War II to detect and read concealed writing in seemingly innocent letters was materially aided by their discovery of the developer-formulae, and so early in the game, at that.

In the meantime, the Germans concluded on their own that the secrecy of their *Geheimtinten* was wearing thin. They decided to develop a novel and unique lock of concealment which, they were confident, nothing and nobody could pry open. This was what became known as the *Mipu* or *Mikropunkt*, the famous "microdot" that J. Edgar Hoover called "the enemy's masterpiece of espionage."

Perfected by Professor Zapp at the Dresden Institute of Technology, the method made it possible to reduce a whole sheet of paper first to the size of a postage stamp, and then, by photographing it through a reversed microscope, to the tiny image of a dot on a typewriter's "i." The negative was covered with collodion, and using a kind of hypodermic needle with a snipped-off point, the "microdot" was lifted out and transferred to a letter or document at the spot where the dot was to be inserted. It was again covered with a dab of collodion to smooth over the uprooted fibers of the paper.

Unfortunately for the Abwehr, and completely unknown to them, the system of microdotting became known to us almost as soon as it was introduced. In early 1940, a double agent the FBI called "S.T. Jenkins" had alerted the Bureau to a startling new "gimmick" that the Germans seemed confident would enable them to "communicate back and forth throughout the world with impunity." The agent could not discover the exact nature of the method except that it used "lots and lots of little dots."

Efforts to crack the secret yielded no concrete results for a year and a half. Then a traveler from Europe arrived in the United States in August 1941. Since he was on the FBI's suspect list he was detained and his belongings were subjected to minute examination. The man was the playboy son of a Balkan millionaire who was making a living by doing such odd jobs as gun-running and drug-smuggling. He was also known to be on the Abwehr roster on which he was carried under the pseudonym "Ivan I."

The examination of Ivan's briefcase produced a suspicious envelope that was promptly forwarded to the FBI labs in Washington. Nothing incriminating was found on it at first glance. But when the laboratory agent held it so that the light slanted obliquely across its front surface, he suddenly noticed a tiny gleam—a dot reflecting the light—"a punctuation period no bigger than a fly speck."

The dot was pried loose and examination under a powerful microscope revealed that it was the infinitesimally reduced image of a full-sized typewritten letter which Ivan was supposed to deliver to a German agent in New York. The secret of the microdot was cracked.

Admiral Canaris was dissatisfied with the whole system of communication. The snail's pace at which the reports of his spies moved threatened to cancel out altogether the effectiveness of his secret service.

The couriers were still coming and going. But they were tied to the increasingly haphazard sailing schedules of their ships, frequently delayed en route. Courier mail was so decelerated that it took a minimum of one month on the average for a report to pass from its sender to its destination.

An occasional spy letter still squeezed through the increasingly dense sieve of British censorship. Suspicious letters were held back on the theory that the passage of time would render useless any intelligence they might contain.

Spy reports are among the most perishable commodities. It is a truism in the business that the best of them are also the most urgent.

The Abwehr became determined to develop shortwave radio circuits throughout the world.

In his book about Michel Hollard's remarkable intelligence *reseau* in the French underground, George Mortelli maintained that clandestine operatives are "better off without signals apparatus, which only draws the enemy's attention." General Sir Collin Gubbins, chief of Britain's Special Operations Executive wrote that radio was the most valuable link in the whole of SOE's chain of operations during the war. Without it, he said, "we would have been groping in the dark." The same was true for the Abwehr.

The so-called Afu apparatus, weighing less than 30 pounds with a maximum power of 20 watts, was not capable of transmitting at such a distance as the United States.

The far larger shortwave morse transmitter was needed to enable the Afu-agents to reach the Abwehr center at Wohldorf. This presented not a single problem but a whole complex of problems, some purely technical, others involving the quintessential question of concealment.

Several attempts had been made to smuggle fully assembled transmitters into the countries of the Western Hemisphere—one concealed in a piano sent with a shipment of household goods to Argentina, another disassembled in diplomatic bags consigned for Bolivia. Both of them were discovered and confiscated. The ensuing embarrassment convinced Admiral Canaris that it was inadvisable to ship the sets ready made. They had to be assembled part by part at the spot where they would operate.

The set had to be simple, compact, with a wide frequency range, and its frequencies determined by removable crystals. The aerials presented another problem. The ideal was a loop antenna—a directional aerial of one or more turns of wire—and the seventy feet of wire that went into it was not easy to hide. The crystals were fragile, difficult to transport, and practically impossible to disguise or conceal.

The perfect spot had to be found where a radio could be hidden to operate with reasonable impunity. Communication agents had to be found, trained, and planted. Replacement of personnel and parts, repair, and maintenance, had to be considered.

Admiral Canaris nevertheless issued orders to organize a worldwide network of stationary clandestine radios. The task was assigned to Lieutenant Colonel Trautmann, chief of the signal service at Wohldorf, who was to be assisted by SS-Sturmbannfuehrer Siepen, director of the Havelinstitut, the radio center of Amt VI at Wannsee. It became one of the rare instances of smooth cooperation between the Abwehr and its Nazi rival.

Technical execution of the program was handed to Telefunken, the huge electronics concern that was Germany's foremost manufacturer of radios, with branches all over the world; and to one of its international subsidiaries, a firm known as Debeg, that contracted with shipping lines to supply radio operators for their vessels. Telefunken was to develop a pilot model. Debeg was to provide personnel from its reservoir of seasoned "sparks" to aid in the on-the-spot assembly of the sets and, when possible, in their operation and maintenance.

The first station in the Western Hemisphere was assembled by Telefunken on the extraterritorial grounds of the German Legation in Mexico City. Called "Glenn," it was to function as the flagship of what was to become the "Bolivar" network, a chain of stations in Latin America strung out from Mexico to Argentina.

Then came the question of the United States. Such a clandestine radio link with this country confronted the Abwehr's communications experts with an especially thorny set of difficulties. "The technical preconditions for a clandestine radio link with the United States are so complicated," Siepen wrote in this connection, "and American radio surveillance is so far advanced, that the projected establishment of such a link requires the most meticulous planning to yield satisfactory results."

Since no previous experience was on hand, experiments had to be carried out. In 1939, Trautmann and Siepen invited two German-Americans to undertake such experiments. One was an Abwehr man named Richard Ernst Weber. The expert delegated by Siepen from the Havelinstitut was an electronics engineer—a radio specialist carried on the roster as US/7 - 368. His name was Dr. Josef Jacob Johannes Starziczny.

Weber tested conditions on the North American, Starziczny on the South American circuit. What they found was discouraging. Atmospheric conditions—geomagnetic disturbances and sunspots recurring in cycles—threatened to interfere seriously with the quality of the signals and with transmission in general. As Starziczny pointed out, even the huge radio stations of the Reichs Postal Administration (which handled the overt traffic) experienced considerable difficulty in sustaining adequate reception, even though they had enormous directional antennas and operated up to 100 kilowatt power. Clandestine radios of secret agents, on the other hand, depended on makeshift aerials and had to operate within a limited power range—they could go neither below 80 nor over 250 watts.

Since the tests showed that the stream of radio impulses flowed much better north-to-south than east-to-west across the Atlantic, the plan was to place relatively low-energy stations in the United States, then beam their signals to high-energy stations in South America for relay to Germany. Glenn became a key station in this relay system. But the stations the Abwehr eventually succeeded in establishing in the United States *by its own efforts* operated on direct beams to Europe.

The building of the transmitter in the New York area confronted the Abwehr with exasperating problems. There was no Telefunken outlet in New York, and no Debeg-men who could come off their ships to help. It was possible but far too risky to buy the parts needed for the assembly of the sets. In the end, the Abwehr found men to whom the building of the sets could be entrusted, and a handful of others to operate them when ready.

Weber was chosen for the job of constructing a transmitter, assisted by a Siepen man, William Gustav Kaercher. Weber (or "Richard Dick," his clandestine name) was a 55-year-old native of Bavaria in the United States since 1908, a radio technician by profession. An ardent Nazi, he had drifted into the Abwehr, which developed him as a communications agent. In 1939 the Abwehr sponsored several of his trips to Germany on each of which he smuggled into the United States parts of the radio he was required to build. He found a job with a radio-parts manufacturing firm in Babylon, New York, that made it simple for him to obtain whatever additional parts he needed.

Kaercher, age 45, was a naturalized citizen, a leader in the German-American Bund, and a machinist by profession. He, too, visited Germany several times during 1938–39, when he was inducted into Hauptsturmfuehrer Carstenn's America department at Amt VI. He returned to the United States early in 1940 in time to aid Weber as the factotum of the venture.

Then it was thought advisable that a portable transmitter be added to Weber's station. This was built by a couple of shortwave amateurs from parts an employee of the Douglas Radio Company of Manhattan pilfered from his firm's stores. One of the hams was a commercial photographer named Josef August Klein, a German-American. The other was his friend Arthur McGee, the only member of both rings who did not know the true purpose of the project. Klein had told him that the radio was needed for a business friend for communication with the Chamber of Commerce in Hamburg to promote German-American trade.

When the sets had been built, men were needed to operate them. One was on tap in New York, a highly trained radioman in Manhattan waiting for the call. He was Felix Jahnke, a 38-year-old Silesian bachelor, naturalized in 1930. This did not prevent him from going secretly to Germany in the late Thirties to be trained as a radio operator at a signal corps unit of the army at Stettin, under a Captain Kerstenn. Jahnke served his internship with another signal unit at Hammerstein, then returned to the United States to wait for instructions.

They came in early 1940. Jahnke was informed that a radio operator would arrive shortly from Germany to take charge of what was called "Operation Jimmy."

"Jimmy" was Axel Wheeler-Hill, a 40-year-old native of Latvia that was still part of Tsarist Russia when he was born. Between 1918 and 1922 he served in the armies of Baltic freebooters fighting the Communists. He emigrated to the United States in 1923, became a citizen and worked as a motorman for the Third Avenue El for ten years. In 1938 the memories of his adventurous youth returned to haunt him. He gave up his job and went to Germany to join one or another of the mushrooming Nazi organizations interested in the United States.

Recommended by his brother, a former functionary of the Bund who was now working for the Foreign Ministry in Berlin, Axel was accepted in the Abwehr for training as a communications agent. Put up in the Klopstock at Hamburg, he attended a seven-week course that was expected to make him proficient "in sending and receiving coded radio messages so that he might establish shortwave communications with (the Abwehr) as soon as possible after his return to the United States."

It was not as easy a path to clandestine glory as he expected. He was a plodding, hard-working man, but had no aptitude whatever for the job. He garbled the test messages, had great trouble with coding, and his reading was slow and faulty. Jahnke, a smart and imaginative young man who was a first-rate radio operator, was amazed that Wheeler-Hill could ever pass muster and be sent into the field on such a delicate mission. "He simply doesn't know," he complained, "how to operate a receiving-sending station designed to send such important material as data about ship movements and sensitive military information."

The Abwehr had no choice. A man was urgently needed in New York, and Wheeler-Hill was the only one available at the moment. His shortcomings were glossed over, and he was dispatched before his training was completed.

If this did not seem to bother his sponsors, it troubled the conscientious Wheeler-Hill. He was not deterred by the perils of his mission, but he was worried about the technical problems of operating the radio. The morning after his arrival in New York in January 1940, he enlisted in a radio class at the West Side YMCA in Manhattan for what he hoped would complete his training and make him a radio-man after all.

The radio Weber had built was set up in a flat on Cauldwell Avenue. Both Wheeler-Hill and Jahnke worked and lived in the apartment, but the agents they serviced were not allowed to contact them there. The agents had to deliver their messages to another apartment on St. Anna Avenue in the Bronx, where Jahnke would encode them, then take them to the other flat where he or Wheeler-Hill would put them on the air.

The idea was to use the portable transmitter at different locations to prevent the American radio sleuths from finding them, a relatively easy thing with a stationary transmitter. But there was no need for such precautions. "Those stupid Americans," Wheeler-Hill said, "will never find us."

Very soon Jimmy had more business than the two men could handle. Elated that their first *Meldekopf*—communication center—was operational in New York, Hamburg grew careless and was enticed into the dangerous practice of what the lingo calls *Traubenbildung*, the "bunching of grapes." Instead of confining access to the radio to the few men of the Reuper ring for whom this outlet was originally intended, one agent after another was referred to the station to be serviced by it. It did not seem to bother either Hamburg or the agents. They held with Wheeler-Hill that "those stupid Americans" would never find them out.

In 1944 the Abwehr had forty-four producing agents working in the United States. The size of the network overtaxed the capacity of the courier service. Their output was proving too much for Glenn and Jimmy to handle.

Something had to be done to expand both the courier system and the radio link, and a number of operators had been recruited for the American wireless net.

As far as the United States was concerned, help was already on the way—a new man had left Hamburg in January 1940. He arrived in New York on February 6, with money and instructions to establish the third *Meldekopf* in North America. Just before his departure, he was given his number—A.3459. Then a code name was to be picked for him.

Captain Hermann Sandel, the Abwehr officer who was his guardian during his training, suggested: "How about calling him Peacock?"

"No," Major Ritter said. "We'll call him Tramp."

Chapter 30

"We'll Call Him Tramp"

SOMETIME in 1922, a 23-year-old German who had served as a teen-age machine gunner in the Kaiser's army and who was now hoboing around the world, sailed into Galveston and liked what he saw of Texas so much that he decided to "immigrate" by jumping ship. His name was Wilhelm Georg Debowski. But now that he was to become an "American," he thought it better to call himself William G. Sebold.

After wandering through Texas he drifted to the West Coast where he worked at all sorts of odd jobs, starting as a dishwasher in sleazy eateries and clubs and working his way up to bartender in the better restaurants. He had his ups and downs. But he was never really out.

Somewhere along his way he acquired a wife and became a citizen. Although this land was not too bountiful to him with its gifts, Sebold came to love it.

By 1938 he was working as a mechanic at the San Diego plant of the Consolidated Aircraft Company. Then he ran into some bad luck. He had had a stomach ulcer from way back and now it began to bother him. Sebold started to drift again, this time eastward. When he reached New York his ulcer was so bad that it had to be operated on. He had the surgery at Bellevue Hospital, and when he was discharged he was alone in the city. Suddenly the United States became a strange and cold land. His family—his mother, his two brothers and sister— lived in Germany. He decided to visit them after all these years and to spend his convalescence with them in a more hospitable environment.

In February 1939, he arrived in Hamburg aboard the Hapag liner *Deutschland* en route to Muehlheim, a sooty, greasy, industrial city in the Ruhr where he was born in 1899, and where the Debowskis still lived. On his landing card he put down his occupation as mechanic with Consolidated Aircraft. Two men in dark green suits questioned him at some length about the kind of work he had done at Consolidated, then permitted Sebold to go on his way.

The war broke out in September, but the United States remained neutral and Sebold was in no hurry to leave Germany. He felt well enough to go back to work and got himself a job with a local factory making turbines.

Then the first letter arrived.

It was from Dr. Otto Gassner, inviting Sebold to visit him in Duesseldorf to talk over, as the writer put it, a matter that could be of some advantage to him while serving the cause of Germany. Gassner was a Gestapo official. He had come upon Sebold in the report of the men who had interviewed him aboard the *Deutschland*. They had marked him down as "a German-American aviation mechanic—of possible interest for some undercover work in the U.S.A."

Gassner was not beating about the bush. His letter was written on Gestapo stationery, and his invitation sounded more like a summons. Sebold became apprehensive, but feeling safe in the protection of his American passport, he decided to ignore the call.

Then came another letter. This time Gassner hinted broadly what might happen if he refused to "cooperate." Sebold wrote back that he was not interested.

Gassner wrote another letter, now warning that "the pressure of the State" would be brought to bear upon him unless he complied, describing "the burial shift" which, he wrote, "we'll give you when you are laid out."

Then Gassner played his trump card. He had made a search for Sebold in the police files of Muehlheim under his family name of Debowski, and found some embarrassing facts in the old papers. Now he told Sebold that he had no choice. He was a man with a criminal record. It dated back to 1920 or 1921, when young Debowski was caught at smuggling and in other felonies, and spent some time in jail. Obviously, Gassner wrote, "Herr Debowski" had neglected to reveal this part of his vital statistics to the American authorities when he applied for his citizenship.

Gassner confronted the man with an alternative—either he agreed to go back to America as a German agent or, if he continued to balk, he would not be able to go back at all; he would be sent to a concentration camp. Means would be found, he wrote, to acquaint the Americans with his past, and that would be the end of his fraudulent citizenship.

"I accepted his proposition one hundred percent after that," Sebold later said.

When he notified the Gestapo that he had seen the light, Gassner forwarded his dossier and their correspondence to Ast VI, the nearest Abwehr office in Muenster. But Muenster was busy with France and was not interested in the United States. A call was put through to Hamburg and an officer calling himself Dr. Rankin arrived in Muenster to take a look at the man. Rankin said he was opposed in principle to recruiting by threats and blackmail, but his colleagues in Muenster told him that Sebold had volunteered his services. Then Rankin said that he took on people only after careful screening by the Gestapo. Dr. Gassner assured him that the man had been checked out and was found to be all right.

A *Treff* was arranged somewhere in the city to give Rankin an opportunity to size up Sebold. It was a friendly meeting but at arms length. Hamburg was looking for people who could operate one of the clandestine radios the Abwehr was planning to set up in America. Rankin, who wanted only American citizens for the job as "sparks," thought that Sebold might do as a wireless operator. He hired the man and said he would have to move to Hamburg to be trained.

"How long will that take?" Sebold asked.

"Well," Rankin said, "maybe three to four months, more or less. It depends on how fast you learn."

"My God," Sebold said. "I was planning to return to the States to take care of my wife. If it takes that long, I'd better make arrangements to send her some money."

Rankin assured him that he could take care of that. But Sebold said: "I think I'd better do it through the American Consul in Cologne. That way we'll avoid all suspicions."

Rankin agreed. Sebold went to Cologne to arrange "things" with the consul, then moved to Hamburg where he checked into the Klopstock. In Hamburg Dr. Rankin handed him over to a man named Heinrich Sorau whose ward he would be during his training.

Sebold was shown how to take microphotographs of documents, and was introduced to the chemistry of secret inks. Mostly, he was taught coding and decoding, Morse telegraphy, and the operation of shortwave transmitters. Unlike Wheeler-Hill, Sebold passed the test with flying colors. At the end of the seven-week course, he was ready to go.

The day before his departure, Sorau handed Sebold a slip of paper with four names and addresses on it. "These are the collectors," Sorau said, "whose reports you will service. Here. Memorize their names and addresses." They were Frederick Joubert Duquesne of 24

West 76th Street and Lilly Stein of 232 East 79th Street, both in Manhattan; Everett Minster Roeder of 210 Smith Street in Merrick, Long Island; and Hermann Lang of 74-36 Sixty-Fourth Place, Glendale, Queens.

Sebold was given an American passport made out to William G. Sawyer and a cover story to go with his new name. He was handed five documents reduced to the size of postage stamps and told to conceal them in the back of his watchcase. These were the instructions for the collectors in New York.

He was given an "advance" of $1,000 and was told that $5,000 an office in midtown Manhattan where you will meet the collectors detailed instructions: "Upon arrival," Sorau told him, "you will open an office in midtown Manhattan where you will meet the collectors and receive their material. You will set up your transmitter and forward their messages by radio."

By this time, Sebold knew as much about the Abwehr as was possible to find out at the Klopstock and on the field trips. He knew that Dr. Rankin was Major Nikolaus Ritter, chief of air intelligence at Ast X, creator and manager of the best spy ring the Abwehr had in the United States. He found out, too, that Heinrich Sorau was Captain Hermann Sandel, Ritter's deputy. An aviator in World War I, Sandel had spent ten years in the United States and returned to Germany in 1938 to join the Abwehr. And, of course, Sebold knew the names of the four stars of Ritter's prize American ring and could barely wait to meet them.

On January 27, 1940, with one of "Papa" Toussaint's faked passports in his pocket—Sebold boarded the SS *Washington*. He arrived in New York on February 6. It was a stormy crossing on the wintry Atlantic, but it did not dampen his enthusiasm. He was approaching his new life like Pip, with greater expectations.

In New York Sebold went to work at once.

He formed a firm called the Diesel Research Company and rented an office in the Knickerbocker Building on 42nd Street in the heart of Manhattan. Shortly afterward he had the shortwave radio set up in a house at Centerport, Long Island. He then made contact with the members of Ritter's ring and found that they were still in harness. Duquesne and the Sperry-engineer Roeder were busy as usual; Lang was still working on the latest developments of the Norden bombsight. The beautiful Lilly was scouting for new agents and acted as a go-between for couriers.

Early in April, Sebold notified Captain Sandel that he was all set to start operations as soon as he was given the green light. A few weeks later a courier brought him the answer with the final details of his instructions.

Beginning May 15, it read, using the call letters CQDXVW-2, he was to try to establish contact by calling AOR in Hamburg every day at 6 P.M. for fifteen consecutive days. "A great deal will depend on atmospheric conditions," Sandel had written. "Don't become impatient even if it should not work for days."

Then, exactly at 6 P.M. on May 31, Sebold put the first message on the air. It was from Duquesne, and properly so. The old Boer was now the doyen of the ring, not merely because he was its oldest member, but because he was the best.

Sebold—or "Tramp" as he was now called in this stealthy part of his life—encoded it in the key picked from the current best-seller by Rachel Field, *All This and Heaven, Too* (which he called *All This is Heavenly* and never got around to reading). The secret of the code was in the date a radio message was sent. The day and month were totaled up and twenty was added to this sum. This indicated the page of the book on which the message was contained. Starting with the first line on that page, the agent worked up and down in a complicated series of squares until the message was completed.

Other reports were sent in from Roeder and Lang. Even Lilly brought in some from the peripheries of the ring where her subagents worked. This was not the only pipeline Ritter had to his agents in America. Longer reports or bulky shipments continued to go out via couriers. Sebold's radio link was used for the most urgent reports or messages that could be compressed into short signals. The one Duquesne sent on June 24, when the operation was only in its fourth week, was relatively long, but had to be sent by radio because it was SSD, *sehr sehr dringend,* very very urgent.

The British had been petitioning Mr. Roosevelt since the outbreak of the war to let them have the Norden bombsight. But the War and Navy Departments were so vehemently opposed to giving it to them that the President had to refuse.

This was the eleventh hour. France had fallen. The Nazis were the masters of Europe. Roosevelt now ruled that Britain, with her back against the wall, should have the precious instrument which could make the difference between defeat and survival.

Duquesne learned of the historic decision immediately.

This was a real scoop.

Intelligence like this was not for the slow boat. It had to go out at once.

Put on the air by Tramp at six o'clock in the evening on June 24, the message read in full in the original English in which Duquesne composed all his reports:

From A.3518 in New York via A.3549 via Afu 24.6.40—1800 SS *Pasteur* carries ten sets drawings Norden and Sperry bombsights to Vickers Co. London for manufacture sight released for use of allies. Vickers Detroit will also manufacture sights. Sperry will make 1200 and Norden 1200. Both firms must spend at least three months in tooling before production in any quantity begins.

The report created a big stir at Ast X. It seemed to justify all by itself the efforts that went into the making of Tramp.

The primary value of a communication center like Tramp's was in the transmission of messages that tolerated no delay—especially intelligence about the arrivals and departures of ships carrying war materiel, to enable the U-Boat Command to chart their course and intercept them en route. Next in importance and urgency were the daily weather reports which the Luftwaffe meteorologists needed in the preparation of their forecasts.

Tramp was always prompt with the weather—it was his own responsibility, not something he was receiving from the collectors. At seven o'clock each morning the necessary data was compiled, and the report went out at 8:25 A.M. each day.

The more important ship movement signals were put on the air during his second transmission, in the evening. It was always pinpoint intelligence. The one he radioed on September 9 was typical of the reports he handled:

According to Fehse the Belgian ship *Ville d'Ablon* departed with copper, machine parts, motors, horses. *Ville de Hasselot* left fully loaded mostly airplanes. Both ships bound for Liverpool. English steamer *Britannic* departs Tuesday with aero-engines and twelve heavy bombers. *Ile de France* and Dutch freighter *Delf Tdyk* loading fifteen fighter planes uncrated on upper deck.

Fehse was a highly-graded regular V-man—No. 2017—who worked not for Hamburg, but for the Bremen subbranch, where he was supervised by Johannes Bischoff. On September 9 he was using Tramp by courtesy of Major Ritter. After the spasmodic operation of Jimmy, the faultless functioning of Tramp had become the talk of the Abwehr. The managers of the other rings—Major Lips of military intelligence at Ast X, Dr. Nautsch of aviation technology, and even officers at the other branches—besieged Ritter with requests that he let their spies use Tramp also for the transmission of their urgent messages.

His performance exceeded the most sanguine expectations. Soon every branch that had agents in America was using him, not merely for the transmission of their own spy reports, but also as a channel for queries to them.

Signals were sent via Tramp asking for the number of Allison motors General Motors was making at its Indianapolis plant; inquiring whether it was correct that the USS *Saratoga* was ferrying planes to Halifax whence they flew to England; requesting data about the Lockheed P-38 and the Bell P-39, how many of them were being produced, how many were going to England; asking for details of the Fairchild, Grumman and Republic Aircraft factories on Long Island; and inquiring about certain ships routed to South Africa, the Persian Gulf, and India.

Ship movements in particular took up most of Tramp's time. New coast watchers appeared to add to the output—a mechanic named Alfred E. Brockhof who was employed on various piers; an ironworker named Paul Bante who was repairing damaged ships in New York Harbor; a shipping clerk named Rudolf Eberling. Hardly a ship entering or leaving through the Narrows escaped attention.

> SS *Kapira* departed for Liverpool . . .
> SS *Southern Prince* leaving in convoy . . .
> SS *Robert H. Locksley* on her maiden voyage to S. Africa . . .
> SS *Charles Trapp* in transit to London . . .
> Unnamed Dutch steamer in port . . .

And from time to time a progress report was sent about the *Normandie* outfitting as a troop ship in New York Harbor.

Still nothing came up to the quality of the material old Duquesne was supplying. Whether it was another arms shipment to England or some development in the General Staff or a decision reached to add a number of new destroyers to the fleet, he was always the first with the information and often the only one to learn about it. On February 1, 1941, for example, he cabled through Tramp:

> Churchill here in battleship *King George V*—visited on shipboard by Roosevelt and Knox.

It was typical Duquesne—part of it true, part of it false, yet amazing even for the semblance of the truth it contained. On January 24, the *King George V* had been in Annapolis—not with Churchill, to be sure, but bringing Lord Halifax, the new British Ambassador, to the United States. Five days before, the Prime Minister cabled the President concerning the ship: "I don't know whether you would be interested to see her. We should be proud to show her to you, or to any of your high naval authorities, if you could arrange that."[1]

Hamburg did not know or care whether or not Churchill had been the mysterious passenger. They were simply astounded by the old man's apparently inexhaustible knowledge of what was going on in the United States and delighted by the insurpassable Tramp line that conveyed his information so promptly to them.

German espionage in the United States had reached its peak. Nothing indicated that it would decline from here. Major Ritter was surfeited with the perfection of the fabulous organization he had built. What more could he do or expect? What new excitement, what greater triumphs could this net of agents hold out for him?

He was looking for new fields to explore and conquer. He now decided to leave Ast X to go to North Africa to pave Rommel's way into Cairo. In February, the legendary Field Marshal had arrived in Libya at the head of a powerful Panzer army. From now on, Ritter thought, that was where the action would be.

There was a major shift in German curiosity about the United States. When it seemed that the Tramp operation had brought espionage against America to the highest level of perfection the country's military and economic secrets ceased to be of paramount interest.

The presidential campaign of 1940 was moving into higher gear. Would Roosevelt run? Who would the Republican's nominee be? How could F.D.R.'s reelection be prevented?

These were questions which now intrigued the Germans and the Abwehr was not the proper agency to supply the answers.

There was still a game of foxes. But now a different game appeared on the scene. Conventional espionage yielded to an unconventional charade of diplomats and politicians.

NOTE

1 The President, accompanied by Secretary of the Navy Frank Knox, did go to greet Halifax and see the ship. Although Duquesne tripped up on Churchill, he still managed to spot the new battleship on her maiden voyage to America and pinpoint Roosevelt and Knox among the visitors through the thickest fog of censorship.

Chapter 31

Target: F.D.R.

AT the height of the Cold War in the Fifties, the American Central Intelligence Agency somehow succeeded in stealing the sample of a key Politburo-member's urine from the laboratory of a noted Viennese urologist, and discovered, by analyzing it, that the Soviet bigwig was suffering from a serious kidney disease to which, it was hopefully assumed, he would soon succumb. Though the man is still alive today, the "procurement," as it was called, of this quaint clue is still regarded as one of the agency's most successful exploits.

But the CIA was not the pioneer in what may be called urological intelligence. The Abwehr was, and we have the documents to prove it. At 8:10 P.M. on June 19, 1941, a top-priority message reached the Abwehr in a roundabout way, going from the United States on the Pan-American Clipper to China, then cabled from Shanghai to Berlin.

"Reliable source confirms," the message read in part, "that Roosevelt is suffering from uraemic condition causing serious disturbances of consciousness as a result of constant application of catheter in urinary tract. Recurrent announcements indicating mild soreness of throat and similar illnesses are made merely to camouflage his true condition."

This was one of a series of messages on the topic of the President's health, supplied by Dinter, the agent in Washington who professed to have a pipeline to Mr. Roosevelt's doctor, with access to his medical charts. Dinter—or Captain Count Sauerma—had ingratiated himself to the capital's notoriously indiscreet "high society" by posing as a scion of the noble Scottish clan of Douglas.

Dinter's latest report, based on gossip he had picked up on Washington's cocktail party circuit, was a vivid illustration of the gradual deterioration of information as it moved along the grapevine. The President *was* being catheterized, but for painful inflammation of his sinuses. Certain Washington physicians, not too well disposed to the President's doctor, expressed the opinion *sotto voce* that Mr. Roosevelt's condition was aggravated rather than alleviated by the harsh treatment he was receiving from Dr. McIntire.

By the time the gossip reached Dinter, the nasal passage became the urinary tract. The rest was conjecture drawn from the confusion. It was not the first or only misrepresentation that could be found in Dinter's usually erratic reports, but, in this case, it did not matter. True or false, the signal created a flurry of excitement in Berlin. The Nazis always reacted to news of Mr. Roosevelt's illnesses, like his domestic foes, in the spirit of Mark Twain's famous quip, "I hope it's nothing trivial."

On the basis of Dinter's report, Abwehr medical experts now diagnosed "the morbid condition of the President's blood caused by his inability to excrete urinary matter." The Nazis hoped that sooner or later F.D.R. would be removed from the scene by an act of God, a victory they craved as much as any triumph of their arms.

One would think that such an important function as the surveillance of the American President would have been given high priority by the Abwehr and handled by handpicked men. Actually no organized effort was made to "cover" Mr. Roosevelt. Hitler's irrational attitude to everything concerning President Roosevelt made it rather risky to come up with data, however factual, that went counter to the Fuehrer's preconceived notions, however fanciful.

Adolf Hitler and Roosevelt had come to power at the same time in 1933, and both embarked on drastic if not revolutionary changes— Hitler with his New Order, Roosevelt with the New Deal. But the Fuehrer paid only the most perfunctory attention to this historic parallel. Inclined to dismiss the controversial President contemptuously as "that cripple in the White House," he saw Mr. Roosevelt as a vague figure in the distance, a lightweight who had neither the guts nor brains to do anything that could slow down the march of Nazism.

When, in 1936, it was suggested that at least some attempt be made, mostly by propaganda appeals directed to American voters of German stock, to prevent the reelection of Mr. Roosevelt, Hitler bruskly rejected all such proposals. He ordered the Foreign Ministry, the Propaganda Ministry, and other organs of the Third Reich's aggressive foreign relations to ignore American elections.

However, he was jolted out of his indifference on October 5, 1937, when the President included in a speech in Chicago his famous call for "quarantining the dictators." Harold L. Ickes, who had inspired and supplied the actual words the President used, called it "the most important [address] on the international situation that [F.D.R.] has ever made."

First in Berlin to react was Propaganda Minister Joseph Goebbels. He heard the speech on his shortwave radio and rushed, late at night, to Hitler with its German translation. The German Ambassador Hans Heinrich Dieckhoff, in Washington only a few months and still trying his best to improve relations, fired off a number of frantic dispatches theorizing that Roosevelt's target was not Germany but Japan (which had just then provoked an "incident" at the Marco Polo Bridge near Peking). Hitler dismissed such a hypothesis. He broke off whatever tenuous personal relations he was willing to maintain with the United States and focused on Roosevelt as his *bête noire*.

From then on his animosity grew by leaps and bounds. Roosevelt, he said at various times, was "an impostor . . . an errant Freemason . . . a sick brain . . . a criminal, tortuous-minded Jew." He refused henceforth to take the President seriously. When the German Ambassador Hans Heinrich Dieckhoff returned to Germany in November 1937, determined to impress Hitler with the importance of Roosevelt as an adversary, the Fuehrer refused to receive him.

Thoroughly obsessed that Roosevelt had at least some Jewish blood, he attributed everything the President was saying or doing to "this basic fact." In the summer of 1939, when war in Europe appeared to be imminent and the United States became a decisive factor in all considerations, Hitler received Lieutenant General Friedrich von Boetticher, his Military Attaché in Washington since 1933, supposedly a shrewd student of the American war potential. Instead of quizzing Boetticher about the possible influence of Roosevelt's policies and plans on a war in Europe, all he wanted the general to give him was "conclusive proof that Roosevelt was Jewish."

Admiral Canaris, in his complex heart, did not share this venomous bias. If anything, he had at least a sneaking admiration for Rcosevelt. But the calculated opportunism that characterized his regime led him to tolerate the President's surveillance according to the Fuehrer's preconceived ideas. Virtually no serious effort was made to procure bona fide intelligence about Roosevelt's intentions, little done to follow his actions and nothing left undone to collect derogatory information about the President and his family that would please Hitler and support the distorted picture he had conjured up.

Coverage was left to a few more or less free-lancing agents. In 1937, Commander Erich Pheiffer boasted to Dr. Griebl during a meeting in Bremen that the tentacles of his subbranch reached into the inner sanctum of the President. Pheiffer did get occasional intelligence from some of his spies who brashly claimed that they had procured it from inside the White House. He bragged to Griebl about recent data describing the reorganization of the United States Navy which his informant had picked up from a member of Mr. Roosevelt's cabinet.

In reality, the Abwehr had nobody in the United States whose *specific* assignment was the coverage of the White House. Most of such intelligence originated with agents like the notorious Dinter. They scavenged in the Washington quagmire of rumor and gossip, producing hearsay evidence which they embellished and doctored to appear as "reliable information" emanating from "absolutely trustworthy sources."

Only two men working for the Abwehr could be called specialists in F.D.R.—one in Bremen conducting his snooping at long distance, the other in Washington.

The man in Bremen was a gregarious entrepreneur named Dr. Nikolaus ("Niko") Bensmann whose activities included espionage at the highest business level.

The fallout of the data Niko was procuring from his American friends before Pearl Harbor included considerable information about the President. Bensmann recognized that this was a neglected field in the Abwehr and that he was practically the only intelligence officer in the Canaris organization who had a line to F.D.R. He made the most of this, and procured as much information as he could, supposedly directly from inside the White House, but actually second- or third-hand, via his gullible associates in a major oil corporation, as we shall see.

It was snooping at long range by the method of the indirect approach. But it did produce valuable information about some day-by-day private activities of the President; some of his policies, especially his support of the embattled Allies; and, most important, the Administration's clandestine manipulation of oil and petroleum products within the framework of Mr. Roosevelt's determined effort to aid Britain long before our entry into the war.

The agent in Washington whom the Abwehr could have characterized as "Our Man in the White House" was "Michael." Although he permitted the impression that he was an American citizen in the confidence of influential political figures in the United States, he was, in fact, an Austrian busybody—con man would be a better term—called Louis A. Matzhold. He was in the United States as the correspondent of the *Berliner Boersen Zeitung*, a conservative Berlin daily supported by a powerful group of Nazi-oriented tycoons. It was not only Hitler's respectable journalistic mouthpiece in financial circles, but, at the same time, a widely used front for all sorts of confidential transactions and the cover for several of the Abwehr's operations.

A suave, intelligent, imaginative Viennese with disarming charm, and a romancer attracted to undercover work by an adventurous streak, Matzhold was eager to work as a V-man in Washington and pulled strings to get into the Abwehr. Canaris, who frowned upon the employment of foreign correspondents as spies, allowed him to function only as a *"Gewaehrsmann"* or *ad hoc* informant, and that only because Matzhold had better than average credentials and claimed close personal relations with influential American politicians.

He inundated the Abwehr with long, effusive, and seemingly well-informed *"vertrauliche Berichte"* (confidential reports) abounding in "inside information" which he insisted he had procured from his highly-placed friends. His circle allegedly included Governor George Howard Earle of Pennsylvania, Senator Burton K. Wheeler of Montana, and many others—even Harry Hopkins. But his *pièce de résistance*, he assured the Abwehr, was his "intimate relationship" with the President himself to whom he was tied, he said, by the bond of their common passion for philately.

According to what Matzhold told the Abwehr, he would meet Mr. Roosevelt in long private sessions, usually on Saturday nights when F.D.R. would spend his lonely hours amusing himself with his stamp collection. Dr. Matzhold would show up at these hobby dates in the Oval Study with sets of rare stamps or recent European issues which the President was supposed to be eager to get. While bartering stamps, or expertly discussing philately with his fellow addict, Matzhold would casually touch upon the burning issues of the day, conning "confidential information" which, Matzhold once wrote to Berlin, the President would share only with a friend he trusted implicitly.

How much of his claim was true, or simply made up to please the Abwehr, is difficult to say. His reports did reflect considerable familiarity with developments within higher levels of the government. But any astute Washington correspondent could pick up this sort of information along the capital's buzzing corridors of power, without direct access to the President himself.

If it exists, no correspondence with or any reference to the President's alleged "friendship" with Matzhold has been available at the Roosevelt Library at Hyde Park. The absence of such documentation does not necessarily mean that Matzhold was lying about his nocturnal sessions in the Oval Study, for not all visitors were recorded in Mr. Roosevelt's appointment diary, especially if their errands were of a strictly private nature.

The Germans found Matzhold's account of his relationship with the President so convincing, and considered their philatelic link so important, that the Abwehr shipped to Matzhold an avalanche of very rare stamps, consigned for F.D.R. Some were purchased from Berlin dealers through middlemen, but some were lifted from collections of Jews which the Nazis had confiscated. It might be possible to trace whether this alleged loot actually wound up in Mr. Roosevelt's collection.

Matzhold operated along these lines until December 1941. His contact was disrupted only by Pearl Harbor, after which he was obliged to leave the United States with the other repatriated Germans. Then, assigned to Hungary in the dual capacity of the Budapest correspondent of the *Boersen Zeitung* and a chief V-man covering the Balkans, he continued his coverage of the President by buttonholing and quizzing "mutual friends" who happened to show up in his area. One of them was Governor Earle who visited Budapest in 1940, on an assignment from the President, and used Matzhold as one of his own "confidential informants," giving him full credit for his "valuable contribution." But this is another story. It will be told in detail in its proper place in this narrative, in the climactic espionage venture of "the spy called Michael."

Tidbits of information about F.D.R. reached the Abwehr from an agent who claimed to be friendly with Mrs. Grenville Emmett, widow of Mr. Roosevelt's former law partner and the American Minister to the Netherlands until his death in 1937. Pauline Emmett continued to be close to the Roosevelts, and was a frequent visitor at Hyde Park where she heard intimate conversations in the relaxed atmosphere of the President's beloved ancestral home. The reports of the agent who alleged to be "tapping" Mrs. Emmett did not contain anything that could be called hard intelligence. But I think his reports reflected faithfully and accurately the historic dilemma with which the President was grappling between 1939 and 1941.

The recurrent theme of the so-called "Emmett Reports" (which the Abwehr was receiving via a go-between in Lisbon and which I found in Abwehr papers) was that Mr. Roosevelt was acting upon principles enunciated in a fireside chat on September 3, 1939: "This nation will remain a neutral nation, but I cannot ask that every American remain neutral in thought as well. Even a neutral has a right to take account of facts. Even a neutral cannot be asked to close his mind or his conscience."

Such reports were valuable, but they were not useful for Canaris's purpose. They were outright harmful in his efforts to ingratiate himself to the Fuehrer, by presenting to him only intelligence about F.D.R. which Hitler liked to hear.

Three men on the roster of the German secret service were "developed" in the only known attempt at creating a nucleus of V-men whose beat would be the White House. One, registered under US/7-376, was an American industrialist of Portuguese ancestry, described in his bio sheet as "a vice president of the Florsheim shoe concern." He was assigned to "the collection of information about American aid to Britain with emphasis on President Roosevelt's activities in this connection."

Another—designated as US/7-362 in the registry—was a "prominent German-American promoter-publisher with vast business interests in America and Europe." According to his German file, his holdings included stock in a German firm manufacturing synthetic silk, and substantial blocks of shares of I.G. Farben and Siemens & Halske, the huge electronic manufacturers. He had a palatial home in Pennyslvania, a sumptuous suite in the Waldorf-Astoria in New York, a château and racing stables in France.

The Germans credited him with "exceptionally good connections in political and economic circles with easy entry into the White House." In his file I found a blue book of prominent and distinguished Americans with whom U/7-362 was supposed to be "on extremely friendly terms." They included Secretary of State Cordell Hull; former Secretary of the Treasury Andrew W. Mellon; Colonel Charles A. Lindbergh; John Hays Hammond; Senators James E. Watson, Henry Cabot Lodge and Robert R. Reynolds; the banker Winthrop Aldridge; John D. Rockefeller, Jr.; Nicholas Murray Butler, president of Columbia University; John Cuddahy of the meatpacking family; Ambassador Joseph P. Kennedy; General Robert E. Wood of Sears Roebuck; Thomas W. Lamont of the House of Morgan; Henry Ford; and Joseph E. Davis, the Washington lawyer who was a close friend of the President and husband of the former Marjorie Post, heiress of the Post cereal millions.

The most promising member of the trio was U/7-375, rated "superb" for his coverage of the President. According to his bio sheet in the files, he was a member of the European aristocracy and claimed to be "married to a half-Jewish lady related to [Secretary of the Treasury] Henry Morgenthau." As a matter of fact, Morgenthau was supposed to have given him the mandatory affidavit when he immigrated to the United States shortly after the outbreak of the war.

The file included the claim that he had been received with open arms by the Morganthaus who, of course, had not the slightest inkling that the new member of the family was a trained and registered German spy. His "continuous reports" to Berlin "about the foreign political aims of Roosevelt and on developments in the world of finance" were given top rating for "reliability and probability," chiefly because he cited as his sources Secretary Morgenthau and even the President himself. He claimed that he was picking up the information during weekend visits to the Morgenthaus' farm in Dutchess County and at the Roosevelts' Hyde Park home to which he frequently accompanied his "relatives" when they called on F.D.R.

I failed in all my efforts to make this agent materialize in the flesh. If there really was such a man, the Morgenthaus profess to have no knowledge of him. However, he survives in the files of the German secret service, with scores of impressive reports revolving around the President, which he sent to Berlin in 1940–41. In fairness, it should be pointed out, that the three so-called "U/7" agents terminated all clandestine operations, and ceased to send any reports after the United States' entry into the war on December 7, 1941. It was gratifying, and remarkable for the basic American patriotism of such men in the upper strata of American society and business, who had agreed to collaborate with the German secret services, that not a single one of them is known to have continued at this clandestine pastime after Pearl Harbor.

The haphazard, opportunistic, inconclusive spying on F.D.R. changed abruptly, and vastly for the better, in October 1939, with the unexpected and unsolicited appearance of "a source" inside the American Embassy in London. Although undoubtedly one of the most serious breaches of security of the American President during World War II, it was not a case of espionage in the usual meaning of the word. A political act of monumental indiscretion, it was "unquestionably," as Richard J. Whalen put it in his biography of the late Joseph P. Kennedy, "one of the strangest episodes in U.S. diplomatic history." The incident arose during the violent emotional atmosphere of the United States in the controversy over war or peace during the period between the outbreak of the European war and the Japanese attack on Pearl Harbor.

Although the case received considerable public airing, in a detailed press release issued by the State Department (No. 405, September 2, 1944) and much data (some of it conjectural, much of it inaccurate) disseminated by Mr. Kennedy, our Ambassador to the Court of St. James's, I am including it in this book because I am able to add considerable unpublished information in rounding out the evidence and placing the case in its perspective.

In October 1939, a 29-year-old fledgling diplomat arrived in London from Moscow where he had served since 1936 as code and cipher clerk in the American Embassy. He was Tyler Gatewood Kent, a clean-cut, studious, handsome young man of average height, quiet and reserved in manner. Despite his youth and brief career in the U.S. Foreign Service (which he joined shortly after his twenty-third birthday in 1934), Kent was not quite an unknown quantity in the diplomatic world, thanks to his family background and apparent competence.

Born in Manchuria, the son of William Patton Kent, a career consul in Newchang, he had a string of illustrious Virginians and Tennesseans among his ancestors of Scotch-English stock, including the frontiersman Davy Crockett. Kent had begun to carve his own niche in life with an impressive scholastic record at St. Albans, Princeton, the Sorbonne, the University of Madrid, and George Washington University. He was an accomplished linguist, fluent in French, German, Greek, Italian, Spanish, and Russian; and an avid reader of biographies, history, and political science.

He had his own unorthodox ideas about the world of the turbulent Thirties.

Two overriding passions, if not obsessions, governed his doctrinarian personal philosophy. By the time he left the Soviet Union, where he "was able to observe firsthand the inside workings of Bolshevism," he was thoroughly imbued with a bitter hatred of the Communists. And preoccupied with the pathology of international relations, he developed into an intense anti-Semite, engendered by a medieval *idée fixe* that "all wars are inspired, fomented, and promoted by the great international bankers and banking combines which are largely controlled by the Jews."

In London, where he was slightly known to Ambassador Kennedy and implicitly trusted by the career men, he was assigned to the Code Room of the Embassy, to handle the most confidential cables, both those originating in London and those passing through. He had access to the Ambassador's correspondence with Mr. Roosevelt and Secretary of State Cordell Hull, as well as dispatches that Ambassador William C. Bullitt in Paris and other American envoys in Europe were sending to Washington.

Then a new super-secret batch of telegrams was added to the traffic handled by the Code Room. At the outbreak of war in 1939, Winston Churchill was appointed First Lord of the Admiralty in Mr. Chamberlain's coalition cabinet. President Roosevelt sent him a personal letter with an unusual proposition that violated tradition and protocol in official relations between the chief of state of one country and a mere cabinet member of another. Contrary to widespread belief, Roosevelt and Churchill had not been friends of long standing at this time, having met only once briefly in London in 1920. But deeply impressed by Churchill's staunch opposition to Hitler during the Thirties, the President now chose him as his foremost confidant in beleaguered Britain.

"It is because you and I occupied similar positions in the World War," the President wrote to the new First Lord on September 11, 1939, "that I want you to know how glad I am that you are back again in the Admiralty. Your problems are, I realize, complicated by new factors, but the essential is not very different. What I want you and the Prime Minister to know is that I shall at all times welcome it, if you will keep me in touch personally with anything you want me to know about. You can always send sealed letters through your pouch or my pouch."

Mr. Churchill responded "with alacrity," as he put it, using the signature of "Naval Person" in what, in fact, was a surreptitious exchange of communications conducted behind the backs of Secretary Hull in the United States and Prime Minister Chamberlain in Britain. But events were moving too fast, the pouches too slow, and the distinguished correspondents were too impatient. Soon the impetuous "Naval Person" began to bombard Mr. Roosevelt with telegrams which he handed directly to Ambassador Kennedy, bypassing the Foreign Office, for transmission to the President, with the admonition that they were meant solely for the President's eyes. The American Embassy merely processed them—enciphering the texts (in the so-called "Gray Code" that was classified as top secret and was, at this time, believed to be "unbreakable"). The encrypted messages were then radioed to Washington directly for the President, avoiding State Department channels.

This telegraphic exchange began at the time of young Kent's arrival in London, and Ambassador Kennedy designated him as one of the clerks in the Code Room to process what was later called "the President's patently unneutral correspondence with Churchill." The coding was done by different clerks in a routine and mechanical fashion. Kent read and reread the messages and, in the solitude of the Code Room, brooded about their meaning and portent.

The British cryptographic establishment had of course been monitoring much of the diplomatic traffic, reading the cables of the chancelleries of the world with the help of the superb crew of analysts under Commander Denniston who succeeded in cracking codes and cyphers with gratifying skill and regularity. Shortly after the Roosevelt-Churchill arrangement had been made, they stumbled upon a series of cables from Hans Mackensen, the German Ambassador in Rome, to his Foreign Ministry in Berlin. When the transcripts of the intercepts were examined in the Foreign Office, it was found that Mackensen was apparently privy to information of an exceptionally confidential nature, some of it known only on the level of Roosevelt and the First Lord.

In one of his reports in January 1940, Mackensen was able to warn his home office that under an order Churchill had issued to the Fleet, "no American ship should in any circumstances be diverted into the combat zone round the British Isles declared by [the President]."

Although this involved only a technical aspect of the war at sea, the information was of the utmost significance. Churchill's order represented a unilateral breach in the blockade, solely favoring the Americans. "I need hardly point out," Solicitor General Sir William Jowitt wrote later, "how important it was that this arrangement remain secret, for if every neutral were to claim the same concessions as had been made to the Americans, the conduct of our war at sea would have been gravely prejudiced."

But it did not remain a secret. Tipped off by the Germans, the other neutrals—including the Italians and the Spaniards—promptly besieged the Admiralty protesting bitterly the "discrimination between various countries" and demanding that their ships be given the privileged treatment enjoyed by the Americans. This threatened the effectiveness of the blockade.

Other reports of Mackensen supplied advance information on practically every arrangement Roosevelt and Churchill were making in their secret covenant to assure American aid to Britain.

The examination of Mackensen's well-informed dispatches convinced the British authorities that there was a serious leak somewhere on the highest echelon of British-American relations. It was obvious from Mackensen's scattered references to his source that he was relaying intelligence given him by the Italians, presumably by Count Galeazzo Ciano, the Foreign Minister, himself.

On the assumption that the Italians were getting the basic information through their Embassy in London, the surveillance of Italian diplomats was intensified. But all the investigation produced was that one of the assistant military attachés, a lieutenant colonel of the cavalry named Don Francesco Maringliano, Duke of Del Monte, was an occasional guest at a Russian tearoom owned by a former Tsarist admiral and his wife, famed for serving the best caviar in London. It then developed that the officer was a friend of the admiral's 37-year-old daughter Anna, a naturalized British subject who made her living as a dressmaker and was a virulent anti-Semite and Fascist sympathizer. Miss Wolkoff was on the suspect list of Scotland Yard and MI.5 as a prominent and active member of the "Right

Club," a Jew-baiting clique of reactionaries, headed by Captain Archibald Henry Maule Ramsay, Conservative Member of Parliament for Peeble, and a distant relative of the Royal family.

A closer scrutiny of the Wolkoff woman revealed incriminating facts of a secret life she led. She was observed slinking at nights usually on the dark side of streets, pasting little labels—called "stickybacks"—on church boards, bus stops, telephone booths, as she walked along. This is a "Jews' War" was printed crudely on one of them, and another bearing the message, "Your willing self-sacrifice and support will enable the War profiteers to make bigger and better profits and at the same time save their wealth from being conscripted." Although they were clearly designed to undermine British morale, one of the Nazis' own objectives, the pasting of these insidious appeals could not be regarded as the work of enemy agents.

While she was under surveillance, Miss Wolkoff was trailed to the studio of a photographer named Nicholas E. Smirnoff, where, it was found, she would rendezvous with her noble Italian friend. Otherwise nothing was found to incriminate her and her companion, certainly not as the sources or conveyors of the high-level sensitive information seeping from London to Rome.

Soon certain information came through another channel that provided an important step forward. It pinpointed the American Embassy as the gaping hole through which classified documents were pouring to the Italian secret service at so massive a rate that sometimes it needed a laundry basket to carry even a single week's shipment. The tip-off came from an anti-Fascist journalist named Luigi Barzini, Jr., son of a noted Italian-American newspaper publisher and former editor of the New York daily *Corriera d'America*. Young Barzini, in Rome as a journalist, had influential friends among likeminded Foreign Ministry officials who freely discussed with him the fantastic influx of the American documents from London.[1]

Was there a link between Miss Wolkoff and the American Embassy? There was. Her conspiratorial circle included a young American diplomat, tied to her by the bond of their common prejudices. He was Tyler Kent.

By this time, the leak had continued for several months, and, judging by Ambassador Mackensen's dispatches, was producing increasingly sensitive information. Moreover, it was found from other sources that Miss Wolkoff was using the Duke of Del Monte and an acquaintance at the Rumanian Legation as channels of correspondence with William Joyce, the Nazis' British mouthpiece in Berlin, beaming his venomous propaganda to Britain. The Wolkoff woman was writing to Joyce regularly, giving the kind of adverse information she thought would make good material for Joyce's morale-shattering broadcasts and offering suggestions that could improve his propaganda appeal.

By the middle of May the British authorities had enough and decided to arrest Miss Wolkoff, simultaneously extending their investigation to Tyler Kent. At ten o'clock in the morning of the 20th, a man identifying himself as a police officer knocked on the door of Kent's apartment on Gloucester Place and asked to be admitted. "No," Kent cried as he tried to bolt the door, "you can't come in!" The door was then forced by four men—two detectives from Special Branch, an officer from MI.5 and a Second Secretary of the American Embassy—that had been notified of the impending raid. A warrant was produced and the flat was searched. Just then, almost on cue, the telephone rang, and the officer who answered the call heard the voice of a man identifying himself as someone from the Italian Embassy—"putting us," as Mr. Kennedy later revealed, "on the trail of [Kent's] Italian outlet to Germany."

In the apartment the security agents came upon some fifteen hundred documents from the files of the American Embassy, stacked in a cupboard, stuffed in a brown leather suitcase, and packed in a crate. Another box contained photographic negatives. They also discovered a pair of duplicate keys—one to the Code Room, the other to the steel cabinet in which the classified papers were kept—and a package of Miss Wolkoff's "sticky-backs" imprinted with anti-war and anti-Semitic slogans.

Kent was asked to accompany the officers to the Embassy for a confrontation with Mr. Kennedy, and there, in the privacy of the Ambassador's spacious office, the sordid story of his inane plot came to light.

During his tour of duty in Moscow, Kent confessed, he became dissatisfied with the foreign policy of the Roosevelt Administration. "I thought," he said, "Roosevelt's policy contrary to the interests of the United States." Alarmed by what he read in the diplomatic dispatches that passed through his hands, and convinced that "the Administration [was] less than forthright with the American people," he "began to acquire evidence of American diplomats . . . who were actively taking part in the formation of hostile coalitions in Europe . . . which they had no mandate to do."

Determined to expose "the plot" to the American people with "evidence" to support his allegations, he decided to remove copies of secret documents, first from the Embassy in Moscow and then in London. He hit upon a method that would make his "indiscretion" safe from discovery. He made copies of documents or salvaged copies that had been discarded. He admitted that he had had duplicate keys made to the Code Room and to its steel cabinets so that he would have access to them if he were shifted to other duties.

When a friend introduced him to Anna Wolkoff he found an immediate outlet for his loot, even before, as he later claimed he had planned, he would have an opportunity of submitting the evidence to members of the United States Congress. He permitted the woman to examine his collection, and allowed her to remove from the flat, scores if not hundreds of the documents which, Anna told Kent, she wanted to show Captain Ramsay.

In March, Ramsay himself visited the flat, examined the collection, and took with him a representative sample of the most sensitive documents, particularly copies of the telegrams exchanged by President Roosevelt and Mr. Churchill.

There, Kent insisted, his "indiscretion" ended. He was adamant in his insistence that he was no party to the channeling of any of the papers to unauthorized persons beyond the Wolkoff woman and Ramsay, and did not know whether or not any of the documents had been sent to Italy or had reached Germany from Italian sources.

Was Kent a spy? Ambassador Kennedy never hesitated to label him as one. "We had to assume," he said, "that week by week these same data went to Berlin by way of Kent." If the United States had been at war, he added, he would have recommended that he be sent home and shot.

That night of May 20–21, the Ambassador said, the United States was hit by a grave communications blackout. "I phoned President Roosevelt," he said, "that our most secret code"—the "Gray Code" in which the Roosevelt-Churchill exchange was encrypted—"had become useless. The result was that just when France was collapsing, the government of the United States had to suspend for weeks its confidential communications with its diplomatic missions throughout the world."

Kent, for his part, did not regard his activities as anything even resembling espionage. He steadfastly maintained that his purpose was "to bring the papers to the attention of the Congress of the United States in time to prevent America's involvement in a war that was being fomented by his own President and the man who was soon to become the Prime Minister of Great Britain."[2]

Two days after the raid on his apartment, in the midst of a spy scare unleashed by the Germans' widespread and effective use of Fifth Columns on the Continent, Kent was formally arrested. When he was already in custody, he was dismissed from the U.S. Foreign Service and his diplomatic immunity was waived in an unprecedented move to give the British authorities jurisdiction over him. He and Miss Wolkoff were arraigned in August and tried *in camera* in October. On November 7, after the Wolkoff trial had ended with a sentence of ten years, Tyler Gatewood Kent was condemned to seven years of penal servitude.

At the time of the discovery of Kent's staggering "indiscretion," the American and British authorities merely *assumed*, as Ambassador Kennedy put it, that a considerable number of the documents which Kent had removed from the Code Room, with the Roosevelt-Churchill correspondence among them, had reached the Germans by way of Italy. In the absence of firm evidence, Kent and the Wolkoff woman were not charged with espionage.[3]

During my research for this book I found the missing link in the case of "Rex vs. Tyler G. Kent." The cables of Ambassador Mackensen, copies of which I discovered in the top-secret files of the German Foreign Ministry, proved beyond the shadow of a doubt that the crucial intelligence he was sending to Berlin had come from the papers Kent had copied and Miss Wolkoff had played into the hands of her Italian friends.

Mackensen's transmission of the intelligence began in January 1940, shortly after Kent had started supplying the documents to Anna Wolkoff. It ended abruptly when Kent was unmasked and the Wolkoff woman was arrested.

The last of the Mackensen dispatches with information culled from the material Kent had misappropriated went out on May 23, 1940, three days after the raid on Kent's flat, its importance attested by the fact that it was addressed personally to Foreign Minister von Ribbentrop. It was virtually a paraphrase of President Roosevelt's response to a plea for aid Mr. Churchill had submitted in a letter, *including the request for fifty American destroyers* to replenish Britain's dwindling naval strength and enable her to cope with the growing U-boat menace.

Mackensen's dispatch read in part:

"I am reliably informed by an unimpeachable source that on the 16th of this month the American Ambassador in London received telegraphic instructions from Roosevelt to deliver a message of reply to Churchill, which deals as follows with various requests presented by the latter in a personal letter to the President.

"1. It would be possible to hand over 40 or 50 destroyers of the old type, but this is subject to the special approval of Congress, which would be difficult to obtain at present. Besides, in view of the requirements of national defense, it is even doubtful whether they could be spared. In addition, in Roosevelt's view, even given approval on the part of the United States, it would take at least six or seven weeks before the ships could take up active duty under the British flag."

This was more than three months before the historic destroyer deal was eventually made on September 3. But the Germans were alerted from the outset to one of the war's most delicate and controversial transactions, details of which Roosevelt and Churchill had every reason to keep confidential, not only from the Germans, but even from the American people, while the deal was pending.

By whatever standards of the game Kent's reckless "indiscretion" is measured, and whatever term of legalistic subterfuge is applied to his actions, it is now abundantly evident that he had injured the British at a time when they could ill afford to be harmed. On the day he was unmasked, the Battle of France reached its grim climax. The German Panzers reached Abbéville and cut off the French and British forces in the Somme estuary. It was also the day when Admiral Raeder first broached the idea of the invasion of England to Hitler. The British were badly shaken by these cataclysmic events, and the Kent case highlighted the precarious nature of their security at home.

The Abwehr had absolutely nothing to do with the case, as, indeed, the entire "operation" somehow eluded the secret services. If it was embarrassing to Canaris, the Abwehr soon redeemed itself by plugging into another gross indiscretion that proved far more harmful to the Allied cause and useful to the Germans, producing valuable intelligence data over a much longer period of time. An Abwehr line to the President was developed through the unwitting cooperation of no less a person than the Vice President of the United States.

In World War II, Switzerland was, as in Ashenden's days, boiling with international intrigue. A considerable portion of the Abwehr's coverage of Britain and the United States had its fountainhead in Switzerland, just as Germany was spied upon by the British and the Americans from that country. (It was from Berne that Allen W. Dulles engineered his two historic coups, the penetration of the German government and "Operation Sunrise," the plot that resulted in the surrender of Italy. It was there, too, that the British and Soviet secret services gained access to the operations plans and tactical dispositions of the Wehrmacht, through Alexander Foote and Rudolf Roessler, the mysterious "Lucy" often called the greatest spy of World War II.)

The Germans enjoyed the advantage in this secret war on Swiss soil for some time because they had broken the codes used by Allied diplomats, even by Mr. Dulles himself. For years the Germans read their confidential correspondence. They also succeeded in penetrating the Swiss secret service, reputed to be the best in the world, by an obscure arrangement with Colonel Roger Masson, its chief, who thought it advisable to play the game with both teams. Also, two German agents were planted: a journalist going by the quaint cover-name of "Habakuk," whose beat was largely the Foreign Ministry, and a writer called "Jakob," who worked part-time in Masson's office.

In the summer of 1941, Habakuk obtained the copy of a long telegram the Swiss Minister in Washington had sent to his home office. It was a detailed account of the historic conference of Roosevelt and Churchill at Placentia Bay that produced the Atlantic Charter. A number of highly confidential deliberations and decisions had been reached at the meeting, including the question of "the line" the Americans should pursue with Japan.

At this time the United States was conducting fateful negotiations with Japan, on whose outcome the issue of war or peace hinged. Churchill, who desperately wanted America to enter the war, was pushing for a firm policy. F.D.R. was inclined to adopt what he called the "medium line."

The document Habakuk had obtained was a review of the Cabinet meeting in the White House, held on August 17, 1941, in which the President acquainted his associates with what had transpired at the conference. On the issue of Japan, he told his associates, that as far as he was concerned, he felt "very strongly that every effort should be made to prevent the outbreak of war."

According to the cable Habakuk procured, Vice President Henry A. Wallace, who kept silent during the Cabinet session, had sent the President a "private communication" after the meeting, imploring F.D.R. to take "an exceedingly firm stand." The paper quoted a sentence from the Vice President's letter, to the effect that "appeasement or partial appeasement" was likely to "bring bad results . . . in the long run," not only with regard to Japan, but also as far as Germany was concerned.

Habakuk obtained another such document a few days after Pearl Harbor. It described in detail two conferences the President held in the Oval Study at 8:30 P.M. and 9:30 P.M. on December 7. The first, with his Cabinet, he characterized as "the most serious Cabinet session since Lincoln met with the Cabinet at the outbreak of the Civil War"; the other was held with Congressional leaders. In both meetings, the President treated his audiences to an unvarnished account of the disaster, giving exact details of the damage the Japanese had wrought on Oahu. The only person other than F.D.R. who was present at both meetings was Vice President Wallace.

In the note that accompanied Habakuk's document to Berlin, the German minister in Berne (who signed all outgoing dispatches emanating from the Abwehr outpost) pointed out that the report contained such "precise and reliable information" because it was based on a cable of the Swiss Minister in Washington, Dr. Charles

Bruggmann, who had obtained the information "in strictest confidence" from "Vice President Wallace."

Dr. Bruggmann (who, of course, was the helpless victim of this pilferage) was the Vice President's brother-in-law, a 52-year-old career diplomat. After service in Russia, Belgium, France, and Czechoslovakia, he had been assigned to the United States in 1923. Here he had met Mary, the sister of Henry Wallace, and married her next year in Paris.

A close family bond developed between Mary's husband and her brother even before Dr. Bruggmann's second assignment to Washington in the Forties. Their tie was deepened by their proximity in the United States. It was Wallace's practice to see his brother-in-law as frequently as possible, and he talked with him daily on the telephone. Mr. Wallace trusted his brother-in-law's discretion implicitly. He had no qualms about sharing with him privileged information to which he had access, and never a thought that even by the wildest stretch of the imagination his candid remarks might reach the Germans.

Now the Germans seized upon this loophole. Habakuk was instructed to monitor all dispatches Dr. Bruggman was sending from Washington to Berne; and Jakob was told to obtain copies of the reports pouring in from the Swiss Military Attaché. Copies of these dispatches were being forwarded practically the morning after they reached Berne, to the Abwehr via the Foreign Ministry in Berlin.

They continued in a steady flow throughout 1942 and 1943—until January 1944, when, as all such good things must sooner or later, this bonanza also came to an end. By then, Allen Dulles had been firmly entrenched in Berne as the representative of the Office of Strategic Services, and was in touch with important members of the German anti-Nazi underground. Through two of their contacts he learned of the activities of the German Foreign Ministry and the Abwehr.

The first man was a mystery-shrouded junior diplomat Mr. Dulles identified in his memoirs only as "George Wood." He was Fritz Kolpe, serving under Ambassador Karl Ritter. Dulles's other informant was a young lawyer named Dr. Hans Gisevius, a member of the Abwehr in the group closest to Canaris. In Zurich he operated with the diplomatic cover of a vice consul using the pseudonym of "Dr. Bernd."

Kolpe removed from the Foreign Ministry literally hundreds of documents, taking them to Dulles in Switzerland whenever he could coax an official trip as a courier. Or he gave them to Gisevius who practically commuted between Berlin and Zurich, for the sole purpose of picking up Kolpe's loot for transmission to Dulles.

Shortly after New Year's Day in 1941, a shipment from Kolpe included the copy of a Habakuk report the Abwehr in Rome had forwarded to Berlin. The paraphrased version of a dispatch Dr. Bruggmann had sent to his home office a few weeks before, it was accompanied by the envoy's note that read: "The reason Dr. Bruggmann's report contains so much concrete information is that, as it is well known to you, Vice President Wallace is talking in the *greatest confidence* with the Swiss Minister in Washington, who is of course his brother-in-law."

Bruggmann's latest cable dealt with a number of burning issues and contained the usual quota of "concrete information." The Germans seemed to be especially interested in intelligence about the conference of the Allied Foreign Secretaries held in Moscow in October 1943. The Swiss Minister represented his brother-in-law as being extremely pessimistic about the turn which Russo-American relations appeared to be taking. He quoted him as expressing the opinion that they had deteriorated to the point where Britain and America would have to win the war "alone" and *"possibly even against the Russians."*

"The main outcome of the Moscow Conference," a paragraph from Dr. Bruggmann's dispatch read in the form the envoy transmitted it, "is not apparent so much in the resolutions adopted as in the realization that the ideology of World Revolution is still alive. Although Russia agreed to a majority of British and American suggestions, there was always a loophole. The assumption was that Russia would endeavor to put the Western powers on the defensive so that after the war the various national Communistic organizations would be guaranteed freedom of action. Since this is diametrically opposed to American ideals for peace," Dr. Bruggmann was quoting Mr. Wallace, "the American Government may be compelled eventually to make momentous decisions."

Just how much aid and comfort the information would give the Germans is a matter of conjecture. It was not entirely without value to them. They always hoped that the unnatural alliance between the Western democracies and the Bolsheviks would not endure, and every scrap of information even hinting at friction in the coalition's camp was welcome in Berlin. The report from Berne, quoting the Vice President of the United States, indicated that a break in the Allied camp was not so far fetched.

Now, through Dulles, two years after it had been sprung, this fantastic leak became known to the Americans, and Dulles immediately alerted Washington to the break.

It was a delicate matter—the patently unconscionable indiscretion of the Vice President. Something had to be done to plug up this incredible hole, perhaps by warning Mr. Wallace to be more careful when he talked with his brother-in-law. It was eventually decided in the OSS to bypass the Vice President and bring the matter directly to the attention of the President. Major General William J. Donovan, head of OSS, took the Dulles cable with its copy of the German intercept to Admiral William D. Leahy, the President's chief of staff and his confidant in security matters.

During his regular daily briefing of F.D.R. on January 11, 1944, Admiral Leahy—who was thoroughly alarmed and scandalized—presented the case to his Commander in Chief, only to find that F.D.R. shrugged it off. As Leahy himself later put it, "The OSS report did not seem to surprise Roosevelt . . . I do not recall that he commented on it at all except to say that it was quite interesting."

There is no sequel, for the story of the incident, if it had been recorded at all, is not available for examination at the Roosevelt Library at Hyde Park. It is possible that the President talked it over with Wallace; and it is not impossible that the Vice President's gross indiscretion had something to do with F.D.R's decision to replace him with Senator Harry S. Truman, who had no Swiss brother-in-law, during Roosevelt's upcoming fourth term.

This was the farthest the Abwehr reached in its systematic spying on F.D.R. It was a military intelligence agency and although the President was also the Commander in Chief, and a fair target for the Abwehr's curiosity, his surveillance was the task of the Foreign Ministry, which was quite jealous in guarding this prerogative.

Inside the Ministry, a small group of experts called the "America Committee" took it upon itself to take a reading of Mr. Roosevelt. Headed by former Ambassador Hans Heinrich Dieckhoff, who had been shunted to the sidelines rather unceremoniously after he had been recalled from Washington in 1938, the nebulous Committee produced a number of so-called position papers, psychoanalyzing the President's policies, and trying to divine his intentions. It had no intelligence function, and Dieckhoff, who had nothing better to do, used the group to develop themes for the propaganda the Germans were beaming to the United States.

In a vulgar campaign devised on Hitler's personal instructions, and aimed directly at F.D.R. and his family, Dieckhoff recommended a number of virulent epithets that Roosevelt should be called in all references to him. "The lunatic in the White House," was one of these gems. "We," he wrote in one of his directives, "shall call the President 'Benedict Arnold Roosevelt,' to mark him as innately and unscrupulously pro-British; or 'Franklin Stalino Roosevelt,' to pillory him as friend of the Bolsheviks; or 'Samuel Isidore Roosevelt' and

'Franklin Finkelstein Roosevelt,' to indicate that he is a stooge of the Jews." This was the intellectual level of German propaganda beamed to the United States and Dr. Dieckhoff's major personal contribution to the war effort.

While the distinguished Ambassador was preoccupying himself with such an inane campaign, the confidential surveillance of the President was left to the Embassy in Washington under Dr. Hans Thomsen, Dieckhoff's successor as Charge d'affaires. We will have a close look at Dr. Thomsen in the role of spymaster later in this narrative.

After the outbreak of the war in Europe, it was a different set of people—mostly Americans—who appeared in this twilight region serving the German cause at this time. It was a hectic period of uncertainty and anxiety—a crisis of unprecedented magnitude and intensity in the United States raging over America's role in the conflict. It produced a number of weird ventures and strange bedfellows, the latter including men who aided the Germans deliberately as secret agents, and a handful of others in high and influential places who permitted themselves to be used as pawns in the game.

NOTES

1 Unfortunately, the Italians got to Barzini and arrested him on August 20, 1940, after learning from intercepted dispatches of the British Embassy in Rome that the journalist had revealed the activities of the Italian secret service in London. He survived the mishap and went on to become world famous as the author of the notable book, *The Italians*.

2 During his trial, Kent told the Court: "Your Lordship, I submit that I have not committed a felony, because I had no felonious intent. I have committed a gross indiscretion, possibly a misdemeanor . . . I am a loyal citizen of the United States of America, in spite of the allegations of the Prosecution in this case . . . [that is] unprecedented in the history of jurisprudence."

3 The indictment against Kent was that "he had obtained documents which might directly and indirectly be useful to an enemy, and . . . had communicated them to Anna Wolkoff for a purpose prejudicial to the safety or interest of this country." The case was fraught with many political and legal complications, involving Kent's status and right to immunity, and the complex issue which he raised with his insistence that he had "copied" the privileged documents when he discovered that F.D.R. was "secretly and unconstitutionally plotting with Churchill to sneak the United States into the war." These controversial aspects of the Kent case are beyond the scope of this book.

Chapter 32

The Strange Case of
John L. Lewis

*T*WO events occurred in North America in March 1938 that shook up Mr. Roosevelt's assiduously cultivated good neighbor policies. On the 17th, the President intervened in Pennsylvania politics by coming out for a Pittsburgh businessman named Charles A. Jones, the State Democratic Committee's candidate in a hotly contested gubernatorial primary race. On the 18th, amid rejoicing in Mexico and consternation in the United States, the government of President Lázaro Cárdenas seized the properties of American, British, and Dutch oil companies.

These two unrelated events produced a strange alliance that could have changed the course of history.

By endorsing Jones, the President affronted John L. Lewis, president of both the CIO and the United Mine Workers of America, who was running his own candidate—Thomas Kennedy, secretary-treasurer of the UMW—in the Pennsylvania primary. By alienating Mr. Lewis, F.D.R. drove the labor leader into the arms of William Rhodes Davis, an independent oil operator, one of the forces of the Mexican coup.

Lewis's frustration had been darkening throughout 1937. As Arthur Krock of *The New York Times* phrased it, Damon had been asking too much of Pythias and gave too little in return. The snub in Pennsylvania propelled Lewis out of his eroding alliance with Roosevelt and hurled him, not only into the camp of the President's domestic adversaries, but also into the orbit of his foreign foes.

Davis, the free-wheeling oil speculator, was an odd choice to replace Roosevelt as Lewis's ally. He was on his way to becoming the most formidable behind-the-scenes operator the Germans had in North America. By joining him, Lewis was caught in the Nazi web,

351

even to the point of coming, as Assistant Secretary of State Adolf A. Berle, Jr., wrote in a confidential memo to the President, "suspiciously close to falling foul of the Logan Act."[1]

During the next three critical years, as Davis developed into a full-fledged German agent representing Hitler and Goering with roots in both the Abwehr and the *Sicherheitsdienst*, Lewis fronted for him and did his bidding in Washington and Mexico City. He played a paramount part in the promotion of three major schemes the Nazis had entrusted to Davis:

• In 1938, Lewis helped materially and perhaps decisively to obtain seized Mexican oil for Germany.

• In 1939, Lewis aided a clandestine effort to ensnare Roosevelt into the promotion of peace in Europe strictly on Hitler's terms.

• In 1940, Lewis worked vigorously for what Herbert von Strempel, one of Germany's diplomatic agents in Washington, called the Nazis' "biggest single scheme involving the United States"—an elaborate and costly conspiracy to prevent the reelection of President Roosevelt for a third term.

The man whose foil and confederate Lewis had become was one of the last privateers in the world of big business. Although he proudly claimed direct descent from Jefferson 'Davis and Cecil Rhodes, the fabulous British "Empire builder," William Rhodes Davis rose from more modest beginnings.

Born in Montgomery, Alabama, in 1889, he moved west on the trains he loved. By the time he reached Oklahoma he had become a fireman, then a locomotive engineer. The restive Rhodes' blood in his veins spurred him faster and higher. In 1913, when he was only twenty-four years old, he organized his own oil company at Muskogee, Oklahoma, and established himself as an independent operator in the mold of Getty.

By 1938, he controlled the Crusader Oil Company and its far-reaching subsidiaries with extensive holdings in Texas, Louisiana, and Mexico. He owned a refinery in Hamburg, an oil terminal in Malmoe, Sweden, and distribution facilities throughout Scandinavia. He had palatial homes in Houston, and Scarsdale, New York, where he entertained lavishly, and was running his growing empire in New York City from a luxurious suite of offices on the thirty-fourth floor of Rockefeller Center.

An expensively dressed, gray-haired, and ruddy-faced man whose Southern courtesy and pleasant Alabama drawl softened the steely hardness of his dealings, Davis looked every bit the estimable executive.

Searching for a foreign market that was wide open for an independent operator in 1936, he zeroed in on Hitler's Germany. The

Nazis needed oil desperately for their fast-growing war machine, but they had none at home and no foreign exchange with which to buy it abroad. The German Navy was especially hard hit. Admiral Erich Raeder warned Hitler that "the High Command [had] completely exhausted all possibilities of buying oil for Reichsmarks."

Davis, who had been doing business with the Nazis on and off since the early Thirties, was keenly aware of Raeder's plight. He conceived the idea of using blocked assets the First National Bank of Boston had in Germany to build a refinery. Then he would ship in crude oil, refine it into fuel oil and gasoline, and sell it to the German Navy on a barter basis, for machinery, other exportable goods, and tankers built in German shipyards.

He prepared a prospectus, went to Berlin, and invited Dr. Hjalmar Schacht, president of the Reichsbank, to join him in the venture. When he was rebuffed by Schacht and given the run-around in the Third Reich's bureaucratic maze, he sent his plan directly to Hitler by special messenger. The result was prompt and dramatic. The next time he was closeted with Schacht and some twenty German financiers, arguing his case and getting nowhere, the door of the board room swung open and in walked the Fuehrer.

"Gentlemen," he said to the startled tycoons, "I have reviewed Mr. Davis's proposition and find it feasible. I want the Reichsbank to finance it."

The deal was quickly made. The refinery, called Eurotank, was built in Hamburg, and Davis was firmly established in Germany, doing most of his business with the navy, which came to depend on him for much of its precious fuel.

When Mexico expropriated the foreign oil properties in 1938 Davis himself had been affected by the seizure. He had an $11,000,-000 investment in the rich Pozor Rica field and was naturally loath to see it totally lost. If he could persuade the Mexicans to grant oil concessions to Germany through him, something could be salvaged.

The Germans thought well of the scheme. Admiral Raeder in particular had long sought such an opportunity. In a memo to Goering, in which he asked for £600,000 from the Reichsbank's meager foreign currency stock to finance Davis's efforts, the admiral endorsed the American oilman's project enthusiastically.

"I intend to use the money," he wrote, "not for the purchase of oil, but for the acquisition of a foreign oil concession." He went on to explain that, at the world market prices of those days, the £600,000 could buy only about 150,000 tons of fuel and Diesel oil, an insignificant amount. "But," he wrote, "by investing the same sum in the acquisition and development of a foreign oil concession—for example in Mexico—it will be possible, in the opinion of experts I have consulted, to bring about 7.5 million tons of oil to Germany—or fifty times as much as in the case of a one-time purchase—without any additional payments in foreign exchange."

Raeder got the £600,000 and gave it to Davis to lubricate his way to the Mexican deal. The admiral appointed Dr. Friedrich Fetzer, the navy's top-ranking fuel specialist, and Goering named Dr. Joachim A. Hertslet, a high official in the Ministry of Economic Affairs, to work with Davis. But someone was needed to plead the case with the Mexicans—a powerful go-between with entry to the Presidential Palace. This was where John L. Lewis appeared behind the scenes.

How, when, and where Lewis first met Davis and became associated with him, and to what extent he profited personally from the deal ultimately involving millions, are secrets buried with the protagonists of the drama. Davis later said that his "connection with Lewis" had been arranged "through various political channels." Davis, who had the born *faiseur's* perfect aim in this kind of target shooting, sought the contact with Lewis because of his close relations with the all-powerful Mexican labor movement.

The blurred record of this collaboration came into sharp focus for the first time in April 1938. Between 5 and 6 P.M. on the 18th, Lewis put in a phone call to Mexico City to Vincente Lombardo Toledano, boss of the Confederation of Mexican Workers. When told that Toledano was not available, he asked for Alejandro Carillo, Toledano's deputy and one of President Cárdenas's closest friends.

Lewis told Carillo that William Davis, whom he described as "a commanding figure in the oil business," had left New York on the 3 P.M. American Airlines plane, flying to Mexico City with a proposition that deserved the most sympathetic consideration. He virtually ordered Carillo to call on Cárdenas that same night, tell him that Davis was "absolutely all right," and make sure that Davis be granted the concession he was seeking. "Germany and Italy," Lewis said, "are the only countries with which it is safe for Mexico to deal."

Thanks to Lewis's introduction, Davis was given the red carpet in Mexico. But it was an intricate and delicate transaction he was promoting, and negotiations—in which he was now joined by Dr. Hertslet—seesawed for several weeks. Lewis invited Toledano to Washington for conferences with Davis. After Toledano's second visit in June, Davis, accompanied by Hertslet and Miss Erna Frieda Wehrle, his confidential secretary, went back to Mexico, convinced that the way was clear to consummate the deal. They saw President Cárdenas and worked out details with Finance Minister Eduardo Suarez and other high officials, but it still took considerable prodding from Lewis to secure the concession. When the papers were finally signed, Mexico agreed to furnish the oil and Germany undertook to pay for it in industrial products.

In September, the first tanker, with some 10,000 tons of oil, left Veracruz for Germany. In that same month Lewis himself went to Mexico City, ostensibly to attend the International Congress Against War and Fascism, in reality to celebrate the conclusion of the agreement. In his public address in Mexico City's bullring on September 17, before 50,000 wildly cheering denim-clad workers waving red flags, Lewis roared against "reactionary groups of employers" who, he said, "would welcome the growth of Fascism in America."

During the next eleven months of 1938 and 1939, some 400,000 tons of Mexican oil, pumped from wells drilled by American and British companies, flowed to Germany. Davis's huge Eurotank plant was operating in three shifts, refining oil for the German Navy.

Davis and Hertslet began to experience difficulties with the Mexicans in their efforts to meet German commitments. Although $8,000,-000 worth of oil was shipped to the Reich, the Germans returned only $3,000,000 in merchandise. One of Davis's biggest barter deals, involving the delivery of seventeen Junkers airplanes for the Mexican air force, fell through when it was blocked by the American Embassy.

The entire transaction then came to an abrupt end with the German invasion of Poland, and the British and French declaration of war. Dr. Hertslet, in Mexico and the United States during July and August, 1939, hurried home, leaving Davis behind to salvage the operation. He tried to keep up shipments through the British blockade, by sending the oil to Italy and Sweden for transshipment to Germany. But the British were not fooled. At the very outset they seized 33,000 tons of oil consigned on three ships for Scandinavia, on the ground that "the supply with reserves on hand was more than the Scandinavian countries would normally require."

Pressed for more and more oil in frantic cables from Fetzer and Hertslet, but able to deliver less and less, Davis was now facing a crisis that seemed to be too big for even the shrewdest operator. In the pinch, he came up with another idea, the boldest and weirdest one yet. He resolved upon a plan to restore peace to Europe by inducing President Roosevelt to arbitrate the conflict.

He cabled details of his plan to Hertslet who carried it all the way up to Goering, then cabled back that the German government was interested. Now all that remained was to get to Roosevelt and win him over. John L. Lewis was put back into harness.

Throughout 1939, the labor leader's relations with F.D.R. continued to deteriorate and by September they were at their lowest ebb.

So strong was his tie with Davis, or so ironclad his commitment, that Lewis swallowed his pride and agreed to get the plan before Roosevelt by foisting Davis on the President.

Late in the afternoon of September 14, Lewis phoned the White House and when Mr. Roosevelt took the call, asked the President to "receive, secretly, Mr. W. R. Davis on a matter which might be of the highest importance to the country and to humanity." Roosevelt was fully aware of the ax that Davis was grinding and had the gravest misgivings about dealing with him. But he could not antagonize Lewis still further with a curt rebuff. He declined to receive the oilman "secretly," as Lewis demanded, and agreed to see him "in normal course." An appointment was made for the next morning.

When he hung up, F.D.R. asked Adolf A. Berle, Jr., of the State Department to be present at the interview because it was "desirable" he said, "that a careful record be had of the conversation."

At 11:45 A.M. on September 15, Davis was ushered into the President's Oval Study and launched immediately into the presentation of his plan. He had been doing business in Germany, he said, for some seven years and had developed close personal relations with Marshal Hermann Goering. Within the past two or three days he had received a cable "from Goering" requesting Davis to "ascertain whether the President might not either act as arbitrator or assist in securing some neutral nation who might so act." "The Germans," Davis said, "desire to make peace," provided certain of their conditions were met.

Even as the oilman was unfolding his oblique plan, Berle was skeptical. "The experience of the State Department with Davis," he noted, "is not such as to suggest that too great reliance be placed on his story." It was up to the President to respond to the invitation, and he, while not rejecting it outright, remained noncommittal. He told Davis that he had had "various unofficial intimations . . . that he might intervene in the European difficulty," but, manifestly, he could not become involved in such a matter "unless requested officially by a government."

Davis was not entirely discouraged. He told Mr. Roosevelt that the German government had asked him to meet its representatives in a secret conference scheduled for September 26 in Rome, and asked F.D.R. whether he could feel out the situation and report back to him upon his return.

"Naturally," Mr. Roosevelt said, "any information that would shed light on the situation would interest me."

Immediately after the meeting, Davis applied for passports for himself, his wife, and Miss Wehrle, declaring that they intended to travel solely to Italy. Miss Wehrle was in the black book of Mrs. Ruth

B. Shipley, chief of the State Department's passport division, and was refused, as was Mrs. Davis. The denial of a travel document to his wife did not bother Davis. He was upset about Miss Wehrle. Again he turned to Lewis and asked him to take up the matter directly with Mr. Roosevelt.

One would think that Lewis might have been embarrassed to bother the President with so petty a matter, but Lewis picked up the telephone again. At 5:20 P.M. he called Mr. Roosevelt and asked him to instruct Mrs. Shipley to issue a passport to Miss Wehrle.

This time the President balked. He referred Lewis to the State Department. He then phoned Berle, told him about the strange call, and asked the Assistant Secretary to make a record of this incident, noting specifically that "the request had come from Mr. Lewis." As far as Lewis was concerned, he must have sensed the significance of the rebuff. He never called Berle, and Miss Wehrle never got her passport.

The next day, however, Lewis was back to the President. Now, frankly playing Davis's game, he sent the President a cable which, he said, Davis had just received from Berlin in reply to his report about his interview with Roosevelt.

Signed "Hertslet," the message read: "Agree completely negotiations Roosevelt on August basis discussed with you. New arrangements Far East important for United States government. Can assure absolute appeasement after Poland war if new combination here is assisted by neutral United States of America government. Try to get Washington remain strictly neutral without any revision of the present Neutrality Act until after your meeting here, because may be impossible change after revision once made. Explain to Washington at once every sale to belligerent nations means destroying of cargo, which may lead to war. Therefore present situation should be held in abeyance until after meeting."

Roosevelt sent for Berle and gave him the copy of Hertslet's telegram, to be added to the dossier he had asked the Assistant Secretary to keep on this transaction. Had it not been for Lewis's puzzling involvement, F.D.R. was ready to dismiss the whole matter. But Berle was shocked.

The State Department had a dossier on Davis going back to 1928. Berle regarded the oilman as close to being a Nazi agent, and so advised the President. Though Mr. Roosevelt was inclined to agree, he could not see his way to do anything about it, if only because of Lewis's involvement.

He thought briefly of asking J. Edgar Hoover to look into the matter, but decided against it. He could not risk the possible consequences should it become known that he had ordered an FBI surveillance of so important and powerful a figure as Lewis. He asked Berle to serve as his personal watchdog, follow developments closely, and keep a record of every move Lewis was making in Davis's behalf. He also enlisted the aid of another confidant, Gardner Jackson, to keep watch on Lewis. One of Lewis's aides during happier days, Jackson carried out the assignment so efficiently that he was able to inform the President of nearly every time Lewis met Davis, even observing his increasingly frequent visits to the oilman's office in Rockefeller Center or at his home in Scarsdale.

Davis left for Europe as planned and went straight to Rome, where Dr. Hertslet was waiting for him with the good news—Marshal Goering was enthusiastic about their peace project and was expecting them in Berlin to discuss it in person. In violation of the travel restriction Mrs. Shipley had stamped into his passport, the oilman flew to Berlin, where he arrived in secrecy on September 28.

During the six days of his stay, Davis was wined and dined by Dr. Fetzer and Hertslet, and participated in four long conferences with Goering, reviewing the Mexican oil situation and discussing details of the peace plot.

The most crucial meeting took place on October 1, in the Marshal's sumptuous Gothic office in the Air Ministry, attended also by Hertslet and Dr. Helmuth Wohltat, an economist on Goering's staff of planners.

The written record of the meeting, prepared by Dr. Wohltat, I discovered among the uncatalogued documents of the German archives. It shows, not only the inventive manner in which Davis misrepresented U.S. policy in these negotiations, but the whole vast scope of this transaction, as well as John L. Lewis's activities in its various phases.

Because of its historic significance, the document follows in full, published here for the first time:

During a one-and-a-half hour conference between President Roosevelt and Mr. Davis in the White House in Washington, on September 15, 1939, the President commissioned Davis to ascertain in Berlin the terms under which Germany would agree to an armistice and subsequent peace. Provided that the initiative comes from Germany, President Roosevelt is prepared to use his influence with the Western Allies to initiate negotiations leading to peace. President Roosevelt needs to know Germany's specific conditions with reference, for example, to Poland and the colonies.

In this connection President Roosevelt also raised the question of the purely Czech territories, a problem, however, the final solution of which could be arranged later. This was mentioned by the President only because he must consider public opinion in the United States, and would have to placate Czech voters and their sympathizers when and if he brings pressure on England to terminate the war.

The conference between Roosevelt and Davis was arranged by the leader of the American labor movement, J. Lewis, because Lewis is convinced that the prolongation of the war would have the gravest social and economic repercussions in the United States. A protracted modern war would result in the total exhaustion of both belligerents and neutrals in Europe. This would redound to the disadvantage of the United States through the loss of its best customers and, indirectly, the lowering of living standards throughout the world. England and France have cash assets in the United States in excess of $4 billion, and investments amounting to $9 billion. The Americans are aware of the danger that would ensue to them from a liquidation of these assets, either by withdrawing the money on deposit in the United States or by selling these holdings to pay for purchases in America.

Originally, up to 1934, Lewis was an opponent of National Socialism, mainly because he assumed that the German working class was suppressed, deprived of the right to safeguard its interests, and pressed into forced labor. However, during the past three years, Lewis was persuaded, mostly by Davis, that the standard of living of German workers has been substantially raised thanks to the economic system of National Socialism.

Davis has developed his oil business mainly in collaboration with Germany. Davis also continued to supply fuel oil to Italy even during the period when sanctions were imposed on that country. Lewis today recognizes the great similarities in the political and social factors that affect the European and American working men. He believes that the economic and social problems confronting the United States cannot be solved on the individualistic English pattern but rather through the working-community and common-good concepts of the New Germany. Lewis accepts the picture of social and political conditions in Germany as Davis paints it. Davis is a generous financial supporter of the labor movement. In addition to the nine million organized members of the trade unions, there are large groups of workers who look to Lewis for leadership, so that Lewis controls a bloc of approximately fourteen million votes. The Democratic Party cannot conduct a successful presidential election campaign without financial aid from Lewis. Lewis is free to choose whether to support either a Democratic or a Republican candidate for President. President Roosevelt can thank Lewis for his reelection in 1937 [sic] but he reneged on his promise to give him a seat in the Cabinet. Should Roosevelt decide to run for a third term, he could win only with Lewis's help. This is similarly true for any other candidate of either the Democratic or the Republican Party. Due to these circumstances, Mr. Davis has extraordinary means to influence the policies and actions of President Roosevelt.

President Roosevelt has a great personal-egotistical interest in initiating peace negotiations even if he decides not to seek a third term. Such a move on his part would make up for all the fiascos of his New Deal and his failures in other fields, and would enable him to leave office in a blaze of glory. Roosevelt believes that similar efforts of Mussolini are insufficient to impress the British. On the other hand, he is convinced that American pressure on England would bring a lasting peace without delay. Roosevelt is worried that the prolongation of the war might end contemporary European civilization through the mutual destruction of the three leading European nations. As another possible consequence of a long war, he envisages the decline and fall of the British Empire with repercussions that cannot be foreseen but would certainly lead to the termination of the white man's paramount rule in the world.

Roosevelt is apprehensive that a protracted war will weaken Germany vis-à-vis Russia which, in turn, will lead to the spread of Communism in Europe and, as a collateral development, to the strengthening of Japan in the Pacific area, which would be intolerable to the United States. He is, therefore, of the opinion that the United States has a vital interest in mediating peace without any further delay and to collaborate with all means at its disposal in efforts to make the peace endure.

In his conversation with Davis, Roosevelt remarked that he had been opposed to the English declaration of war against Germany. He was not consulted by England beforehand. He found out about it only through a telephone call from Ambassador [Joseph P.] Kennedy in London eight hours before the expiration of the ultimatum England presented to Germany. He believes that England is not so much concerned about the Poles and that the English declaration of war on Germany had other, more dangerous motivations. He has reasons to believe that England drove France into the conflict not merely against the will of the French people but also against the policies of the French government. As he sees it, the real causes of the war can be found in the one-sided dictates of Versailles that made it impossible for Germany to sustain a viable standard of living comparable to those of its neighbors. He believes that if he could gain the German government's support for it, he would be able to arrange immediately a just, equitable, and enduring peace on the following terms:

(The following statement was made by Roosevelt on September 15)

a) Germany should receive Danzig, the Polish Corridor, and all its former provinces ceded to Poland by the Versailles Treaty.

b) All overseas colonies which Germany had before 1914, and which are now administered by other countries either under mandates or other forms of control, should be returned to Germany forthwith.

c) Germany should receive substantial financial aid to enable her to procure all raw materials and goods necessary to adjust her level of economy to that of her neighbors.

Roosevelt proposed to name Davis as his personal plenipotentiary to conduct the negotiations in his name. Davis declined in view of the fact that it would interfere with his freedom of action in his business activities in which he has to meet great private responsibilities. Roosevelt and Davis agreed that Davis will report back to him immediately upon his return. Should an understanding be reached between Germany and the United States on the basis of a fixed program, Roosevelt is prepared to send Davis to Paris and London to sound out the British and French governments on his proposals for peace. Should it develop that Daladier and Chamberlain opposed the plan, Roosevelt would be prepared to put pressure on France and England along the following lines:

Roosevelt would advise France and England that he would support Germany in efforts to gain a just, equitable, and lasting peace. In the interest of this, he was prepared to conclude an agreement with Germany under which the United States would supply goods and war materiels. As a last resort he would threaten that he would send these shipments to Germany under the protection of the armed might of the United States.

Roosevelt is especially anxious to make use of the present moment to break the English monopoly in world trade. As far as the lifting of the arms embargo was concerned, Roosevelt expects the debate to last several more months. He considers it unlikely that the embargo will be lifted along lines recently proposed. He views the handling of the question in the Senate as a political maneuver to gain time. He expects that should his efforts at mediation fail, the lifting of the embargo would lead to incidents that, in the present psychological atmosphere, would induce Americans to side with the Allies, supported as they are by world-wide public opinion.

Davis acquainted Lewis with everything that transpired during his conference with Roosevelt. If his position found support in Germany, Lewis was prepared to mobilize the resources of his entire organization behind the move for peace. He believes that should it become necessary, his organization would, thanks to its influence on public opinion even in France, ensure the acceptance of the peace proposals. If there is an understanding between Germany and America, Lewis can create a situation in which American working men would simply refuse to produce war materiels for England and France.

Knowledge of the negotiations with President Roosevelt should be confined to only a few individuals. No other power must be told about them. President Roosevelt on his part excluded the State Department from these talks in order to guard against indiscretions.

It would be advisable to send a German representative and Herr Hertslet back to America with Davis to avoid any possible misunderstandings that could arise through the divergent interpretation of the language and in order to present authoritatively to Washington the actual position of Germany.

On October 3, when Goering authorized Davis officially to pursue the peace plan with Roosevelt, he instructed Hertslet to accompany the oilman to the United States as his own personal representative. For Davis, who remained refreshingly naïve throughout the deepening melodrama, this was merely another complicating factor in a difficult business transaction. But for Hertslet, a saturnine young man in a hurry, the assignment represented the pinnacle of one of those meteoric careers which the Nazi era produced for so many bright, high-reaching, and unscrupulous young Germans. A native of Halle in Prussian Saxony, he had joined the Hitler Youth movement in 1929, rose rapidly in its hierarchy, then worked for Dr. Goebbels in the Propaganda Ministry. Now, at the age of twenty-five, and a protégé of Marshal Goering, he was recognized as "one of the three or four most skillful Nazi officials" specializing in the economic penetration of Latin America.

Small and slight, his blond hair cropped close in the Prussian version of the crew cut, his pale blue eyes concealed behind the thick lenses of horn-rimmed glasses, he spoke English fluently and persuasively in a soft voice. Unquestionably he had a highly resourceful mind and a great background of expert knowledge in his specialty. This, now, was the big break in his already fast-moving career. Goering told Hertslet that if Davis's efforts succeeded and the President agreed to arbitrate a peace with the Allies, he would be appointed to the vacant post of German ambassador in Washington, as the youngest envoy in the history of German diplomacy.

Up to this point, Hertslet was acting more or less overtly as an accredited official of the Ministry of Economic Affairs. For the mission to Washington, however, Davis suggested that he be given a "cover." Davis was developing qualms and decided to conceal his intimate association with the young German economic wizard while peddling his scheme to the President of the United States.

Davis's suggestion was accepted by Goering. In a quick-change act, even while Davis was still in Berlin, Hertslet was transformed into a secret agent. Taken over by the Abwehr, he was supplied with all the usual appurtenances of cloak-and-dagger, including a complex cipher especially designed for him. His associates were given code names: Goering became "Harold" and Dr. Fetzer "Fritz"; Davis became "Agent No. C-80," and John L. Lewis was listed as his H-man (or *Hintermann*, sub-agent), with the number C-80/L, and was also referred to as "Charlie."

A go-between was established in Madrid in the person of an oil operative named Janssen, whose first assignment was to book passage for Davis and Hertslet on the American Clipper, scheduled to depart from Lisbon on October 8.

The Abwehr found a passport for Hertslet, one that was originally held by a Swedish citizen named Carl Clemens Bluecher, who had turned it in upon becoming a German national a short time before. Espionage experts substituted Hertslet's photograph for Bluecher's and stamped the forged seal of the Swedish Consul in Berlin on the picture. When an American visa was obtained for the doctored passport, the German secret service felt confident that Hertslet's metamorphosis was foolproof.

But even on the first leg of Hertslet's journey a hitch grounded him. Although Davis had tried to keep his detour to Berlin under cover, his presence there became known to Sam E. Woods, the commercial attaché at the American Embassy, and a well-informed report was cabled to the State Department. The Department made Woods's dispatch available to the Foreign Office in London. British Intelligence quickly picked up the trail of the travelers, identified "Bluecher" as Hertslet, and tipped off the United States Legation in Portugal that the younger member of the duo was "traveling on a passport that was not his own."

When Davis and Hertslet checked in for the flight at the Pan American office in Lisbon, the German was challenged by a clerk, who pretended that he knew him by his real name from previous trips. Hertslet was flustered. This was not his first voyage on a bogus passport. But it was the first time that he had been found out.

Davis intervened vigorously, although awkwardly. He berated the clerk, insisting that Hertslet *was* Bluecher, an executive of his Scandinavian subsidiary. When it became evident that the clerk could not be swayed, Davis changed his tack. He hinted broadly that he himself was on a secret errand for the President of the United States and it was the nature of his mission that necessitated Hertslet's masquerade. The clerk remained adamant, however, and Davis appealed the case to the American Consul General, Samuel H. Wiley, who, on instructions phoned from Washington, refused to honor Hertslet's visa.

Davis left alone, arriving in Port Washington, Long Island, on the afternoon of October 9, one of thirty-five passengers cleared for the trip on the American Clipper. Confronted on his arrival with a United Press dispatch revealing that he had been in Berlin, he glibly assured the reporters that he was "only in Rome two weeks on business," and denied rumors that he had negotiated the sale of oil to Italy for transshipment to Germany.

Immediately upon his arrival, he asked John L. Lewis to call the White House and arrange an appointment with the President. This time Lewis got General Edwin M. Watson, Mr. Roosevelt's appointment secretary, on the line, and was told that the President had no time to see Davis. Davis remained undaunted by the snub. He wrote two long letters to Mr. Roosevelt—one on October 11, another on the 12th—describing on seventeen closely typed legal-sized pages his "impressions of Europe" and giving a warped account of his negotiations with Marshal Goering.

Unable to wrest an appointment from the President, Davis went to the State Department instead. He saw Assistant Secretary Berle in a meeting that proved highly embarrassing. Berle reproached Davis for what he charitably described as "numerous misrepresentations" in his letters to Mr. Roosevelt. When he brought up the matter of Hertslet's bogus passport, Davis tried to lie his way out of it.

Lewis, on October 23, 1939, called Berle for an appointment but refused to accept the invitation of the Assistant Secretary to see him in his office at the State Department. They agreed to meet at Berle's home.

In a strange and ominous meeting, Lewis launched threats-by-innuendo, the cutting edge of which were unmistakable. As Berle recorded the conversation, Lewis began by reminding the Assistant Secretary that "the resolution passed at the CIO convention in support of the President . . . could just as easily have been passed in opposition to him."

Then he switched to Davis. He had seen the oilman, he said, and understood that he had brought back from Europe "an important message" from "high German officials." The time had come, Lewis insisted, for a general peace, exactly along the lines Davis had outlined to the President on September 15. Davis's message "afforded such a possibility." But the President had made himself inaccessible. Did this mean that he was not interested in doing his part in the interests of peace?

Berle responded sharply, by telling Lewis that the United States government could not consider any such suggestion unless it came from a government through recognized channels. Moreover, he said, Davis had misrepresented himself and his capacity in Berlin, and was not considered the proper liaison in any matter between the American and German governments.

"Would you like the German government to say officially," Lewis asked, "what Davis is saying unofficially?"

"The German government," Berle said, "has a thoroughly competent representative in Washington to convey any messages of this character."

When the meeting broke up in a chill that was keenly felt by both men, it must have been abundantly clear to Lewis that Davis was *persona non grata* with the Roosevelt administration and that his own role in this affair was viewed with grave misgivings. For a week after the acrid session, Lewis, his pride deeply hurt and bristling with anger and contempt, huddled with Davis, seeking ways and means by which he could either compel Mr. Roosevelt to adopt the Davis plan or, if the President refused, to punish him.

Perhaps at no time in his remarkable regime of power and influence was John L. Lewis so sure of his power and so doubtful of his influence. In the end, fervently convinced of the excellence of his own case and, with equal piety, of the callous indifference of the President to the cause of peace, he concluded that he was left with no choice: Mr. Roosevelt had to be punished.

Davis was delivering on his commitment to Goering sooner than had been expected. The second act in this incredible drama had begun.

NOTE

1 Enacted in 1799 during the presidency of John Adams, this Act outlawed unauthorized contact of United States citizens with a foreign government "for the purpose of influencing its conduct in a controversy with our government or to defeat measures of our government."

Chapter 33

The Big Deal

*I*N a press conference on May 4, 1940, Under Secretary of State Sumner Welles was subjected to what sounded like, and was probably intended to be, an embarrassing inquiry. The State Department correspondent of a Detroit newspaper questioned him about an article published a few weeks before "by a usually responsible journalist," stating that William Rhodes Davis, "who has made a number of oil arrangements for the Mexican Government," had given "a gift of $250,000" to the Democratic Party, "divided between the National Committee and an organization in Pennsylvania."

The question of Davis's alleged contribution was embarrassing to the Roosevelt Administration which was then conducting a quiet campaign to discredit the oilman in an effort to end his collaboration with the Nazis. Secretary Welles managed to dismiss it casually. The matter, he said, was "entirely political," and, therefore, he was "not in a position to comment on it."

The news happened to be relevant and timely, but not in the context in which it was pursued. Davis had been an ardent supporter of the Democratic Party and a generous donor to its campaigns in the past. By now he had broken with Roosevelt. Unknown to the correspondent and, for that matter, to Mr. Welles, he had recently given, not $250,000 as it was rumored, but the sum of $160,000 to the Democrats. It had been paid not to the National Committtee but under the counter to "a representative of the Pennsylvania Party organization."

This was how Dr. Hertslet accounted for the money and explained the payment in a report to Marshal Goering. The $160,000 had come from a slush fund of millions which Goering had appropriated for Davis and Hertslet, to finance their anti-Roosevelt lobby. According to Hertslet, it had been paid to "promote the candidacy" of a Pennsylvania politician (whose name was garbled in the transcript of Hertslet's coded cable) in "opposition to the anti-German Senator [Joseph F.] Guffey"; and "for the purpose of . . . buying approximately forty Pennsylvania delegates at the party convention in Chicago, to be held on July 17."

In making the payment, Davis and Hertslet hoped to conceal the tainted source of this contribution. The German records indicate that they used a middleman, a millionaire oil operator from Pittsburgh and a potent figure in Pennsylvania politics. His name was Walter A. Jones.

Who the Pennsylvania bagman was and how he expected to "buy" those anti-Roosevelt votes we do not know and need not care. But Walter Jones is another matter.

The Pittsburgh oil operator was neither a business buccaneer nor a political opportunist like Davis. He was anything but pro-Nazi. Nor was he hostile to the Democrats. On the contrary, he was one of the handful of super-rich independent oilmen who supported Roosevelt. Reputed to be "the largest single contributor to the President's campaign in the 1936 election," he was close to F.D.R. and had free entrée to the White House. He also enjoyed the confidence of Secretary of the Interior Harold L. Ickes, the watchdog of the oil industry.

What, then, motivated Jones to act as recipient of the Davis contribution? He did it not as a favor to Davis, but because he had been asked to do so by John L. Lewis.

The hard-boiled, cool-headed oilman was spellbound by the formidable labor leader, whom he regarded as the greatest living American. As long as Lewis and Roosevelt saw eye to eye, Jones had no problem concerning his loyalty. He was for Roosevelt because Lewis was for him. When Lewis turned against the President, Jones also turned. But unlike Lewis, he was no fanatic and did not quite have the courage of his convictions. He kept his change of heart under cover, willing to perform critical services for Davis, while pretending that his devotion to Roosevelt remained undiminished.[1]

Hertslet revealed that Davis was also interested in the defeat of "the anti-German" Senator Joseph F. Guffey. For many years the Senator from Pennsylvania had been one of Lewis's closest allies on Capitol Hill and the beneficiary of his union's munificence. Although a devout Roosevelt man, Guffey supported Lewis in all his controversies with the President and had sided with him in the bitter gubernatorial primary fight in 1938, which saw the Democrats' official nominee pitted against Lewis's candidate. When Lewis had made his arrangements with Davis, Guffey had become one of the oilman's chief senatorial supporters.

Guffey's relations with Davis had reached a crisis on June 15, 1939, when Marquis W. Childs, Washington correspondent of the St. Louis *Post-Dispatch*, wrote an article linking the Senator with "a freelance oil operator" who, as Childs reported, had been instrumental in obtaining the expropriated Mexican oil for his German clients. The material for the article had been "leaked" to Childs by Assistant Secretary of State A. A. Berle, Jr., as part of his campaign against the oilman. Guffey, in turn, was used by Davis and Lewis in an attempt to discredit Childs. In a vitriolic rebuttal, Senator Guffey charged that Childs "had been paid by someone other than his employer" to write the article.

Guffey's cooperation with Davis had now gone too far, and Berle was determined to put an end to it. Assuming that the Senator's support of the oil operator was based on his ignorance of Davis's background and motives, Berle resolved to enlighten Guffey and also to reveal to him the part Lewis was playing in his machinations.

A meeting was secretly arranged and Guffey was shown the evidence the State Department had accumulated. It was so persuasive and disturbing that the Senator promptly discontinued his support of Davis and rearranged, as he put it, his association with Lewis, at considerable jeopardy to his own political fortunes. In the wake of his session with Berle, he retracted, both on the Senate floor and in a statement issued to the press, the charges he had made against Marquis Childs. He conceded that the "facts of Mr. Childs's story are substantially correct."

Retribution was prompt. Guffey was included in the purge Lewis was mounting in the critical election year of 1940. All support he had previously received from Lewis and the UMW suddenly evaporated. Part of the funds given Jones to "bribe" the Democrats in Pennsylvania was allocated for an anti-Guffey campaign. Lewis put up a candidate of his own, none other than Walter A. Jones. In one of the strangest maneuvers in American politics, Jones passed on Davis's tainted money, not merely to defeat his good friend Guffey, but also to have himself nominated in his place. Despite his break with Lewis and the German money spent on unseating him, Guffey retained the Democratic nomination and was reelected, carrying even the coal mining regions where Lewis's influence was assumed to be paramount and decisive.

Guffey, of course, was not the primary target of Lewis's vendetta. Although this was the first time that German funds had been disbursed clandestinely to influence American domestic politics, it was not the first move in the implementation of the Davis plan.

When Davis had met Goering in Berlin in the early fall of 1939, "the defeat of President Roosevelt for reelection in 1940," as Goering later put it, was discussed as well as the peace plan. Davis had assured him, Goering said, that "he could swing the election against Roosevelt" by using the influence of John L. Lewis. The oilman was effusive and almost eloquent in explaining to Goering the labor leader's enormous power and the decisive nature of his influence in American domestic affairs. Lewis's mind was firmly made up, Davis had told Goering, to thwart whatever plans the President had to remain in the White House in 1940.

"He presented himself as a very good friend of John L. Lewis," Goering said later when asked about the conference. "He told me that Lewis was not tied up with either of the political parties but was a free-lance as far as political decisions were concerned and was one of the few people who understood Germany's position. . . . Davis told me that by using his influence on Lewis, he could influence the elections in such a manner that the reelection of Roosevelt, which in his opinion would mean war, would be prevented."

When Davis literally guaranteed Lewis's participation, Goering became interested. "At the time of the American depression," he told his interrogator, "I had been desperately looking for someone who would have been useful to me in the United States in exploiting the economic situation." Lewis was now such a man, he thought, to whip up political unrest that the tradition-defying third-term issue would create in the States.

Davis told Goering that he himself would be willing "to put up a million of his own money . . . to have Lewis help him defeat President Roosevelt." Substantial additional funds would be needed because, as he put it, an effort to elect a President "who was favorably inclined toward Germany" might cost as much as $5 million, if not more.

Goering said that it could cost as much as $100 million to $150 million, but, he added, he would be willing to spend any amount for such a purpose. As for himself, Davis said, he expected no financial gain from the project. In the event he was successful in defeating Roosevelt, he hoped to become Secretary of State—a prospect he thought would make the plot even more palatable to Goering.

Goering discussed the matter with Hitler and obtained the Fuehrer's consent. In their final meeting on October 3, he told Davis to go ahead—make his "agreement" with Lewis and "arrange" the defeat of F.D.R., should the President decide to run again. He also promised to send millions of dollars to the United States in cash, as soon as the project got off the ground. Immediately after the meeting, probably to impress Goering (whose *Forschungsamt* was monitoring all such telephone conversations), Davis put in a call to Lewis in

Washington and reported to him in guarded language the details of his negotiations.

When the President refused to participate in the peace maneuver whose plan Davis had brought back from Germany, the alternate anti-Roosevelt drive began right away. Lewis launched the campaign in October 1939, at a time when F.D.R. himself had not yet resolved the third-term issue.

His opening salvo, although not of the megaton power of his later blasts, was shrewdly designed to produce maximum effect. It took for granted that a surreptitious third-term move was already afoot, and Lewis now moved to expose it as a conspiracy.

His first thrust was apparently directed at two middle-echelon government officials—Norman M. Littel of the Justice Department and Marshal E. Dimock of the Department of Labor—who were said to be planning to summon liberal Democrats from eleven Western states to a political conference in California. New Dealers had become increasingly disturbed by F.D.R.'s apparent drift from left of center toward the center and even slightly to the right of it. The meeting was subtly designed to put pressure on Mr. Roosevelt to "adopt a straight liberal course and keep to it."

Mr. Lewis preferred to read a sinister intent into the move. In a statement issued in Washington on October 30, he spoke ominously of "a secret agenda" which the organizers had drawn up for the purpose of "promoting the candidacy of President Roosevelt for a third term." And he deplored, in similarly ominous terms, "the *surreptitious* manner" in which the conference was being prepared, "the *doubtful* source of its financing" by "an *anonymous* individual in California," and "the *secret* plans to use the conference to launch a third-term boom."

In an aside—for he had not yet completely broken with F.D.R.—Lewis absolved the President of complicity in the California episode. "I doubt," he wrote with obvious tongue in cheek, "that the President has knowledge or would approve the plans of these overzealous individuals responsible for this program." Lewis scored with his very first blast. The conference was abandoned.

During the rest of 1939, Lewis embarked on his course, leaving no doubt about its direction. On January 24, 1940, he delivered a scathing indictment of the President and a vitriolic attack on the New Deal. A third-term movement was gaining momentum within the labor movement and even inside his own United Mine Workers. At this time, forty-seven drafts advocating the reelection of President Roosevelt were before the Resolutions Committee of the UMW convention held in Columbus, Ohio.

Using his enormous prestige and making the most of his dazzling eloquence in his presidential address to the 2400 delegates of the convention, he recommended that the mine workers "refrain from endorsing President Roosevelt for a third term." He went so far as to "predict" that F.D.R. would go down in "ignominious defeat" if the Democratic National Convention "could be coerced or dragooned into renominating him."

The UMW convention adjourned on January 30. Five days later, Davis handed over the $160,000 to "buy" the Pennsylvania delegation's vote against Roosevelt. The campaign he had sold to the Germans was on in earnest, and John L. Lewis was, in keeping with the commitment Davis had made to Goering, carrying the ball.

In the wake of the UMW convention, Lewis confided to Robert Kintner, who was then writing a syndicated column with Joseph Alsop, some of the features of his activities. He told Kintner that he had turned against Roosevelt and was backing Senator Wheeler for the Democratic presidential nomination, that he had "more than a million dollars" in the bank "to be put on Wheeler," and that he had already shifted the Railroad Brotherhood and Dan Tobin, head of the Teamsters, "one of the roughest branches in the whole labor movement" away from F.D.R.

Davis now asked Hertslet to arrange the transfer of the Germans' share of the "campaign funds" as soon as possible; and suggested that Hertslet join him in the United States, despite his previous failure to do so.

Hertslet carried Davis's dunning letter to Goering. What with the acute shortage of foreign currency in the German exchequer, it needed much of the Field Marshal's considerable ingenuity to scrape up the money for financing the plot. He did not have anything like the $100,000,000 which he thought would be needed either to elect or to defeat a presidential candidate. He was, in fact, apprehensive that the entire scheme might fail because it would be underfinanced. But he managed to scrape up $5,000,000 from his various secret funds, and place it at the disposal of Davis and Hertslet.

It was an enormous sum. At about this same time, only $50,000 in a "special fund" was appropriated for the German Embassy in Washington when the Foreign Ministry decided that Dr. Hans Thomsen, the Charge d'affaires, should undertake a similar anti-Roosevelt campaign. As we shall see, the Embassy's fund proved too little and the millions Goering gave Davis too much. Even today, when all the details of the plot are available in the documents, this multi-million dollar "campaign fund" remains the only mysterious feature of this conspiracy.

Hertslet insisted after the war that Goering had raised it; that it was taken to the United States by a trusted Italian courier named

Luigi Podesta; and that Podesta had turned it over to Davis, who deposited it in various accounts at the First National Bank of Boston, the Irving Trust Company in New York, the Bank of America in San Francisco, and the Banco Germano in Mexico City. But Hertslet did not profess to know how the money was used, how much of it was spent, and what became of the remainder. He conceded merely that the anti-Roosevelt campaign had swallowed up only a fraction of this sum. "It became possible for Davis," he said, "to conduct the campaign on a shoestring because he had a trump card in his deck and expected to win the game with it alone. It was John L. Lewis."

As far as it was possible to ascertain, Davis, Hertslet, and Lewis spent about $1.5 million of this clandestine campaign fund. Approximately $3.6 million was discovered in December 1941 among the hidden assets of the German Embassy in Washington, with nobody in authority able or willing to explain this particular hoard.

As for Davis's invitation to Hertslet to come to the United States, it was no simple matter. The State Department was alert to any attempt of his to enter the country on a fake passport. Travel through the tightening British blockade in the Atlantic had become increasingly risky.

But Goering insisted that he go, and Hertslet set out. The Abwehr supplied him with a Danish passport for the transatlantic crossing, which he made on a Portuguese ship to Argentina. Then he worked his passage up to Mexico. There he discarded his camouflage, and entered the United States at Brownsville, Texas, under his own name and with his own diplomatic passport, on which the State Department could not refuse a visa.

Hertslet arrived in Washington on March 18, 1940, and checked into Davis's suite in the Mayflower Hotel. His close association with Goering, the monumental nature of his secret mission, and his access to that $5,000,000 fund had turned the head of the brash young German. Davis did not like this new Hertslet, who was now seizing the reins and giving orders, even instructing him regarding Lewis's future activities.

During this first of his two visits, Hertslet spent twenty-six days in the United States, meeting associates of Davis. March 27 was the high point of his sojourn. Though he and Davis went to considerable length to keep the major event of the day a secret, they could not conceal it from the State Department.

Back in the fall of 1939, when Assistant Secretary Berle had proposed that the FBI keep Lewis under surveillance, the President had rejected the proposition with horror. No sooner had Berle returned to his office than he called Director J. Edgar Hoover and asked him to put a discreet watch on the Svengali-Trilby act of Davis and Lewis.

None was put on Lewis. Only Davis was shadowed but, in this manner, every confluence of his and Lewis's movements was established.

Hertslet's trail had been picked up when he set foot on American soil. On this Friday in March he was followed by special agents to Davis's home in Scarsdale, where it was discovered that the oilman had still another houseguest—John L. Lewis.

Hertslet later revealed that this was his first full-scale meeting with the famed labor leader. Davis had introduced him to Lewis immediately upon his arrival in Washington, and Lewis had granted him several audiences in his office in the massive Florentine building of the United Mine Workers on 15th Street, but they had had no opportunity to discuss serious business.

At Davis's home, Lewis could stay only for the night and part of Saturday, but they had ample opportunity to review their project and plan their course. Lewis propounded his ideas and Hertslet listened to the rumbling exposition of the great Welshman.

According to Hertslet's account, Lewis sealed their alliance. Davis repeated what he had told Goering, that Lewis could count on the support of ten million workers and would use this enormous following against F.D.R. Lewis agreed. They discussed the coming elections, and Lewis said that if Roosevelt became a candidate, he would formally come out against him.

It was an exhilarating session, as all encounters with Lewis invariably were, dominated by his overpowering personality and ennobled by the obvious sincerity of his fierce pacifism. Hertslet, too, came under Lewis's irresistible spell. But he was too cynical to be completely taken in. What he had found upon his arrival in Washington neither pleased nor satisfied him. It did not take him long to realize that Davis's glowing reports to Berlin were based solely on what Lewis had done rather than on anything Davis had undertaken. The sophisticated young Nazi found out that Davis was bluffing, and told the oilman so to his face.

Hertslet concluded that the base on which Davis was developing the project was too narrow to assure its success, even with Lewis's formidable aid. He decided to involve the German Embassy. In this way he could make use of the Embassy's widespread contacts. What Davis had neglected to do, Hertslet himself would undertake.

The Monday morning after his return to Washington from Scarsdale, he went to the German Embassy on Massachusetts Avenue to see the man Berlin had designated as his official contact in the United States—Captain Robert Witthoeft-Emden, the Naval Attaché. He produced his passport, then introduced himself as Goering's personal envoy and his plenipotentiary in "a certain project." He so impressed the naval officer that he was promptly taken to Dr. Hans Thomsen.

What Hertslet had to say in the privacy of Thomsen's study left the Charge d'affaires, himself a shrewd practitioner of diplomatic skulduggery, literally breathless.

As Thomsen recalled the interview during his postwar interrogation, "Hertslet said that he knew John L. Lewis personally very well, and that he could exercise a lot of influence on the trend of American politics. . . . He said that his influence with Mr. Lewis was strong enough to make the election run against Roosevelt. He said that through Lewis he could swing the election against Roosevelt."

Hertslet told of the huge fund at his disposal and suggested that "it would be a practical political idea" if the Embassy would join him and Davis "to boost Mr. Lewis."

Until Hertslet showed up, Thomsen later claimed, the idea of intervening in the presidential election had never occurred to him. The very concept of such a campaign seemed preposterous—or, as Heribert von Strempel, Thomsen's crack aide, later described it, "too fantastic and impossible to be realized."

Thomsen did not dare turn Hertslet out. He cabled Berlin, inquiring about the man's credentials. "The answer came," Strempel recalled, "that he was an accredited agent of the German Navy. Furthermore, Berlin answered that if he wished to communicate by way of the Embassy code to the Foreign Office, he was entitled to do so."[2] Hertslet had a faster and presumably safer line of communication. He was authorized to use the Naval Attaché's secret crypto-system, which was different from the crack-prone diplomatic cipher that, as Hertslet correctly suspected, had been compromised by the British.

After Hertslet had left, Thomsen discussed the matter with Strempel and, as he told his American interrogators after the war, they decided to have nothing to do with "the adventurous plot." Not only did he refuse to join Hertslet, he claimed, but he also urged the Foreign Ministry to abort the scheme and intercede with Goering to disavow Davis and recall Hertslet.

This, however, was not what actually happened. Far from objecting to the plot, Thomsen merely protested the encroachment of an interloper on his own prerogatives and suggested that he and his embassy would be far better qualified to organize such a campaign, with or without Lewis. There the matter stood on April 12, when Hertslet, his spadework completed, returned to Mexico City to turn his attention to smuggling more Mexican oil through the British blockade.

Much of this was mere shadow boxing. Less than three months before the political conventions and only seven before the election, the Democratic candidate was still anybody's guess. While Lewis thundered in public against a third term and conspired behind the scenes against Roosevelt, the subject of his wrath remained exasperatingly aloof and elusive. Nobody—not even Mrs. Roosevelt—seemed sure of the President's intentions. He himself appeared to be struggling to reach a decision.

Then the situation changed. While Hertslet was plotting in Washington, the ominous calm of what Senator William E. Borah had dubbed the Phony War ended with dramatic suddenness. On April 9, Germany invaded Denmark and Norway. A month later German troops crossed into Belgium and the Netherlands, then launched the attack against France.

Walter Lippmann wrote in his column: "Our duty is to begin acting at once on the basic assumption that the Allies may lose the war this summer." This was clearly the eleventh hour, and Roosevelt responded to its challenge.

NOTES

1 By continuing to pose "as a liberal" and "talk like a New Dealer," Jones even fooled Secretary Ickes. On August 10, 1939, when Ickes asked him point-blank how he stood on the third term issue, Jones said that he "ought to be [opposed to it] but . . . would find it impossible to be against the President." While he claimed to be a staunch supporter of F.D.R., he was actually working for the nomination of Senator Burton K. Wheeler, who had become Lewis's candidate against the President.

2 The papers of the German Foreign Ministry show that Hertslet traveled under the special orders issued by the Abwehr. The Canaris organization also provided whatever cover he needed and assured a line of communication for him from Mexico City. But that was the extent of the Abwehr's involvement.

Chapter 34

The Thomsen Formula

*T*HE German Embassy in Washington, D.C. was an ugly old red brick building on Massachusetts Avenue, looking like the barracks of cuirassiers in the staid capital of a Graustarkian principality. Most of the time it was the sedate seat of that plodding, colorless Teutonic diplomacy which Bismarck regarded with such consummate contempt.

For two decades after World War I, the mission was engaged in the collection of intelligence (political by the career officers, military by the service attachés) strictly within the boundaries of proper diplomatic usage. The clean climate changed somewhat in 1937 when Dr. Hans Heinrich Dieckhoff was named ambassador.

He was no stranger in Washington, having served there as Counsellor in the Twenties, then in London in the same capacity. Most of his professional life abroad had been spent in America and England assimilating some of the principles and the manners of the Anglo-Saxons.

With one foot in Germany's proper diplomatic past and with the other not quite yet in current Nazi conspiratorial dealings, Dieckhoff preferred to get his information straight from people he thought were best qualified to dispense it. In Washington, however, he was narrowly restricted in his efforts to obtain facts he needed. Representing Nazi Germany, he could not very well cultivate progressive politicians, liberal professionals, trade union leaders, and prominent Jews, usually the best sources. He was ostracized by influential Americans in public life who would have nothing to do with Hitler's envoy. The people he could associate with, or who sought him out, were either far removed from the Roosevelt Administration or reflected Nazi prejudices of the new Germany.

376

Dieckhoff was a complex and weak man. Though never a Nazi himself, he drifted steadily in the direction of Germany's masters who could make him or break him. With this careerist an entirely new atmosphere began to permeate the Embassy.

In 1938, in a crude gesture of mutual loathing, Germany and the United States recalled their ambassadors *sine die* and left their embassies in care of Charge d'affaires. Dr. Dieckhoff left Washington for temporary oblivion at home. Much as the mood of the play darkened with the entry of Cassius in the second act of *Julius Caesar,* the climate of the Embassy changed abruptly. It became a bastion of Nazism, with all the conspiratorial trimmings reminiscent of the cunning of medieval Venetian envoys. In a real sense, the Embassy went underground.

Spying and plotting became the established practice behind the walls of the house on Massachusetts Avenue. It was, in fact, Dr. Dieckhoff who had inaugurated the change. Apprehensive that information sent to Berlin by the inexperienced crew of mediocre diplomats he left behind would be far too inadequate and unilluminating, he began looking for someone to remedy this situation. A seasoned professional who would act as secret agent-at-large was needed to procure intelligence under the counter.

In the summer of 1938, while vacationing at a German spa, Dr. Dieckhoff bumped into a man who was, of all things, seeking exactly this kind of a job. He was the notorious George Sylvester Viereck, a gifted poet in the mold of his idol Oscar Wilde. The most industrious and insidious German agent in the United States through World War I, he was bent on making his living as a propagandist and panderer of political secrets.

Dieckhoff accepted when Viereck offered to serve as V-man for the Washington Embassy. Viereck was given a cover job as a correspondent for a Munich paper, which would also act as the conduit for the funds paid to Viereck from the Foreign Ministry's unvouchered "Special Account J."

Thus, when the Embassy came under the authority of Dr. Hans Thomsen, after only six months as Charge d'affaires, he also obtained the services of a spymaster. Viereck became just that in everything but name, if only because Thomsen, on his own authority, expanded Viereck's functions beyond what Dr. Dieckhoff had had in mind when he hired the man. Thomsen used Viereck as "the cuckoo of propaganda," as the man once actually called himself, "to lay its eggs in every nest." His assignment was no less than influencing members of Congress and the opinion makers, dividing the nation, spreading confusion and chaos. But that was only part of it. Viereck was also required to keep Berlin posted "on what was really going on in the

United States"—to collect privileged information and secret intelligence. "This was his main task," Ambassador Dieckhoff conceded after the war.

Under Thomsen, Viereck succeeded in spinning a web of confidential informants in key and strategic places in Washington, especially on Capitol Hill. He developed close relations with a number of lawmakers whose isolationism and anti-Roosevelt bias made them easy prey. However, he was shrewd enough not to compromise these public figures. For this, he established a network of paid spies inside the offices of the friendly senators and Congressmen.

Thomsen was keenly aware of the impropriety of his action and of the risks he was taking as a diplomatic plotter. In several dispatches he pleaded with Berlin to let him conduct his secret campaign at his discretion, without requiring him to explain its details, and even to suspend the bureaucratic rule that obliged him to account for all expenditures.

The war had disrupted his courier service and he was compelled to use commercial facilities almost exclusively. Thomsen assumed that his telegrams would be monitored "by the enemy," that his cipher had been compromised, that the British were intercepting his cables and providing transcripts for the American authorities. On July 3, in an extraordinary appeal to his Foreign Ministry, he requested permission to destroy all records relating to his "expenditures for political purposes," as their seizure would "mean political ruin" for Germany's friends "despite all camouflage."

In order to step up "to maximum efficiency" his efforts "to prevent [the United States] from entering the war and to exert direct political influence," he had to employ "special methods," and disbursements "for these purposes" had to be made to the recipients "through trusted go-betweens." It was obvious, he wrote, that "in the circumstances . . . no receipts can be expected." He received the authorization on July 8. Henceforth all correspondence relating to his campaign was destroyed by the Embassy and all payments were made without receipts.

Thomsen believed that he succeeded in concealing his activities, but his secrecy did not prove as enduring as he had hoped. On July 18, for example, he sent by cable a top-secret report describing how Senator Gerald P. Nye of North Dakota had consented "after lengthy negotiations" to distribute "to 100,000 specially selected persons" one of his speeches which the Germans regarded as an extraordinarily effective piece of propaganda attuned "to the American mentality." Thomsen went out of his way to emphasize the importance of this coup. "This undertaking," he wrote, "is not altogether easy and is particularly delicate since Senator Nye, as a political opponent of the

President, is under the careful observation of the secret state police here [*der hiesigen geheimen Staatspolizei*]." He concluded his dispatch with what had become his stereotyped postscript: "This telegraphic report . . . [has] been destroyed here."

It was *not* destroyed in Berlin, and is now on file under Serial No. 897, Folio 291872 in our own National Archives among other papers of the German Foreign Ministry captured by the Allied forces. So are innumerable other documents Thomsen thought had been destroyed in Germany. It is, therefore, possible to reconstruct the Thomsen conspiracy in its entirety, from its inception to its bitter end in December 1941, when the attack on Pearl Harbor and Hitler's declaration of war closed this chapter in German-American relations.

How did this fantastic campaign originate; how was it conducted; and which people knowingly or unknowingly lent themselves—their prestige, their enthusiasm, their prejudices—to Dr. Thomsen's scheme?

It began tentatively enough on March 30, 1940, when Thomsen reported Hertslet's visit and suggested that he, Thomsen, be allowed to match the Davis operation with his own efforts. Berlin replied on April 8, authorizing him to go ahead, allocating $50,000 to finance the project. It was a mere pittance compared with the millions Davis and Hertslet allegedly had.

Immediately after receipt of the $50,000, Thomsen commissioned Viereck to design a campaign, first to influence the political conventions of 1940, and then to manipulate the election. Viereck presented his plan early in June, and Thomsen forwarded it to Berlin for approval on the thirteenth.

Unlike the Davis plan, which had its origin in John L. Lewis's emotionally charged loathing of Franklin D. Roosevelt and was aimed exclusively at the "destruction" of the President, the Thomsen-Viereck plan was supremely realistic—it opposed Roosevelt's reelection, but more important, it promoted American isolationism. The emphasis Viereck placed on the latter theme made the campaign extremely effective. It coincided with the overwhelming sentiments of the vast majority of the American people, and brought into Thomsen's orbit many prominent and influential Americans who abhorred Hitler but overcame their distaste for the Nazis in their sincere and vehement opposition to this country's involvement in the European war.[1]

Proceeding from a relatively small core of pro-Nazis, Thomsen claimed on dispatch after dispatch to Berlin that he was able to expand his campaign into a huge and lively movement, broaden and articulate it, and bend it to German interests. Its implementation was a *coup de maître,* stage-managed by the greatest virtuoso of political propaganda, George Sylvester Viereck.

When Thomsen submitted Viereck's detailed campaign plan to Berlin, he demanded immediate action, since the Republican Convention was to open in Philadelphia in less than two weeks Thomsen told Berlin that Viereck had designed a special plot for the convention. It was what the Nazi envoy called "a well-camouflaged blitz propaganda campaign," for which he took the credit, consisting of two major parts:

1. A well-known Republican Congressman who works in close collaboration with the special official for press affairs [Heribert von Strempel, the Embassy's political and press attaché], will invite fifty isolationist Republican Congressmen on a three-day visit to the Party convention, so that they may work on the delegates of the Republican Party in favor of an isolationist foreign policy. Three thousand dollars are required.
2. In addition the Republican in question is prepared to form a small ad hoc Republican Committee, which . . . during the Party convention would publish in all the leading American newspapers a full-page advertisement with the impressive appeal "Keep America Out of the War." [The cost of this advertising campaign was estimated at $60 to $80 thousand, but Thomsen reassured Berlin that half of it "will, in all probability, be borne by our Republican friends."]

Berlin cabled its approval on June 17. Only two days later, Thomsen told the Foreign Ministry that "some fifty Congressmen will be going to Philadelphia to explain our views to the delegates at the Party convention." In fact, such a "delegation" had been assembled from among members of the Wednesday Night Club, an informal caucus of first-term Republican Congressmen who met regularly each week.

The club was united mainly on the issue of opposition to American involvement in the war. Representative Hamilton Fish of New York succeeded in persuading Representative (later Senator) Karl E. Mundt of South Dakota to lead the group to Philadelphia. Its isolationist plank, drafted by Viereck, according to Thomsen's claims, was pitted against one proposed by Christopher T. Emmett, Jr., of New York. The Committee to Defend America by Aiding the Allies, headed by William Allen White, editor of the *Emporia Gazette,* urged the inclusion of this plank for "all possible aid to the Allies."

Representative Mundt himself did not know that the German Embassy was claiming that it was behind his bid. "We were mostly against Wendell Willkie," he later said, "because he was an interventionist." He added that his group had paid its own way to Philadelphia. Thomsen told his superiors that he had paid $1,350 to cover its travel expenses.

Simultaneously, an ad appeared in *The New York Times* on June 25, the day before the convention was scheduled to adopt the platform. Addressed to "the Delegates to the Republican National Convention and to American mothers, wage-earners, farmers and veterans," it read in part: "Stop the war machine! Stop the interventionists and warmongers! Stop the Democratic Party which we believe is the War Party in the United States, and is leading us to war against the will of the American people!"

The ad was supposedly paid for by a front-organization called National Committee to Keep America Out of Foreign Wars. The German documents assert that it had been put together by Viereck.[2]

The Republican Convention produced the astounding nomination of Wendell L. Willkie of Indiana on the fifth ballot. Thomsen proved his skill as a shrewd observer of the American scene with an appraisal he cabled to his home office on June 28: "From the standpoint of foreign policy, Willkie's nomination is unfortunate for us. He is not an isolationist and . . . his attitude in the past permits no doubt that he belongs to those Republicans who see America's best defense in supporting England by all means 'short of war.' "

Thomsen asserted that he had sneaked several planks into the platform that were clearly favorable to the Germans. "By making skillful use of all tactical openings," he wrote on July 3, in the first of a series of brilliant postmortems, "the isolationist wing of the Republican Party succeeded . . . in anchoring the foreign policy of the Republican Party on principles, to the observance of which the presidential candidate Willkie had formally pledged himself during the convention. The two most important read as follows:

1. The Republican Party is firmly opposed to involving this nation in a foreign war.
2. The Republican Party stands for Americanism, preparedness, and peace.

Thomsen bluntly claimed credit as the author of these planks "taken almost verbatim from the conspicuous full-page advertisements in the American press published upon our instigation."

On July 19, he smugly concluded his dispatch: "Nothing has leaked out about the assistance we rendered in this."

The Republican Convention was barely over when Thomsen, Strempel, and Viereck turned their attention to what they regarded as the easier nut to crack—the convention of the Democrats. "The special officer for press relations [Strempel] has seen to it," Thomsen wrote, "that several reliable isolationist Congressmen went to Chicago in order to exert influence on the delegates with the purpose of including, at least formally, in the Democratic platform as well, a pledge of non-participation in the European war."

In addition, he went on, "the Congressmen used for the purpose the tried and proved promotion aid of a sensational advertisement in the leading Chicago newspaper." Thomsen claimed that the special ad which Viereck allegedly had prepared for the Democrats was similar to the one he had written for the Republicans, except for a pinpointed appeal: "Don't let the Democratic Party, historically the Party of non-intervention, become the Party of intervention and war, against the will of 93 percent of the American people." It appeared in the July 15 issue of the *Chicago Tribune,* in the name of Hamilton Fish's committee.

In his preoccupation with his own campaign, Dr. Thomsen paid only passing attention to the competition represented by Davis & Company.

The rush of events—the nomination of Willkie and indications that Roosevelt would be the Democratic nominee—moved John L. Lewis to put his own campaign in high gear. Davis thereupon urged Hertslet to hurry back to the United States to rejoin the plot. He arrived by plane in Washington on June 26, but this time he was able to spend only four days in this country.

The surveillance of Lewis had tightened considerably. It was done indirectly by trailing Davis, tapping his telephone, even tampering with his mail. Hertslet was kept under close observation. Exasperated and frightened, he became convinced that he had outlived his usefulness.

Even aside from the FBI's interest, a feeling of frustration was creeping up on him. The euphoria of his March-April days had evaporated. The relatively small return of the investment in Davis had caused Goering to reevaluate the plan. While Hertslet continued to bombard Berlin with highly optimistic reports from Mexico City, Berlin's responses were less than enthusiastic. By June, they stopped altogether, compelling Hertslet, now in a vacuum of his own creation, to shift for himself.

On July 1, snubbed by the Embassy, he advised Berlin that he was returning to Mexico City. The tone of his farewell message reflected his melancholy mood:

"Depart for Mexico today, since continued presence here unadvisable due to strictest surveillance. . . . This [presumably the surveillance] proves that the value of my activities are better appreciated and rated higher by the American government than by Berlin."

Davis was considerably relieved when Hertslet vanished from the scene.[3] He had come to dislike intensely the exuberant young Nazi and to regard him as a liability, likely to embarrass him. While Hertslet was gone between April 12 and June 25, Davis had strengthened his own position with the Germans, and no longer needed his support. As a matter of fact, he had added a new dimension to his collaboration with the Nazis. He became a registered *Haupt-V-Mann* (senior secret agent). Now he operated his own ring of spies, using Hertslet's line of communication via the German Naval Attaché in Washington and the German Legation in Mexico.

Davis exploited his own international business organization, tapping his contacts in England and France. He could do this with impunity under the cover of American neutrality, which gave him mobility and entry into countries from which the Germans were barred.

His new line of business began on May 16, 1940, when an associate, called "MacDonald" in the documents (the cover-name of one of his business associates) took encoded secret intelligence on a seemingly legitimate business trip to Europe. "MacDonald" succeeded in smuggling the material through the British blockade and censorship, and delivered it to the German Consul General in Genoa, who forwarded it to the Abwehr in Berlin.

At about the same time, Henry Warren Wilson, senior vice president of the Davis organization and chief of its foreign operations, was in Paris and London on the first of a series of fishing expeditions. On his way back to the United States Wilson vanished for a couple of days while he sneaked into Rome to deliver the information he had collected in France and England to "an innocuous cut-out" the Abwehr had sent from Berlin.

On May 25, in Mexico City, Wilson met with a high-ranking Abwehr operative identified only by his code name "Fritz," to receive a list of high-priority items which the Germans were eager to procure from France and England. Accompanied by Fritz, Wilson flew to Lisbon and then on to Madrid, where he and the German parted. While Fritz remained in the Spanish capital, Wilson went to Paris (which was just beginning to receive the first lashes of the Battle of France) and then on to London to procure intelligence the Germans needed at this critical juncture of the war.

On this, as well as on subsequent trips, London proved an especially fertile field for Wilson, thanks to Davis's close relationship with Lord Inverforth of Southgate, senior member of the Weir family of

Scottish munitions makers and aircraft manufacturers. His Lordship's home in Hampstead was a gold mine of information. Not only was Inverforth extremely well-informed about conditions in Britain and the plans of His Majesty's Government—indeed, about every phase and aspect of the hard-pressed country's strained war economy—but he had a son-in-law, a retired officer of the Royal Navy, who had a wide range of knowledge of military and naval matters.

Lord Inverforth and Commander Ronald Langton-Jones knew Wilson only as Davis's chief lieutenant and had no reason to suspect him as a German spy. Each time Wilson visited London he stopped in Madrid on his return to the United States, long enough to deliver the newly collected data either to Fritz or to a cut-out named Jenssen, who was posing as Davis's representative in Spain.

On June 17, Wilson was instructed to fly to Madrid and await instructions from Berlin. They arrived on the 29th, directing him to go to London again. By then Paris was no longer of any interest, France having sued for an armistice four days before. His mission accomplished, Wilson stopped in Lisbon, this time for a *Treff* with a man he knew as Albert von Karsthoff, who was really Major von Kramer-Auenrode, station chief of the Abwehr in Portugal.[4]

John L. Lewis was now committed to Senator Burton K. Wheeler, and was spending as much time in promoting the Montanan's presidential candidacy as on forestalling that of F.D.R.'s. The Lewis-Wheeler covenant, long in the making, was sealed on June 8. As Dr. Thomsen reported the deal, Lewis was to "organize a third party of disgruntled Democrats, the Peace Party."

What Lewis designed as his decisive pre-convention haymaker was a carefully constructed speech he prepared for delivery in Philadelphia even as the delegates to the Republican National Convention began to assemble there. He chose for his audience the conference of the pro-Roosevelt National Association for the Advancement of Colored People, lambasting F.D.R. "Mr. Roosevelt," he told the bewildered delegates, "made depression and unemployment a chronic fact in American life." Then, on the eve of the Democrats' convention in Chicago, he delivered another blast, now depicting Roosevelt as a warmonger, a would-be dictator, "a man on horseback." It proved of no avail. F.D.R. was nominated on the first ballot.

Lewis reacted with a series of increasingly vehement and bitter attacks, beginning on July 30 in St. Louis, in an address before the convention of the United Automobile Workers of America.

The two campaigns—those of Thomsen and of the Davis-Lewis combine—converged in October, when the election campaign reached its shrillest pitch and provoked a grave crisis in the United

States, exactly as Viereck had claimed. Dirty campaigns were nothing new or rare in American politics. But the fear of war was another matter. "It was something new and unreasoning," wrote Robert E. Sherwood in his masterly postmortem of the 1940 campaign, "and tending toward a sense of panic."

Much of this "panic" was the natural backlash of events in Europe, where Hitler had conquered virtually unchecked and was, at this time, punishing England with his air blitz. But much of it was generated by the Germans. The strident slogans of the campaign sounded homemade and American. Actually many of them unknown to their users were coined by Viereck, as reported in the German documents, before he had supplied them to politicians. Two of the most often quoted incendiary catch-phrases had been invented by Viereck, broadcast by politicians, and eventually appeared on millions of American lips. One was the slogan that Roosevelt's intervention would "plough under every fourth American boy." It was first used by Senator Wheeler, who was perfectly capable of making up his own slogans, but who unknowingly accepted this one. The other was the canard that "American boys are already on the transports."

By October twenty-four Senators and Representatives were inadvertently giving Viereck's ideas and phrases both an American ring and the widest distribution.

It was the mail that carried the brunt of the message and reflected most of the fear. Hundreds of thousands of letters were going out to the voters—with the Congressional frank—spreading the warning that Roosevelt's reelection would mean war and war would mean "the end of America as we know it."

In several secret dispatches to Berlin, Thomsen boasted that he had "instigated" the distribution of "millions" of such letters and broadsides, using the frank of legislators who either collaborated with Viereck or had been "used" by him. What he described as an "incomplete list" of such reprints from the *Congressional Record*, sent out by or in the names of twenty-four members of Congress with their frank, totaled 1,173,000 copies of thirty-seven tracts. According to Thomsen, they were written by Viereck and inserted into the *Congressional Record* by his friends and dupes.

By the middle of October it was obvious that the President was badly hurt by the isolationist attacks. Now a new kind of mail was added to the venomous flood. The White House was swamped with pleas from the party faithful with variations on the same theme—say something, do something, Mr. President, before it is too late. The plea was echoed by Roosevelt's cronies, his friends, and speechwriters. In a telegram, Edward J. Flynn, the astute Bronx boss who had taken over as national chairman, demanded that Mr. Roosevelt "provide absolute guarantee to the mothers of America that their sons would not fight."

The President was scheduled to make a number of speeches on a tour of New England, culminating in a major address in Boston on October 30. He was working on the latter in his special train that had just passed Meriden, Connecticut, when the telegram from Flynn was brought in. It irritated him. "But how often do they expect me to say that?" he asked. "It's in the Democratic platform and I've repeated it a hundred times."

"I know it, Mr. President," said Robert E. Sherwood, one of his principal speechwriters, "but they don't seem to have heard you the first time. Evidently you've got to say it again—and again—and again."

It was then that they put into the draft of the Boston speech the words "And while I am talking to you mothers and fathers," the passage read, "I give you one more assurance. I have said this before, but I shall say it again and again and again: Your boys are not going to be sent into any foreign wars."

Judge Samuel I. Rosenman, Roosevelt's friend and adviser, reminded the President that the Democratic platform had added the qualifying words, "except in case of attack." Mr. Roosevelt sensed that the hour was too late for any such qualifications. "Of course we'll fight if we're attacked," he shot back. And in the jammed Boston Arena, he uttered the words exactly as they stood in his typescript.

It was in this cruel climate of tension and suspense—as Roosevelt was slipping and Willkie was gaining in the polls—that John L. Lewis poised to fire the shot that would administer the *coup de grâce* to Roosevelt's chances of reelection. It was again the beginning of a weekend in Scarsdale. Lewis was closeted with Davis to plan the climactic stage of their campaign. Lewis was not entirely pleased. He had lost out on Wheeler and had failed to drum up support for a third party. Now he was under extreme pressure to endorse Willkie. It was from Davis's home that he called Willkie in New York to arrange a meeting at which he could size up the man, feel him out, and perhaps make a deal. They met the next morning, a Saturday.

In a desperate last attempt to patch up the feud with the President and keep Lewis from bolting, Walter A. Jones arranged a private meeting for him with Roosevelt, in the hope that the President could charm Lewis back into the fold. It proved a futile gesture. The next morning Lewis advised Davis that he would come out in support of Willkie.

On October 21, somebody called the Columbia Broadcasting System, the National Broadcasting Company, and the Mutual Network and bought time on 322 radio stations for an address by John L. Lewis. The man who made the call was not an official of the CIO, the UMW, or Labor's Nonpartisan League, which would have been expected to make such an arrangement. The caller identified himself as a *personal* representative of Mr. Lewis. He was William R. Davis. When asked who would pay for the broadcast, Davis said curtly: "Send the bill direct to Mr. Lewis."[5]

The same day Lewis issued a terse statement that he was ready to announce his stand on October 25, in a radio speech. At nine o'clock that evening, as many as 25,000,000 people listened to his words over the three networks.

He came to the heart of the matter in the crucial sentence: "His [Roosevelt's] motivation and his objective is war."

There was but one concession Lewis made, repeating the very argument with which Davis had recruited the Germans for the plot. "If he is, therefore, reelected," Lewis said, "I will accept the result as a vote of no confidence, and will retire as president of the Congress of Industrial Organizations at its convention in November."

It was pure threat—a calculated intimidation to drive the fear of Lewis into the hearts of millions of American working men and turn their votes away from Roosevelt.

It was Lewis's final blast. But the Germans were not yet through. On October 30, just six days before the election, Foreign Minister von Ribbentrop decided to get into the act. He had watched Dr. Thomsen's campaign with admiration. Now he thought he had something that would assure his envoy's success. When Poland was overrun and the Germans captured the archives of the Foreign Ministry in Warsaw, they found a number of reports which Count Jerzy Potocki, the Polish Ambassador in the United States, had sent to his government before the war.

Potocki, whose mind was blighted by anti-Semitism, was a diplomatic chatterbox.

The document Ribbentrop regarded as potentially devastating to Roosevelt's chances of reelection was dated March 7, 1939. In it Count Potocki reported an alleged conversation he had recently had with William C. Bullitt, the Ambassador to France, who, apparently with Roosevelt's approval, assured the Pole that the President was prepared and ready to give the Allies—including Poland—"all-out support in a possible war."

Here, Ribbentrop concluded, was definitive proof that Roosevelt was a warmonger, and conclusive refutation of his assurance given to the fathers and mothers of America in the Boston speech, exposing F.D.R. as "a criminal hypocrite."

The document was cabled to Dr. Thomsen in Washington with Ribbentrop's personal instructions that he secure for it the widest possible circulation in newspapers and on radio. Thomsen, who had been scattering bits of Potocki's indiscretions from time to time, did not think much of the Polish Ambassador as a character witness against Roosevelt. But he had no choice.

All of his efforts to persuade the press associations to pick up his release with the text of the document met with contemptuous refusal. As a last resort, he turned to a yellow journalist named William Griffin, publisher of a scandal sheet called the *New York Enquirer*, which appeared on Sundays. The *Enquirer* was one of the very few American newspapers that carried the propaganda of the German Embassy, simply because Griffin was on Viereck's payroll. For a bribe of $5,000, Griffin was now quickly induced to print the Potocki document, and it appeared on November 1, with bold front page headlines, exposing "Roosevelt's preparations for America's entry into the war."

"The precautions taken," Thomsen wrote to Berlin, "in launching this item will, as far as technically possible, ensure concealment of the role of the Embassy." This "role" included Thomsen's arrangement with Griffin to print a special issue of the *Enquirer* in "a greatly enlarged edition of 250,000 copies" because, as he told Ribbentrop, New York held "a decisive role in the presidential election, and publication [of the item] in New York on the eve of the election may, therefore, be regarded especially effective."

The article did create a brief flurry, but it did not prove to be a "bombshell," as Thomsen described it to Ribbentrop. The Potocki statement was disavowed by Roosevelt and Secretary Hull, and the incident was left at that. The campaign was too far advanced for any more such "exposés" to make any difference. This was the finale of Thomsen's campaign.

Then it was all over—the speeches, the campaign, the election. At the next convention of the CIO, in a tearful, jut-jawed speech to 600 delegates in the ballroom of the Chelsea Hotel in Atlantic City, Lewis resigned, as he had said he would. Nine months later, William Rhodes Davis died of a heart attack, a broken, disillusioned, discredited man. He had made millions in his wheeling and dealing, but lost out in his biggest deal.

The first round of the Nazis' bid for support in America—what Heribert von Strempel called their "biggest single scheme"—ended in defeat. Looking back, the Davis plot in which John L. Lewis became entangled seems foolish, futile, contemptible and anti-climactic. But the Embassy's campaign yielded some dividends. It was a victory of sorts, for Dr. Thomsen in particular.

Even if he could not topple Roosevelt, he had challenged him for a whole unbelievable month. He pushed him into a corner where the President was forced to wage an odious fight whose equivocations he himself despised. "Perhaps," Sherwood wrote "he [Roosevelt] might have done a better and more candid job of presenting his case. For my own part, I think it was a mistake for him to go so far in yielding to the hysterical demands for sweeping reassurance. . . . It left a smear on his record which only the accomplishments of the next five years could remove."

NOTES

1 When the war broke out in September 1939, the Roper Poll showed that Hitler had little to fear from the United States—the country was thoroughly isolationist. Only 2.5 percent were in favor of America's immediate entry into the war; 14.7 percent voiced support of England and France, 2 percent of Germany; 67.4 percent either took no side or wanted to have nothing to do with either belligerent.

2 After the war, Thomsen and Fish presented conflicting claims about the sources of the money for the ad. Fish insisted that it had been paid entirely by his committee, while Thomsen said that the Embassy had contributed $3,000 toward its cost.

3 Shortly after his departure from the United States, Hertslet was forced out of Mexico, too. His pretty young wife stayed behind for a few months, supplied with funds and filling in for her husband. But all she could do was to wind up the complex operations Hertslet had built up in three years of hard labor, only to see them go up in the smoke of the war. The end found Hertslet stranded in the part of Germany that was occupied by the Red Army. There he was discovered by an American team of intelligence experts under United States Attorney O. John Rogge, investigating Nazi penetration of the United States. His interrogation supplied much of the data contained in the Davis-Hertslet part of this story.

4 Davis had still another sideline in his multifarious business with the Germans. An elaborate attempt was made by the German Navy's U-boat command to establish hidden oil depots on secluded islands in the West Atlantic and the Caribbean at which the German submarines could refuel. Davis was to charter several cargo vessels in Mexico, buy hundreds of drums of oil, and ship them to the out-of-the-way islands. British and American authorities found out about the project. They aborted the scheme by preventing him from chartering ships and by cutting him off from funds he needed to pay for the oil.

5 Lewis himself paid only $15,000 of the bill, which came to $60,000. The rest was paid by Davis from the multi-million dollar slush fund, one of the few disbursements that could be traced definitely to it.

Chapter 35

Edge of Treason

*I*N the morning of November 11, 1940, the officer code-named "I.M.6" at Ast X in Hamburg reported to his superiors that he had received a personal cable from a friend in Madison, Wisconsin. It was brief, consisting of only seven words—"Heartiest congratulations on job well done, Phil"—all of it in plain English.

According to him, it was a pre-arranged message.

If "Phil" had cabled only "congratulations," he claimed it would have meant that the United States was contemplating "active intervention in the war *at some future date*." But "*heartiest* congratulations" was designed to indicate that "intervention had been decided upon" and was *"imminent."*

This was a startling bit of intelligence to the Abwehr. The air blitz over England had subsided somewhat, and it was quiet again on all the remaining fronts. The only major action occurred off Taranto, where an attack by British torpedo-bombers was decimating the Italian battle fleet.

Though the United States had adopted the Selective Service Act a few weeks before and had just reelected "the warmonger Roosevelt" to a third term, nothing in its recent actions appeared to bear out the cable's ominous prognosis. Puzzled as they were but reluctant to dismiss the information, the Abwehr high command directed I.M.6 to find out from his source in the States what had made him sound the alarum.

The officer who handled the contact was Lieutenant Gerhard Joachim Metzger, a lawyer in civilian life serving as a *Sonderfuehrer* (special officer) in the Naval Intelligence Division of the Abwehr.[1]

The American friend who allegedly sent the cable was Philip Fox

La Follette, member of the great Middle-Western dynasty of progressive politicians and three-term Governor of Wisconsin.

Lieutenant Metzger later reported he flew to Italy where the Abwehr usually originated transatlantic calls in situations like this, and put in a call to La Follette in Madison, only to be told that he was en route to New York to make an anti-war speech. Metzger was given a number where he could reach his party, and contact was made the next day in a static-marred telephone conversation that, as Metzger put it, "had to be conducted with extreme caution in consideration for La Follette's prominence and exposed position."

As reported by Metzger it was a revealing talk nevertheless, not for what was actually said, but in the way certain phrases were given emphasis to indicate what they were really intended to mean. After telling his friend that he was in New York "campaigning for peace," La Follette was supposed to have said: "Whether the situation will become worse, in other words, whether America will interfere is very hard to say—right now." He paused before and after uttering the words *"right now,"* and pronounced them with deliberate emphasis.

Then he allegedly added, in a lugubrious tone, "I wish we could meet soon, but we do not need to, because our friendship will not change . . ." He paused again, then finished the sentence, with pointed emphasis: *". . . even if the time that will pass by in between [will be] long and hard."*

Metzger claimed that the circumspect way in which La Follette expressed himself was calculated to reiterate his message. He asserted that "right now" in the first sentence did not mean that "at this particular moment" it was difficult to say whether the United States would interfere with the war, but, indeed, that the United States was planning to interfere *"right now."* He further assumed in his report that the nostalgic theme of the second sentence—that their friendship would survive unchanged the *"long and hard time"* ahead—was intended to mean that the United States was about to go to war against Germany, thus erecting a barrier between them for some time to come.

When Metzger returned to Hamburg he prepared his report. "The conclusion," he wrote, "one must draw from La Follette's cable; from the fact that he had gone to New York to 'campaign for peace'; and from what he said on the telephone is clearly that America's attitude toward the war in Europe is ripening toward a final and definitive decision during these days."

Metzger later claimed that he had never "explicitly" told La Follette that he was I.M.6, an executive of the Abwehr; and insisted that the Governor had "never set foot inside any of the Abwehr premises." But he said that when he introduced him to Captain Wichmann in Hamburg and Commander von Bonin in Berlin, there could have been little doubt in La Follette's mind that they were high officials of the German secret service and what the nature of their interest in him was.

Like his father and brother, Philip La Follette was a liberal and a reformer, a vigorous bridge-builder between farmers and workers, opposed to the financial and industrial power held by what today is called the Eastern Establishment. A prodigy of politics, he left his indelible mark with a progressive program in Wisconsin that influenced the economic and social fabric of the nation.

But then, in the second half of the Thirties, something snapped in his progressive soul.

What made him change and what psychological factors produced his political metamorphosis is difficult to say. He made the journey from the far left to the far right in great secrecy and never accounted for its reasons to anyone. It is possible that it was his way of creating a distinct identity for himself, of at last breaking out of the oppressive shadow of a great statesman-father and a suave, sophisticated, brilliant elder brother lionized in the nation's capital. Perhaps it was his creeping disillusionment with President Roosevelt and the New Deal, which had so advanced by 1935 that he shocked the President with the suggestion that he "forthwith suspend relief, PWA, WPA, and other Recovery Program projects" to appease "the businessmen of the country."

It was in this new frame of mind that La Follette began to receive letters from a Hamburg lawyer who had been his best friend on the campus of the University of Wisconsin. He was Gerry Metzger. Their friendship was revived in the late fall of 1937, when Metzger sent him a letter of congratulations on his reelection as governor and invited "dear Phil" to visit the New Germany. Even before, while watching the metallic march of the Fascists and the Nazis from afar, La Follette had found himself somewhat impressed. When he accepted the invitation and Metzger introduced him to the Third Reich, and "explained" to him "the true meaning of Hitler's New Order," he was impressed.

On his return from his first visit to Italy and Germany, in April 1938, he mortified friends with his new political stance. Shortly after his arrival in Wisconsin, he held a rally of his Progressives in Madison and people were startled to see how much its staging resembled the ritualistic pageantry of the Nazi mass meetings. "Just as Hitler does," an observer reported, "he appeared absolutely alone on a big platform. Phil is under medium size and in order to make up for this deficiency the newspaper photographers were required to take his picture from below instead of on a level or from above, in order to make him look bigger. No one was allowed within fifty feet of him. There he stood on the big vacant platform, aloof and apart from his audience. There was a white flag used as a decoration which had on it a black cross in a red circle—not far removed, it will be noted, from the German swastika. His gestures were also Fascist or modifications of those the Fascists use."

Max Lerner, the political scientist and a close friend of the La Follettes, attended the rally and came away "not only disturbed but disgusted." On May 12, when he heard that F.D.R. was toying with the idea of appointing the La Follette brothers to his cabinet (Bob as Secretary of State and Phil as Secretary of Agriculture or Attorney General), Lerner went to see F.D.R. to warn him that "Phil La Follette . . . apparently came back [from his European tour] with some Fascist bugs in his system."

His term had ended on January 1, and he planned another visit to his friends in Germany, this time as a private citizen. He apparently had a grandiose idea developing in his mind, a new movement of the young people of America somewhat on the pattern of the Hitler Youth. When he arrived in Rome on February 2 and was met by Metzger, La Follette asked his friend to set up an appointment in Berlin with Baldur von Schirach, the Reich's Youth Leader. Protocol required that the meeting be arranged through the Foreign Ministry, but the diplomats were not enthusiastic about it. They knew only of the Governor's "ultra-radical" past and nothing of his recent conversion. Finally a meeting was arranged at the insistence of the Abwehr. Cautioned by the Foreign Ministry, Schirach treated his visitor at arm's length, and the meeting disappointed La Follette. But Metzger saw to it that there were compensations.

By this time, Metzger had completed his own metamorphosis. He was now officially "F.3059," a scout of the Abwehr and collector of secret intelligence from his clients and contacts in the United States. So it was neither a gesture for old times' sake nor patriotic pride that motivated him in reviving the old friendship and in acquainting the distinguished visitor from Wisconsin with the glories of Nazism. He was determined to win over La Follette for the Abwehr. Prominent politicians were by no means at a premium in the German secret service. Some of Europe's leading statesmen had been seduced, bribed, or compromised to work surreptitiously for the Nazis. Metzger shrewdly realized that it would be invaluable to the Abwehr, and a feather in his own cap, if he succeeded in enlisting La Follette not only as a friend of the New Germany but as a confidential informant. When La Follette returned home after meeting the Nazi intelligence chiefs, he had been designated as *H-Mann* or *Hintermann* (back-up source) with a number of his own—A.3059/LaF.—in the Abwehr's secret registry of V-men, although he himself may not have known this.

Then, according to Metzger certain complications appeared. Transatlantic communication was precarious because all mail had to pass through British censorship in Bermuda. To overcome this difficulty, Metzger said that he set up a mail drop in Italy for some of his friend's letters. Then he established a faster and much more intimate link by calling La Follette on the transatlantic telephone from Italy, sometimes as frequently as every ten days.

Metzger's log states that his first wartime call from Rome was made at 6:15 P.M. Central European Time on September 21, 1939. La Follette had gone to Washington to be present at the Senate debate on an amendment to the Neutrality Act. Roosevelt had asked the legislators to call a special session to repeal the embargo on American arms shipments to the belligerents, because, as he said, "the embargo hurt Britain and France but helped Germany."

Metzger wrote in his report that the phone conversation of the 21st was devoted wholly to this topic. La Follette was lobbying "against the shipment of arms and thus against Roosevelt's plan" and told the German that no decision could be expected for at least two weeks. But he assured him that, for the time being, "there [was] no reason to be worried." When they spoke again ten days later Metzger claimed he was no longer so confident. He told Metzger that things were going badly—Congress would respond to Roosevelt's challenge and repeal the arms embargo, an event that came to pass two weeks later.

The failure to forestall the amendment disturbed La Follette as much as it annoyed the Germans. He began to devote himself to United States neutrality in what was a coincidence of German interests and his own sincere sentiments. The La Follettes were traditionally pacifists. Although in 1916 the father had approved armed intervention in Mexico, he vehemently opposed Wilson in taking the United States into the war in 1917. Now his younger son followed in his footsteps.

When the America First Committee came into being in the summer of 1940, Philip La Follette was one of the first prominent Americans to join it, and then became its most energetic and eloquent spokesman. More and more of his energies were devoted to spreading the gospel of nonintervention.

By early 1941, he had become one of the most diligent, hardest-hitting spokesman of the diehard isolationists. When the popular panel show "Town Hall of the Air" scheduled a debate for January 30, 1941, on the pending Lend-Lease bill with Secretary of the Interior Harold L. Ickes representing the affirmative, George Denny, Jr., producer and moderator of the program, invited La Follette to oppose Ickes. He was chosen over Senator Wheeler and Senator Wayland Brooks of Illinois (whom Ickes had called "the office boy of the *Chicago Tribune*") from a list of prominent anti-war advocates.

Within a few months, La Follette completed his political metamorphosis when he made common cause with Father Charles E. Coughlin, the Jew-baiting founder of the Christian Front. He became the respectable front man of a movement to turn the America First Committee into a political party.

His preoccupation with isolationist propaganda (in which, according to Metzger, he acted entirely on his own) cut the flow of his correspondence with Metzger. The Abwehr was not entirely displeased by this. The intelligence La Follette had been sending to Metzger was disappointing and his erroneous phone call of November 11, 1940, did nothing to enhance his standing as an informant. La Follette was, therefore, considered far more valuable as a propagandist.

They continued their correspondence. But the Abwehr instructed Metzger to discontinue all transatlantic conversations, which were being monitored and transcribed by both the British and American authorities.

In a communication sent to Metzger on December 2, 1941, five days before Pearl Harbor, La Follette advised him that the new leadership of the America First Committee would reorganize as a political party. La Follette, was oblivious of the Japanese armada sneaking toward Hawaii. In his last letter to Metzger a few days later he labeled the crisis produced by the breakdown in Japanese-American negotiations merely the product of Roosevelt's war of nerves. He took heart from the fact that, shortly before, a shift of but ten votes in the House would have killed the bill repealing Section 6 of the Neutrality Act which forbade the arming of United States Merchant ships—the latest of the President's thousand-and-one-steps to-war.

Then came the attack.

Philip F. La Follette got the message. Although he believed to the day of his death that it was F.D.R. who had brought the war upon the United States, he accepted the verdict of this historic December. He had used his contact with Lieutenant Metzger as one weapon in his struggle to keep the United States neutral, but he would never stoop to trafficking with the enemy.

A few days after Pearl Harbor he donned his old uniform and accepted a captain's commission in the United States Army, with one proviso—he insisted on fighting this war in the Pacific. He fought it well. He was a full colonel when he returned four years later, not yet fifty years old, after distinguished service in a war which he loathed.

NOTE

1 The "I" in I.M. 6 indicated that he was attached to Section I, the secret intelligence and espionage section of the Abwehr; "M" stood for *Marine-achrichtendienst* or Naval Intelligence Service; and "6" was shorthand for his rank in its North American Branch.

Part V

THE SPIES ON
EMBASSY ROW

Chapter 36

... Some of Man's Best
Friends Are Spies

ON June 26, 1940, the day after France capitulated, an array of distinguished, rich men assembled in a private dining room of the Waldorf-Astoria Hotel in New York to celebrate the triumph of the Germans. They came at the invitation of Gerhard Alois Westrick, a German international lawyer, now in the United States on a diplomatic passport that identified him as the Commercial Counsellor of the Embassy. Actually, as his secret instructions showed, he was here on a special mission to "build up goodwill for Germany among American industrialists and financiers."

In a report to Berlin, Dr. Westrick later referred to his guests merely as "prominent businessmen," adding that "in the interest of our operations" they did "not want to be further identified in any circumstance at this time."

Among those discreetly unidentified by the Germans were Colonel Sosthenes Behn, chief executive of the International Telephone and Telegraph Company; Ralph Beaver Strassburger, millionaire Pennsylvania financier, publisher and sportsman; James D. Mooney, chief of General Motors' overseas operations; Edsel Ford; Eberhard Faber; and certain executives of Eastman Kodak, the Underwood Elliott Fisher Company, and the International Milk Corporation.

These tycoons were not Nazi sympathizers or even pro-German. They were rather what are called business realists, and realism now demanded that they do business with Germany through Westrick. Each had a different ax to grind. Strassburger, for example, held considerable stock in German companies. But now he warmed up to Westrick to make certain that his palatial residence and racing stables in occupied France would remain safe. Colonel Behn was in the fold to protect IT&T's subsidiaries in Germany and the Nazi-occupied countries; and James Mooney was doing the same for General Motors.

The guest of honor at the dinner—indeed, the tycoon who had assembled this crowd representing some of the biggest American corporations—was Captain Torkild Rieber of the Texas Company. His interest in Westrick was both professional and personal. It was he who had paved the German's path to the United States and who was now chaperoning him on his mission to "build good will for Germany."

Of those present, "Cap" Rieber had the biggest stake in what Westrick called "our operations." He was not merely protecting existing investments but busily building up enormous new business. He collaborated personally with Reichsmarshal Hermann Goering, on the pattern of the "deal" William R. Davis had made with Goering.

Rieber, too, was no "Nazi" by any means. Occasionally he even censured the Fuehrer, especially for his raging anti-Semitism. ("Why," he would say in his Norwegian-accented English in a characteristic paraphrase of the old saw, "some of my best friends are goddam Jews, like Bernie Gimbel and Solomon Guggenheim.") But he was a martinet and an authoritarian, and the Nazis appealed to him. He liked to do business with them, both overtly and covertly, so much so that he wound up as one of the Germans' gold-plated agents in the United States.

Torkild Rieber brought to this sideline of his multifarious activities the tough traits and spectacular talents of the born adventurer. Born in Voss, Norway, in 1882, he had gone to sea in sailing vessels as a fifteen-year-old cabin boy, reached the United States in 1898, and was naturalized in 1904. That same year, at the age of twenty-two, he had his first command, as master of one of the first tankers to load oil from the vast new Spindletop Field in Texas, at the dawn of the oil-drilling age. The next year he joined the fledgling Texas Company, and went on to build up its tanker fleet. He reached the pinnacle of his career in 1935 when, as newly-elected chairman of the board, he embarked on deals to increase Texaco's oil holdings all over the world.

His shrewd and daring projects made the rough, tough ex-sailor something of a legend among oilmen. He developed the million-acre General Virgilio Barco oil concession in Colombia; built a 263-mile pipeline across the Andes from the new city of Petrólea to the port of Covenas through a 5284-foot high pass which the amazed Colombians named Paso Capitan Rieber; and wangled a half-interest for Texaco in the rich Bahrein fields on the Persian Gulf. Lesser men would have been satisfied with the sole task of building the Barco pipeline, a superhuman undertaking that required the air-lifting of entire suspension bridges and labor camps over impassable jungles and mountains. Rieber was looking for more worlds to conquer. No business was too big or too small for him, and he did not care what happened in his conquests. The Germans nicknamed him *"Leichen-gaenger,"* a man who walked over corpses of his own making.

Once when he reviewed his deal with the Nazis in seemingly candid terms, he stressed that it was "simply good business" and had "no political significance." But it was somehow typical of Rieber that he preferred to do business with people and governments on the far right of the political spectrum.

He first attracted the unwelcome attention of the United States Government with a deal he had made with General Francisco Franco's insurgents early in the Spanish Civil War. In the summer of 1937, Rieber smuggled oil and other petroleum products to the rebels. Texaco tankers would leave Galveston with oil apparently consigned to Antwerp, Belgium. When they reached the open sea, their masters would open sealed orders directing them to Franco-held ports in southern Spain.

The operation was reported to President Roosevelt and he instructed the Attorney General to put a stop to it. Rieber was warned that if he persisted in this "clear violation of [the] Neutrality Law," the license of his guilty captains would be revoked and the Texas Company would be indicted for conspiracy. But Captain Reiber continued to ship oil to Franco, now by way of Mussolini's northern ports, where the cargo was reloaded for transshipment to the Spanish insurgents.

It was in connection with this undercover operation in Spain that he first met one of the two obscure Germans who became instrumental in drawing him into the Nazi orbit. He was the same Dr. Friedrich Fetzer, the German Navy's chief oil manipulator, who had initiated the pact with Davis. At a meeting in Rome, in December 1938, Fetzer persuaded Rieber that it would be "good business" for Texaco to do business with the Germans. The Captain agreed and began to ship oil to the Third Reich even though the Germans could pay for it only in currency on blocked accounts. During the first nine months of 1939, thousands of tons of oil and other petroleum products were sent to Germany from the Barco fields in Colombia, and millions of Reichsmarks piled up in Texaco's account in a Hamburg bank.

The outbreak of the war in September did not put an end to the shipment of the oil—Rieber defied the British embargo and avoided the blockade by continuing to send his tankers to neutral ports in Europe whence the oil would be transshipped to Germany. His hopes of ever getting the money out of Germany seemed shattered until he hit upon what he envisaged as a barter deal. "His genius for business," an admirer of Cap said later, "was marked at this time by his success in getting the Nazis to turn over to his company three tankers in payment for oil purchased by Germany before the present war."

But it was not so simple and not so cheap. To arrange the barter Rieber met Fetzer again in Italy shortly after the outbreak of the war, and agreed to accept three tankers, then under construction at the Deutsche Werft in Hamburg, in payment for the sum the Germans owed him. Fetzer told him that the contact would have to be approved by Goering and around Christmas he took Rieber to Berlin supposedly to consummate the deal. In a two-hour session in the Reichsmarshal's office, Goering, who was cordial but sharp, told Rieber that the Germans expected a little more from him for those tankers and the release of the blocked funds. They insisted that Texaco continue the shipment of oil through the British blockade; and they wanted Rieber to aid them in "certain operations" in the United States similar to those that Davis was undertaking at the same time.

Rieber was not required to cooperate in the plot against Roosevelt, because the Germans knew he was a dullard in politics and had nobody like John L. Lewis to help him. But he was asked to try where Davis had failed, and use his influence in the White House to win Roosevelt over to Goering's stubborn peace plan. Finally, he was invited to participate in another project the Germans were initiating. It was designed to proselytize American businessmen to cooperate with Germany in defiance of Roosevelt's policies, in violation of the Neutrality Law, and in the face of the increasingly effective British blockade.

On January 24, 1940, shortly after his return to the United States, Rieber went to see the President and submitted Goering's half-baked peace proposal. It was not a pleasant session. Rieber himself was ill at ease—he was out of his element in the rarified air of high diplomacy, and the President seemed irritated by this clumsy resuscitation of the inane Nazi project. Lasting less than half an hour, the meeting convinced Rieber that the President would be willing to arbitrate only if asked formally and officially by all parties concerned, and it was not likely that Churchill would agree to anything like that.

F.D.R. loathed Davis but somehow he had taken a fancy to the two-fisted, hard-swearing ex-sailor. Now he considered him with bemused condescension. "Cap," he told him, "if I were you, I'd keep out of this thing."

That ended one part of Rieber's assignment. He still had to take care of the others, in order to get his tankers and continue his precarious business with the Germans. Just as Goering had assigned Dr.

Hertslet to cooperate with Davis, it was now decided to delegate a special emissary to assist Rieber in spreading "good will for Germany." The man chosen was Dr. Westrick, the lawyer who represented a number of major American corporations in Germany, including the International Telephone and Telegraph Company. The idea of sending Westrick to the United States as a good-will ambassador had originated at a meeting between Colonel Behn of IT&T and Westrick in the summer of 1939, in the office of Wilhelm Keppler, a high Nazi attached to the Foreign Ministry as Secretary of State for Special Tasks. "You have good connections in the United States," Westrick was told, "and therefore you would be an ideal person to foster good relations by using your friends in commercial and industrial circles of the United States."

Nothing more was heard of the project until December 1939, when Colonel Behn happened to be in Europe again, and the idea of sending Westrick to the United States was revived. At a secret meeting at The Hague in Holland, Behn urged Westrick to undertake the mission. It was then left to Rieber to arrange the sojourn under the deal he had just made with Goering.

Westrick left Germany and, traveling via Siberia and crossing the Pacific on a Japanese ship, arrived in San Francisco on April 17, 1940. He had been given diplomatic cover for the trip, as Commercial Counselor supposedly attached to the Embassy at a salary of $3,000 a month. He had received $4,449.70 from secret funds of the Foreign Ministry to cover his expenses. It was a paltry sum considering the nature of his mission, the lavish entertaining he would be required to do, and the bribes he was authorized to dispense. But it did not bother Westrick. "He had plenty of money," Heribert von Strempel, the political attaché at the German Embassy, later recalled. "He had access to funds in a multiple way. He had a dollar account waiting for him on which he could draw. And he could get anything he needed from his prominent business friends who had money on blocked accounts in Germany."

Most of his money came from Texaco. Old "Cap" had agreed to underwrite the expenses of the mission, to pay Westrick's monthly salary, to finance his entertaining, and to set him up in the style becoming an ambassadorial counselor on a secret mission, all from the Texaco's treasury.

Westrick was given an office at the New York headquarters of Texaco. Rieber leased a big house for him and his attractive blond wife in Scarsdale, New York, where Davis also lived; and bought a Buick for him for $1,570. He even paid for the dinner at the Waldorf.

With Rieber's assistance and the vigorous help he was receiving from James Mooney of General Motors and his other clients in New York, Westrick seemed to be succeeding beyond expectation. On June 27 he was able to report to Berlin that the influential group headed by Mooney had agreed to "put pressure" on President Roosevelt to improve relations with Germany by "immediately sending an American ambassador to Berlin" and especially by "suspending shipments of armaments to Great Britain."

In mid-July, Westrick saw Henry Ford and his son Edsel in Detroit about a plan to coax peace from Britain on the familiar terms. He also began a campaign to secure for Germany a five billion dollar loan from the United States, to be floated immediately upon the conclusion of such a one-sided peace.

This phase of Westrick's operations was, while not completely above board, not illegal. He was doing neither more nor less than the British did at this time, promoting their political and business interests with the help of influential friends in the United States. And, if Westrick succeeded in enlisting men like Behn and Mooney to promote his project, it merely showed how little certain American businessmen understood the true nature of Hitlerism.

But Rieber had another role to play aside from promoting the nebulous Westrick project. At the time he made his deal with Goering and Fetzer, in December 1939, he had also met another German. It was no chance meeting, and this man understood how to complete the corruption of Captain Rieber. He was none other than the employee of Texaco, Dr. Nikolas Bensmann, who spied on Roosevelt through various connections. He was a partner in the Bremen firm of Hermann Bensmann & Co., which represented Texaco's patent interests in the Third Reich.

"Niko" Bensmann was an expert concerning the oil industry of the United States. He had studied at Columbia University in New York, worked at several automobile plants around Detroit, and spent some time roughnecking in the oil fields of Texas and Louisiana. He was a big and ruddy-faced man who spoke English fluently in the American idiom—a delightful companion with exquisite taste for beautiful women, good food, and vintage wines, an especially wonderful escort for tired businessmen relaxing on trips to Germany.

He acted and sounded like a hearty American of the salesman type, quick with a wisecrack, a backslapping, guffawing fellow. He had none of the uncouth air and repulsive swagger of the bigshot Nazis. As a matter of fact, he did not seem to be unduly impressed with Hitler, and entertained his friends with jokes ridiculing his antics.

Rieber was personally fond of Niko. He not only used him as his patent attorney but also drew him into his inner circle as a general consultant, until Bensmann became a kind of supermanager of all of Texaco's business ventures in Germany.

There was, however, something that Captain Rieber did not know about his man in Germany—that Dr. Bensmann was an officer of the Abwehr and its foremost oil specialist. He had joined the Bremen subbranch in 1936 as scout No. F.2359, and at the outbreak of the war enlisted formally and full-time as a *Sonderfuehrer,* F.2531. He was now I.M.3, the third-ranking member of the Bremen subbranch, directly under Commander Carls, the outpost's brilliant chief of overseas operations. Everything he now did—his diligent care of Texaco affairs and the services he was rendering to Rieber personally —was part of his official function as well as a cover for his clandestine job.

He functioned well as an intelligent executive, interrogating homecoming travelers, culling intelligence from American newspapers, magazines, and trade journals, and even managing a handful of his own spies in the field, operating a full-blown intelligence service.

As the captured records show, he produced more first-rate intelligence than any other member of the Bremen subbranch. He was not too scrupulous about his means. He was rarely slowed down by difficulties.

During Rieber's visit to Germany in December 1939, when the jovial Niko was his constant companion, he was invited by Bensmann to "broaden" his collaboration with the Germans by also cooperating with the Abwehr. Niko did not reveal his own membership, which would have been a violation of his rules. But he hinted broadly that he had excellent connections in the secret service which, he told Rieber, could be very useful to Texaco.

At this time, Rieber was beginning to experience growing difficulties with the Germans, caused mostly by the complexity of their vast bureaucracy and the stupidity and arrogance of the officials he had to deal with. He had almost lost one of his tankers as a result. The sailing of the *Scandinavia,* the first to be delivered under the barter deal, was so badly bungled that, temporarily at least, it wound up as a British prize. Bensmann assured Rieber that no such thing would ever happen if the Abwehr handled the transfer of his tankers. Rieber agreed, and the departure of the second tanker, the *Nuova Andalucia,* was managed smoothly by the secret service.

In his memorandum arranging the transfer, Dr. Bensmann paid a left-handed tribute to Cap Rieber. He urged the other German agencies involved in the transaction to cooperate with the Abwehr, "in recognition," as he wrote, "of the considerable services Captain Rieber [was] rendering to the German cause."

In his eagerness to develop this extraordinary source, Bensmann waited for a nod from Rieber to arrange the technicalities of the operation. Using the name "Dr. Bremer," he rented an office at 212 Schwachhauser Heerstrasse in Bremen as a blind and mail drop. He then planted his own representative, a certain Linzen, inside Texaco's headquarters in New York, to manage the operation at its source, assemble the material, and take care of its prompt shipment to Bremen. Most ingenious in his arrangements was a cipher he devised to conceal the nature of the communications he was expecting to receive from the United States via cables which, he properly assumed, would be monitored by the British and perhaps even by the American authorities.

In the regular course of his overt business, he frequently exchanged cables with Texaco in New York concerning patent matters, and such communications contained the multi-digit numbers of patents.

On January 29, 1940, signing as "F.2531," Niko Bensmann submitted to his superiors in the Abwehr the outline of an ingenious code system that, he suggested, would enable him to keep up his correspondence with his friends in America without letting the British in on their secrets.

His memorandum read as follows:

"In my capacity as the trustee and representative of American patent interests I found in the course of my business correspondence that British Censorship regularly passes letters sent to my address in Bremen.

"I am enclosing herewith a sample copy of a letter [from a New York firm called Process Management Corporation, dated November 2, 1939] which contains a long list of patents. This one letter by itself produced hundreds of numerals. It seems to me possible, therefore, to communicate safely and confidentially with our agents in the United States and vice versa, by so camouflaging our correspondence as to make it appear that it involves some sort of patent transaction.

"As it is well known, all international codes use digits as substitutions for code words. If, in a letter supposedly referring to a patent transaction, the numbers of pre-arranged code words are represented as the digits of alleged patent-numbers, even lengthy espionage reports can be transmitted without running the risk of discovery by British Censorship."

Bensmann's proposal was accepted on March 28. He then proceeded to devise a *Satzbuch* or "Code Book" for the Abwehr's special needs in this particular correspondence, based on the old Rudolf Mosse Code which was still in general use. In this way, Bensmann was able to outwit the British censor and receive and send messages, some with invaluable intelligence.

Shortly after the introduction of his code, the first such letter was received through British censorship, from one of his agents using a dummy firm in Jersey City, New Jersey, as his blind. The letter read as follows:

"Subject: *Our Opposition Filed Against USA patent applications.*

"Against the various claims claimed by these patents we think that the following issued patents can be used:

"Claim No. 1—USA patent	528	127
DRP	505	985
DRP	561	836
French patent	529	727
"Claim No. 2—USA patent	662	001
USA patent	611	095
British pat.	531	937
USA patent	626	197
"Claim No. 3—British pat.	552	830
USA patent	616	606

"We furthermore think that in general USA patent 552 205 and USA patent 557 010 will be found noxious by the examiner but we think that these two patents should not be mentioned, etc."

All patent numbers were substitutions for Bensmann's code words. When he decoded the letter, Bensmann found it contained the following message: "[528 127] *March 10th* [505 985] *departed* [561 838] *Genoa* [529 727] *Marseille* [611 095] *American liner* [531 937] *President Polk* [626 197] *carrying* [552 830] 2500 *crates* [616 606] *inflammable goods* [552 205] *1000 barrels* [557 010] *gasoline.*"

On March 31, 1940, a New York agent cabled Bensmann as follows:

The German patents listed below will become due for renewal shortly:
"D.R.G.M. 106,585
"D.R.G.M. 517,008
"D.R.G.M. 661,619
"D.R.G.M. 775,777
"D.R.G.M. 518,119
"D.R.G.M. 675,843
[Etc.]
Please undertake the necessary steps and advice.

There were no such numbers listed in the German Patent Office; the cable was one of Bensmann's coded communications that actually read:

During recent visit with Roosevelt, Rieber learned personally from President that he was absolutely determined to keep USA out of war under any and all circumstances. Rieber obtained same assurance from presidents [sic] of Democratic and Republican Parties.

Bensmann also established a transatlantic telephone link with his contacts in New York to obtain information he needed in a hurry. Unlike Lieutenant Metzger, he did not have to go to Italy to place these calls. After all, he was the bona fide Texaco representative in Bremen and could phone his home office in New York as he pleased without the risk of compromising himself or his sources. According to the transcripts of these calls, Bensmann frequently phoned two vice presidents of Texaco, whom he identified as R. J. Dearborn and H. W. Dodge; a man named William L. Moore, whom he described as the company's general purchasing agent; and a chief engineer called Oldis. None of them, of course, suspected that he was a German agent.

Rieber was impressed with what the Abwehr could do for him and agreed to reciprocate. Although he was a shrewd businessman he never attained any sophistication in matters like this. It is unlikely that he intended this sordid by-product of his deal to be a close and continuous cooperation. Certainly he did not visualize himself as a German agent. What he had in mind was to let Bensmann have confidential information mostly to help Niko repay the help he received from his "friends." He did not think that any of this would seriously harm the United States. As he explained on August 12, 1940, when he was challenged about his cooperation with the Nazis: "Though I was born in Norway fifty-seven years ago, I have spent practically my entire life in the United States. This country has honored me with its citizenship and under no circumstances could I be identified with, or sympathetic to, any un-American activity." He seemed to be deeply moved and was probably sincere when he said this. But he issued the statement at a time when both oil and intelligence were still secretly flowing from Texaco to the Germans.

The intelligence reports of the "Rieber ring" were invaluable to Bensmann. The information they contained was concentrated, authoritative, and up-to-the-minute. From these reports, like stones going into the making of a mosaic, the whole vast petroleum industry of the United States could be pieced together—capacity, output, research and development, transportation facilities, the myriad details of a pulsating, growing, changing industry so vital in both peace and war. It was the exclusive property of Niko Bensmann. Aside from him, the Abwehr had no other means of procuring this intelligence. None of its numerous agents in the United States was capable of collecting, collating and analyzing such massive data from his own resources. As it functioned, the "Rieber ring" was, in effect, an outpost of the Abwehr, not only producing high-grade intelligence but also evaluating and analyzing it.

If there was one special gem in this generally high-quality output, it was a report, sent in the summer of 1940, presenting a detailed and uncannily accurate projection of American aircraft production based on an analysis of its eventual requirements in fuel and lubricants.

It came in the form of a dossier that a representative of Texaco (who had come to Germany to take possession of the third barter tanker) had brought along. It included a 58-page study reviewing the impending expansion of the American aircraft industry, designed to establish what 50,000 planes would require in fuel, lubricants, and other petroleum products.

The paper was the distillation of several studies, classified and unclassified, official and unofficial. It included estimates prepared by George W. Holland and Edward B. Swanson, chiefs of the Interior Department's Petroleum Conservation Division; excerpts from a paper prepared by a Danish-born oil expert named Jacobsen for Assistant Secretary of the Navy James V. Forrestal; the summary of an analysis by the prodigy of oil research, a young German refugee who free-lanced for the Government; and, even a report drawn up by Captain Rieber, for the White House. It was synthesized by the economists of Texaco, who concluded that the production of 50,000 planes President Roosevelt envisaged was entirely within the capability of American industry.

The report stirred the Abwehr to instant activity. Admiral Canaris, not yet intimidated by Hitler's scornful rejection of intelligence reports that did not bear out his own calculations or confirm his intuition, personally handled this particular project. He took the paper to Hitler. It was of no use. The Fuehrer shrugged it off, and even threatened to punish those who believed or circulated such "defeatist rubbish."

"Did you say 50,000 planes?" he asked Canaris. "You must be out of your mind to take such crap (*Dreck*) seriously. Fifty-thousand rubber tranquilizers maybe, for the poor little babies of America. But 50,000 planes! Don't be ridiculous!"

This incident ended Bensmann's primary usefulness in the Abwehr, for the strangest possible reason as far as an intelligence officer could be concerned. He continued for some time to procure authentic information about the growth of the American war potential, and it impressed him and his associates in the Abwehr with the titanic power of the United States. But there was no place to which he could take this intelligence. It was "defeatist rubbish," and nobody who knew what was good for him ever dared again to cater it to the Fuehrer, or even to circulate it in lower echelons.[1]

Shortly after the receipt of this paper, the "Rieber ring" blew up as abruptly as it had come into being only a few months before. If its establishment represented a singular coup for the Abwehr, its demolition was an even bigger one for MI.6, the British Secret Intelligence Service, thanks to the alertness and efficiency of its branch in the United States.

In all his bold and stubborn ventures, "Cap" Rieber had never experienced defeat. Now, he tumbled all the way, within a single week. His sudden downfall was not brought on by what he was doing for Niko Bensmann. Neither the American nor the British security organs ever caught on to his *clandestine* activities. His loaded cables were never so much as suspected, his simple cipher was never discovered and cracked. He was tripped up by the debonair freeloader, the elegant missionary he was treating to the good life in the sumptuous underground of American big business: Counselor Westrick.

Unfortunately for "Cap," just when Westrick reached the United States, another operator also arrived, bent on precluding the very skulduggery the German had come to practice. He was William Stephenson, the diminutive Canadian millionaire we have seen before in the act of destroying the Abwehr's huge Mexican outpost by hijacking its funds. Stephenson, chief of MI.6 in the Western Hemisphere, had been sent to the United States to put an end to German "espionage . . . and other subversive activities, particularly propaganda directed against Britain and designed to frustrate projected American aid and keep the country out of the war."

"Little Bill" Stephenson brought along a blacklist. Captain Rieber was prominently featured on it, not because the British knew anything about the aid and comfort he was giving the Abwehr, but because he was "suspected of supplying the Axis with oil through the British blockade." Rieber became one of the first to attract Stephenson's attention and it did not take long to discover Westrick behind his broad back.

The Rieber-Westrick axis was thinly camouflaged. Stephenson's investigation soon revealed that Westrick had his office at Texaco headquarters; that his car was owned by Texaco; that when he applied for his driver's license he gave the company's office as his address; and that the lease of his house in Scarsdale was in the name of the corporation.

Then Stephenson's sleuths found out that Westrick, who looked somewhat like the late actor Herbert Marshall, also had an artificial leg but had concealed this infirmity in his application for a driver's license; and that he had lied when he claimed ownership of the Buick he was driving. Stephenson placed the Scarsdale house of the Westricks under surveillance and by jotting down the license plates of the cars that ferried a chain of "guests" to the hospitable couple, he established that their visitors included, not only some of the "most important American businessmen," but also "a number of comparatively obscure young Americans of German descent who were employed in strategic factories."

Stephenson decided to put an end to Westrick's activities in the United States by exposing them. He passed the evidence his agents had accumulated to the *New York Herald Tribune*, which splashed the sensational story on its first page, then expanded the Westrick saga into a series of articles. The scandal that erupted hit Captain Rieber with hurricane force. Westrick was declared *persona non grata* by the State Department, and so was Rieber by an irate public and then by the embarrassed board of directors of Texaco.

The end was quick in coming. On August 12, even as Westrick was sailing home via Japan and Siberia, Rieber was asked to resign as the company's chief executive officer. He promptly complied "in view of the harm," he said, "that might be done to the company by reason of the unfair and unjust criticism which appeared recently in the press."

Rieber vanished from the scene and, as Stephenson put it, "presented no further problem to British security intelligence." But unknown to Stephenson, probably to this day, was the other facet of his complex cooperation with the Nazis. Undaunted by Westrick's debacle, Bensmann stayed in business. Now behind the back of W. S. S. Rodgers, Rieber's successor at the head of the Texaco, his man Linzen continued to syphon information to Bremen. And Bensmann kept on calling his old contacts at Texaco on the transatlantic telephone.

At the height of the air blitz against England in the fall of 1940, more than a month after Rieber's downfall, Niko was on the phone calling Vice President R. J. Dearborn, inquiring how England's chances of survival were seen in the United States and what plans Texaco had for a postwar world without Britain. According to Bensmann's transcript of the conversation, Dearborn said: "We anticipate the war to be over soon and are making our dispositions in the light of this expectation."

It was Bensmann's brazen persistence to abuse his business associates in America that kept the line open, however tenuously. Dearborn, Dodge, and Oldis, who knew Niko as the Texaco factotum in the Third Reich, were not aware of his association with the Abwehr.

When Niko brought up topics that had no bearing on business matters, they assumed that he was personally and not professionally curious, and that such small talk would die as soon as they hung up.

By 1941, Bensmann's opportunities to sustain the contact had become sharply curtailed. Vice President C. H. Olmsted, who succeeded Rieber in charge of overseas operations, frowned upon any collateral shoptalk whose usefulness to the Germans he instinctively recognized. More important, President Rodgers first cut back and then stopped entirely whatever business the Company still conducted with Germany. As if to atone for Rieber's dangerous blunder, his successor took Texaco to the opposite extreme, making it the most patriotic of all oil companies and going out of his way to cooperate with the new Petroleum Coordinator of the Roosevelt regime. He curtailed the shipment of Texaco oil to Japan even though the State Department was still raising no objections and the other companies kept pouring their oil into the tanks of the Imperial Navy's stockpile. Without even informing the Administration, Vice President Dodge raised $250,000 and organized a newspaper advertising campaign urging consumers to save gasoline.

The support the Nazis had received was valuable and effective while it lasted. But it lasted only until December 7, 1941. The moment the Japanese bombs began to fall on Pearl Harbor, all such cooperation ceased.

"Cap" Rieber, too, had learned his lesson. The Old Viking continued for some time to be labeled the "pal of Nazis" in the tabloids and stigmatized as a "pro-Nazi." He no longer cared. He joined his friends the Guggenheims, and went to work to "beat the hell out of those Nazi bastards." Less than six months after the scandal, he was building certain "special type vessels" for the United States Navy, so secret in design and construction and so confidential in purpose, that the Navy refused to reveal any of their details. Rieber was praised for undertaking what Captain N. L. Rawlings, the officer in charge of the Navy's shipbuilding program, characterized as "a complex and risky enterprise."

When the Westrick scandal broke, Captain Rieber sought solace in the indomitable faith of the old sailor. "No matter how fierce a storm may come," he would tell his friends, "it always calms down in the end." He did not have to wait long. By March 1941, he was back in the big time as the new president of the Barber Asphalt Company, a Guggenheim subsidiary, whose name he promptly changed to Barber Oil Corporation and which his managerial sorcery rapidly developed into one of the most flourishing companies among the independents.

He was still the chairman of its board twenty-seven years later—on August 10, 1968, when he died serenely in his Fifth Avenue apartment in New York City, at the patriarchal age of eighty-six.

NOTE

1 It was this intelligence that first convinced Canaris of the hopelessness of the German cause and of the certainty of his country's eventual defeat. The material was instrumental in turning the admiral into "a defeatist" and a plotter of peace behind Hitler's back.

Chapter 37

The Purloined Pell Papers

*D*URING World War II, the embassies and legations of the belligerents were supposedly the most secure of all diplomatic outposts. Yet there was hardly a British or American mission throughout the world, even in places as exotic as Afghanistan or as remote as Lourenço Marques, that was not under intimate observation by at least one German agent.[1]

The Abwehr had a direct line into the British Embassy's mailroom in Lisbon through one of the King's Messengers who was on the German payroll. The courier would stop just long enough on his route to deliver the pouch he was carrying to a man he knew as "Duarte." He was really Herbert Dobler of the big Abwehr bureau in Portugal. In Dobler's house the bag was pried open, the envelopes were steamed open, and their contents microphotographed.

Probably one of the most productive diplomatic agents the Germans succeeded in planting was in the American Consulate in Antwerp, headed by Consul William H. Beach. She was one of the secretaries, a Belgian hired locally because of the shortage of clerical personnel the State Department was able to send from the United States.

Called "Jenny" in the V-man roster, she was Jennie LeMaire, an attractive, industrious, and conscientious young woman who served both of her masters with equal zeal. Never suspected of treachery in the consulate, she was gradually given greater responsibilities with access to classified information that few non-Americans were allowed to handle. Literally everything that passed through her hands, and much that she could pick up besides, went out through the secret line that endured until the Germans invaded Belgium in the spring of 1940, occupied Antwerp, and the American missions had to close

down. Developed by Major Ritter of Ast X, Jennie proved most useful to the Abwehr by stealing blank passports from the consulate for
use by V-men. So active was she in this respect, that Ritter once
circulated a sort of prospectus to other branches of the Abwehr,
offering Jennie's loot to others who needed U. S. passports for their
overseas operations.

In Ankara operated a wayward man, variously called "the spy of
the century" and "the greatest spy of World War II," who was im-
mortalized, by himself and others, in books and motion pictures. He
was "Cicero," an egomaniac adventurer named Elyesa Bazna, the
most famous, or notorious, son of rugged Albania since Skanderbeg,
her fifteenth-century national hero. Bazna was the valet of Sir Hughe
Knatchbull-Hugessen, the British Ambassador to Turkey, a veteran
diplomatist who was unusually susceptible to encroachment upon his
secrets.

When Knatchbull-Hugessen, then in his forties and not yet
knighted, was His Majesty's Minister to the Baltic States at the Legation in Riga, between 1930 and 1934, he had another valet who was
a young native with credentials and references which seemed to be in
perfect order, but with somewhat questionable habits. This man,
remembered only as Tony in the secret German documents, was also
the gay Estonian capital's highest priced male prostitute, much
favored by the city's coterie of wealthy homosexuals. His antics, of
which the Minister was totally ignorant, did not escape the attention
of the Abwehr representative in Riga, and Tony was seduced into
working for the Germans. Then, as later, it was Knatchbull-Hugessen's practice to take to his quarters a black dispatch box with secret
papers, which he liked to pore over late at night in the privacy of his
bedroom. Tony managed to produce a duplicate key to the box, open
it when the Minister was not around, photograph the documents, and
deliver the negatives to the Abwehr contact.

From time to time Tony was careless enough to entertain his boyfriends in his chamber at the residence, and in so doing attracted the
attention of the S.I.S. stationhead, Captain Arthur Leslie Nicholson,
a career intelligence officer. Nicholson soon suspected that the valet
was working for the Germans, warned the Minister and also reported
the case to London. But these were the carefree, careless days of
peace. Captain Nicholson's warnings were pigeonholed both in Riga
and London. Nothing was done either to check up on Tony or, indeed, to remove him. He stayed on until 1940 as the valet of other
ministers and as one of the Abwehr's best spies in Riga, until the
Soviet occupation of Estonia forced the closing of the Legation.

In the meantime, Knatchbull-Hugessen had been posted to

Teheran. There he had no one sharing the secrets of his dispatch box as he did later when Cicero appeared in 1943, by which time the ambassador was stationed in Turkey. The story of how Bazna stole top secret documents from his employer's dispatch box and sold them to Ludwig C. Moyzisch, a quiet, diligent, subtle Austrian who was Schellenberg's station chief in Ankara (only to find later that the Germans had paid him in counterfeit Bank of England notes) is far too well known to need retelling.

Another diplomatic spy in the guise of a valet was Livio, planted by the Italian secret service in the household of D'Arcy Godolphin Osborne, Britain's Minister to the Holy See from 1936 to 1947. Osborne's legation was a key mission during World War II, when the British embassy in Italy was closed down, but England was left with the listening post on Vatican soil. A devout, ascetic bachelor of trusting disposition, Osborne saw no reason to suspect Livio until the S.I.S. was apprised of the man's sideline by one of its own agents who, in turn, had been insinuated into the Italian secret service. Unlike Tony, Livio was fired. While he lasted, the Germans benefited from his activity under the agreement Canaris had made with General Mario Roatta in 1935.

It is one of the remarkable features of the spy game that most of its major successes result, not from the fastidious work of professionals, but from the frivolous feats of amateurs like Cicero, Tony, and Livio.

Such an amateur was a young woman I will call Ilonka Szabo, a pretty Hungarian chambermaid in the Ritz Hotel in Budapest.

She stumbled upon her great moment not by any design or yen for adventure, but merely by a whim of fate. Her great opportunity came in February 1941, when a new American Minister arrived in Budapest. He was Herbert Pell, a fifty-seven-year-old New Yorker, offspring of rich and influential families whose roots, old and sturdy, ranged from Rhode Island to the South.

Pell belonged to the small fraternity of wealthy or wellborn irregulars so resented in the State Department because they easily reached the peaks of the profession toward which the Foreign Service regulars have to climb slowly and laboriously. President Roosevelt favored such influential men at critical posts around the world, hoping to receive directly from them the kind of straight-forward reports he never expected to get from the circumspect, and mostly conservative, career diplomats.

In 1937, the year after Pell had served as vice chairman of the Democratic National Campaign Committee during Roosevelt's bid for a second term, the President appointed him Minister to Portugal, not as the customary reward for his political contribution, but because Lisbon was one of Europe's best listening posts. F.D.R. expected the astute New Yorker to pick up valuable information about the Germans and Italians aiding General Franco in the Civil War in Spain. "Bertie" Pell thus took his place as a "presidential envoy" with such other stars of Roosevelt's personal diplomacy as William C. Bullitt in Paris, Anthony Drexel Biddle in Warsaw, and Joseph E. Davies in Brussels.

Herbert C. Pell had everything—looks, pedigree, status and money, a family he loved, and friends he cherished. But favored as he was, Pell was no playboy emeritus. He worried and cared about people, about the bad repair of great institutions and the rapid deterioration of hallowed principles, about the war in China and poverty in India. And, especially, he worried about the Nazis and the Fascists who conquered unchecked.

Pell was grateful for his assignment. Although it seemed humdrum, for the State Department regarded the post in Portugal as one of the secondary missions, he performed brilliantly in the personal part of his job. He sent to his friend Roosevelt innumerable long reports in which he described the quickening march of the Nazis. He could never put his worries and cares into notes to Secretary Hull, but he could pour all his misgivings and forebodings into his letters to the President. Mr. Roosevelt understood and appreciated him. "It is much more valuable to me than perhaps you realize to have you in Lisbon at this time," the President wrote in one of his "Dear Bertie" letters on October 30, 1940. "I know, of course, that you feel duty bound to remain at your post that, in my opinion, is the best watchtower we still have in Europe under these difficult circumstances."

In 1941, Roosevelt moved Pell to Hungary. In that handsome, sophisticated and gaily corrupt capital of Budapest he would have a ringside seat to observe Hitler's intrigues in the Balkans. Mr. Pell was in Hungary on borrowed time and he knew it. Instead of renting a house for his private residence, he took a suite at the Dunapalota, the famed Ritz Hotel in Budapest, fronting on the Danube. He relied on the hotel staff for service, except for Ilonka Szabo. She was hired as Mrs. Pell's personal maid and also to keep the suite in order, and help with the serving when the diplomatic couple entertained.

Although the Pells arrived in Budapest only in February, 1941, they already had more friends there than some of the diplomats who had spent years in the city. "Our rooms in the Ritz," the envoy wrote in his notes on his brief sojourn in Hungary, "were always full of flowers sent us by Hungarians who hated the Germans. We continuously

had visitors from all walks of life, from archdukes to small businessmen. Members of Parliament and cabinet ministers came frequently
to dine or lunch with us."

Ilonka was the perfect chambermaid—a pretty, fresh-faced girl,
breezy and gay, properly humble without being servile. She quickly
became popular, not only with the Pells, but also with the members
of the mission who did their business with the Minister in his study at
the Ritz.

But Ilonka was neither artless nor unspoiled. Early in her employment she discovered that Mr. Pell was keeping files in his study,
and she could not resist the temptation to inspect them whenever she
was alone in the room tidying up. The files contained Pell's entire
correspondence with President Roosevelt—carbon copies of his own
many letters and the originals of the President's answers. Ilonka was
no expert in international affairs, but she was smart and sophisticated. She immediately recognized that she had come upon a gold
mine. All she needed now was someone who would be interested in
these papers.

While she was pondering how to go about this business, her opportunity came with unexpected help from the Minister himself. Early in
October, acting on a premonition of an imminent break in American
relations with Hungary, Mr. Pell began to review his files and destroy
carbon copies of his voluminous correspondence which he didn't care
to preserve. Usually diplomats burn their papers on the eve of wars
or diplomatic breaks, but Pell had no facilities for the time-honored
ritual, not even a fireplace in his suite. Instead of burning them, he
simply tore up the papers and threw the scraps into his wastepaper
basket.

The morning after, while Ilonka was cleaning, she could not help
noticing the basket full of torn papers. Instead of dumping it with the
rest of the trash, she carried the basket to her room, emptied it, and
hid its contents. It was at this point, by one of those strange coincidences that occur frequently in a profession in which so much depends on chance, that Ilonka found a customer.

A minor diplomatic crisis had blown up around the brisk social life
of the popular American Minister, which did not escape the attention
of Wilhelm Hoettl, a young Austrian with a doctorate in philology. A
member of Walter Schellenberg's inner circle of adventurous intellectuals who saw in the spy business a shortcut to a meteoric career in
the Nazi bureaucracy, he functioned as Schellenberg's personal
envoy at the SD outpost in Budapest. Irritated by the Pells' popu-
larity, he sent a report to Berlin about the gregarious diplomatic
couple, and Schellenberg persuaded Heydrich to ask the Foreign
Ministry to do something to dampen the Hungarians' enthusiasm for

these Americans. Ribbentrop, who himself was quite touchy about such things, instructed Dietrich von Jagow, the German Minister in Budapest, to "bring the matter to the attention of the Hungarian Ministry of Foreign Affairs." It was an unusual complaint as diplomatic protests go, but Jagow, himself a rabid Nazi who held the post on leave from the SS, promptly sent a junior member of his staff to deliver the tactless protest. The official at the Hungarian Foreign Ministry shrugged it off politely. They deplored it, he said, if more Hungarians visited the American Legation than the German. But then, he added, Hungary had duly established relations with the United States, and the American Minister was properly accredited. There was little he could do beyond admonishing his own colleagues in the Ministry to avoid the Pells' bountiful hospitality.

Heydrich, dissatisfied with the outcome of the protest, then shifted the case back to his man Hoettl and ordered him to keep an eye on the Pells. From then on, the Minister was constantly shadowed by SD agents. Hoettl also bribed the room-service waiters on the Pells' floor in the Ritz to observe their guests and eavesdrop on their dinner talks. When he invited Ilonka into this ring encircling the Pells, he was rewarded with an unexpected bonus. The shrewd chambermaid showed him the pile of scraps she had salvaged from the Minister's wastepaper basket and told Hoettl that she could get more of the same if he would make it worth her while.

Hoettl recognized at once that he was on to a major espionage break. A deal was made, and Mrs. Pell's personal maid became a Nazi spy. From then on, no time was wasted in waiting for the Minister to supply mere scraps. Whenever the Pells were absent from the suite, an SD technician would help Ilonka pry open the Minister's filing cabinets. Dossier after dossier was removed to her room where their contents were photographed sheet by sheet. The rifling of Mr. Pell's files continued for several weeks, even after Germany had declared war on the United States and coerced Hungary to follow suit.

One of the dossiers Ilonka was able to borrow contained the correspondence with F.D.R. The letters went back to September 11, 1937, to one in which, writing from Lisbon, Mr. Pell thanked the President for his appointment, described Portugal's peculiar dictatorship under Dr. Antonio Salazar, and suggested boldly that the President name Frank Knox, Republican publisher of the *Chicago Daily News*, to his cabinet (a recommendation that was heeded three years later). The dossier contained fifteen letters, most of them long, including an incisive report, dated January 8, 1940, from Spain. Mr. Pell had visited there to check up, as he put it, on the somewhat pro-Franco American Ambassador whose "impressions" he seemed to be eager to correct. The report, meant for the President's eyes only, dwelt at length on Franco's delicate relations with the Nazis and the Fascists. Although at this time it was widely assumed that he would, sooner or later, join the Axis, Mr. Pell predicted that no matter what happened Franco would stay out of the war.

Among the gems was also the copy of a five-page letter to an anonymous friend in the United States reviewing in the frankest terms the controversial role Colonel Charles A. Lindbergh was then playing in American politics; confidential instructions from President Roosevelt to Pell to do everything in his power to keep the Hungarians from becoming too deeply involved in the war against the Soviet Union; penetrating political and economic reports about people and events, not only in Portugal and Hungary, but also in Germany, Italy, Spain, and France; and literally scores of what passed for straight political, economic, and military intelligence reports.

Shortly before the outbreak of war with the United States, the Hungarians found out about the SD's access to Mr. Pell's filing cabinets. Since they had a sense of proportion, if nothing else, and detested the Germans even more than they liked the Americans, they regarded their forced declaration of war as a foolish act in general and a personal affront to the respected American Minister in particular. They dared not warn him directly that the Nazis were stealing his papers. But they did come upon an ingenious idea of putting an end to the pilferage. They refrained from interning members of the American mission and so the people of Budapest were treated to the spectacle of seeing enemy diplomats moving freely about in the streets, stores, restaurants, and nightclubs, all except the envoy and his wife. The Foreign Ministry confined the Pells to their suite in the Ritz and forbade them to receive any visitors. In this way the Hungarians satisfied Jagow (who kept complaining that "the influx of visitors to the Pells almost made it appear that Hungary was at war with Germany in alliance with the United States and not the other way 'round") and also terminated the thievery. By keeping the Pells in their suite they deliberately put a lid on Ilonka's lucrative sideline.

The last document Ilonka was able to steal was taken from the Minister's study in January 1942. Written in longhand shortly before his departure from Budapest, it was an eighteen-page memorandum to himself in which Mr. Pell summarized his experiences and impressions during his stay in Hungary. He worked on it late into one night, then left the draft on his desk. Ilonka found it there when she went into the study to tidy up after the Minister had retired. She called her SD man at once. He rushed to the Ritz and photographed it page by page. She would not pass up a single scrap, for Hoettl was paying her on a piecework basis.

This plunder of an American diplomat's private and official papers lasted only a few months, yet yielded hundreds of photostats. As Schellenberg advised Heydrich, the loot included:

A. Pell's exchange of letters with President Roosevelt.

B. Voluminous correspondence with members of his family and friends in which he gave free expression to his thoughts about past, present, and future political and economic developments in America and Europe.

C. Numerous official reports which Pell, in his capacity as American Ambassador [sic] in Lisbon and Budapest, sent to his government in 1938-41.

D. Copies of private correspondence with Senator [Robert Rice] Reynolds [of North Carolina] and his daughter; Secretary of State Cordell Hull; etc.

It was an unprecedented coup. Never before had access been gained almost *in toto* to the confidential correspondence of a ranking diplomat who, moreover, was the confidant of his country's chief executive.

The entire contents of Pell's filing cabinets had been copied. Although much of it was vintage stuff, little of it was stale. "The material," Schellenberg wrote to Heydrich, "provides abundant information about political and economic matters, and of Pell's views of conditions in Europe, exactly as he communicated them to President Roosevelt and Secretary Hull personally, and to the Department of State officially."

Amazingly, this gold mine of intelligence was never properly exploited by the Germans. By a stroke of exceptional good luck for the United States and the Allied cause, the Pell papers got caught in an internecine feud raging at the top of the Nazi bureaucracy, between Schellenberg and Ribbentrop's Foreign Ministry, his prime client.

Schellenberg decided that the glory should be all his. He would stage the presentation of the Pell material as if it were a theatrical performance, working for dramatic effects with a succession of climaxes. He plotted his course with special care and cunning, determined to make the utmost of the coup, benefiting the *Sicherheitsdienst,* but mainly promoting his own career.

It took some time to prepare the material—to translate the letters, collate them, analyze them—and for Schellenberg to decide what to do with them. Then, instead of forwarding the whole dossier, Schellenberg selected individual items from the hundreds of letters and documents to prolong the impact of his triumph. It was February 1942 before the first submission was made. It consisted of a letter President Roosevelt had written to Pell in the summer of 1941 acknowledging a report Pell had sent to F.D.R. on June 23, the morning after the German invasion of the USSR, discussing its broader implications knowingly at some length. In the letter, Roosevelt reiterated his confidence in Pell and expressed satisfaction that his friend was "spreading the democratic message so well in so hostile an environment."

Schellenberg's teaser arrived at the Foreign Ministry with an accompanying letter signed by Heydrich himself, to emphasize the importance of the item. Although addressed personally to Ribbentrop, it was delivered into the hands of Schellenberg's liaison officer at the Foreign Ministry, an SS-Standartenfuehrer named Werner Picot. Picot was not unduly impressed with this particular exhibit and hesitated to forward it to Ribbentrop, who could be extremely unpleasant when bothered with trivia. Picot had burned his fingers before.

A few weeks earlier, Schellenberg had sent to the Foreign Ministry what he described as "a most reliable agent's compilation of confidential information from exceptional sources in the United States" about the American war potential with emphasis on aircraft production. The report, exquisitely typed and handsomely bound in Moroccan leather, its cover emblazoned with the great seal of the *Sicherheitsdienst,* was greeted with great expectations because by this time, as Picot wrote to Schellenberg, the Foreign Ministry could no longer procure "directly from the United States any of the intelligence we need." At first glance it seemed quite erudite, studded as it was with tables, charts and statistics, and spiked with the *lingua franca* of the secret service. On closer scrutiny it turned out to be what Secret Counselor Dr. Davidsen, chief of the Ministry's United States desk, called it—"a piece of junk."[2] He told Picot bluntly: "The submission of this report to the Foreign Minister is, in my opinion, not advisable."

And now the Pell papers! Since Pell was an American stationed in Hungary; and since his writings concerned Portuguese and Hungarian as well as American affairs, Picot called a meeting of the Ministry's experts in these fields, to advise him on the best procedure he should follow with the distribution of the material. Their verdict was discouraging. "Since the letters," the experts told him, "contain little except a categorical refutation and rejection of the National Socialist and Fascist ideologies, it is considered inadvisable to bring them to the attention of the Foreign Minister."

Actually, the papers abounded in hard facts from which a skilled political analyst could have culled invaluable information. Such an effort was ruled out *a priori.* His underlings did not dare to antagonize the sensitive Foreign Minister with such outpourings of the most articulate anti-Nazi sentiment. Rather, they allowed precious intelligence to fall by the wayside, much in the manner they eventually discarded the material "Cicero" pilfered from the British Ambassador in Turkey.

In the final analysis, the joke was not on Pell but on the Germans. If he had planned the whole affair and had deliberately allowed his letters to fall into Nazi hands, he could not have achieved a more devastating effect. Through his pilfered correspondence, the American envoy was holding up a mirror to the Nazis so they could see themselves at their worst. By courtesy of Schellenberg, Pell was able to tell the Nazis what otherwise he could never tell them to their faces.

But Mr. Pell involuntarily helped Schellenberg move a giant step forward in his career. The papers had come into his hands early in this precarious phase of his advancement, when he still held only an interim appointment, while apparently Heydrich was searching for someone more mature and experienced to head Amt VI of the *Sicherheitsdienst*. Now he sensed that Heydrich would search no longer. Schellenberg had been made acting chief on June 22, 1941. In December, after the first batch of the Pell papers had reached Berlin, his appointment was made permanent.

In 1940, the Abwehr already had a spy in the American Embassy in Berlin. Agent No. F.2631 was a middle-aged typist at the American Embassy whom I shall call Frau Herter. Her job was not sensitive by any means—she was but one of the typists in the emergency department which the Embassy, representing Britain since the outbreak of the war, had set up for the care of British prisoners of war. Her office on the second floor of the Embassy building was a passageway which Foreign Service officers and service attachés crossed on their way to their own offices, frequently stopping for small talk, making phone calls in transit, and escorting their visitors. She thus became privy to some inside information.

Frau Herter also became quite proficient in eavesdropping, memorizing offbeat conversations, listening in on phone conversations, even drawing out people on specific topics. She worked under Mrs. Frederick C. Oechsner, the wife of the chief of the United Press bureau in Berlin, and claimed that she was picking up many an interesting item from Mrs. Oechsner who, she reported, was exceedingly well-informed.

On February 4, 1941, for example, Frau Herter overheard two officers on the staff of the American Military Attaché, Colonel Bernard R. Peyton. They were discussing a German experiment with a new type of smoke screen that could conceal major ground targets, probably even parts of Berlin. She was able to inform the Abwehr that several of the attachés had made reconnaissance excursions to places where the new screen was tested. She also tipped off the Abwehr to certain American employees in the Embassy who apparently had more important assignments than their seemingly modest jobs indicated. She mentioned a "Dr. Spencer," who was with the field service of the P/W-care section, but was filing reports on such sensitive installations as a shipyard in Stettin constructing U-boats, which he "happened to observe" on one of his inspection trips to the various camps. Another man she denounced was a certain "Mr. Howard," working as a simple operator in the wireless room. But she claimed that "Howard" was in reality a scientist on loan from the California State Observatory. His actual function in the Embassy was, she said, to collect meteorological information and radio it to America whence it was forwarded to the British.

Since the American Embassy was virtually impregnable on its political side, the service attachés rated primary consideration in the Nazi scheme. This was partly designed to prevent them—"official spies," as they were regarded and treated—from getting too close to the Wehrmacht's secrets, and partly to obtain from them information about American, and even British and French, plans and intentions.

At the *Sicherheitsdienst,* the U.S. desk was receiving copies of F.2361's second and thirdhand intelligence about the American Embassy, but was not satisfied with such trivia. Its chief, a man named Carstenn, planned to collect what he called "high-level policy intelligence" from which he could deduce the course the United States would be taking in its relations with Germany. Determined to plant his own agents within the walls of the Embassy, he put out feelers for Americans who would be willing to cooperate with him. He found in Berlin a seemingly impeccable young man who seemed to fit the bill—a native-born American but pro-German and, discreetly, even pro-Nazi. He had good credentials, and was doing nothing in particular that could not be dropped in favor of something better that came along.

As it turned out, the young man was not so impeccable after all. At Carstenn's suggestion he applied for a job at the Embassy, was promptly hired, and assigned to a desk in the political section. He began his work for Carstenn's bureau by delivering each day a copy of the mimeographed *Radio Bulletin.* It was a daily compilation of current news which the State Department was sending from Washington to the missions abroad. Since the outbreak of the war, it also contained some restricted material.

It was not much but Carstenn made the most of it. He put one of his aides, a man named John, on the job to compose a daily intelligence report in which items culled from the *Bulletin* were skillfully elaborated upon until the end product appeared to be an original, penetrating, and comprehensive survey of American affairs that neither the Foreign Ministry nor the Abwehr could match. Between September 1940 and December 1941, a total of 355 such reports were forwarded to the Foreign Ministry. The deliveries were terminated only by Germany's declaration of war against the United States.

This was only a beginning. Very soon this agent was procuring for Carstenn some of the confidential dispatches Leland Morris was sending to Washington, as well as copies of communications from the State Department to the Charge d'affaires.

Carstenn also had in his stable at least two V-men who specialized in spying on the American Embassy service attachés. One of them— described as "the head of the Distribution Center for Knitted Goods," of all things—claimed to be on friendly terms with Major William D. Hohenthal, one of Colonel Peyton's assistants. The other V-man was identified in Carstenn's roster as "a relative of Prince Bernhard of the Netherlands," and was also said to be close to Peyton. Elsewhere in the mission, Carstenn had working for him a "part-Jewish business-man" and "an aristocratic lady of American extraction who used to know President Roosevelt." They mingled with American diplomats, invited them to their homes, and attended their parties. By pretending to be critical of the Nazis, they induced their American acquaintances to let down their guard and discuss with them confidential topics they would otherwise have thought twice about before sharing with strangers.

The American ambassadors in Madrid—first Alexander W. Wedell, and then Professor Carlton Hayes—were kept under a dual surveillance. Schellenberg's agents were regularly reading their confidential correspondence, through a Spanish contact Amt VI had in the section of the postal administration that handled the diplomatic mail. A high official in the Spanish Foreign Ministry (who shows up in both the Abwehr's and the SD's papers with the nickname "Guillermo") reported practically everything that came to his attention about Wedell and Hayes.

Guillermo not only forwarded to the Germans the findings of the Spaniards' own close surveillance of the American and British embassies in Madrid, but also produced copies of the minutes of the conferences they held with Foreign Ministers Count Jordana and Ramon Serrano Suner, and with Generalissimo Franco.

This went on until Dr. Hayes's retirement in 1944, when he called on Franco and the new Foreign Minister to bid them farewell just before his return to the United States. On this occasion, it seemed, the American Ambassador was especially outspoken and, from the German point of view, informative. But this was so late in the war that whatever intelligence they could cull from the Ambassador's candor was not exactly reassuring.

NOTES

1 All this coverage was in addition to the continuous eavesdroppings of the *Forschungsamt,* Goering's private "black chamber," that was systematically tapping the telephones of members of the diplomatic corps, "bugging" the embassies and the living quarters of certain diplomats, and opening the diplomatic mail in transit. Access was also gained to pouches by suborning a number of couriers, or by intercepting and unsealing bags going by mail or rail. In addition, the telegraphic communications of the Allies were monitored, recorded, and deciphered, primarily by the *B-Dienst,* the code and cipher bureau of the Naval High Command that broke every one of the American diplomatic and several naval codes and ciphers, and was reading our encrypted signals most of the time during World War II.

2 Dr. Davidsen phrased it more diplomatically in his assessment of the report prepared for Schellenberg. "I found," he wrote, "hardly a single one among these papers that would not be on file here from our own sources. As a matter of fact, I think I recognize the sources from which the agent supposedly received his data. They are not much more reliable than, alas, our own sources."

Chapter 38

"Fetch the Devil
from Hell"

KURT Frederick Ludwig arrived in New York in March 1940—coming home, in a sense, for he was an American. But it was a mischievous homecoming. His German parents had immigrated to the United States fifty odd years before, and settled briefly in Fremont in northern Ohio, where Kurt was born. Things did not work out as expected, and the Ludwigs moved back to Germany, taking the boy when he was only two years old.

Although he held onto his American citizenship, was fairly fluent in the English language, and visited the United States from time to time in the Twenties and the Thirties, he was a German in all but name. He had none of the native son's attachment to the land of his birth.

An attractive, intelligent man, living comfortably in Munich, he was successful in business—a mature person with solid roots in the community and many very important persons in his circle of friends. Dr. Robert Ley, the Nazi labor boss, was one of them; Reichsfuehrer Heinrich Himmler of the SS was another. It was, in fact, Himmler who had inspired his journey to the States shortly after the outbreak of the war. When Ludwig once told him that he was eager to do something for the German war effort in spite of his American citizenship and forty-eight years, Himmler suggested that he could serve the Fatherland best by organizing an espionage ring in the United States.

Taken over by the Berlin headquarters of the Abwehr and groomed for the new job (for this was Ludwig's maiden venture in espionage), he was sent on his perilous journey in the usual stages. In Spain he received his final instructions from his case officer Major Ulrich von der Osten, a top executive of the Abwehr outpost. Ludwig called the Major "Konrad" and he was "Joe" to von der Osten.

Although his back-up base would be in Spain, arrangements were made for a line directly with Himmler who would periodically receive reports from Ludwig addressed to "Lothar Friedrich" at 1 Helgolaender Ufer in Berlin. Himmler's personal interest in the project and Ludwig's apparently exceptional qualifications, caused this mission to be one of the most ambitious and important operations ever mounted in North America.

His instructions called for the assembly of his own ring from among members of the German-American Bund, "for the purpose of gathering and sending to Germany, via mail drops in Spain and Portugal, detailed information on the size, equipment, location and morale of United States Army units; on aircraft production; and on the routings of convoys as well as the movement of single ships between the United States and England." His reports were to be forwarded by airmail via the transatlantic clipper, addressed to Señor Emanuel Alonzo in Madrid and Señora Isabell Machado Santos in Lisbon. Ludwig was also expected to operate his own clandestine radio, either a stationary long-range transmitter capable of direct contact with Hamburg or a portable shortwave set hidden in his car (to change location with each transmission). On the latter, he would be sending his signals to stations of the "Bolivar" net in South America, or to U-boats off the United States coast for relay to Germany.

In the United States, Ludwig needed only a couple of months to build up a ring of eight dedicated confederates, among them Paul Theodore Borchardt-Battuta, a retired major of the German army. Posing as a former inmate of a concentration camp and a refugee from the Nazis (because, he claimed, he was of Jewish extraction), Borchardt-Battuta (using the cover-name of "Oakland") had served as an agent-at-large on the Abwehr's payroll. When Ludwig arrived in the United States, he was assigned to act as military adviser to "Joe" and other members of the ring. These consisted of a 30-year-old soldier on active duty at Fort Jay on Governor's Island, Rene Charles Froehlich by name; Karl Hermann Schroetter; Karl Victor Mueller; and a woman Ludwig called "the Young Lady" (26-year-old Helen Pauline Mayer). They supplied shipping information and order-of-battle data, together with two lads in their late teens covering the Brooklyn waterfront—tall, blond Frederick Edward Schlosser and swarthy Hans Helmuth ("Bubi") Pagel.

The ring had a full-time "secretary" to take care of clerical chores, a pretty 18-year-old blonde named Lucy Boehmler of Maspeth, Queens, in Long Island. It was her regular duty to maintain the card file on United States army camps, disposition of American military forces, troop movements, and armament production. Despite the youth and inexperience of most of its members, this was a very active and efficient ring, thanks mainly to Ludwig's inspiring leadership, administrative talents, and the bold spirit that his adventurous mission had brought out in this normally sedate and unromantic businessman.

From time to time, when touring the country in search of information, he would challenge fate by driving at breakneck speed, at the risk of being hauled in by the very police that spies normally are most anxious to avoid. Once going to Baltimore, to check up on ships in the harbor, he drove the stretch between Newcastle and Wilmington at 80 miles an hour. Then, in a letter describing his findings, he bragged about his bravado, drawing a sharp rebuke from his mentor.

On a trip to Washington, he ventured into the White House on a regular guided tour, and produced one of the most vivid personal observations of a secret agent from inside the President's house. He put fast automobiles to excellent use, collecting much information by cruising in the vicinity of Army camps and picking up soldiers he spotted hitchhiking on the roads. He visited war factories and harbors all along the Eastern Seaboard. Aside from these personal inspection tours, he collected stores of material clipped from newspapers, magazines, and trade journals.

Although he proved incapable of assembling a stationary radio, Ludwig did have a powerful shortwave set built into one of his automobiles to receive coded instructions from Berlin and Hamburg. Judging by the sheer volume of his correspondence he was an extraordinarily industrious spy. Almost daily, he would write long typewritten letters to his wife in Munich (to whom he was also sending copies of the *Saturday Evening Post* and *Ladies Home Journal* solely for her entertainment, with no ulterior motives). Several times a week he mailed letters to his "customers" in Madrid and Lisbon, giving the impression that he was running a thriving export firm in leather goods.

When read in a cursory fashion, the letters seemed to be innocent enough, containing either family chitchat or the business communications of a busy New York exporter. But every letter he ever sent contained at least some coded information intended for the Abwehr.

His letters to his wife were solicitous, even nostalgic. "How are you and the children?" he wrote in one of them. "Do you think the children, especially the younger ones, will still recognize me when (and if) I should return?" Such sentiments of a homesick husband and father might mellow the British censor sufficiently to distract attention from the other side of the letter, with its damaging message written in secret ink.

"British have," he wrote in such a letter, typical for the mass of data and his concise, businesslike style "70,000 men on Iceland #

The S.S. *Ville De Liege* was sunk about April 14—many thanks #
Types of airplanes flown to England (continued from letter 693.)
Boeing B-17C (model 299T) twenty were released by the U.S. Navy
to Britain on Nov. 20, 40 # 13 B-17C were at McChord Field,
Wash. with British markings—later some B-17C were seen at Van-
couver, B.C. en route to Gandar Lake, N.F.—arrived in England
some weeks ago." And so on, ad infinitum.

The fine expertise of Major Borchardt were often evident in these
reports, enabling Ludwig to elaborate on or correct information
available in the public domain. "According to British publication,"
he reported in dubious English, "Boeing is since months manufacturing B-17B what I doubt very much—apparently newer models are
meant—either B-17D or B-17E of which the U.S. Army ordered
50."

With Ludwig firmly established, his ring growing and his production increasing by leaps and bounds, the Abwehr reached its peak
period in the United States. It had four major rings fully operational,
with two communications centers (those of Sebold on Long Island
and Wheeler-Hill in the Bronx) servicing more than forty high-
grade producing agents and scores of confidential informants.

Commander Pheiffer's organization had been rebuilt after the collapse of the nebulous Rumrich ring and the disintegration of the
Lonkowski-Griebl operation in New York. Major Ritter's phenomenal network—whose stars were still Duquesne, Roeder, and
Lang—was working at capacity, its value enhanced by the vastly
increased speed of its transmissions thanks to the facilities of "Tramp."
And Reuper, using the Wheeler-Hill radio set-up, broadened the
base of his operations, collecting far more information than he could
put on the air, sending blueprints and other bulky material via the
new courier system on neutral ships. It was an unprecedented bonanza, supplying more than adequate information to enable the
Wehrmacht High Command to assess this country's war potential and
our aid to Britain.

Suddenly a totally unexpected incident threatened to destroy this
remarkable organization, not by the intervention of the American or
British security organs, but by misgivings and jealousies rampant in
this vast German secret underworld. It was characteristic of the way
σ⁻ ⁻rnment was conducted in the Third Reich. Nazi bureaucracy (a
ʼend of Prussian pedantry, Hitler's Austrian *Schlamperei* and
ᵔds of the League of the Assassins) had more than the usual
onfusion and duplications. It was nowhere more chaotic
intelligence establishment. Hitler's regime was conspira-

torial *per se*, and this was reflected in every department of the government and the Party.

Every agency that dabbled in espionage was disregarding the Fuehrer's ban on spying in the United States. The Himmler-Heydrich *Sicherheitsdienst*, various foreign offices of the Party, all had agents in America. While others were left to do as they pleased, the Abwehr was singled out for scrutiny, and denounced all the way up to Ribbentrop and Himmler for its vast espionage organization in the United States.

Most outspoken and energetic in objecting to these Abwehr operations was Dr. Hans Thomsen in the Washington Embassy. Glossing over his own illicit clandestine activities, he embarked on a campaign against the Abwehr in America, bombarding the Foreign Ministry in Berlin with complaints and admonitions. His argument was sound even if hypocritical.

"In complete agreement with the service attachés," Thomsen wrote to Berlin in the spring of 1940, "I repeatedly and gravely called attention to the danger which such activities, if discovered, would represent to German-American relations, especially during the current period of tension. I would like to bring to mind again that the American Government had used such activities to justify this country's entry into World War I, and to gain popular support for the intervention. The service attachés and myself recognize the need for an intelligence apparatus. However, the agents who are known to this Embassy do not seem to be suited for such activities . . . Lacking in expert knowledge and savvy, we doubt that these agents could ever make a contribution valuable enough to compensate for the risk of jeopardizing German-American relations. I request, therefore," Thomsen concluded, "that the responsible agencies be persuaded to terminate the machinations of their representatives."

Nothing was done until an incident that exploded the whole problem. On May 20, 1940, a man named Walter von Hausberger appeared in the Embassy, identified himself as an agent of the Abwehr, and claimed that he was in the United States to organize sabotage on a substantial scale. He had decided to contact the Embassy, he told Thomsen, because he was destitute—his funds had run out and the Abwehr was not responding to his pleas for more money.

A few days later, another self-styled saboteur calling himself Julius Bergmann, also contacted Thomsen because he, too, had run out of money. The Charge d'affaires was mortified and scandalized. It was bad enough that the Abwehr had stupid spies running around in the United States, but saboteurs! This was an inexcusable blunder!

Thomsen cabled the Foreign Ministry to check out the two men, and received an answer by return cable. "They are totally unknown in the Abwehr," the Foreign Ministry told him. "Nobody with an assignment to conduct sabotage has ever been sent to the United States."

The exasperated Thomsen shot back another telegram. If the Abwehr had nothing to do with these men, he asked, how was it that they had "received their training from Dr. Hohenstein, chief of the Abwehr's Sabotage Laboratory, and instructions for their missions from Lieutenant Colonel Margueree, Lieutenant Colonel Stoltz, Lieutenant von Meerheimb and Dr. Wolfgang Blaum," all of them known to these men as functionaries of Abwehr II. "If their claims are nothing but lies," Thomsen cabled again on June 2, "it still remains to be clarified: (a) who gave them the explosives which I now have to store; (b) who impersonates Major von der Osten, who, according to them, issued to them separately and individually their final orders to undertake sabotage operations in the United States."

The "clarification" arrived on June 4. Lahousen suddenly remembered that the men mentioned by Thomsen had been sent to America by his department, but merely as "observers." They had strict orders to refrain from doing anything that even remotely resembled sabotage.

The Foreign Ministry was so disturbed by this incident that Under Secretary of State Ernst Baron von Weizsaecker called Admiral Canaris to his office and read to him Thomsen's latest cable: "Since I now have conclusive evidence of the activities of numerous agents here, most of whom are totally unsuited for the job, I deem it imperative and urgent that the Abwehr refrain from any such activities in the United States. I would be much obliged if you would intervene accordingly." Canaris pursued Lahousen's line, pretending that he did not know what Thomsen was talking about.

In actual fact, the Abwehr was up to its neck in sabotage operations in the United States. A whole string of such plots was under way, masterminded by three special agents of Abwehr II and carried out by an assortment of Irish, Polish, and Ukrainian desperadoes. Considerable mischief was in progress and the United States was substantially damaged, long before Hitler declared war against this country on December 11, 1941.

Defeated people are loath to admit that they have done anything atrocious during a war, and not merely because it may have been a violation of international agreements or fear that such admission might provoke retribution. Abwehr-directed sabotage in the United States and Britain is a moot question, mainly because the Germans later disputed everything on this count. As head of Abwehr II, Colonel Lahousen was in charge of what his directives called "sabotage, insurrections, sedition, and destructive propaganda" between 1939 and 1943. It was natural, therefore, that he should be the loudest and most eloquent in denying that the Abwehr was "directly involved" in the perpetration of such outrages.

During his first interrogation as a prisoner of war in 1945, he conceded merely that Abwehr II had "agents in North and South America," but dismissed them as "unimportant and ineffectual." He claimed that he himself had never had anything to do with them and "did not even know their names," except for a single saboteur in the United States whom he had ordered to drop everything and return to Germany in the summer of 1940.

After that, Lahousen claimed, no sabotage was attempted, except for a single effort in June 1942 which, he said, turned out to be "the biggest blunder that ever occurred in Abwehr II." Eight agents were sent to the United States in a pair of U-boats, their mission designed to cripple American aircraft production by blowing up a cryolite factory in Philadelphia (manufacturing materials essential in the production of aluminum) as well as the plants of the Aluminum Company of America at Massena, New York, East St. Louis, Illinois, and Alcoa, Tennessee. Lahousen insisted that the mission was undertaken on Hitler's explicit orders, but it was deliberately so arranged by the Abwehr as to make it fail from the very outset.

This was the notorious "Operation Pastorius," named after Daniel Pastorius, a decent Teutonic pioneer who was among the first German immigrants to try his luck in this country. The operation hit the headlines in the United States when four of the saboteurs were spotted by a young Coast Guardsman as they landed from a U-boat at a secluded place on the coast near Amagansett on Long Island. One of the "dark intruders" got cold feet. A greedy and unscrupulous young man named Georg Dasch betrayed the mission to the FBI, hoping that he could keep for himself the slush fund of $160,000 Lahousen had given him to finance the venture. Their military trial was held in secret.

Aside from this ill-fated mission, Lahousen insisted that the United States—or, for that matter, Britain—never figured as targets for major sabotage operations. As time went on, and after the war, his disclaimers became ever more positive and sweeping. In 1953 he stated categorically that sabotage in America "amounted to next to nothing."

The impression was reinforced in Heinz Abshagen's biography of Admiral Canaris. According to Abshagen, Canaris actually engaged in what he called the "sabotaging of sabotage," by instructing Lahousen that "nothing must be done that contravened international law"—a rather strange and inherently contradictory injunction coming from a Chief of Intelligence.

It is true that Canaris, as Abshagen claimed, would become sick at the mere thought of blood and violence, and tried to ignore this one function of the Abwehr. Yet it was early in his regime that Abwehr II was established. It was he who organized the largest and most elaborate organization of this kind in modern history—the so-called "Brandenburgers," an elite military force of saboteurs. Starting at company strength, they developed into a whole division that was sent into action before the commencement of hostilities without the slightest concern for "international law," which allegedly Canaris had admonished Lahousen to respect so scrupulously. "The Division fought on all fronts, on three continents," wrote Will Berthold in his excellent history of what Canaris himself called the "arsonists of the war." "Its soldiers dressed as Bedouins or as British officers . . . isolated fighters beyond the protection of international law, liable to be strung up from the nearest branch if they got caught . . . They were Admiral Canaris's own troops." In 1939 their first commander told them: "The Chief wants you to become a band of robbers—ready, if need be, to fetch the Devil from Hell."

When Canaris could not exclude himself from the actual plotting of such operations, he made it known that he himself did not "think much of sabotage and assassinations."

Occasionally this aborted such missions. In October 1940, Canaris deliberately bungled a project based on Hitler's directive to prevent the French fleet from leaving Toulon by sabotaging the ships in port. He circumvented the Fuehrer's orders to assassinate Generals Maxim Weygand and Henri Honoré Giraud. He saved the life of the British envoy in Berne, Switzerland, marked for murder in a weird and senseless plot hatched by his friend Heydrich of the *Sicherheitsdienst*. In another instance, he countermanded a Gestapo operation aimed at killing five French generals in German captivity.

On the other hand, the widely advertised story that Canaris personally intervened to foil a sabotage plot against the Pan-American Clipper while moored in the Tagus River in Lisbon is contradicted by the documents. On July 19, 1941, when the United States was still neutral, Lahousen himself drafted a plan to blow up one of the Clippers during a stopover there. The top-secret document, prepared only in the original draft and a single carbon copy, bore number 1588-41G. KBOS. ABW II-WS, and was captioned, "Sabotage-Attack on Traffic by Air Between USA-Portugal-England."

Since the Abwehr was under strict instructions to clear with the Foreign Ministry all operations that would take place in neutral countries, the copy of the plan was submitted by Lahousen personally to Assistant Secretary of State Ernst Woermann. Woermann forwarded the plan to Ambassador Karl Ritter, the Foreign Ministry official in charge of liaison with the OKW, and Ritter submitted it to von Ribbentrop.

When preparations were completed and nothing had been heard from the Foreign Ministry, Lahousen's deputy asked Secretary Woermann what was delaying the approval of the plan. On October 1, an unqualified objection was received. The "S-Attack" on the Clipper had to be abandoned in the face of the Foreign Ministry's vehement opposition.[1]

The war in Europe was still a year away when Colonel Lahousen first began to draw up plans for sabotage operations in the United States. The so-called "scheme of sabotage" was to be implemented in three stages.

As a first step, Major Dr. Richard Astor, an economist specializing in target intelligence in Abwehr II, was to compile a catalogue of "focal installations" to be sabotaged.

Second, a number of "American citizens of German extraction [were] to be enlisted by a scout," brought to Germany and trained in sabotage and subversion. They were to be planted in the U.S. at strategic spots such as power plants, water works and reservoirs, factories, and telephone exchanges.

Highly-trained master saboteurs were to be sent here to organize separate networks and direct their operations.

The execution of the plan was assigned to a quintet of American experts—Lieutenant Colonel Stoltz, Major Ulrich von der Osten, Lieutenant von Meerheimb, and a couple of civilian specialists named Wolfgang Blaum and Walter Kappe. The latter, a former press chief of the German-American Bund and influential editor of its official organ, was now serving in the Abwehr as a scout. He was to supply names of German-American citizens "suitable for carrying out sabotage in the United States."

Lahousen asked his colleague Colonel Piekenbrock of Abwehr I to obtain from his agents in the United States lists, descriptions, and maps of all big cities, and "strategic spots along the country's railroad nets," such as the Hell Gate Bridge over the East River in New York, and the Horseshoe Curve of the Pennsylvania Railroad at Altoona. The destruction of this key target was supposed to "paralyze Pennsylvania's entire anthracite coal industry by depriving it of rail transportation."

The agents responded promptly and avidly. One of them sent to Berlin the layouts of "the water supply system of New York," another that of Los Angeles, complete with maps of reservoirs and blueprints of their filter plants. Another came through with a listing of "all war-essential factories located in the eastern United States," adding, as a bonus, a map showing the location of fifty-two golf courses on Long Island which would "provide ideal landing places for German aircraft."

The first field agent sent to the United States to mastermind the execution of the Lahousen-Astor plan was Walter von Hausberger, an obscure operative about whom little is known even today except that he was Lahousen's personal protégé as a man of some hidden violence. Prepared for the mission at the Abwehr's sabotage schools and laboratories on the Quenzsee and in Tegel, he was seen off by Major von der Osten via Lisbon early in 1939. Hausberger carried the addresses of German-Americans who, according to Lieutenant Kappe, had agreed to carry out sabotage operations for which Hausberger would train them.

Hausberger's journey had rather strange undertones. He carried only meager funds, with the promise of more, and he was accompanied by his wife and child. This philistine serenity about Hausberger's migration was useful to "cover" his missions, but not necessarily conducive to efficiency in its execution.[2]

In the United States, Hausberger procured some fifty pounds of high explosives which he stored in his apartment where he made the fuses and containers his agents would need. In the meantime "Fritz" Duquesne, the old pro Ritter recruited in 1937, had decided that he could be more effective as a saboteur than as a spy, and kept pestering Hamburg with messages recommending specific sabotage operations he could carry out either alone or in association with some anonymous friends. One of his schemes involved blowing up the General Electric plant in Schenectady, and he also suggested that a bomb be placed in the church at Hyde Park where President Roosevelt worshipped.

He proposed "a bomb could be made from Chiclets," by "chewing the gum thoroughly, then folding it around a phosphorous compound." It would, he added, "make an excellent incendiary device which could then be scattered on docks, ships, or elsewhere through a hole in the pocket of one's coat." Its greatest advantage, Duquesne said, was the "inability [of this Chiclet bomb] to explode in temperature under 72 degrees." Moreover, it could be planted easily, "while speaking to the boss." He also asked for a supply of "lead-coated bombs" because, he conceded, it was likely to be more reliable and effective than his Chiclet bomb.

Greatly impressed by such enthusiasm and apparent expertise, Hamburg transferred Duquesne to Abwehr II. He headed the list of people Hausberger was to see upon his arrival in New York. Promptly contacted, Hausberger assured him that he would supply him with everything he needed—explosives, dynamite caps, fuses, lead pipes—but no Chiclets.

One by one, Hausberger approached the people on Kappe's list, only to find that most of them refused to collaborate. Others, Hausberger reported, were "totally unqualified for the task." Yet enough candidates agreed so that by the end of 1939, Hausberger started his cells in New York and New Jersey and on Allied ships loading at piers on the New Jersey side of the Hudson.

He planted saboteurs at the Harrison Gas Works of the Public Service Corporation of New Jersey; a team at the New York Liquidometer Plant; teams at the four Brewster aeronautical plants (as well as thirteen "sympathizers" who were to create slowdowns); two men in Kearney; and operatives at the Ford, Chrysler, Hudson, and Packard plants in Detroit. He also had a man at the Bausch & Lomb factory at Rochester, New York. The infiltration of the last was considered so important that a special assistant was sent from Germany to aid Hausberger in this particular operation. This individual, a foreman at Karl Zeiss in Jena, was trained as a saboteur at Tegel, then sent to New York where a job was waiting for him at the Zeiss branch on Fifth Avenue. From there it was one easy step to Bausch & Lomb.

Colonel Lahousen then picked a second sabotage master to carry out Major Astor's plan, a music publisher and fanatical Nazi named Georg Busch. Lahousen had known him when he was with the Austrian Secret Service and Busch had worked for him as an agent in Czechoslovakia and Rumania.

As the first step toward his conversion, Busch had been thrown out of the Party on drummed-up charges, then quietly absorbed in the Abwehr, and trained at both Tegel and Quenzsee. When he graduated Busch was resurrected under the alias of Julius Georg Bergman. According to the legend concocted for him, he was supposed to have been an Austrian industrialist with interests in Rumania. Since he was part Jewish, so the cover story went, he had to emigrate to escape the Nazis. He managed to obtain a visa to the United States (even when genuine, Jewish refugees found it next to impossible to get one), and unlike Hausberger, was amply provided with funds. Arriving in New York City in January 1939, he plunged immediately into his mission. He bought a large house in the suburbs and built a sawmill there which he considered an excellent front for sabotage enterprises. He procured explosives, made containers and fuses, and looked around for men who could help him in the venture.

If espionage is an art, sabotage is a science, requiring the precision and techniques of the engineer. Bergman possessed neither. He had grown up in the Bohemian world of musical artists and Viennese coffee houses, so he was dependent on others who were both skilled and trustworthy. All of Lieutenant Kappe's prospects whom he accosted recoiled from his offer. At last he found an apprentice for his macabre sawmill, a wayward stolid Polish handyman called Mike. Bergman put him to work making homemade bombs by packing dynamite into tin containers and sawed-off lead pipes. But one day Bergman lit a cigaret while watching Mike at work and detonated one of the half-filled canisters. The explosion tore several fingers from the Pole's hand and gave him second degree burns.

The explosion threatened to blow up the whole mission. Bergman panicked. He should, of course, have phoned for an ambulance and taken poor Mike to the nearby Grassland Hospital in Valhalla, or at least summoned a doctor. But Bergman could not compromise himself. The accident would be reported and the cops would take a good look at his "sawmill," with all the dynamite and lead pipes lying around. Questions would be asked, an investigation would be made, the FBI would be called in. He quickly bandaged the man's maimed hand, smeared Unguentine on his singed skin, and went looking frantically for a friendly physician. At a nearby Bundist camp, he found an elderly German doctor; the fact that he was a dedicated Nazi with Hitler's picture in his waiting room did not discourage him from collecting $350 for this particular house call.

Mike had had no idea that he was part of an illicit operation. When he now saw Bergman scurrying about for surreptitious help, doing all he could to hush up the accident, he became suspicious. "How about workman's compensation?" he asked pointedly. "Haven't you insured me?" He was not too bright, but he saw the light. He began to shake down Bergman. Before long he was paid $1,500—practically all the cash Bergman still had. With the money he had spent on the house, the sawmill, and buying "raw materials," his exchequer was amost exhausted.

When Mike continued to blackmail him, Bergman did what he was told never to do—he asked Lahousen for funds to be sent "by return cable." The money arrived promptly, in the form of a £500 check drawn by a Bucharest bank on the Chase Bank in New York—made payable to "Mr. Georg Busch," the name he had discarded for his *nom d'espion*. Hard pressed as he was, he was loath to cash the incriminating check. He sent another cable to Lahousen, asking for a check made out to Julius Georg Bergman.

While waiting for the replacement and nursing Mike, Bergman continued the build-up of his apparatus, planning to sink ships in the harbor. From Kappe's list, he selected two stevadores with whom he made several reconnaissance visits to vessels tied up in the Hudson and the East River. The going was easy. He boarded the *Independence Hall* and the *Effingham*, and spent a half hour on each without being challenged. "It's nothing short of amazing," he wrote to Lahousen, "this total absence of any precautions anywhere along the waterfront. I'm not surprised that the Americans don't care about security. But English and French ships are also wide open, longshoremen are coming and going without ever being stopped, whether or not they have any business on them. I was unobserved several times and could have placed bombs right and left that would have blown the ships to high heaven. I am eager to start operations as soon as the funds arrive."

They never arrived. In desperation, Bergman took his plight to the Consulate in New York, but the sum he needed, mostly to keep Mike quiet, was too large for the Consul to advance. He was referred to the Embassy in Washington, and so came to Dr. Thomsen's attention.

On June 4, 1940, in answer to Dr. Thomsen's vigorous protests, Lahousen ordered Bergman and Hausberger to return to Germany; Hausberger left as directed, but Bergman decided to stay. From then on, he lived on borrowed money and on borrowed time.

Even so, he endured at large until the summer of 1941. Then, hunted and penniless, he had no place to turn to except the FBI. He went.[3]

Just when it seemed that sabotage operations in the United States would have to be suspended, in the face of Thomsen's stubborn objections, another plan was proposed to Colonel Lahousen. It provided an entirely different tangent with different people, without compromising the Abwehr.

The originator of the idea and the *spiritus rector* of potentially the most dangerous sabotage campaign in the United States and Canada was one of the original band of Dr. Griebl's "undercover boys." He was Oskar Karl Pfaus, the closest a devout Nazi would come to being a Renaissance man, an anachronistic intellectual adventurer with an impetuous, inquisitive soul. His vast talents for mischief-making were destined never to be properly rewarded. But he gave his best to the cause.

Pfaus had come to America in the Twenties in the flood of disillusioned, frustrated Germans of the World War I generation. A hobo, a forester, a prospector, a cowboy, and a newspaper columnist at various times, he was once nominated for the Nobel Peace Prize by an admirer carried away by Pfaus's missionary zeal in expounding a pseudo-religious movement of "Global Brotherhood." He also served in the United States Army and was a cop in Chicago where he learned tricks of undercover work on assignments against the Capone-Arcado mob.

In Nazism he found the cause worth fighting for. Dr. Tegeliss Tannhaeuser, the German consul in Chicago, invited Pfaus to return to his native Germany in 1938, and he went home to work for the Abwehr.

At first nothing seemed commensurate with his talents, but then a niche was found for him. On February 1, 1939, he was sent to Ireland to recruit I.R.A. terrorists.

He returned after completing arrangements for I.R.A. espionage and sabotage in the United Kingdom. More important, he learned that a lively Irish underground was active in New York and Boston, and that Sean Russell, the former chief of staff of the I.R.A., was living in exile in New York.[4]

Canaris and Lahousen remained impressed with Pfaus's project and chose Karl Franz Rekowski, an apparently respectable 48-year-old Austrian businessman who had worked for years as a wholesale paper salesman in the United States, to harness dissident Irishmen for sabotage there.

Now he was taken on as a *V-Mann* with the cover-name of "Rex" (later changed to "Richard I"). He was supplied with the exceptionally large sum of $200,000 (by then, Berlin realized that the Irish were expensive). He was instructed to commute between the United States and the Abwehr's big outpost in the Legation at Mexico City.

Rekowski arrived in New York on June 6, 1940, only two days after Hausberger had been called home, and contacted leaders of the I.R.A. whose names and addresses Pfaus had supplied. In one of his first reports, Rekowski identified three of them with the fictitious names of "John McCarthy, Jim Conaty and Tony Cribben." McCarthy was the key man, called "the roving ambassador of the Irish Republican Army in the United States," who played a prominent role in the Russell affair. This patriot was "the organizer of sabotage."

"The Irish have agreed," Rekowski advised Lahousen, "to undertake sabotage on a substantial scale . . . against British ships in American ports as well as warehouses filled with supplies for the enemy war effort; also to interfere with lines of communications, and to attack all military and economic objectives essential to the Allies. The Irish organization has, for the time being, adequate S-material at its disposal. . . . All the active saboteurs are Irish Nationalists."

Rekowski triumphantly enumerated a number of outrages his Irish friends had already perpetrated: the explosion on September 12 at the Hercules Powder Plant at Kenvil, New Jersey, which killed 52 persons and injured 50, causing damage that "ran into millions of dollars"; the "tremendous explosions" on November 12, in three war production plants at Woodbridge, New Jersey, and Edinburg and Allentown, Pennsylvania. He sent along newspaper clippings, one with a statement of Secretary of War Henry L. Stimson that "the precision of the explosions might suggest Teutonic efficiency", to substantiate his claims.

Rekowski used these "successes" shrewdly to support urgent requests for additional funds. Lahousen wrote on March 7, 1941, in an inter-office memorandum: "According to Rekowski, the money is not available there. The need for the funds is explained by the fact that the active saboteurs are almost all working men and minor employees, who cannot raise the money these operations require from their own resources.

"The forwarding of money and instructions is assured by the employment of non-German couriers," Lahousen went on. "Connection between Abwehr II and Rekowski is maintained, for the time being, through reliable V-men of Spanish nationality." One of these Spaniards was Eduardo Penja Martin, who had been recruited by Dr. Blaum in Madrid for his mission to Rekowski. Lahousen managed to transfer $50,000 through a chain of South American banks.

In the meantime, Rekowski expanded activities considerably from Mexico. In one message, he asked for the formulae of stinkbombs "to disrupt political meetings in the United States." By then he had to conduct himself with great circumspection to cover his trail to the Irish, and told Lahousen that he could not safely leave Mexico City to supervise actual operations. He kept in touch with McCarthy and his cohorts through a go-between in Roma, Texas, identified as "a Roman Catholic priest named Father Charles." Rekowski would journey to Ciudad Juarez and Matamoros on the Mexican side of the border for periodic meetings with Father Charles, and to meet McCarthy or Cribben coming from New York. In the midst of the growing difficulties the Abwehr organization was experiencing in Mexico, Rekowski's reports represented the only bright spots.

"Friends in the North," he wrote on March 9, 1941, "report successful attacks against seventeen steamers. Explosives partly supplied from here, hence the necessity for occasional trips to the border. Expansion of network proceeds satisfactorily, now operates also in Canada, Only difficulties experienced are with supplies and personal supervision. Northern friends enthusiastically active."

The smuggling of explosives and the other paraphernalia presented problems of bulk. Rekowski urgently requested that his Northern friends be provided with the formulae of explosive compounds they could concoct themselves. "They must have at least comparable incendiary and explosive power to those now used," he wrote, "and whose export is becoming increasingly difficult from here."

This was not the only hardship Rekowski experienced. The transfer of $50,000 temporarily rescued him from the bankruptcy of the rest of the Abwehr apparatus in Mexico. But British and American agents had come upon his trail, and he felt their hot breath down his neck. On March 19, he complained about the tightening of the net around him, attributing it to "recently improved collaboration" between the Mexican and American authorities. "Anticipate," he wrote, "that continued work from Mexico would be impossible in the event of war with the United States."

He had been in Mexico a little over six months when he urged Lahousen to let him shift headquarters to Guatemala or Uruguay, leaving an assistant in Mexico City, "a naturalized Mexican of German descent named Carlos Vogt." But Lahousen ordered him to remain as long as possible. In his next report, brimming with confidence, Rekowski supplied the usual newspaper clippings to prove that his Irish network was performing with impunity.

"Operation Rex," as the Rekowski mission was called, seemed to be spreading disaster from coast-to-coast, leaving disabled ships, charred forests, damaged factories, and derailed trains in its wake. The fantastic venture dazzled Lahousen and elicited nothing but praise from Canaris. Much of it was probably Rekowski's imagination.

Lahousen was not the best judge of men. He was especially unfortunate in his choice of senior saboteurs. If Hausberger was a spendthrift and Bergman was a *Pechvogel*, a sorry bird of bad luck, Rekowski was a fourflusher. When he undertook the mission, he hoped to squeeze substantial sums from his gullible bosses in Berlin, with doctored reports and newspaper descriptions of routine accidents.

In turn, Rekowski was the helpless victim of his own Irish accomplices whose contributions were mostly the product of their lively imaginations. Their need of money was so insatiable that, in the end, Rekowski gave them most of the funds he was receiving. His expectation of becoming rich from this venture (and using his new fortune to establish himself in some legitimate business in Mexico) remained a dream.

By this time, Rekowski was no longer the Abwehr's only ace saboteur in North America. Late in 1940, at a secret conclave in a Chicago motel called by Gerhard Kunze, the prominent Philadelphia Bundist and agent-at-large for Abwehr II, a new avenue opened up. In 1938, Kunze had established contact with the head of a rambunctious Ukrainian underground group in the United States that effectively obscured its pro-Nazi orientation by emphasizing its anti-Soviet activities. "The Millionaire," as he was called in his circle of dubious revolutionaries, was Anastase Andreyevich Vonsiatsky, the self-styled *Vojd,* or leader, of a world-wide exile organization whose membership he modestly put at "20,000 loyal followers."

One of the truly romantic figures connected with German subversive activities in the United States, Vonsiatsky was a member of that fraternity of penniless but handsome playboys from around the Donets Basin who bestowed nobility upon themselves and struck it rich by marrying American millionairesses.

He was nineteen years old when his native Ukraine was engulfed in the Bolshevik revolution. For a while he fought with the White Russian armies of General Denikin and Admiral Wrangel, in a vain effort to keep southern Russia out of the Communists' claws.

After their collapse he escaped to Paris where he worked as a chauffeur until he met Marion Ream, heiress to the fortune of Norman B. Ream, the Chicago financier. They were married six months later in the United States, Anastase having given himself the title of Count to impress his rich wife and her social circle.

Vonsiatsky then worked briefly at the Baldwin Locomotive Works in Philadelphia, but later he and his rich wife retired to the seclusion of the huge Ream estate at Thompson, Connecticut, where, on his wife's money, Vonsiatsky went to work developing the global Ukrainian conspiracy. He founded the International Russian Fascist Party and was elected its *Vojd* at the convention held in 1934 at Harbin in Manchuria, under the aegis of the Japanese secret service.

Back in the United States Vonsiatsky used the Party as a front for a rapidly growing clandestine military organization trained on his wife's vast estate, guarded by detectives and a pack of bloodhounds. There he kept an arsenal of rifles, guns, pistols, ammunition, tear-gas cannisters, uniforms and enough high explosives to blow up every factory in Connecticut. The avowed purpose of the Party was, as its constitution phrased it, "the overthrow of the present Russian government by force and violence."

Soon the rambling estate at Thompson began to swarm with German agents before whom Vonsiatsky paraded his goon squad of young Ukrainian desperadoes, training in sabotage and assassination behind its guarded gates. Among the veteran terrorists, Vonsiatsky has resuscitated Fedior Wozniak, the most notorious saboteur of World War I, who had earned the nickname of "Firebug."

Kunze made a deal with Vonsiatsky for espionage-sabotage activities by his group. The contact proved extremely lucrative. Vonsiatsky not only financed his own activities out of his wife's fortune, but when it became increasingly difficult for the Abwehr to funnel money to its agents, he also gave Kunze substantial loans "to finance the work of German agents in the United States."

As his link with the Japanese weakened, Vonsiatsky's relations with the Germans became increasingly intimate. Other Abwehr agents joined Kunze in plotting with Vonsiatsky, especially when its scope was broadened on orders from Berlin to include the Midwest in addition to the East, and to prepare for sabotaging the American aircraft industry on the West Coast. Kunze's deputy in this conspiracy was the Reverend Kurt E. Molzahn, a Lutheran minister, who was receiving funds and instructions directly from Berlin via the German Consul in Philadelphia.

The Vonsiatsky ring had orders to lay low so far as sabotage was concerned. In 1938 it was already actively engaged in espionage, supplying intelligence "relating to the numbers, personnel, disposition, equipment, arms and morale of the [United States] army; the location, size, capacity, and other features of the United States fleet; the location, size, equipment and other features of military establishment, naval establishments, essential to the national defense of the United States."

The secret meeting in the Chicago motel was called by Kunze in December 1940 to activate the Ukrainians also for sabotage. The conference was attended by Vonsiatsky, the wayward Lutheran clergyman Kurt E. Molzhan (who was thus extending his nonclerical activities far beyond his base in Pennsylvania), and the Chicago Bund leader Otto Willumeit ("serviced" by the same Consulate). It produced an operations plan for sabotage of war installations. Now straining at the leash, Vonsiatsky volunteered to execute the "Chicago Plan" with the help of young desperadoes he had trained for this eventuality at his rich wife's secluded estate in Connecticut.

The United States was still at peace, and internal security quite lax. Mercenaries like the Ukrainian gang could operate effectively; this seems to be borne out by a number of industrial disasters that occurred *after* Vonsiatsky had at last been given his marching orders.

According to figures published by the Hartford Fire Insurance Company, forty "mysterious accidents and disasters" occurred between January 10 and December 24, 1941, involving the burning of British and French ships, shipyards, warehouses, grain elevators and cranes, government ammunition factories in Philadelphia, Acton, Massachusetts, Indian Head, Maryland, as well as privately-owned plants in Massachusetts, Virginia, New York, Pennsylvania, Wisconsin. Hardest hit was New Jersey, where five factories were believed to have been sabotaged. In Washington, a mysterious fire broke out at the Navy Department building; in San Francisco, army barracks under construction at Ft. McDowell were destroyed by a "fire of undetermined origin"; and an explosion shattered the new naval air base on Japonski Island, Alaska.

How many of these "disasters" had been man-made; how many had been perpetrated by Rekowski's Irish or Kunze's Ukrainian friends, neither the FBI nor the insurance companies could establish with certainty. The FBI denied categorically that any of them had been sabotaged, just as Scotland Yard insisted that none of the outrages in Britain had been caused "by enemy action on the ground."

In his semi-official, authoritative book, *The FBI Story*, Don Whitehead wrote: "Throughout the war years [presumably 1939 to 1945] the FBI investigated 19,649 cases in which sabotage was suspected, but there was not a single case of enemy directed sabotage to be found. . . . The suspected sabotage cases were, for the most part, industrial accidents caused by fatigue, carelessness, spite, a momentary burst of anger or horseplay among the workers."

Yet, on April 20, 1942, the United States Navy had to take over four plants of the Brewster Aeronautical Company, at which Abwehr II had no fewer than thirty-two agents, because the plants had "failed to deliver a single plane to the United States Armed Forces." Suspected workers, including an assortment of Bundists and at least two Ukrainians, were then investigated and, when their pro-Nazi record was established, dismissed. After this there was no more delay at Brewster.

Similarly slowdowns and "accidents" ceased at the sensitive Liquidometer plant in New York (manufacturing crucial warship and plane pipes) after a machinist, a foreman, and a department supervisor were discharged because close scrutiny revealed their pro-Nazism.

Whether the claims of the Rekowski and Vonsiatsky gangs were true or false, the German documents show indelibly that, contrary to all indignant protestations and phony disclaimers, the Abwehr was in the sabotage business in the United States on a substantial scale throughout the war.

Canaris and Lahousen sustained these operations with subterfuges and equivocations. On June 3, 1941, in a letter to Baron von Weizsaecker, Lahousen acknowledged that for about a year the "aim of the collaboration of Abwehr II with the Irish organization is the conduct of sabotage operations *solely in Canada*." The Foreign Ministry countered this disclaimer with a recitation of a number of sabotage cases that occurred *in the United States* during this same period and for which the Abwehr, in reports to others, had claimed credit. The Ministry had "incontrovertible evidence" that in February 1941, a freighter in Boston Harbor had been sabotaged by the Irish on German instructions. Lahousen's reply to this charge was that "the blowing up of the ship was either an unfortunate mistake or probably an operation our chief V-man [Rekowski] could not anticipate or prevent."

When in 1942, Gerhard Kunze developed the jitters and bombarded Berlin with frantic messages of dire premonition (he expected to be arrested momentarily), the Abwehr instructed him to go underground, then helped him to escape to Mexico. Lahousen ordered him to continue his activities from there, under the supervision of "Natus," the mysterious Abwehr chief who had taken over the outpost after the smashing of the Schleebruegge apparatus. When Kunze was caught by the Mexican authorities on a tip from the FBI, "Natus" hastened to reassure Berlin that "Kunze [had] revealed nothing [during his interrogations] of his close connections with and work for Abwehr II."

Also forced to abandon his precarious foothold in Mexico City, Rekowski reached greener pastures in Croatia, where, as a reward for his successes in America, he was given a pseudo-diplomatic assignment. Operations he had initiated with his Irish friends were continued on explicit orders from Berlin. His successor, the German-Mexican Vogt called "Richard II," went on reporting successes throughout 1942: "Ship destroyed in Baltimore Harbor" and "forest fires" in New Hampshire, Vermont, and New Jersey. Lahousen renewed his appeals to the Foreign Ministry to sanction his activities aimed at "installations which serve the war effort of the United States." Even when the Foreign Ministry turned him down, as usual, he went ahead with his plans, ordering "Richard II" to "interfere with oil deliveries from Mexico to the United States."

As late as 1944, an interesting episode in the peculiar German-Japanese relations of this war revealed that Abwehr II was still planning sabotage operations in the United States. On January 25, Admiral Canaris invited Lieutenant Colonel Higati, who represented the Military Intelligence Division of the Japanese Imperial General Staff in Berlin, to a conference to "explore the possibility of joint sabotage enterprises in the United States." On February 3, after consultation with Tokyo, Higati returned to the Tirpitz Ufer to tell Colonel von Freytag-Loringhoven, Lahousen's successor at Abwehr II, that the Japanese were prepared to cooperate. Such activity, Higati said, was impossible when first proposed two years before. But it had now become practical "provided the Abwehr would send agents to America under the German-Japanese espionage agreement."

The negotiations continued for months, long after Canaris's departure from the Abwehr in February 1944. By then, the Japanese, desperate to damage the United States at home and grasping at straws, implored the Germans to live up to the old agreement. In the end, the Abwehr complied in what became the last sordid scene of the final act in the grand guignol of German sabotage in the United States.

At 11 P.M. on November 29, 1944, during a blinding snowstorm, two men landed at Crabtree Point, Maine, from a U-boat. They were Erich Gimpel, a highly-trained operative, and William Curtis Colepough, an American ex-sailor, bearing $60,000 and orders to resume espionage and sabotage.

They did not get far. Young Colepough made his way to a friend's house in Richmond, New York, exposed himself as a German agent, and was turned in by his friend on December 26. With leads supplied by him, the FBI trailed Gimpel, who was trying to pass on false identification papers made out to "Edward Green," to a newsstand in Times Square, and arrested him there.

The mission of these two men was far too little and much too late. In summing up the story of German sabotage in America during World War II, it is illuminating to reread Canaris's protestations and Lahousen's disclaimers in the light of this hapless pair, lost on the windswept wintry Maine coast, pitting themselves against the United States.

Master saboteurs were still arriving when the men who had sent them knew that everything was lost. If the design did not work out quite as planned, it was not due to any lack of effort and investment on the Abwehr's part, but to circumstances over which Canaris and Lahousen had no control.

NOTES

1 According to the legend, Canaris first heard of the plot during a chance visit to Lisbon when the bomb was already on the Clipper. He summoned the Abwehr officer in charge and ordered him, in some heat, to have the bomb removed. The saboteur then sneaked back to the Clipper and removed the bomb, at even greater risk than he had incurred when originally planting it.

2 When Hausberger's funds ran out and no more arrived, he subsisted on his wife's earnings as a secretary.

3 The case of Busch-Bergman remained a mystery to the end. Although he was included among the defendants of the mass spy trial in the fall of 1941 he vanished during the proceedings and was never heard from again. Only the FBI might clear up the mystery, but it remains silent about the odyssey of Georg Bush alias Julius Georg Bergman.

4 One of Pfaus's first assignments was to arrange Russell's surreptitious return to Ireland to organize an anti-British uprising. Russell, an emaciated man burned out as a revolutionary, was smuggled to Germany by way of Italy, and sent to Ireland in a U-boat. But he had an ulcer hemorrhage en route and died aboard the submarine. The whole ambitious project was buried at sea with him.

Chapter 39

Tramp in a Trap

*T*HE chronic difficulties of his American agents convinced Admiral Canaris that something had to be done to improve the organization *at the top*. It had become abundantly clear that the shift of control to Mexico did not work out; that the umbilical cord had to be cut.

The United States was covered from coast-to-coast with a web of high-grade agents, unique for its size, diversity, and talent. The various networks and rings extended to practically every Army camp, Navy Yard, and critical industrial installation, as well as to the highest echelons of the American Government. Canaris needed a Resident Director in the United States itself, a seasoned professional who would coordinate the independent efforts of scattered V-men, to see that they performed at the peak of capacity, and, if possible, assemble others.

The man he chose for the job was Kurt Ludwig's case officer, Major Ulrich von der Osten. A career intelligence specialist descended from an old patrician family whose members traditionally distinguished themselves in secret service work, he is remembered merely as a shadow, probably because he was but an obscure corpse when he was found out. Before his mysterious demise he had been a fixture in the Abwehr for nearly twenty years.

When Canaris took over, von der Osten rose rapidly in his hierarchy. Sent to Spain in 1935 to aid the ill-fated General José Sanjurjo and then General Francisco Franco in clandestine preparations for the overthrow of the Azana regime of left-wing Republicans, he was instrumental in unleashing the rebellion on July 19, 1936, with a brilliantly plotted uprising at Burgos. Thanks to von der Osten's spadework, Burgos became the first important Spanish city to fall to the rebels.

He appeared in Burgos under the name of Don Julio Lopez Lido, in the guise of a merchant living in one of the city's rambling old monasteries, the Convento de las Enclavas. Among his triumphs during this period was also the quaintest—he succeeded in enlisting Kim Philby in the German secret service.

In his own brash account of his years as a double agent for both the British and Soviet secret services, Philby mentioned in passing his brief encounter with von der Osten. Assigned by *The Times* of London to cover the Civil War on Franco's side, Philby waited to be accosted by the British secret service which he had orders from his Soviet friends to penetrate. But his own compatriots ignored him.

"The only intelligence officer," Philby wrote, "who took the slightest interest in me during my Spanish days was German, a certain Major von der Osten, alias Don Julio." He dismissed this contact lightly. "It emerged in due course," Philby wrote, "that his real interest in me was to get an introduction to a lady of my acquaintance. When I obliged him, he propositioned her forthwith, both espionagewise and otherwise. She turned him down indignantly on both counts, and his manner became distant."

In reality, Philby worked for von der Osten, too, in the brief span of his best years, as the most gregarious of the commuting spies. He served the Germans mostly by denouncing fellow correspondents and others of his local acquaintances whom he suspected as anti-Franco, or simply disliked.

When the Civil War ended in 1939, von der Osten remained in Burgos as the Abwehr chief in Castile. His interests ranged far, to South America and especially to the United States where he had connections. His brother lived in Denver, Colorado, and a cousin was married to a German-American in New York, both rendering occasional secret services.

To broaden coverage of the United States, von der Osten recruited Spaniards and Portuguese as agents or couriers. He processed V-men like Hausberger and Ludwig when they stopped briefly in Spain en route to New York; and debriefed couriers and itinerant spies to avoid jeopardizing them with journeys to Germany. He remained majestically independent even of the huge *Kriegsorganisation*, the major base in neutral Spain.

Now Major von der Osten was to go to the United States via Shanghai, stopping in Hawaii just long enough to "reconnoiter Pearl Harbor for our Japanese friends." He had his fake Spanish passport, and though it was no secret that Don Julio Lopez Lido was really von der Osten, the American State and Justice Departments apparently remained ignorant of his true identity. He received his American visa without difficulty, and landed in Los Angeles in March 1941.

He arrived in New York on the 16th, and checked into the Taft Hotel as Don Julio. Waiting for him was the vast network in urgent need of a spymaster who would bring order into this extraordinary apparatus.

In New York, Major von der Osten found the ground well prepared for the expansion of Ludwig's splendid little ring into a pivot for all operations in America. Although he had no reason to suspect that anything was wrong, and was reassured by his intrepid agent that the FBI had no inkling of his activities, von der Osten's mission was to begin most inauspiciously.

Ludwig was no longer as obscure as he liked to think as his correspondence had not escaped British censorship in Bermuda. Two months before the arrival of the new Resident Director, a long typewritten letter addressed to "Lothar Frederick" in Berlin was intercepted by Miss Nadya Gardner, a young censor with a sixth sense in spotting telltale mail. Signed "Joe K" and stamped in New York, it contained a list of Allied ships in the New York Harbor, giving dates of their arrival, departure, and auxiliary armaments.

Although written in English, Miss Gardner thought that certain expressions in the typewritten text (such as the word "cannon"—from the German *Kanone*—for "gun") indicated that the writer was neither an American nor a Briton. From this first incidental clue Miss Gardner concluded that the writer was a German and a spy.

Captain H. Montgomery Hyde, Security Officer at the censorship station, submitted the intercept to William Stephenson, chief of the British Secret Service in the Western Hemisphere. Stephenson, whose sense of melodrama was easy to ignite, after only a moment exclaimed, "This might turn out to be a most important letter. Keep a lookout for any more like this."

The mail sorters, guided by the suspect's handwriting, soon came up with a number of letters from the prolific "Joe K." All originated in New York but were sent to different addressees in Spain, Portugal, and Switzerland. Miss Gardner sent samples to the laboratory to be tested for writings in secret ink, but the results proved negative. The writer was not using any of the Abwehr's new chemicals which the British censors could develop.

Was it possible, Miss Gardner pondered, that "Joe" was using one of the old fashioned secret inks of World War I such as a solution of the headache powder, Pyramidon, that responded to the simple iodine reagent? It was a long shot but she was proven right. When the next "Joe" letter was tested with iodine, it was found to contain the latest information on aircraft production and ship movements, written in secret ink.

In January 1941, Stephenson gave a collection of the intercepts to

J. Edgar Hoover, and the FBI began a search for the writer. In March
the plot thickened considerably, as the intercepts suddenly showed
"Joe's" activities gaining in scope and momentum. A letter marked
"c/o Joe" was signed "Konrad," the work of an astute military observer. Now two agents were involved in this correspondence, one a
trained professional, probably an army officer.

Despite these additional clues the FBI was still unable to track
down the writers. Then, still in March, came the big break. A communication in "Joe's" awkward English, five days later, contained
this piece of startling news:

> This week something terrible happened. Phil, whom you know, too
> —had a fatal accident. One evening he wanted to cross Broadway.
> He stepped at the middle of the street, as he could not go on further,
> on account of heavy traffic.
>
> I was with him all evening—but I did not try to cross the street
> with him as I thought it too risky. The moment he turned around, he
> was first hit by a taxi—thrown to the ground, and then hit again by a
> passenger car which knocked him unconscious by injuring his head
> very badly.
>
> At once policemen surrounded the place of the accident, and
> stopped the northbound traffic. Phil was carried to a store—his face,
> especially around the mouth was terribly injured, and where his head
> lain on the street, blood (with broken teeth) remained. The taxi driver
> was immediately taken into custody, and the driver of the passenger
> car arrested. Both were apparently Jews.
>
> After my urgent request the police called an ambulance, and only
> about 15 minutes after the accident he was taken to a hospital where
> he died the next day without regaining consciousness.
>
> As his condition was, according to information received by tele-
> phone very critical, and I myself could not do anything, I notified
> "his" consulate (through an old friend) which acted at once but it
> was impossible to save his life—the injuries were too serious.
>
> You will easily understand that I did not get in touch with the
> police—nor gave them my name. Today I went up to the consulate,
> and there I was assured of their support—especially in the matter of
> the burial and settling of his bills. Even if I have not much money,
> some of my friends are willing to advance the necessary funds.

The reverse side of the letter revealed the following in secret ink:

> Date of the accident 18 March about 20.45 o'clock. The passenger's
> car had the number 5U 57-35. The hospital where he was taken to
> and where he died is Saint Vincent's Hospital. Phil died on Tuesday,
> 16.30 o'clock (March 19, 1941). The Consulate mentioned is the
> Spanish.

It was bad news, indeed, for the Abwehr. "Phil," of course, was Ulrich von der Osten. Only two days after arriving at his crucial new post, he was a battered corpse refrigerated in the Bellevue Hospital's morgue. This gory accident marked not merely the beginning of the end of the Ludwig operation, but of the Abwehr's apparent monopoly of espionage in the United States.

Von der Osten had spent the morning in his room in the Taft Hotel composing a long letter to a certain "Mr. Smith" in China, via Señor Manuel Alonso in Madrid, giving a detailed description of the Hawaiian island of Oahu, with a series of maps he had drawn of Pearl Harbor. He had picked up the information during his recent stopover in Honolulu en route to the United States, and was now writing it up—"as of certain interest to our Yellow allies," as he put it—for "Smith" who was Louis Siefken, chief of the Abwehr station in Shanghai.

Ludwig had joined him in the early afternoon, for a review of his operations and a discussion of future plans. At half past eight in the evening, the two spies left the hotel to dine modestly at one of the Child's restaurants on crowded Times Square. Fifteen minutes later von der Osten was lying in his own blood, barely alive.

Ludwig phoned the Taft Hotel, told an assistant manager that "Mr. Julio had met with a serious accident," and said that he would call for his luggage. When the manager asked him to identify himself, Ludwig panicked and hung up.

The strange call with its abrupt ending aroused the manager's suspicion. He notified the police and the case wound up with the FBI where "Mr. Julio's" belongings were subjected to the most meticulous scrutiny. Some letters found among his effects were addressed to Carl Wilhelm von der Osten in Denver, Colorado, and it was then learned that the dead man was his brother Ulrich, an "officer attached," as he put it, "to the German military intelligence service."

Obviously "Joe" of those enigmatic letters was the key to the mystery, and now the chase began in earnest to find the elusive spy. Among the dead man's papers the FBI found a telephone number of a shop owned by an elderly couple, David and Loni Harris. Their interrogation produced half of the solution. Only two days after the accident, Mr. Hoover was able to notify "Little Bill" Stephenson: "Investigation has disclosed that 'Joe J' is identical with one Fred Ludwig."

With this important clue on tap at last, the FBI pieced together the vital statistics of Kurt Frederick Ludwig. But that was as far as the Bureau could get. The quarry of this feverish inquiry remained as elusive as ever.

Was the Bureau really as inept as it seemed, incapable of finding a fugitive spy so badly compromised and eagerly sought as "Joe"?

In 1933, still far from being the country's paramount civilian counterespionage agency, the FBI had its first brief encounter with Nazism as an element of conspiracy in the United States. In Germany, Hitler was just beginning to practice the violent anti-Semitism he had been shouting about for some time. His very first acts of repression provoked a man calling himself "Daniel Stern," into sending a warning to German Ambassador F. W. von Prittwitz in Washington, that unless President Roosevelt publicly rebuked the Hitler government for its atrocities against the Jews, he would "go to Germany and assassinate Hitler."

At the request of the Ambassador, the FBI undertook an investigation of the case. "Stern" was never found, but the incident afforded Hoover an opportunity "to conduct an intensive and confidential investigation of the Nazi movement, with emphasis on anti-American activities having any connection with German government officials." It was the first "general intelligence investigation" made by an American government agency into Nazi activities in this country. After that, Hoover and the FBI continued this pursuit, free-lancing more or less in counterespionage, without any explicit authority or real professional qualifications.

Between 1933 and 1937, the FBI "investigated" an average of thirty-five espionage cases each year. The Bureau had failed to penetrate Commander Pheiffer's lively and lucrative espionage organization, even after its two master spies, Lonkowski and Griebl, had surfaced momentarily in 1935. By 1938, with the rapid deterioration of the international situation, these "investigations" increased to 250 cases, and resulted in cracking the first German espionage ring, that of Guenther Gustave Rumrich, as we have seen, but the Bureau was still far from hitting its stride in counterespionage. The Rumrich case was initially broken by the British; Rumrich himself was handed to the Bureau on a silver platter by a team of State Department security agents and New York City policemen who had tracked him down while Hoover's special agents were still looking for him.

When the war broke out in Europe and President Roosevelt issued his confidential directive on September 6, 1939, establishing the FBI as the country's senior civilian counterespionage agency, the Bureau was still—or seemed—both naïve and inefficient in the coverage of German espionage in the United States.

There was a flurry of excitement but mostly in the public relations sectors of the White House, the Department of Justice, and Capitol Hill. President Roosevelt pointing an accusing finger at potential

spies, asked the local police authorities all over the country to aid
the FBI in finding them. The popular and liberal Attorney General
Frank Murphy proclaimed open season on spies and saboteurs and
appealed directly to the citizenry for help. Hoover gave specific
details on how the people could cooperate with the FBI in what
amounted to anti-spy vigilantism. The American Legion got into
the act by voicing all-out support for "the FBI's anti-espionage
drive" and demanded that Congress appropriate substantial funds for
the hunt.

The Bureau was flooded with tips and denunciations, but not a
single agent was apprehended at this time. Only through the common
sense of the American people did the country escape a dangerous
period of spy hysteria.

The clamor continued unabated. President Roosevelt warned the
nation melodramatically that "secret emissaries are active in the
United States and the neighboring countries." Specific charges were
launched from Capitol Hill. The mimeographing machines of the
House Committee on Un-American Activities, which had switched
temporarily from haunting Communists to the pursuit of Nazis, were
busy turning out spy-thrillers reporting sabotage at an unnamed California plant which manufactured a British plane of secret design;
claiming evidence that "Axis agents in the United States are working
to disrupt American aid to Britain"; and linking the German-American Bund with "news-leakage of convoy departures from Canada."

The Committee published the testimony of J. E. Edmonds, a self-
styled double agent, stating that he had been hired by the Nazis in the
United States to report ship movements. Congressman Martin Dies of
Texas, chairman of the Committee, painted a lurid picture of German agents operating from United States soil against Canadian targets in hit-and-run raids, trying to blow up a munitions train in a
tunnel between Port Huron, Michigan, and Sarnia, Ontario; and
planning to wreck the Consolidated Mining and Salting Company
plant at Trail in British Columbia. All of this was mere shadow
boxing. Canadian authorities countered the Dies' revelations by insisting that not a single case of sabotage had occurred there; and the
FBI found no such perpetrators. Was the country overrun by spies
and saboteurs or not?

The question was answered conclusively very soon, leaving little
doubt how the Bureau was faring in the secret war.

The impunity with which the galaxy of German spies was operating in the United States appeared to be too good to be true to the
spymasters in Berlin and Hamburg, who simply refused to believe
that the FBI was as bad as it seemed. There was momentary uneasi-

ness early in 1941. A seaman named Paul Fehse, one of the Abwehr coast watchers using the facilities of "Tramp," vanished abruptly the morning after he had sent a signal via Sebold, reporting the departure from New York of the Belgian ship *Ville d'Ablon*, carrying copper, machinery, aero engines, and horses to England. The Abwehr was relieved when it transpired that he had been caught accidentally and was tried on the relatively minor charge of failing to observe the Alien Registration Act. Fehse avidly pleaded guilty and was sentenced to a year and a day. He was safely tucked away in Atlanta, Georgia. Hamburg queried Sebold as to whether Fehse could have betrayed the secret radio at Centerport, Long Island. Sebold promptly responded that Fehse did not know enough about the setup to compromise it.

No new crisis flared up in the immediate wake of Major von der Osten's fatal accident in mid-March. Ludwig reassured his home office that nothing indicated, that the FBI had come upon his trail, despite clues they might have found in von der Osten's orphaned belongings. Berlin was anxious to protect the invaluable "Tramp" and, on March 29, instructed "Duarte"—Herbert Dobler of the Lisbon Abwehr—to inform Ludwig to "observe extreme caution in [his] relations with 'Tramp'" and to avoid anything that could jeopardize his or "Tramp's" security.

Then the roof fell in.

On Monday morning, June 30, 1941, Counsellor von Grote of the Foreign Ministry, who served as liaison with the Abwehr, called 21-81-91 on the telephone and asked for Lieutenant Colonel Scholz on extension 2656. Grote had before him a pile of intercepts of the Associated Press, the United Press, Reuters, the Transocean agency's foreign service, and even transmissions of the "United States Navy News." All announced that twenty-nine Germans had been taken into custody in New York on charges of "espionage for a foreign power." Von Grote asked what the Abwehr knew about the downfall of so many of its agents. The diplomat drew a blank from the colonel. "I think," he said, "you better discuss this with Major Brede or Captain Busch." Brede, head of the air intelligence branch at the headquarters of Abwehr I and employer of the majority of the German spies in America, proved totally ignorant of the fate of some of his best spies. "Perhaps you could get some information for us," Brede told von Grote, "from your people in Washington."

Several times during the 30th, and again and again on July 1 and 2, von Grote was on the telephone to Brede and Busch, his chief aide, giving details of "the spy scandal in America" from intercepts coming to his desk. At first everything was exasperatingly vague. No names were mentioned by J. Edgar Hoover who, on June 29, was the first to announce "the greatest spy roundup in a series of sudden raids." A Boston shortwave station broadcasting in German described the network as "the biggest of its kind in the history of the United States."

Then, as the dispatches kept tumbling in, one fallen agent after another was identified. At 7:25 P.M. on the 30th, the AP reported the arrest of Hermann Lang and Everett Roeder. An hour later the UP announced that Fritz Duquesne was also in custody. On another transmission, the AP raised the number of arrests to thirty-two, and named Conradin Otto Dold, Adolf Walischewsky and Heinrich Clausing, three stewards on American ships of the Atlantic run, among those taken into custody.

"Have you heard from the Embassy in Washington?" Brede asked, but von Grote had to admit that Dr. Thomsen was strangely speechless. All of the Foreign Ministry's lines with its missions in the United States seemed to be dead. The silence of the German diplomats in America indicated their embarrassment.

On July 4, a top-priority cable was sent to Thomsen ordering him to report. At long last, the Chargé d'affaires bestirred himself, but only to send a one-page dispatch:

(1) Arrests confirmed.
(2) Seven of the accused have confessed espionage for Germany.
(3) Among them Axel Wheeler-Hill, who operated clandestine radio for military employer, known to FBI since inception.
(4) Arrested men charged with violation of espionage laws for transmitting information about American armament production, ship movements, deliveries to England, and preparation of sabotage.
(5) FBI acted after approximately two-year long surveillance of all those arrested.
(6) Embassy, consulates, services attachés uncompromised.
(7) Max Blank was, until fourteen days ago, temporary employee at Information Library in New York.
(8) Big play in press and radio, but as yet not comparable to sensationalist treatment of case of [Rumrich], Hoffman, Glaser, etc. Prolonged exploitation aimed at us is certain.
    More as soon as possible.

It was a petulant message, reproachful between the lines, as though Thomsen were reminding the Foreign Ministry that he had warned often and amply enough that the rampage of "those misfits" would come to this dismal end. By the time his cable reached Berlin, as the incredible story of the debacle unfolded in headlines throughout the world, the Abwehr was in a state of shock. For decades the Germans had made fun of the American security organs. "Those idiotic Yankees," wrote Captain Franz von Papen to his wife in 1915. "Those stupid Americans," said a spy named Walter Koehler in April 1941, only a few weeks before the blow-out.

Feeling smug, the Germans did as they pleased in open challenge to the FBI and the counter-intelligence services of the Army and the Navy. More and more agents were planted in the United States, and they operated with increasing arrogance. They violated all the cardinal rules of espionage. Every member of one ring knew everybody in the other rings. The whole organization, the largest ever assembled in any one country, resembled a brotherhood whose members met from time to time at convivial picnics, got drunk together on imported Wuerzburger beer and Mosel wine, and celebrated their exploits in open conventions, exchanging notes and regaling one another with tales of their adventures.

A spy frequenting the Staten Island ferry to watch the movement of ships through the Narrows, became so chummy with the Italian-American bootblack on the boat that he confided to him the real purpose of his trips and invited the man to join the club. Another spy, emboldened by his immunity and envenomed by his hatred of the United States, could not resist the impulse of writing an abusive letter to an American major general, signing it with his real name and giving his address, censuring the officer sternly for some anti-Nazi remark he had made.

Now that the FBI had struck, the entire structure was a shambles. Spies and saboteurs caught in the dragnet operated in five different rings built around two communications centers. One—that of Wheeler-Hill—was smashed. Nothing was heard of the other.

When Admiral Canaris examined the list of the fallen agents compiled for him by Colonel Piekenbrock, he asked: "What happened to Tramp?"

"That's one of the mysteries we're trying to solve, Excellency," Piekenbrock replied. "His name isn't mentioned on any of the lists, and, for all we know, he may still be at liberty. It could be the only redeeming feature of this blasted disaster."

The Abwehr waited with bated breath until July 7, expecting to hear about Sebold or possibly even from him on the direct line, for miracles do happen in the spy game. When nothing was received, Colonel Trautmann, the chief of Abwehr communications in Wohldorf, tried to raise "Glenn" who operated "Max" which was the code name of the third clandestine radio station in North America located in Mexico City. It was incapable of direct communication with Germany, over six thousand miles away, and Tramp was normally working it in relay. When Trautmann could not raise Max, he queried R.3757, his liaison with Glenn in Mexico City.

R.3757, a Mexican-German named Fernandez, responded promptly, but had nothing encouraging to report. "Total Hamburg traffic including Max-messages now handled by Glenn," he cabled. "He is not arrested but under close surveillance. He suggests you warn Tramp that U.S. had twenty and Mexico three direction finders trained on him. 'Glenn' is destroying his papers and is standing by to dismantle station. Transmissions temporarily impossible. Hopes to resume operations with mobile transmitter as soon as conditions improve."

As soon as the signal was received, Colonel Trautmann put one directly to Tramp on the air. "Suspend contact with Hamburg until further notice," it read, "in the interest of your security."

No answer was ever received. CQDXYW-2 was dead.

Nothing was heard about William Sebold for the next two months, and all efforts to contact him through cut-outs or to track him down through the Embassy (if, indeed, he was still at large) remained unsuccessful. So tightly insulated was the investigation by the FBI that nothing seeped back to Germany.

By September, the American government was ready to try the spies—so many had confessed and revealed so much during their interrogations that the authorities had all the evidence needed to convict those—including Duquesne and Lang—who persisted in their "not guilty" pleas.

Admiral Canaris followed developments like a doting father whose children were in trouble with the law. Using Foreign Ministry channels, he syphoned Abwehr funds to America to pay a kind of dole to the families of the defendants. He had Hans von Dohnanyi of his legal staff aid the defense at long-range.

The defendants had counsel chosen by themselves or engaged by their families, but Canaris arranged what came to be called a *"Vertrauensanwalt,"* or confidential attorney, to be hired to represent the Abwehr, so to speak, and deal with the more delicate aspects of the case which could not be confided to the other lawyers.

The attorney chosen to hover unobtrusively over the proceedings was a distinguished New York lawyer. He dealt directly with Dr. Thomsen who had his instructions to do his utmost to lighten the burden of the spies in their predicament.

The trial began on Tuesday, September 3, 1941, in the Federal Court in Brooklyn, with nineteen of the 33 arrested agents arraigned before Judge Mortimer W. Byers, an eminently fair and learned jurist. As Dr. Thomsen put it in the first of his daily cables to Berlin in which he summarized the day's events, "it is played up enormously by the entire American press to the utmost detriment of Germany."

The tension of the atmosphere was heightened by the coincidence of a collateral event. A few days before, the FBI picked up the trail of the fugitive Ludwig as he was trying to race across the country to the West Coast where he hoped to sneak onto a Japanese ship undetected. Hotly pursued from the moment he vanished from New York, he was traced to the State of Washington where he was trapped near Seattle. Still carrying several bottles of Pyramidon tablets for his secret ink, he was probably now taking them internally to alleviate his acute headache. At the same time, five members of his ring were found and arrested, swelling the fantastic collection of fallen agents, their mysterious presence in the background casting a shadow on the case.

The trial itself started off with a bombshell. United States Attorney Harold M. Kennedy charged in his opening statement that "the secret of the Norden bombsight, this country's most jealously guarded air defense weapon, has been in the hands of the German Government since 1938." He pointed an accusing finger at Hermann Lang as the man who had stolen it.

Nothing was heard of Sebold—until September 8, when special dispatch No. 3110 sent "extra urgent" by Dr. Thomsen, suddenly brought him out of the dark. "According to V-man," the Chargé d'affaires cabled from Washington, "arrests were made possible through the collaboration of an engineer named Seebold [sic] who is said to be an agent of the American secret service."

The next morning in Court, Sebold materialized in the flesh, introduced with a flourish by Mr. Kennedy as the government's star witness.

"For sixteen months," the prosecutor told the jury, "the Federal Bureau of Investigation has been in constant communication with the Nazi secret service in Hamburg, Germany, by means of a shortwave station on Long Island, exchanging worthless 'information' about the American defense program for accurate reports on the activities of Nazi spies in this country. It was the German espionage system itself that had conceived the idea of a shortwave station here that would enable it to check on American defense preparations and at the same time regulate the activities of its secret agents in this country.

"The plan boomeranged," Mr. Kennedy went on, "because William G. Sebold betrayed the operation to agents of the FBI on his return from Germany early in 1940."

Sebold's own testimony on September 9 and 10 exposed the operation in all its detail and ramifications, and pinpointed the two spymasters in Hamburg who had conceived it, one as a "Dr. Rankin," the other as "Heinrich Sorau."

If the arrests in June sent shock waves through the Abwehr, the dramatic appearance of their Tramp as an FBI informer created unmitigated panic in Berlin and Hamburg. In a war that was producing some of the strangest deceptions in the history of espionage, "Operation Tramp" was revealed as the biggest hoax of them all.

Canaris was besieged in his office (from which he could not absent himself now as he usually did whenever the heat was on) by frantic inquiries and demands from the Foreign Ministry, Heydrich's office, and even from the Reichs Chancellery. He was ill prepared to stave off the frequently malevolent probings of his enemies, because it was not his habit to familiarize himself with the activities of even his best agents in the field. To set the record straight, he summoned Captain Herbert Wichmann, and quizzed him mercilessly about the defunct operation.

"Who is this man Sebold," he asked," and what did he have to do with the Abwehr?"

Captain Wichmann identified him as the V-man Tramp and related how he had come back to Germany in February 1939, and was, as he put it, "introduced to Ast X by the Gestapo via the Muenster outpost." He then told Canaris of Sebold's employment and training, described his mission to America, and the deceptively phenomenal success of the operation.

The admiral then asked: "Who is this Dr. Rankin? And where does this Heinrich Sorau come into the picture?"

He was told that Rankin was Major Nikolaus Ritter, chief of air intelligence at Ast X, and Sorau was Captain Hermann Sandel, his deputy, the two officers who had "developed" Sebold for the job. Ritter had acted as the agent's case officer until his separation from Ast X, leaving to stage a special intelligence operation for Field Marshal Erwin Rommel in North Africa, plotting the defection of a top-ranking Egyptian politician and the commander in chief of the Egyptian army. After that, Sandel was handling Sebold, to the bitter end.

When Canaris asked for Ritter, to get his version of the story, a frantic search began for the elusive officer. The mission in North Africa having failed (for the Egyptians developed cold feet and did not show up), Ritter was named resident director in Brazil where the Abwehr had its most flourishing outpost in South America. The major was on his way to his new post, where he was to function in the guise of an Assistant Air Attaché, but was still in Rome waiting for a L.A.T.I. plane to take him to Rio de Janeiro. Called back for the confrontation with Canaris, he unfolded the incredible details of the monumental mishap—truly a comedy of errors—in the admiral's barren office.

The sensational prosecution in New York was putting the Abwehr on trial in Berlin. Hitler's cabinet office, the Foreign Ministry, and Himmler's monstrous Amt all clamored for explanations. The morning after the trial opened, the Abwehr chief was summoned to the office of General Keitel to brief his superior in the OKW about Sebold in preparation for a report Keitel was scheduled to make to Hitler in the afternoon. Canaris came prepared with a two-and-a-half page *Vertragsnotiz* (aide memoir) in which he represented the man who was the cause of all his troubles as a charlatan and an impostor whose double game had been discovered at the earliest stages of his employment and who had been used after that as a conduit to the Americans for misleading information. It did not matter that anything Canaris told Keitel and wrote in the paper for Hitler had no relation to the facts of the case. It was the line he would adopt, and to which he would stick throughout the emergency.

A top-level inter-agency conference was held at the Foreign Ministry on the 18th to review the situation on the basis of a report the Admiral was expected to submit personally. He did not show up, but sent Captain Hermann Menzel, one of his deputy directors, to present a shrewdly concocted and carefully rehearsed variation of the theme the Admiral had played for Keitel. Menzel's self-serving report —too transparently designed to vindicate the Abwehr—was not accepted, and Canaris was asked formally to submit a written report, sticking to the facts.

The admiral delayed the submission of the paper as long as he could, hoping that the passage of time would mitigate his predicament. Prodded repeatedly, he finally sent a long memorandum to Under Secretary Baron von Weizsaecker, in the expectation that his old friend would know how to soothe Foreign Minister von Ribbentrop who was out for Canaris's scalp.

"The employment of agents for the reconnaissance of military objectives had become necessary," he wrote in the paper dated October 11, "because the Abwehr was pressed by the Luftwaffe Staff, the Admiralty and the Army General Staff to produce information the collection of which was possible only at the source. . . . The development of a large and swift network [in the United States] was demanded vigorously by the various high military staffs, when the closing of [German] consulates [in America] and limitations imposed upon the movements of our diplomatic representatives in Washington would impair their collection of intelligence data; and when it had to be anticipated that the break of diplomatic relations would terminate altogether the procurement of intelligence through accredited channels. It became imperative to leave in the United States a clandestine apparatus after the break.

"As pointed out in memorandum OKW A Aus/Abw (ZR I) B. No.899-41, Top Secret, dated July 23, 1941, the agents planted by the Abwehr supplied a flow of valuable and important information, as shown by laudatory communications from all three branches of the armed forces on file in the Abwehr."

He then acknowledged that "about a dozen of the altogether 45 persons" eventually caught in the big FBI roundup had been producing agents for the Abwehr at the time of their arrest. He conceded that the others, too, could have been working for his organization as sub-agents, although they were not carried in the registry.'

After that he took up the matter of Sebold, presenting an expediently falsified version of the factual information Captain Wichmann and Major Ritter had given him.

"Shortly after the commencement of his activities in the United States," he wrote, "and though his reports were in part highly praised by the Luftwaffe Staff, and were not disputed by the Admiralty, the suspicion arose that the intelligence he was submitting could not be trusted implicitly. Thus, for example, a report about certain projected developments in the American Air Force was recognized as worthless. Several of his reports were not deemed worthy of dissemination and were discarded.

"The Abwehr's suspicion of his material, that soon also extended to the person of Seebold [sic], was aggravated when the agent attempted to obtain from us the code used by another clandestine transmitter (Max) for which he was supposed to act merely as a relay station. Despite several requests, the code was not made available to him. Seebold then distorted the cipher in which certain instructions were radioed to Max through him. This, too, was quickly discovered, resulting in the deepening of our distrust of Seebold. . . . Moreover, despite urgent and pressing demands of several outposts, the Abwehr categorically refused to attach to Seebold other agents working in the United States, in order to avoid possible jeopardy to the agents and their contacts.

"From this point on, communications to Seebold included deliberately misleading information, to deceive the adversary about the status of our operations or to create confusion in his mind about our true objectives."

Canaris went on to insist emphatically that "Seebold" knew the Abwehr officers he was in touch with only by their cover names; and denied that the agent was aware that the officer he knew as Dr. Rankin was in reality Major Ritter.

He concluded the long memorandum by going over to the offensive, complaining pointedly that none of his agents in America had ever received any support or enjoyed the protection of the diplomatic and consular missions, while such aid and comfort was given to American agents freely and fully by their diplomatic representatives abroad.

The Canaris memorandum, with its seemingly factual data and candid review of the situation, was received well in the Foreign Ministry and elsewhere. His explanations and justifications were accepted at face value, and the case was closed. The Abwehr survived what threatened to become its lethal crisis, and Canaris had vindicated himself.

It was a remarkable performance, far more interesting for what he suppressed than what he disclosed. Aside from such petty lies as the claim that Sebold did not know Dr. Rankin and Heinrich Sorau by their real names; and the assertion that he had been suspected as a double agent from the outset, the document was brazenly mendacious from beginning to end.

What was the true story of the affair in contrast to the Admiral's pretty tale?

When in the fall of 1939, Major Ritter accepted Sebold into the fold, he permitted the new agent to pay a visit to the American Consulate in Cologne, accepting the man's word that he went there merely to arrange for the support of his wife in New York while he would be staying in Hamburg to be trained as a radio operator.

It was never thought necessary to screen the new V-man even superficially. His wife—presumably stranded in America—did not even exist.

In Cologne, Sebold met Vice Consul Dale W. Maher behind the closed doors of his office, confided to him that he was in the process of being hijacked into the Abwehr for a mission in America as a radio operator, and asked the consul what he should do. Mr. Maher, unquestionably the unsung hero of this major coup, did not hesitate for a moment to give Sebold the benefit of his advice.

Fearful that his own cipher might be compromised, he refrained from letting Washington know or asking for instructions. After sizing up Sebold with a keen eye, and satisfying himself that this ex-gunner of the Kaiser's army was a glowing American patriot risking his life with this precarious visit, the consul told his visitor to accept the offer and pretend that he was going along enthusiastically with the Abwehr.

It was then agreed that Sebold would return to the United States after the completion of his training, but would be taken in tow upon arrival by special agents of the State Department. Only then would the FBI be taken into the department's confidence and the custom-made double agent handed over to the Bureau.

Sebold went back to Hamburg, and Consul Maher journeyed to

Lisbon whence he felt safe to alert the State Department to the coming of this prodigal son. Then on February 6, 1940, in an elaborate masquerade, Sebold arrived back home. The Abwehr sent him on his journey with a fake passport made out to "William G. Sawyer." To the State Department and the FBI he was "S. T. Jenkins."

How he could manage to remember all his various names; to keep his allegiances apart; and perform his complex assignments to the satisfaction of his different employers, I do not know and cannot explain. Sebold was an unsophisticated, almost illiterate man. Yet he performed with the dexterity and brilliance of a quick-change artist, gaining the unquestioning confidence of the Germans (whom he was betraying) and the gratitude of the Americans (whose bidding he faithfully carried out).

In his bugged office in the Knickerbocker Building on 42nd Street in New York, every move was filmed by FBI cameras hidden behind two-way mirrors and peepholes; "his" radio station, built on Long Island, he never even visited throughout his adventure. It was operated by Special Agents J. C. Ellsworth and M. H. Price of the FBI, who had learned to simulate his touch on the Morse key with perfection.

It was the unfailing efficiency of this spy (which in fact was the technical perfection of the FBI) that trapped the Germans in their second fatal mistake. Contrary to what Admiral Canaris claimed, they attached one of their agents after another to this perfectly functioning electronic conduit. By June 1941, after Sebold had been seventeen months back in the United States, every single agent of the Hamburg branch, and an assortment of other spies, such as Ludwig and Reuper, was an ornament dangling on Sebold's overloaded Christmas tree. This was why the FBI could make such a clean sweep when it decided to strike.

Sebold was the FBI's trump card, but not its only ace in the hole. Another young German-American was the Bureau's short-cut to the ring of Karl Alfred Reuper, that enormously dangerous busybody of a spy from New Jersey. He is also an unsung hero, the forgotten man in the FBI's great coup. But there is a special testimonial extant, spelling out the intrepidity, efficiency, and patriotism of this little known American double agent. It was written by Dr. Thomsen in utter consternation on September 27, 1941.

"Not only Sebold," he wrote, "but also another man, a certain Walter Nipken, was in the service of the Abwehr while working simultaneously for the American secret service. Born in Muehlheim Ruhr, Nipken has been an American citizen since 1936, a lathe operator with Air Associates in Bendix, New Jersey, manufacturing plane parts. On December 21, 1940, he made the acquaintance of

Karl Alfred Reuper who asked him, on January 4, 1941, to procure sketches and blueprints of aviation instruments for transmission to Germany.

"Reuper told Nipken on this occasion that he had served in the German army for six years, and had been trained afterward especially for espionage work in the United States. Arriving here four months after the outbreak of the war [in Europe], he was commissioned to ferret out the secrets of America's defenses, and to instigate discontent and unrest in this country's defense plants.

"He showed Nipken a number of drawings, the kind he expected to obtain through him. On January 5, Nipken delivered these samples to the FBI and agreed to serve henceforth, exactly as Sebold was, as a counterspy. . . . On January 11, Nipken gave Reuper antiquated drawings of certain secret pumps, and was told that they would be microphotographed at once and sent to Germany by courier with the next shipment."

Thanks to Nipken, Reuper and his ring were also blown up in late June, and the FBI was put on the trail of Axel Wheeler-Hill and Felix Jahnke, the Siamese radio-twins of the Bronx, who serviced Reuper's radio traffic. Since Nipken was able to tip off the FBI to the Wheeler-Hill operation practically the day his radio went on the air in the apartment on Cauldwell Avenue, special agents could monitor the station and record its traffic from its inception. Much of the apparent incompetence of the awkward Axel, about which Felix complained so bitterly to Dr. Thomsen, was not really due to the novice operator's notorious incompetence. It was caused by interference by the FBI, a kind of synthetic static.

The FBI—which even a few months before seemed so indolent and ineffective—was now suddenly revealed as the world's most formidable counterespionage force.

It was lucky as well.

In June 1941, almost simultaneously with the smashing of Operation Tramp, the German consulates in the United States were sent packing by order of President Roosevelt because, as their expulsion note diplomatically put it, they "have been engaged in activities wholly outside the scope of their legitimate duties."

Early in July in downtown Manhattan, the Consulate General was sorting out its papers—all of those bearing on its illicit trafficking with the spies and saboteurs—to be burned. Consul Lurtz, who was the resident spymaster in the office, assembled all the documents the Americans might regard as "inimical to the welfare of this country," then called in the janitor of the building to help him get off his hands this embarrassing encumbrance.

It was a hot summer day, but Consul Lurtz asked the janitor to start a fire in the furnace in the basement. The janitor did as he was told, but set the fire at one side of the furnace. Then, watched by Lurtz and a confidential clerk of the consulate, he threw in the bundles one by one—into the area of the furnace that was free of the fire.

When the Germans left the basement, satisfied that the paperwork of their guilt had been consumed by the flames, the janitor put out the fire altogether, and sent for the FBI to collect the unburned loot. The next morning the bundles were all in the possession of the FBI, slightly singed. Among the documents thus saved for posterity the FBI found the complete roster—names, addresses, vital statistics, pertinent notes—of every German agent in the New York area who was ever serviced by the consulate, and some who were not.

This seemed the end of German spying in the United States, but the halcyon days were not quite over. Every single agent managed by Berlin and Hamburg had been exposed to the FBI. The operations directed by Berlin headquarters and Ast X had been paralyzed.

But two important areas remained untouched. One was Dr. Thomsen's spy apparatus, now gaining, as we shall see, paramount significance for more reasons than one. The other was the network whose strings were pulled by the indomitable Bremen subbranch.

Chapter 40

The House on Massachusetts Avenue

*I*N early January 1938, at a cocktail party in Washington attended mostly by prominent pro-German Americans, an elegant gamine of a young woman accosted Dr. Herbert Scholz, counselor of the German Embassy on Massachusetts Avenue, and asked him for what sounded like a date. Scholz was not immune to such advances. A handsome, debonair man with exquisite cosmopolitan manners, the young diplomat, married to the beautiful and rich daughter of a senior executive of I. G. Farben, the great German chemical trust, was enormously popular with the capital's top social set, despite ugly rumors that he was really a glamorized Gestapo bully on some sinister errand in the United States.

He was, in fact, the resident director in America of Heydrich's *Sicherheitsdienst*, the Nazis' own secret service locked in deadly rivalry with the Abwehr, and knew how to conceal his true mission beneath the gloss of his diplomatic cover. He was a fixture at the affairs of Washington's most flamboyant hostesses, attending them chiefly to meet the people who mattered and to eavesdrop on the loose talk of Washington insiders.

The chic young woman who sought him out had no amorous designs on the good-looking, blond, blue-eyed Continental. She asked Scholz for a *private* meeting to discuss a *confidential* project she had in mind.

Scholz knew the lady only slightly, but was aware that she was one of the country's richest playgirls, heiress to the American fortune her father amassed in the leather business. She was Merry Fahrney, featured almost daily on the society pages for her many antics, escapades, and marriages.

In the carefree, careless atmosphere of the capital there was no

467

need to arrange a *Treff*. Scholz invited Miss Fahrney to luncheon upstairs at Pierre's on Connecticut Avenue, one of Washington's uppercrust French restaurants, and was startled to hear the vivacious heiress offer him her services as a spy even before they finished the hors d'oeuvres.

"Already during our first meeting," Scholz recalled, "she went out of her way to protest her pro-German and also pro-Nazi sentiments which, in my opinion, were strongly motivated by her bitter hatred of the Jews. I immediately recognized from the way she talked that she was exceptionally intelligent, well above the average one finds in her circle, although her ideas were somewhat marred by her erratic way of thinking."

Then—between the entrée and dessert—Miss Fahrney placed herself, as Scholz put it, "at my disposal to collect for us intelligence of all kinds, emphasizing that she expected no remuneration for her services."

A deal was made, and it proved enormously lucrative for the Germans. "I actually received from her," Scholz wrote, "invaluable intelligence material both during my tenure as Counselor of Embassy [until December 1938] and as the German consul to the New England states [from March 1939 to July 1941]."

This glowing testimonial to Miss Fahrney was written on February 16, 1944, in a letter recommending her for secret German employment in Argentina. A similar report was offered simultaneously by Heribert von Strempel, who was chief political officer of the German Embassy in Washington until December 1941. "She was especially effective," he wrote, "thanks to her prominent position in American public life, in establishing contact for me with influential American personalities who were politically or economically interested in Germany."

In the spring of 1939, when Dr. Scholz was transferred to Boston, he gave up Miss Fahrney, first to von Strempel, and then to Dr. Hans Thomsen himself. From then on she worked in Washington at the highest German level of intelligence collection.

She continued to move in the circle of her well-informed friends, where it was fashionable to be eccentric. Merry's pro-Nazi foibles were dismissed as the whim of a spoiled young lady who otherwise had everything. She proved to be a prolific and valuable spy, but she was not the most discreet of the breed. Her work for the Germans, zealous and florid like everything she did, was becoming so conspicuous that it attracted the interest of the American authorities.

When it seemed that she was outliving her usefulness because of her gentle surveillance by the FBI, Dr. Thomsen suggested to her that she leave and, taking her money along, move to a country like

Argentina where she could continue to work as an agent unmolested by the authorities. Miss Fahrney—by then a contessa through her marrage to a member of the aristocratic Fascist family named Berlingieri—heeded the advice and emigrated to Buenos Aires.

Her employment in Argentina ran into a snag. The chief of the German secret service there, a rabid Nazi named Siegfried Becker, did not know her even by reputation, and balked at taking an American heiress into the fold. It was then that Miss Fahrney decided to buttress her credentials with references from Thomsen, von Strempel, and Scholz. They did the trick. Her clandestine career that began in 1938, was terminated only by Germany's defeat in 1945. Her activities left a legacy of bulging folders in the secret files, full of sensitive data detrimental to the war effort of her native land, which she collected with ease and gusto from her fine-feathered friends in high society.

No diplomat worth his salt could survive in his "dreary trade" without at least a small coterie of so-called confidential informants. In the United States, Miss Fahrney's appearance under cover had the added touch of piquancy of ushering in, by coincidence, a dubious period of German-American relations.

These were the beginnings of German diplomatic espionage in the United States. Before long Thomsen's mission blossomed out as a hothouse of intrigue and a den of spies—the most conspiratorial the Nazis had anywhere in the world, with the possible exception of their embassy in Argentina and their legation in Rumania.

The blond Viking who was in charge of the German Embassy was not dependent on George Sylvester Viereck. He turned out to be a smart spymaster in his own right. When the war broke out in Europe, Hans Thomsen assumed that the United States would quickly join Britain and France against Germany or at least break off diplomatic relations with the Reich. He created two separate secret networks for what he called the continued protection of German interests.

He quickly organized a group of foreign correspondents representing newspapers of countries Thomsen expected to remain neutral. Promising each a monthly subsidy of $350, a huge sum for those days, he invited them to serve as ad hoc agents, mostly in Washington and New York.

He had already begun to spin a web of regular V-men from coast to coast to "supply by covert means the kind of information the embassy and the consulates will no longer be able to provide," as he soon expected the United States and Germany to be at war. He subdivided the United States into four districts and appointed groups of "comptrollers" and "reporters" in each. A total of 47 "trustworthy agents" were handpicked by Dr. Thomsen to act as V-men—four in

Washington, D.C., 13 in Illinois, one in Indiana, three in Wisconsin, four in Minnesota, one in Nebraska, one in Iowa, three in Louisiana, five in Texas, one in Florida, one in Georgia, one in the State of Washington, six in Missouri, and three in New York. The United States stayed out of the war for two more years, and when the FBI roundup of 1941 came, so abruptly and unexpectedly, Dr. Thomsen had no time to activate his dormant networks.

Thomsen also excelled personally in clandestine operations. In his "secret diplomacy," he regarded the continuous surveillance of the President in his third term as his chief function and primary responsibility, and rightly so. F.D.R. was emerging as the most powerful leader of the great anti-Nazi coalition long before the American entry into the war. Some of the most crucial policies and decisions directly affecting Hitler's war effort were made by this nominally neutral Chief Executive. It was up to Thomsen to monitor F.D.R.'s plans, intentions, and movements, and gain access to his critical decisions even while they were in the making.

Thomsen's reports dealing with Mr. Roosevelt were remarkable for their accuracy, lucidity, and objectivity. Unlike Dieckhoff, Thomsen gave no thought to Hitler's and Ribbentrop's blind Roosevelt-phobia. He concentrated rather on facts, procuring them partly by the conventional diplomatic means and partly by espionage.

He assembled whatever information he could from Americans in high places who were bitterly opposed to F.D.R.'s domestic and foreign policies. Many of them actually sought Thomsen out, not necessarily in flagrant conspiracy to aid and abet the Germans, but to promote their own determined efforts to keep the United States out of the war. In a highly personal sense, they sought to alleviate the frustrations of their own long and losing opposition to the President. Much of the material Thomsen obtained from them consisted of "inside" coverage of the Washington scene known to resident correspondents and syndicated columnists. His undercover snooping was a different matter.

Combing the Washington jungle for people who had access to state secrets and were willing to sell them (either for love of Hitler or love of money), Thomsen succeeded in stirring up a number of "stringers" far better posted than the gregarious Miss Fahrney and closer to the corridors of power even than Viereck and his political hacks.

One of the most important among them was "a friend of [Attorney General Homer S.] Cummings who is at the same time my reliable confidant." Thanks to this agent, he procured a mass of hard intelligence, including considerable information about what was going on at cabinet meetings. On June 11, 1940, for example, Thomsen enlightened Berlin with some of the President's innermost thoughts, on the basis of a conversation the Attorney General had with the President. The report, paraphrasing one given him by his "reliable confidant," read as follows:

1. In the present war situation the President will use every legal trick in order, by circumventing the Neutrality Law, to furnish the Allies with every possible material help.

2. Should the war last long enough to make it possible to build up American armaments and the American army, he will place both on the side of the Allies.

3. Should the war end within a short period with the defeat of England and France, then America would "be sweet and polite toward Germany for two years"; during these years America would build up her army, navy, and air force, regardless of cost and waste.

4. Should Germany at any time attack Canada or the West Indian possessions of England or France, this would mean immediate war with Germany, irrespective of the state of American rearmament.

"I have no reason," Thomsen added, "to doubt the authenticity of these statements. They are also worthy of note because the President thus lets it be known that he takes for granted a prolongation of his term of office, that is, his reelection."

Thomsen had an even better source of intelligence—the kind that comes straight from the horse's mouth—which covered the top echelon of the American government.

The President's sacrosanct security had been breached by a lowly Foreign Service officer making copies of the top-secret cables that passed through the London Embassy Code Room. As we have seen, Tyler Kent was found out and arrested in May 1939. Yet the Germans continued to receive almost verbatim transcripts of some of Mr. Roosevelt's telegrams, especially those he exchanged with Ambassador Joseph P. Kennedy in London. Two in particular reached them direct from Washington while Kent was still at large and working. Since they were not included in the mass of cables Kent had copied, they obviously came from another source. Moreover, similar intercepts continued to pour in long after Kent had been unmasked.

They came from Dr. Thomsen in Washington.

On August 19, 1940, he forwarded to Berlin a telegram of the utmost topical interest in which Ambassador Kennedy complained to the President that an American military and naval mission had been sent to London without Kennedy being consulted in advance. Thomsen described the "indignation" of the ambassador, who "asked to be recalled when he was informed by Churchill about the arrival of American officers. It required a personal telephone conversation on the part of Roosevelt to dissuade Kennedy from his intention to resign."

The Kennedy telegrams enabled Thomsen to monitor Britain's power of resistance, as well as the physical and morale damage that the savage air blitz was causing in Britain in the fall of 1940. Thomsen forwarded a whole string of them, in which Kennedy described "the devastating effect of German air attacks on England's ports, fields, and armaments industry."

On September 30, 1940, Thomsen sent to Berlin the telegram in which the panic-stricken Ambassador warned Roosevelt that "England is"—quoting Kennedy's actual words—"completely through"—in the original English.

He gave his source as "the reliable informant known to you."

This was by all standards one of the greatest coups of German espionage in the United States during the whole of World War II. And it is also one of the most mysterious of any such operations, never revealed by the State Department in its postwar investigation of the case.

However, independent research by this author—including a moderately productive interview with Dr. Thomsen himself in 1966 —brought to light at least the contours of this incident.

Thomsen had succeeded in penetrating the State Department Code Room in Washington and procuring *firsthand* information about some of this country's most precious secrets.

How was it done?

The Code Room of the State Department, a part of the Division of Communications and Records, was housed on the second floor of the old rococo State, War, and Navy Building on Pennsylvania Avenue, perennially (since 1910) headed by David A. Salmon, a former archivist of the War Department.

Under Salmon, cryptographic security was so lax that American diplomats had to conduct their business in a goldfish bowl. "The United States," wrote David Kahn, "must have been the laughing-stock of every cryptanalyst in the world." Salmon was persistently tardy in tightening the Department's communications security even when code books were stolen right and left; and when it became known that most (and probably all) of the Department's ciphers had been compromised by both friend and foe.

According to Thomsen, it was a "reliable and tried confidential agent" who kept him posted. The man was "very friendly with" what he called "*Leiter Chiffrier-bureaus*," the head of the cipher bureau. He revealed that this friendship was extremely close—so intimate, indeed, that "the director of the code room" permitted his "friend" to see for himself and probably even to copy "the relevant telegraphic reports."

The man responsible for the leaking of these crucial secrets was the technical operating chief of the code room, Joseph P. Dugan.

In the emotional climate of those days, when isolationist sentiment was pronounced, Mr. Dugan permitted himself to be trapped in a fateful indiscretion. He freely discussed Ambassador Kennedy's cables with a friend, an American with whom he felt close kinship in his convictions. He went so far as to take home copies of certain cables that had relevance to the great issue of peace or war.

He had no idea that his friend was anything but a concerned citizen. Nothing in his conduct or comments indicated to Dugan that he was a German agent. Dugan even permitted him to copy certain key dispatches, because his friend told him that he wanted to show them to sympathetic legislators on the Hill who, he said, "were entitled to know what's going on."

Most of the German papers bearing on this loophole in American diplomatic security have been destroyed. But five major documents survived to show that this particular operation involving the State Department's code room lasted for a minimum of seventeen months. During this period Thomsen supplied transcripts of critical Kennedy dispatches, one dated October 22, 1939, two on April 3, 1940, and one each on August 19 and September 30, 1940.

Then, on April 29, 1941, Thomsen's "confidential agent" made it possible for him to score another, perhaps even greater scoop.

In the fall of 1940, American cryptologists succeeded in compromising the highest-grade Japanese diplomatic cryptosystem based on a supposedly unbreakable cipher machine, called the "B-machine." As all of Japan's other codes and ciphers had been successfully penetrated before, the cracking of the secret of the B-machine meant that the American government could read Japan's entire diplomatic correspondence that could be intercepted.

It was an historic accomplishment, unprecedented in cryptology. No network of spies could have procured Japanese intelligence in such profusion, in such a steady flow, and so promptly.

The United States actually did not have a single spy in Japan at this time, and did very well without any. The American code-breaking operation, called "Magic," was guarded with exceptional security measures. It was assumed that the Japanese were totally unaware of this comprehensive breach of their security and that no unauthorized persons had even an inkling of the existence of "Magic."

On April 29, Thomsen shattered this assumption with a cable to Berlin. "As communicated to me," it read, "by an absolutely reliable source, the State Department is in possession of the key to the Japanese coding system and is, therefore, also able to decipher information telegrams from Tokyo to Ambassador Nomura here regarding Ambassador Oshima's reports from Berlin."

It is beyond the shadow of a doubt that the "absolutely reliable source" was the "reliable and tried agent" who was "very friendly with the director of the State Department Code Room," as Thomsen had reported to Berlin on April 3, 1940.

The State Department was on the most restricted distribution list of the "Magic" intercepts, under an agreement of January 23, 1941, that confined State Department access to the Japanese cables solely to Secretary Cordell Hull. But Mr. Hull violated this restriction. He shared the Magics with at least six of his closest associates. They in turn let four lower-ranking officials in the Far Eastern Division see them. None of them was responsible for the leak, but so many copies of the intercepts were needed by this arrangement that the Secretary's office had certain important cables run off on a mimeograph machine by an employee who had not been cleared even for restricted documents, much less for the Magics.

The duplicating machine used was located in the code room. In this way, others found out about the American possession of the key to the Japanese coding system. Eventually, the critical indiscretion reached Dr. Thomsen.

His warning was relayed immediately to the Japanese in Tokyo. The Germans promptly tightened security in their relations with the Japanese ambassador in Berlin. But in Tokyo, after a perfunctory investigation of "the alleged leak," the Japanese decided to do nothing. It was possible, they mused, that several of their lower-grade systems had been compromised by the Americans. But they concluded that their top-secret cipher based on the B-machine "remained absolutely safe."

Inside the house on Massachusetts Avenue, Dr. Thomsen had another young attaché who, behind his diplomatic mask, was the full-time manager of his own ring of spies. Sometimes called "the Baron," probably because he looked like one, he was an arrogant, cynical young Berliner who had been a dedicated Nazi since he was fifteen years old when his Prussian family had first met Hitler and became enamored of him.

For all his rabid associations, Ulrich von Gienanth had the innate elegance and charm of the born aristocrat and the easy manners of high society. It was his best cover. He had first come to the United States in 1930 as an exchange student, then joined the SS on his return to Germany. He was immediately appointed to Himmler's own Praetorian Guard of handpicked young men chosen for their Nordic good looks and distinguished family backgrounds. In 1934, Gienanth was transferred to the SD, and Heydrich, his new boss, sent him back to the United States as his personal representative in the guise of an attaché at the Embassy.

He was to act as the Gestapo watchdog to keep the Ambassador under surveillance. He was also required to observe closely Dr. Ernst Meyer, one of the counselors about whose politics Heydrich had some derogatory information and who *horribile dictu*, was rumored to have some Jewish blood in his veins. Gienanth was absorbed in his Gestapo duties (which made him rather than the Ambassador the political boss at the Embassy) until the outbreak of the war in 1939. He was then instructed to broaden his activities and to operate also in the political field, not so much to collect information as to subvert people.

As spymasters can be judged best by their stable of agents, it is safe to say that Ulrich von Gienanth was not a virtuoso of the craft. He was familiar only with people on the lunatic fringe, a coterie of American eccentrics who saw in Nazism the wave of the future.

In this crowd of misfits he had only one person worth mention. She was Laura Ingalls, American-born madwoman of the skies, a pasty-faced, cherry-lipped hysterical female whose antics were financed by Gienanth with occasional handouts that never exceeded $100 at any one time. Miss Ingalls was extremely conspicuous for a secret agent and caused a lot of commotion by haranguing pre-conditioned audiences at Nazi rallies, and once even flying low over the White House to scatter crude propaganda leaflets.

Others in young Gienanth's weird "network" were shrill in their Nazi clangor, but added nothing to his meager collection of information. As far as Amt VI was concerned, this supposedly top SD-man in the United States was a flop.

Within the German Embassy, the traditional figures of espionage *per se* were the two service attachés. Emboldened and invigorated by Thomsen, they now added a new dimension to the old system under which military and naval attachés were tolerated as "official spies."

The Naval Attaché was Captain Robert Witthoeft-Emden, a stiff, tight-lipped, self-effacing officer whose double name stemmed from his gallant service in World War I on the cruiser *Emden*.

Witthoeft-Emden took seriously his informal designation as an official spy, but refused to participate in any espionage over which he did not have full control. Occasionally he consented to the use of his cable facilities by Abwehr agents, but this was unavoidable as the

Navy's Cipher M was the only cryptosystem considered unbreakable. It was advisable to use this highest-grade cipher whenever a spy report had to be forwarded through the Embassy, to assure that such a breach of proper diplomatic usage would not leak out.

In September 1939, Witthoeft-Emden received instructions to keep certain ports on both the East and West Coast under close surveillance. He acted promptly and in these two maritime zones his spies operated as well as, if not better, than the Abwehr's ubiquitous coast watchers.

In New York, Witthoeft-Emden had a man by the name of Rehmel, working under one of the New York Consuls. Rehmel is one of the few remaining mystery men of German espionage in the United States. He may have been a shipping expert who had, by virtue of his job, access to the records of all ships passing through New York Harbor.

On the West Coast, Witthoeft-Emden had a man named Oscar Haber, recruited and developed for him by Consul General Gyssling of Los Angeles, to do what Rehmel was doing on the East Coast. Since Gyssling had to leave Los Angeles shortly after Haber had been installed, Witthoeft-Emden found it difficult to sustain him from as far away as Washington. He decided to abandon the responsibility for the Pacific Coast to the Mexican outpost of the Abwehr operating out of the Legation in Mexico City. It had a lively and efficient network consisting of scores of agents, thanks mainly to the superb work of the best naval observer the Germans had anywhere in the Western Hemisphere.

He was Alfred Johann Woehler, purportedly working for a firm called Vos de Pueblo at Mazatlán in Sinaloa Province, a sultry Pacific port on the trunk line between the United States and Mexico City.[1]

Captain Witthoeft-Emden had still another ring of maritime agents who plumbed crew members of ships going to Mexico from the United States for information, including naval intelligence about the American fleet on the Pacific coast. This organization was headed by Walter Schmiedehaus. The organization was finally destroyed in October 1942, when Schmiedehaus was arrested by the Mexican secret police on evidence supplied by the FBI. By then Captain Witthoeft-Emden had left the Washington scene.

Friedrich von Boetticher was the first and only German Embassy military attaché accepted by the United States between the World Wars. He arrived here in April 1933, in the third month of the Hitler regime, also a memorable year in his own life. As the chief military envoy for the whole of North and Central America, he was promoted to *Generalleutnant* (major general).

Born in 1881, trained as an artillery officer, Boetticher was a dabbler in history, military philosophy, and geopolitics. He wrote articles and several books on these topics that gained for him a reputation in the German military establishment as a shrewd observer and a deep thinker. This record as a writer and analyst, rather than any practical accomplishments in the army, recommended him for the key Washington post.

During his tenure of more than eight years in the United States, Boetticher was the most prolific reporter on the American military scene, sending to his home office, the *Attaché-Abteilung* of the Army, tens of thousands of words about the army of the United States and its military potential. But his reports, written in a fancy style of apparent erudition, did not bear out his reputation (especially in Hitler's eyes) as a shrewd observer.

An amiable extrovert with easy drawing-room manners, he was really a pompous ass, an archaic soldier burdened with rampant prejudices. He was a vitriolic anti-Semite, his bigotry seasoning even his professional estimates. His Jew-baiting, in fact, endeared him to the Fuehrer as a good Nazi.

After the war, a high anti-Nazi official in the Foreign Ministry, called Boetticher one of the grave-diggers of Germany. He charged that his biased reports materially contributed to Hitler's fateful misconceptions about the United States.

The woeful quality of his reportage was due no doubt to his methods of collecting information. His circle of informants was a volatile but small coterie of American General Staff officers and their associates whose ideas and beliefs seemed to coincide with his own.

There was in Washington before the United States entered the war, a military clique overly impressed with the precision and might of the German war machine, and perhaps even with Hitler, that tended to view developments with a distinct pro-German bias. It was a tight little group, loosely organized as an isolationist lobby of military pros. Its members met regularly at the home of Colonel Truman Smith, a former American military attaché in Berlin, with Smith acting as the ideologue and *spiritus rector* of the group. He was one of the most obscure and enigmatical forces that moved quietly behind the Washington scene of those days. His influence radiated to both the policy makers and the public, and fanned the frenzied controversies that raged over the great issues of war or peace, and aid to the Allies. Smith, who suffered from a serious gastrointestinal ailment that made him abrasive and impatient, was a sincere patriot, a loyal and competent officer, and an original thinker of absolute integrity. He was respected and frequently consulted by General Marshall who regarded him as the best expert of the Germans in the United States Army.

Smith, a strong conservative with a subliminal admiration of authoritative ways, was inclined to give the Germans the benefit of the doubt. To his inner circle of military reactionaries and political isolationists belonged a handful of brilliant but politically unsophisticated younger officers. Also in the group was a captain of the Army air corps who worked on what was called the "Victory Program," the basic strategic war plan of the United States. The Navy was represented in the well-meaning cabal by Rear Admiral Stanford C. Hooper, intense, opinionated and querrulous, and highly regarded nevertheless for his pioneering work in naval communications and radar.

These men were motivated, not so much by any pronounced pro-German sympathies, although such sentiments may have played a part, as by their wish to keep the United States out of the war. When Colonel Charles A. Lindbergh made his determined stand against this country's involvement in the quarrels of Europe, even if it meant the defeat of Britain, he, too, was drawn into this circle and attended many of its conclaves. He derived considerable inspiration from their firm opposition to war. And he procured the ammunition he needed for his campaigns from their inside knowledge of German strength and Britain's alleged weakness, of American preparedness, and the supposed "warmongering plots" of the Roosevelt administration.

This was no mere study group, no private debating society of concerned citizens. It had all the characteristics of a cabal. Their meetings were held in circumspect secrecy. The subjects of their deliberations were kept confidential. Classified documents were brought to these gatherings and privileged information was exchanged. Contact was maintained surreptitiously with influential isolationists on Capitol Hill, especially Senator Burton K. Wheeler of Montana. He was visited from time to time by members of the group to acquaint him with the "facts" he needed to expose Roosevelt as a warmonger. Secret papers were smuggled to him to enable the Senator to document his exposés with incontrovertible evidence that, as Admiral Hooper once told him, "the man at the other end of the Avenue [was] going to get us into the war."

This was the circle of informants to which General von Boetticher pegged himself, not merely to monitor the mood and morale of the United States Army, but to procure the most reliable factual information he could get. He regarded this "connection" as both proper and prudent. Like many of the German service attachés who emerged into the twilight region of secret diplomacy, he was vehemently opposed to espionage and actually fought the Abwehr on this score. This drew upon his head the wrath of Admiral Canaris who complained bitterly to Field Marshal Keitel, charging bluntly that Boetticher was negligent "in his duty to promote the interests of the Reich" by "sabotaging the work of the secret agents."

The controversy erupted in full force in March 1940, when Boetticher was admonished by his home office to refrain from hampering the work of Abwehr agents in the United States. In a handwritten letter to the chief of the German Army General Staff, Boetticher protested indignantly that he was acting "solely in the best interests of the Fatherland" when he objected to the planting of the Canaris spies who were "a sorry lot," in the United States. His own reports, based on the best sources, provided far more reliable coverage. Moreover, he added, such an influx of spies threatened to provoke the United States into still greater aid to Britain.

General Halder reassured Boetticher on May 6, but also ordered him to cease his interference with Abwehr agents, who were "indispensable" in "procuring certain classified information about air and naval armaments" and were needed "to observe the flow of strategic supplies to Europe."

Boetticher remained steadfast in his opposition. He reported that he was meeting individually and relatively often with members of the Smith group and the "circle about Lindbergh," especially with those who, like Smith and Major (later General) Albert C. Wedemeyer, had served or studied in Germany. Such contacts produced the assurance in Berlin that key officers in G-2 and the War Plans Division supported the cause of Germany in contrast to, if not actually in defiance of, the official policies and plans of the Roosevelt administration.

Actually Boetticher did not have to go out of his way, as he had three "contacts" close to the group who supplied in abundance whatever he thought he needed. They were not bound by the discretion that guided officers in their relations with Boetticher. They were civilians and could do as and say what they pleased.

Most important of the trio was Major Alford J. Williams, Jr., a former naval aviator who held his commission in the Marine Corps Reserve. An aviation writer for the group of Scripps-Howard newspapers, his exceptional usefulness to Boetticher stemmed from his close proximity to the group in whose deliberations he frequently participated. He was a charter member of "the circle about Lindbergh" that was trying, as the general advised Berlin on July 20, 1940, to "impede the fatal control of American policy by the Jews."

His other informant closely linked both with the Smith and Lindbergh circles was Charles B. Allen, another prominent aviation writer who, according to the same report, had been "on close terms with [Boetticher] for years and until recently held an important government position in civil aviation." Allen was, Boetticher added, doing what the general discreetly called "independent research" for him.

So eager was he to protect these two informants that on several occasions between May and August in 1940, he pleaded with Berlin never to mention them in any German publications. "I repeat my recommendation," he cabled on July 20, "to avoid strictly any discussion in the press and also in conversations with Military Attachés, etc., of relations with Lindbergh and other Americans fighting the Jews." He repeated his recommendation on August 4. "It would paralyze the activities of [Alford Williams] this indispensable contact, the importance of whose work on our behalf I cannot sufficiently praise and emphasize."

The man the Smith-Lindbergh group used as a go-between to forward confidential information to prominent isolationists on Capitol Hill and influential places elsewhere in the United States, who acted as a kind of public relations man to get their ideas and facts into print, was Chesly Manly, Washington correspondent for the *Chicago Tribune*. His main congressional contacts were Senators Wheeler and David A. Walsh of Massachusetts, the chairman of the Naval Affairs Committee of the Senate. Manly also had close relations with Heribert von Strempel, the Embassy's political attaché who conceded after the war that the *Chicago Tribune* correspondent was "probably his most valuable source of information."

The secret dispatches of General von Boetticher demonstrate that either his American officers were very badly informed about their own nation and military matters or their knowledge was distorted. Their friendship with the Washington representative of a potential enemy, and the protestations of their isolationist creed and anti-British feelings deceived poor Boetticher into believing that the majority of American army officers was essentially disloyal, at least to the extent of refusing to be drawn into a war against Germany at Britain's side.

Whatever hard intelligence Boetticher received from his informants was badly mishandled by the German general whose attention was focused on the supposed influence of Jews with the American government. He was, for example, accurately informed of the negotiations with Japan going on behind closed doors, but his dispatches disclosed an opinion that Roosevelt was hellbent on provoking the Tokyo government into an attack in Asia, "a design his Jewish advisers had concocted to pave the way to America's entry into the war."

He assured Berlin that the Japanese would not stumble into this trap and that there was no prospect of a war with Japan "in the foreseeable future." He was as surprised by Pearl Harbor as everybody else was in Washington.

In May 1940, Admiral Hooper began to feed to Senator Wheeler information culled from classified Navy documents that the Germans had no "capacity for launching an air invasion against" the United States. He also supplied what Wheeler called facts about the rapid growth of American aid to Britain.

Then something more exciting happened. On June 8, a young army captain of the clique—"in uniform, and clean-cut and intelligent-looking"—called on Wheeler to ask whether he "wanted some facts" about the defenses of the United States. He proceeded to tell the senator that the country did not have a single plane fit for overseas service.

"You've got to have three things," the captain said, "armor-plate, self-sealing fuel tanks, and fire power. We haven't got a single, solitary plane that has all three. Some of them have one of those essentials, some have two, but not one has all three."

The captain told Wheeler that U.S. aircraft "were good enough to fight in Cuba or Mexico but not against the modern German Air Force." He assured the senator that when the administration claimed "over four thousand planes ready for combat service, twenty-six hundred of them in the Army Air Corps," it was "lying to the American people."

The captain continued to pour information to Wheeler; the senator continued to review it with Manly or Viereck's man in his own office; and the latter continued to discuss much of what they heard with Boetticher and von Strempel.

Then, frustrated by the apparent hopelessness of his efforts to stop Roosevelt, the captain decided on a desperate action.

At the direction of the President in the summer of 1941, the planners of the army and navy staffs drew up what the captain described as "a master plan for a gigantic American Expeditionary Force." In reality it was a set of staff studies and estimates, trying to establish, as Wedemeyer, the chief planner phrased it, "the overall production requirements to defeat our potential enemies."

The Wall Street Journal revealed on October 21, 1941, that work on such a project was going on. But it could not produce any detail of the program. The author of the article, Eugene S. Duffied, refrained from divulging any specific data beyond stating that the plan's basic aim was to "beat Hitler."

Members of the clique regarded this so-called "Victory Program" as "irrefutable evidence," as Wedemeyer put it, "that American intervention in the war was planned and imminent, and that President Roosevelt's promises to keep us out of the war were only campaign oratory."

Now it was decided to stop Roosevelt on his march to war by exposing details of the "program." It fell to the captain to commit the grave indiscretion it entailed. On December 3, when his office in the War Plans Division closed down for the day, the captain removed the document labeled "Secret" from the safe and took it home. It was a bulky folder, "as thick as an average novel," and he carried it out of the Munitions Building concealed as an ordinary package wrapped in brown paper.

From his home he called Senator Wheeler and asked him for an appointment, this time in the privacy of the senator's home on Kalorama Road. The meeting was arranged for that evening. When the captain showed up he had with him what Wheeler called "the most closely guarded secret in Washington."

"Aren't you afraid," the senator asked, "of delivering it to me?"

The captain shot back: "Congress is a branch of the government. I think it has a right to know what's really going on in the executive branch when it concerns human lives."

This actually was the motivation of the officer. The delivery of the copy of the "Victory Program" was intended merely to convince Wheeler that such a plan—"contemplating an attacking army aggregating five million men" out of armed forces planned to total 10,045,658 men—had been drawn up on the President's orders. He told Wheeler that it was now on the President's desk.

The idea was to give the senator the facts which might result in a speech delivered on the floor of the Senate, in which Wheeler would expose the program without divulging any of its specific details.

Wheeler was "startled and fascinated." It was a bulky document and he needed time to study it. He asked the captain whether he could leave it with him overnight, and the officer said he could, if Wheeler would get it back early next morning to return it to its niche in the War Department before his office opened.

When the captain left, Wheeler pondered his course. But when he finally decided on one, it was quite different from what the captain expected him to take. It was a senator of the United States who deliberately aggravated what was merely an indiscretion on the part of an irresponsible but sincerely motivated young American. Wheeler moved all the way to the edge of treason by "releasing" the document to a journalist whose "paper," he later wrote, "would give the plan the kind of attention it deserved."

He called Chesly Manly of the *Chicago Tribune* bureau in Washington to come to his house right away. Manly arrived shortly after eight o'clock and stayed until midnight, making verbatim extracts and selecting "the most important sections" which Wheeler's personal secretary, summoned to this nocturnal plot, copied *in extenso* in shorthand.

That same night Manly turned everything into a blistering article. It appeared, under banner headlines, next morning in the *Chicago Tribune,* the *Washington Times-Herald* and the *New York Daily News,* flagships of the anti-Roosevelt press in America.

"A confidential report," read Manly's lead, "prepared by the joint Army and Navy high command by direction of President Roosevelt . . . is a blueprint for total war on a scale unprecedented in at least two oceans and three continents, Europe, Africa, and Asia.

"The report"—he added the subtle isolationist slant—"expresses the considered opinion of the Army and Navy strategists that 'Germany and her European satellites cannot be defeated by the European powers now fighting against her.' Therefore, it concludes, 'if our European enemies are to be defeated it will be necessary for the United States to enter the war, and to employ a part of its armed forces offensively in the eastern Atlantic and in Europe and Africa.' "

Accordingly to Manly, July 1, 1943, was fixed as "the date for the beginning of the final supreme effort by American land forces to defeat the mighty German army in Europe."

The exposé of the "Victory Program" created an enormous sensation. It drew from Secretary of War Henry L. Stimson the most succinct comment among all the stunned and appalled statements issued by members of the Roosevelt administration. "While the publication," he said, "will doubtless be of gratification to our potential enemies . . . the chief evil of their publication is the revelation that there should be among us any group of persons . . . willing to take and publish such papers."

It was later disputed that the publication of the purloined program had given aid and comfort to the Germans who, within a week, would be this country's enemies.

Such disclaimers were refuted persuasively by Mark Skinner Watson, the late military editor of the Baltimore Sunpapers, in his authoritative book, *Chief of Staff.* They can be demolished conclusively on the evidence of the German documents and the interrogation of the principals involved in the aftermath of this fantastic incident.

This was the sequence of events that followed:

In the early afternoon, General von Boetticher received the material in an unmarked envelope, but with elaborate comments by Alford Williams based on his own intimate knowledge of the program.

At 4:05 P.M. Chargé d'affaires Thomsen sent a long cable to the Foreign Ministry in Berlin, summarizing the Manly article.

"This secret report," Thomsen wrote, "is doubtlessly an authentic *war plan* drawn up at Roosevelt's request. It probably served as the reason for the special Cabinet meeting about which I reported in my No. 3545, of October 14."

At 4:36 P.M. General von Boetticher cabled his more detailed report to the German High Command. And one of Karl Eitel's Spanish couriers was contacted to take a copy of Manly's notes and Wheeler's transcript to Germany.

The salient intelligence features of Boetticher's summary were as follows:

1. American combat power was not to be expected before July 1943 the earliest.

2. Germany can be subdued only by an American expeditionary force of several million men.

3. To activate, arm, and transport such a force would require enormous sums of money and would be a serious shock to the American economy.

4. The thesis that Germany could be starved into defeat was refuted; and the American propaganda theme that Roosevelt merely wanted to do away with the "Nazi regime" was demolished.

5. Military measures against Japan would be by necessity of a defensive character.

6. In the event of a two-ocean war, America would make its main offensive effort in the direction of Europe and Africa.

7. The elimination of the Soviet Union and the collapse of the British Empire by the summer of 1942 was taken seriously and regarded as a distinct possibility.

In Berlin, the information was regarded as having "the most profound intelligence value conceivable, enabling [the German High Command] to adapt [its] arrangements to the American program." The planning staffs at Fuehrer Headquarters were called in and instructed by General Alfred Jodl, Hitler's chief of staff, to examine and, if necessary, revise existing German plans "in the light of the incontrovertible intelligence that had become available."

It was a fantastic coup scored by the Germans—without any Abwehr spies, without Boetticher exerting himself too much—by the strange interpretation of "patriotic duty" by a captain in the American armed forces.

This was Thursday, December 4, 1941, two days before Pearl Harbor.

The Embassy in Washington had also supervised brisk espionage and sabotage operations which had spread to all parts of America like the spokes of a wheel.

In the fall of 1941, beset by a series of setbacks his organization had suffered in the United States, Admiral Canaris formally complained to Field Marshal Keitel, his superior in OKW, that his difficulties were due largely to the hostility of the German diplomats there. Keitel took the matter to Foreign Minister von Ribbentrop who, afraid that the complaint might reach Hitler and redound to his own disadvantage, ordered an investigation.

By then the American government had ordered the closing of the German consulates, and the consuls were back in Germany. One by one, on Ribbentrop's orders, they wrote out long accounts of their close and wholehearted cooperation with the Abwehr. Their stories presented a picture of widespread espionage under consular protection. Their memoranda, composed in two separate sets, were captured during the closing weeks of the war. The following is the first published account based on their revelations.

The Germans maintained a large number of honorary consulates throughout the United States as well as regular consular missions as Consulates General in major cities.

The Consulate General at 17 Battery Place in downtown Manhattan was suspected as a den of subversion but even in the fall of 1945, Consul General Heinrich Franz Johannes Borchers told W. Wendell Blancke, his American interrogator at the elite Oberursel prison camp, that his consulate in New York "neither spied nor propagandized." If his office had any live connection with the Abwehr, he personally knew nothing of it.

This disclaimer sounded hollow in the face of hundreds of messages involving espionage (and even some sabotage) that passed between the consulate in New York and the Abwehr via the Foreign Ministry's liaison office. All of them were signed, "Borchers." Of course such dispatches are always sent out over the signature of the mission chief, whether or not he actually sent them or was familiar with their contents.

If Borchers himself was not acting as a spymaster, others in his office were—practically his entire staff. The consulate performed a dual function—it was a base of operations for the Abwehr under a young consul named Siegfried Lurtz, and headquarters of Nazi espionage and propaganda under consul Friedhelm Draeger.

Among the agents Lurtz listed as having received support from him at the consulate were Count Douglas, "Duenser," Walter Koehler and "a V-man planted at E. Leitz Inc. in New York,'" the firm that made the Leica camera. He also acknowledged that he regularly "serviced" the agent named "Rehmel" already mentioned as the chief coast watcher for the Naval Attaché. More than that, Lurtz boasted that he had recruited "several longshoremen in New York and a lieutenant of the Royal Canadian Navy" to work for Rehmel, supplying "invaluable intelligence about the routing of convoys."

Not mentioned by Lurtz, but brought to light by other documents, were even more important agents. The saboteur Hausberger was one of them. Fred Ludwig, head of the potentially most dangerous ring of German spies in the United States, was another. Both received their funds from Lurtz and used his cable facilities for their reports.

Lurtz was a first-rate spymaster of his own, responsible for at least three major contributions to the Abwehr. Quite early in his lucrative career as a manager of agents, he recruited two men working at the Sikorsky aircraft plant on Long Island, and obtained from them, among other things, samples of aluminum and what he called "special alloys" (*spezial-legierungen*) used in the making of fuselage, empennage, wings, and engine mounts.

He also made "a very profitable deal" with an American engineer who, as Lurtz phrased it, "proved to my satisfaction that he was intimately familiar with the British aviation industry, and thanks to his influential position in America had entry into all aircraft factories in the United States and was personally acquainted with leading managerial figures in the aviation industry." Paying the man $500 a month he received from him "information that could not have been obtained otherwise." The engineer once gave him "the original blueprints of a fighter plane as it had been drawn by its designers at the factory that was producing it."

Lurtz found for the Abwehr "an American pilot ferrying warplanes to England." For such sums as $30 to $50 at a time, the man, a native American from a New England state, sold him "tabulations showing the times postulated for flights, maps, and the so-called flight orders issued to the pilots."

When Germany had to close their Consulates, Lurtz transferred his contacts to the Military Attaché in Washington who remained in the United States, though on borrowed time.

With Lurtz went Draeger, who did for the Nazis what Lurtz did for the Abwehr; Theodore von Knoop, who specialized in economic intelligence; and a romantic figure in Lurtz's office, destined to die as a spy. In 1943, this man was chosen to come back by U-boat and act here as a radio spy. The mission was aborted when the U-boat was hit by a bomb dropped from an American plane in the west Atlantic and sent to the bottom with its entire crew as well as the hapless tourist.

In New England, the espionage foothold was Boston, under the debonair SS-man Herbert Scholz who had started the ball rolling by enlisting Miss Fahrney as early as January 1938. He blossomed out as a full-fledged spymaster after his transfer to the banks of the Charles River. Instantly popular, he succeeded in fooling even such an authentic liberal as Edward Weeks, the distinguished editor of the *Atlantic Monthly*. Scholz sneaked into the *Atlantic* an article, entitled "Germany and World Trade After the War," that took for granted that Germany had already won the war.

It was published under the by-line of a German industrialist, Dr. Georg von Schnitzler, member of the board of directors of I. G. Farben who happened to be Scholz's own father-in-law. Unknown to Mr. Weeks, and, for that matter, to the readers of the highly respected, influential journal, the article had been concocted in the German Propaganda Ministry. On January 23, 1940, the Foreign Ministry sent the English translation of the essay to the Embassy in Washington, with a confidential note requesting Dr. Thomsen to forward it to Scholz who would then submit it to "Herr" Weeks "through an appropriate V-man." The article was published in the June issue of the magazine.

Soon after his arrival Dr. Scholz had a widespread net of confidential informants. After the outbreak of the war in Europe, he branched out into sabotage, by establishing contact with men who claimed to be members of the Irish Republican Army's branch in the United States.

The plan was to sink or damage ships in Boston harbor, and to destroy warehouses holding supplies consigned for England. A considerable number of marine accidents occurred at this time, and the Irishmen insisted that they had been the perpetrators. With a single notable exception—the sinking of a freighter in the Charles River—these seemingly wanton acts were mere fragments of the men's imagination, "perpetrated," if that is the right word, to coax money from Dr. Scholz. However, his reports to Berlin were resplendent with lurid accounts of these outrages, repeating the colorful description of the explosions exactly as related to him by his Irish friends.

This mixed activity—the diplomat out front and the master saboteur behind the scenes—lasted until October 15, 1940, when the consul was tipped off that he was in trouble. One of his informants was an American reserve officer attached to the Intelligence Office at the First Naval District in Boston. He warned Scholz that serious charges were being prepared against him, based on a sworn statement given the FBI by a crew member of the *Columbus*, bottled up in U.S. waters by the British blockade, which the consul used as a supply base in his sabotage operations. Moreover, his American friend told him, another witness—a former counsellor of the German Embassy,

Dr. W. Ernst Meyer—was supposed to have identified him as the chief of the Gestapo in the United States.

Scholz reported this ominous development to his friend Himmler and asked the *Reichsfuehrer*-SS what to do when the charges were formally pressed. In great panic, Thomsen in Washington advised the Foreign Ministry to recall Scholz before the case broke open.

Himmler ordered Scholz to deny everything and stand pat. Scholz's indignant denials and disclaimers filled whole columns in the Boston newspapers. He left only in July 1941, going home with the other consuls, and was rewarded with an assignment as counsellor to the embassy in Rome, this time to spy on the Italians.

Publicly both the embassy and the consulates steadfastly and vigorously denied that they ever participated in any activity that even remotely resembled espionage and sabotage. After the war consuls like Johannes Borchers, Captain Fritz Wiedemann, and Carl Windels protested indignantly that they never had anything to do with any such activities.

This was correct only in the case of Windels. As far as it could be ascertained, neither he personally nor anybody on his staff engaged in espionage either in Canada or in Philadelphia, where he served as consul general. The closest he came to such an involvement in the game occurred in 1940, when he was contacted by the chief V-man the Abwehr had in the Philadelphia region, one of the most energetic and productive agents in the United States.

He was the Rev. Kurt E. B. Molzahn, a Lutheran clergyman, who worked for the Third Reich on two levels—aboveground as a shrill propagandist and underground as the sub-agent of R.2601, a New Yorker named Guenther Orgell, traveling organizer of the Bremen branch in the eastern United States. Molzahn had recruited several V-men for the Abwehr and, after the outbreak of the war in September 1939, he worked as a producing spy under registry No. 2320.

By July 1940, Molzahn felt strong enough to divorce himself from Orgell and establish himself as the manager of his own ring. What he needed was money and a line of communication. He demanded that Windels finance his operation "with a subsidy of several thousand dollars," and find for him "a reliable radio technician" to establish "a secret wireless connection with Germany."

Rev. Molzahn was notorious for his Nazi activities and, by then, German representatives in the United States had a standing order to avoid all contacts with branded Bundists, so Windels refused Molzahn's demands.

In Chicago, a consul named Krause-Wichmann functioned merrily as a spy executive with jurisdiction in the Midwest. Several Abwehr and SD agents—including the notorious Otto Willumeit of Chicago

—enjoyed his support. Wichmann himself developed at least one secret agent who regularly reported "the place and time of the departure of American bombers for England."

Consul General Carl Kapp of Cleveland ran what amounted to a branch of the Abwehr as early as the fall of 1938, when one of Canaris's traveling salesmen sold him the plan. He was given a list of items in which "the OKW was especially interested." It enumerated factories of "special military significance," mostly those which produced "aluminum, magnesium, and rubber, essential for the production of aircraft."

Kapp boasted that half of his staff was engaged in the collection of confidential information about those plants, and that he went out of his way to procure intelligence data from his own numerous contacts in Ohio. He hired several agents and set them up in Canada, going and coming by way of Detroit. They supplied "a great number of up-to-date Canadian newspapers, the careful reading of which yielded important information, and also furnished original material that could not be published because of censorship."

In the summer of 1940, Consul Kapp intensified his secret collaboration with the Abwehr, procuring "invaluable information that was not otherwise or normally available about new factories and older ones in the process of being converted to the production of engines, tanks, ammunition, chemicals, machines, and machine tools." He once made an extra special effort to infiltrate the civil defense system in the Cleveland area, and to probe developments in chemical warfare, even succeeding in procuring a novel type of GI gas mask one of his agents stole.

So voluminous was his output that Kapp sent out a shipment each evening via the diplomatic pouch from Washington.

Georg Gyssling, the consul general of Los Angeles, had acquired some notoriety as the rabid Nazi district leader *(Kreisleiter)* for California. Gyssling ran one of the most active espionage outposts. He processed a senior agent named Eugen Lahr from Abwehr headquarters in Berlin, who arrived in Los Angeles via Japan in 1940, in the guise of a correspondent for the *Muenchner Neueste Nachrichten*, to collect high-grade intelligence along the West Coast which Canaris's Japanese business partners were clamoring for.

Lahr needed a cover, money, guidance, a safe house, and a line of communication, and Gyssling supplied it all. The agent managed to stay in the United States through the Democratic and Republican political conventions, then returned to Germany, his presence in this country revealed here for the first time.

Gyssling also took care of a man named Carl Riedel, for whom the Abwehr had big plans on the West Coast and hoped to establish as the resident director of a ring covering the area from San Diego to Seattle, though he could hardly speak English. Riedel was not as lucky as Lahr. When he had reason to suspect that the FBI was on his trail, Gyssling arranged his sudden escape, and even paid for his girl friend's trip as far as Mexico.

After Riedel's departure, Gyssling scouted for a replacement and found a man named Klinge to specialize, even as Riedel did, in the rapidly growing aircraft industry in California. Klinge proved a vast improvement over Riedel. At least he could speak English. And while Riedel was a drunkard and a womanizer, financing his escapades with Gyssling's unvouchered funds, Klinge seemed clean-living, hardworking, and fully dedicated.

In northern California, the spy business flourished at first under Consul General Manfred von Killinger, a high-ranking Saxon Nazi and SA commander, also a *Kreisleiter* for the West Coast. He was, indeed, the most rabid Party man ever accredited as a diplomat in this country. He worked closely with George E. Deatherage of the American Nationalist Confederation who was later under indictment for sedition; and used a White Russian adventurer to organize a kind of free corps of hoodlums to conduct sabotage "when the time was ripe."

Killinger was recalled because he was needed in Rumania to soften up that Balkan country for easy conquest. Captain Fritz Wiedemann, Hitler's company commander in World War I and later one of the Fuehrer's adjutants, was appointed his successor.

Under the mild-mannered, petit bourgeois Wiedemann the conspiracies von Killinger had promoted with such gusto gradually subsided, and San Francisco lost its importance as an espionage base. A handful of agents still remained in the area, tied to his consulate by the familiar umbilical cord—money and communications.

Wiedemann's sideline was exposed in August 1940, when an Abwehr agent identified as E. Wolff was caught in the Canal Zone with spy material in the false bottom of his suitcase. Actually, Wiedemann was an innocent bystander in this case. Wolff had been his ward only in transit through San Francisco. He was an Abwehr courier taking a set of new codes and ciphers to German agents in Buenos Aires on the long Pacific route, making the trip by way of San Francisco on a Japanese ship.

Wolff's arrest mortified Wiedemann. He begged the Foreign Ministry to save him from such embarrassments in the future. But while he was not plotting for the Nazis, he was knee-deep in a quaint conspiracy against them.

On December 11, in a totally unexpected gesture to his Axis ally and contrary to his stated policy, Adolf Hitler, whose shivering divisions were spending their first winter along a 2000-mile front in Russia, declared his own war against the United States.

From coast to coast FBI agents descended on enemy aliens. By the week's end, 1002 Germans were in custody, picked out of a secret list of suspected spies and saboteurs. The authorities in Norfolk, Virginia, did not even wait to hear from the FBI. At the news of Pearl Harbor, they rounded up every Japanese they could find and clapped them in jail.

That left only 1,124,000 Germans, Italians, and Japanese at large —among them two of the Abwehr's top spies who had escaped Tramp's trap.

One of them was a resident of New York City. The other lived in Norfolk, Virginia.

NOTE

1 Woehler headed what was called the *H-Dienst* or *Hafendienst* (Harbor Service), the special organization of coast watchers. This was the best-organized and widest-spread maritime spy organization in North and Central America operating with observers at Tampico (three men), Vera Cruz (three men), La Paz (one man), Acapulco (one man), Puerto Angel (a maritime agency), Salina Cruz (one man), and of course Mazatlán where Woehler had two accomplices.

Chapter 41

After the Fall

*T*HE obscure man the FBI missed in New York was my favorite German spy of World War II, because he seemed to be that rare specimen—the perfect secret agent. I stumbled upon him in the Abwehr papers early during my quest, identified only by his registration number—"A.2011."

Numbers alone did not tell much in the Abwehr. They were mere administrative symbols. In this case, the prefix "A" indicated that he was one of the regulars, a professional. The "2" in "2011" meant that he worked for the Bremen subbranch; and "011" showed his place in the registry, the low number indicating that he was an early bird.

But his file told a lot, by the sheer size and diversity of material it contained. His folders were among the bulkiest of all agents who worked in the United States; his field of inquiry seemed to have been the most catholic; and his life span as a producer, the longest.

He impressed me with his apparent guile, with the ingenuity he displayed in procuring some of the hardest to get items with the softest of touch, and with his resourcefulness in covering up his trail. I was able to follow his movements practically from day to day.

At last, when I was more than two years at it, having scanned thousands of frames of microfilm of secret documents, I hit upon my first clue to the identity of the man from a single line in the fiscal records of the Bremen subbranch which I found intact among the uncatalogued papers. It was a $200 item, listed as the "monthly stipend" paid to an agent in the Abwehr ledger. Behind the number "A.2011" the paymaster in Bremen added in parantheses, with the pedantry of the conscientious accountant, the word "Koedel" that could have been either his name or his pseudonym.

492

The search for "A.2011" was over. Now the quest for "Koedel" began.

All official inquiries failed (the FBI and the CIC refrained from cooperating), and a dozen contacts in the United States and Germany could not illuminate the mystery. I found him at last where I should have looked from the start, in the morgue of *The New York Times.*

In a long discarded folder from the warehouse, I discovered a single clipping, dated October 24, 1944, announcing the arrest of a German spy named *Simon Emil Koedel*. Suddenly, the vague spirit assumed bodily form, the arcane shadow became a man, with Christian names, a family and friends, a past, and several addresses in the United States.

Now I learned that Koedel was an old-timer, sixty-two years of age at the time of his arrest, born in Wuerzburg, Germany. He had come to this country on April 4, 1906, and had become an American citizen six years later; served in the Army attaining the splendiferous rank of corporal; was separated from his native American wife Anna, and had a foster daughter, Hedwig Marie, a 26-year-old comely brunette.

The clipping contained little to enlighten the dark area of his life except to state that the FBI had arrested him at dawn on October 23, 1944, in a rooming house at Harpers Ferry, West Virginia, where he had recently taken a job as a motion-picture projectionist.

The story in *The Times* was a stunning find nevertheless, not for what it said but for what it left untold. The Bureau charged him with "conspiracy to commit espionage . . . between October 1, 1939, and October 25, 1941." The record I found in the Abwehr's files revealed that he was at the game from the spring of 1936 to 1943, and probably longer.

The complaint filed upon his arrest accused him of acting as a coast watcher, and cited a single overt act against him, his attempt to observe the loading of lend-lease supplies on a ship at the teeming Busch Terminal in Brooklyn, on October 9, 1941. But I knew that he was a one-man general store of espionage, whose interest encompassed everything from Washington politics to the manufacture of arms, and whose observations ranged from the United States Army's Chemical Warfare Center in Bel Air, Maryland (which he reconnoitered in his own name and overtly) to the Army's motion picture establishment in Queens, Long Island, (where he procured classified training films, and movies showing tanks, ships, all sorts of equipment, and the confidential testing of new weapons).

The indictment did not connect him with the Abwehr. It failed to mention that any of his intelligence ever reached Berlin. Yet among his papers, I found in excess of six-hundred reports forwarded by him.

There were just two bits of incidental information that added to my knowledge of the case. As I related before when describing the careless bravado of German agents in the United States, one spy had the temerity to write an abusive letter to an American general, and another spy felt so immune that he tried to enlist the bootblack of a Staten Island ferry. Now I learned that Koedel was the man in both incidents. He had written to Major General Morris B. Payne of the 43rd Division, Connecticut National Guard, assuring him that Germany was certain to win the war no matter what the United States did, because, he fulminated, the average American was "a double-crosser, a chronic draft dodger and crooked at heart" and "carried these qualities into the Army."

It was Koedel who had made the offer to Carmine d'Andrea, the shoeshine man on the Staten Island ferry. After observing Koedel as he watched the traffic of ships through powerful binoculars, d'Andrea once asked him why he was taking notes. "I'm sending them to Germany," Koedel told him bluntly, then asked the bootblack to do for Italy what he was doing.

Koedel continued to have his shoes shined on the ferry by d'Andrea for some time afterward, for it was five years later—on February 10, 1940—before the bootblack came out with the anecdote.

When Koedel realized how little the Americans knew about his secret past, he quickly pleaded guilty. He expected lenient treatment if charged merely with a minor trespass of the Espionage Act. On March 1, 1945—when the war in Europe had only ten more weeks to run—he was convicted on the charge of "conspiracy to commit espionage," and sentenced to fifteen years in the penitentiary at Milan, Michigan.

I have not the slightest doubt that Simon Koedel was the best all-round spy the Abwehr had in the United States—in *two* world wars. The story of "A.2011" began, not in 1937, as his Abwehr record showed; not in the fall of 1939, as the FBI asserted; but in 1915, when this ex-corporal of the United States Army became a captain in the German army, stationed in the United States as a spy.

His clandestine career in World War I began not too auspiciously. After a brief span of watching ships come and go in New York harbor, Koedel could not resist the lure of the sea. He suggested that he be sent to England—a cinch on his American passport—to collect military intelligence. But when he reached Southampton he was met by a reception committee of detectives from the Special Branch, who had been tipped off by MI.5 whose agents in America had spotted him at his new pastime. The British did not have enough on Koedel to take him into court, so they merely deported him back to the United States. After that he somehow managed to reach Germany again, where, with his rank of captain at last made official, he worked in intelligence. So well did he manage to hide his crooked trail that he remained an American citizen in good standing, even when he joined Hitler's new crop of intelligence officers.

Showing up at the Bremen subbranch of the Abwehr in 1936, he again volunteered his services in the United States. He was referred to Johannes Bischoff, the dubious cotton merchant with one foot firmly in the Abwehr, already engaged in constructing the global network that became the legendary CHB network of fifteen first-grade agents on whom the sun never set. They were developed specifically against the "Anglo-Saxons" to be stationed in every part of the British Empire from Northern Ireland to Australia.

Bischoff picked Koedel (listed as "CHB-7" in his special roster), confident that the old pro would do the job of a whole ring in the United States all by himself. One by one, Koedel was introduced to all the luminaries of the Bremen outpost—to the ubiquitous Niko Bensmann (who later shared control of him with Bischoff), and other "Anglo-Saxon" specialists.

He also made the acquaintance of a certain R. A. Hambourg of Milan, Italy, whose home at 46 Via Gran Sasso was designated as his mail drop. And he met another American citizen, a certain Waldemar Othmer from Trenton, New Jersey. In training under Bischoff and Bensmann, Othmer was slated to act eventually as Koedel's back-up man, to watch the Eastern Seaboard between Baltimore and Cape Hatteras from Norfolk, Virginia, which was to be his base of operations. Koedel arrived in the United States early in 1937, rented a large apartment on Riverside Drive in Manhattan, and went about his operations boldly, on a substantial scale. Although he was paid only $200 a month as his regular salary, Bischoff was giving him a big allowance, enabling him to put up a front of respectability and affluence. He needed it as part of the scheme he devised to worm his way to the innermost secrets of the American defense industry and the War Department itself.

He had hit upon the idea of applying for membership in the American Ordnance Association, a semi-official, quasi-confidential trade organization of armament and munitions makers which was practically a branch of the War Department's Ordnance.

In his letter of application he told L. A. Codd, secretary of the AOA, that he was a chemical engineer by profession and a large stockholder in such defense industries as Sperry Gyroscope, Curtiss-Wright, and a number of factories making ammunition. He enclosed his Army discharge papers, and though they dated back to 1909, they duly impressed Secretary Codd. "You can be justly proud of your service to our country," he wrote in the letter returning the dog-eared yellowing papers. "Take good care of them!"

He was accepted without a hitch in AOA, enjoying all the privileges that membership in this organization entailed. He was placed on the War Department's confidential mailing list for all releases involving ordnance, a gold mine for a spy. These publications, although not explicitly classified, contained much that was confidential. He was given free entry to all meetings of the AOA, including those held behind closed doors, and permitted to listen to lectures and the discussions of all phases of the entire American weapon system. By simply showing his AOA membership card, he was allowed to visit any defense plant in the United States, both privately and government owned.

Even in 1937–38, when security was still woefully lax in the United States, this represented a remarkable accomplishment, virtually assuring success for Koedel. The AOA was considered so sensitive an organization that it was constantly "monitored" by the FBI for attempted espionage. Membership in it required screening and clearance by the Bureau, but nothing indicates that his World War I spying had been investigated at all before taken into the AOA.

Koedel broadened the base of his operations by writing letters (on the stationery of the American Ordnance Association) to the chairmen of the military and naval affairs committees in both houses of Congress. Again introducing himself as an investor with considerable stake in the American defense industry, he invited their aid and cooperation "in the interest of our nation's preparedness and security."

He struck pay dirt with the letter he wrote to Senator Robert Rice Reynolds, member (later chairman) of the Senate's Military Affairs Committee. So impressed was the gentleman from North Carolina with the fervor and concern of this sincere patriot that he invited Koedel to call on him personally in Washington. Koedel's visit in the Senate Office Building the following week began the enormously profitable friendship that was to last for years.

The shrewd process of building his sources and establishing his *bona fides* continued unabated. In the effort to establish himself as a trusted citizen, he wrote to Mr. Codd, editor of AOA's journal, objecting to an article which had recently appeared, complaining that it revealed too much. From time to time he would send recommendations to the AOA on how to improve security measures in defense plants. Once he reproached the War Department for too great laxity in protecting its secrets in the private sector—offering recommendations to tighten security each time he himself visited one of the plants whose deficiency displeased him.

Simon Koedel nevertheless remained a "sleeper," standing by for activation on a moment's notice. The call came on September 5, 1939, in a cable from Bischoff with the prearranged code word "Alloy" in the text and the name "Hartmann" used as the signature. It was the combination "Alloy-Hartmann" that told him to start spying.

By now a lean, sinewy, gray-haired, smooth-skinned man with thin lips and piggish little eyes, Koedel looked as hard and cold as he actually was. A sense of humor was not among his traits. That very day he made his first inspection trip on the Thirty-ninth Street ferry to Staten Island, a trial run to ascertain how much he could observe of the stores piled high on the Fort Hamilton docks. He had with him his foster daughter Marie, just turned twenty, a doe-eyed creature whose girlish figure was just filling out. She was also fast becoming the "Waterfront Mata Hari," the title which Koedel would later coin for her in one of his rare light moments.

He was training Marie in the art of spying on ships and docks from ferry boats, taking her to taverns frequented by merchant seamen to let herself be picked up so she could pry shipping secrets from them. Simon Koedel was a harsh disciplinarian, a demanding, short-tempered parent. He would slap her in the face at the slightest provocation and beat her with his leather belt whenever she happened to be a few minutes late coming home from her dates. Afraid of her foster father, Marie meekly did as she was told.

Koedel's vigil on the river, loitering in waterfront bars with an ear bent for unguarded talk was part of the job but humdrum and tedious. Koedel was made for greater things. His first opportunity to send to Bremen better stuff than bare reports about docks and transient ships came just after the outbreak of the European war. On November 11, the American Ordnance Association invited him to attend a hush-hush lecture about the infantry rifle issued to the British Expeditionary Force in France. An ordnance colonel of the North-Humberland Regiment spoke freely, demonstrating the rifle, and answered probing questions about the equipment of British infantrymen.

That same night, Koedel sent to Bremen his first solid intelligence report. Before the year was out, he would forward scores of such reports, including two of the most remarkable scoops of his entire career.

For some occult reason, chemical warfare has always held a special fascination for spies. Mystery shrouded and controversial, it provokes their liveliest imagination. I recall that during World War II, we were inundated in ONI with highly-rated intelligence reports from the Polish secret service dealing with poison gases whose use in action was invariably described as "imminent."

Koedel, too, was fascinated by the spectre of chemical warfare, but he was a sensible, responsible spy. Instead of concocting scare reports about this bugaboo of modern warfare, he decided to inspect the Edgewood Arsenal, where the United States Army had its Chemical Warfare Center, and give Bremen the indisputable facts.

Twice in November 1939 he tried to gain entry by simply walking up to the sentries at the gate, showing them his membership card in the AOA, and demanding ingress. Twice he was turned away. Undaunted, he phoned the Association's headquarters in Washington and entered a formal complaint about his exclusion from Edgewood. They phoned the War Department and obtained permission for this distinguished member in excellent standing to visit the Arsenal.

When he arrived at Bel Air on the morning of December 7, he was given the red carpet treatment. The description of the tour he sent to Bischoff afterward left nothing in question. He even included in his reports labels he had stealthily peeled off boxes loaded on railroad cars, one of them reading: "*25 Hand Grenades—Irritant M 7—Fuse M 200—Gas.*" His report also contained a potentially useful tip for Bischoff to follow up. "The major suppliers of the Arsenal are Baker in Philipsburg, the General Chemical Co., and a factory in Lodi, New Jersey. However, its biggest source of raw material is the firm Eimer & Amend, located between 18th and 19th Streets on Third Avenue in New York, controlled by German-American interests. Penetration probably possible."

His long report, sent from a hotel in Havre de Grace, Maryland, where he stayed during this trip, gave a mass of scientific and technical data, statistics of the storage facilities, and information about some of the latest development in the laboratories—by courtesy of the United States Army.

Koedel's other coup concerned the *Admiral Graf Spee*, blown up on order of its captain in Montevideo harbor as the result of crippling damage inflicted upon her by Commodore Henry Harwood's lightly armed British cruisers, and by the concentration of superior British forces that bottled her up. The Battle of the River Plate that led to the *Spee*'s demise had completely unnerved Hitler. He demanded to know every minute detail of the action, and urgent orders were sent to Captain Dietrich Niebuhr, the Abwehr's chief of naval intelligence in Buenos Aires, to forward at once every scrap of information.

Niebuhr's hastily compiled report failed to satisfy the irate Fuehrer. Then a dispatch arrived that answered every question Hitler was asking, and some that did not occur to him.

It came from Koedel! How did he get it?

In the immediate wake of the battle, the American Ordnance Association was designated by the authorities to conduct an investigation of the circumstances of the *Spee*'s destruction. A special delegation of experts was sent to Montevideo to undertake an investigation on the spot. It was their final report which Koedel managed to procure by virtue of his membership in AOA that eventually told Hitler the whole grim story, enabling him to assess the humiliating disaster in the light of irrefutable facts.

Koedel's industry in collecting his data and his ingenuity in getting them to Bremen knew no bounds. As usual with Abwehr agents overseas, communication with his home office was his biggest problem. Waterfront intelligence was highly perishable. Data about the departure of eastward bound ships singly or in convoys had to be flashed to Germany to guide marauding U-boats and surface raiders. For this, and this alone, Koedel was allowed to use the cable facilities and the code of the German Consulate in New York. Otherwise he was restricted to slow-moving mail, subject to all the vicissitudes of wartime conditions, especially the vigilance of British censorship.

When the censors in Bermuda threatened to put an end to the flow of his reports, Koedel found a way that effectively circumvented them. Several times each week, he was receiving War Department information designed for privileged members of the AOA who had to be kept abreast of developments. It arrived in large Manila envelopes marked "Official Business," addressed to "Mr. Simon E. Koedel, 660 Riverside Drive, New York, N.Y."

Koedel steamed open the envelopes, added to their contents his own reports, resealed them. Then he crossed out his name and address, and substituted those of his mail drop in Milan, on the assumption that such official-looking letters in envelopes marked "War Department, Washington, D.C." would pass the censor unmolested.

He proved absolutely right. Every one of these particular letters wound up on the desk of Dr. Bensmann in Bremen. In this manner the Abwher was receiving, not only its agent's own reports, but the confidential releases of the War Department, virtually straight from their original source in Washington. Never in the history of espionage was a secret service serviced directly by the victim it was spying on.

His methods for procuring guarded information were nothing short of breathtaking. In late March 1940, when the Germans were concluding their campaign plans against France, they found themselves hampered by the absence of certain information. They had little if anything on the strategic French ports of Nantes, La Rochelle, and La Pallice. Anxious to ascertain whether these ports could handle ships other than tankers and colliers, the Abwehr was asked to query its agents on this score. A round robin was sent out quickly. Koedel was included among the addressees—but how could a chemist in New York get hold of such data?

He solved the problem in a manner that, after the highly gratifying results of the first such attempt, became his standard procedure in such cases. He contacted his friend, Senator Reynolds in Washington, explained that he needed the data to make arrangements for the shipment of supplies to France, and asked the chairman of the Senate Military Affairs Committee to get the information for him. Helpful as ever, he suggested that the United States Maritime Commission might be the best place to inquire.

Senator Reynolds promptly wrote to the Commission on his official stationery. Thanks to his request, Koedel was able to inform Bremen on April 9 that "according to the U.S. Maritime Commission, these ports are not limited in their facilities, but are capable of handling ships loading oil and coal, as well as general cargo."

To the letter which Reynolds received from the Commission in reply to his query, the original of which he forwarded to Koedel in New York, the helpful Senator appended a little personal note: "Glad I was able to help." The cover of the folder into which Koedel's report was put in Bremen carried this interesting notation: "Owing to the current uncertainty of mail going by Clipper, agent, in a praiseworthy manner, forwarded this urgent report via the Naval Attaché in Washington, using his M cipher. He sent a duplicate to another mail drop with which British censorship is apparently unfamiliar."

Thanks to the help Koedel was getting from his friend on Capitol Hill, he scored a number of such scoops. He thus regularly obtained through the Reynolds office a confidential weekly report issued by the Munitions Board of the State Department enumerating permits granted for the export of war material to England.

In August, a cryptic message from Bischoff queried Koedel about the apparently mysterious voyage of the U.S. Army transport *American Legion* from Petsamo in Finland to New York. The Abwehr was intrigued on two grounds. First, the ship had ignored German warnings and sailed through supposedly mine-infested waters in the war zone. It was assumed, therefore, that she must have been familiar with the pattern of the minefields. Second, it had made an unscheduled stop in a Scottish port, probably to take aboard a passenger or passengers whose identity the Abwehr was curious to find out. Could Koedel obtain the passenger list of the *American Legion*?

At the spy's request, Senator Reynolds wrote to the State and War Departments demanding that his Committee be furnished with the list. The State Department fielded the request, referring Reynolds to the "proper authorities." The War Department declined to make the list available. Koedel refused to give up. He persuaded the Senator to insist that the passenger list be released to him, and the War Department complied. It took some time to straighten out things. But the success of Koedel's efforts was clearly indicated by a report sent to Bremen on December 4, 1940, in which he was able to assure the Abwehr that "no passengers boarded the ship in the Scottish port where the *American Legion* made an unscheduled stop."

In the meantime, Marie Koedel was covering the waterfront. She had no choice. Whenever she balked at harbor snooping or squeezing information from her growing collection of talkative boyfriends in the merchant marine, her foster father would beat her mercilessly. For all her apparent second thoughts, Marie had become extremely proficient in assembling information. From one of her daily trips to Staten Island, for example, she returned with enough data to enable Koedel to send the following typical fact-studded report to Bremen on January 3, 1940, via a courier traveling on the steamship *Saturnia*:

> Hamilton Dock in Brooklyn the Finnish ship *Wilja*, loading general cargo.
> Norwegian ship *Berganger* loading great quantity of iron poles, approximate length 20-30 feet, in addition to other cargo.
> Massive supplies piled up on Hamilton Dock, waiting to be loaded on just-arrived *Protopapa*, due to sail for Liverpool; *Emmy* and *Adamas*, bound for Le Havre. According to inscriptions on crates, supplies originated with following firms: Sundsbrand Machine Tool Co. of Rockford, Illinois, shipment consigned to Burton Fils. at 68 Rue de Marais in Paris, each crate weighing 2 to 3 tons; 100 black-painted metal barrels containing Sadonia oil, to be loaded on *Emmy* for F.A.H. Co., Ltd. in London; U.S. Navigation Co., 17 Battery Place, to Hubert Davies Co. Ltd. in Johannesburg, South Africa via Port Elizabeth.

Marie's boyfriends made it possible for her foster father to prepare two enormously important reports for the German Navy. One was entitled: "Report Concerning American Ships Inspected by England on Suspicion of Contraband." The other, probably the most valuable intelligence he would ever send, was called: "Report on the Conduct of Enemy Ships in Convoy at Sea in the Atlantic, Based on Conversations with British Seamen." The latter included interrogation of one British sailor who had jumped ship in New York and offered his services to the Abwehr through Koedel.

He was Duncan Alexander Croall Scott-Ford. Taken into the fold at Koedel's recommendation, he worked for the Abwehr's shipping expert in Portugal, where Ford was eventually entrapped by British counterspies working under the supervision of Kim Philby. Spirited to England by a ruse, he was arrested and ended on the gallows only a few months after he had made Koedel's fatal acquaintance.

Shortlived though his career was, Ford proved to be a most dangerous spy in the brief span of his collaboration. Revealing convoy routings, he enabled U-boats to ambush the ships. The records of MI.5, which are rather stingy with praise of German spies, accorded Ford the dubious distinction of being the spy who did the greatest damage to British shipping in the whole war.

Simon Koedel continued snooping with his magic wand, the membership card of the AOA. In September 1940, he inspected the U.S. Arsenal in Waterfleet, New York, which was then making guns for Fort Monroe on Chesapeake Bay, Fort Moultrie in South Carolina, and Fort Hancock in Massachusetts. In April 1941, after visiting a factory manufacturing new types of military explosives at Radford, Virginia, he forwarded a set of five photographs of the installation with his detailed report. Two more such factories were later added to his list, one at Charlestown, Indiana, the other at Childersburg, Alabama.

Even a partial list of his targets would fill pages: such as new speedboats of the Navy, the cruiser USS *Tuscaloosa*, the defenses of the Caribbean. In 1941, Koedel was hitting his stride. On May 17, Johannes Bischoff notified him that the Fuehrer had been pleased to promote him to major.

After March 11, 1940, the reports of another agent were filed with Koedel's in Bremen, indicating that he had acquired a full-fledged colleague rather than just another stringer.

The agent was listed as "A.2018," and I had as much trouble as with Koedel in making him emerge in the flesh. After almost a year of searching, I found the critical clue to his identity in the log of the Bremen subbranch. A laconic entry dated January 25, 1940, stated: "Othmer sends postcards from Brooklyn signaling arrival in USA." Then another notation. "In long letter from Brooklyn, A.2018 reports via mail drop, describing his trip to the USA." "A.2018" was "Othmer." A search for this name revealed that, during the Thirties, Waldemar Othmer was leader of the German-American Bund in Trenton, New Jersey, collaborating closely with Gerhard Wilhelm Kunze and the Rev. Molzahn of Philadelphia, two Nazis identified long before as agents of the Abwehr.

Othmer was never as faceless as Koedel. Born in the mountainous Harz region in Saxony in 1909, he immigrated to the United States in 1919, and was naturalized in Trenton on April 13, 1935. One day later, he joined the Bund and became the local "Fuehrer" in Trenton before the year was out.

His Nazi activities got him into the papers, which a future spy should have been careful to avoid. On March 25, 1938, *The New York Times*, described a Bund meeting in Trenton that broke up in a riot, noting this quaint item about one man's effort to quell the uproar: "As the stage curtain was drawn, Waldemar Othmer, representing the Trenton unit of the Bund, directed the playing of 'The Star-Spangled Banner.' The audience arose and sang this." It was a futile attempt. A moment later, when Othmer tried to introduce his friend Kunze from Philadelphia, the catcalls resounded louder than before.

When Othmer resorted to this patriotic gesture, he was already an Abwehr spy. The bio sheet of "A.2018" found among the Bremen papers rounded out his curriculum vitae. On a visit to the Fatherland in December 1936, he volunteered for service in the Abwehr, was assigned to the Bischoff-Bensmann team, but asked to return later for his training. In early 1937 he was traveling back and forth, getting his training on the run.

He was, like Koedel, a "sleeper." Unlike Koedel, he did not enjoy the Abwehr's generosity. During this waiting period, he received $300, then $500, sent him from Shanghai via the Chase National Bank, but he managed to eke out a living. He was an electrician by trade, and supplemented his income during those depression years by selling Electrolux vacuum cleaners.

A handsome, personable blue-eyed young man with blond hair parted in the middle, he looked at the world with quizzical eyes from behind a pair of rimless spectacles. Though he had neither Koedel's dazzling brilliance nor his gift of the born mixer, and never grew out of his artisan background, he made an excellent spy.

On November 25, 1938, he went to Germany again, this time for a long stay, getting married, his wife bearing him a son, and spending the whole of 1939 in training with the Abwehr. Next time he returned, he came as a secret agent. After a short stay in Brooklyn, he was directed to move to Norfolk, to supplement Koedel's coverage of the Eastern Seaboard by watching the Atlantic coast, south of Chesapeake Bay. He spent his brief period of acclimatization in Norfolk by casing the great naval base, then worked at the Naval Operating Base as a plumber's helper, at Camp Pendleton as an electrician, and at the busy harbor as a stevedore, for 45 to 65 cents an hour.

In one of his reports, he would merely list the ships he had observed in port; but in the next, he would give hard-to-get details of a departing convoy. From enumerating the damaged British warships undergoing repair in the Norfolk shipyards, he would jump to alerting the Abwehr to the imminent increase in the production of American 50-ton tanks for the British, on information he had procured about a $10 million dollar contract the War Department had awarded the Mack Truck Co. for the manufacture of special transmissions.

Nothing seemed to escape his attention, whether it was the drastic increase of the range of certain 15-inch guns capable of firing up to twenty shells a minute to 12,000 yards, or the development of a new amphibian tank by the Trenton firm of John A. Roebling's Sons.

"Attention!" he signaled on October 29, 1940. "Two brand new six-inch coastal guns installed in northwest corner of Norfolk Naval Base."

"Light cruiser *Omaha* back in Norfolk after nineteen-day cruise Portugal, Africa, South America. Sailing soon Halifax with Admiral Richardson aboard. He is new CO American destroyers North Atlantic, replacing Admiral Brenton. *Omaha*'s engines produced average 22 knots on cruise, vessel returned with enough fuel left for only ten miles."

"Sold to England," he wrote on January 28, 1941, "by J. M. Winchester & Co. of New York: SS *Bellemine*, 9786 tons: SS *West Raritans*, 5703 tons; SS *Clairton*, 9808 tons; SS *Western Ocean*, 8800 tons; SS *Willimantic*, 7615 tons; SS *Winon County*, 9808 tons, all of them anchored in James River."

His method of collection had none of the shrewdness of Koedel's; his signals lacked spectacular quality. But in the long run, Othmer was probably the more valuable of the two, for it was from the routine little items of his reports that the Abwehr was able to piece together the mosaic of America's naval aid to Britain and this country's growing preparedness at sea.

On the day the Tramp operation blew up in June, Othmer was going about his business as usual, advising the Abwehr that construction had begun at forced speed on a string of new barracks at Camp Pendleton and Fort Story.

Both he and Koedel escaped arrest in the FBI roundup of June, not by sheer good luck, but thanks to the astuteness of their handlers, Johannes Bischoff and Niko Bensmann.

While Hamburg and Berlin had been jumping helter-skelter on the wonderful bandwagon of Tramp and attached their agents to Sebold's and Wheeler-Hill's supposedly clandestine radio centers in what the Abwehr lingo called *Traubenbildung*, the bunching of grapes, Bremen refrained from participating. Not a single agent of the subbranch was ever permitted to use those facilities and not a single Bischoff or Bensmann agent was compromised.

The collapse of the fabulous New York networks in the summer of 1941 came at a time when the Abwehr could ill afford such a disaster. And when the moment of truth arrived on December 7, 1941, the Germans had not even a skeleton of their once phenomenal organization in America. Hitler's declaration of war took Canaris by surprise. This was reflected in a breathless directive issued on December 12 by Colonel Piekenbrock, ordering the Abwehr to undertake the immediate construction of a string of networks in the United States.

"This is a new war," Piekenbrock wrote. "We must create a new organization for its prosecution."

Only five months before, the United States was swarming with German spies. Now all the Abwehr had for the gigantic task of spying here were six agents in the United States and a spy operating from Cuba watching American activities in the Caribbean area.

The man in Havana was the most romantic and intriguing of the group, remembered in the folklore of espionage by a romantic epithet. He was called "the Bird Man of Morro Castle" because he kept a flock of canaries in his room in Señor Emilio Perez's shabby boarding house, hoping that their singing would drown out the clickety noises of his clandestine radio; and because he ended his life facing a firing squad in the old fortress.

In the boarding house on Teniente Rey he was known as Enrique Augusto Luni. Others in Havana called him Rafael Castillo. In reality he was Heinz August Luning, a 40-year-old Honduran of German-Italian parentage who joined the Abwehr in 1937. Sent to Cuba four years later, his job was to keep watch on the big American naval base at Guantánamo, note the ships in the Caribbean Sea, and military and naval activities around the Florida Keys.

A hapless, lonely, mysterious figure, Luning was born to be a loser. He was up to only his forty-eighth message when the FBI came upon his trail and the Cubans arrested him. Just three weeks short of his first anniversary in the game, this unknown soldier of the secret war was dead.

The Abwehr had left only one more old-timer like Koedel, who also had his start as a spy in World War I, and was reactivated in 1938. He was Ernst Frederick Lehmitz, a tall, lean, taciturn naturalized American living at Tompkinsville on Staten Island, a vantage point from which to watch the movement of ships.

Trained in Hamburg in 1939 as a coast watcher, he returned to the United States on the liner *Siboney* in March 1941. He went into harness immediately, specializing in shipping intelligence. Although he had been a rubber salesman, Lehmitz became a handyman in a waterfront tavern frequented by seamen. He sent his data to mail drops in Lisbon and Bilbao, and to his major link with the Abwehr, a man named Walter Hirzel in Winterthur, Switzerland, signing his letters as "Fred Lewis" or "Fred Sloane."

Hirzel had other pen pals in the United States, a certain "R. O. Gerson," one "R. L. Erskine," and somebody who signed his letters simply as "Rogers." On closer scrutiny the three turned out to be the pseudonyms of a single person whose real name was long enough to fit three men: Wilhelm Albrecht von Pressentien Genannt von Rautter. He was the black sheep son of a German count and an aristocratic British lady (related to the famed Admiral Lord Fisher of World War I fame).

Turning his back on (or more precisely having been turned out of) his family's vast estate in Pomerania, he entered the United States illegally in 1920 by jumping ship, reentering legally in 1926, becoming naturalized twelve years later. He also promptly turned on his adopted country by enlisting in the Abwehr soon after he received citizenship and became eligible for an American passport.

He became indispensable after Pearl Harbor, partly because the charming rogue who never did well in anything turned out to be a splendid spy, and partly because he was in harness while his predecessors were in jail.

The odd man of the sextet was a Colombian linguist, Roberto Lanas Vallecilla, working under the cover-name of Gabriel Reyes. A former translator with the International Labor Office in Geneva, he arrived in the United States in September 1940 under the auspices of the Abwehr. He did exceptionally well in this country, as a linguist, as a spy, and even as an eligible bachelor—actually combining the three vocations on behalf of his German employers.

As a linguist, he succeeded in getting a job in Nelson Rockefeller's new Washington plum, the Office of Co-Ordinator of Inter-American Affairs. As a spy, he used this exceptional opportunity to procure classified information about Pan-American affairs. And as a handsome, seductive, wavy-haired Latin bachelor, he courted (and later married) the secretary of Rear Admiral Charles E. Rosendahl who commanded the United States Navy's fleet of dirigibles. The end results of his combined efforts went out in reports to the Abwehr via Gonzales de Azevado, a Portuguese the Germans used as one of their mail drops is Lisbon.

These men remained in harness for some time—von Pressentien during four long war years. Others arrived from time to time, some as late as the end of 1944, such as the hapless Erich Gimpel and a Johnny-come-lately "super-spy," a French engineer named Jean Marie Cavaillez. But the halcyon days of the Abwehr in America were over. The quality of the agents the Germans enlisted was a far cry from the virtuosity of a Lonkowski, a Duquesne, a Lang, and a Reuper.

As we will see, the FBI was never again completely absent from any of these later operations. And the Fuehrer would fly into a rage whenever he was shown yet another report from America speaking of 10,000 more tanks, 100,000 additional tons of ships, thousands of more planes—spelling out in facts and figures the miracle of American war production that was surpassing all expectations.

Part VI

THIS IS A NEW WAR

Chapter 42

The Iberian Black Market

ON December 20, 1941, a fortnight after Pearl Harbor and nine days after Germany's declaration of war against the United States, Colonel Hans Piekenbrock, sent a letter to the Foreign Ministry that read:

> The entry of the United States into the war further shrinks the basis on which the Wehrmacht's secret intelligence service functions.
>
> It will be necessary, therefore, to expand the collection of secret intelligence in the remaining neutral countries [Portugal, Spain, Sweden, Switzerland, and Turkey]. This will require a considerable increase of Abwehr personnel in these countries.
>
> The Abwehr deems it necessary to call attention to this situation and must reserve the right to apply for permission, as circumstances demand, to "build" additional personnel into the German diplomatic missions in these countries.

The top brass of the Foreign Ministry frowned upon the system of harbouring spies in the embassies and legations, and considered Piekenbrock's letter insolent. The Abwehr was already crowding the missions with spymasters and secret agents, frequently assigning incompetent goldbrickers with diplomatic covers, whose indiscretions resulted in embarrassing scandals.

When the Foreign Ministry balked, Canaris enlisted the aid of General Wilhelm Keitel, Hitler's chief of staff, and even that of the Fuehrer himself. Citing Hitler's interest, Keitel addressed a letter to Ribbentrop (actually drafted by Canaris), demanding that the Abwehr be permitted to plant its people in the missions. After that, their gates were opened wide to let in a flood of bogus diplomats.

Before long, personnel at the German Embassy in Madrid grew to

391 men and women of whom only 171 were bona fide diplomats and members of their secretarial and clerical staffs. The rest were Abwehr agents, many of them enjoying the immunity and other privileges that went with their status.

Canaris had good reasons for expansion of his bases abroad. As early as January 1940, when the war was only in its fifth month, it had become evident that Hamburg or, for that matter, any place in Germany, was not the ideal spot from which to conduct espionage against an island stronghold like Britain to which even authorized ingress was becoming increasingly difficult.

Ast X in Hamburg and its subbranch in Bremen were by no means idle. They were stamping out a new crop of agents for Britain. It was a time-consuming and tedious effort, and very risky. There were no guarantees that German agents of whatever nationality could be insinuated into England from points of departure within Germany.

Admiral Canaris anticipated the difficulties the Abwehr would encounter after the outbreak of war. He created well in advance a number of what he called *Kriegsorganisationen*, KO for short, major branch offices located in countries which were likely to remain neutral. They were opened for business immediately after the commencement of hostilities.

In the end, the Abwehr had six major KO's—in Spain, Portugal, Switzerland, Sweden, Turkey, and China, all of them, even the outpost in Shanghai, spying on Britain.[1]

The first KO to be made operational was in Madrid, for sentimental and practical reasons. It was in Spain, the only foreign country Canaris really liked, where he had had his beginnings in clandestine manipulations. As early as 1939 the Abwehr had become a fixture there, covering the whole country with a dense net in close collaboration with Canaris's colleague and friend, General Campos Martinez, chief of the Spanish secret service.

The cordial relations with Campos Martinez and the intimate relationship with Franco's secret service harked back to the Civil War which Canaris was instrumental in unleashing. He built up an intricate web of agents, spun a vast line of communications, and created several dummy firms—including Rowak Hisma, Carlos Hinderer & Co., and Transmare—to serve as blinds and handle the financial transactions of the combine.

Transmare was by far the biggest, with tentacles reaching to Spanish Morocco and all the countries of South America. It was managed by Canaris's sole truly intimate friend in the world, an obscure Russian exile known as Baron Ino, whose real name was Baron Roland Kaulbars.

Thanks to Canaris's personal influence in Spain, which extended all the way up to Generalissimo Franco, the Spanish intelligence service (known as "Sirene") was, for all practical purposes a branch of the Abwehr.

Another reason for the primogeniture of KO-Spain was the availability there of a man Canaris regarded as his alter ego—his old comrade Wilhelm Leissner—to whom he felt he could safely entrust his favorite outpost. Leissner had been a naval officer in World War I, passed over for transfer into the postwar navy, and had migrated to Nicaragua to sit out his civilian life as a publisher. No sooner was Canaris made chief of intelligence in 1935 than he sent for Leissner, reinstated him in the navy with the rank of commander, and sent him to Spain as his personal representative. Leissner became "Gustav Lenz" in the process, a businessman representing a firm called Excelsior, one of Canaris's dummy commercial enterprises. In 1936 the Civil War broke out and "Papa" Lenz was activated. He managed the enormous Abwehr contingent backing Franco, then stayed on at the head of a skeleton organization after the triumph of the dictator.

Commander Leissner was a strange old buzzard in this exotic aviary. Wearing conservatively cut, ill-fitting somber dark-gray suits and white shirts with high starched collars, and sporting carefully groomed handlebars, he looked like the man in the old ads selling pomades for moustachios. He was an old-fashioned gentlemen in his fifties, ponderous, pedantic, and correct. Despite Canaris's unqualified faith in his competence as a super-spymaster, he turned out to be not quite the right chief for such a key post. He could be easily outfoxed, since he was a parochial, fastidious bureaucrat, more concerned with the forms than the substance of the game.

When it became necessary to reorient the coverage of Britain with operations mounted from neutral soil, Canaris chose Leissner in Spain to take over from Hamburg. Another big outpost was then set up in Portugal with a KO in Lisbon under a former intelligence officer of the Austrian General Staff, Major von Auenrode alias Albrecht von Karsthof, a foppish, fastidious Viennese. He was remarkable as chief of intelligence mainly for his talent for spending vast sums of secret funds on inane, mostly stillborn enterprises.

By May 1944 on the eve of D-Day, the Abwehr's peak period, Lenz had 717 regular full-time and over 600 part-time employees on Spanish soil. Aside from the Madrid center, with the so-called Lenz Office and eight additional "bureaus" (including several radio listening stations and cryptographic agencies), the KO-Spain also maintained outposts in San Sebastian, Barcelona, Seville, Algeciras, La Linea, Tangier, Ceuta, Tetuan, and Melilla.[2]

The Lenz Office was organized in five branches—Central Office, secret intelligence, sabotage and counterespionage, and a number of technical bureaus. Among the "diplomats" were espionage and sabotage masters; a senior recruiter, the general manager of agents in the field, a collector of technical air intelligence, and a lieutenant colonel responsible for penetration of the British and American secret services.

"Authenticators" worked under Dr. Kuenkele, a scientific manufacturer of all sorts of forgeries, faking documents and passports, handling microphotography, secret inks, and other paraphernalia, including explosives. A huge staff of clerks was headed by Leissner's confidential secretary, Fraülein Haeupel.

The Lenz Office had in the field 360 spies and 60 saboteurs. The organization was duplicated in Portugal under Auenrode-Karsthof. With headquarters in the Legation in Lisbon, the tentacles of the KO extended to all Portuguese territories overseas.

They were formidable bodies, but more in quantity rather than quality. As we will see, they proved no match for the networks the British had in the Iberian black market.

From the outset, both KO's had instructions to develop secret agents in their own bailiwicks for missions in England and the United States. Leissner was not content with what he was getting from "Sirene" under the agreement Canaris had made with Campos Martinez; nor was Auenrode satisfied with what he could procure under the counter from pro-Nazi or corrupt members of the Portuguese Foreign Ministry and secret service. The Spanish intelligence establishment, in particular, was outdated, sluggish and highly vulnerable. The Spaniards had the most insecure crypto-system in Europe, relying on methods already out of fashion in World War I.

They had few secret agents stationed abroad. Shortly after the fall of France, instructions were sent to Ambassador Eberhard von Stohrer in Madrid to explore the possibility of closer collaboration by drawing Spanish agents stationed in England into the Abwehr's orbit. The ambassador took up the matter with Foreign Minister Colonel Juan Beigbeder y Atienza, who bluntly told him: "We have no spies in England."

Canaris was undaunted by the rebuff. On his insistence, the matter was discussed with Franco who proved more accommodating. On September 6, 1940, Franco instructed all Spanish consuls in England to act as secret agents for the Germans by sending "detailed reports on the morale of the population and the effects of the [German] attacks by air." Four days later, the Duke of Alba, the Spanish Ambassador at the Court of St. James's, was ordered to "extend this reportage beyond the inquires at Spanish consulates," and to report on a number of topics, a list of which Canaris had submitted to General Franco—on the targets and effects of the German air attacks;

effects on the morale of the population, the trade unions, members of Parliament, British airmen (especially pilots), and the Royal Navy, as well as food supplies and industrial production.[3]

The results were disappointing. The Spaniards agreed to give the Germans copies of their Ambassador's dispatches, but they were not of much help. According to Ambassador von Stohrer the Spanish ambassador confined himself "merely to forwarding statements made by English governmental departments."

Commander Leissner relied on the vast reservoir of native Falangists who, for one reason or another (mostly ulterior, as it turned out) expressed willingness to go to England to spy for the Germans.

For the difficult task of building an independent network of Spanish nationals in Britain, a Falangist journalist named Don Angel Alcazar de Velasco was chosen. Called "Guillermo" by his covername and carried as "V.312" in the KO's registry of agents, Don Angel was sent to London in the early fall of 1940, partly to reconnoiter the terrain, and partly to act as a producing spy on his own.

Using the cover of a Press Officer attached to the Spanish Embassy, Alcazar de Velasco established himself as a spymaster, sending the Germans highfalutin reports mostly on political topics. His chief source, he claimed, was a rising star in the Conservative Party with a consuming ambition to become its leader and Prime Minister. He was strategically placed for Don Angel's quest—an under-secretary in Mr. Churchill's National Government.

Alcazar de Velasco returned to Madrid briefly in February 1941, to report his accomplishments. Described as "the Abwehr agent . . . in whom the English have the greatest confidence," he brought with him "a number of military intelligence reports" which went directly to the Abwehr in Berlin. His political reportage was summarized by Ambassador von Stohrer in a long dispatch dated February 28, saying that:

> The secret agent confirmed the report of [Spanish Interior Minister and Falangist leader] Serrano Suñer regarding the idea of a possible leasing of Gibraltar after the war. According to the report of the secret agent, his highly placed British source did not come out quite clearly in favor of a cession of French Morocco to Spain but spoke only of a revision of the frontiers in favor of Spain.

Arrangements were then made for Don Angel to return to London as a *Haupt-V-Mann*, chief espionage agent, to start his work for Leissner, managing a ring of a dozen Spaniards. For a brief time, his output was indifferent, but then two scoops established him as one of the most valuable panders the Abwehr had in England.

In March 1941, he submitted a comprehensive report on the damage of the Luftwaffe raids which was so detailed, pinpointed, and sanguine that it pleased the Luftwaffe Intelligence no end. It was circulated by Goering, shown to the Fuehrer, and the agent was given a fat bonus.

Within six months he came through with another scoop. The British Army had been practically destroyed during its brief stand in France, and had to be completely reorganized from the remnants left after Dunkirk. Only inadequate information was available in Berlin about the table of organization and order of battle of this brand-new army. Great efforts were made to collect information on this score, but it met with little success.

Then everything changed. The General Staff's intelligence division came into the possession of a copy of the actual order of battle of the British Army through a windfall. Alcazar de Velasco claimed he had bought the precious document from a corrupt lieutenant of the British Army.

Don Angel was suspected of the theft. Now, Kenneth Carter Benton, MI.6's resident director in Spain camouflaged as an official at the Embassy, decided to make the evidence conclusive. On his orders, de Velasco's apartment was searched as if some intruders had burglarized it. They found and copied his diary, which proved beyond a doubt that the man was the chief of a dangerous ring of Spanish spies working for the Abwehr.

In the meantime, de Velasco had returned to London, with orders to get from the lieutenant additional "originals." When he was notified from Madrid that "burglars" had ransacked his flat, he realized at once that the British counterspies were on his trail. He left London in a great hurry, naming as his successor Luis Calvo, the London correspondent of ABC, the big Madrid daily, as resident director of the V-ring of Spanish spies. He also saw to it that his line of communication remained intact, making arrangements with a member of the Spanish Embassy office, Don Jose Brugada Wood, to continue sending information by diplomatic pouch.

But Don Jose was "Peppermint," an agent of the Double-Cross System, with whose aid MI.5 had succeeded in penetrating the Spanish Embassy to keep tabs on its extracurricular activities. He promptly advised Major Liddell of MI.5 of the change of the guard, and Calvo was picked up. By this time Calvo was senior agent (*Haupt-V-Mann*) V.319, the manager of a ring of seven Spaniards in England and Wales, some of them strategically placed in hotels and war plants. He was taken to Ham Common where he quickly caved in, and he, too, became a controlled agent.

In April 1942, the Germans were tipped off that Calvo had

been arrested by MI.5, and urgent queries were sent to Madrid and London to ascertain the circumstances of his apparent downfall. The inquiries produced the information that Calvo was at large and safe. So reassured was the Abwehr by this gratifying end of the investigation that V.319 was left at his post as chief of the Spanish V-men in England. He was still firmly believed to be on the job in 1944, during the hectic period preceding D-Day, palming off doctored intelligence on his German friends.

The genius behind this phenomenal coup who disposed of Don Angel, netted Peppermint and Calvo, and gained control over the entire so-called Spanish group of agents operating in England, was Harold Adrian Russell Philby. Son of Harry St. John Bridges Philby, the famed Arabist, Kim moved from Cambridge into a career in journalism that was, from time to time, not entirely above board. He enlisted in the Red Army Intelligence Service in June 1933 and, according to his own confession, served his Red masters to the best of his ability.

In 1934, on orders from Moscow, he became one of the first propaganda agents the Nazis dug up in England. He joined the Anglo-German Fellowship to publish a pro-Hitler magazine with Nazi funds, and was active in pro-German organizations, getting instructions and secret funds on visits to the Propaganda Ministry and the Foreign Ministry in Berlin. Later, sent by *The Times* of London to report the Civil War from the Franco side, his work so pleased the General that he personally pinned Rebel Spain's most coveted decoration, The Red Cross of Military Merit, on Kim's soiled tunic. Then—after groping in Britain's secret underworld—which he later called "an old-established racket"—he found a niche in Section V of MI.6, as Major Cowgill's chief assistant in charge of counterespionage on the Iberian desk.

Although Section V was not the only British security organ battling German agents in Spain, Philby was given virtually unrestricted authority and he made the most of it.

Under his management—as imaginative as it was efficient—this branch blossomed out as the best in Section V. His Iberian episode stands out as a perplexing intermezzo in the sordid career of this notorious double agent. At this time, he had been a Soviet spy for more than a decade, but the job he was doing for the British secret service left nothing to be desired. Now it was due largely to his ingenuity that the enormous German organizations on the Peninsula were brought to a standstill. As more and more Spanish and Portuguese nationals were sent to England, they fell invariably into the trap Philby set for them.

The triumph of Section V was especially remarkable in that it was scored by a handful of amateurs pitted against the seasoned German professionals. Philby's chief assistants in the coverage of Portugal were two newcomers to the intelligence game—Graham Greene, the novelist, and Malcolm Muggeridge, the former *Punch* editor. Both were groomed for their clandestine duties—hastily and perfunctorily, at that—by a pixyish old S.I.S. hand, my late friend Captain Leslie Arthur Nicholson—"kindly, twinkling and unassuming," as one of his pupils described him, "a sort of Father Brown of espionage."

The job proved too much for Muggeridge. Posted to Lourenço Marques in Portuguese East Africa (Mozambique), he became so unnerved by the task of combatting the relatively large Abwehr contingent there that he once tried to drown himself in the Indian Ocean. Greene's innate cynicism and sardonic approach to the game made him the perfect adversary to cut the Auenrode organization down to its true size.

Such British activities in the Iberian black market of espionage and counterespionage were not confined either to MI.6 or to the ubiquitous Kim Philby in particular. Although MI.5 was not supposed to be operating abroad, its Section B.1.A (the "XX" System) maintained a major agent, "Nettle," in Spain, running a feedline to him from London through a French double agent called "Shepherd."

In Portugal the Abwehr was running a kind of extension service, an autonomous ring of agents in direct, and often acrimonious, competition with Auenrode-Karsthof's regular KO organization. By the same token, more or less, MI.5 utilized this same ring in rivalry with the MI.6 organization in Lisbon.

The chief of the Double-X operation was the Abwehr's trusted head V-man, a highly respected German expatriate living in Lisbon. A prosperous industrialist who had originally come to Portugal to represent Nazi business interests in war-essential materials, he was also a close personal friend of Major Kremer von Auenrode, the local KO chief.

Called A.1416 in the Abwehr, and "Hamlet" in Double-X, his service of two masters in an Elizabethan play of intrigue was so smooth that both of his contacts had every reason to be satisfied. Hamlet had made his way to Double-X in 1941 as representative of certain high-ranking anti-Nazi officers in the Wehrmacht for whom he solicited British aid. While no such assistance was forthcoming (the memories of Venlo were still too fresh), the German was enlisted as a conveyor of bogus intelligence on the Double-X pattern.

His group in Lisbon worked for the Abwehr under the elaborate cover of a flourishing export-import business. MI.5 maintained contact with the man through two of his business associates—a British subject who represented the firm in England (called "Mullett") and an Austrian (going by the cover name of "Puppet"). The latter was allowed to visit England periodically as the representative of Hamlet's Portuguese company. His moves were so well camouflaged by Double-X that the Abwehr never had any reason to question the purposes of these trips.

Mullett and Puppet (who were called "Famulus" and "Budny" in the Abwehr) were supplied by MI.5's Double-Cross organization in London with doctored intelligence for transmission to Hamlet, who then passed it on to the Abwehr. In order to sustain this vital link (whose tentacles reached to the highest echelons in the Wehrmacht, including Colonel General Nikolaus von Falkenhausen, military governor of occupied Belgium), Double-X had to engage in commercial activities on a substantial scale. It was buying and selling, importing and exporting via the prosperous business organization large quantities of soap products, impregnated paper, and even degreasing patents and lemonade powder.

It was probably the most complex of all operations Double-X ever had to tackle, and undoubtedly the most direct penetration of the Abwehr on a high plateau. Hamlet's elevated position in the Abwehr assured the Double-Cross organization that all Double-X-information channelled through him reached its destination and would be accepted as authentic.

Most active among the Abwehr rings in Portugal was the one called "Ostro." Managed by a mystery man from Lisbon, it had agents—such as Bischoff's and Schaerenbeck's CHB organization— throughout the British Empire and in the United States. Three of them were supposedly posted in the United Kingdom.

Section V made a special effort in Portugal to track down the mastermind behind the Ostro ring. Philby personally went to Lisbon to conduct the operation. The ringleader was discovered to be a chemist named Paul Fidrmuc, managing director of a reputable international firm doing business in Allied countries. He was using these footholds, not merely as a blind for his agents, but as a direct means of procuring secret intelligence.

A closer scrutiny of Senhor Fidrmuc revealed some interesting facts. As access was gained to more and more of the reports he was forwarding to the Abwehr, the British security organs concluded that Ostro was a hoax. Far from having agents in England, Fidrmuc did not have a single spy anywhere in the world. Even in Lisbon, he was the whole of Ostro.

The highly-evaluated reports he submitted to Major von Auenrode, for which he was receiving the highest fees that KO was paying, were all composed by him alone. Most contained intelligence he either culled from Allied periodicals, or were produced from his imagination.

When MI.6 succeeded in establishing the true colors of Ostro, it was decided to leave him alone, so he could continue to fool the Germans.

By the late summer of 1944 Fidrmuc reached the conclusion that the great gold rush was over—Germany was losing the war. He decided to leave Portugal to escape the authorities in Lisbon who had come upon his trail and were taking a rather dim view of his activities.

By this time, there were not too many places left in the world where a scoundrel like Fidrmuc could find a safe haven. Going to Madrid he found himself completely discredited inside the Abwehr, and was saved only by Canaris's downfall. He made new friends in the Schellenberg empire, but his days as the Germans' biggest and most prosperous contractor in espionage were definitely over. Fidrmuc was one of the last big-time Iberian spies to fall by the wayside.

Already in 1943, when Philby began to make his presence felt in Iberia, the brass at Abwehr headquarters somehow sensed that Spain and Portugal had outlived their usefulness. Another neutral country had to be found from which the espionage offensive could be continued against England.

Sweden promised to be that spot.

NOTES

1 The Shanghai outpost was also engaged in espionage operations against China and the Soviet Union, even against Germany's allies, the Japanese. Another set of semi-autonomous branches, called "Walli" and based in Vienna and Warsaw, were established against the Soviet Union.

2 Among "Papa" Lenz's phony diplomats were Lieutenant Colonel Kiekebusch, his deputy; Major Kuehlenthal, the senior recruiter of secret agents; Lieutenant Dr. Schoene, the manager of V-men in the field; and Captain Naumann zu Koenigsbruck, chief of sabotage operations. The penetration of the Allied secret services (IIIF) was the responsibility of a colonel named von Rohrscheidt.

3 The Germans told the Spaniards that they could deduct the extra expenses incurred in these activities from the 372 million marks the Franco regime owed Germany for services rendered during the Civil War.

Chapter 43

The Swedish Cockpit

"*W*HO," Macbeth asked Macduff, "can be wise, amazed, temperate and furious, loyal and neutral in a moment?"

The Swedes tried. They fought their last war in 1813–14 (against Napoleon, at that), then made a fetish, not of peace, but of neutrality. In World War II, far more Swedes were pro-British than pro-German; but they were so much closer to Germany than they were to Britain, they subordinated sympathies to expediencies, hoping that the war would pass them by if they played it cool. Like Shaw's Englishman, they thought they were moral when they were only uncomfortable.

After the occupation of Denmark and Norway in the spring of 1940, and the eviction of the British from their last footholds on the Continent, their neutrality was somewhat rearranged, until it seemed that they were neutral *against* Britain.[1]

The lopsided golden means was nowhere more evident than in the official Swedish attitude toward spies. As professional neutrals usually are, the country was inundated by them, both the belligerents' secret agents and privateers free-lancing for personal profit.

Did Stockholm—or, for that matter, the whole of Sweden—have enough secrets to satisfy the craving of all these scavengers? Obviously not. The Swedes were extremely security conscious about their defenses, sensitized by the ostentatious Soviet interest in them. The Russians maintained a huge contingent of spies inside their Legation and in the bustling Communist Party. Within the mission, a troika of pseudo-diplomats—called Semenov, Vetrov, and Yartsev by their cover-names—managed a motley assortment of secret agents. Yartsev's pseudo-wife, Kruglova, acted as liaison to the local Communist Party. The importance of military intelligence was attested by the fact that it was masterminded by one of the Soviet Union's ranking spymasters. He operated on a false name as an assistant naval attaché. His *pièce de résistance* was the theft of the Swede's sacrosanct military crypto-system.

Aside from the Russians, the spies who flocked there during World War II were not interested in Sweden's secrets; espionage became a big and grim business of the various camps opposing each other.

The Norwegians were the most numerous and ubiquitous, having the great advantage of being almost at home, so their secret service in exile, headed by Colonel Roscher Lund, made the most of it. The Gaullist French operated perfunctorily, under the Comte de Fleurieau who masked his true sympathies and activities by serving as a Vichy diplomat.

The Americans were in the game with the controversial double agent, Eric Siegfried Erickson, a Swedish-American businessman who became famous after the war as "the Counterfeit-Traitor." They also had an astute operative at Göteborg in the person of Vice Consul William Corcoran, an unconventional diplomat with a keen eye and an adventurous bent of mind.

The Japanese were even more ubiquitous than the Norwegians and more persistent than the Russians, thanks to Major General Makoto Onodera, the wiry little military attaché who was chief of the Japanese secret service in Europe. As an Oriental posted to plumb the Occidental mind, Onodera was completely dependent on three Europeans, a quaint collection of continental con-men who found in him the ideal boss, for he was both generous and gullible. One of them was an Italian *faiseur* known in the espionage community as "Egghead," not because he was an intellectual but simply for the shape of his head. Another of his henchmen was the defector Dimitriewsky, a former counselor of the Soviet Legation, who was also working for the Germans behind his benefactor's back.

Onodera's real factotum with a Svengali-like influence on the rotund Japanese was a mysterious Pole whose activities caused considerable strain in German-Japanese relations. Onodera was snooping on Germany with greater curiosity than on its enemies, and the "Pesky Pole," as I shall call him, was supplying vast amounts of information about his Axis allies. Heinrich Himmler, who once described the Pole as "the world's most dangerous espionage operative," protested to Tokyo against "the ranking collaborator of the [Japanese] military attaché." The Gestapo contingent in Stockholm repeatedly tried to kidnap him to Germany. When the Pole escaped all such attempts, Himmler denounced him to the Swedish Minister in Berlin and offered to exchange two Swedish sailors, who had been caught in Germany spying for the Russians, for the Pesky Pole.

He continued at Onodera's side as his most trusted lieutenant, while working simultaneously for the British, who used him as a conduit to convey doctored intelligence to the Germans via the Japanese.

The widespread and efficient Polish secret service operated under a unique arrangement with a group of powerful Swedes doing business with the Germans in Poland. Organized by Sven Norman, the 51-year-old Warsaw manager of the big Swedish industrial concern ASEA, and Colonel Carl Herslow, a former Swedish military attaché in Berlin and Consul General in Warsaw, this fantastic ring was not at all mercenary. Its members were reputable industrialists, businessmen, and bankers. They agreed to act as spies because they witnessed the Nazi terror at close quarters.

The Polish-Swedish ring represented an indispensable link in Britain's overall coverage of German activities. It was the first to alert the British to the impending German invasion of the Soviet Union. And thanks to its efforts, the British obtained a working model of the "Enigma" machine, which the Germans used to encipher their top-secret messages.[2]

When the Gestapo uncovered the ring in 1942, fifty-one Poles were arrested in Warsaw and dealt with summarily, and the Swedish members were dragged off to Nazi prisons with death sentences hanging over their heads. Actually, the Nazis kept them as hostages to assure immunity for their own colony of spies in Sweden. Whenever the Swedish authorities made a move to clamp down on their spies, the Germans revived the case against the captive Swedes and threatened to chop off their heads.

The British, by and large, found their activities in Sweden badly clogged. Aside from a rampant anti-British bias in certain high places, two incidents at the outset placed them at a distinct disadvantage in the secret war. In the twilight of 1939, the British found out that the Germans had only about nine months' supply of the high-grade phosphorus ore they needed for the manufacture of steel, and were almost entirely dependent on Swedish supplies shipped via Lulea in the Gulf of Bothnia and Oxelösund in southern Sweden. They decided that they could drastically damage the German war effort by cutting off the flow of this ore. William Stephenson, the diminutive Canadian millionaire-industrialist, thought up a scheme of preventing this critical raw material from leaving Sweden by blowing up the cranes and other facilities used in the loading of the iron ore on German ships.

He volunteered to arrange the ambitious sabotage operation on the spot. His offer was accepted on the highest level of His Majesty's

Government and Stephenson reached Sweden, accompanied by a sabotage expert of MI.6, a man named Alexander Rickman. The latest type of plastic explosives was shipped to them in diplomatic bags in care of the British Legation in Stockholm. The explosives were stored in the cellar of the Legation and in the studio of a friendly Swedish sculptor.

The project was not without risk. Stephenson expected to be kidnapped or murdered by the Germans. He and Rickman carried on with such a sinister air, and with such leaky discretion that, before long, the project became the talk of the town. The Germans did not have to murder Stephenson to frustrate the plot. They simply saw to it that King Gustaf V learned of the plan. The King then wrote a personal letter to King George VI of England, beseeching him to order the immediate cancellation of the project.

Stephenson had to leave Stockholm in a hurry, but Mr. Rickman was arrested. The scandal rocked the country. The Swedes were startled to learn that the project involved not Nazis, who were notoriously suspect of plotting such outrages, but two apparently impeccable Britons as master saboteurs.

Far worse was an incident early in the war that turned the high command of the Swedish Navy vehemently against the British and gained for the Germans influential protectors. The Swedes had ordered three destroyers in an Italian shipyard. When they were completed, with the war already on, the Swedes planned to sail them home through the British and German blockades. The Germans raised no objections and even offered to aid their passage. But the British intercepted and impounded the vessels, interned their crews in a Scottish port, and even subjected them to some indignities.

The ill-advised action kicked up a storm of indignation. It so embittered a number of Swedish flag officers—among them Admirals Stroemback and Tamm (whose sympathies leaned to the Germans anyway)—that they remained vigorously anti-British throughout the war, while lavishing special favors on the Germans. Under their prodding, Major Walter Lindquist, the Defense Staff's No. 1 spybuster, made life difficult for British agents while allowing German spies a relatively free run.

Before the war, MI.6 had a foothold in Stockholm in the British Legation, camouflaged as the Passport Control Office, headed by an S.I.S. veteran named Martin. One of his operatives in Stockholm was a Hungarian poster painter, Emery Geroe, who had a friend, young Carl Christian Albrektsson Ellsen, a Swedish journalist with ostentatious pro-Nazi sympathies. The Germans employed him as an itinerant propagandist to send spot-news items to broadcasting stations in neutral countries. Paid 500 marks a month and expenses, Ellsen wrote articles about the advantages of being occupied by the Germans.

Early in 1941, Geroe succeeded in persuading Ellsen to join him as a collector of secret intelligence. For a year and a half, the Swede supplied "invaluable information from inside German-occupied Europe." It included timely reports about troop movements eastward on the eve of the German attack on the Russians.

In November 1942, Ellsen and Geroe were arrested. This was a serious blow to the British, but it had a silver lining. Ellsen exposed the Stockholm outlet of Radio Mundial as a Nazi spy front, with a clandestine transmitter to send secret information to Germany.

The prime target of the Swedish admirals' wrath and the chief victim of Major Lindquist was Captain Henry Mangles Denham, the naval attaché, acting as the senior representative of the Naval Intelligence Division.

With the appointment of Rear Admiral John Godfrey as Director of Naval Intelligence and the transfer of Lieutenant Commander (later Vice Admiral Sir) Norman Denning, life was breathed into the moribund Naval Intelligence Division. The venerable agency blossomed out as a huge secret service with its own agents and code-crackers scoring a number of coups.

This was due partly to the influx of romantic-minded, adventure-bent young civilians, one of whom was Godfrey's own chief assistant, Ian Fleming by name. The imagination that later produced the James Bond novels flowed freely with new ideas and bold ventures. His spirit, initiative, and energy made naval attachés like Commander Alan Hillgarth in Spain, Commander Wolfson in Turkey, and Captain Denham in Sweden both decorous diplomats out front and busy spymasters behind the scenes.

A handsome and dashing officer with independent means, Denham had his ups and downs. The informant he regarded as his best agent was the Swedish master of a merchantman who regularly supplied intelligence about German naval units in the Baltic Sea and such key ports as Stettin, Kiel, Sassnitz, and Pillau. He was an authentic mystery man, and Denham still does not know his real name.

The skipper, who seemed to be so staunchly devoted to the British cause that he refused to accept any money for his services, was in reality the German agent "Balzac," carried in the Abwehr registry under No. F.3243. His real name was Fritiof von Barth, and he had been planted on the naval attaché to palm off misleading information on him. Mishaps like this were unavoidable, but Denham's accomplishments far outweighed his failures. He was the original architect of one of the war's historic victories.

It was Captain Denham who had alerted the Admiralty when the *Bismarck* passed through the Kattegat and the Skagerrak toward her imminent doom.

In the early morning of May 20, 1941, the Swedish cruiser *Gotland* spotted the *Bismarck* and the cruiser *Prinz Eugen*. The sighting was mentioned by an officer of Sweden's Combined Intelligence Service to the Norwegian naval attaché who, in turn, passed on the information to Denham. He immediately cabled the Admiralty in London: "Most Immediate—Kattegat today 20 May. At 1500 2 large warships escorted by 3 destroyers, 5 escort craft or 12 a/c passed Marstrand course northwards."

It was correctly assumed in London that the *Bismarck* was preparing to break out into the Atlantic. After that the vigilance was never relaxed until the late May day when the battleship was sunk.

The Germans were painfully aware of the danger Denham's presence in Stockholm presented, and tried to remove him. His natural adversary, the German naval attaché, Paul von Wahlert, who had been the Hamburg representative of General Motors, did practically nothing to interfere with Denham's undercover pursuits. He did not have to, because the Swedes did their utmost to obstruct the British naval attaché. Denham was hounded at every turn by Major Lindquist's gumshoes, and was also the *bête noir* of another security officer, an enigmatic colonel named Adlercreutz.

His visitors were constantly harassed. He was trailed wherever he went, and his office bugged with microphones suspended in the chimney of his fireplace. Once a lip-reader was set up in the window of an apartment across the street from Denham's home, with the aid of a pair of binoculars, to catch conversations which the bugs could not pick up.

When Denham provided no opening, his enemies sought to compromise him by planting agent provocateurs on his neck, hoping that one or another would entrap him in a situation that could then be seized upon as reason for his expulsion. They could neither intimidate nor get rid of him. He was discreet by nature and knew how to elude embarrassing situations. Also, his opposite number in London, Captain Oxenstierne, the Swedish naval attaché, was digging for classified information and, as we shall see, getting quite a bit of it. The Swedish admirals were loath to kill off this valuable source by risking his expulsion in retaliation for Denham's eviction.

The Abwehr set-up ultimately became a huge, rambling establishment comfortably housed in numerous offices in the elegant Karlaplan district of Stockholm. But it was only late in 1940, when the

British had already set up their shop, that the Germans decided to move to Sweden in force. On the urging of Colonel Piekenbrock, who recognized Sweden's importance in the secret war, Admiral Canaris agreed to put up a branch office in Stockholm, and picked the Abwehr chief in Bucharest, 47-year-old Major Hans Wagner, a full-fleshed native of Zweibruecken, as its chief.

Lieutenant Colonel Rudolf Rohleder was designated as his "control" in Berlin, using the cover-name of "Axel." The country was henceforth to be referred to as "Schwerin" for purposes of camouflage in Abwehr communications. Wagner was to be "built into" the Legation with the cover of a civilian economist on the staff of the military attaché, to be known as "Hans Schneider" in the Abwehr, with a revolving fund of 400,000 marks. He was to use the facilities of the Legation, its courier system and codes, sending his reports via the Foreign Ministry, marked to the attention of Lieutenant Commander Wieckmann in Room 320 at Abwehr headquarters on the Tirpitz Quay.

On November 28, "Doctor" Wagner reported to the German Minister and was, at first, given a couple of rooms in the Legation, for himself and Lieutenant Albert Utermark, his aide, and Alice Fischer and Erika Wendt, his secretaries. Then he was in business—resident director of the flagship of German espionage in Sweden.

Wagner was chosen because his specialty was counterespionage and Piekenbrock envisaged work against the enemy's mushrooming secret organization as his primary function. He had strict orders to refrain from spying on Sweden, an injunction he initially observed but later violated wholesale.[3]

Wagner was unique among the spymasters in Stockholm. He had neither the lean elegance of Captain Denham nor General Onodera's contrived geniality. A jowly, pouchy-eyed, humorless man always carrying a heavy briefcase like a sacred burden and walking officiously with a lumbering shuffle, he looked comical in his ill-fitting civilian suit and long overcoat—like an unfrocked Brother Juniper.

He was all business, a strict disciplinarian, and such a punctilious, demanding bureaucrat that he drove poor Miss Fischer, a sensitive redhead who went by the cover-name of "Bertha," into suicide.

He turned out to be a formidable foe, not by getting any valuable intelligence about the British, but by effectively blocking them from their sources. He quickly identified Captain Denham as the most important adversary, and found out that his enviable efficiency was due in a large measure to his friendship with Colonel Bjoernstierna, chief of the Swedish High Command's Combined Intelligence Bureau.

For all practical purposes, Bjoernstierna was a British agent. He gave Denham abundant data about the Germans from his own considerable collection—copies of reports sent by the Swedish military attachés, the dispatches of secret agents, staff studies and estimates. He also supplied intercepts of "Gray House," the mysterious bureau of the Swedish Defense Staff hidden in a drafty old building on Karlaplan, where two dozen cryptanalysts "translated" some of Germany's most secret communications, including messages sent on the supposedly unbreakable Siemens Cipher Machine. In a real sense, during the Denham-Bjoernstierna cooperation, Swedish Intelligence served as an arm of the British secret service.

The material Bjoernstierna was able to funnel to Denham was extremely valuable, thanks to the exceptional competence of the Swedish military attachés in Berlin and Vichy. The Berlin post was held by Colonel C. H. Juhlin-Dannfelt, while Lieutenant Colonel Constanz Edouard du Rietz stood watch in Vichy. Dannfelt not only supplied his own observations and those of his aides, but had a number of agents in the Waffen-SS, the armed force of Heinrich Himmler's blackshirts. They were patriotic young Swedes who had infiltrated the Nazi movement of Per Lindblom, then "escaped" to Germany and joined the Waffen-SS, all the while serving their country as spies against Germany. Dannfelt also had a barter arrangement with his colleague, the equally well-informed Swiss military attaché in Berlin, giving the British as rounded a picture of the German military establishment as was obtainable in times of war.[4]

Now Wagner put this "problem" of Denham-Bjoernstierna at the top of his agenda.

With the help of a young captain in Major Petersen's Secret Intelligence Bureau, he assembled enough evidence to leave no doubt of Colonel Bjoernstierna's association with the British. Instead of forwarding the evidence against Bjoernstierna through channels and letting Berlin launch a formal protest through the Legation, he sought out the Swede who would personally benefit from the exposure of his brother officer and thus become indebted to Wagner.

He thought of Major Walter Lundquist, the Swedish military security chief, a counterespionage expert like himself, and bitterly anti-Red. Long before Wagner's appearance on the scene, Lundquist cooperated closely with Colonel von Bentivegny, chief of the Abwehr's counterespionage group, exchanged notes with him on Soviet spies and benefitted from the Germans' superior coverage.

Major Lundquist presented Wagner's evidence to Lieutenant General Olov Thoernell, chief of the Defense Staff. Aroused and embittered by the revelations, Thoernell ordered a purge in Combined Intelligence. Bjoernstierna was not only dismissed but threatened with court martial. Others who cooperated with Denham were arrested and sentenced. The fabulous "ring" was a shambles.

It was a fantastic coup. But Wagner's victory was not yet complete. The man General Thoernell appointed to take Bjoernstierna's place at the head of Combined Intelligence was not Major Lundquist but Captain B. Landquist, a not too bright but rather vain officer in the Operations Division of the Naval Staff. Wagner was on as friendly terms with Landquist as Denham had been with Bjoernstierna. "The new chief of Combined Intelligence," Wagner wrote to Colonel Piekenbrock, "is prepared to cooperate with me closely." He persuaded Admiral Canaris to invite Landquist to Berlin where he was given the red carpet treatment.

Not to be outdone, Captain Denham arranged for Captain Landquist to visit London, and the delicate balance seemed to be restored. But the Swedish Combined Intelligence was no longer the major source of information for Denham that it had been.

Wagner's close friendship with Major Walter Lundquist served the Germans well during the war's most difficult period. Not only was the Major seeping information to Wagner about British agents in Sweden, but he set himself up as the protector of German agents. "There can be no doubt," Wagner wrote to his home office, "that secret agents in our service, who have strict orders not to work against Sweden, will enjoy complete immunity."

The shield provided by Major Lundquist made Wagner greedy and careless. Wagner employed scores of "shadows" to keep tab on spies in the other camps, and double agents to infiltrate the rival secret services. He felt so safe that he communicated with them more or less openly, and even employed several in his office. His chief V-man was a 40-year-old German pastry cook, married to a Swedish woman, whom Wagner employed in his office supposedly as a translator.

Three of his shadows regularly tracked down British spies and served as agent provocateurs, receiving their instructions and salaries at Wagner's office and reporting to him there. A cameraman, a ship's steward, and a customs official were observed coming and going by the detectives of the Secret Police headed by Martin Lundquist.[5] No protection from Wagner's influential friends then saved them from arrest.

When the arrests produced screaming headlines, the embarrassed Swedes summoned Dr. Hans Thomsen, the German Minister at the time to the Foreign Ministry, where he was told by a high official of the Political Department: "We do not intend to make an issue of this case. But we would appreciate it if you asked Colonel Wagner to conduct his business with a little more discretion." It was but a slap on the wrist, but the German Minister professed to be scandalized. He asked Wagner to move. The Abwehr director then rented office space on Nyborgsgatan where he continued his careless practice. It was there, two years after the scandal, that Wagner's pastry-cook-translator was eventually trapped by Martin Lundquist's sleuths.

What Wagner neglected to do or did not know how to do—conduct *positive* intelligence against the British—was accomplished by others.

Dr. Paul Grossmann, veteran German correspondent in Sweden and now the press attaché of the Legation, sustained venal newspapers with secret subsidies, corrupted publicists, and engaged in spying on the side. His chief "consultant" in these activities was a mysterious "T.K." frequently cited in Grossmann's confidential dispatches. In actual fact, "T.K." was Thorsten Kreuger, brother of the ill-fated match king. A shy, retiring millionaire, who wielded his considerable power through the big newspapers he controlled, Kreuger aided Grossmann's propaganda efforts and served as chief adviser in his cloak and dagger sideline.

In September 1942, the normally reticent, cautious Kreuger agreed to lend a hand in a melodramatic "mission" which Ribbentrop thought up and Grossmann was instructed to organize. The plan was to "pick a reliable Swedish journalist whose pro-German sentiments were not widely known" to be sent to London from where he would send back secret reports in addition to his open dispatches. In the privacy of his hunting lodge, Kreuger recommended the man he thought ideal for the mission. But the correspondent sorely disappointed his mentors. The dispatches he filed in London were, as Grossmann bitterly complained to T.K., "invariably slanted in favor of our enemies, and totally useless to us."[6]

NOTES

1 Some manifestations of this strange correctness was quite petty and uneven, like the disciplining of Swedish newspapers for printing "un-neutral" articles. In 1941, seventy newspapers were punished for featuring reports which the Germans regarded as objectionable, but only eleven were chastised for articles presumably slanted against the British.

2 Invented by a German engineer named Arthur Scherbius, the "Enigma," a rotor machine, was sold by its manufacturers to anybody willing to pay the price. During World War II, the battery-powered, typewriter-sized device (which required three men to operate) was the Wehrmacht's top system. It was to pick up one of these machines that Commander Denniston went clandestinely to a secluded Polish castle on the eve of the war. Dilly Knox later solved its keying, exposing all Abwehr signals encoded by this system.

3 In September 1944, for example, he commissioned two Swedes to collect information about "the fortifications and garrisons of the Swedish-Norwegian

region east of Oerje (65 km southeast of Oslo)." At the same time, he sent a spy to the vicinity of Schonen in south Sweden to observe exercises which the Swedish army was holding there. Wagner also had on his payroll a colonel, a captain, two lieutenants, a sergeant, and six corporals of the Swedish army, and an NCO of the Swedish Army Signals Corps.

4 The work of du Rietz was cut short in June 1942, when Colonel Karatsonyi, the Hungarian military attaché in Vichy, denounced him as "an enemy agent" serving the British "as a courier on the Vichy-Madrid and Vichy-Stockholm circuit." Du Rietz was declared *persona non grata* and had to leave Vichy. Dannfelt endured until 1945 when a quaint mishap terminated his services. During the move of his office to safer quarters, he lost his brief-case bulging with copies of his most secret reports to the Swedish Defense Staff's Foreign Department.

5 Since it may be difficult to keep these men apart, we repeat that Captain Landquist was the chief of Combined Intelligence; Major Walter Lund-quist was the chief of military security; and Martin Lundquist was the ascetic and dedicated head of the secret police.

6 In March 1942, a *Sicherheitsdienst* cell was established inside the Legation under the SS-Sturmbannfuehrer, Dr. Finke, a 38-year-old, tall, heavy-set Nienburger with dark blond hair and gray-blue eyes, disguised as an assistant to the Commercial attaché. His chief V-man in the field was a Swedish Nazi paid 18,000 marks per month to do the legwork for Finke. Other agents in his stable included a Latvian journalist, a Swedish engineer whose girl friend was a secretary of Mme. Kollontay, the Soviet Minister; the Consul General of Slovakia; a White Russian who also worked for the Rumanians, and many more.

Chapter 44

The "Baron" Goes North

*W*HEN Canaris and Piekenbrock decided finally to send others to Sweden to collect "positive" intelligence about the Allies, it was left to two operatives in particular to raise the level of German espionage. One was an international banker from Cologne, the other a Danish nobleman.

Waldemar Baron von Oppenheim, the banker, was born in 1894, at Castle Schlenderhahn in the Rhine province, a member of one of Germany's great Jewish dynasties. He chose the career of professional soldier and served with distinction as a lieutenant of the exclusive 3rd House Regiment in World War I. After the war, he married Gabriela von Goldschmidt in a "merger" of two rich, aristocratic families. Then, at his father's request, he resigned his commission and joined the venerable family bank in Cologne.

A handsome, slender, tall man, conservatively groomed, with the bearing of the military officer he was, Baron von Oppenheim, like so many German Jews of his caste, felt far more German than Jewish. In fact, he had joined the NSDFB, the Nazi Party's banking group, in July 1932, months before Hitler's seizure of power. Although his generation was only part Jewish by this time, the Nazis rated him "second degree bastard," an official label that reflected on his origin and not on his character. Oppenheim got the message. After 1933 he thought it better to refrain from any participation in Nazi activities, and concentrated on his business, managing his bank's widespread international transactions.

The war forced his bank to shift its foreign operations to Sweden, where the Oppenheims had intimate ties with the powerful Enskilda Banken owned by the legendary Wallenberg brothers, Jacob and Mark. Oppenheim was closely linked to the Wallenbergs and related to them by marriage.

532

It was this relationship, his international connections, his impressive background, and proven patriotism that brought him to the attention of the Abwehr as a potentially valuable secret agent. Recommended by F.2371, himself a banker who scouted for spies, as a "purposeful personality with considerable experience abroad and many excellent foreign connections," he was approached by Captain Driessen of the Abwehr's outpost in Bremen. Introducing himself as "Herr Druisenberg," Driessen met Oppenheim in the Hotel Excelsior in Cologne and invited him to work for the Abwehr, chiefly to collect economic intelligence about England and the United States.

Oppenheim balked at first. He did not think, he told Driessen, that he with his Jewish ancestry should become involved in anything as delicate as this. But Driessen reassured him. The Abwehr had many people like the Baron among its V-men, "including some who are full-blooded Jews."

An "arrangement" was then made at a *Treff* in the Hildmanns Hotel in Bremen. On June 23, 1941, Waldemar von Oppenheim was checked into the Abwehr as a full-fledged secret agent with the cover-name of "Baron" under Registry No. A.2408. Driessen gave him a *Fadenzaehler*, a coding device, and set up a mail drop in Bremen to which to send his reports. He then handed him his first set of instructions on a typewritten sheet reduced to the size of a postage stamp which, Driessen suggested, Waldemar could easily conceal under the back cover of the heavy gold watch he had inherited from Grandfather Oppenheim.

His first mission was to Holland, a test field trip. When he returned with useful material, he was sent to Sweden to lay the foundations for his overseas snooping through the unsuspecting Wallenbergs. He produced five long reports on this excursion (Nos. g4086-89 and g4098 in the log) and they seemed to justify Driessen's most sanguine expectations. One was a general report on the growth of the American armament industry. The others contained much specific data about the production of tanks and aircraft, and the construction of merchant ships even before the United States direct involvement in the war. Report No. g4089 described the methods used in the United States to train crews for ships traveling in convoys, information Oppenheim had obtained by quizzing the First Officer of an American cargo vessel in Stockholm.

Oppenheim made four trips to Sweden in 1941, and returned with sixteen reports, all rated "valuable," several of them "excellent." Their captions spoke for themselves: "English Tonnage in the Atlantic," "Norwegian Ships in Enemy Service," "Production of Tanks and Armored Vehicles in the United States." He submitted an incisive report on "Japanese-American relations" on the eve of Pearl

Harbor, and a detailed study, with schedules and types, of American aircraft going to Britain.

The year 1942 promised to be even more productive.

His earliest reports dealt with the American armament industry, the construction of cargo ships, and the production of aircraft. Later he supplied the specifications of an American fighter plane and details of "Anglo-American convoys in the Atlantic." On February 6, he submitted the "inside story" of *Arcadia*, the Washington conference of Roosevelt and Churchill, in which the decision was reached to make Europe "the center of gravity in the Anglo-American war effort."

On April 8, on a passport and visa procured by the Abwehr, he left for Sweden on another fishing expedition, staying as the guest of the Wallenbergs in the Grand Hotel. Suddenly an incident in Stockholm struck the Germans with the impact of a bombshell. Ralph Hewins, correspondent of the London *Daily Mail*, had cabled a story to his paper about an anonymous "banker from Germany" who was in Stockholm "as Hitler's personal emissary to contact English and American friends and explore with them the possibilities of a separate peace."

The timing of this alleged peace feeler was embarrassing to the Germans, just when the Fuehrer was flaunting his power with massive preparations for what he proclaimed would be the showdown offensive against the U.S.S.R. Hitler was furious when told of the Hewins report and personally ordered the Gestapo to uncover what he regarded as "a vicious plot." A quick check established that, between October 25, 1941, and April 2, 1942, five different "bankers from Germany" had been in Stockholm, but none of them was there when the Hewins story broke.

The *Daily Mail* story created a sensation throughout the world, adding fuel to Hitler's wrath, and intensifying the search for the mysterious banker. He was discovered through one of what the Germans called "Brown Friends"—the copy of an intercepted telegram from Victor Mallett, the British Minister in Stockholm, to the Foreign Office in London. The Germans had compromised the British diplomatic code and were reading Mr. Mallett's dispatches regularly, including this one in which the envoy identified Waldemar Baron von Oppenheim as the banker.

Inquiries then brought out that, during his stay in Sweden, the Baron had met "people with Anglo-American connections" at the estate of Mark Wallenberg in Malmvik, and also at an auction of race horses at Ulriksdal.

When Oppenheim returned to Cologne he found waiting for him a summons to Berlin, where he was instructed to check into the Bristol

Hotel. Inspector Clemens of the Gestapo confronted him with the accusation that he had "abused the Fuehrer's name" and engaged "in unauthorized maneuvers detrimental to German interests."

It was a grave charge and Oppenheim denied everything.

But how did Mr. Hewins know, Gestapo-man Clemens asked, that he happened to be in Stockholm? He was there on a mission from the Abwehr, Oppenheim said, and had conducted himself with the utmost discretion. The only "leak" he could think of might have occurred by what he called an unfortunate inadvertence. One evening, in the company of "the Wallenberg children," he went to a nightclub where the Chilean singer Rosita Serrano was appearing, and he asked for her autograph. Since he had nothing else for her to write it on, he had given her his calling card, and it was possible, Oppenheim said, that she thus found out who he was and tipped off Hewins.

Oppenheim was quizzed for several days, not only by Clemens, but by Gestapo chief Heinrich Mueller himself. However, no hard evidence could be produced to incriminate him. He was allowed to return to Cologne, but his passport was taken away and he was told never to go to Sweden.

It was a blow to the Abwehr.

By this time, Oppenheim had established himself as a high-grade agent, and Colonel Piekenbrock refused to let him fall by the wayside. He intervened with the Gestapo and Oppenheim was allowed to return to the spy business. He was now the indispensable man. The Germans had on order in Sweden forty-five "fishing boats," built according to the specifications of the German Navy which planned to convert them into gunboats. Oppenheim had been instrumental in persuading the Swedes to permit their construction over vehement British objections.

At this same time, the Germans were eager to unload portfolios of foreign stocks and bonds they had captured in their rampage through Europe, and Oppenheim was acting as a go-between with the Wallenbergs. He was no longer a minor cog in the Abwehr apparatus managed by a mere subbranch. Now working for the Abwehr in Berlin, he enjoyed the protection of Colonel Piekenbrock, and even of Admiral Canaris himself.

In letters sent to the Foreign Ministry and the Gestapo, demanding that Oppenheim be allowed full freedom of movement, Piekenbrock attested that the agent's reports "about the American and British armament industry were exceptionally valuable," adding that "thirty-one of them in particular [had drawn] highest commendation from the Navy."

Between July 23 and 30, Oppenheim was in Paris negotiating the transfer of the sequestered foreign stocks and bonds to the Wallenbergs. On September 10, he received orders to return to Stockholm to interrogate "a high Scandinavian personage who will be returning from the United States with valuable secret information." The man was a Swedish diplomat stationed in Washington who had intimate links to American financial and industrial circles.

Oppenheim went to Stockholm on the 20th. His contact provided new data about the construction of Liberty ships; a few interesting figures about aircraft production; and a memo which Oppenheim captioned "The Supply and Production of Rubber." Most of this was "old stuff," and much of it was "slanted in favor of the Allies."

Deeply hurt by his treatment in April, Oppenheim himself was no longer the eager spy he had been. It was obvious that A.2408 had burned out. After a heart-to-heart talk with Canaris and Piekenbrock, he was allowed to retire. The "Baron" was removed from the roster of agents on November 6, 1942, and it seemed that his clandestine career was over.

Then, in the Nazi gloom of early 1945, he was suddenly remembered as the man involved in those mysterious peace feelers three years before. By this time, when Canaris no longer headed the German intelligence establishment, his successor Walter Schellenberg and Heinrich Himmler himself were, behind Hitler's back, plotting peace through Sweden with the help of Count Folke Bernadotte. They thought of Oppenheim and dug him up on the theory that he might be useful in these efforts.

On February 6 the "Baron" was resurrected in the secret underworld, but quickly filed and forgotten when he could not or would not produce any results. As a final gesture of goodwill, as an Allied army approached Bremen, the subbranch ordered that the Oppenheim dossiers be burned, to keep the evidence of his past from the Allies. A quaint document bearing on this last-minute whitewash survives: two witnesses attesting that sixty-seven intelligence reports submitted by Oppenheim and all his personal papers on file had been destroyed. Like so many similar documents marked for burning, the Oppenheim papers also escaped this auto-da-fé. They were captured intact by an American intelligence team, enabling us to reconstruct the strange case of "the Jewish banker from Cologne" who was a Nazi spy.

Even while Oppenheim was establishing himself as a secret agent, another suave aristocrat was being developed to procure important intelligence about England. It was a brazen plot, involving a certain Nazi-minded Danish gentleman who was said to have close ties to the Swedish royal family and court officials. He seemed to be on especially friendly terms with Crown Princess Louisa, the sister of

Lord Louis Mountbatten, who, the Count told his German employers, was in close contact with her relatives in Buckingham Palace. He also professed to be an intimate of Count von Essen, a high official at King Gustaf's court—a confidant of the King himself.

Drawn into the German secret service shortly after the occupation of Denmark, the gentleman was sent to Sweden in the fall of 1940, on an entry visa which he obtained through the intervention of the Crown Princess. The report he submitted on his trip, dated November 11, seemed exciting and important, with an account of his interviews with the King and the Crown Princely couple. It recounted his heated political discussions, especially with the Crown Princess, whom he characterized as "a 100 percent British patriot who hates Nazi Germany."

The Danish gentleman was again in Stockholm around Christmas time in 1941, for a fortnight of conversations with the King, Foreign Minister Guenther, and other "old friends," including F. J. Ronald Bottrall, the British Consul, and a number of English newspapermen.

This time he managed to coax some pro-German statements from his Swedish contacts and a modicum of what could pass for "intelligence" from his British friends. But his usefulness was at an end. The Crown Princess was told confidentially that her friend's visits had ulterior motives. When the gentleman experienced more difficulties in obtaining an entry visa for still another trip, the Princess intervened again, but only to keep him out of Sweden this time, and for good.

With Oppenheim in limbo and the Danish gentleman barred, the Germans had no agent of distinction left to spy on Britain and the United States from the Swedish cockpit.

This was a sorely felt gap. A young man from Hamburg now moved quickly and ingeniously to fill it.

Chapter 45

The Affairs of Josephine

WAR or peace, Stockholm is nine hundred miles from London as the crow flies. But in World War II the two cities seemed light years apart. Neutral ships had to brave two blockades—the British west of the Skagerrak, the German in the Baltic. The few commercial planes still in service risked anti-aircraft fire if they strayed from the narrow corridor charted for their flights. And yet, one of the best spies against the British the Germans ever had lived in Stockholm. Neither distance nor restrictions prevented him from snooping for English secrets as if he lived just off Marble Arch in London.

He was called "Josephine," the only secret agent of the Abwehr singled out for specific mention in the more than 5000 pages of the German High Command's monumental War Diary.

Even the cover-name was sparingly used. Most of the time, the spy was referred to as the *S.Z.V-Mann* ("very reliable confidential agent") or as *bekannte Quelle* ("familiar source"). I found a number of intelligence reports attributed to Josephine, but only a single document—an evaluation sheet of the Luftwaffe Staff—in which the cover-name was used with an identification: "the military attaché of a neutral country stationed in the capital of one of the belligerents."

I was already two years into my research for this book when I discovered that the identification, authoritative though it seemed, was misleading. The "neutral military attaché" was connected with the operation without knowing it, but was not himself Josephine.

Then, one by one, the fragments of the puzzle began to fit. I found that the pseudonym was not the code name of a single individual but that of an operation. It was the collective cover-name of two super-agents called "Pandur" and "Hasso," and of two espionage rings re-

538

ferred to as "Siegfried A" and "Siegfried B." "Pandur" was Heinrich Wenzlau, a captain in the Luftwaffe Reserve, and "Hasso" was a lawyer in civilian life—Karl-Heinz Kraemer, a member of the Abwehr throughout World War II.

The search for Wenzlau led me into a blind alley. I traced him to Godesberg on the Rhine, only to be told that he was dead. Kraemer, the surviving member of "Josephine," at first proved most difficult for me to track down. His development as a master spy, his every movement, the mass of material he produced in nearly three years of top-level espionage—all these clues were preserved intact in hundreds of documents which mention his real name, with no connection to Josephine. The evidence leaves no doubt that he was one of the truly authentic geniuses among the spymasters the Germans had in the field. The documents presented a fascinating, tantalizing apparition— a man in his late twenties moving sure-footedly in this world of shadows, producing strategic intelligence at the highest echelons.

The profusion of documentary evidence would have made it possible to reconstruct his activities, but not the man himself. It became a game within the game to identify him, which I was finally able to do. When he agreed to see me, our meeting confirmed the image I had conjured up from clues in the documents.

Still youngish-looking in his fifties, he was tall, handsome, and in firm control of his thoughts and actions. I could see even at our first session what had made this extraordinary man such an exceptional secret agent. He left no doubt that I was meeting the individual I had been seeking so eagerly and tenaciously, for he told me right at the outset: "You need not look any longer. I was the 'Hasso' of 'Josephine.' "

He had been reluctant to see me, he explained, because he regarded his wartime career as a closed chapter and did not care to revive this relatively brief episode of his past. The young lawyer-spymaster had become a tycoon in the international shipping business. "My friends might misunderstand the part I played," he said with a wry smile, "although I did it in the service of my country even as any Englishman or American would do in similar circumstances."

Then, in long meetings lasting several days, he unfolded the story of what I have no hesitation in describing as the most ingenious and effective clandestine operation of the Second World War.

He had joined the Abwehr when he was only twenty-five years old, a native of Oberkirchen living in Hamburg. Although trained for the law, he planned to become a diplomat and was attached to the German Embassy in London when the outbreak of the war cut short his promising career in the Foreign Service.

A friend introduced him to the Gauleiter of Hamburg who, impressed with the bright young man-of-the-world, sent him to Colonel Dr. Hans Dischler. Kraemer, who spoke English, French, and Spanish fluently, and had lived abroad where he had many friends, was exactly the kind of urbane young man the Abwehr was looking for. Taken into the fold as a *Sonderführer* (a hybrid rank, not quite military, but not altogether civilian either), he was assigned to the air intelligence section whose chief, the studious, punctilious Major Nikolaus Ritter, was assembling a small staff of sophisticated officers with a fresh approach to the old profession.

Given a desk on Sophien Terrace, but little to do aside from listening to Ritter's lectures on the demands and intricacies of his new job, he was straining on the leash. Espionage may be a grand adventure but, like any bureaucracy, it has its boring side—in fact, most of it is just plain undramatic drudgery at its administrative end. Kraemer yearned for the melodrama of the craft, and went roaming in search of it.

He did not stay long in a desk job on Sophien Terrace. Shortly after his arrival in the Abwehr, Ritter sent him to Holland and Belgium, to participate in the crash program laying the groundwork for the invasion of the Low Countries. In November 1940 Hitler dispatched General Ritter von Thoma to Libya to plan a possible joint German-Italian campaign against the British in Egypt. The Abwehr decided to get into the act then and there. Captain Thoran of the air intelligence branch of the Abwehr in Berlin called Ritter in Hamburg and tipped him off to a Hungarian explorer and aviator named Count László de Almásy who might be useful in suborning the Egyptians. For the Egyptian Government, the Count had surveyed the Western Desert through which the Axis campaign would be conducted and knew the area better than any man alive.

Major Ritter sent young Kraemer to Budapest to recruit Almásy for the Egyptian project as well as three diplomats in the Hungarian Foreign Ministry—the "Cairo clique." The Cairo clique was up to its neck in anti-British conspiracies in Egypt, and now they delivered to Kraemer on a silver platter their contacts in Cairo, among them Masri Pasha, Squadron Leader Hussein Sulficar Sabri, Abdel Raouf of the Moslem Brotherhood, and two "born revolutionaries," Gamal Abdel Nasser and Anwar Sadat, who was then a junior officer in the Signal Corps.

In Budapest, Dr. Kraemer made surreptitious deals with a number of Hungarians who had access to the British Legation, even enlisting in his ring of V-men the dentist who cleaned the British Minister's teeth.

The enterprise yielded considerable information about secret British arrangements in North Africa. A British captain named

Frederick Smith who worked in the Movement Control branch of the British General Headquarters in Cairo had become enamoured of an attractive Yugoslav girl, Zorka. On his visits to her apartment, Freddy would take along his briefcase filled with classified papers which his hectic schedule prevented him from processing in the office. While the captain napped, Zorka photographed the documents.

Zorka's loot for the Germans was minor compared with what the Abwehr was getting from Almásy's top-ranking dupe in Cairo, Masri Pasha. The bitterly anti-British general gave the Germans the complete set of the British plans for the defense of the Western Desert. Copies were found by the British among papers they captured during their offensive in December 1940, and Masri Pasha was fired. His dismissal merely deepened his alliance with the Germans. He was set up as the leader of a group of rebellious Egyptian officers, preparing an anti-British uprising in Cairo. The Abwehr was ready to strike when the war flared up in one of the strategic areas of the British Empire.

Since the fall of France, British and German land forces had met only in brief encounters, mostly in Commando raids, while Hitler was looking to the Luftwaffe and the U-boats to force Britain to her knees.

The land war, farmed out to the Italians in North Africa, ended in unmitigated disaster for the Axis. The cream of Italy's colonial army, led by Marshal Graziani, was smashed by the British in Libya. On January 19, Hitler and Mussolini met in an emergency conference, and the Fuehrer told the Duce bluntly that henceforth Germans would do the fighting for both of them, and that he was sending his own troops to North Africa to save the day.

By March 1941, Rommel was ready to mount the decisive offensive that promised to take the Axis all the way to the Suez Canal. The Ritter task force was ordered to pave the way, and Kraemer joined Almásy in Libya to make the last-minute arrangements. Masri Pasha was alerted and agreed to abscond to Rommel's headquarters.

Ritter and Kraemer tried to get the general out of Egypt, attempting to pick him up by U-boat near the Suez Canal, but the waters of Lake Burullus were too shallow for a submarine and the plan had to be abandoned. Next, a Luftwaffe plane disguised with RAF markings was sent to an abandoned airfield at El Khatba, but the general's car broke down on the way to the *Treff* and he missed the connection.

Now Almásy and Kraemer set up Masri Pasha's escape so that nothing could go wrong. Masri was to fly out in a two-engined bomber of the Egyptian Air Force piloted by Squadron Leader Zulficar, one of the chief plotters, taking off from the Almaza airfield. Ritter, Almásy, and Kraemer were waiting for the Egyptians at Rommel's headquarters in Libya, but the plane failed to show up. This time the

British penetrated the conspiracy. Captain A. W. Sansom, the British Chief Field Security officer in Egypt, intercepted the defectors just as they were leaving Almaza and arrested them *in flagranti*. Instead of heading a liberating army marching with the Germans, General Masri Pasha and his fellow conspirators spent the rest of the war locked up.

The only beneficiary of the stillborn plot was Count de Almásy. Rommel rewarded him with the Iron Cross First Class, and kept him at his headquarters as his guide through the tricky deserts of North Africa. But the African operation was broken up.

Major Ritter was recalled, to be sent to Brazil with the cover of an air attaché. Young Kraemer was moved again, this time to Istanbul, straight into the hottest cauldron of espionage in Europe. He fitted quickly and snugly into this congenial environment and shed his amateur status for good.

Instead of hitching a hike on the existing Abwehr appartus in Turkey, he made a working alliance with a super-agent named Karl Friede. Friede appealed to Kraemer because he specialized in procuring most of his intelligence either from or through the foreign diplomatic missions in Turkey. Friede's specialty matched Kraemer's own designs. When organizing the Egyptian plot and the Hungarian coverage of the British in Budapest, Kraemer learned his basic technique of espionage. By plugging his own intelligence-gathering activities into the services of foreign ministries of other countries he could harness diplomats for the benefit of the Abwehr. With Friede's help in Istanbul, Kraemer developed footholds inside the Spanish and Japanese Legations. He soon obtained the cooperation of Marquis de Prat, a Spanish diplomat, and the Italian Dr. Emonotti, known as "Egghead."

A brilliant linguist, "Egghead" worked for the Japanese secret service in Turkey as a general factotum—tout, translator, and evaluator. He had unrestricted access to the mass of usually high-grade intelligence the Japanese were collecting in Europe, especially about England and the U.S.S.R., the two countries in which the Germans had the keenest interest. He copied the best reports and sold them to Dr. Kraemer.

Kraemer also aligned himself with a mysterious Austrian called Klatt or Klatterer, a seasoned operator who free-lanced on a huge scale as a collector of information on Britain and the Soviet Union. But Kraemer was by no means completely dependent on his new friends. In Istanbul he evinced his flair and rugged independence, and scored his first respectable success, establishing his reputation as the fastest rising star in the Abwehr's firmament.

The Turkish telephone and telegraph net had been built by a German firm and one of its men, a certain Karl Wester, had remained in Turkish employ as the chief engineer of the system. Kraemer befriended Wester, and hit upon the idea of putting taps on the telephones of all the Allied agencies in Istanbul.

The engineer agreed to collaborate and since he had easy access to the cable maze of the system, Kraemer listened in on the phone conversations of the important members of the British mission, and tapped the wire of René Massigli, the French delegate. The phones of the British secret service yielded far more than just tidbits of incidental intelligence. Surveillance of the British wire, in one fell swoop wiped out their entire directorate managing sabotage operations in Rumania and occupied Greece. But by then Kraemer was gone from Turkey. The scoop gained from the project he had initiated became a feather in somebody else's cap.

Until this time, the struggle with England was mostly peripheral, and so by necessity was Kraemer's private war with the British Empire. When the Japanese attacked Pearl Harbor and Hitler declared war against the United States, Dr. Kraemer recognized at once that the British Isles had suddenly become the center of the war in the west.

It was one thing to irritate the British with pinpricks from a safe distance, and another to assault them from closer quarters. He became determined to go west, and in the spring of 1942 developed a plan that would enable him to scoop the whole Abwehr in its coverage of England and establish himself as the master spy of the war.

England had become a vast cemetery of German espionage. The Abwehr was doing worse than ever. Johnny was but a fond memory. Attempts at building a new network on the ruins of his venture petered out. The debacle of the pathetic Sea-Lion spies was matched by the fiasco of the Lena team.

No sooner did the Abwehr succeed in recruiting one or another agent for the British beat than he was unmasked, hanged, or worse, turned into a double agent. Admiral Canaris was told candidly by his top lieutenants that it had become next to impossible to organize espionage against England, except for the inferior crew of spies the Abwehr outposts in Madrid and Lisbon were sending to the British Isles.

It was into this intolerable vacuum that Karl-Heinz Kraemer burst with his idea. He was thinking of a novel method that would enable the Abwehr to procure the highest-grade intelligence about Britain without the need of keeping even a single of its own V-men in England, but simply by tapping the secret services of other countries which still maintained agents in Britain.

To some extent, his contact with Emonotti was the inspiration of his bold plan. Dr. Emonotti had been unmasked in Istanbul as a Japanese spy and was expelled at the insistence of the British. He moved to Bucharest, but merely in transit, planning to join Major General Onodera in Stockholm in the same capacity as he served his colleague in Turkey. With the Egghead restored to the pot of secrets, he could continue to supply the intelligence the Japanese were still procuring in Britain, despite the fact that the two countries were now at war.

Then Kraemer discovered an even better source. Back in Germany, he had seen a batch of reports the Abwehr had received in the fall of 1940 and the spring of 1941. The haphazard manner in which those reports had been obtained, he thought, could be organized on a regular basis, and produce a vast amount of the most reliable information about the British. During the air blitz it was imperative for the Luftwaffe to have a string of agents on station in England, to get from them indispensable target intelligence before their air raids, and damage reports promptly in the wake of them.

Between August 13 and October 31, 1940, more than 17,000 planes dropped 17,831 tons of bombs and 13,472 incendiary devices on England. In September alone, London was hit 268 times with a total of 6224 tons of bombs and 8546 incendiaries. It was inconceivable to Goering and his Luftwaffe satraps that the British would be able to survive this savage punishment.

However, the Reichsmarshal was in his blind fury. He knew how hard he was hitting, but did not know how badly the British were getting hurt. Aerial reconnaissance proved inadequate and insufficient. A system organized by Colonel Josef Schmid, chief of Luftwaffe Intelligence, to obtain information from all possible sources, near and far, proved unsatisfactory. For the results of the raids against nearby Britain "Beppo" Schmid had to rely on reports from observation posts as far away as Washington, Tokyo, and Buenos Aires. German air attachés obtained as best they could the reports from London air attachés of the United States, Japan, and Argentina sent to their home offices.

In this crisis, help came from an unexpected quarter. It was known in Berlin that Major S. E. Cornelius, the Swedish air attaché in London, was sending to Stockholm detailed reports about the raids with a daily assessment of the damage they were supposedly causing. Urgent instructions were sent to 41-year-old Colonel Reinhard von Heimann, the German air attaché in Sweden, to procure the Cornelius reports by all means, fair or foul. But Heimann was a correct and punctilious officer who would not stoop to any skullduggery to obtain information. When he could not get the Cornelius reports overtly, he refused to procure them covertly.

Fortunately for Schmid, Heimann had on his staff a captain named Heinrich Wenzlau whose *raison d'ètre* in Sweden never ceased to intrigue the straight-laced air attaché. Wenzlau was, in fact, "Pandur," the "Josephine" officer sent to Stockholm for the explicit purpose of spying on the RAF from the Swedish cockpit. What Colonel von Heimann either could not or would not procure, Wenzlau now obtained in abundance. With the surreptitious help of a pro-German member of the Combined Intelligence staff of the Swedish High Command, he received pilfered copies of the daily reports of Major Cornelius. When they reached Berlin on the *G-Schreiber* (the air attaché's cipher teletype) they pleased Goering no end, if only because the devastation Cornelius reported to have seen in England exceeded the Reichsmarshal's most sanguine expectations. As a matter of fact, he was so pleased with these reports that he chose them for presentation to Hitler to impress him with the devastating effectiveness of the Luftwaffe.[1]

When Kraemer stumbled upon the "Pandur" dossier in the Abwehr's files, he concluded that it was possible to gain access to the confidential correspondence of neutral service attachés stationed in London. The question now was which of the neutrals would be the most productive and the best to be tapped.

Admiral Canaris had a formal alliance with the Spanish Intelligence Service under which the Abwehr was receiving copies of all reports sent to Madrid by three attachés in London. They were regularly forwarded to Schmid who found them "not too good," probably because the attachés assessed the damage as "great but not critical."

Another tap on a neutral diplomatic pipeline, also arranged by Captain Wenzlau, was in Lisbon, secured by corrupting an official in the Portuguese Foreign Ministry. Its consuls around the world were required to send regularly to Lisbon listings of the ships which moved in and out of the harbors where they were posted. Their dispatches were sneaked to Pandur by the man on his payroll, enabling the Abwehr to assemble at least some of the intelligence that the U-boats needed.

Called "Globus," the operation had several disadvantages. The corrupt Portuguese was very expensive and, suffering from some apparently incurable disease, was too often on sick leave. Also, most of the consular reports were sent by mail, and the ships they listed had come and gone by the time the Abwehr received information about their movements.

In the summer of 1942 Wenzlau was sent to Lisbon again, to explore the possibility of making better use of the Portuguese facilities in the coverage of England. He came up with a plan to plant a man inside the Portuguese Embassy in London, and persuaded a young diplomat to take on the job. He was supposed to copy the confidential reports of the Ambassador, and forward them to the Abwehr via a mail drop in Lisbon, actually in the diplomatic bag, which he was permitted to use for his private correspondence.

Although this contact was much cheaper than Globus, it endured for only a short time. British security, tipped off by Kim Philby's superb counterespionage organization in Lisbon, arrested the young man, and effectively discouraged any more such violation of the traditional Anglo-Portuguese alliance by getting the death sentence for him.[2]

Although beautiful Lisbon and elegant Estoril held out the promise of an exquisite good time, Dr. Kraemer abandoned the idea of corrupting Portugal. The country was Britain's oldest ally, its ranking officials generally pro-British.

Kraemer also dismissed the other neutrals, such as the Turks, because their diplomatic code had been broken and their reports were regularly read in Berlin. The correct and prudish Swiss, also pro-Ally in their sympathies, would never be susceptible to his kind of persuasion.

This left only one neutral country whose secret resources he could tap. So young Kraemer did like Peer Gynt in a perilous pass to eke a measure of his days. He chose Sweden.

Since Kraemer was a member of the Abwehr he had to abide by the rules and amenities of the organization and make his arrangements for his transfer to Stockholm with Colonel Hans Wagner, the senior Abwehr representative in Sweden. He saw him on August 1, 1942, but what transpired during their conference convinced Kraemer that if he became a mere cog in the Wagner Bureau on Nybrogatan it would grind him up.

He could not very well take his misgivings to Admiral Canaris or Pieckenbrock, so he carried his beef to a friend, Major Friedrich Busch, who was "Ludwig" in the Air Intelligence Section of the Abwehr in Berlin. A prosperous sardine importer in civilian life, Busch was an ambitious newcomer unawed by sacred cows. He recognized that Kraemer's plan represented an entirely new approach in penetrating the Royal Air Force and the British aviation industry, promising to be a shortcut to the target intelligence Goering was constantly clamoring for. Busch obtained Canaris's approval to let Kraemer function on his own, together with all the authority and money he needed. To him, Kraemer appeared to be the indispensable man Germany needed in Sweden. In a memorandum to Foreign Minister von Ribbentrop, Ambassador Karl Ritter, who handled all

Wehrmacht matters in the Ministry, wrote in support of the young outsider's application for the coveted diplomatic cover:

"Dr. Kraemer works for the Luftwaffe. He has long-standing connections in Britain and is receiving continuous reports from inside England about factories engaged in war production. The authenticity and accuracy of his reports has been proven. At this time his information is regarded as the most valuable contribution to the target intelligence the Luftwaffe Staff needs in planning its campaign against British war industries."

Ribbentrop assigned him *pro forma* to the Press Bureau in Stockholm with the rank of Secretary of Legation. On October 29, he was formally accredited at the Swedish Foreign Ministry as a diplomat. Two days later, traveling on Diplomatic Passport No. 2769 issued to him on his real name, Kraemer arrived in Stockholm and plunged into his secret mission at once.

Thanks to Busch's efforts he had all he needed to succeed. He occupied a desk in the air attaché's office and had an office of his own where he could do as he pleased. He was authorized to use the couriers of the Legation and GLYST, the scrambler teletype of the air attaché with a direct line to the Luftwaffe High Command. He had Minister Prince zu Wied's daughter as his private secretary. No member of the Abwehr hierarchy enjoyed such privileges and was allowed such autonomy. And he had his wish—he had nothing to do with Colonel Wagner, the burly spymaster was left out in the cold.

His first shipment, too bulky for the teletype, went out by special courier on November 12. It consisted of eleven separate reports, listing and describing as many industrial installations in Britain. It created a sensation, not only in the Abwehr, but also in Luftwaffe Intelligence where the information was hailed as the most valuable target intelligence they ever received.

"Josephine" was off to a flying start.

In actual fact, "Josephine" was a vast espionage cartel of several interlocking enterprises, with Wenzlau as "Pandur" acting as a kind of chairman of the board and Kraemer as "Hasso" as chief executive officer. Wenzlau commuted between Stockholm and Lisbon.

Kraemer was making the most of his opportunity. The year 1943 was his peak period. His bulging dossiers in the files of the Luftwaffe High Command, where his dispatches wound up, show that he forwarded nearly a thousand different intelligence reports during this most productive year. Dealing with every phase and aspect of the Allied war effort, they contained both strategic information—about the Allies' invasion plans—and pinpointed tactical data—about the

RAF and the growing American air power in Britain, the concentration of Allied warships, and about major plants of the British war industry as targets for the Luftwaffe.

Some of his reports demonstrated uncanny knowledge of what was going on in the highest Allied councils, even within 10 Downing Street. They quoted strictly confidential statements of an air vice marshal, a member of Parliament, high-ranking officials of the Air Ministry, other civil servants, and an officer serving as one of the King's aides at Buckingham Palace.

His coverage had breathtaking scope. It ranged from the purchase of twenty copies of the latest *Who's Who* to the minutes of a top secret conference held in the office of Sir Stafford Cripps, then Minister of Aircraft Production, attended by only five individuals—one of whom Kraemer called "Hektor," described as his informant. According to his report, it was at this meeting that the decision was reached to intensify the aerial bombardment of Germany to hit any target, military or civilian, indiscriminately. "Please," Kraemer noted on his report about the conference, "refrain from making any propaganda use of this information, for my source could be traced easily if our knowledge of this decision became public." Actually the British concentrated on skilled workers' districts as well as war production buildings.

How was a single man capable of accomplishing so much? What and where were his sources? The enterprise was unique in the enormous industry and ingenuity which Kraemer invested in the effort. He was tapping a number of feedlines going by different covernames, each gushing intelligence of a different variety. Kraemer found one of them, called "Siegfried A," functioning in Stockholm under an Abwehr agent who was a local representative of the Lufthansa at Bromma Airport.

As early as 1940, the Lufthansa representative monitored the shipment of strategic materials on leaving for or reaching Bromma for England, and also reported passengers of special interest to the Germans. He enlisted two Swedes—a mechanic and a freight manager, to assist him in this venture, paying each 7500 kroner.

The trio supplied daily copies of the lading bills of all outgoing shipments, listing such essential war items as ballbearings from SKF, machine parts from Bolinders and Atlas Diesel, electrical machinery and spare parts from ASEA, and special steel drills manufactured by Sandviken, all of which were indispensable for the British war effort. Passenger lists of every plane arriving or departing at Bromma on the British route were checked out. This proved fatal in the end for a number of young Norwegians going to Scotland via Sweden to be trained as resistance fighters and returning to Norway by the same route to join the underground.

Air traffic here was indispensable to the Josephine operation. Kraemer moved his correspondence with his mysterious contacts in Britain on the Swedish ABA airline. This ring of spies, called "Siegfried B," was the backbone of his enterprise, the precious source from which emanated the most valuable intelligence he was able to collect, such as the report on the Stafford Cripps's conference.

British security was aware that a leak existed somewhere in Whitehall, and that spies were using the ABA planes to ship their strategic information out of Britain, probably in the privileged pouch of the Swedish Legation in London. But no matter how hard they tried, neither MI.5 nor Scotland Yard succeeded in identifying the elusive agents.

A clue to at least one of them was then found in the summer of 1943, in a painful incident involving Captain Count J. G. Oxenstierna, the Swedish naval attaché in London. Bearer of one of his country's most revered historic names, the ebullient, debonair aristocrat and his wife were popular at St. James's Court. Commander Cyril F. Tower, head of the Scandinavian branch of the British Naval Intelligence Division, did not quite like Oxenstierna's avid interest in the Royal Navy and the aggressive manner in which he went after sensitive information. The naval attaché, astute and exceptionally competent, seemed completely wrapped up in his job. He was in the habit of buttonholing friends in the Admiralty and pumping them for information. On frequent inspection trips to the fleet bases and naval installations, he was always asking pointed technical questions which revealed that he already knew a little too much and was trying to find out more.

Tower was mortified when some hard evidence suddenly turned up to indicate that his worst apprehension seemed to be justified. It was discovered that certain data about the armament of a new type destroyer had seeped to Germany shortly after one of Captain Oxenstierna's tours of the naval base in Portsmouth.

The British were monitoring the overworked teletype in the German air attaché's office whose cipher they had broken. In one of the intercepts they came upon the exact information which Oxenstierna had prevailed upon his hosts in Portsmouth to divulge to him. In another intercepted signal they found him mentioned by name as the originator of certain intelligence Josephine was forwarding.

Commander Tower no longer doubted that the Swedish officer was responsible for the embarrassing crack in British security, and demanded that he be declared *persona non grata*. Apprehensive that the Swedes might retaliate in kind by booting out Captain Denham, the Foreign Office refused, but the Count was asked politely to go home. He left under a cloud, hurt, puzzled, and protesting, incapable of comprehending how the British could ever mistake him for a German spy.

Tower's suspicion seemed to be borne out when Commander Prince Bertil, a grandson of King Gustaf V, was named Oxenstierna's successor as acting naval attaché. Suddenly, the leaks dried up. No more information about the British Navy passed through the monitored teletype, nothing at all attributed to Prince Bertil. Oxenstierna was not a German agent. Information he collected in England in the line of duty was exclusively for the Swedish Admiralty. But if he was not personally involved in his security breach, how did the Germans succeed in getting hold of his dispatches? This was one of Josephine's great mysteries. Kraemer had penetrated the Foreign Department of the Swedish Defense Staff, which had jurisdiction over the service attachés, and the intelligence establishment (both Combined Intelligence and Secret Intelligence Services). Without their faintest knowledge, Captain Oxenstierna and every other Swedish service attaché stationed in London (and Moscow) were fountainheads of Josephine's information. Kraemer had access to their reports no matter how closely they were held in the vaults of the Swedish Foreign Department.

Kraemer befriended a whole bevy of pretty Swedish girls who rewarded him with copies of attaché reports. Moreover, he used them as his most expedient cover, giving the impression to anybody who would become too closely interested in his surreptitious activities that he was romantically involved with these young ladies while actually he was merely tapping them for first-rate intelligence material.

Kraemer did not waste any time after his arrival in Stockholm before plunging headlong into the whirl of the Swedish capital's jet set. One beautiful young woman would introduce Kraemer to her friends, and he then cultivated those among them who seemed most likely to be useful. Three of them became most useful—Inga Britt Ollson, Monica Ahlstroem, and Siv Hoeglund.[3] They had a lot in common. They were beautiful, vivacious, and outgoing, fond of a good time, enthusiastic dancers, and all of them worked in the Defense Staff; Siv was a secretary in the department where files of the attaché's reports wound up.

When Kraemer's perambulations aroused the interest of the National Police Board, whose responsibilities included counterespionage, it became impossible to overlook the link between him and these young women. They were seen dining or dancing with him at fashionable restaurants and smart nightclubs, and were traced to one or another of his bachelor flats which he maintained for his *Treffs*. For a while the detectives let them come and go. When it became obvious that Kraemer was not what he pretended to be—a diplomat working at his Legation's Press Office—these young women were gently questioned about the nature and extent of their relations with the dashing young German. As the minutes of their quizzing show, they succeeded remarkably well in leading their interrogators down the primrose path. They admitted readily and cheerfully that they were friendly with Dr. Kraemer, but they insisted that they had violated none of the security regulations of their sensitive jobs. Those *Treffs* in his hideouts, they claimed with bashful indignation, were trysts. All they gave Kraemer on those occasions was a good time, not any secret information.

Had the detectives pressed them a bit harder, scrutinized them more closely and searched their handbags on their way to those trysts, they would have found that they were bearing gifts. Siv Hoeglund was the most indignant and eloquent in protesting her innocence, so far as it went. In actual fact, she was Kraemer's chief accomplice, or dupe, in this part of the Josephine operation. It was Siv who smuggled to him Oxenstierna's invaluable dispatches, together with reports from the Swedish air attachés in London who succeeded Major Cornelius.

But this was one-way traffic. It was also necessary for Kraemer to procure specific information from time to time. His customers both in the Abwehr and Luftwaffe Intelligence drew up shopping lists for him—items seeking elaboration of the attachés reports, and original information which, the Germans assumed, one or the other of the attachés could get.

In due course, Kraemer supplied the items one by one, indicating that he had the means of forwarding queries to London and getting them answered. He himself had realized quite early in the game that he would have to win over one or more members of the Swedish Defense Staff through whom he could plant his own questions. Such a contact was readily available in the person of the officer who helped Captain Wenzlau get the Cornelius reports in 1940–41. This old relationship was now revived. A few weeks after his arrival in the fall of 1942, Kraemer arranged a trip to Berlin for the officer to make his own deal with Busch and others. After that, the officer became a regular German agent inside the Defense Staff. He was exceptionally well placed for the job: he was the aide of the head of the Swedish Secret Intelligence Service, and could easily plant the questions to which Kraemer sought answers for Berlin.

There was more. Probably to impress his home office, Kraemer practically paraded his other sources in his dispatches. It was an unusual and risky feature of his operation; intelligence reports are usually intercepted in transit, and such blunt disclosure of sources often terminates their usefulness. His colleague Wilhelm Schierenbeck of the Bischoff Bureau in Bremen claimed to have at least three super-agents in England and referred to them as CHB 1, CHB 2, and CHB 3. He steadfastly refused to identify them even to his most important client, Colonel Alexis von Roenne, chief of the Army General Staff's intelligence division.

Kraemer had no such qualms. His reports explicitly indentified his informants, usually by their real names. He even included those he claimed he had inside Britain, who were as innocent of wrong doing as Captain Oxenstierna. Among them the names of three distinguished Britons recurred most often. His chief source within the RAF thus seemed to be an Air Commodore (later Air Vice Marshal) who served during the war with the Fighter Command. Another major source he identified as a member of the family that owned a large group of tearooms, restaurants, and other related enterprises. The third man at the top of his list was a high-ranking civil servant to whom he attributed the intelligence he gathered about the goings-on in Downing Street.

It is beyond the shadow of a doubt that none of his so-called sources either knew that they were being bugged or had even the faintest inkling that they were mentioned so frequently and prominently in Kraemer's dispatches. It was possible that information attributed to them had been picked up from Kraemer's regular sources with whom they were on friendly terms, and that such important individuals let an occasional indiscretion slip off their lips despite the tight security they imposed upon themselves.

The actual conveyors of the intelligence Kraemer allegedly gained from these men were masked by cover-names—such as "Hektor" and "Fink" and "Monogram"—and he still refuses to reveal the identity of the people behind these pseudonyms.[4] His line of communication with them was much simpler than one would think possible. Kraemer gave Hans Schaefer of "Siegfried A" sealed letters addressed to his mail drop in London, and the Lufthansa man at Bromma then found someone in the crews of the planes to Britain who agreed to take them along and post them, leaving delivery to the regular mailmen at the far end of the line. Other mail was handed to a man he had in the Foreign Ministry's mailroom, who included these letters in the pouch he was preparing for the next courier going to London. The system worked in both directions, on the Stockholm-London as well as the London-Stockholm routes.

For all the galaxy of his key sources and mysterious go-betweens, Kraemer's chief source was Egghead, now firmly entrenched in Stockholm, where he was running General Onodera's outpost. Whether or not the Japanese had agents in England during this period cannot be ascertained. However, Onodera was procuring first-rate intelligence about the British, partly from spies, but mostly by cryptanalysis. He was reading the encoded dispatches of the British Foreign Office, the War Office, and the Admiralty, whose cryptographic security left much to be desired. Onodera's specialty was codes and ciphers, through which he obtained some of the Allies' most sensitive dispatches, culling from them invaluable intelligence.

This explained Kraemer's apparent omniscience. He himself was on excellent terms with General Onodera to whom he gave copies of practically all the reports he collected from the two Siegfried groups. Onodera was not quite so generous, but that did not matter. Under the old deal arranged by Klatt, Kraemer received the entire output of the Japanese secret service in Europe from Dr. Emonotti, including translations of the intercepts.

In the fall of 1944 the Josephine operation suddenly appeared in a new light. Unexpectedly in early November, Kraemer was asked to return to Berlin for consultation. When he reported to Lieutenant Colonel Ohletz of the Air Intelligence Station, he was told bluntly that he was under investigation as a possible faker, misusing official funds by financing non-existent intelligence operations.

Ohletz then escorted him to Heinrich Mueller, the dreaded chief of the Gestapo, in whose office he was quizzed mercilessly for the whole day and into the night. Kraemer emerged from his ordeal unscathed. He succeeded in persuading Mueller that his activities were beyond reproach, and that no fakery whatsoever was ever involved in his operations. When they left the Gestapo chief's office, Ohletz was visibly relieved. "I don't know," he told Kraemer, "whether you're aware of it, but this was the most critical day in your life. If you had failed to convince Mueller and vindicate yourself, you would be on your way to a concentration camp."

The ending of this crisis proved that he was the master spy he claimed to be, and that his activities were on the level. But by this time his usefulness was nearing its end. In an evaluation report dated October 5, 1944, prepared by the new masters of intelligence under Walter Schellenberg who had succeeded Admiral Canaris in the shake-up of the Abwehr earlier in the year, the high rating Josephine had invariably received before was drastically revised.

"The evaluation of this operation by the Abwehr," the report stated, "is no longer valid. The quality of the Josephine material, especially those concerning army matters, is generally inferior."

Of ten reports chosen at random from his 1944 output for the purpose of this evaluation, one was rated "very good," another "good," and a third "usable." But four were dismissed contemptuously as "nonsense," and two were described as "fakes." The evaluator called the tenth report *Spielmaterial*, raising the possibility that Kraemer was a double agent peddling misleading information planted by the enemy.

The inevitable dénouement, coming at a time when Germany was staring into the face of ruin and defeat, did not invalidate the fantastic contribution Josephine had made to the German war effort, nor did it diminish Kraemer's accomplishments.

What made Kraemer such a good and hardy spy was that he seemed unaffected by the clandestine hokum. He lived a normal, though lively life in Stockholm with his pretty wife Eva and his infant daughter Heidi, in a handsome villa at Stora Essingen, an elegant residential suburb. He was the perfect specimen of the gifted amateur who gives the seasoned professionals a run for their money—bright, sharp, ambitious, eager, and smooth. He was always on the go, full of original ideas, with a real knack for doing boldly and easily what others found difficult or impossible.

Terribly good-looking—a blue-eyed giant with the pink complexion of a baby—enormously attractive, and a brilliant gabber, he oozed cheer and charm, and, as far as the ladies were concerned, considerable good will.

In a letter to me, a high-ranking official of the Swedish secret police wrote with grudging admiration:

"His activities came to our attention early in February 1943. After that, up to the end of the war, he was continuously subject to covert surveillance.

"Kraemer had no fixed working time. In the morning, he usually spent a few hours at the Legation. He also paid a daily visit to the office of the German air attaché on Karlawegen. . . .

"He was fond of painting the town red. Among his favourite restaurants were three in the center of Stockholm and an inn in one of the western suburbs. He used to take his 'contacts' to one or another of the three flats he had at his disposal in the northern part of the city. These circumstances made it relatively easy for our men to shadow him, identify his 'contacts' and come on his trail again whenever it was lost."

He needed some camouflage, of course, for no spy of even lesser stature could function without it. But he eschewed all the familiar gimmicks and hoary melodrama that usually goes with the spy game.

"Kraemer lived dangerously," I was told in Stockholm by one of the detectives who had the thankless task of keeping him under surveillance, "but not because he was a secret agent. He had a souped-up DKW which he always drove at breakneck speed."

Spies are anxious as a rule to avoid anything that might bring them to the attention of the cops. Kraemer was different. His reckless driving made him a familiar figure to every policeman in the city. Involved as he was in a number of accidents, he had a "record." During the regime of Admiral Sir Hugh Sinclair, there was a popular maxim in the British Secret Service. Newcomers to the game were usually given but one piece of advice when sent on their initial mission: "Always be friendly with the policeman," they were told. "He's the only friend you have." It is doubtful if Kraemer knew about this quaint injunction, but he lived by its principle, going out of his way to befriend the detectives assigned to keep tabs on him. Invariably they were sporty young men who needed vim and zest to keep up with him. And they had to be daring drivers or they would have been unable to stay on his tail.

"He really puzzled us with his conduct," one of the detectives told me, "so different from the usual ways of spies. Take, for instance, those three little flats he had. It is customary in the spy business to meet confidential contacts in so-called 'safe places,' in out-of-the-way houses or in hidden apartments, usually in buildings with several entrances, where such surreptitious meetings can be easily concealed. But not Kraemer! He would drive straight to one or another of his flats whenever he had such a date and park his conspicuous little car in front of the building. We could watch him as he came and went. He was the easiest quarry to stalk, except that he was such a fast driver."

When he came under surveillance, he did not resent their interest in him, not even when it became somewhat awkward, because one could never tell whether he was on a *Treff* or a tryst. He once blocked the path of the detectives' car, got out and accosted his pursuers in his best drawing-room manner. "I like to know the people," he said, "who have such generous interest in me. My name is Kraemer. What's yours?"

On one of his frequent visits to the Opera Grill, one of the town's most expensive restaurants, he spotted another set of shadows at a nearby table. He ordered a bottle of champagne for them, then raised his own glass in a toast to the startled detectives.

He felt perfectly safe in Stockholm because he never spied on the Swedes. His undivided attention was devoted to the British. And he managed his business so well and so discreetly that the secret police, who accumulated a bulging dossier about this mercurial young man, had come to know all about his amorous escapades, but precious little about his espionage activities. The police regarded him as a playboy, a four-flushing big-spender of the Abwehr's money, and dismissed him as a harmless phony.

This became his best cover.

If Ian Fleming had known him, I would say that Kraemer was the original model for his James Bond—except that the German was not licensed to kill. All of his pent-up violent instincts were vented in sporting exercises—his vicious serve in tennis, for example—or in his fervid, reckless bidding at bridge.

He abhorred violence, not because he was a coward by any means, but because it was so messy. And Karl-Heinz Kraemer was the neatest, nattiest, most fastidious buccaneer of them all.

NOTES

1 There is reason to believe that the British themselves fed exaggerated data to Major Cornelius and other neutral attachés through the "Double-Cross System" of MI.5. They assumed that at least some of their reports would reach Berlin and induce Goering either to temper the raids in the light of the damage he had already wrought or divert his attention from strategically important targets supposedly destroyed.

2 The man was still listed as "hanged" in the roster of executed German spies the Home Office published in the fall of 1945. In actual fact, he had been reprieved and allowed to return to Portugal after the war.

3 Although the real identity of these women is known to me, I have chosen to conceal them behind these pseudonyms.

4 Kraemer endured in Stockholm until April 1945, when he was compelled to return to Germany, in the last throes of its final agony. Captured by the British in Flensburg, he was flown to MI.5's maximum security detention center at Ham Common near London, together with three dozen key Abwehr officers scooped up in various hideouts after the collapse of the Third Reich. Although he was kept in custody for over two years, longer than any of his fellow inmates, and was interrogated continuously during that time, he succeeded in concealing both his modus operandi and the identity of "Hektor" and "Fink," who allegedly served him as producing agents inside England.

Chapter 46

The Road to Casablanca

*E*XCEPT perhaps for Sir Francis Walsingham's spies who spotted the approach of the Spanish Armada in 1588, secret services have a genius for overlooking hostile fleets on their course to sneak attacks. What the Abwehr overlooked in the fall of 1942 was an armada of 104 American ships on a 3000-mile march from Norfolk, Virginia, to the Atlantic beaches of French Morocco. It also failed to notice British convoys sailing from Loch Ewe and the Clyde estuary in Scotland to Algiers through the U-boat infested Bay of Biscay and the Strait of Gibraltar. They carried the forces of "Torch," the Allies' first offensive in the war, on their laborious roundabout journey to the Nazi-occupied continent.

The Abwehr, senior member of the German intelligence community, was so completely unaware of this massive flow of ships, and of what it portended, that on the day the Americans and the British reached their destination and went ashore in North Africa, Admiral Canaris and Colonel Piekenbrock were on a leisurely visit to Copenhagen, more than a thousand miles from where the action was. They were as stunned by the news of the invasion as Southwell must have been when beholding the Burning Babe in the snow.

There may have been some extenuating circumstance for their failure to anticipate the blow. Only three months had brought a dramatic change in the war. The Allies were still hard pressed throughout the summer of 1942, the apparent ebb of their fortunes highlighted by the mauling of convoys to Malta and Murmansk, the Canadians' disaster at Dieppe, and the rapid advance of Rommel toward Cairo.

But their summer of discontent was followed by their most glorious November in this war. By the 4th, Rommel was in full retreat and Egypt was cleared on the 8th. On the same day, the compact Anglo-American expeditionary force started operations in North Africa.

The comeback of the enemy was so sudden, and reverses represented such a novel experience for the Germans, that they had no time to climb out of their conceit and complacency. With their eyes focused on the war in Russia, they ignored the threat from the Western Allies, especially at such *outré* places as Morocco and Algiers.

In the wake of the fall of France, the region south and north of the western Mediterranean moved simultaneously into the ken of two implacable adversaries—Adolf Hitler and Franklin Roosevelt. In July 1940, provoked by the determination of the British to continue the war single-handed, Hitler decided to "drive the English out of the western Mediterranean" by "taking Gibraltar and closing the Strait." Almost simultaneously, President Roosevelt reached the conclusion that the best road to the Continent (and to the defeat of the Nazis) led through the same general area, though the United States was not yet at war.

Hitler was charting his course formally. An ambitious operation plan called "Felix" was drawn up with the attack on Gibraltar scheduled for November. Because of his close relations with the Spaniards and supposed influence on General Franco, Hitler assigned to Admiral Canaris the spadework for Felix, essentially to reconnoiter the Rock for the assault and to coax Spain into the venture.

For once, Canaris was seized by a delusion of Napoleonic grandeur. He embarked on a grandiose plot of his own that quickly exceeded his limited assignment. He sought to reserve to himself control over the whole of Felix, from the menial task of spying on the Rock to the exalted prize of commanding the assault forces.

On July 22, Canaris personally led an intelligence team to the outskirts of Gibraltar "to study the terrain, the possible difficulties of the assault, and develop a basic attack plan." At the same time, he began to assemble the expeditionary force from the Brandenburgers, his private army of Hell's Angels.

Canaris's reconnaissance venture developed into a farcical tour. Never in the history of espionage was a mission like this mounted by such distinguished spies—the Chief of Intelligence in person, flanked by his top-ranking aides, Colonel Piekenbrock and Commander Wilhelm Leissner (alias "Gustav Lenz"), the Abwehr chief in Spain. In a manner typical of his way of doing such things, he also sent another team of snoopers to the Rock, practically behind his own back. Assembled in greatest secrecy, it was headed by a dour, no-nonsense sabotage expert, Captain Hans-Jochen Rudloff, who had conducted highly irregular operations during the French campaign.

The initial double mission was followed by a veritable avalanche of reconnaissance ventures, until Spain became the popular tourist attraction of the Abwehr. All one had to do to get himself a vacation was to think up an idea that had some bearing on Felix and he was assured of a holiday in Andalusia. One intelligence unit after another was dispatched to the area around the coveted Pillars of Hercules, one ignorant of the other and working at cross purposes, during a brief period of manly hilarity in the Abwehr which was not otherwise noted for its sense of humor.

The feverish action was reminiscent of a Mack Sennett comedy, with people rushing through doors, bumping into one another, stepping on each other's toes and getting banged on the head by unidentified falling objects. Once when Canaris dispatched two such separate teams simultaneously, he issued strict orders to them to operate independently with the utmost discretion and take pains to avoid each other. Stopping in Madrid en route to the mission, craving a little good time on this unexpected junket, members of one of the groups, carrying bulky briefcases, visited a cabaret which catered to German guests, to find their colleagues from the other team at the place, also lugging their bulging portfolios.

Somehow characteristic of the frivolity of the enterprise was an incident that led to the discarding of the best photographs Captain Hans Roschmann from another team managed to shoot of the Rock's formidable fortifications to the east. They were taken from the balcony of a house in La Linea, Roschmann posing two comely young ladies in the foreground to camouflage the true purpose of his picture taking. The prints were rejected with disdain when General Jodl of the High Command found out that the house from which the snapshots had been made was a notorious bordello and the women in the picture were two of its inmates.

Canaris himself would return from time to time to direct the activities personally. He was doing it so conspicuously that British agents, who were as numerous in the area as were the Abwehr spies, could not help spotting him wherever he went. He celebrated New Year's Eve in a tavern in Algeciras which was also a favorite of the competition. The admiral's choice of this particular place gave birth to the legend that it was his first effort to make contact with the British secret service for a joint struggle against the Fuehrer.

If all this had been done for some ulterior purpose—to deceive Hitler, for example, by feigning feverish activity merely to sabotage Felix (as it was later claimed by Canaris's apologists), or to lighten the war's deadly seriousness, the comedy could be appreciated. But this was no hanky-panky. The actors were blissfully unaware of how funny they really were in this parody of espionage.

By the end of 1940, the area was completely charted, a wasted effort on a grandiose scale. After some teasing and fooling, the Spaniards backed out of Felix and in January 1941 the plan was shelved. What was left of it was an enormous intelligence organization on both shores of the western Mediterranean, stationed in a crescent extending from Spain to French Morocco.

At its northern terminus in Algeciras, the Abwehr maintained a contingent of handpicked specialists under Major Fritz Kautschke and Albert Carbe, observing the Rock and watching the Strait from two villas equipped with the best instruments of surveillance that the German optical and electronic industries could produce.[1] One of the leaders of the Strait-watchers in Tetuan was Colonel Johann Recke, in Spanish Morocco since 1937 as the Abwehr's resident director. The Bureau Recke had senior agents and innumerable stringers. In Tangier alone, a crew occupying two houses watched the Strait in three shifts day and night.

Inside Canaris's friendly Spanish intelligence service, which cooperated in the preparations of Felix far more zealously than General Franco, a contingent of spies was assigned to the job full time. The network extended to Algiers and Casablanca, with a senior V-man camouflaged as a member of the German Armistice Commission directing a ring in French Morocco.

It was assumed that nothing could escape the vigilance of this enormous network consisting of some of the Abwehr's keenest spymasters and 357 secret agents (by actual count) in the field, backed up by the huge Abwehr outposts in Madrid and Lisbon.

But they were not alone. In Spain and Portugal the British had a splendid organization of their own, headed by Commander Hilgarth, the naval attaché in Spain, and Kim Philby who managed the operation by remote control from Section V of MI.6. Intelligence was not the primary purpose of this clandestine expeditionary force dispatched by S.I.S. to the Iberian Peninsula. They were engaged in a war of their own, fighting the Abwehr on what was practically its own home grounds. The British won this particular battle, as they were to win the whole secret war eventually. They penetrated the Abwehr network, tripped up its agents, kept them under constant surveillance, and fed misleading information to them in a campaign especially designed to frustrate Felix and mess up the Germans' frenetic scrutiny of the Strait. The result was devastating for the Germans. The Canaris organization appeared to be at the peak of its preparedness and efficiency in November 1942, but it failed totally and dismally in this case. The Allied invasion of North Africa actually reached its destination undetected.

Gross as the Abwehr's oversight was, Canaris's efforts to cover it up afterward was even worse. He worked overtime to confute his critics with random and manufactured evidence to show that he had warned the High Command. He was so glib and convincing that he succeeded in befuddling even as shrewd and skeptical a man as Goebbels. On April 9, 1943, Goebbels wrote in his diary: "Admiral Canaris reported to me about the work of the Abwehr service. From this I gather that the Abwehr has operated better than I had supposed. For instance, it reported the Anglo-American operation in North Africa and the Casablanca meeting in good time, but these facts were not reported to the Fuehrer with sufficient emphasis. . . ." "I have arranged with Canaris," he wrote in July 1943, "that in the future we shall work more closely together. He will now make regular reports to me so that I in turn can work on the Fuehrer.

"In general," he added (as the ultimate proof of Canaris's power of persuasion), "Canaris makes a good impression—or at least, better than I had expected."

Although it took some time to become fully evident, the undetected allied landing in North Africa was the fatal blow to the Abwehr. The High Command viewed the fiasco with grave misgivings. Canaris's own position deteriorated so suddenly and badly that his enemies now dared to criticize him to the Fuehrer and even recommend his dismissal.

A formidable rival, Walter Schellenberg, appeared on the scene plotting to seize this plum of the intelligence establishment from the discredited Abwehr chief. How formidable he was can only be shown by tracing his rapid climb in typical Nazi competition with Canaris, especially in penetrating the United States and Britain.

The situation was characteristic of the ways the government's business was conducted in the Third Reich. The arcane maze of Nazi bureaucracy had more than the usual quota of confusion and duplication. It was nowhere more chaotic than in the intelligence establishment in which Canaris's Abwehr and Heinrich Himmler's *Reichssicherheitshauptamt,* as monstrous an institution as was its name, vied for supremacy.

Within the RSHA, the Party's elaborate intelligence apparatus, the *Sicherheitsdienst* had been carefully cultivated by Canaris's friendly gestures to its boss, Reinhard Heydrich. Of the various units of RSHA, a special branch of Amt IV called "E" for the surveillance of foreign agents abroad, was headed by Walter Schellenberg, Heydrich's protégé and ranking specialist in matters of foreign intelligence. Still in his twenties, he was an ambitious and gifted man, a fledgeling lawyer with intellectual pretenses, a gift of gab and an uncommon flair for the murky business of the secret service. Planning his own advancement with the same sagacity with which he plotted the descent of others, he boldly bypassed Gestapo chief Heinrich Mueller, his rapacious boss in Amt IV, and cuddled up to Heydrich. Schellenberg slyly apprised Heydrich of the sordid state of affairs in Amt VI, the foreign intelligence branch, and was promptly given the job, exactly as he had anticipated.

He immediately began to build his empire, creating a huge section for South America and a USA desk to which he appointed SS-Hauptsturmfuehrer Wilhelm Carstenn, mostly because Carstenn had a couple of friends who spoke English. This was, of course, in direct competition to Canaris. Carstenn paid high tribute to the FBI which by the end of 1940 was, as he put it, "applying its enormous experience gained in undercover work against the gangsters to the tracking down of secret agents." He listed some of the prophylactic measures the American government had introduced to stem the influx of spies and saboteurs, such as the mandatory registration of all aliens, stricter rules in the issuance of passports and visas, and restrictions placed on the movement of funds.

Even so, Carstenn wrote, he had succeeded in assuring a more than adequate coverage of the United States. According to his report he had a number of shortwave radio technicians attempting to build up a line of rapid communication between the agents in the United States and Berlin. Eight agents were active in diplomatic circles, six of them spying on the American Embassy in Berlin. Six of the agents were said to be on station in the United States.

Walter Schellenberg, however, was totally ignorant of things American. And Carstenn, too, was baffled by that complex land so far away. They needed someone better informed than either of them who could provide guidance for their agents and make sense of their incoming messages. Schellenberg found such a man in Kurt Jahnke, the only old-timer of real stature left from the small crop of German master spies in World War I. He was a heavy-set, thick-skulled Protestant from Pomerania, with a huge, round, bony face, looking impassively at the world with droopy eyes. But under his gruff, stolid exterior throbbed the spirit of grand adventure. The son of a country squire with a large estate on the Baltic Sea, Jahnke had been driven from his ancestral home, going to the United States shortly before World War I, where he served in the border patrol of the United States Immigration Service, guarding the Mexican frontier; then made a fortune in San Francisco among the Chinese. After the war he drifted to China where he was taken into Sun Yat-sen's household, all this time being a secret agent. In China he helped Dr. Sun's revolution, then hired himself out to an assortment of war lords, trained spies at the Whampoa Military Academy, and simultaneously worked for the Japanese secret service in Manchuria. With the Japanese holding first mortgage on his services, Jahnke returned to Germany to join the personal staff of Rudolf Hess.

Schellenberg sought out this colorful oldster when he needed an expert to guide him through the maze of problems presented by the United States and Japan. With Schellenberg's approval, he funneled information to the Japanese secret service, in exchange for intelligence about the United States and the U.S.S.R.

Guided by Jahnke's shrewd analyses, Schellenberg had become convinced that the United States would intervene in the European war sooner or later, and this was the recurring theme of Schellenberg's reportage about the United States. In December 1940, he announced to his clients that, "according to an absolutely reliable source," F.D.R. would take the United States into the war by the spring of 1941.

When the spring came and went, and the United States was still neutral, Schellenberg simply updated his timetable. Now basing his prediction on a conversation one of his American agents allegedly had with Mrs. Granville Emmett, widow of President Roosevelt's former law partner and a frequent guest at Hyde Park, Schellenberg reported on June 14: "Answering the pointed question of Mrs. Emmett when he—Roosevelt—believed the United States would enter the war, [the President] stated that formerly he thought it would occur during the Spring. Now, however, he is convinced that it will be possible only in the Summer of 1941."[2] Like an evangelist always predicting the end of the world, he continued to report American intervention as imminent. By late summer, however, his emphasis shifted from intervention in Europe to involvement in the Pacific.

After the Tripartite Pact of September 1940 that brought Japan into the Axis, Japan and the United States continued negotiating in Washington to resolve their differences. Little hard intelligence was available in Berlin about these talks. None could be procured by Thomsen in Washington, and the Japanese refused to keep the German ambassador in Tokyo posted.

"Hitler," Schellenberg wrote, "was rightly displeased about this insulting behavior by a member of the Three Power Pact. In spite of all the pressure Ribbentrop had brought to bear, they had made no response to the suggestion that they should enter the war against the Soviet Union. Nor was it clear whether Japan planned an attack in the South Pacific or whether they would content themselves with continuing their campaign in China."

Snubbed by his ally and left to grope in the dark by his Foreign Ministry, Hitler ordered both Canaris and Heydrich "to use every means to secure information" about the negotiations in Washington and especially about the intentions of the Japanese. Canaris was ill-equipped to carry out the order, having only tenuous relations with the Japanese secret service. Recognizing Hitler's burning interest in "the unfathomable Japanese" and exploiting Canaris's chronic inability to satisfy it, Schellenberg decided to concentrate his efforts on the Japanese problem. He set up Jahnke to monitor the Japanese-American negotiations to discover what Tokyo intended to do if the talks yielded no results.

Jahnke managed to secure for Schellenberg some cooperation with the Japanese in Stockholm. They used the same sources that proved so valuable to Klatt and Kraemer. In addition, Schellenberg had the services of the Italian Egghead who worked for Onodera as a translator, and gained access through him to some of the dispatches the envoy was exchanging with Tokyo. Jahnke did not rely entirely on these ties. Via Dr. von Ritgen, chief of the official German News Agency, he was in touch with Dr. Richard Sorge, correspondent of the *Frankfurter Zeitung* in Tokyo. Sorge was the chief agent of the Red Army General Staff's intelligence bureau in the Far East, but he was keeping a back door to the Germans open to cover up his work for the Russians. By this time Ritgen had some reason to suspect that Sorge was "a Communist spy." But he and Jahnke kept up a line to him nevertheless, "to profit," as Ritgen put it, "from his profound knowledge of the situation in the Far East."

By October 1941, Jahnke had most of what Schellenberg wanted. Sorge had repeated to him the crucial information he had given the Russians—that the Japanese did not regard themselves as bound by the Tripartite Pact to attack the Soviet Union. Warning that "under no circumstances would Japan denounce her non-aggression pact with the Soviet Union," he informed Jahnke that "their strategic planning . . . envisaged an advance into the South Pacific, but nothing more."

When on October 17 General Hideki Tojo succeeded Prince Konoye, Jahnke learned from his Japanese contacts that "the new premier . . . believed that Roosevelt and Churchill would never yield in [the] negotiations." He advised Schellenberg that war between Japan and the United States (and, for that matter, Great Britain) had become a foregone conclusion and was but a matter of months, if not only weeks, away.

Up to this point Hitler, who had begun to feel the pinch in his campaign in Russia, hoped that the Japanese would join him in the war against the Soviet Union. When Schellenberg submitted to him the intelligence Jahnke had gathered, the Fuehrer decided that "after all it was immaterial where Japan entered the war as long as she definitely did so."

While working for the Germans, Jahnke also continued to serve the Japanese. In mid-November they used him to clarify what seemed to be a moot point in their considerations—"whether," as Schellenberg phrased it, "in case of war between Japan and the Anglo-Saxons, Germany would commit herself not to conclude peace without Japan," and whether Germany would follow suit if and when Japan declared war on the "Anglo-Saxons."

At Schellenberg's request, Heydrich personally queried Hitler on this issue. Around November 15, Jahnke was able to reassure his Japanese friends that "Germany was anxious to secure Japanese participation in the war, no matter what its nature and direction."[3]

"I believe," Schellenberg later wrote, "that I am not wrong in assuming that [Jahnke's] message played a decisive role in Japanese policy, for immediately after its receipt, and without having received any official guarantees, the Japanese completed their mobilization, and at the end of November ordered their entire fleet to sail to the South Pacific on amphibious operations."

In the wake of Pearl Harbor, after a brief period of increased influence, Jahnke's star began to wane. At the initiative of the Japanese, he plotted a separate peace between Germany and the Soviet Union; on German initiative, he tried to arrange an armistice in China. But though Schellenberg continued to stand by him, he was *persona non grata* with Hitler, Himmler, and Heydrich. Since he had been close to Rudolf Hess, Hitler suspected him of complicity in his deputy's startling flight to Scotland on the eve of the invasion of the Soviet Union. And he was denounced to Heydrich in a Gestapo report that asserted that Jahnke was a British agent.

In March 1942, while he was in Switzerland reviewing with his Chinese friends the possibilities of a separate peace with Japan, Gestapo chief Heinrich Mueller gave Heydrich a 30-page report detailing Jahnke's association with the British secret service. The report stated categorically that Jahnke was in Switzerland at that very moment, not to work on a Sino-Japanese peace, but to receive new instructions from his British contact.

On his return from Switzerland, Jahnke was confronted with the accusation by Heydrich and Schellenberg, but they drew from him only an enigmatic rejoinder. "Your whole life," he said, "has inclined you toward systematic suspicion, but I think you are big enough to overcome that. What is important is a man's real character—and there you can trust your instinct."

After that, Jahnke was placed under Gestapo surveillance and Schellenberg was forbidden to have anything more to do with him. Jahnke faded out of the picture[4] and Schellenberg was abandoned to his own resources in the management of his secret agents in the United States.

Yet Jahnke still performed a last great service for his young mentor, even though he himself was no longer able to play an active part in it. One of Jahnke's major contacts was a certain Kijuro Suzuki, a Japanese secret agent in Lisbon. Through a venal official in the Portuguese Ministry of Foreign Affairs, Suzuki had gained access to the confidential dispatches of the Portuguese envoys in London and Washington, and had shared with Jahnke the information. Since both diplomats were exceptionally well informed, much valuable intelligence could be gained from their reports.

After Jahnke's downfall, Suzuki continued to forward this intelligence through Erich Schroeder, head of the SD mission in Portugal. On December 17, 1942, for example, he passed on to Schroeder the copy of a dispatch from the Portuguese ambassador in London giving details of a top-secret meeting the Allied War Council had held on the night of December 11 to 12, after the Allied invasion of North Africa.

On January 19, 1943, Suzuki gave Schroeder a brief dispatch from the same convoy. It contained the information that Churchill had left London by air, presumably for a meeting with Roosevelt in Casablanca. Since the movements of such statesmen are shrouded in utmost secrecy in wartime, there is a high premium on intelligence about them. Schellenberg tried frantically to follow the perambulations of Churchill and Roosevelt, especially since the Abwehr was either unable to procure such information or had no interest in it.[5]

When the Schroeder telegram from Lisbon reached him, Schellenberg immediately informed Hitler in a top-priority signal (marked *Blitz—RSHA-Amt VI—No. 1201/Kr-VI 85—19.1.43—Top Secret*) that another Roosevelt-Churchill conference was in progress. This was a superb feat of timely intelligence. It pierced the supposedly ironclad secret of what, in fact, was the Casablanca Conference of January 14–24, 1943.

The Allied security organs had gone to extreme lengths to conceal the historic excursion of the two statesmen. Roosevelt had left Washington on the 9th, and Churchill had departed from London on the 12th, veiled in secrecy and censorship. The unprecedented precautionary arrangements seemed to be holding up until February 1, when the story of the conference was presented to the world officially as a "dazzling *fait accompli*." Yet the Germans had managed to find out about it on the fifth day of the meeting, when Roosevelt was to spend six more days in Morocco.

The great scoop fell short of being perfect, and Schellenberg could blame only himself for spoiling it. He was afflicted by the one cardinal fault that is fatal in a spymaster: he allowed his creative imagination to intrude on a job that demanded absolute adherence to stubborn facts. Rarely satisfied with leaving well enough alone, whenever a report had gaps he would fill them with conjecture, guesswork, or simply the fumes of his fancy. He edited his agents' reports, elaborating and embellishing them in the process, to make even the best bit of intelligence seem better. A man with a more rounded education and familiarity with the international scene might have been able to get away with it. But Schellenberg's knowledge of the world was limited. As a result, his doctored reports were not merely useless but misleading and deceptive, often actually harmful.

The bare facts of the telegram did not satisfy Schellenberg, and the reference to "Casablanca" tripped him up. He could not imagine that the President would risk a journey to the combat zone, going all the way to French Morocco where his troops had landed only two months before. Assuming that "Casablanca" must have meant "casa blanca," Spanish for "white house," Schellenberg decided that Churchill had gone to the United States to meet Roosevelt in the White House.

So when his report reached Hitler, it read: "Portuguese ambassador in London advised his government that Churchill had left London by air for another conference with Roosevelt in Washington."

Then he compounded the marvelous blunder—he contrived a report of his own by inventing the "inside story" of this summit conference. Sent out at 7:15 P.M., January 23, 1943, as another Blitz signal, it read: "From several reports just received, details of Churchill's current visit in the United States have been learned. The following information is based on dispatches of Portuguese chiefs of missions to their Ministry of Foreign Affairs.

"The Portuguese minister in Washington advised his government that during his stay in Washington Churchill will address the Senate urging increased deliveries to England. In connection with Churchill's departure for America, the Portuguese ambassador in London confirmed on the 19th that the United States is expected to demand further territorial concession, e.g. Trinidad and Jamaica, in return for additional supplies. According to the Portuguese ambassador, friction over North Africa and the question of supreme command aggravate the strain in Anglo-American relations. The Americans are said to be insisting on the exclusion of the anglophile de Gaulle from North Africa, while England refuses emphatically to accept Giraud."

Schellenberg's reports created a flurry of excitement both at the Fuehrer's headquarters and in Berlin. A Roosevelt-Churchill meeting had been expected to take place shortly. This, however, was the first definite word that it was being held and to give details of its agenda.

The excitement endured for several days and Schellenberg was congratulated on his phenomenal scoop. On January 27 a telegram arrived from Ambassador Eugen Ott from Tokyo. "According to information just communicated to me confidentially by the Foreign Ministry," it read, "Roosevelt and Churchill are meeting in Casablanca. Stalin and Chiang Kai-shek have also been invited but declined. . . . Foreign Ministry would be much obliged for any information as it becomes available about alleged conference in Casablanca."

The initial sensation the Schellenberg reports had created turned into bewilderment. Who was right—Schellenberg, who reported Churchill in Washington, or the Japanese who placed him in Casablanca with Roosevelt? In the light of such conflicting reports, was there any truth to their meeting at all?

On January 28, by which time the Germans had accepted the information from Tokyo that the conference had been held in Casablanca, Schellenberg tried to wiggle out of his predicament by circulating a dispatch he had allegedly just received from Lisbon. Again citing Portuguese diplomatic sources, and again inventing the "intelligence" he so badly needed, he still insisted that Churchill had been to the United States. He now told his clients that the Prime Minister had gone to the United States to pick up the President. Then, he claimed, they *sailed* together to Casablanca. "The Portuguese consul in Casablanca," Schellenberg wrote, "reported to his Ministry on January 26 that . . . both [Churchill and Roosevelt] had traveled to Casablanca together behind a tight screen of extreme security measures."

Still ignorant of the proceedings in French Morocco, yet eager to show how well informed he really was, he improvised another piece of "intelligence" that backfired with a resounding crash. "The English participants at the conference," he wrote, "are reported from Tangier to be annoyed that the Americans had featured [General Henri Honoré] Giraud by including him rather than [General Charles] de Gaulle in the negotiations, the latter not even being allowed to go to North Africa."

Only three days later, on February 1, when the front pages of the world gave the official story of the Conference, his exposure came in the form of the historic photograph showing Roosevelt and Churchill.

They were looking on in apparent bliss while Giraud and de Gaulle were shaking hands for the benefit of the cameramen during an off-the-record press conference held on January 24—in Casablanca.

NOTES

1 Carbo or Karbe, as he was variously called in addition to his cover-name of "Caesar," never ceased to intrigue the British, chiefly because he seemed to have an enigmatic sub-agent who could not be identified beyond his name of "Axel." The mystery was solved when the British read in one of the intercepts from Bletchley: "Caesar in hospital, bit by Axel." The "agent" was a police dog guarding one of the Abwehr stations in Algeciras. The real boss of this Mediterranean watchtower of the Germans was a certain "Fehleisen," another mystery-shrouded person until found to be Kautschke's determined, domineering wife using her maiden name in her spirited espionage pursuits.

2 This conflicted with a report of Hans Thomsen, the German Charge d'affaires in Washington, who cabled on June 19, 1941: "I have just learned reliably that in a cabinet session held on June 14, President Roosevelt replied to the question of a member of his cabinet whether or when the United States would enter the war, 'That is definitely out.' "

3 Tokyo's concern on this score was reflected in repeated efforts to seek "clarification." Apparently not quite persuaded by Jahnke's assurances, the question was raised bluntly by the Japanese ambassadors in Berlin and Rome, the latter asking Mussolini point-blank on December 3: "Should Japan declare war on the United States and Great Britain, would Italy do likewise?" The question was answered in the affirmative in both capitals.

4 Although no evidence was produced to bear out Mueller's charges, Jahnke was banished into forced residence at his estate near Stralsund in Pomerania, where he was captured on April 26, 1945, by a unit of the 53rd Army of General Fedyuninski's Ukrainians. Nothing was heard from him again.

5 Canaris was fearful that such intelligence might lead to direct attacks on the President and the Prime Minister by the assassination-minded Nazis, and did what he could to forestall them by banning the collection of this kind of intelligence or withhholding from distribution whatever information of this nature reached the Abwehr.

Chapter 47

The President's Agent

ALTHOUGH the war of wits is supposed to have its own battlefields on which secret agents fight with gun or dagger, frequently dying bizarre deaths, the theater of German-American clandestine operations was not littered with corpses. Possibly the only casualty in a head-on clash between these operatives was a hapless Nazi in Bulgaria. Even he got out of the brawl with nothing worse than a lacerated scalp. Responsible for the injury (which added to some previous insults) was a flamboyant politician from Pennsylvania who was the American Minister in Sofia at the time of the barroom brawl. A combination troubleshooter and trouble maker, he seemed determined to take on the Nazis and defeat them single-handed.

His private war with the Germans produced the quaintest spoils in the conflict. It enabled the Germans to ferret out the secret of "Husky," the projected Allied invasion of Sicily; and at the same time enriched President Roosevelt's famous collection with a 1941 set of overprinted Croatian stamps. This is essentially the tale of those stamps (today valued at about $7.50). They were donated by the Abwehr, whose motives for the friendly gesture were not exactly philatelic.

Istanbul . . . 1943 . . .

The erstwhile capital of the Ottoman Empire on the Golden Horn, long a center of Oriental splendor and corruption, had been scrubbed clean by the austere regime of the great Ataturk. The famed landmarks of old Constantinople—the Topkapi and the Dolmagchi Palace, the Yeri Batan cistern and the Spina, around which the chariots of Constantine the Great once raced—had become sightseeing attractions where starry-eyed tourists could marvel at the power, wealth, and depravity of ancient regimes.

By now, the fourth year of the war in Europe, much of the city's quondam corruption had returned. Turkey was a strategic neutral country of the first order, coveted by both camps. Since the city was the best observation and listening post in the eastern Mediterranean, Istanbul acquired a Byzantine underworld in which foreigners out-spied the natives, though the Turks themselves were no pikers at the game. Every secret service of the world was represented in this enchanted city on the Bosporus, swarming through its elegant hotel lounges and best restaurants where between enemies there were no barriers. At cocktail time, at *thé dansants* and even at private parties, American, German, British, Russian, French, Italian, Polish, Yugoslav, Greek, and Japanese agents could be seen at adjacent tables or bumping into one another on the dance floor, sharing feminine partners and, via them, some of their secrets. There were just so many accommodating comely ladies to go around. The demand being far greater than the supply, swains of rival secret services scrambled not only for the same secrets, but also for the same dark, sloe-eyed beauties, frequently interchanging and bartering them in a demonstration of sex-across-the-war.

Never was secret service rendered so openly. Hardly a day passed without some incident of the boisterous presence of these supposedly clandestine operators. The Russians as usual had the largest contingent headed by a troika of spymasters, Comrades Yakhimov, Matchkanelli, and Moharadze. They were the most conspicuous, if only because they made the biggest noise. Firm believers in direct action—the euphemism for sabotage and assassination—they were forever blowing up things and people, somewhat indiscriminately, but always in keeping with their alliance of the moment.

Every branch of His Majesty's Secret Services was conspicuous with ace operatives. MI.6 had the courteous Commander Wolfson and the mysterious Gibson brothers, the foremost specialists of S.I.S. on the Balkans and the Soviet Union. Others could be seen flitting in and out of town—vanishing for a few weeks to sabotage the Ploesti oilfield in Rumania, or to organize the Greek resistance movement, then reappearing to rest up in the Taxim Kasino with the delightful Hungarian girls of the chorus line.

The most gregarious and fractious group was the German colony, which worked in rival agencies—the *Sicherheitsdienst*, the *Auslandsorganisation* and, of course, the Abwehr. Its chief, a major named Schulze-Bernett, was himself as sedate as his head office in Ankara, the capital; and so was the main SD bureau under Ludwig C. Moyzisch, a soft-stepping, lugubrious Austrian who gained world fame after the war as the mastermind of the "Cicero" operation. The action was in Istanbul where Dr. Paul Leverkuehn—who had come to Turkey from considerable mischiefmaking in the Persian Azerbeijan —headed the bustling Abwehr outpost. He covered the whole of Turkey with a dense net of agents, including a ring of Greeks, one of whom was a wireless operator in Britain's Middle Eastern intelligence bureau in Cairo.

Virgil's quip that vice is nourished by secrecy was given its acid test in Istanbul. Personal loyalties and national allegiances criss-crossed and interlocked. An American broadcaster aided the Russians; the bureau chief of a Nazi news agency comforted the British; Cicero was betraying his British employer to the Nazi Moyzisch until he was betrayed to the Americans by young blonde Elizabeth Kapp, Moyzisch's confidential secretary. Turkish officials were supposed to keep tabs on the alien spies and choke them off; but the chief of the Turkish secret service cooperated with the Germans, while his deputy kept the British posted. Two of their aides worked for both the Germans and the British, as well as the Russians.

Into this cauldron arrived on the morning of January 23, 1943, the remarkable American who would add his own consummate skill at skullduggery and a touch of humorous relief. He was Lieutenant Commander George Howard Earle III, a rich Philadelphia Main Liner, former Governor of Pennsylvania, now an assistant naval attaché on special assignment.

The moment he arrived in Istanbul, Earle filed a personal but irregular telegram from neutral Turkey to Hungary, a country with which the United States was at war. The wire was addressed to Miss Adrienne Molnar, at 12 Muskátli Utca, a street in Budapest whose name was aptly romantic under the circumstances. "Muskátli" means geranium and the wire was intended to revive a flowering friendship which the war had rudely interrupted. Signed "Hefty," the pet name by which Adrienne called George, the message was in Hungarian; an English text would have complicated things for Miss Molnar. It advised her that he was staying in the Park Hotel, where he expected her arrival at her earliest convenience.

This was the Governor's second visit to Istanbul. The first was over a year before under circumstances vastly different from his quiet entry this time. On the previous occasion he came from Bulgaria, where he had been the American Minister until two days before. The rugged Balkan country had fallen to the Nazis, ending Earle's tenure as the envoy of the United States at King Boris's court in Sofia. The Bulgarians had hustled him out amidst rumors of a Nazi plot to murder him in the commotion of the occupation by Field Marshal

List's German troops. He had arrived on December 27, 1941, traveling like an Oriental potentate in the private car of the Bulgarian monarch, escorted by His Majesty's private secretary. According to the Istanbul correspondent of the official German news agency, who met him with a huge contingent of reporters and foreign correspondents, his thirty-eight pieces of luggage, bags and boxes contained over a hundred bottles of toilet water, distilled especially for him from Bulgaria's fragrant rose petals, and an enormous collection of jeweled cigarette cases, old gold coins, antique icons and other church artifacts. Although he had to leave behind Pussy, a tamed cheetah, he had brought his three dachshunds and another kind of a pet, a willowy blonde the German reporter identified as "a Jewish cabaret dancer named Adrienne."

The German's article was deliberately overdrawn and calculatingly insulting. Earle was at the top of the Nazis' blacklist as a dangerous enemy. The correspondent had orders from the Propaganda Ministry to leave no gibe unturned in his slanderous article to assassinate at least the American's character, now that they had been prevented from bumping him off physically.

Big, burly, good-looking Earle was in his forties, an attractive and able man, an astute politican at home and a better than average diplomat abroad, generating both good and bad will. His dispatches from Vienna, where he was the American envoy in 1933–34, were considerably livelier than those of political appointees whom Washington usually sent abroad. Some professionals of the State Department dismissed them even when they contained keen observations and sound opinions. They frowned upon him as a man hankering for notoriety, a congenital troublemaker, as gauche in the diplomatic drawing rooms as he was nimble in the nightclubs. They sighed with relief whenever circumstances beyond Earle's control terminated his assignments and removed him from their necks.

During his first tour of duty in Vienna, he scandalized the staid Foreign Service officers with his outspoken official utterances and escapades. It was there that the Nazis first became interested in George B. Earle the Third, as the Germans called him in the bulging dossier they invariably filled with scurrilous reports.

As an entry in one confidential report put it, "He used the occasion of the presentation of his credentials [to the President of Austria] to abuse National Socialism, telling Herr Miklas, 'I loath the Nazis.'"

In Sofia, a few years later, Earle mortified the State Department even as he scandalized the Germans, with an unbridled display of his anti-Nazi sentiments. He was generally popular with the Bulgarians, and the personal favorite of King Boris among foreign diplomats. But his violent anti-Hitler stance created one incident after another. When he once found a German spy in his Legation, it became known that he obtained a confession from the man by giving him the full third-degree treatment. On another occasion he had to be forcibly restrained by an aide to prevent him from firing out of his bedroom window at a noisy Nazi demonstration against him.

His crowning triumph (or disgrace, as the Germans preferred to view it) was when he provoked a bloody brawl with a German in a Sofia nightclub, by ordering the band to give a rendition of "Tipperary" after some Nazis in the place had asked the musicians to play the "Horst Wessel Lied," the Nazi anthem glorifying a Berlin pimp. The incident even upset a Congressman, who demanded that Earle be recalled and sacked. In Sofia he became acquainted with a beautiful Hungarian girl appearing in one of the city's better nightclubs, and often took her out. She was the "Adrienne" whom the German reporter called a "Jewish cabaret dancer."

After returning to the United States, Earle was blackballed by the State Department. Though the President suggested that his good friend and political crony be assigned another diplomatic post (in Ireland, for example, where he could continue his private war with the Nazis), Secretary of State Cordell Hull categorically refused. F.D.R. was not only politically indebted to the rambunctious Pennsylvanian but was personally fond of him, for exactly the same reason that made him so disliked in the State Department—for his muscular opposition to the Nazis. The President was eager to find another berth for his friend, especially since Earle was forever pestering him to send him to some neutral country, preferably not too far from Hungary, where Adrienne was waiting out their enforced separation.

From time to time in 1942 President Roosevelt was told about groups of Germans who supposedly plotted the overthrow of Hitler in diffuse conspiracies. F.D.R., who doubted even General de Gaulle's potency as a resistance leader, discounted the German opposition as a possible aid to the Allies. But when those reports multiplied, most of them coming from Turkey, he decided to send his own confidential observers to size up the dissidents.[1] The existence of an anti-Nazi cabal in Turkey gave Roosevelt the opportunity to find a niche for his friend. Since the Department still refused to give Earle another diplomatic post, the President (who deferred to Secretary Hull in such matters) commissioned the Governor a lieutenant commander in the Naval Reserve, appointed him an assistant naval attaché, and sent him to Turkey as a Presidential Agent to monitor the anti-Nazi movement.

As a final gesture of the high regard in which he held Earle, F.D.R. invited him to travel in his entourage as far as Casablanca where the President was going in January 1943 to meet Prime Minister Churchill.

From there Earle flew to Istanbul where, as the first act of his new assignment, he sent that dispatch to Miss Adrienne Molnar on Geranium Street in Budapest. Overjoyed but bewildered by the complexities of the situation, Adrienne did not know what to make of the telegram and how to respond to it. Then, however, she thought of Frau Asta Matzhold, the wife of the Austrian journalist previously stationed in Washington, now assigned to Budapest. Asta had befriended the young woman and repeatedly acted as her adviser whenever her problems proved too complicated for her to solve all by herself. Earle's telegram created a situation in the Matzhold household, setting off the chain reaction of a melodrama far surpassing anything that Upton Sinclair invented for Lanny Budd, his fictitious Presidential Agent.

Asta left the solution to her husband Louis. He was, she concluded, much better qualified to deal with a relationship that had such international undertones. Moreover, he had known Earle both in the United States and in the Balkans.

As in Washington, Matzhold was in Budapest in a dual capacity. Overtly he represented the *Berliner Boersen-Zeitung*, a big Berlin daily patterned on the *Wall Street Journal*. Covertly, he was "Michael," an all-purpose German agent catering to the Abwehr, Heydrich's SD, and Foreign Minister von Ribbentrop's private intelligence bureau. The latter was headed by an SS-officer and former journalist named Rudolf Likus, a friend of Ribbentrop's from their school days. Matzhold was not doing too well in Budapest in his covert job. The city was quarantined by the war. From time to time, therefore, he would visit Istanbul and Ankara, posing as a correspondent but actually collecting intelligence, largely for the Likus Bureau. On these occasions, he buttonholed prominent British and American correspondents he had known in happier days—such as Ward Price of the *Daily Mail* (who was known for his pro-German sympathies before the war) and young Cyrus L. Sulzberger, roving foreign reporter of *The New York Times*. These interviews produced little of real value and only modest rewards for Matzhold-alias-Michael. Now he saw a bonanza in the predicament of Adrienne.

On January 24, the day after "Hefty" had sent his wire to Adrienne, Matzhold fired off to Likus an urgent communication in the German Legation's secret cipher. He informed him of Earle's brash invitation to Miss Molnar and suggested that it could be exploited for what might become a real intelligence scoop. With Ribbentrop's blessing Likus flew to Budapest, where he and Matzhold devised a plot for using Adrienne as a pawn and Earle as a dupe, to obtain high-grade information from the personal representative of the American President. It was an ingenious scheme, playing on Adrienne's eagerness to rejoin her distinguished friend and on Earle's interest in the girl.

For the time being, they decided, they would use their influence with the Hungarian authorities to delay the issuance of an exit permit to the Molnar woman. Matzhold would go to Turkey, contact Earle and offer his services as Adrienne's father confessor, using the blind to pump Earle for information. Matzhold flew to Istanbul on February 4 in a German courier plane and got in touch with Earle the same evening in his suite at the Park Hotel. He presented himself in a dual capacity—as Adrienne's doting guardian and as a secret anti-Nazi who was in an excellent position to dispense interesting information about the movement against Hitler. It was no secret in Istanbul even at this initial stage of his mission that Earle had come to Turkey for the official purpose of renewing his contacts with his old anti-Nazi friends.

At their meeting, Matzhold was most accommodating and Earle seemed openhearted and accessible. He gave the journalist 7530 pengoes in Hungarian currency for Adrienne and some juicy information which Matzhold considered so important that he decided to fly immediately to Berlin to report to Likus.

Earle revealed that he had accompanied Roosevelt to Casablanca, and told Matzhold details about some of the items on the agenda of this summit meeting of the Big Two. Among numerous items he divulged the decision reached at Casablanca—that the Allies had decided to start their return journey to the European continent by first invading Sicily immediately after the Germans and Italians had been cleared out of North Africa.

The information Matzhold brought back proved a bombshell. What began as a tentative contact now became a major secret mission. Ribbentrop personally authorized Matzhold to develop his source, using Adrienne as a decoy and later as a go-between. The Foreign Minister recognized in this unexpected link with Governor Earle an opening to Roosevelt through which he could funnel his thoughts and views to the President, perhaps even persuading him that aid to the Soviet Union would establish the Bolsheviks as the rulers of the world in which, as Ribbentrop put it in his briefing to Matzhold, "there would be no place left for millionaires like Roosevelt and Earle."

On February 28 Matzhold flew to Ankara to see Earle again. This time they met at midnight in Matzhold's hotel room. After conveying Adrienne's greetings and the assurance that she was as eager to see "Hefty" as ever, Matzhold gave Earle an envelope "for the Mister

President personally," as he put it. It contained a few sets of postage stamps, mostly recent issues of the German-occupied countries, including a number of new Croatian stamps which, he said, were "rather rare."

"When I was stationed in Washington," he said, "I used to exchange stamps with the Mister President. Please give him the regards of an old philatelic friend and these stamps with my compliments. I am sure he cannot collect them easily these days when the United States is cut off from Europe."

The Foreign Ministry had obtained the collection from the Abwehr for Matzhold, as a gesture to play upon the philatelic passion of F.D.R. and soften him up for future approaches. Written on the envelope . . . actually that of the Abwehr . . . was the notation: "Property of Louis A. Matzhold, for the Mister President of the United States."

Earle sent the envelope to Roosevelt with his next dispatch, without obliterating what was printed or written on it.[2] Matzhold then drew the Presidential Agent into a discussion of Ribbentrop's pet theme concerning the Bolsheviks. He knew that "the Red menace" was also the favorite subject of Earle. The Governor loathed the Nazis and Communists with equal ardor, and made no bones about it.

Earle launched into a bitter tirade elucidating his violent hatred of the Bolsheviks in no uncertain terms. This was at the time of the Russo-American alliance when such loose talk was frowned upon by Washington and could be embarrassing to the President.

In the heat of conversation, Earle tried to persuade Matzhold that Germany had already lost the war. "As soon as the campaign in North Africa will end," he said, according to Matzhold's report to Likus, "we will land in Europe in 34 different places, beginning with Sicily. I know—I've been with the President in Casablanca and am familiar with everything he and Churchill have discussed."

Matzhold again regarded the information he had coaxed from the American as so important that he took the next plane to Budapest. He composed a fifteen-page report on the way, and forwarded it to Likus by courier.

Then a crisis developed, its portents hinted at in a telegram Earle sent to Matzhold the day after his departure. He asked the journalist to return to Istanbul at once. Matzhold was back on March 3, and Earle called on him at his hotel at noon the next day, coming in evident consternation.

"I am in trouble, Louis," the journalist reported him as saying. "The day after our last meeting, our mutual friend Gedye, the former *New York Times* correspondent who's now a big shot in the British secret service here in Turkey, visited me in great confidence and told me that your room in this damned hotel has been bugged by the Russkies. They recorded every fragment of our conversation."[3]

He produced a couple of phonograph records. "Gedye assured me that the British wouldn't stoop to such low methods against me, but somehow they managed to steal these damned records from the Communists. I don't know what is to become of me if our conversation gets to the President, especially since I have expressed such strong views about those blasted Bolshies to a German."

According to Matzhold's account of this incident, Earle said they would not be able to meet again in the future because the Russians and British were probably keeping him under surveillance. However, Earle added, he would be grateful if he would keep up his efforts on behalf of Adrienne, who was still in Budapest waiting for her exit permit. Matzhold reported this strange turn of events to Likus. They decided to ask the Hungarians to grant the permit so that the Molnar girl could join Earle in Turkey. If Matzhold could no longer tap this fantastic source, they thought, Adrienne would still be there to maintain a line to Earle, and they could syphon off information through her.

At first the Turks balked at issuing an entry visa to Adrienne, and the connection with Earle seemed to be cooling off, but at last Adrienne wired Earle that she was leaving after all, on April 24. The Presidential Agent now appeared to have grown tired of waiting for the girl, and was seen going out with a young Belgian lady. Earle sent Adrienne a wire imploring her to remain in Budapest and forget him. He promised to take care of her, finding means to transfer funds in intervals of six months. Adrienne rushed to Matzhold with the wire. He advised her not to pay any attention to it. "Pretend you never got it," he told the sobbing girl. "Leave as planned and keep in touch. If everything goes well, I'll follow you to Turkey in a week or two."

Traveling on the Orient Express, Miss Molnar arrived in Istanbul without a hitch. Despite the telegram he had sent, Earle seemed overjoyed to see her. They celebrated their reunion with a feast. "We are in seventh heaven," Adrienne wired to Matzhold on April 26. That was the last he heard from her.

If Earle was really glad that Adrienne had come, inclined to take up where his sudden departure from Sofia a year and a half before had left them, he now acted strangely. He tried to persuade the girl to fade quietly into the background, and then arranged a job for her at the Taxim Kasino.

Matzhold reported all of this. In a series of frantic letters to Likus, he assured the German that it would still be possible to salvage the connection. Adrienne was in Istanbul, he wrote, to act as a conveyor belt on which information of the greatest significance could still be obtained from Earle. But even as he was getting rid of Adrienne, Earle also dropped Matzhold for good.

Was the Governor really so naïve as to accept the Austrian busy-body at face value? Was he really so reckless as to confide to him such top-secret information as the goal of the Allies' next giant leap on their return to Europe?

"Perhaps indiscreet and certainly unorthodox," wrote Cy Sulz-berger of *The New York Times*, "Earle was nevertheless a true friend, quite fearless and a gay companion."

For all his ebullience, and far from being a fool, Earle was a shrewd judge of men and situations. His long experience in politics and diplomacy made him cagey and sharp, holding with Rabelais that machination was worth more than force. He could be just as crafty and devious as his enemy, and certainly Matzhold's superior in cunning. Although he had a penchant for getting himself into hot water, he usually found the right solution for the knottiest problems in the clinch. In Matzhold's special case, Earle had no illusions about the man. He was well aware that his friend was a German agent, and considered him only a little better than a nincompoop.

He had known Louis from his days in Washington,. and had been in touch with him in 1941, during his tenure as American Minister in Sofia. Twice he had visited Matzhold in Budapest on fishing expeditions for inside information about the Nazis' future plans for the Balkans, because he knew that the man had excellent inside sources and liked to flaunt his supposed omniscience. Most of the time he used Matzhold to get his views to the Germans and plant information that would mislead them. In Istanbul he seized the opportunity of befuddling the Germans through this obvious pipeline. He was wary of snaring Matzhold by involving Adrienne. He chose the "intelligence" he was dispensing carefully, to impress the man with the hopelessness of the German cause and, in specific terms, to deceive them about the Allies' true intentions. By telling Matzhold that it had been decided at Casablanca to invade the Continent at thirty-four different places, he intended to induce them to scatter their defenses. As it turned out, the Germans were sufficiently distracted to miss his reference to Sicily, and were just as surprised and unprepared for the invasion when it came on July 10, 1943, as they had been in North Africa exactly eight months before.

After Adrienne's arrival in Istanbul he seized the initiative and went over to the offensive, turning the table on Matzhold. He had succeeded in worming himself into the circle of anti-Nazis in Turkey, and even held clandestine sessions with Ambassador von Papen himself, plotting the overthrow of Hitler. He became instrumental in the demoralization and eventual smashing of the Abwehr apparatus in Istanbul. He accomplished it in the little coup in which Adrienne figured prominently. He had kept in touch with her for the purpose of penetrating the German secret service in Turkey. Since nothing remains secret in the world of the secret services, it had become quickly known that Earle's job as an assistant naval attaché was merely a cover, and that he was President Roosevelt's personal representative in Turkey. In due course, every intelligence outpost in Istanbul focused in on Earle, to tap this pipeline leading directly into the White House. Since Adrienne was his confidant, she came to be regarded as an excellent channel to the Presidential Agent.[4]

She soon blossomed out as Istanbul's most coveted *femme fatale.* Every secret service—Russian as well as British, Italian as well as French—assigned their best looking young men to approach her. The British secret service delegated a dashing lady-killer who made the charge dressed in the garb of his Highland clan, calling himself Lord Campbell. Dr. Leverkuehn of the Abwehr detached a handsome, sociable young Viennese, Dr. Wilhelm Hamburger, to do the snooping via courting. Valuable gifts were suddenly showered on the young woman. She was decorated with necklaces, bracelets, and a six-karat diamond ring by her eager suitors, for services rendered beyond the call of duty.

Only Hamburger was not so generous. Dr. Leverkuehn was keeping a tight rein on the budget of his outpost, so Hamburger could not give Adrienne anything but love. It soon became obvious that she appreciated it more than the large decorative sapphire brooch Lord Campbell had given her. Willy and Adrienne became inseparable, so much so that when Hamburger found out that Adrienne was doing her cooing at the behest of the Presidential Agent, he abdicated from the Abwehr and defected to the Americans via Earle, in order that he could stay with the woman he loved. He was Earle's first conquest in his secret war. Others followed as more and more deserters from the Nazi cause beat a frantic path to the best escape hatch in town.

Late in 1944, Louis Matzhold arrived in Istanbul again, this time on a secret mission of his own. He looked up Adrienne for old time's sake—she had become a soigné young lady, a Hungarian version of Eliza Doolittle perfected by her shrewd Pygmalion. They celebrated their reunion at a champagne dinner in Tokatlyan's.

"How is Hefty?" Matzhold asked, and when Adrienne assured him that Hefty was fine, he came out with the question he had come to Turkey to pop.

"Do you think you could arrange a secret meeting with him for me?" he asked. "I would like to make my arrangement with the Americans."

NOTES

1 Early in 1943, F.D.R. sent Archbishop Francis Spellman of New York to Madrid, the Vatican, Istanbul, and Ankara as his special envoy—Ankara in particular—to consult with Cardinal Roncalli (later Pope John XXIII). The Papal Nuncio in Turkey was reputed to be Hitler's most spirited foe in the hierarchy, with his own connections with the anti-Nazis.

2 According to Matzhold, Earle later conveyed to him the President's greetings and thanks for the stamps, suggesting that he send more of the same. F.D.R. asked his fellow hobbyist that he refrain in the future from forwarding the stamps in Abwehr envelopes.

3 G. E. R. Gedye, "a testy, vain Englishman" (as Cyrus L. Sulzberger called him), represented the London *Times* in Central Europe and *The New York Times* in Prague and Vienna, during the *Anschluss* and the Sudetan crisis. During the war he was stationed in Vienna as an operative of MI.6.

4 According to Cedric Salter, the Istanbul correspondent of the *Daily Mail* of London, Earle even met Canaris in 1943, when the Abwehr chief tried to find out "what terms of peace the Americans would be prepared to consider." No such meeting ever took place, but Earle was quite popular with a number of restive members of the Canaris organization.

Chapter **48**

Tapping the Roosevelt-Churchill Hot Line

ON May 20, 1943, while listening to one of his special agents who had just returned from Italy and was reporting on his findings, all bad, Adolf Hitler sighed and said: "One has to be on the watch like a spider in its web. Thank God, I've always had a pretty good nose for everything so that I can generally smell things out before they happen."

His nose failed him nine weeks later when it did not "smell out" the fall of Benito Mussolini.

On Sunday afternoon, July 25, the Duce went to see King Victor Emmanuel III at the royal villa, his mind, as he later put it, "completely free of any forebodings." He found the King, wearing the full dress uniform of the chief marshal of the realm, waiting for him in the doorway of his drawing room. When they were seated inside, the King, "his face livid and looking almost dwarfish," told him in a solemn voice: "My dear Duce, it's no longer any good. Italy has gone to bits. . . . The soldiers don't want to fight any more. . . . At this moment you are the most hated man in Italy." Then he fired Mussolini and appointed 72-year-old Marshal Pietro Badoglio as his successor. The old marshal went on the air to announce the "resignation" of the Duce and the end of the Fascist regime. His broadcast broke the first news of Mussolini's penultimate disgrace.

At this time, by the Italians' actual count, the Germans had nearly 10,000 secret agents in Italy, distributed everywhere from the Quirinal to the lowliest police station. Yet Hitler had received not a scrap of hard information from his vast intelligence establishment to warn him of the imminent events. The first hint of trouble came in around noon of July 25th, in a telegram from Ambassador Hans von Mack-

582

ensen in Rome, reporting that "according to a flood of rumors" the Fascist Grand Council had met the night before and "invited the King to emerge from obscurity and assume his responsibilities."

It was enough for Hitler to summon his staff to an emergency conference to review the situation. "Any news, Hewel?" he asked Minister Walter Hewel, the Foreign Ministry's representative at his headquarters.

"Nothing yet," Hewel said. "It's clear that there is a real crisis there, and Mackensen thinks that we should do nothing and be very careful in this crisis."

Hitler interrupted him: "What's going to come out of this anyway?" was all he could say.

At 9:30 P.M., four hours after Badoglio had broadcast the news of Mussolini's downfall, Hitler held another hastily summoned briefing session. "Do you know about the developments in Italy?" he asked his bewildered entourage in great excitement. "The Duce has resigned. It is not confirmed yet. Badoglio has taken over the government. The Duce has resigned."

It is obvious from the transcript of the session that the Fuehrer was completely unnerved. His thoughts raced as he contemplated the abrupt emergency. General Alfred Jodl was no help. "We should," he kept saying in different ways, "really wait for precise reports of what's going on before we do anything."[1]

In the end Hitler fell back on his innate conspiratorial inclinations. "We can play the same game," he ranted. "We'll get everything ready to lay hands on the whole boiling, the whole crew. I'll send a man down tomorrow to the commander of the 3rd Panzer Grenadier Division with an order to drive into Rome with a special detachment and arrest the whole government, the King—all that scum, but primarily the Crown Prince—to get hold of this rabble, principally Badoglio and the whole gang."

The heavy pall of confusion and uncertainty hovered over the proceedings as one briefing session followed another. The intelligence community was conspicuously absent. "The quick windup of the acute crisis," the War Diary noted in an aside, "shows conclusively that the coup was meticulously prepared and that these preparations remained effectively concealed from our military and intelligence agencies in Italy."

For once Hitler was stunned. He had held the initiative in every crisis since 1933, and now was tricked by events over which he had no control. On July 27, he issued special orders to Admiral Canaris and Colonel von Roenne, chief of intelligence of the Army General Staff, to make "extraordinary efforts" to procure definitive information about the Italians' plans and intentions. All he would get from them was a rehash of the first reports and no impending change in Italy's alignment. Nothing indicated, wrote General Enno von Rintelen, the military attaché in Rome, that Badoglio intended to turn his back on the Germans and go over to the Allies. There were no signs of peace negotiations.

Canaris's agents had infiltrated the circle of the conspirators and monitored the preparations for Mussolini's ouster.[2] Canaris was in personal touch with General Cesare Amé, chief of Military Intelligence, and had been told in so many words that the Duce's days were numbered. An Abwehr agent had reported that enormous pressure was being exerted on Mussolini to loosen his ties with the Germans and that the Duce showed signs of weakening.

Canaris personally screened such reports. Determined as he was by this time to work for peace, he welcomed anything that would weaken Hitler's ability to continue the war. He regarded Italy's collapse as a major factor and would do nothing to impede the course of events. Absent from the scene when the crisis broke, he was at Wiener-Neustadt near Vienna with Field Marshal Erwin Rommel. When Rommel was sent to Greece, Canaris accompanied him to Salonika and was there on July 25 when the blow fell.

Only four days later did he bestir himself to get closer to the quickening events. He contacted General Amé—who was, in fact, one of the conspirators—and arranged a personal meeting to "get the facts." They met in Venice on July 30, by which time it was crystal clear that the Italians meant to seek peace. Yet Canaris confused the issue in a report he prepared for the Fuehrer.

"The Italians' will to resist the Allies," he wrote, in the face of all evidence to the contrary, "is unbroken both so far as the people and the armed forces are concerned. The government is determined to apply firm domestic measures in order to continue the war. Peace negotiations are out of the question, nothing along these lines is being undertaken, not even by the Pope. On July 27, rumors averred that Germany was planning to march into Rome and restore Mussolini to power. General Vittorio Ambrosio [head of Comando Supremo], pays no attention to these rumors. On the other hand, there is apprehension in Rome about certain unregistered and undisciplined German units and what they might undertake on their own."

This was the precise line the Italians were following to camouflage their true intention—to leave the Axis and conclude a separate peace.

During these critical four days in July, with advisers like these, Hitler did not know what was going on, what to expect, and what to do. Eight German divisions could be trapped on the Italian mainland, with an expeditionary force of 70,000 troops in Sicily and the huge Afrika Korps in Libya, now in danger of being hopelessly cut off.

Signals to the Germans multiplied. A report came from Merano that plans were made to trap all German forces at the Brenner Pass when they attempted to cross the Alps. The commanding general of the Fourth Italian Army, deployed on the Franco-Italian frontier, refused to let two German divisions pass on their way to new positions in northern Italy.

Then a report from Siegfried Kasche, the SD-chief in Zagreb, supplied additional evidence of the mounting Italian double-cross. Citing Ante Pavelic, the Croatian Fuehrer, Kasche signaled that General Roatta, chief of the Italian General Staff had confided to Sincuc, the Croat plenipotentiary with the Second Italian Army, that "Badoglio's assurances are designed merely to gain time for the conclusion of negotiations with the enemy."

The signal, sent on July 27, reached Hitler's headquarters only on the 30th.

On the morning of the 29th, General Jodl received a sealed envelope from the Reichs Minister of Post, marked "U" to indicate that it was a "deciphered" intercept of the "USA-England radio telephone circuit." The historic incident that changed the course of events was recorded in a special entry of the German War Diary:

"At 1:00 A.M. [Central European Time, on July 29], a radio telephone conversation between British Prime Minister Churchill and President Roosevelt of the United States of America was intercepted, and was found to have dealt with a proclamation of General Eisenhower [to the Italian people] and the impending armistice with Italy. Churchill: 'We do not wish to come forward with any specific armistice terms before we are asked in so many words.' Roosevelt: 'That is right.' Churchill: 'We can wait one or two days.' Roosevelt: 'Right.' By then the problem of British prisoners of war in Italy will be reviewed in order to forestall their transfer 'to the land of the Hun.' Churchill intends to address a direct communication to the King of Italy in this matter. Roosevelt undertook to communicate with 'Emmanuel' also on his part. 'I do not quite know yet how I will go about it.'[3]

"Thus," the War Diary entry concluded, "incontrovertible evidence has come into hand to show that secret negotiations between the Anglo-Americans and the Italians are already under way."

It is necessary to digress here from political events to the fascinating scientific communications warfare that had been fought.

The President and the Prime Minister had reason to feel secure in their probing chat on their "hot line." They had been assured by their communications experts that their radio telephone link was absolutely safe from eavesdroppers, thanks to a device that so scrambled their voices as to become unintelligible in transit. Transatlantic telephone was the most convenient and expeditious means of communication between Washington and London. Both Roosevelt and Churchill preferred it because "it cut through red tape and diplomatic routine and the delays of coding and cabling," and provided for greater intimacy in their personal contacts. Precautions had to be taken to mask such conversations by the interjection of some mechanical means. A device had been developed by the Bell Telephone System to split the frequency band into smaller bands and jumble the normal tones of a voice, making it sound like "a recording of a Mah-Jongg game played too fast."

Called A-3 by its technical name, such a scrambler had already been installed in September 1939 on the radio-telephone Mr. Roosevelt used for his talks. It was later improved with a system called inversion that turned the voice upside down, so to speak, until it sounded like "a thin squawking, ringing with bell-like chimes."

Other special security measures were observed in all transatlantic phone conversations, particularly those conducted by the President. Mr. Roosevelt used a special scrambler-phone the Signal Corps had installed and operated in the White House. The President's words went by wire to the overseas switchboard in an A.T.&T. building at 47 Walker Street, New York. There, with all other transatlantic phone calls in a special security room, the A-3 equipment "mangled" it. Engineers watched the dials to be sure that speech was properly distorted. At the transmitter, channel mixers continually shifted the transmission from one frequency to another, so that anyone listening on one circuit would hear it go suddenly blank.

How, then, was it possible for the Germans to pick up the scrambled Roosevelt-Churchill conversation, unscramble it, and prepare its translation for Hitler?

To answer this question, we must go back to October 1939 and the mailing of a letter by a German agent in New York. Simon Emil Koedel had just finished his regular daily study of *The New York Times* and clipped a number of stories he thought would interest his friends at the Abwehr subbranch in Bremen. He mailed them on the chance that his letter would slip through the British censorship in Bermuda. His letter reached "Niko" Bensmann, the intelligence officer in Bremen, with one intriguing headline: "Roosevelt Protected in Talks to Envoys by Radio 'Scrambling' to Foil Spies Abroad." The article revealed that a "scrambler" had been installed in a soundproof room in the White House basement to assure privacy for the President's transatlantic phone conversations. It went on to describe how Mr. Roosevelt had used it on September 1 for the first time, when he received word of the German invasion of Poland from Ambassador William C. Bullitt in Paris.

Dr. Bensmann brought this to the attention of Commander Carls, who sent it to a special inter-departmental committee that was struggling with the problem of intercepting overseas communications. The committee had explored the possibility of tapping the transatlantic cable, not by a direct method—that was considered far too difficult if not impossible—but by induction instruments that would pick up the high-frequency impulses running through the cables. In his posthumous memoirs, Walter Schellenberg asserted that "the main cable between England and America had been tapped," and yielded considerable intelligence which produced precious data about armament production and supplies. "A great deal of information on convoys and shipping could also be deduced," he wrote, "which was invaluable for our U-boat raids on Allied shipping."

Nobody, it seemed, throughout the German high command's vast communications[4] establishment had sufficient interest in Koedel's tantalizing clue to undertake efforts to unscramble the American scrambler and thus open up an exceptional shortcut to the secrets it concealed.

The job went begging until it was adopted by an agency that was, strictly speaking, far from the intelligence community. As common to most European postal organizations, the *Deutsche Reichspost* also administered the telephone and telegraph service. Its own research facilities, not unlike the Bell System's famed laboratories, were engaged in the development and improvement of the technical means of telephonic and telegraphic communications.

Reichs Post Minister Wilhelm Ohnesorge, a man in his late fifties, had already proposed that the transatlantic cable be tapped by the induction system. Now he focused on another solution—to "decipher," as he put it, the scrambled conversations moving on the England-America radio circuit. This did not involve "deciphering" in the usual cryptological sense of the term but what is called *ciphony*, a term concocted from "cipher" and "telephony." In his endeavor to crack the scrambler, Ohnesorge's research chief, Engineer Vetterlein, faced a task similar to that confronting the American codebreakers in 1939–40, when they had to crack the Japanese diplomatic cipher by first reconstructing the mysterious machine which produced it. Neither the Americans nor Vetterlein had anything tangible to begin with—no models, blueprints, or wiring patterns of the machines. Yet both succeeded in reconstructing the complex devices. It took Vetter-

lein much less time to grope his way to the design of the A-3 scrambler than the Americans needed to build their replica of the famous
Japanese B-machine, which they then called "Magic."

Vetterlein began to work on the project in the summer of 1941. By
September he had pilot models of both the scrambler and the de-
scrambler. It took a little longer to build a pilot monitoring station
and manufacture the intricate equipment needed to intercept, record,
and unscramble the conversations on the England-United States circuit. The whole project was completed by March 1, 1942. A monitoring station with giant directional antennae was erected at a secluded
spot near Eindhoven on the coast of occupied Holland. Its equipment was so efficient that the intercepted conversations could be
"deciphered" instantaneously, losing only a few syllables after each
key change (which occurred at intervals of twenty seconds) until
the proper key was found automatically. The German transcripts
were sent to Berlin on a *G-Schreiber*, a classified teletype that had its
own scrambler system. The entire operation, from the interception to
the arrival of its transcript in Berlin, usually required only a couple
of hours. It was probably the fastest means of intelligence procurement in secret service history.[5]

In the experimental stage, Minister Ohnesorge and Engineer Vetterlein surrounded the project with utter secrecy. By March 1942 it
was functioning with such perfection and was yielding such significant data, that Ohnesorge thought the time had come to acquaint the
Fuehrer himself with this fantastic new implement in the intelligence
arsenal of Germany. On March 6 he addressed a top-secret letter to
Hitler, informing him that his Research Bureau had "completed . . .
an installation for the interception of the telephone traffic between
the U.S.A. and England," with proper pride that his was "the only
agency in the Reich that [had] succeeded in rendering conversations, that had been made unintelligible, intelligible again at the instant of reception."

This was a Nazi triumph, and it was to remain a Nazi operation.
Distribution of the intercepts was strictly limited. A single copy of the
original transcript was sent to Heinrich Himmler, to be distributed at
his discretion. The Abwehr was bypassed, as were the intelligence
departments of the Army, Navy, and Luftwaffe.

Himmler received the first batch of transcripts on March 22. From
then on, a steady stream of intercepts flowed into his office. The
choicest intercepts were forwarded to Hitler, with copies occasionally
going to Ribbentrop in the Foreign Ministry.[6]

Dr. Ohnesorge's operators quickly learned how to plumb even the
most bowdlerized and harmless-sounding conversation for valuable

information. The roster of the Allied officials on whose conversations the Ohnesorge apparatus eavesdropped reads like a Who's Who of the Anglo-American war effort: Harry Hopkins; Anthony Eden; W. Averill Harriman; Sir John Anderson (when he was Chancellor of the Exchequer); John Miller Martin, Mr. Churchill's principal private secretary; Sir Ronald Ian Campbell, the British Minister in Washington; Ross Campbell (later Lord) Geddes, a Scottish shipping magnate who headed the British Merchant Shipping Mission in Washington; Sir Frederick William Leith-Ross, chief economic adviser to His Majesty's Government and director general of the Ministry of Economic Warfare; Sir Wilfred Griffin Eady and Sir David Waley, high-ranking officials of the Treasury; Lord Keynes; and a great number of lesser officials representing the War Office, the Minister of War Transport, the Ministry of Supply, and other key war agencies in London and Washington.

With abiding faith in the inviolability of the scrambler system, the Prime Minister called Mr. Roosevelt, his other friends and associates in Washington and New York, at all hours of the day or night, from his bomb-proof shelter under Whitehall where his transatlantic telephone was installed.

It was Mr. Churchill who, on July 29, put in the fateful call to the President to review person-to-person the exhilarating events in Italy. Although the British secret service had a lively net of high-grade agents in Rome, the coup was so well guarded that nothing leaked to them in advance. "We had," Mr. Churchill wrote later, "no definite knowledge of the inner stresses of Italian politics."

Churchill received the news of Mussolini's downfall shortly before midnight on July 20, and promptly fired off a telegram to Roosevelt, celebrating the event in properly Churchillian phrases. "The present stage may only be transition," he wrote. "But anyhow Hitler will feel very lonely when Mussolini is down and out."

Roosevelt's message, which crossed Churchill's cable, was not too encouraging. "It is my thought," the President wrote, "that we should come as close as possible to unconditional surrender, followed by good treatment of the Italian populace. . . . In no event should our officers in the field fix on any general terms without your approval or mine."

The President was in excellent spirits and so both men let down their guards. They joked and talked freely about the ramifications of Italy's plight—and about the terms of an armistice.[7]

At this time, Italy had not yet made any formal move to seek even a cease-fire. Peace feelers in Tangier, Lisbon, Barcelona, and Bern were informal and unofficial. The President and the Prime Minister, in their justifiable exuberance, spoke of an Italian armistice as an imminent reality.

It was the transcript of this fateful telephone conversation that General Jodl handed to Hitler at eleven o'clock in the morning on July 29. Indecision about what to do in Italy had been still rampant at the Fuehrer's headquarters. Now the uncertainty ended dramatically. The clue was the one Hitler had been waiting for but could not get from any of his other intelligence agencies. It galvanized him to immediate action. Before the day was out, the Fuehrer issued orders to occupy Italy. German troops began to roll through the Alpine passes, until Hitler had twenty divisions in Italy, all the way from Calabria to the Alps.

In his postmortem, Churchill viewed this move into Italy as the crowning error of Hitler's strategy and war direction. "There was no need," he wrote, "to consume his strength in Italy and the Balkans, and the fact that he was induced to do so must be taken as the waste of his last opportunity."

It may be true that the occupation of Italy was the wrong disposition to make, and that it enabled the Allies a year later to launch their main direct assault in Normandy. But in Italy the war went on with unrelenting fury and horror, as the Allied troops were forced to hack their way up the peninsula, fighting for every square inch as they went.

When it came at last on April 15, 1945, the end was almost two years overdue.

If there is a moral in this story, it may be put in a paraphrase of the Bell System's famous slogan: When it comes to state secrets, write, don't telephone.

NOTES

1 Jodl later confessed to a gathering of Party bigwigs that he had been completely dumbfounded by the events. "This was the one time throughout the war," he said, "when I was at a loss for advice to be given the Fuehrer."

2 They were difficult to overlook. By July 23–24, arrangements for the coup were almost conspicuous. The telephone exchanges, police headquarters, and the Ministry of the Interior were quietly occupied. A special detachment of police was deployed near the royal villa. Carabinieri were reinforced at every key spot. Mussolini's personal musketeers were relieved of their duty to guard the Palazzo Venezia, and their place was taken by handpicked police armed with submachine guns.

3 As no American or British record of this conversation could be found (none is on file at the Roosevelt Library at Hyde Park, New York), the

remarks attributed to Churchill and Roosevelt had to be reconverted from their German translation.

4 Even as late in the war as August 1944, the head of the British section in Schellenberg's bureau, bemoaned the "gap" that was left in the collection of intelligence by the failure to tap the cable directly. He suggested that a number of U-boats be assigned to the task of tampering with them. Several other communications agencies had also tried, including Goering's Research Bureau.

5 The first interception was made at 7:45 P.M. on September 7, 1941. It reproduced the conversation of a British official who had just arrived in Washington and phoned his office in London to send him an assistant.

6 The unimaginative Foreign Minister recognized little of intelligence value in these intercepts. To be sure, most of the time the parties on the line were sufficiently alert to the dangers inherent in telephone conversations, even when scrambled, to observe special care in what they were saying. The circumspect tone of these conversations so exasperated Ribbentrop that he once penned a deprecating note on the margin of one of them: "Owing to the fact that these conversations are camouflaged," he wrote, "there is very little one can learn from them."

7 The German's electronic eavesdropping continued unabated—until May 5, 1944, when, as Schellenberg put it, "we hit a bull's eye." Eyndhoven unscrambled a five-minute conversation between Roosevelt and Churchill in which they discussed the build-up of the Allied forces in Great Britain. The intercept was hailed at Hitler's headquarters as yet another scoop of the Ohnesorge apparatus. It corroborated on the highest Allied authority the many scattered reports about the impending invasion. And it persuaded the Germans that it was now imminent. "Had the two statesmen known," Schellenberg wrote, "that the enemy was listening to their conversation, Roosevelt would hardly have been likely to say goodbye to Churchill with the words, 'Well, we will do our best—now I'll go fishing.' "

Part **VII**

TWILIGHT OF
THE FOXES

The Riddles of Overlord

*I*N the early morning of January 15, 1944, when Major Hermann Sandel arrived in his office on Sophien Terrace in Hamburg, he was handed an unsigned telegram with a message of only ten words.

"Hoerte, dass Eisenhower am 16. Januar in England eintreffen wird," it read. "Heard that Eisenhower will arrive in England on January 16."

This was the fifth year of the war, yet the telegram had come straight from Britain. The sender of the signal was A.3725, Sandel's best spy, still at large in England, the young Danish industrial draftsman, Hans Hansen. This was Hansen's 935th message in a clandestine career that seemed to have miraculously endured since that late summer day in 1940 when he first parachuted in the vicinity of Salisbury.

The timid winter sun rose sluggishly on a dreary day, the air chilled by a nipping wind from the North Sea, sweeping through the rubble left by "Gomorrha," the heaviest air raid of the war which the Allies launched on the great Hanseatic port. It had reached its apocalyptic climax during five frightful days and nights in July 1943, when a total of 6889 tons of incendiary bombs left the city (including eighty Wehrmacht installations) in ashes. Sophien Terrace was badly hit, but work continued in the wrecked Abwehr offices behind shattered windows and battered desks.

Major Sandel, a reserve officer in his late forties who had lived in America for years and was considered the Abwehr's best expert on the Anglo-Saxons, was overcome by gloom. Privy as he was to all the war's secrets which Dr. Goebbels was trying to keep from the German people, he could view the war as a whole.

The day before, the Red Army had launched a major January offensive against Field Marshal Georg von Kuechler's shivering Army Group North on a front stretching from the Leningrad sector to Novgorod.

The telegram from England deepened his apprehension. It was no secret that the Western Allies were feverishly preparing the enormous massing of men and materiel on the British Isles for the historic leap to occupied Europe. The terse message from A.3725 indicated that these vast preparations had now reached the terminal stage.

At face value, the report represented a remarkable feat. Ike's appointment as Supreme Commander had been announced on Christmas Day, but he had vanished from North Africa on December 31, flying to the United States for conferences with General George C. Marshall and a reunion with his family. His coming and going securely hidden—the stars of his overseas cap removed and those on his shoulder covered by his overcoat collar, he had left Washington at 7 P.M. on January 13, and reached London at 11 P.M. on the 14th. The lid was on. No announcement of his arrival was to be made until the afternoon of the 16th.

Hansen had word of it on the morning of the 14th, even while Ike was still inside "Bayonet," his private railroad car, which was taking him from Prestwick to London through thick English fog and dense censorship. The agent radioed the news seven hours before Ike's arrival at his new command post and forty-eight hours ahead of the official announcement.

Major Sandel regarded the signal sufficiently interesting and important to warrant distribution to Group I at "Belinda," the secret Abwehr headquarters in a suburb of Berlin. It was put on the *G-Schreiber*, the direct-line cipher teletype; then Sandel drafted a message to the agent. "Many thanks for excellent No. 935. Keep us posted on Eisenhower's movements in context of invasion preparations."

It went out at 8:30 P.M. on the regular schedule of Hamburg's daily contact with Hansen.

On October 21, 1940, in a broadcast to the French people held in the Nazi yoke, Winston Churchill taunted Hitler for delaying "Operation Sea Lion," the grandiose but stillborn plan to cross over to Britain in the wake of France's defeat. "We are waiting for the long-promised invasion," he said. "So are the fishes." Now the fishes were waiting on the other side.

Churchill later described the awesome problems of choosing the safest and most direct assault across the Channel on the German sea front in France. "I knew that it would be a very heavy and hazardous adventure."

Somehow Adolf Hitler had no such doubts. In an astounding demonstration of his famous intuition, the Fuehrer anticipated in 1941 exactly when and where the invasion would eventually come. Only a week after Pearl Harbor he issued a remarkable directive called "Construction of Coastal Defenses." Envisaging what he called *die Grosslandung der Alliierten* ("the decisive landing of the Allies"), he expected them to hit "the protruding parts of Normandy and Britanny," where the excellent harbors "would make ideal beachheads."

The Fuehrer propounded a vast scheme to "thwart any attempted landing." In March, 1942, he recalled from retirement old Gerd von Rundstedt, the most unflappable and dependable among his field marshals, appointing him Supreme Commander West, responsible for the defense of France, Belgium, and Holland.

It was like living in a haunted house where the slightest sound is charged to an elusive ghost. By 1942 any random noises from the direction of the English Channel made Hitler jumpy. The bold Commando raid on St. Nazaire, he told his staff, was actually an "invasion probe." The ill-fated assault on Dieppe, he regarded as "an invasion pure and simple." He continued to insist that "those British were fully determined to stay," even when a General Staff study, based on the raiders' captured operations plan, showed conclusively that the Canadians had explicit orders to return to Britain after the completion of their mission.

The Atlantic Wall went up, mounted with batteries of 16-inch naval guns stripped from idle warships. Some of the Wehrmacht's best units were kept in the critical region. During one of his periodic panics in 1942, Hitler ordered two crack infantry divisions—the "Adolf Hitler" and the "Grossdeutschland"—transferred in great hurry from Russia, where they were desperately needed, to the Atlantic front, where they were not yet needed.

Two years went by and the Allies did not show up. Their absence made the "invasion" the war's most tantalizing enigma. The fantastic investment in manpower and money, in steel and concrete, was made in a vacuum. It is fascinating to note the shadowboxing of the Germans during this period. Never in history was a high command so uninformed about their opponent at the most critical stage of a conflict. Documents of this time paraded their ignorance.

"The enemy," wrote Field Marshal von Rundstedt on November 19, 1943, in a directive called *Preparations for the Struggle*, "is on the eve of the completion of his arrangements for the offensive against the Western sector. *Where* he will come we do not know; neither do we know *when* he will come."

On December 23, a conference was called by Hitler at his headquarters, but the meeting merely compounded the confusion. Another directive came from General Alfred Jodl, the Fuehrer's personal

chief of staff, conceding his woeful want of knowledge by listing six different places where the landing could take place. Two of
them were in the West, two in Italy, and two in the eastern Mediterranean, henceforth to be referred to by their code names—Flower I
and II, Marten I and II, and Trout I and II respectively—which Jodl
coined for these areas.

Such blind groping at the top, less than six months before D-Day,
was astounding. It cast grave doubt on the astuteness of Admiral
Canaris and the efficiency of his Abwehr, which was supposed to
know what was going on inside the Allied camp.

In an attempt after the war to rationalize the defeat, diehard reactionary circles in Germany insisted that the Abwehr not only failed to
provide the indispensable information the High Command needed
but deliberately misled it with bogus intelligence. Admiral Canaris
was represented as the arch villain actually working for the Allies
and it was pointed out that the German Army's own senior intelligence officer was a prominent member of the attempt to kill Hitler on
July 20, 1944.

The Canaris organization was certainly not as good as its apologists now claim, but neither was it as abysmally bad. It managed to
sustain a respectable surveillance of the United States and the British
Isles under exasperatingly difficult conditions. It procured reliable
information and enabled the German High Command to follow the
evolution of the Anglo-American strategic concept of the invasion
plan, from its inception in early 1942 to the arrival of the Allies in
Normandy in 1944.

The surveillance began in December 1941, in the immediate wake
of the Japanese attack on Pearl Harbor. Colonel Hans Piekenbrock
immediately alerted the whole Abwehr apparatus. The distinct possibility of a cross-Channel return to the Continent by formidable
Anglo-American forces was one of the overriding problems the Abwehr was expected to monitor.

Enemy intentions, developed on the highest echelons in circumspect secrecy, are the most difficult to probe. Yet the Abwehr succeeded from the outset in ascertaining the basic intention of the
Anglo-Americans—the premise on which the entire Allied strategy
was constructed.

Only a fortnight after Pearl Harbor, President Roosevelt and
Prime Minister Churchill met in Washington in a conference code
named "Arcadia," to determine the conduct of the war both in the
Atlantic and the Pacific. Twenty-three days of deliberation behind
closed doors produced a stunning, momentous design. Major Lionel
Frederic Ellis, the official British historian of the war in the West,

later referred to "the essential features of their strategy," cloaked by what their authors hoped would be ironclad secrecy.

Yet, only a few weeks after the conclusion of the conference, they were on Hitler's desk, presented to the Fuehrer by Admiral Canaris in person. The 20-page report, spelling out the policy decisions reached at Arcadia and "the steps to be taken" to implement them, had been procured from a source described discreetly as "the well-known reliable V-man of our friends." He was Colonel José Carlos Garcia, the Spanish military attaché, who was de facto the Abwehr's top agent in the American capital.

The document was smuggled out in the Spanish diplomatic pouch and reached Madrid on February 1, addressed to General Campos Martinez, chief of the Informacia Militar, Franco's secret military intelligence service. The Spaniard personally handed the document to Commander Wilhelm Leissner alias Gustav Lenz, chief of the Madrid outpost of the Abwehr and it was then flown by special courier to Canaris in Berlin.

Simultaneously, the Abwehr obtained supporting data from other sources. The Italians gave Canaris the decoded intercept of a cable sent to Ankara by the Turkish Ambassador in London, reconstructing a lengthy conversation he had with Colonel Robert Lees, the American military attaché, about the implications of Arcadia in regard to Turkey. The *Forschungsamt* deciphered several reports of the exceptionally well-informed Portuguese Ambassador in London,who had been briefed on the conference upon Mr. Churchill's return to Downing Street. Another agent, described as "our trusted and tested V-man inside the Swiss General Staff," gave the chief of the Abwehr outpost in Bern a copy of the Swiss military attaché's analysis of Arcadia cabled from Washington.

Probably the most specific strategic intelligence reports were submitted to the Bremen branch by A.2248. This agent was Waldemar Baron von Oppenheim, the Cologne banker, who had a string of high-level informants in influential financial circles in New York and Washington. In three reports (Nos. 4097/41/IH, 308/42/IH, and especially 573/42/IH), the "Baron" (his code name) was able to inform the Abwehr in no uncertain terms that, according to the minutes of Arcadia, "notwithstanding the entry of Japan into the war," the Atlantic and Europe were regarded as "the decisive theater," Germany "the prime enemy," and her defeat "the key to victory."

The dossier about Arcadia which Canaris presented to Hitler left little to the imagination.

The German transcript revealed (in chronological sequence, step by step) every operation the Allies planned to launch up to 1943, beginning with "a limited land offensive" in 1942, to gain "possession of the whole North African coast." The way was to be cleared by 1943, if possible, "for a return to the Continent across the Mediterranean, from Turkey into the Balkans, or by landings in Western Europe."

At Arcadia, too, the Allied staffs were instructed to "take steps immediately for the assembly in England of the Allied forces," and to draft plans for launching "a full-scale attack by Allied forces landed in France." The military intention of the Allies was spelled out in unmistakable terms; their operations plan was enunciated in specific detail; their timetable was drawn up in exact order.

The gradual implementation of this grand strategy was observed closely by German intelligence. In May 1943, the Spanish military attaché in Washington supplied more strategic information to the Abwehr. Now he forwarded what purported to be a transcript of the minutes of "Trident," the Roosevelt-Churchill conference at which the invasion of the Continent was first reviewed in specific detail. Operational and tactical intelligence was obtained in abundance through monitoring by German signal intelligence of the Allies' wireless communications whose codes and ciphers had been cracked; by the examination of captured documents and interrogation of prisoners taken in North Africa, Italy, and in the St. Nazaire and Dieppe raids; and from a network of secret agents specializing in what came to be called "invasion" intelligence.

Yet the vast mass of ominous information which these elaborate efforts yielded either did not reach the top echelons of the Wehrmacht High Command or failed to make the proper impression on them. Such was the situation in January 1944, when the report from A.3725 began its bureaucratic passage to Zossen, the rambling concrete compound of bunkers to which the Army General Staff had been moved in Berlin.

Although the signal was marked SSD, the symbol for "very, very urgent," it passed through channels before reaching the man most keenly interested—Colonel Alexis von Roenne, the army's senior intelligence chief of *Fremde Heere West*, the German equivalent of the American General Staff's G-2.

On the afternoon of the next day, Reuters (one of Roenne's main sources of information, assiduously monitored throughout the war) carried the official communique, still worded so as to conceal Ike's detour to the United States. "It can now be announced," it read, "that General Eisenhower has assumed the duties in the U.K. assigned him by the Combined Chiefs of Staff. On his journey from the Mediterranean to the U.K. he had conferences with the President and the Prime Minister."

In the meantime, A.3725 came through with another variation on his new theme. "There are now," he radioed on the 16th in signal No. 937, "more than 7000 American officers and men in London, in addition to those who come here temporarily on their furloughs. Most of those on duty here work at various invasion headquarters, one of which is located on Berkeley Square in Mayfair."

Remarkable though the agent's accomplishment seemed, this was nothing spectacular in itself. Colonel von Roenne was starved for any hard news from England, and so, when he drew up his situation report for January 17, he took his cue from the spy.

"The arrival of Eisenhower in England," he wrote, "is by now featured prominently in numerous news items in the press and on the radio. Another agent signal simultaneously reporting the installation of the Allied high command in Gibraltar was presumably referring to a second top-level command post in the process of being organized, to direct operations in the Mediterranean, especially attacks against the south of France.

"Another report," he went on, "announcing the arrival in England of Eisenhower's deputy, British Air Chief Marshal Tedder, demonstrates the rapid progress in the build-up of the Anglo-American command apparatus for the pending operations. As far as the naming of General Bradley as 'commander of the United States field army under Eisenhower' [American Army Group No. 1] is concerned, it is notable that Bradley at one time commanded the 82nd Airborne Division [whose partial transfer to England from Italy had become known from the 'unimpeachable source'], and was subsequently in command of the 28th Infantry Division, whose arrival in southern England had been reported by another agent."[1]

This was not one of Roenne's better situation reports. Even at this late stage, Roenne had very little really hard intelligence at his disposal.

If any one man could be singled out as the key figure in this sideshow of the great pre-invasion drama, it was Alexis von Roenne. It was his mission to produce for the High Command the definitive intelligence they needed to make their dispositions. All the bustling secret services, the code-crackers and intelligence analysts worked for him. It was at his desk where the buck-passing ended.

A mere colonel in the glittering coterie of field marshals and super-generals around the Fuehrer, he headed a relatively small bureau in the General Staff. Roenne was recognized even by his internal enemies (he had many because he was a proud and outspoken man with abundant courage and strong convictions) as the ideal man for the critical job. He was erudite, imaginative, level-headed, and an excellent administrator. Only a captain in 1940, he created a sensation and earned unstinting praise for his superb collection of data about the French army, spotting its fatal weaknesses even when all the other experts regarded it as a formidable fighting force. Roenne's contribution to the Battle of France was hailed by General Franz Halder, then chief of the General Staff, as a decisive factor in the stunning success of German arms.

When the Chief of the intelligence bureau was retired in 1942, Colonel von Roenne was the natural choice to succeed him. Promoted three times in less than three years, he was now facing not only the supreme challenge of his career, but also a chance to improve on his phenomenal coup of 1940, by charting the mystery of the Allies' course toward the Continent. But it seemed that this was overtaxing Roenne's resources.

"Until well into 1942," wrote Professor Percy Ernst Schramm, keeper of the OKW's war diary, "the German High Command could by and large confine its efforts [in the West] to the safeguarding and controlling of the occupied territories, and to the build-up of coastal defenses. Since the summer and fall of that year (Dieppe, El Alamein, and the landings in French North Africa), it had become obvious that the Anglo-Americans were determined to establish a 'second front' somewhere along the German-held coastline of Europe . . . [with] a thrust aimed at the heartland of 'Fortress Europe' to force the decision."

The remarkable feature of the situation, according to Schramm's analysis, was that Roenne's so-called *Feindbild*, or picture of the enemy, produced no clues for the precise landing of the Allies' second front. Moreover, the picture became increasingly clouded in the winter of 1943–44. In a situation report prepared for Hitler himself, a Brigadier General of Jodl's planning staff wrote: "We occupy the inner line in the strategic defensive for 'Festung Europa,' without being able to take full advantage of the inner line, since numerous loose (*ungebundene*) forces of the enemy, in the Mediterranean, the Middle and Near East, in Africa, America, England, and Iceland, whose participation in the major assault on the coast of Europe must be expected at any time, pin down considerable portions of our reserves."

This was an intolerable situation and nobody felt it more keenly than Colonel von Roenne in his concrete-encrusted ivory tower in Zossen.

Throughout 1943, he had pondered, probed, and projected the momentous problem. As the Allies were moving relentlessly through the Mediterranean to their foothold in southern Italy, Roenne was carefully weighing the strategy contained in this tactical chain—the great invasion that sooner or later would climax the campaigns in

North Africa, Sicily, and Italy. He had little firm evidence on which to base his estimates.

"Our ignorance of the Allied aims," wrote Professor Schramm in the War Diary, "was aggravated by their skillful manipulation of the news. From the summer of 1942 on, they released periodic waves of 'invasion rumors.' " Though most of them were, as Schramm put it, patently transparent, they nevertheless added to the ambiguity of the situation.

Several times Colonel von Roenne was forcefully reminded of what topside expected from him. General Jodl, expected by Hitler to draft German countermeasures, was handicapped by the stubborn absence of strategic intelligence. The usual contingency plans, which higher staffs routinely draft to meet any and all eventualities, would not do. How could he devise such plans when he remained in the dark on the direction and timing of the invasion?

On January 3 he drafted instructions for all intelligence agencies, listing specific queries to which he expected unequivocal answers. On the 6th, he called Roenne and Admiral Canaris to his office, and impressed upon them what they already knew only too well. Then he showed how far his own estimate strayed from the true situation. "I demand," he told them, "that you give the Mediterranean area far greater attention than has hitherto been the case. What happens there is not only indicative of the enemy's intention in the Mediterranean, but is likely to supply invaluable indices for the sum total of the Anglo-Americans' strategic intentions and plans elsewhere."

He mentioned the ferment that was evident in the Mediterranean basin. The Allies apparently had ceased to withdraw any more landing craft from the area, and several major units had been removed from the front, vanishing without a trace. The items he cited were correct, but the conclusion he drew was wide of the mark. "As I see it," Jodl said, "these moves indicate that the main effort of the Allies will be in the general area of the Mediterranean."

"And, incidentally," he added, "I discussed the matter with the Fuehrer several times in recent days, and he questioned emphatically the seriousness of any Allied intentions. He's envisaging a series of diversionary moves which the Anglo-Americans are likely to make before risking a full-scale invasion. In particular, the Fuehrer expects them to land in Portugal or somewhere on the Spanish coast or, if in France, then north of the Gironde."

This was a far cry from Hitler's inspired guess of 1941–42, when he singled out the Normandy-Brittany area as the most likely goal of the Allied *Grosslandung*. Now in 1944, when he had to deceive himself in order to sustain his faith in a German victory, he became so imbued with the impregnability of the fortifications he had conjured up on the Channel coast, that he did not think it possible for the Allies to dare venturing against them.

Roenne was dismayed when he left Jodl's office. He no longer doubted that the Allies meant business and would waste their resources on "raids" or "landings" in places like Portugal or Spain. As a matter of fact, two major intelligence coups scored at this time enabled Roenne to see through the Allied smokescreen.

On December 16, 1943, he had received an intercepted message in which an American colonel, identified as an influential member of Eisenhower's staff, spoke freely of a pending operation called "Overlord," which had all the earmarks of the major Allied attack across the English Channel.

At about the same time, the war's greatest intelligence scoop made it possible for Roenne to identify Overlord definitively as the code name of the main Allied thrust. He obtained details of the operation from a most authoritative source—top-secret documents of the highest Allied authorities.

Since October 26, 1943, the *Sicherheitsdienst*, had a super-agent in Turkey supplying information straight from the safe of the British Ambassador in Turkey. He was the ambassador's valet "Cicero," —again—with a duplicate key to the private strong box His Excellency kept in his bedroom.

"Out of the blue," wrote Ludwig C. Moyzisch, the SD chief in Ankara who managed this operation, "there dropped into our laps the sort of papers the Secret Service agent might dream about for a lifetime without believing that he could ever get hold of them. Even at a glance I could see that the valet's service to the Third Reich was unbelievably important."

The edge of this unique coup was nevertheless badly blunted. While Moyzisch was satisfied that Cicero was genuine and the documents authentic, his superiors in Berlin were inclined to believe that the whole windfall—Cicero had come to the Germans unexpectedly and unsolicited—was but another of the Allies' deceptive maneuvers. Instead of acting on the information, Cicero shipments were held up while ponderous committees debated in endless conferences whether or not to accept the documents for what they seemed to be.

The great debate was still going on when, on December 14, 1943, Cicero gave Moyzisch what seemed to be the most important of all of his pilfered papers. It was the transcript of the Teheran Conference, the November meeting at which Roosevelt, Churchill, and Stalin reached agreement on the future course of the Allied war effort and decided on the means that would accelerate their push toward victory. Much of it revolved around the operation "Overlord"—the same code-name Colonel von Roenne had encountered in the intercept of the American colonel's indiscreet message.

Now that he knew what Overlord meant and what the Allies were planning, Colonel von Roenne breathed more easily. Henceforth he had only to assemble the operational and tactical details through whatever channels he had.

He conferred daily with Admiral Canaris and his chief lieutenants. He prodded General Fellgiebel, the Wehrmacht's chief signal officer, and the others in charge of cryptographic espionage, to keep the most intensive watch on the Allies' communications, trying to gain the kind of data that not even the best spy could procure. Roenne himself toured the vulnerable areas of the French coast to conduct personal reconnaissance, conferring wherever he went with the intelligence officers of the armies in the field.

Now, at last, in response to his prodding, Abwehr reports about the Allied build-up began to multiply. A signal identified the First United States Army in southern England; another located one English airborne division in the Salisbury-Yeovil-Taunton area, a second between Aldershot and Guilford, and a third "forming" near Hull. Still another report pinpointed Reading as "the new headquarters of the VII Corps." A spy saw the 49, the (British) Infantry Division, moving out of Scotland and rolling southward in the direction of Harwich and Lovestoft. Another agent reported "considerable activity around Poole and Bournemouth." One place-name after another appeared in the reports. Troops coming from all over the United Kingdom, Northern Ireland, Iceland, the Mediterranean basin, and America were spotted in assembly areas. Command posts were being set up. Eastbourne, Brighton, Worthing, Wye, and Wemouth were most prominently mentioned.

Reports revealed distinctly that the bulk of the Allied forces was assembling in the south, facing the lower part of the English Channel, below the Strait of Dover. This was the direction from which the main thrust should be expected to come.

Still Roenne had no satisfactory clues for two burning questions:

Where *exactly* on the long coast of France did the Allies intend to land? On what *exact* date was the climactic attack to be launched?

It was clearly the eleventh hour.

Roenne concluded, as he stated in his estimate of January 19, "that the attack in the West must be anticipated to begin at any time from the middle of February on, when the weather is expected to be favorable for landing operations."

There was no more time for equivocation, no margin for error, and he so informed his staff. Since the inconclusive November conference at the Fuehrer's headquarters, which had produced Jodl's proliferating alternatives, Roenne had kept in his desk drawer an ordinary 1:6,000,000 scale map of Europe. He would take it out from time to time, pore over it, follow the coastline from northern Norway to the Dardanelles, trying to insinuate his thoughts into the Allied plan.

By the end of January, he assumed the Allies might launch the historic operation in little more than a fortnight. In his office in Maybach II, he took out the dog-eared map and studied it more intensely than at any time before. He had lined up a set of colored crayons on the desk, and with his mind suddenly made up, he began to mark the map.

With a green crayon, he drew a thin arrow to mark what he concluded would be one of the diversionary thrusts, pushing through the Dardanelles into the Black Sea in the direction of Odessa. A thin dotted arrow in blue (with a question mark next to it) went through the Adriatic, curved eastward over Croatia, and aimed at Budapest in Hungary. A couple of dotted arrows in yellow pointed at the sector between Marseilles and the Italian Riviera. He drew a somewhat thicker black arrow up the Italian boot in the direction of Milan.

For the major, decisive thrust, he painted a red arrow, almost an inch wide, from England in the direction of the French coast. Its base resting on Manchester, it left England through the Dover-Folkstone area, and crossed the Channel where it was narrowest—its head pointing clearly and unequivocally to the Pas de Calais region in northern France.

It was a strange conclusion, for none of the incoming reports had referred to any massive concentration of troops and equipment, or even any unusual activity, behind the white cliffs of Dover. But Roenne told Major Soltmann, his deputy and chief of his British desk: "Why should the Anglo-Saxons risk the long passage from Portsmouth, for example, when they can dash across to Calais from Dover where the Channel is only 20 miles wide?"[2]

The Pas de Calais, of course! This slightly hilly rural region of Artois and Picardy, bulging into the Dover Strait, was the historic region over which fought the Counts of Flanders, the Dukes of Burgundy, and the Bourbons, Frenchmen, Spaniards, Austrians—and was the famous battleground of World War I!

His mind made up, Roenne invited Canaris to a day-long conference, to arrange the Abwehr's final effort to guide a defense. He was not yet home by any means. He still needed myriad pieces of final tactical intelligence—the enemy's exact order of battle, data about equipment, intelligence about combat tactics, the innumerable facts to make up a conclusive *Feindbield*.

They met on February 2, in the General Staff's bunker at Zeppelin, and their conversation was recorded in a captured report of the event. Roenne as a General Staff officer shared with Canaris a disdain for the Nazi regime, but he also did not think too highly of the Abwehr. He realized that it was extremely difficult to maintain effective espionage on the British Isles, but thought nevertheless that the Abwehr should have done better in its on-the-spot surveillance.

He was therefore pleasantly surprised when Canaris now sketched for him the network of spies he still had inside Britain who could obtain the missing information. "The fact," the admiral said somewhat smugly, "that we have any V-men at all in Britain, and have had several for as long as three to four years, is undoubtedly the most remarkable feat in the history of espionage." After more unnecessary bragging about how ingenious and ruthless the British security measures were, Canaris came to the point, describing his network of V-men from Bristol in the south to Glasgow and Aberdeen in the north. "We have succeeded in sustaining them so well that we are receiving even at this stage . . . an average of thirty to forty reports each day from inside England, many of them radioed directly on the clandestine wireless sets we have operational in defiance of the most intricate and elaborate electronic countermeasures."

Canaris was satisfied in his own mind that he was not exaggerating the Abwehr's coverage of Britain. At the outbreak of the war he had only a single uncaptured agent (A.3504) there. In 1944, he told Roenne, he had several rings, as well as scattered V-men working on their own, altogether some 130 secret agents at large. The Abwehr branches of Hamburg, Bremen, Wiesbaden, Paris, and Brussels each had operatives inside Britain—including Hamburg's phenomenal A.3725, (Hansen) and a mystery agent, going by the cover-name of "Tramp." This was not the same "Tramp" previously captured, but a woman who commuted between London and Bristol. "She's sending us absolutely first rate military information, although," Canaris added blandly, "she is only a woman."

In addition, the big Abwehr outposts in Madrid, Lisbon, and Bern had agents at key posts. Madrid maintained a whole network, called "Arabal," consisting of seven producing V-men, and a ring managed by Sp.-319, smuggling information, collected by his group of five more V-men, in the Spanish diplomatic pouch. The Lisbon office was represented by "Ivy," another woman producing "first-rate military information," and a ring managed by "Ostro," a Portuguese businessman who had contracted with the Abwehr to gather intelligence through the branches of his big international firm located in England and the United States.

High-grade intelligence was coming via Stockholm through "Josephine," still tapping the resources of the Swedish Legation in London. Via Bern, "Banta," an employee of the Swiss Legation, had access to the reports of the well-informed Swiss military attaché in London.

Some of his lines were reaching into high places. Canaris promised Roenne that at 10 Downing Street one of Churchill's private secretaries "could be persuaded to work for the Abwehr." At Eisenhower's headquarters he had a girl named "Mary" whom the intrepid and gregarious A.3725 (Hansen) had recently succeeded in "seducing." In General Bradley's FUSAG headquarters, the liaison officer of the Polish General Staff doubled as an Abwehr agent.

This enormous apparatus, built with meticulous care during the war years, had been kept going. All of these agents could be alerted immediately and instructed to concentrate on invasion intelligence. Moreover, Canaris assured Roenne, a number of additional V-men would be insinuated into England from Spain and Portugal. Several of them, fully trained, authenticated, and briefed, were standing by to leave on a moment's notice.

If this was to be his spies' finest hour, it was also Canaris's final challenge and the Abwehr's acid test. For the first time in its existence of a quarter of a century, after years of trifling with largely tactical matters, it had a supreme strategic mission. Its place in history, its final rank among the great secret services of the world, depended on how it would carry out this assignment. The Abwehr would be responsible for the preparedness of Hitler's hard-pressed Third Reich. It was no exaggeration to say that on its ability to pierce the Allies' tight security screen hinged the issue of victory or defeat.

This moment of truth was rendered much more hazardous by a factor which Canaris dreaded in his secret heart but refused to admit even to himself. In England, Canaris was defied by an adversary who held some of the trump cards of the game.

NOTES

1 Unimpeachable source (*sichere Quelle*) was the code by which clients of Signal Intelligence referred to intercepts of the Allies' wireless communications.

2 The area became firmly implanted in Roenne's mind, and he stubbornly persisted in regarding it as the primary goal of the main Allied attack, even on June 6, 1944 when the Anglo-American forces invaded in overwhelming force the Cotentin Peninsula of Normandy.

Chapter 50

Pawns of Fortitude

ADMIRAL Canaris's serious dilemma was resolved by a rush of events that made him personally expendable just when his Abwehr was needed most desperately. Soon after the Roenne meeting, on February 19, 1944, Canaris was fired. The blow was cushioned by his appointment to another job in the OKW. He was made chief of the Department of Economic Warfare, moving his headquarters to one of the High Command's scattered camps near Potsdam.

The manner in which Hitler got rid of him indicated that the Fuehrer still retained vestiges of his old fondness for the opaque little man, but the Abwehr itself was in deep trouble. The small group of its anti-Hitler dissidents had been spotted by the Gestapo, including general Oster and the lawyer Dohnanyi. The Old Fox continued his precarious balancing act as best he could, politicking with insurgents who believed the war was lost, while doing business with the Nazis.

Canaris's political schizophrenia and the inroads of the anti-Nazi opposition, as well as the wear and tear of the long war, were reflected in the performance of the Abwehr. Though bigger than ever, complaints multiplied—its coverage of the enemy was erratic, its reports were increasingly equivocal and ephemeral. Adversaries in the armed forces and the Nazi apparatus dug up old beefs. Walter Schellenberg, the young SD leader squatting like an eager suitor in the background, brought out the "munitions box" brimful of all the damning evidence he had been collecting against Canaris and the Abwehr. The time was ripe for the lethal blow that would at last give him control of the long-coveted agency.

It was, however, not Schellenberg's steady intrigue that brought on the first tremors of the devastating quake. For the time being, the

609

young spymaster sat back smugly to wait for the Abwehr to crumble, hammered to pieces by another of its foes, the Foreign Ministry.

The rivalry between Joachim von Ribbentrop and Admiral Canaris was keenest in two Latin countries where German influence was strongest throughout the war. In Argentina, the only major power in South America that remained steadfast in its pro-Axis "neutrality," the Abwehr had one of its super-spies subverting the government practically single-handed, an outstanding *coup* which no other German secret agent succeeded in scoring anywhere in the world during the war. The feat of this operative, Hans Rudolf Leo Harnisch, was the more remarkable because he was an amateur at such skulduggery, a respectable 46-year-old executive of Boker & Co., one of the Argentine's largest export-import houses.

Recruited for the Abwehr in the summer of 1941 during a brief vacation in his hometown of Hamburg, Harnisch (under the cover-name of Erich Viereck) was supposed to collect economic information about the United States. Carried away by the thrills and opportunities of his secret career, this "sober, sensible, reserved, and coldly calculating" fellow applied his talents to the game with unmatched skill and gusto, going far beyond his limited assignment. He had a hand in the overthrow of the neutralist Castillo regime in June 1943 by a junta that established the corrupt pro-Nazi General Pedro P. Ramirez in power. Harnisch then succeeded in suborning the Ramirez government until Argentina became Germany's ally in all but name.

The other country was Spain where the Abwehr's influence was based almost entirely on Canaris's connections in Madrid and his supposedly hypnotic powers over General Francisco Franco. The admiral's hold on Franco was believed by Hitler to be the last rein keeping Spain in line.

Both of these Abwehr strongholds collapsed almost overnight at the worst possible moment for Canaris. The Harnisch operation was exposed on January 27, 1944, by the joint efforts of British and American security organs. Argentina was forced to break off diplomatic relations with the Germans, knocking out their last viable base in the Western Hemisphere. The sudden and unexpected break threw Hitler into one of his wildest tantrums, screaming for scapegoats. The Foreign Ministry could throw the blame on the Abwehr for the Harnisch exposure, which enabled the Allies to put the heat on General Ramirez, himself one of the conspirators who was trying to save his own skin.

Almost simultaneously, Canaris's influence in Spain was revealed to Hitler as pure imagination. In November 1943, Ambassador Eberhard von Stohrer, a punctilious career diplomat who was reasonably friendly with Canaris, was replaced by Hans Heinrich Dieckhoff, brought out of the limbo to which he had been banished after his recall from the United States in 1938.

When Dieckhoff presented his credentials to General Franco, he was startled to be greeted with the words, "I am glad that in the future I will be able to deal with a genuine representative of the Third Reich rather than with that busybody Canaris." This, at least, was what Dieckhoff eagerly reported to Foreign Minister von Ribbentrop. Ambassador Dieckhoff followed up the first salvo with sharp frontal attacks on the Abwehr outpost in Spain. In dispatch after dispatch, he described it as top heavy with overbearing, incompetent goldbrickers whose awkward manipulations drove the Spaniards into the Allied camp. The ambassador also hinted broadly that Canaris was playing a double game by assuring Hitler that he was working to preserve Franco's collaboration for Germany, but telling the Generalissimo that the Germans were losing the war and urging him to abandon the sinking ship.

By 1944, the crisis Dieckhoff whipped up required Canaris's personal intervention in Spain, in a desperate effort to expose the ambassador's campaign as a selfish intrigue. Dieckhoff received word that Canaris was planning to pay a secret visit to Madrid to rally his old friends to his defense—Chief of the General Staff Vigo and General Campos Martinez, the head of the secret service, among them. Just when the impending Allied invasion dominated all problems with which the hard-pressed Abwehr had to struggle and Canaris needed his wits to cope with the greatest challenge in his career, Dieckhoff decided to bring his campaign to a head.

"Have just learned confidentially," he advised Berlin on February 5, 1944, "that Admiral Canaris has under consideration a plan to come to Spain next week. As much as I would welcome the opportunity of reviewing with him the Abwehr apparatus here, I believe it is incumbent upon me to advise emphatically against such a trip by Admiral Canaris at this time. His visit, which could not be kept secret, would not only give the Anglo-Saxons opportunity to intensify their pressures, but would also embarrass our Spanish friends."

Dieckhoff's advice was heeded. Canaris was forbidden to go to Spain, though he was permitted to meet Dieckhoff on French soil near the Spanish border to thrash out their differences. The fashionable resort of Biarritz on the Bay of Biscay was chosen for the rendezvous. When Canaris arrived in that lovely city, flanked by the chiefs of his Madrid and Lisbon outposts, he found a young pseudo-diplomat named Herbert von Bibra, an SS-man doubling as the SD representative in Spain, waiting for him with a note from Dieckhoff.

"I appreciate your assurance," it read, "that you place the utmost importance on my presence at the conference in Biarritz. Unfortunately, my responsibilities here make it impossible for me to absent myself from Madrid at this time. I have, therefore, delegated Herr von Bibra to act as my representative with full authority to speak for me."

The cards were already stacked against Canaris. In the crisis, Campos Martinez declined Canaris's invitation to meet him in France.

Prior to the Madrid crisis, a similar situation had developed in Spanish Morocco where General Orgaz, under pressure from the Anglo-American forces at his eastern border, demanded that the Abwehr move out. Not only was the resident organization demolished with the forced departure of its key personnel, but a special Abwehr network, called "Anti-Atlas" was also smashed.

At this critical juncture, Canaris suddenly lost his most powerful protector in the Nazi camp. Heinrich Himmler turned against him, not to hijack the Abwehr like his underling Schellenberg, but to take his own secret service off the hook in a situation far more ominous in its ramifications than the diplomatic imbroglio.

The exodus from Hitler's buffeted ship began long before it started sinking. Even minor intelligence officers were better posted than most people at the top as to the total picture and the true seriousness of Germany's position.

The earliest rats to leave helter-skelter were members of the Abwehr. Defections were brewing in Switzerland and Portugal, but it was in Turkey that the floodgates first broke. At the Abwehr branch in Istanbul, three officials went over to the British. A far more serious breach occurred similtaneously in the office of Ludwig C. Moyzisch, the SD-man who handled the Cicero operation, when Moyzisch's confidential secretary, a young woman named Nellie Kapp, defected to the Americans and exposed Cicero.

The *Sicherheitsdienst* was badly compromised. To minimize the scandal in his own backyard, Himmler went out of his way to magnify the damage done by the Abwehr's defectors by making Canaris personally accountable for the debacle. Suddenly, the admiral found himself under multiple attack. To meet it, he would have to extricate himself by marshaling all of his old cunning at bamboozling the Fuehrer. His foothold in Spain could have been held and the fatal blow to the Abwehr averted if Canaris had had the will to fight. But he was almost completely burned out. His closest associates—Piekenbrock, Lahousen, and Bentivegni—had left him for service on the Russian front, and he was uncomfortable with the new men who had replaced his intimates. Held on February 10th, the conference at Biarritz ended with Canaris's total and irrevocable capitulation. He no longer cared what happened to the Abwehr or to himself.

In his report to Berlin, describing the meeting in unabashedly exultant terms, Ambassador Dieckhoff wrote: "Admiral Canaris has agreed to revamp the Abwehr in Spain in accordance with my wishes and also to please the Herr Foreign Minister." Yes, he will reduce personnel to an absolutely indispensable minimum! Yes, he will move his bureaus out of the Embassy! Yes, he will turn over his radio center and monitoring units to the Foreign Ministry!

Only once did the ghost of the old Canaris flicker up during the meeting, when he testily told von Bibra: "It will, of course, be my duty to advise the high commands of the Army, Navy, and Luftwaffe that, in the light of the changed situation, it will be impossible in the future to carry out any of the intelligence operations they may want the Abwehr to undertake." It was an empty threat.

Biarritz was Canaris's Waterloo. Although he had gone to the conference prepared merely to reorganize the Spanish outpost, he gave up so much that his successors, headed by an ill-starred colonel named Georg Hansen, could salvage little if anything from the ruins. A week after his return from France, Canaris was out in the cold. Three months later, the battered remnant of the Abwehr was transferred lock, stock, and barrel to Nazi control by Hitler's special decree establishing a centralized intelligence service. Schellenberg was appointed to preside over the new all-inclusive organization in which parts of the Abwehr survived under the name of *Militaerisches Amt* or Military Bureau.

Canaris's dismissal was more than just a change at the top. The Abwehr was his creation and he was the creature of what he had wrought. After his departure it became a ship without a rudder, drifting aimlessly, even dangerously. Its demolition at Germany's critical hour was an act of Hitler's suicidal psychosis that began to dominate all of his decisions as the great drama approached its finale. With the Allies poised for their decisive stroke, the collection of intelligence became a matter of *qua non*, and the Abwehr the Germans' first line of defense. Without it Hitler was as eyeless as Samson in Gaza.

The immense task of probing Allied intentions and preparations shifted dramatically and drastically, but not to Schellenberg, who was not quite in the saddle as yet. It became the responsibility—or burden—of the man to whom Canaris had promised so much intelligence on the invasion—Colonel von Roenne of the General Staff. He now had to run the whole gamut, from the assembly of raw intelligence to the prognostic estimates for nailing down the invasion.

Roenne's conclusion that the Pas de Calais would be the terminus of the main Allied effort was not as self-induced as the colonel had come to think. It was planted in his mind, in a process akin to thought transference, by the most elaborate deception scheme ever concocted—a complex "cover plan" perfected with as great care and ingenuity as the grand design of the invasion itself.

"Our major deception was to pretend that we were coming across the Straits of Dover," Mr. Churchill later wrote. "It would not be proper even now [1955] to describe all methods employed to mislead the enemy, but the obvious ones of simulated concentrations of troops in Kent and Sussex, of fleets of dummy ships collected in the Cinque Ports, of landing exercises on the nearby beaches, of increased wireless activity, were all used. The final result was admirable."

The cross-Channel part of the enterprise was masked by the code name "Neptune." "Overlord" properly referred to the operation that commenced at the water's edge in France and continued until the two beachheads, "Omaha" and "Utah," were secured. The intricate cover plan was drawn up in two separate schemes, one called "Bodyguard," the other "Fortitude."

"Bodyguard" was designed to misrepresent the Allies' strategy in Europe and to induce the German high command to make faulty dispositions. "Fortitude" was the "cover plan" to persuade the Germans that "the narrower waters of the Channel would tempt the Allies to launch their main assault on the nearest French coast."

The elaborate deception campaign was prepared with care and finesse and at enormous cost. It was managed centrally in the Cabinet Office from 10 Downing Street by John ("Johnny") Bevins under the personal supervision of General "Pug" Ismay, Mr. Churchill's chief of staff.[1] From this nerve center flowed the ruses designed to befuddle the enemy. All the organs of Bodyguard and Fortitude had to report to Bevins's cluttered, busy command post. This was a world of make-believe—conjuring up events that would never take place; people who never lived; situations that would never occur, except in the belief of the Germans.

The plan revolved around the pretense that the campaign would open with an attack on southern Norway launched from Scottish ports, while the main attack would come at the Pas de Calais (where Roenne was convinced that it would come). Normandy, where the Allies would actually land, was represented as a diversionary attack. As for the date of the invasion, the deception scheme set D-day for the third week of July, about forty-five days after the actual deadline.

A "Fourth Army" was conjured up in Scotland, presumably to mount the preliminary attack on Norway, but it consisted of nothing more than headquarters with elaborate signal equipment filling the air with contrived radio traffic to simulate the communications of three entire corps, which were, of course, imaginary. At the same time, another army of twelve divisions was assembling in the south for the assault on the Pas de Calais. It was a phantom force, made to appear even more formidable by a large volume of fake radio traffic linking it with other "formations" which were also entirely fictitious.

The Allied air forces were used extensively to back up the deception. Enemy airfields, radar installations, batteries, railway centers and bridges were attacked all over western Europe. But anything which could have pinpointed the Normandy coast as the probable center of the invasion was avoided. For every target attacked in the prospective assault area two were simultaneously raided outside it.

At the same time, infinite care was taken to avoid any leakage of information about real forces, genuine arrangements, or any activities to meet *actual* requirements. Regular civilian travel between the United Kingdom and Eire was halted. In Great Britain, a coastal belt ten miles deep on either side of the Firth of Forth and stretching from the Walsh to Land's End was closed to all visitors.

Only the German spies seemed to be able to come and go as they pleased.

When in February 1944, Admiral Canaris saw Colonel von Roenne at what was destined to be their last confrontation, he probably felt that he was not exaggerating the Abwehr's coverage of Britain, but he was living in a fool's paradise. His vaunted secret agents were all the pawns of "Fortitude."

Several agencies were entrusted with the execution of the maneuvers the Bevins office devised; or with the task of developing their own campaigns within the framework of this giant conspiracy. Field Marshal Sir Bernard Montgomery's 21st Army Group, the original invasion force, had its own organization for this purpose, in care of a brilliant scholar, Roger Heskith. He had developed three counterfeit spies—a Dutchman ("Paul"), a Spaniard ("Cato"), and a Frenchman ("Talleyrand")—to feed misleading intelligence to the enemy. He also used other means and people in a super-secret effort (that did not end at the water's edge on June 6, 1944), details of which are described in Mr. Heskith's unpublished narrative of one of the most bizarre military operations in the history of war.

The British secret services were an integral part of the cover plan, playing a decisive role in the deception maneuver. Abroad, MI.6 was disseminating misinformation through the purposeful indiscretion of diplomats, service attachés and people seemingly in the know. Much of it was planted straight in German ears with the help of double agents in Spain, Portugal, Switzerland, Sweden, and Turkey, the great eavesdropping posts of the war.

In one of the brashest episodes of the maneuver, appropriately enough on April 1, MI.6 sneaked an informant to the Spanish General Moscardo in Barcelona with pinpointed intelligence about the Allied invasion plans. In Moscardo's prompt report to the Germans, the man was identified as a colonel of the Red Army named Nikolai Putiloff Budyenny, "a confidant of Stalin," who had been parachuted into France to prepare the Communist forces of the resistance movement for D-day. Spotted by the Gestapo, so the story went, the colonel had to flee before he could complete his mission. He reached a safe haven in Gibraltar where he not only gained additional details of the Allied designs but also revealed what he knew to a Spanish Communist who was a double agent working for the Spanish secret service.

According to this agent, quoting Colonel Budyenny, the invasion would take place on a front running from Amiens in the north through Orléans, Limoges, and Montauban all the way to Toulouse in the south, and on a crossline between Bordeaux and Tarascon. It was to be mounted by 150,000 airborne troops flown to France in gliders or dropped by parachute, to attack the German coastal fortifications from the rear. Simultaneously, Spain would be invaded to establish an Allied base there for a march into France across the Pyrénnées.

As with all planted intelligence, the report contained some kernels of fact. Even so, Colonel von Roenne dismissed it in its entirety as "utter nonsense." He preferred to believe another agent from Switzerland who reported that, according to Major General West, the British military attaché in Berne, all plans of an invasion in 1944 had to be shelved because the British and the Americans could not agree on details of Overlord.

Some of the information MI.6 was spreading abroad contained elements of truth; much of it was plausible. But the Germans proved incapable of separating fact from fiction. They conspicuously failed to recognize accurate intelligence in the reports of a handful of independent agents who had not been affected by Fortitude. When Josephine in Stockholm intercepted information sent home by the Swedish military and air attachés in London, pinpointing Normandy as the target of the Allies' main thrust and reporting that the date of the invasion had been definitely set for the period between May 15 and June 15, his reports were ignored. His information simply differed from the preconceived notions of Hitler and his aides, and from the basic conclusion of Colonel von Roenne.

On January 1, 1944, the entire apparatus of Section B.1.A. of MI.5 was pressed into servicing the deception campaign from inside the United Kingdom. This fantastic finale had been prepared with an effectiveness that exceeded the fondest expectations of Major Robertson, its *spiritus rector* and general manager. From 1941, when the System formally took shape in Colonel White's B-Division within MI.5; through 1942, when it began to hit its stride; to 1943, the entire apparatus was honed and tuned for its role in the Overlord drama. Looking at this unique effort in retrospect, it is no exaggeration to say that—by befuddling the enemy and compelling him to make the wrong dispositions—Robertson's B.1.A made a historic contribution to the success of the invasion, and saved the lives of thousands of Allied soldiers. Not many cogs of the Allied war machine could make such a claim, certainly not one that operated in utter secrecy with only a few hundred faceless "combatants."

By this time, in 1944, hardly a German agent was either at large in Britain or beyond the reach of MI.5. Not only were double agents run on a long-time basis but they were run so extensively that B.1.A. could think not in terms of a number of isolated cases but in terms of a double-agent system. In fact, by virtue of this system . . . these men did much more than practice a large-scale deception through double agents: by means of the double-agent system they *actively ran and controlled the German espionage system in Britain.*

This may at first blush sound like a staggering claim. Nevertheless it was true, and was true for the greater part of the war. By 1944, the entire stable of controlled agents were employed on behalf of Fortitude. It was a motley crowd, their ethnic composition mirroring the mixed bag of wayward Europeans from which the Abwehr was drawing its secret agents. Among them were Spaniards, Scandinavians, an Austrian woman married to an Englishman, a French woman of Russian parentage, a Frenchman, four Yugoslavs (bunched together in a ring of their own), a Czech, a trio of Poles, a Belgian, even a couple of British subjects—but only one solitary German specializing in naval intelligence.

Their ranks were swelled by a late influx of newcomers, the special drop of so-called "invasion spies," such as the members of the "Arabal" group, sent to Britain from Spain and Portugal between November 1943 and May 1944 to monitor invasion preparations. MI.5 captured and held those who would not cooperate in Ham Common, the converted lunatic asylum used for prisoners. But well over a hundred had been won for Double-Cross, and now, forty men and women were in harness broadcasting invasion intelligence, including two who had been fooling the Germans since 1940, and five deceiving them since 1941.

Working on a meticulously written scenario, each double agent was given a different part to play. Four in particular had stellar roles, because their influence with the Abwehr was accurately gauged to be the greatest. The leading man was Hans Hansen, the young Danish draftsman who had begun his promising career in the summer of 1940 as Abwehr agent No. A.3725, only to wind up promptly in the clutches of Double-X, where he was called "Tate." The chief supporting player was called "Brutus" in MI.5 and "Hubert" in the Abwehr. The leading lady was "Tramp," so much more appropriately called "Treasure" in MI.5, if only because she was proving to be priceless.

"Garbo" was the masterpiece of Double-X, if only because the operation (involving up to twenty scattered agents) was conceived within the organization. The Germans contributed to it their faith in the veracity of intelligence pouring in to them from this group of mostly non-existent Spaniards.

Hubert was a gallant Polish staff officer who suffered the bitter humiliation of defeat twice within ten months—in Poland in 1939, in France in 1940. Undaunted, he organized one of the first underground groups in France after the surrender and managed it so well that this one *reseau* grew into a formidable resistance force of sixty-four activists within the first year of its existence.

Betrayed to the Germans in 1942 by Mathilde Carré, the notorious "Cat-woman" whose fragile allegiance was controlled by her infatuation with Hugo Bleicher—the most intrepid of German counterspies—Hubert was accosted by Lieutenant Colonel Oscar Reile, Bleicher's boss at the head of the Abwehr's Section III/F in France. Colonel Reile visited him in his cell with an attractive proposition. If he agreed to work for the Abwehr in England, Reile would arrange his "escape" and guarantee on his honor as an officer and gentleman that his underground associates would not be turned over to the Gestapo, a change of venue which in this case meant rescue from torture and death.

Hubert accepted the offer and the covenant was sealed in his cell in a formal written contract which Hubert and Reile solemnly signed. Oscar Reile then engineered his "escape" on Bastille Day in 1942; Hubert then rejoined the resistance movement which smuggled him into England. Exposing his dubious mission the moment he reached London, the double spy (who was also to function as Reile's E-man or penetration agent, as No. GV-7615) wound up in MI.5 as a valued guest of the Double-X system, cover-named Brutus.[2]

Though acting as Hubert, communicating with the Abwehr, he actually served in a Polish squadron of the RAF with the rank of wing commander. Inside the Double-X System, his case officer managed his secret business without so much as consulting him. His British spy shadow was endowed with status and given vantage points whence he could feed the Germans information of seemingly exceptional value. Guided by the deft hands of the Double-Crossers, Hubert was attaining chimerical but increasingly important positions in the Allied war effort, until he was able to inform Reile that he had been made liaison officer of the Polish General Staff at General Omar N. Bradley's headquarters in London. His mission was connected with a key project within Fortitude to persuade the Germans that the American army under Bradley would remain in England after the British forces of General Montgomery had landed in Normandy, to mount the main assault in the Pas de Calais area.

The woman of the trio was one of the great ladies of espionage in World War II that produced so many remarkable female spies in the Allied camp.[3]

She was Lily Sergueiev, a chic 26-year-old French girl of Russian birth. Her rough-hewn Slavic face was marred by a square chin but mellowed by her gently sloping brow and sensitive eyes. She wore her rich auburn hair down to shoulders that were firm and broad, giving her a somewhat masculine appearance. But Lily was all woman—tender, skittish, vital, highly-strung, and set in her ways. She was a suffragette to whom adventure was the staff of life. At the age of seventeen, she made her way from Paris to Warsaw on foot, then back again as a stowaway on a German freighter. In 1937 her personal life was touched by the melodrama of the secret world, when her uncle, Eugen de Miller, a former Tsarist general plotting the overthrow of the Communists from exile in Paris, was abducted and killed by his Red foes.

The outbreak of the war caught Lily in the Lebanon on the first leg of a bicycle tour to Indochina. Instead of going on to Saigon, she returned at once to Paris with the plot of her life's greatest adventure pat in her mind. She was determined to become a secret agent.

"The idea had come to me one night in Beirut," she wrote in her diary on December 27, 1940. "I turned it over for two days. At night in bed with the lights out, it all seemed so simple! But in the morning in broad daylight, my scheme seemed mad and childish—the sort of thing one reads about in books, but which does not happen in real life."

During her walking trip to Warsaw in 1932, she had met one Felix Dassel, a shady journalist from one of the Baltic States, then bumped into him in Berlin six years later and discovered that Felix was a recruiting agent for the Abwehr. When France collapsed, Lily thought of Felix. "Could I," she wrote, "through him, get enlisted in the German Secret Service and then perhaps be able to help those who were carrying on the fight?"

Felix was in Paris, still working for the Abwehr, and she now asked him to introduce her to "Moustache," a big, heel-clicking, hand-kissing sybaritic Austrian whom she knew was Major Emil Kliemann, second in command of the big Abwehr office in the Hotel Lutetia on Boulevard Raspail. Kliemann screened Lily at exquisite dinners at Maxim's, Prunier's, Fouquet's, and La Maisonette, and courted rather than recruited her. In the end he agreed to take her into the fold. By early 1941, Lily was an agent of the Abwehr with the cover-name of "Tramp," which Kliemann had chosen for her in a moment of inebriated whimsy. "Now my holiday is over," she wrote, "and I must start on my enterprise. If I succeed, from now on I shall be alone, utterly alone."

Kliemann did not quite know what to do with her in Paris, and thought of sending her to Lisbon to fish for information among the English around the Estoril. Lily proposed to go straight to the lion's den; this had always been her plan—to enter England as a German agent, then turn and work against the Germans.

In 1943 she got her wish. She went by way of Madrid where she promptly checked in with the British and was flown on a visa, presumably granted to visit relatives in Cambridge and friends in Bristol, to London from Gibraltar, to become a classic double agent under the aegis of MI.5.

Lily played the game for extraordinarily high stakes, with unbounded courage and ingenuity, despite (or perhaps because of) being marked for death by an incurable disease. In March 1944, when the part assigned to her in the scenario of Fortitude called for fast communication, she lured the major to Lisbon and persuaded him to give her an Afu set to speed up transmission of the information the Germans valued so highly. Kliemann could never resist her. She became the only woman in the Abwehr entrusted to operate her own clandestine radio.

Back in England, MI.5 used her transmitter to broadcast a flood of misleading information to the Germans, so broad in scope and so convincing, that she became a star performer. In the eyes of the Abwehr no agent was more important, none more deserving of their trust. This was what made Lily invaluable to the British, and she became the most important single cog in the elaborate ruse distracting the Germans' attention from Normandy.

It would be absurd to give her sole credit for the success of this phase of Fortitude. But her part was vital; the Germans' ace in Britain, who never faltered in her loyalty to the Allied cause. "All around her," an admirer wrote in a testimonial to her great contribution, "she could sense the invisible army of the Allied soldiers whom she would save from death on the bloodstained beaches of the Normandy landing."

A few weeks after her work was done, when the Allies were firmly established in Normandy, Lily thought back on her part in the gigantic venture. "I'm Number 75.054," she wrote in her diary on July 1, 1944. "I've lost my personality. With it, I've lost my solitary state. I'm no longer alone. I've got the whole army with me."

Although he was personally absent from the secluded house in a London suburb where Double-X had its headquarters, Brutus's contribution was by no means less than that of Lily. He, too, had his own Afu set which B.1.A. operated, sending reports, as his German contact wrote on his evaluation sheet, which were "uniformly highly rated by *Fremde Heere West.*"

Conceived by Roger Heskith, Field Marshal Montgomery's deception wizard, the part Brutus played in the grand maneuver was potentially the most important. He was to persuade the Germans that the invasion would take place in several installments, the real blow to follow an initial feint. Brutus was meticulously built up for his crucial role. In the care of his handlers, he apparently had a meteoric career during the war, advancing steadily in rank and occupying an increasingly responsible position as the liaison officer of the Polish army in England.

Purporting first to be at his key observation post inside General Bradley's headquarters, he claimed in the eleventh hour to have been moved up to General Eisenhower's own supreme command post. In May 1944, seven of his reports struck the Germans as so persuasive that they marked the batch as "uniformly excellent," with the notation: "The intelligence supplied by this agent is contributing materially to the clarification of the enemy's order of battle."

The "clarification" was not doing the Germans any good. His reports fortified their belief that Normandy would be merely a secondary target, and that a huge American army was being kept in England under General Bradley for the major effort further north. The result is a matter of history. The German Seventh Army defending Normandy was surprised on June 6 and overrun before it could do anything, largely because the much more powerful Fifteenth Army was waiting for the invaders on the cliffs of the Pas de Calais.

As for Hans Hansen, beginning with his report of January 15 that General Eisenhower was arriving in London the next day to take over the supreme command of Overlord, this intrepid agent sent to Hamburg scores of messages reporting the quickening rhythm of the preparations. He reached the ultimate stage of his long double game in May, with daily reports about troop concentrations in places where there were none, providing an order of battle that was pin-

pointed and plausible but largely fictitious, and identifying commanding generals—such as one named "Friedenhall" and another called
"Ashland"—who existed only in the imagination.

During May, he described visits to Wye in the "restricted Dover
area," where he claimed to have seen 20,000 Canadians; to Ashford,
where he "found" the 83rd U.S. Infantry Division; to Folkstone,
which he described as, "the U.S. headquarters city" and where he
allegedly saw "many trains overcrowded with newcomers from the
United States." He visited Newmarket, Thetford, Cromer, and Norwich, identifying one division after another, wandering with total
impunity through what he called the "*Sperrgebiet*," the restricted
zone to which, it seemed, no unauthorized person but he had managed to gain access.

As his sources he quoted an air chief marshal, a captain of the
Royal Navy, and another high-ranking RAF officer he identified as
"Spekeman." Nobody at the German end apparently wondered how
it was possible that such prominent Britons had taken this itinerant
young Dane into their confidence and revealed to him some of the
innermost secrets of Overlord.

Garbo was Double-X's cover-name for the German super-spy
V.319, the Spanish journalist Luis Calvo. He had been turned into a
controlled agent after his exposure in February 1942 as Don Angel
Alcazar de Velasco's successor at the head of the Abwehr's Hispanic
contingent in Britain.

The operation named for his cover-name, by far the most elaborate and sophisticated hoax ever attempted by MI.5, was the
brainchild of Thomas Harris, the ebullient, bilingual painter-antique-
dealer-gourmet who could uncannily empathize with the hapless
Spaniards "Papa" Lenz was dumping on England. When Don Angel's
group was smashed, all that was left was Calvo—safely ensconced in
the "cage" at Ham Common. Would it not be possible, Harris queried,
to construct a new network around him, its members supposedly recruited by the trusted chief V-man of whose downfall the Abwehr was
blissfully unaware? The idea was welcomed enthusiastically by
Colonel Robertson, and Harris went to work, building a wholly
fictitious espionage organization supposedly covering the whole of
Britain.

It taxed even Harris's rich imagination and unbounded energy to
create and sustain such an enormous phantom network, designed to
deceive the Germans about the invasion in 1944. He succeeded in
developing it bit by bit—an agent here, another there—until V.319
had more than a score of people allegedly working for him, every
one a fantasy.

The Germans were completely overwhelmed by this bonanza. They named the organization the "Arabal Network," and as its membership was so numerous, subdivided it into three rings for which they coined the cover-names Alaric, Benedict, and Dagobert. Here is a partial list of these agents based on their dossiers in the Abwehr, with the official evaluation of their performance *on the eve of D Day*:

V-217, operating out of Bedford, N.Y. in the United States—"fair."

V-303, clerk, stationed in London—"reliable but capable of carrying out only minor assignments."

V-305, traveling salesman, Southeast England—"tested & reliable."

V-308, businessman, London—"apparently reliable."

V-314, shipping clerk, London—"tested & reliable."

V-315, merchant, London—"tested & reliable."

V-316, government employee, Bristol—"tested & reliable."

V-322, pilot officer, London—"tested & reliable."

V-337, unemployed, at large in England—"nothing special."

V-372, employee, Liverpool—"tested & reliable."

V-373, Venezuelan student, Glasgow—"tested & reliable."

V-374, Venezuelan student, Aberdeen—"tested & reliable."

V-377, hotelier, London—"tested & reliable."

V-392, salesman traveling in U.S.A.—"good reports."

V-1239, technician, London—"new [in 1944], not yet tested."

V-1241, London—"useful."

V-1245, London—"tested & reliable."

The Garbo operation of Tommy Harris, that started in April 1942 in earnest, was in full bloom by the spring of 1944. This was exactly as Colonel Robertson and Harris had planned it, to have the organization fully established by then, for its strategic *raison d'être*—to funnel deceptive invasion intelligence to the Germans. Relevant "information" was sent by the Garbo spies from every spot where the Allied forces were supposedly staging.

How was the flood of information and misinformation reflected in the *Feindbild* in May 1944? The Germans were not entirely dependent or, for that matter, relying on intelligence supplied by their agents. The "enemy picture" was pieced together from information produced by aerial reconnaissance, radio intercepts, captured documents, prisoner interrogation, previous knowledge on file, and intelligence procured from neutral diplomatic missions in England. And yet, because of the flood of data from the agents, this source dominated all considerations and estimates, often in preference to such hard intelligence culled from photographs which the Luftwaffe's reconnaissance planes were bringing back.

By May, the German estimate of the situation had boiled down to the definitive assumption that the Pas de Calais area would be the focal point, preceded or followed by the launching of "subsidiary assaults" in Norway, on the Mediterranean coast of France, even in Portugal, and "probably in Normandy and Brittany."

Field Marshal von Rundstedt had recognized Normandy as early as October 1943, as "one of the primary danger points, because of the Allies' need to win large and capacious harbors like Le Havre and Cherbourg." Now he went along with the conclusion that the Pas de Calais was "the most probable place of attack."

For the date of the invasion, the Germans were groping completely in the dark. As of June 4, the sum total of all German guesses was expressed by Vice Admiral Krancke, the naval commander in France. "It is doubtful," he wrote in his estimate, "whether the enemy has yet assembled his invasion fleet in the required strength." Next morning, Field Marshal von Rundstedt echoed Krancke's optimism. He concluded his weekly situation report with the unqualified statement, "As yet there is no immediate prospect of the invasion."

All was serenely quiet on the Western Front.

Naval patrols in the Channel which Admiral Krancke had ordered for the night of June 5 were canceled. Local leave for officers was open. A leisurely war game was scheduled for the 6th by General Friedrich Dollmann, to be held at Rennes for commanders of the Seventh Army. As for Field Marshal Rommel, he feared an immediate attack so little that he left his headquarters in France on June 5, to spend a night with his family in Thuringia celebrating his wife's birthday, after which he planned to visit Hitler.

The befuddlement of the German high command and their stubborn inability to dispel their ignorance was illustrated most graphically by General Walter Warlimont, Jodl's deputy at the head of the Fuehrer's highest staff. "On June 5, 1944," he wrote in his memoirs eighteen years after those historic days, "the day before the invasion, German Supreme Headquarters had not the slightest idea that the decisive event of the war was upon them. For twenty-four hours more than five thousand ships had been on the move across the Channel toward the coast of Normandy but there had been no reconnaissance to spot them."

In spite of all the Allies' elaborate security and deception measures, one piece of incontravertible evidence slipped through to indicate that the invasion was a matter of days if not hours. "We did not know," Warlimont wrote, "that as early as January 1944, Admiral Canaris had discovered the text of a two-part radio message to be transmitted from England shortly before the invasion as a standby signal to the French Resistance. . . . On the afternoon of June 5, the

Intelligence Service informed Jodl that during the night of June 4 the second of these two sentences had been heard by the Security Section of Fifteenth Army. But no action was taken."

As Warlimont remembered the incident, none of those involved, including General Jodl himself, paid even the slightest attention to the warning. "It may have been," he wrote, "that, unlike Admiral Canaris, who had meanwhile fallen into disfavor and been dismissed, they did not realize its import; alternatively they may have been waiting for some more definite confirmation."

One would assume that General Warlimont described this curious incident on the basis of his personal observation, from his high perch at Hitler's headquarters. But no! His account, inaccurate in part, cited as his source neither his own recollections nor any documentary evidence, but Cornelius Ryan's book, *The Longest Day,* which in 1959 was the first to mention the incident.

According to Ryan, "in January [1944] Admiral Wilhelm Canaris, then chief of German intelligence, had given [Lieutenant Colonel Helmuth] Meyer [intelligence officer of General Hans von Salmuth's Fifteenth Army] the details of a fantastic two-part signal which he said the Allies would use to alert the underground prior to the invasion." He went on to describe the incident, substantially as Warlimont later presented it in his memoirs. But Ryan gave Colonel Meyer credit for actually intercepting the signal when it was broadcast and sending it on to General Jodl, an unlikely act if only because it would have been a crass violation of the sacrosanct chain of command which no German staff officer would care or dare to commit.

In view of the historic interest in this episode of the war and the nebulous nature of its belated presentations, I undertook a special search for the actual documents which I hoped would bear out this remarkable exploit of the Abwehr, giving the High Command the definitive clue to anticipate the invasion. I found them intact in the captured archives of the Army General Staff, three separate papers in all. The first was dated, not January, 1944, as Ryan and Warlimont asserted, but October 14, 1943, numbered Abw.4508/43; the second, No. RSHA IV-A2/478/44, was issued at 9:37 A.M. on June 2, 1944; and the third, with the dateline of June 4, 1944, was numbered RSHA IV-A2/573/44.

Although the first report was signed "Huebner" and the other two "Dr. Kaltenbrunner," they actually originated with Lieutenant Colonel Oscar Reile, the studious and highly efficient Abwehr officer in charge of Section IIIF in Paris, engaged in the thankless task of combatting the French underground. The document dated October 14, 1943, was based on an event which occurred on October 3. A man described as "the leader of a sabotage organization directed from England" was caught by Reile's agents, and revealed during his interrogation that "the password to announce the impending Ango-American invasion of France had been established to read as follows: *'Les sanglots longs des violons/de l'automn blessent mon coeur/ d'une langeur monotone.'* "

Reile, himself a gifted poet, recognized the passwords as lines from one of Paul Verlaine's sonnets.

A few days later, another resistance leader arrested under similar circumstances confirmed that the password had been established, and that it was the passage from Verlaine. Colonel Reile incorporated the information in a special report, together with additional data produced by his interrogation of the two Frenchmen.

"The first part of this signal," he wrote, "up to and including the word *'l'automn,'* will be broadcast by the English radio on the 1st and the 15th of given months, while the second part is scheduled to be broadcast to mean that the landings would ensue during the next 48 hours, the time counted from midnight of the day of the initial transmission of the signal."

Then, on June 2, 1944, when the Abwehr was already in Nazi hands and all such top-secret, top-priority messages were signed by Dr. Hans Kaltenbrunner, Himmler's deputy, Colonel Reile sent an urgent message to his clients, informing them that the moment of truth was on hand.

According to Reile's dispatch, radio station Daventry had broadcast the *first* segment of the password (*"Les sanglots longs des violons/de l'automn"*) several times between 1:30 and 2:30 P.M. on June 1, to five resistance groups in France, alerting them to stand by.

On June 4, Reile notified the addressees of his previous dispatches that the *second* part of the alert had been put on the air by Daventry fifteen times between noon and 2:30 P.M. on June 3, together with the following additional signals which Reile recognized as last-minute warnings:

"Le quoup d'envoia quinze heures."
"L'heur du combat viendra."
"Messieurs, faites vos jeux."
"A mon commande met garde à vous."
"L'électricité date du vingtième siècle."

Colonel Reile had distributed his first report to twenty-three addressees on his mailing list, including Field Marshal von Rundstedt's headquarters, the commanding generals in France, Belgium, the Netherlands, Denmark, and Norway, and Field Marshal Rommel's

Army Group B whose headquarters were at Château La Roche Guyon. The second and third messages were sent by scrambler teletype to Colonel von Roenne at the intelligence division of the Army General Staff, and to Colonel Wilhelm Meyer-Dietring, Field Marshal von Rundstedt's chief of intelligence.

In each case, copy No. 1 was sent to General Jodl's office at the Fuehrer's headquarters.

Receipt of the first Reile report in Jodl's office was acknowledged on October 15, 1943, by an officer named Hallbauer who apparently neglected to record its arrival in the log of incoming reports. Reile's communication of June 2, 1944, was received at Jodl's staff at 7:55 P.M. on the same day, by Captain Henkel who duly logged it in under No. WFSt/IC/II 771747. The third report reached the same staff at 11:37 P.M. on June 4. The message was received by a Major Cranz in the office of Colonel Krumacher, Jodl's intelligence officer, and filed under No. WFSt/IC/II 772174.

These, then, became the pigeonholes in which Colonel Reile's messages wound up. Contrary to Ryan's assertion that "at OKW the message was delivered to Colonel General Alfred Jodl," none of the reports was in fact ever submitted to him.

In Colonel von Roenne's office in Zossen, the messages were filed and forgotten.

At Rundstedt's headquarters in France, Colonel Meyer-Dietring forwarded copies of the second and third reports to the intelligence officers of the armies which comprised Rundstedt's command. This was how Colonel Meyer received his copies at the Fifteenth Army. He paid no attention to them, however, partly because General von Salmuth, his chief, was attending a stag party when the copy of the Reile report arrived and Meyer did not want to spoil his fun with such ominous nonsense. Also, the final warning of June 4 was accompanied by a note from Meyer-Dietring, that read: "Now as before, the Scheldt-Normandy-Brittany line is regarded as the most likely invasion front. However, the immediate 'invasion' is not yet apparent." It was indicative of what he was thinking of the Allied threat that he put the word "invasion" in quotation marks.

Convinced that nothing unusual would happen during the next few days, Meyer-Dietring decided that this was a good time to go on a short leave. Immediately after he had dutifully distributed Reile's last warning and his own disclaimer, he left. He was absent from his desk and maps and telephones when, a few hours later, the Allies arrived —in Normandy.

The invasion began between 1:30 and 2:00 A.M. on June 6, with the dropping of parachutists and the landing of airborne troops, after which thousands of planes began bombardment of the German batteries and coastal fortifications.

The Fuehrer slept late that morning, and nobody dared to disturb his slumber with the news. It was not until 5 P.M. when 130,000 Allied soldiers had already landed with 20,000 tanks under an umbrella of fire from hundreds of naval vessels, that Hitler bestirred himself to order the first countermeasures.

In Zossen, Colonel von Roenne was unfazed by the Allies' arrival in Normandy instead of the Pas de Calais. The area had become so firmly implanted in his mind that on June 9, when the Anglo-American forces had been in Normandy for seventy-two hours, he made a special appeal to General Jodl through Colonel Krumacher to consider the Normandy landings merely as a diversionary attack. "The main thrust," he said, "must be expected momentarily in the Pas de Calais."

On June 21, fifteen days after the landings when the two beachheads were firmly in Allied hands, German intelligence scored what, on the face of it, was the outstanding accomplishment of its invasion snooping. An agent in England forwarded what purported to be an actual copy of the "Neptune" plan.

When it reached Colonel Meyer-Dietring through the usual channels, he scribbled this comment on the margin of the cover page of the lengthy document: "This is a masterpiece of espionage. However, it would have been even better if it had reached us *before* June 6."[4]

NOTES

1 The founder of this group in the Cabinet Office was one of the war effort's most original "idea man," Dennis Wheatley.

2 The playful intellectuals of Double-X indulged themselves in displaying their sympathies and antipathies in the cover-names they were assigning to their pawns (without their knowledge, of course). An especially obnoxious character was burdened with the pseudonym "The Worm," and others in this class of pariahs were saddled with nicknames like "Freak" or "Puppet" or "Washout." On the other hand, favorites were honored with ornamental designations like "Meteor," "Rainbow," and "Brutus."

3 The only feminine agent of the first rank tolerated by Canaris was Paula Koch, a German nurse in Turkey where she tried to emulate Florence Nightingale. She headed the Adana office of Captain Paul Leverkuehn's Istanbul outpost, assigned to the frustrating job of dealing with the fickle Arabs.

4 The copy, a carefully bowdlerized paraphrase of the original "Neptune" operations plan and obviously useless *post festa,* had been made available to the Germans through one of the double agents, in an effort to enhance the man's standing in German eyes and raise his credibility rating for future operations.

Chapter 51

Mr. Churchill's Spy
in the Family

ON August 25, 1944, Paris was liberated by Major General Raymond O. Barton's American infantrymen and General Jacques Leclerc's French tanks—and so was 27-year-old Jacqueline Marguerite Princess de Broglie, one of the most *recherché* members of the international *beau monde*. She and her husband, a handsome, lighthearted 30-year-old Austrian named Alfred Kraus, welcomed the conquerors with a precious gift—two officers of the Royal Air Force. The flyers had parachuted to safety when their planes were shot down near Paris a few days before and had found their way, with the help of the Maquis, to Jacqueline's hospitable home on Rue Galilée.

Jacqueline de Broglie was a Parisian original in whose delicate veins flowed the blood of European aristocracy and American plutocracy. Her father was Prince Jean Amadée de Broglie whose feudal Piedmontese title predated the Middle Ages. Her mother, Marguerite Severine Philippine Duchess de Gluecksbierg, was the granddaughter of Isaac Merritt Singer, the American inventor who, in 1851, patented a practical sewing machine and amassed a fortune as its leading manufacturer.

In 1865, Singer, the son of a New York millwright, gave up his flourishing business in the United States and moved with his money to England where he took up residence in Torquay in Devonshire, the elegant spa on the north shore of Tor Bay. His two daughters married scions of European nobility. Their descendants became cousins of the Churchills of Blenheim and established themselves at the very top of continental society. With châteaux in France and stately homes in England, they lived lavishly on the enormous Singer fortune.

The American sewing-machine king's French granddaughter Marguerite (who was called plain Daisy by the chic set), married her Prince with whom she had three daughters—Emmeline, Isabelle, and Jacqueline. The Prince was killed in 1918, the year Jacqueline was born. His young widow, a ravishing and poignant figure in the deep mourning that was fashionable at that time, then married the Hon. Reginald Fellowes, a tall, dark, dashing British banker, younger son of the second Lord de Ramsey.

From then on, she commuted between her palace in Neuilly-sur-Seine, her spacious Villa Zoriade on the Riviera, and Donnington Hall in Berkshire, once the residence of Beau Brummel, now decorated with Daisy's magnificent collection of eighteenth-century furniture. She lived so sumptuously that even the walls of her boathouse on the Côte d'Azur were lined with drawings by Giovanni Tiepolo, the great painter of Venetian baroque whose frescoes adorn the Doge's Palace. With apartments also in Belgravia and Tangier, she was always on the move, allegedly to dodge taxes on the vast Singer fortune.

Daisy Fellowes de Broglie Ducasez, acclaimed as the world's best-dressed woman, was the outstanding hostess of her age, more devastatingly smart and witty than beautiful. She entertained prodigiously at her many homes and aboard her 250-foot yacht, the *Sister Anne*. Her circle of friends included not only such blue-blooded fixtures of high society as the Duke and Duchess of Windsor, the Lady Castlerosse, Lady Diana Cooper, Sir Oswald and Lady Cynthia Mosley, and the Aga Khan, but also Somerset Maugham, the great ballet master Serge Lifar, Coco Chanel, Cecil Beaton, Yvonne Printemps, and Sacha Guitry.

She was especially close to her cousin Winston Churchill. Once in Cannes, when the great man had a session scheduled at the Grand Hotel with a group of European statesmen, who traveled to the Riviera especially for the meeting, he canceled it at the last minute because he preferred to go yachting with Daisy Fellowes.

Jacqueline, a pudgy, auburn-haired, serious little girl with the round face of a Massaccio angel, lived in the shadow of her glamorous mother. Educated at the exclusive Heathfield School in Ascot, she spent her adolescence amidst the Anglo-Saxon splendor of Donnington Hall and the Gallic grandeur of her mother's French homes. In 1936, at the age of eighteen, she established her own court at a little château in Surenne—a lively, independent, darkly beautiful, rich young woman called "Little Daisy" by the jet set of those days.

Her townhouse and cosy château were always teeming with interesting people. Nothing could dampen her bounce and good cheer, it seemed—not even the fall of France. The collapse in the summer of 1940 caught her in Paris. Her sister Emmeline immediately joined the underground with her husband, Count Alexandre de Castija, who later spent six months in a Gestapo prison. But Jacqueline, whose circle of friends included many Germans before the war, apparently had none of her sister's dedicated patriotism. The air had barely cleared after Compiègne when she reopened her salons. High-toned fops of the uppercrust eager to be *en rapport* with the new masters mingled at her parties with bushy-haired opportunists from Montmartre. She also had a new set of guests—impeccably groomed German officers whose boots were as highly polished as their manners, tentatively adapted to the easy *bienséance* of Paris' unflappable smart set.

Her link to her new friends was Freddy Kraus, then still but one of her many beaux. But in 1941 Jacqueline startled her set by marrying Freddy on special dispensation granted by the German authorities. It was a mésalliance, and not only because she married a man way below her state whom the Germans considered a citizen of the Third Reich. Freddy had entrenched himself in Parisian society and was regarded as a man of wealth. Actually the Sarajevo-born young man was the son of an impoverished Austrian officer and his Hungarian wife, one of those heel-clicking, hand-kissing Middle European swains who understood how to parlay their good looks and exquisite manners into social success.

Jacqueline was infatuated with her man. On June 10, 1942, a daughter was born to the couple, destined to become a pawn in the later fate of her parents. Jacqueline's gaiety and conviviality seemed callous and flippant in a city occupied by the enemy. There was, however, a noble motif in all this apparent frivolity. Her seemingly indiscriminate hospitality was a cultivated pretense.

After the fall of France she could have escaped with the help of her powerful cousin, the British Prime Minister. But she decided to stay, determined to become a cog in the slowly assembling resistance movement. She established contact with MI.6, the first of the British secret services to appear underground in France after the surrender. When Special Operations Executive took over the management of French resistance in 1941, she placed herself completely at its disposal.

Aided by Freddy, who professed to be a staunch anti-Nazi, she serviced the underground's secret mail. Jacqueline would collect clandestine correspondence consigned to SOE headquarters in England; Freddy would carry the mail to Marseilles where the office of Savon Gibs, the soap-manufacturing concern, was the final relay point on French soil for these risky communications.

Her most highly valued contribution was her willingness to hide downed Allied flyers waiting to be smuggled back to England on the underground railroad. From 1940 until the day Paris was liberated, she was personally responsible for helping sixteen French and British aviators to escape from the Gestapo.

After the liberation, the gallant couple became extremely popular with members of the British missions in Paris who knew about their activities in the Resistance. Freddy was as charming and gregarious as ever. Now he cultivated the company of Allied officers who replaced the departed Germans at their parties. So close did he become to some of them that he was invited to serve the Allied cause still further by enlisting in the British Army "for special employment." Made a captain, he moved about in Paris wearing his new British uniform which his friends had given him as a token of their appreciation, somewhat prematurely.

The ebullient Mrs. Fellowes, who sat out the war in the Dorchester Hotel in London, established contact with her daughter immediately after the liberation. Although she was startled to learn that Jacqueline had married an Austrian during the war, she invited them both to join her in England. She intervened with Mr. Churchill to permit her new son-in-law to enter Britain.[1]

Jacqueline was ill and could not make the trip with her little daughter. Freddy was going alone. Thanks to Mr. Churchill, all red tape was cut. In late August, "Captain" Kraus was taken to England by sea, wearing the uniform his new friends had given him.

Mrs. Fellowes welcomed Freddy with open arms and introduced him to the Churchills, who invited him to spend weekends with them at Chartwell, their famous country place. The Prime Minister took an instant liking to his charming new relative. Freddy confided to Mr. Churchill that certain highly-placed anti-Nazi friends of his in the Wehrmacht and government had entrusted him with the mission to establish contact with the British to speed the end of the war by getting rid of Hitler. He offered his services to promote the conspiracy by acting as the liaison between the German dissidents and the British authorities. The Prime Minister put him in touch with the people who handled such delicate matters.

Freddy was lionized in Mayfair and Belgravia. A dashing figure, he was introduced to some of the best clubs around St. James's Street. Then in October, he vanished from sight. Those who knew about the "plot" he was hatching asumed that he had gone on some secret mission in pursuit of the plan he had submitted to the Prime Minister. Nothing was heard from him for months.

On April 8, 1945, Edgar Granville, Independent Member of Parliament representing Eye, was tipped off by a war correspondent of the *News Chronicle* that a "handsome German officer" identified as a "Captain Klause" had flown to Britain from the Continent, probably from Sweden, and landed by parachute "in a country area about a month ago." According to the reporter's story, "Klause" then made his way to London where he hoped to remain in the guise of a refugee. His plan was, the reporter told Granville, "to use information he gained in Paris during the German occupation as his bargaining point to enable him to change sides at this late stage of the war."

Although he was familiar with only the barest contours of the case, and in badly garbled form, Granville rose in Commons to question Herbert Morrison, the Home Secretary, and Sir James Grigg, the Secretary of War, about the mystery-flyer whom he described as "a Reichswehr officer."

"Did this man," he asked, "bring various proposals with him and did he make certain contacts in this country?" He queried pointedly why the man was receiving "special treatment not usually afforded to Nazi prisoners."

The questions were answered by Miss Ellen Wilkinson, the Labor Member of Parliament who was serving in Mr. Churchill's coalition government as Parliamentary Under-Secretary of the Home Office. Now Freddy abruptly emerged as a character in a mystery thriller. Miss Wilkinson set Mr. Granville right. The gentleman the distinguished Member referred to, she said, was not "Captain Klause," but a man named Alfred Ignatz Maria Kraus, a former employee of German firms in France, rather than an officer of the German army. She conceded that Freddy was not exactly what he appeared to be when welcomed so enthusiastically upon his arrival in London. "In 1944," she said, "after the liberation of Paris, he claimed to have rendered assistance during the occupation to the Allied cause and offered to join the British Army. In September 1944, he was brought to this country on insufficient information about him and without proper authority."

As a result of inquiries made, she said, it had been decided that he was a person "who should not be at liberty" and "he was accordingly interned." Miss Wilkinson sought to reassure the House by stating that "Herr Kraus was not receiving any preferential treatment."

Mr. Granville was not satisfied with the explanation. He pursued the matter on the 24th, with another set of intriguing questions. The incident threatened to develop into a *cause celèbre*. This time the questions were answered by Herbert Morrison, the Home Secretary himself, in an obvious attempt to take the sting out of the inquiry and dispose of it once and for all. Morrison admitted that Freddy had been brought to London "without explicit permission to leave France," and that he had been given the British uniform "which he was not entitled to wear." He revealed that the officer responsible for this unusual treatment of an enemy alien had been court-martialed.

Two days later more light was shed on the Freddy affair by Mr. Morrison. Kraus had been left at liberty for only a month after his arrival in England, he said, and was detained in October, but not as a refugee. He was interned, the Home Secretary said, as a civilian alien of enemy nationality. "There are no grounds," he added, "for suspecting that this alien engaged in any harmful activities in this country."

How come, Mr. Granville asked, that Kraus was permitted to run loose in Britain for a whole month before he was apprehended?

"It was admitted," Mr. Morrison said, "that there were irregularities in his arrival. We got track of him as quickly as we could and put him 'inside.' "

"But is my Right Honorable Friend quite sure," Mr. Granville asked, "that he has the fullest information about this man?"

Mr. Morrison was smiling confidently as he said: "I think we know all about him; in fact, the honorable Member would be surprised how much we know about all sorts of things."

This was as far as the questioning went. The case appeared to be closed.

Today we know that Herbert Morrison was overly confident when he assured Mr. Granville that the British authorities knew "all" about Freddy Kraus. The elusive Austrian remained a mystery man for almost three decades, and it required long and difficult investigation to bring him out of his cloak. My attention was first attracted to his case by a passage in the memoirs of the famous Colonel Giskes who smashed the British Continental secret service on the eve of the war. Giskes also engineered the most successful German measures to counter the operations of Allied agents in occupied Europe. In a stunning coup variously called "Operation North Pole" and the "England Game," he devastated the Dutch circuit of SOE by securing practically complete control of the Dutch spies and saboteurs that London was sending to Holland. He operated up to eighteen clandestine radio stations exchanging messages with the Dutch Section of SOE, between May 1941 and November 1943, handing the Allies their worst defeat in the secret war.

Before going to Holland to take charge of the Abwehr's Section IIIF (counterespionage), Giskes, then still a major, served in the same capacity in Paris, engaged in efforts to penetrate the British secret service in France. It was there that he scored his greatest triumph by developing a secret agent who would eventually insinuate himself into Mr. Churchill's personal entourage.

Freddy Kraus was that spy.

The operation—if a private matter between a superb intelligence officer and his cat's paw can be called that—began shortly after the collapse of France, at one of the social functions of the American Embassy in Paris. Among the guests was Jacqueline de Broglie and a young German living in Paris whose association with the Abwehr was completely unknown to his American hosts.

While dancing with the Princess, and smiling affably as he spoke sternly, he warned the young woman that her continued presence in Paris depended entirely on the good will of the German authorities. He was well aware that Jacqueline was related to Winston Churchill and had her roots in England where her mother lived.

"Why don't you help us," the man told her, "in exchange for our protection? It isn't much we would expect you to do. Just go on with your entertaining. The rest you could leave to us. We will know how to get the most out of the arrangement, and nobody but us will know anything about it."

"What do you want me to do?" Jacqueline asked.

"Well," the man said, "if you want me to put it bluntly—let us use your places as our listening posts."

"How dare you . . ."

"I'm only trying to help," the man said and changed the subject.

Jacqueline was mortified. In her helpless panic she related the strange incident to Freddy Kraus, the Austrian among her acquaintances she thought she could trust implicitly, and implored him to do something to protect her from the man's sinister scheme. Kraus was genuinely moved by the young woman's plight. Since he himself had no connections in the Abwehr, he enlisted the aid of a certain Count Kreuz, a mysterious Balt who was rumored to have a pipeline to the Hotel Lutetia. Kreuz took Kraus to Major Giskes because, he said, he was the kindest, most compassionate of all Abwehr officers in Paris, had the courage to act forcefully and independently, and was the most likely to help.

Kreuz was setting a trap. He was one of Giskes's operatives at large, an unscrupulous informer deep under cover. And Giskes himself was not quite the good Samaritan Kreuz had presented him to be, who would help a lady in distress out of the sheer goodness of his heart. Far from being scandalized by the invitation extended to Jacqueline to become a blind for the Abwehr, Giskes actually liked the idea. He proposed that Freddy deepen his relations with the Princess, become her suitor in earnest, and worm himself into her confidence so that he could keep her under surveillance. It was a preposterous proposition. But Freddy did not have the guts to throw it back at Giskes with contempt.

At the major's suggestion, that sounded more like an order, he began to cultivate Jacqueline and before long, they were in love. Whether his feelings for her were sincere or feigned, only Freddy could tell. However, this tender attachment did not prevent him from spying on her for Giskes. Jacqueline fell completely under his spell. Freddy managed her whole life, influenced her every action as proxy for the Abwehr. Jacqueline's connections with MI.6, SOE, and the French underground were constantly monitored by him, his findings promptly reported to Giskes. Kraus also betrayed the resistance fighters in Jacqueline's circle, the very people he was pretending to aid as the woman's trusted partner in the underground.

The parties at her residences were henceforth arranged, and partly financed, by Giskes. He attended many of them personally to direct the collection of information from the chatterboxes of Jacqueline's set. The major was an honored guest at the Krauses. The grateful Princess liked him. Freddy had told her that it was Giskes who had saved her from the Abwehr.

It was in his role as a secret courier that Freddy proved most useful to the major, and did the most serious damage to the Resistance. The mail entrusted to him in transit all went to Giskes first. The major gained the opportunity of reading some of the underground's most confidential communications long before their proper addressees had a chance to see them. The letters were steamed open and censored by Giskes. Anything he decided SOE should not get was removed from the shipment. He rewrote reports to confuse and mislead. He substituted false information for accurate intelligence. He used the mail to disrupt and disorganize the Resistance movement.

All this was the doing of the man who paraded his pro-Allied sympathies and anti-Nazi sentiments behind the back and in direct betrayal of the woman he professed to love. To gain absolute hold over Jacqueline and to establish Freddy inside the de Broglie and Churchill families, Giskes smoothed the lovers' path to marriage. He personally prepared the necessary papers Freddy needed to marry a Frenchwoman in occupied France, and acted as his best man at their wedding.

When the tide began to turn after the invasion, and as the Allies were approaching Paris, Giskes hit upon the boldest idea of his whole career. He decided to plant Freddy as a spy on the neck of Prime Minister Churchill himself. Giskes talked it over with Freddy and the Austrian agreed to go along with the project. When, in due course, he arrived in England as Jacqueline's husband and the father of her child, Giskes had accomplished the impossible. He had his man in London. And he was Mr. Churchill's private spy.

Details of the arrangement are still unknown, except for the fact that Kraus did mail to Giskes a number of intelligence reports via a mail drop during his brief sojourn at liberty in England. During the war, several Abwehr agents professed to have contacts within the Prime Minister's intimate circle. Josephine, for example, claimed categorically that one of his "direct sources had an affair with the secretary of Churchill and we received the most interesting and thrilling information through this love affair." The Falangist functionary, Alcazar de Valesco, spying in London for the Abwehr in 1941 in the guise of a Press Officer attached to the Spanish Embassy, also asserted that he had "someone inside 10 Downing Street."

But these claims can be taken with a grain of salt. Kraus was the only Abwehr contact known to infiltrate the Prime Minister's circle, and get close to him. British security organs undertook the most elaborate investigation of the case, but never succeeded in unraveling the whole story or proving conclusively that Mr. Churchill had a German spy in his family. Even when there was reason to believe that Freddy did not come to England with clean hands, he was merely interned, and not arrested on suspicion of espionage.

His ordeal promised to end well for Freddy. It seemed certain that he would be released from internment at the end of the war in Europe, and permitted to return to his wife and little daughter in Paris.

But that was not what happened.

After the war, from telltale tips British intelligence officers picked up in Paris, contours of Freddy's sordid services to the Nazis appeared in scattered reports to MI.5. He came under suspicion of having been a double agent who betrayed to the Germans a number of underground fighters and Allied airmen. Mr. Churchill was apprised of the increasingly serious imputations and he agreed that his second cousin's husband be formally detained pending the clarification of his case. Kraus was arrested and taken to Ham Common, the MI.5's maximum security prison.

Freddy steadfastly denied any wrongdoing on his part. He insisted that his friendship with Giskes was uncorrupted by any ulterior designs. He cited the help he had given the downed RAF flyers, and reminded his interrogators of his valuable contribution to the Resistance movement—how he had risked his life in carrying his *réseau's* mail to Marseilles.

Giskes was brought to Ham Common, kept under harsh, humiliating conditions in solitary confinement, was quizzed continuously, forced to stand for hours at a time, often stripped, facing relays of interrogators. He was willing to divulge all the details of his part in the "North Pole" operation. But he insisted that his relations with Freddy were impeccable and irreproachable. Yes, he enjoyed the young man's company and attended his parties as often he could, even chipping in occasionally with a few thousand francs to share in their costs. That was the money he had given Freddy, not for any secret services rendered.

Mrs. Fellowes was kept posted by the Prime Minister of her son-in-law's gradually deteriorating status in England in the light of increasingly incriminating evidence the investigation was turning up. It was still circumstantial—a rumor here about his involvement with the Nazis, some gossip there about his work for the Abwehr. Although all efforts failed to harden the evidence, it was assumed that Freddy Kraus had been a Nazi spy. His future in British hands did not look rosy.

The family lawyers were alerted. The news was gently broken to Jacqueline. On April 28, 1945, in Paris, the Princess instituted divorce proceedings against Alfred Ignatz Maria Kraus, asking for the custody of their 3-year-old daughter Rosamond. But they counted without Freddy. From Ham Common, professing his innocence, protesting his devotion to his wife and child, he contested the action. If Jacqueline wanted the divorce, he sent word, she could have it. He absolutely refused to give up Rosamond.

The tug of war over the little girl became one of the strangest international domestic struggles ever to reach the courts.

Then suddenly the crisis was resolved.

Freddy was taken on mysterious errands from Ham Common, always in the same huge black limousine calling for him and bringing him back. The detention center was abuzz with questions. What was Freddy doing on these outings? Was it Mr. Churchill he was seeing? Was a deal in the making?

The usually voluble Kraus was glum and taciturn. The questions remained unanswered. One day in June, Freddy was picked up again, but this time he did not return. He was never again seen at Ham Common.

Jacqueline got her divorce and the custody of little Rosamond. Freddy Kraus got his freedom. And the Churchills no longer had a spy in the family. Was it a deal? All the protagonists of the drama who could answer the question—Churchill, Jacqueline, Daisy Fellowes, even the solicitors and *maîtres* who handled the case—have been silenced by death. Freddy alone is alive, living in seclusion somewhere in Austria. And he is keeping mum.

NOTE

1 As an Austrian, Freddy was not officially an enemy national, but security in England was so tight that even alien refugees were interned before their future was determined.

Chapter 52

Operation Heinrich and Josephine's Last Report

*A*FTER the demolition of the Abwehr, Field Marshal Keitel and General Jodl insisted that combat intelligence be left under the jurisdiction of the OKW, with one of Canaris's old aids and confidants, Colonel Georg Hanson, in charge. It proved to be a brief interregnum for Hanson. Implicated in the *putsch* of July 20, 1944, he was arrested, executed, then succeeded by an obscure naval officer at the head of this broken fragment of the Abwehr. Its hastily organized units—the so-called *Frontaufklaerung-Kommandos* or combat intelligence troops—had to shift for themselves, operating well-nigh autonomously under their commanding officers.

When the great retreat began in the face of the rapidly advancing Allies, the gigantic battlefield became chaotic. Any intelligence activity on the fluid fronts became extremely difficult. An ambitious effort was made belatedly to recruit a new crop of spies and leave them behind the Allied lines. Hastily and perfunctorily trained, a few hundred such cannon fodder were rounded up and scattered more or less indiscriminately in areas that the British and American forces had just liberated. These agents were equipped with radios to report their observations to the combat intelligence teams for which they were supposed to be working.

While the Wehrmacht was still fighting with grim determination, prolonging the war in a wasteful sacrifice, the spies regarded the issue as already decided. Most of them refused to risk their lives in a lost cause. Both the combat intelligence teams and the R-spies, as the leftover agents in the Allies' rear were called, produced very little information. The handful of R-agents who took their missions seriously, and pursued haphazard spying behind the lines, were quickly rounded up by American and British security organs. Nothing in the captured records indicates that any of these makeshift efforts produced even minimal combat intelligence that harassed and confused German commanders needed on fronts that changed by the hour. Nothing demonstrated the rapid disintegration of the German war effort more dramatically than the decomposition of the OKW's intelligence establishment.

Nothing showed the utter incompetence of Walter Schellenberg as Admiral Canaris's successor more than the total ineffectiveness of his *Militaerisches Amt*, which had been formed on the ruins of the Abwehr. Only once in the post-Canaris era did the Abwehr's old zeal and efficiency flicker up, in an operation designed and executed by one of its spymasters, the indomitable Lieutenant Colonel Hermann J. Giskes. He had been named commanding officer of one of the front intelligence groups, presiding over five combat intelligence teams in the field and pulling tenuously a few dozen hapless R-spies on his strings. Giskes's opportunity in this eleventh hour occurred during preparations for the Battle of the Bulge, Hitler's single trump card.

Military intelligence service produced shrewd observations in support of the planners of this desperate Ardennes venture of December 1944, correctly identifying the strength and disposition of American forces in the onslaught between the Hautes Fognes in Belgium and Northern Luxembourg.

The Fuehrer's favorite stormy petrel, the scarfaced SS-bully Otto Skorzeny, aggravated the momentary confusion in Allied camps with improvised "special operations" behind the lines. Employing infiltrators clad in British and American uniforms, their inane intervention proved little more than a pinprick. These goon squads forced General Eisenhower to take cover when rumors spread that he had been marked for assassination.

Giskes came up with an ingenious plot. Dubbed "Operation Heinrich," it was designed to divert the Allies' attention from the impending offensive by disseminating a mass of misleading information within the intelligence staffs of the First U. S. Army of General John N. Hodges, whose Fifth and Eighth Corps bore the brunt of the attack.

For Heinrich, Giskes chose a number of bedraggled men from among the alien slaves held at forced labor camps. Planting false intelligence on them, he sluiced them across the lines, giving the impression that they had succeeded in escaping. Most of these Giskes stooges actually believed that they had managed to break out by their own efforts, so shrewdly had he arranged their sudden departure. Most did not know that they carried forged documents and other telltale data smuggled into their belongings before their getaway.

The Heinrich operation proved a success, but only with very

short impact. Giskes's hapless messengers added to the rampant confusion in Brigadier General Edwin Luther Sibert's badly unhinged intelligence division of the 12th (United States) Army Group. But the Americans quickly recovered both their senses and their equilibrium. Two days after its start, the German offensive came to an abrupt stop. By December 24, it was halted for good.

Operation Heinrich, the swan song of German military intelligence, proved as futile as the Ardennes offensive it was supposed to serve. Nothing more was undertaken. The battle of intelligence was lost months before Germany lost the war.

"It is sad," Field Marshal Sir Alan Francis Brooke, chief of Britain's General Staff, wrote in his diary, "that this date will not return for another hundred years."

The date was March 12, 1945—a sweet day in London. After the furious winter weeks of the Battle of the Bulge and the angry counteroffensive of the Allies that carried them to the Rhine, it was quiet on the Western front. But the massive air bombardment of Hamburg, Bremen, Dortmund, Essen, Kassel, Swinemünde, and scores of other cities was driving home to the Germans that the war had moved into its terminal stage. Hitler's Thousand Year Reich was crumbling everywhere. In the general disarray caused by the crisis, and befuddled by the complexities of the task, Walter Schellenberg had lost control of his organization. Each of its segments was left to shift for itself in dispersed emergency shelters where their bewildered staffs hoped to survive the holocaust.

On this nice day an air vice marshal of the Royal Air Force found time off from his duties for a visit to his club on St. James's Street, to talk in congenial company about the last spasms of the war. Someone in the group around him mentioned certain recent changes in the RAF and asked the officer what was happening to the Balloon Command—was it true that it was about to be disbanded?

It sounded like a silly question in the current context of the war. Obviously, this branch of the RAF (set up in 1937 in preparation for the conflict that was running out its course) was no longer needed. The officer said so, adding a few details about the pending deactivation of the Balloon Command.

It was a harmless conversation. There was little if anything of a confidential nature that should have counseled greater discretion. Anyway, the sedate halls of these clubs, to which Britons-in-the-know kept flocking throughout the war, had heard far graver confidences bandied about. Yet this bit of seemingly innocuous shoptalk was not as impromptu or casual as it sounded. The man who had raised the question had a more than perfunctory interest in the matter.

He was one of the V-men of Josephine, the Swedish attaché group which young Karl-Heinz Kraemer of the Abwehr had succeeded in tapping. By now, of course, the war had bypassed Josephine. The great military secrets were no longer spawned in London but at General Eisenhower's headquarters in France. But Josephine was kept in harness.

Major Fritz Brede, the air intelligence officer who had made the original arrangements with Dr. Kraemer and guided the operation through its most productive period, was no longer with the Abwehr. Josephine was now working for Major Ludwig Kleyenstueber of the Luftwaffe General Staff, a punctilious and obtuse officer with an excess of bureaucratic zeal to do something, just about anything, even when there was little more anyone could do. The major insisted on pestering Josephine with queries about petty matters to which he demanded prompt and detailed answers.

On March 10, Kleyenstueber had sent a signal to Josephine inquiring about the fate of the Balloon Command. In response to this query, an agent in London had gone to the club where he expected to pick up the answer. Then, later in the day with the intelligence on hand, he drafted his report, encoded it, and sent it through the Swedish pouch, that channel the British still left open in that strange and inscrutable protocol of international espionage.

"According to Air Vice Marshal Ambler," the signal read in its full plain text, "Air Ministry directive of March 5 ordered transfer of 3000 men from Balloon Command to Army. Affected are staffs and ground crews, as many as 15,000 May 1."

The dispatch of his last spy still at large in England reached Kleyenstueber in the morning of the 13th. It was remarkable only for the speed with which it traveled at a time when most lines of communication were down. That morning the Russians' Third Ukrainian Army hit the Fourth German Army of General Vincent Mueller so hard that it virtually disintegrated on the first day of the battle; that night RAF bombers obliterated the Ruhr city of Dortmund; the 8th U.S. Air Force showered 1435 tons of bombs on Swinemünde; and on the Rhine, the 78th U.S. Division held the Remagen bridgehead in the face of desperate German counterattacks.

But Kleyensteuber continued to be intrigued only by the imminent demise of the Balloon Command. He was not satisfied with Josephine's reply. He fired off another signal, demanding that he find out why the RAF had decided to dismantle the balloons.

Josephine answered on the 14th with a signal that contained the obvious. "Queried about the reason for disbandment of Balloon Command," it read, "Ambler stated that it was no longer needed. Units still left in Great Britain will be absorbed by Fighter Command."

The report arrived at the message center at Belinda II in the early morning of March 15, and Kleyenstueber forwarded it immediately to the intelligence chiefs of the Army and Luftwaffe General Staffs. In the chaos of those days, it took until April 15 to reach them. It did not matter. It created none of the excitement that reports from Josephine once stirred up in those quarters. It was filed and forgotten.

And yet, the report, with its trivial tidings, had a certain historic significance. It was Josephine's last; it marked the end of an era.

Chapter 53

The Spy Who Fooled
J. Edgar Hoover

*F*RIDAY, April 26, 1945. We did not know it yet but the end in Europe was only a fortnight in coming.

The Third Reich was a shambles.

The United States was emerging from the war unscathed. No enemy soldier set foot on its soil. No hostile planes ever as much as approached its coasts. The war was as far away as Iwo Jima and Berlin and Budapest, and yet it was as near as a secluded estate on Long Island.

What was going on behind its locked and guarded gates symbolized the fact that the United States was not as inviolate from enemy attack as it seemed. The big house on the estate, hidden from sight by the trees and bushes of the park, concealed a clandestine radio station servicing a German spy.

He was a Dutchman named Walter Koehler, or at least that was the name by which he was carried on a dossier in the Central Registry of the Abwehr. At the age of fifty-one, balding, myopic, and pudgy, he was neither a romantic figure nor a hot-headed adventurer. He had come to the United States in the summer of 1942 on a special mission. One of the last of the *Grossagenten*, the few super agents the Abwehr still had in reserve, his assignment was to collect whatever information he could about nuclear developments. He was to assemble his own secret shortwave set, and radio his reports to Germany on a schedule calling for transmission regularly at 8 A.M. each Friday.

Koehler did rather well, it seemed, for he was still in harness. His radio never missed any of those weekly transmissions.

On this cheerless April morning he was standing by again to put on the air his report of the week. It was "Message No. 231," going out a little over two years after that cold winter day in 1943, when

645

his new transmitter had made the first contact with the Abwehr's overseas listening post.

His latest message had little relation to his original assignment. What he now tapped out on the Morse key was a humdrum dispatch, giving away no greater secret than the description of the shoulder patch of an American infantry division which, it was claimed, was about to embark for Europe. They kept playing the game—as if the battered Wehrmacht could still benefit from such trivia and turn the tide with it.

This particular game began as a straight intelligence matter some time before Koehler had any part in it. On November 12, 1940, a spy report arrived in Bremen from the United States. It seemed a routine message but it started a chain reaction that ended four and a half years later.

In the report—checked into the log under No. 6079/40/Ig— agent No. R.2232 informed his home office that several helium plants in America were being expanded to increase the production of the strategic gas of which the United States had a world-wide monopoly.

The agent pointed out that helium production at its normal rate had been more than sufficient to meet the normal needs of the United States. The United States Navy used the gas for its fleet of dirigibles and as a component of the "air" supplied to deep-sea divers and caisson workers. The sudden increase, R.2232 wrote, must therefore have some other purpose. Calling attention to the fact that "the alpha rays which emanate from radium are composed of the nuclei of helium atoms," he ventured the opinion that the increase in helium production "could be connected with some significant development in nuclear physics." Probably, he wrote, experiments to harness atomic energy for military purposes could be the reason.

R.2232 was the registry number of a German chemist named Alfred Hohlhaus. A long-time resident in the United States working in a well-paying job, he was here to procure technical intelligence for the Abwehr. The "R" in his numerical designation indicated that he was one of the *Reiseagenten*—traveling agents—who collected classified data on seemingly bona fide business trips.

Hohlhaus's cover job enabled him to visit important American installations throughout the country. He sent in his report after such a visit to Amarillo, Texas, where the Interior Department maintained one of the biggest helium producing plants. The agent thus sent to the Abwehr what, in retrospect, may be singled out as the first spy report that heralded the coming of the atomic age. During the rest of November and in December, he forwarded to Bremen a number of follow-up reports. He was guessing, to be sure, but not in a vacuum.

On May 5, 1940, an article in *The New York Times* by William L. Laurence, the science writer, first described work in this country on "the utilization of atomic energy" by a number of distinguished scientists. Then in a long article in *The Saturday Evening Post*, entitled "The Atom Gives Up," on September 7, Laurence described how, on May 4, "a new source of power" had been discovered "millions of times greater than anything known on earth." Just one pound of the substance used, he wrote, "would be equal to 15,000 tons of TNT," and he identified it as U-235, "a veritable Prometheus bringing to man a new form of Olympic fire."

Not yet persuaded by its agent's reports, but impressed by his contagious excitement, the Bremen branch circulated his reports to their clients in the Army, Navy, and the Luftwaffe. The response was tepid. Typical of the skepticism was the Admiralty's comment on December 17, 1940. "The agent's assertions about helium production," it read, "contained in B.No.6079/40/Ig and subsequent submissions, represent nothing new. Nothing known here indicates any connection between an increase in helium production and the possible industrial manufacture of heavy uranium. This agency is interested merely in information about the export of helium, in what quantities and to which countries."

In the spring of 1941, Hohlhaus was ordered to return to Germany. Back in Bremen he summed up what he knew and what he only assumed in a long paper with the provocative title, "Production of heavy uranium from helium, probably for the U.S. Air Force," and urged Commander Carls, the head of the subbranch, to circulate the memo to those of his clients who had received his previous reports.

The Army failed even to acknowledge receipt of the paper. The Navy again shrugged it off, and actually asked Carls to stop bothering them with any more of the agent's fantasies. "The increase in helium production," they wrote back, "far from having anything to do with nuclear developments, is caused by a considerable enlargement of the United States Navy's fleet of dirigibles and especially by the need to supply a substantial number of barrage balloons with the gas."

On January 19, 1942, almost six months after the distribution of the original paper, Colonel Josef Schmid, chief of Luftwaffe intelligence, sent a belated but positive reply to Commander Carls. "As far as it is known," Schmid wrote, "work in the field of nuclear physics is already so far advanced, especially in the United States, that, if the war were prolonged, it could become of considerable significance. It is, therefore, desirable," he added, "to acquire through the Abwehr additional information about American plans and of the progress made in the United States in the field of nuclear research."

Schmid forwarded the Hohlhaus dossier to Colonel von Roeder, chief of research and development in the Wehrmacht's Bureau of Ordnance. And suddenly Hohlhaus acquired a fan. To be sure, the colonel, himself a competent scientist, questioned the facts. "The agent's reports are very unclear," he wrote, and asked Carls to quiz the chemist for more specific information about "these experiments in the United States." But he went along with the man's bold conclusions. "It would be advisable," von Roeder wrote, "to find out, if possible, from other agents still in the United States: (1) what processes are used in the production of heavy uranium, (2) where such experiments are conducted (including private industrial laboratories) with large quantities of uranium, and (3) what other raw materials are used in the various processes."

Colonel von Roeder concluded his memorandum by proposing that "a special secret agent (preferably a physicist) be employed" and sent to the United States to "pursue the matter on the spot."

In the meantime, both Canaris and Piekenbrock had become interested in the topic and also endorsed Roeder's suggestion that a "special agent" be assigned to the project.

This was Koehler's cue to go on stage. He was not the ideal man for such a big job, far from it. But he would do in the pinch, especially since he had other qualifications that recommended his employment. Koehler was no newcomer to the game. He was a veteran spy who had worked for the Germans in World War I, and on and off between the two wars. He was a bona fide Dutchman and a Roman Catholic, two good reasons to flee from the Nazis and pass as a refugee. Although he was a jeweler by trade, he had been trained as an engineer and had a smattering of technical knowledge. And he was familiar with the United States.

As a matter of fact, he had lived in New York for some time as an Abwehr "sleeper"—until June 17, 1941, when he was suddenly ordered home. An audit of his accounts had revealed some irregularities in his "expenses" and the fiscal bureau of the Abwehr insisted that he be recalled to explain the discrepancies.

One of Koehler's greatest assets was his ability to work himself out of a tight situation. He managed to vindicate himself by persuading the comptrollers at Ast X that he had spent every penny of the funds entrusted to his care in the proper pursuit of his espionage business. He did not quite succeed in convincing his bosses, but it did not matter. They needed the man, warts and all. The Abwehr was relieved and elated when Koehler agreed to go back to the States and try his hand again, this time as an atom spy.

He was given a cram course in the elements of nuclear physics. His old cover story was slightly revamped. But his best disguise was, now as before, his innocuous appearance, the prototype of the harmless little philistine. A swarthy, somewhat corpulent, shy man looking at the world with squinted eyes behind thick-lensed glasses, he had no trait that would draw attention to him as a possible spy.

Accompanied by his wife, he was to go to the United States by way of Argentina on a visa which the Abwehr's dispatcher was to get for him in Madrid. It was left to the organization in Buenos Aires to arrange his northward trek to the United States.

Koehler agreed to the plan even though he had grave misgivings about the wisdom of this new beginning in his long career as a German spy. He felt he was stretching his luck too far. He had managed to escape detection in his previous involvement. But he could not be absolutely certain that he was as unknown to the FBI as it seemed.

Moreover, he had a criminal record. Once between his tours of duty in espionage, when he was penniless in his native Holland, he had stolen the briefcase of a friend with several thousand guilders in it, and had spent six months of an eighteen-month sentence in a Dutch prison. He assumed that his fingerprints had been distributed to every police department by Interpol, and might be on file in the United States as well. If nothing else, they could betray him by opening a path to his true identity.

He overcame his qualms. He had been promised substantial funds for the mission, and he could never resist the lure of money. He accepted the assignment almost avidly, mainly because he had hit upon a brilliant idea. He would take the money, go as far as Argentina, then get lost.

No sooner had he arrived in Madrid en route to the mission than a hitch developed. The Abwehr dispatcher in Madrid could not procure his Argentine visa. His itinerary was revised. He was to take a Portuguese ship from Lisbon straight to the United States, traveling on an American visa which he himself—the little, hapless Dutch-Catholic anti-Nazi—was to coax from a kind-hearted American consul always willing to help such refugees.

He agreed to go through with the mission, taking the slow boat directly to New York, because he now had a better plan than the one he thought up for Argentina. It was with this ingenious scheme that Walter Koehler—equipped with doctored credentials—appeared in the office of an American vice consul in Madrid to present his request for visas for himself and for his wife. What he then told the young consul was the most bizarre story ever offered in support of a visa application.

"Actually, sir," he told the consul. "I'm an employee of the Abwehr. They are sending me to the United States as an espionage agent on a special mission. According to my instructions, I am to set up a clandestine radio station and send my reports by wireless, because of their importance and urgency."

The consul asked him what was so special about his mission.

"I have to report on troop movements," he said.

He had ample proof that he was a German agent en route to America. In a battered little cardboard suitcase he carried with him all the paraphernalia the Abwehr had given him. He brought out his manual for the assembly and operation of the wireless set, and his cipher, reduced to small films by microphotography. He produced a music sheet of the Dutch national anthem on which was written with invisible ink his weekly transmission schedule and the set of his call letters. He showed a prayer book on which, he said, his code was to be based. He produced chemicals for the making of secret inks and developers; and a powerful magnifying glass that had become a familiar tool carried by all Abwehr agents.

As his last piece of evidence, out came the funds the Abwehr had given him—$6,230 in cash, travelers checks, and gold coins, some valuable jewelry, and a small collection of rare stamps. When he had established his secret mission, Koehler blurted out the part of his cover story he had concocted.

He told the consul that he had accepted the assignment solely to escape from the clutches of the Nazis, who were looking for him because he was a patriotic Dutchman and a devout Catholic. "I'm eager to serve the Allies," he said. "If I am admitted to the United States, I would be prepared to prove my loyalty by serving as an agent for you while pretending that I'm carrying out my mission for the Abwehr."

The unusual offer was reported to Washington and the FBI agreed to take the calculated risk. The State Department was asked by J. Edgar Hoover to authorize the granting of the visa. The consulate in Madrid was instructed by cable: "Send him along."

Koehler was puzzled by the aftermath of his visit to the American consulate. While he was in Madrid and Lisbon waiting for his ship to sail, no effort was made by the consul or, for that matter, by anybody representing the American authorities to take him up on his offer. He was inclined to think that the naïve consul blithely swallowed his sob story and gave him the visa without any strings attached. This was exactly how he hoped things would work out—to enter the United States with the knowledge and approval of the FBI. It was August 1942 when he boarded a Portuguese ship in Lisbon and a reception committee of the FBI was waiting in New York to take him in tow the moment the ship berthed. But when she arrived after a stormy crossing, Koehler was not abroad. He was in a hospital in Florida.

A week or so before, a Coast Guard boat patrolling the east coast of Florida had spotted a Portuguese ship flying the distress pennant and requesting assistance. When a boarding party went to see what the trouble was, the naval intelligence officers were told that one of the passengers was critically ill. He was Koehler, suffering from pneumonia. The Coast Guard rushed him to the Florida hospital where, after some frantic search, the FBI was relieved to find him.

When he was nursed back to health, the FBI took over Koehler as a German spy at large in the United States and insisted that he act accordingly. The plan was to establish as fact what had become the fiction of Koehler's mission—to pretend that he was free to operate as a German agent while actually serving as an FBI conveyor belt for the transmission of bogus intelligence.

It took some time before the spy could be set up and given a radio station for the transmission of his messages. It was eventually built in a rambling house on Long Island. In all the time the FBI maintained this estate as its "communicating station," no stranger was allowed near the place. The grounds were guarded day and night by police dogs. Three FBI agents who operated the station slept and ate at the house, standing tours of duty of eight hours each at the radio apparatus.[1]

Koehler himself was not present at 8 A.M. on Sunday, February 7, 1943, when his first signal went on the air. The clandestine radio was operated in his name by a team of special agents, German linguists, and radio technicians of the FBI. The agent who transmitted the first signal and would continue to send out Koehler's messages had groomed himself by meticulously adopting the Dutchman's peculiar touch of the Morse key.

"I am now ready to begin operations," the signal read. "Necessary to be very careful, but feel I am safe. Will listen for you at 1900 o'clock. If contact not made then, will listen following day at the same time."

Koehler's rearranged new schedule called for transmission by him at 8 A.M. on Saturdays or Sundays, and for the reception of his incoming signals at 7 P.M. on Fridays or Saturdays. On the next Friday, February 12, the FBI was rewarded for its trouble. The reply came in from Hamburg. "Uncle is highly pleased," it read. "He sends his thanks and good wishes. Henceforth please observe caution and discretion in the execution of your assigned tasks."

From then on, for over two years, the messages crisscrossed the Atlantic on schedule. "Week by week," Mr. Hoover wrote later, "we fed the Germans military and industrial information (cleared with the armed services), for the most part true"—and most of the time trivial. The information included weather reports (which were classified during the war), ship movements in American ports, the names of warships undergoing repair, and data about new ship construction. From the spring of 1944 until the invasion became imminent, intelligence about the departures of army units for Europe, was sent out, together with descriptions of their insignia. The latter was what Koehler had told the consul in Madrid he had been instructed to collect.

The only information that was conspicuous by its total absence was what he had actually been sent to procure—data about those mysterious nuclear developments. To the FBI, the Germans seemed to be quite pleased with what they received. Their replies abounded in laudatory comments and congratulations. They remembered him on his birthdays, and even on the day of his patron saint. They sent him Christmas and New Year's greetings, and a good-cheer message at Eastertime in 1944. The FBI responded in kind, closing many of the outgoing messages with some friendly salutation. It was a very chummy correspondence, as far as it went, full of little pleasantries and amenities.

The whole thing was the familiar hoax, what the Germans called *"Funkspiel,"* a picturesque term for which "radio game" is a pale translation. The game the FBI played with Koehler was but one of literally hundreds of such shots in the dark. Both sides excelled in this tricky doubleplay.

The FBI was not playing this game for its own entertainment. This outlet was used with several serious objectives in mind. "We wanted to find out," Mr. Hoover wrote, "whether any other spies were operating in America. Hamburg might tell [Koehler] to get in touch with them. We wanted to know how the Germans paid their operatives in the Americas. And, most important, we hoped to mislead the [German] High Command by feeding them false information"—especially about the timing and the direction of the Normandy invasion.

As Mr. Hoover put it, "we succeeded on all scores."

In the meantime, Koehler was made comfortable and helped "in every possible way" to enjoy his stay in the United States. Put up in a good little hotel in midtown New York, and endowed with a fairly generous allowance (out of his confiscated funds) he was seemingly on his own, free to come and go and to do as he pleased. Koehler lost no time to make the most of it. He became demanding, rather arrogant, and considerably less candid with the FBI than he had been when he had surrendered himself to its care and feeding.

There was something furtive about his manners. Several times he was caught in attempts to deceive the agents who supervised him. At the very outset, his wife tried to smuggle into the United States the entire spy paraphernalia which he had displayed to the consul in his eagerness to establish his *bona fides*—the magnifying glass, a special Leica camera, chemicals needed for making and developing secret inks.

The funds the Abwehr had given him—as well as the jewelry and the stamps—had been taken away, but he appeared to have additional funds which he chose not to divulge, as well as money hidden with an accomplice. Although he professed to be a jeweler, he demanded that the FBI let him open a radio repair shop, insisting that this was part of his original deal with the consul.

He played ball, to be sure. But, as Mr. Hoover put it, "with 'a pistol' in his back."

Between February 7, 1943, and April 26, 1945, a total of 115 different messages went out in Koehler's name under the FBI's aegis. All told, his reports in the Abwehr files were sent in 231 signals, as the serial number of his last dispatch indicated.

When I came upon Koehler's papers in the flotsam of the German archives, I discovered every one of them neatly transcribed on the familiar Form 0448-32831 of the *Herren-Fernschreibenetz* (Army Teletype Service). In an article, entitled "The Spy Who Double-Crossed Hitler," published a year after the war, Mr. Hoover quoted one of them verbatim—a lengthy message transmitted on March 3, 1944—and it was quite a thrill to find it in Koehler's dossier in the original German as Hamburg recorded it.

But the dossier held a stunning surprise. The number of transcripts preserved in it far exceeded the 115 which the FBI had put on the air on those 231 transmissions.

For example, on March 4, 1944, the FBI was up to Nos. 63–65. Around the same date the dossier held transcripts of messages numbered as high as 129–137.

Then another surprise awaited me.

The messages the FBI was sending in Koehler's name went out in the cipher the Abwehr had concocted for him, keyed to the Dutch prayer book he had shown the consul and then surrendered to the FBI. When I examined some of the undeciphered transcripts, I found that their messages—Nos. 137, 140, 178, 229, and 240, for example—had gone out in a totally different cipher.

Still another clue was found to indicate that the Koehler operation apparently moved on several separate tracks. In February 1944 when Admiral Canaris was fired and most of the Abwehr's functions were taken over by Walter Schellenberg, the latter moved fast to revamp the old Abwehr. Convinced that most of the spies had outlived their usefulness and some of them were outright harmful, he subjected its entire V-man roster to merciless scrutiny. A malignant dilettante, he trusted nobody (and trusted the Canaris foxes the least), so he devised an ingenious system to evaluate them.

Schellenberg ordered that a separate sheet be drawn up for every V-man, with two columns—one to list reports which time had proven "good," the other to list reports proven "bad" or even misleading. By simply glancing on this double ledger of a spy's accumulated output, it was possible to determine who among the agents were useful and reliable, who were useless and who were double agents.

Schellenberg had such checklists compiled at intervals of four months. He assumed that four months were sufficient to ascertain whether the events, dispositions and moves the spies had reported had proven true or false.

By this time most of the secret agents with whom the Abwehr had embarked on the war had fallen by the wayside anyway. The roster Schellenberg was now drawing up contained mostly replacements, novices at recently developed outposts, the third or fourth casts in this long-running play.

The list of agents still active in the United States showed most graphically the shrinkage in both quantity and quality. Even in August 1942 (when Koehler first arrived in America), the secret register of V-men at work against the United States listed nine senior agents and scores of minor spies and ad hoc informants, sending in "very good" or "mostly accurate" reports.

The Schellenberg Bureau now carried only about a dozen, most of them Spaniards and Portuguese whose work, as the roster showed, left much to be desired. There were only two senior agents enduring valiantly, it seemed, in the face of rapidly worsening odds. One of them was A.3778, a German merchant doing business in the Western Hemisphere, who had been recruited for the Abwehr way back in 1941. His original assignment was to go to Uruguay and set up a clandestine radio station to relay to Germany "intelligence concerning [American] war production and military installations," which he would be receiving from three spies in the United States.

When he arrived in Montevideo, he contacted an American diplomat and volunteered his services as a double agent. On instructions of the FBI, he moved to New York, explaining to the Abwehr branch in Hamburg that his efforts to establish his radio link in Uruguay had proved unsuccessful. Checked into the FBI on the number ND 98, his first signal from Sebold's old radio center on Long Island was put on the air on February 20, 1942. From then on, during the whole war, he was feeding information "carefully prepared by the FBI and screened for security or furnished by the Joint Security Control operated under the direction of the Joint Chiefs of Staff."

His work so satisfied the Germans that they smuggled to him $55,000 in salary, bonuses, and expenses, sufficient to pay for the whole hoax. A.3778 alias ND 98 also participated in the deception maneuver on the eve of the invasion of 1944, telling the Germans that "a number of infantry and armored divisions originally slated for the United Kingdom are being diverted for a special operation"— in the Mediterranean area—to distract attention from Normandy. He was kept in harness to the end. By late spring of 1945, there was nobody left at the Wohldorf radio center either to receive his messages or answer them.

Aside from him, the only other major agent in the United States was Koehler. He was no longer as prolific as he had been, it seemed, but he was still rated first class. His ratio of "good" versus "bad" reports was consistently running three to one, a respectable accomplishment by any standards used for the assessment of agents.

If Koehler was only a bystander idling away his days in New York while the FBI was doing his job, I wondered, how was it possible that so many of his reports survived Schellenberg's acid test?

To be sure, most of the messages the FBI concocted for him were either true or had some basis in fact. Even that, however, could not have been the whole answer to Schellenberg's puzzling recognition of Walter Koehler.

I began to suspect that the man who was called "Albert van Loop" by Mr. Hoover and described as "the spy who double-crossed Hitler," had somehow succeeded in double-crossing the FBI as well. I assumed that he had managed by some fantastic ruse to send his own genuine reports to his German employers while the FBI was radioing to Hamburg bogus intelligence in his name.

It proved difficult to assemble the data that would bear out my suspicion. My search in Germany yielded three survivors among the top-ranking Abwehr officers who were familiar with the Koehler operation, and they solved the mystery.

According to them, "Koehler" was a native of Gouda, in the Netherlands, where he was born on October 15, 1885. They described him as a heavy-set man with graying hair, an oval face with squinting blue-gray eyes, and conspicuous for his bad teeth, with a couple missing in the front.

An effective spy of the Germans in World War I, he was re-enlisted in August 1939, to spy on his native Holland. After the conquest of the Low Countries, he was sent to the United States on his first tour of duty as a "sleeper."

When preparing his return appearance in 1942, the man was developed as a double agent from the outset. In order to facilitate his re-entry into the United States, Dr. Praetorius had agreed to his plan to "surrender" to the Americans already in Madrid, and to participate in any "radio game" his pro-forma treachery would entail.

At the same time, he was set up as a genuine producing agent. In this capacity he worked, not for Hamburg, but for the Abwehr's huge outpost in Paris where, for some time, a colonel named Waag, a nephew of Admiral Canaris, acted as his case officer.

The phony messages the FBI was sending to Hamburg were, of course, recognized for what they were.

On June 9, 1944, for example, three days after the Allied landings in Normandy, he risked his security and wasted his strictly rationed radio time on a two-part message that read: "According to rumors circulating here, the invasion appears to be a success. It does not look good for our cause. I am convinced that this is gross exaggeration and that all will end well. I hope Uncle will not forsake me and will do everything he can to keep supplying me with working capital. Barometer reading at 9 o'clock this morning 30 point 29. Greetings, Koe."

"We would have recognized it as a 'flower,'" one of the Abwehr officers said when I showed him the transcript, "even if it had not gone to Hamburg with the rest of the fake messages."

How did he manage to outwit the FBI despite the close surveillance under which he was presumably kept? The watch on Koehler was not as tight as one would expect. Such a surveillance can never be. Since a suspect like Koehler had to be watched day and night, and the FBI invariably employed agents in pairs on such assignments, he would have taken up the full time of at least six special agents to keep him covered. The Bureau simply could not spare the men.

Also, Koehler was a shrewd operator who knew how to slip out of an even tighter noose. He managed to outwit the FBI in a number of ways. He had been given a little over $16,000 for his mission, but he surrendered only some $6,000 of it. The rest was smuggled into the United States sewn into the girdle of his ample wife. Using the money, and contacts in this country whose existence he also concealed from the Bureau, he assembled his own clandestine radio station with the help of an associate in Rochester, New York. It was cautiously and sparsely used, to escape detection. His man in Rochester would make special trips to New York to pick up the copy of Koehler's messages, mostly perishable items that had to be forwarded by the fastest means. Otherwise, he was sending his reports through a small net of couriers the Abwehr had organized especially for him on Spanish and other neutral ships.

While his misleading information was going out from Long Island, Rochester was beaming his authentic signals to Paris. When the liberation of the city closed down the huge Abwehr radio center there, the messages continued to be sent nevertheless, now beamed to the third big radio station the Abwehr had at Sigmaringen in southwestern Germany, for communications with agents at long distance. It was servicing the outpost in Wiesbaden where a lieutenant colonel named Rauh had become Koehler's last case officer.

The indomitable triple agent failed in his basic mission. He never supplied any intelligence about atomic developments. This, however, was less his fault than the remarkable accomplishment of the American security organs created especially to safeguard the stupendous secrets of the Manhattan Project. But Koehler's failure to work as an "atom spy" did not diminish his standing in German eyes, not even a quarter of a century later when I discussed his case with the three former Abwehr officers. "He was the greatest V-man we had in the war," Colonel Waag told an American interrogator in 1945 when questioned about this wandering Dutchman.

"He was the best man we ever had in the United States," Colonel Rauh said later, but he added with a sigh: "Alas! He was also our last."

NOTE

1 According to Don Whitehead, "the first long Island radio installation was established on December 4, 1941," but though his book, *The FBI Story: A Report to the People,* was based on data he obtained from Hoover, this—as, indeed, much in his narrative—was in error. The first station was set up for William G. Sebold at Centerport, Long Island, in the spring of 1940 and kept operational until July 7, 1941, when the arrest of German agents it had serviced terminated its usefulness.

Epilogue . . . More Than Just the End

On April 26, 1945, Koehler's final signal sent under the auspices of the FBI was beamed as usual to the Overseas Message Center, three-thousand miles away in a tree-shaded Hamburg suburb called Wohldorf, the enormous, severely camouflaged installation built around a concrete subterranean hall, the nerve center of the German secret service for nearly a decade. Even a few weeks before, it was jammed with intelligence officers, radio operators, cryptographers, secretaries, and messengers, humming with the crackling sounds of wireless correspondence with hundreds of agents in Britain, the Americas, Africa, and in places as far away as Patagonia and Afghanistan.

Now there were barely a dozen listless men in the big hall. Above them, all around them, the great city of Hamburg had been crushed. Completely surrounded by British troops, its fall was but a matter of hours.

The huge bunker held up, and the radio station was still operating on its emergency generators. But the traffic had diminished to a mere trickle. Where hundreds of signals had been handled on each watch, efficiently, mechanically, impassively, now every incoming call startled and stunned the handful of "sparks." Who would still want to contact Wohldorf? German espionage had run its course.

The radioman who picked up Koehler's signal was stunned by its anachronism and futility. He wrote down the five-digit groups of the message on a pad but did not bother to decipher any of it. He recognized the peculiar "fingerprint" of the sender, whose dots were almost as long as his dashes. He handed it in the raw to a Lieutenant Roehr, one of the young officers of the watch, who was now the senior officer in charge. Roehr looked at the rows of numbers with bleary eyes, then tore up the sheet and threw the scraps into a wastepaper basket.

"He expects an answer, sir," the radioman said.

"Sign him off tomorrow," the lieutenant told him.

The prearranged sign-off signal went out on May, 1945, just as Koehler was expected to find it on his old schedule.

"Conditions compel us to suspend communications," it read, "but please continue to stand by on schedule once a week. Do not despair. We will look out for you and protect your interests as usual."

It was signed, "Uncle."

Later, during that Tuesday, the order arrived from Flensburg, where the executor of Hitler's testament, Grand Admiral Karl Doenitz, had his headquarters, to destroy everything. The men set the charges, then scrambled out of the bunker and ran, watching from a safe distance as the earth shook and the heavy roof of the bunker erupted in myriad scraps of concrete.

Wohldorf went off the air with a bang, never to return again.

Just two weeks before, in another symbolic event during these chaotic days, Admiral Wilhelm Franz Canaris was hanged by a Nazi goon squad at the Flossenbuerg concentration camp, on a meat hook with thin piano wire.

Now even what little was left of his Abwehr was also dead.

Bibliography

GUIDES, BIBLIOGRAPHIES, AND SUMMARY SHEETS

American Historical Association. Committee for the Study of War Documents, *Guides to German Records Microfilmed at Alexandria, Virginia*, 41 vols., Washington, D.C., 1959–1965

Bibliothek fuer Zeitgeschichte, Weltkriegsbuecherei, *Jahresbibliographie*, Frankfurt, 1960–1970

Fritz, S., "Die schwedische Literatur ueber den zweiten Weltkrieg. Eine Bibliographie," in *Jahresbibliographie*, q.v., 1963, pp. 573–603

Gunzenhaeuser, Max, *Die Bibliographien zur Geschichte des zweiten Weltkrieges*, in *Schriften der Bibl. f. Zeitgesch.*, Frankfurt, 1966

Kent, George O., *A Catalog of Files and Microfilms of the German Foreign Ministry Archives*, 4 vols., Stanford, Cal., 1966

Koehler, Karl, *Bibliographie zur Luftkriegsgeschichte*, in *Schriften, etc.*, Frankfurt, 1966

National Archives and Records Service, *Summary Sheets of Captured German Documents*, Washington, D.C.

Roeseler, J., "Die deutschen Plaene fuer eine Landung in England und die Luftschlacht um England in der Literatur," in *Jahresbibliographie*, q.v., 1962, pp. 541–553

The following documentary material and other sources and references have been consulted in the preparation of this book:

PRIMARY SOURCES

Unpublished Documents

Abwehr: Ast X (Hamburg) and Nest Bremen, ML-Series, microfilm rolls in the author's collection

Abwehr II, War Diary (August 12, 1939 to April 12, 1941), copy in the author's collection

Bredow, General Ferdinand von, Papers, in Bundesarchiv

Canaris, Wilhelm, Papers (1924–1926), in Militaergeschichtliches Forschungsamt

Central Criminal Court No. 334, Rex v. Tyler Gatewood Kent, transcript of the shorthand notes of the trial, in Charles B. Parsons Collection, Historical Manuscripts Division, Yale University Library

Gempp, General Fritz, *Geheimer Nachrichtendienst und Spionageabwehr des Heeres*, 14 vols., on microfilm in T-77 Series, National Archives and Records Service, Washington, D.C., copy in the author's collection

Heinz, Colonel Friedrich Wilhelm, *Von Wilhelm Canaris zum NKVD*, unpublished manuscript, copy in the author's collection

Hiles, C.C., "The Case of Tyler Gatewood Kent," manuscript

Huppenkothen, Walter, transcript of trial record, February 4–14, 1951, 3 vols., 1613 pages, copy in the author's collection

Huppenkothen, Walter, "Canaris und Abwehr," in the collection of Prof. Harold C. Deutsch

Johnson, Thomas M., *The C.I.C. in World War II*, research data and manuscript

Kriegstagebuch (War Diary) der Kriegsmarine, in U.S. Department of the Navy, Naval History Division

[Masterman, Sir John], *The Double-Cross System in the Second World War 1939–1945*

Mueller, Dr. Josef, affidavit concerning the death of Admiral Canaris, in the collection of Prof. H.R. Trevor-Roper

National Archives and Records Center, Washington, D.C., T-Series:

    T-70:   Records of the Reich ministry for Public Enlightenment and Propaganda

    T-73:   Records of the Reich Ministry for Armaments and War Production

    T-77:   Records of Headquarters, German Armed Forces High Command

    T-78:   Records of Headquarters, German Army High Command

    T-81:   Records of the Deutsches Auslands-Institut

    T-82:   Records of Nazi Cultural and Research Institutions, and Records Pertaining to Axis Relations and Interests in the Far East

    T-83:   Records of Private Austrian, Dutch, and German Enterprises, 1917–1946

    T-84:   Miscellaneous German Records Collection

    T-120: Records of the German Foreign Ministry

    T-175: Records of the Reich Leader of the SS and Chief of the German Police (Heinrich Himmler)

    T-177: Records of the Reich Air Ministry

    T-178: Records of Miscellaneous Reich Ministries and Offices

    T-179: Records of German and Japanese Embassies and Consulates, 1890–1945

T-253: Records of Private German Individuals
T-311: Records of German Field Commands
T-312: Records of German Field Commands
T-321: Records of Headquarters of the German Air Force High Command
T-354: Miscellaneous SS Records
T-405: German Air Force Records

Nicholson, Leslie Arthur, *21 Queen Ann's Gate*, unfinished manuscript

Nicholson, Leslie Arthur, Papers, Diaries and Transcript of interviews

Niedermayer, Oskar Ritter von, Papers, in Bundesarchiv

National Socialist German Labor Party (NSDAP), complete records in the Berlin Document Center

Reichstagsuntersuchungsausschuesse, Protokolle ueber die Semeorganisation und die Fememoerder (1926–1928), in the collection of Emil G. Gumbel

Reile, Oscar, manuscript

Reile, Oscar, Papers and transcripts of interviews

Ritter, Nikolaus, Papers and Diaries, 1937–1945

Ritter, Nikolaus, *My Name Is Dr. Rantzau*, manuscript

Ritter, Nikolaus, Ast X, Luft/I, 1937–1941

Smith, Colonel Truman, "Air Intelligence Activities, Office of the Military Attaché, American Embassy, Berlin, Germany, August 1935 to April 1939," manuscript, in Yale University Library

U.S. Department of State, Special Interrogation Mission (1945–46), transcripts of the interrogation of the following individuals in the author's collection: Field Marshal Werner von Blomberg; General Friedrich von Boetticher; Ernst Wilhelm Bohle; Baron von Bieberstein; Heinrich Franz Johannes Borchers; Ambassador Hans Heinrich Dieckhoff; Ambassador Herbert von Dirksen; Hanna Feldtange; Ulrich von Gienanth; Ernst Adolf Hepp; Philip Prince of Hesse; Ambassador Walter Hewel; Baron Oswald von Hoyningen-Huene; General Alfred Jodl; Dr. Ernst Kaltenbrunner; Field Marshal Wilhelm Keitel; Wilhelm Keppler; Paul Koerner; Fritz Kolbe; Dr. Erich Kordt; General Erwin von Lahousen; Constantin Baron von Neurath; Captain Dietrich Niebuhr; Wilhelm Ohnesorge; Theodor Paeffgen; Franz von Papen; Ambassador Friedrich Wilhelm von Prittwitz; Carl Berthold Franz Rekowsky; Joachim von Ribbentrop; Ambassador Karl Ritter; Paul Otto Gustav Schmidt; Heribert von Strempel; Wilhelm Ernst August Tannenberg; Dr. Hans Thomsen; Dr. Edmund Wesenmayer; General Walter Warlimont.

Volksgerichtshof, complete records in Berlin Document Center

Published Documents and Official Publications

Battle of the Atlantic. The Official Account of the Fight Against the U-Boats, 1939–1945, London, 1946

Boberach, H. (ed.), *Meldungen aus dem Reich. Auswahl aus den geheimen Lageberichten des Sicherheitsdienstes der SS*, 1939–bis 1944, Neuwied/Berlin, 1966

Boelcke, Willi A. (ed.), *Kriegspropaganda 1939–1941. Geheime Minister-*

konferenzen im Reichspropagandaministerium, Stuttgart, 1966

Butler, Sir James (ed.), _Grand Strategy_, in United Kingdom Military History, 6 vols., London

Collier, Basil, _Defence of the United Kingdom_, in United Kingdom Military History, London, 1957

Combined Operations, London, 1943

Confidential Records of the French General Staff, Berlin, 1940

Derry, T.K., _The Campaign in Norway_, in United Kingdom Military History, London, 1952

Ellis, L.F., _France and Flanders, 1939–1940_, in United Kingdom Military History, London,

Ellis, L.F., with G.R.G. Allen, A.E. Warhurst, Sir James M. Robb, _Victory in the West_, 2 vols., London, 1962, 1968

Enquetecommissie Regeringsbeleid 1940–1945. _De Nederlandse Geheime Diensten to London. De Verbindungen met het Bezette Gebied_, vol. 4A/B, The Hague, 1950

European Resistance Movements 1939–1945. Proceedings of the Second International Conference on the History of the Resistance Movements, Milan, March 26–29, 1961, Oxford, 1964

Foot, M.R.D., _S.O.E. in France_, in United Kingdom Military History, London, 1966

Groscurth, Helmut, _Tagebuecher eines Abwehroffiziers, 1938–1940_, ed. by H.C. Deutsch and H. Krausnick, Munich, 1966

Hayes Confessions. Special communique issued by the Army Council of the Irish Republican Army, Dublin, Sept. 10, 1941

Heibur, Helmut (ed.), _Hitler's Lagebesprechungen. Die Protokollfragmente seiner militaerischen Konferenzen, 1942–1945_, Stuttgart, 1962

Hubatsch, W. (ed.), _Hitler's Weisungen fuer die Kriegsfuehrung, 1939–1945. Dokumente des Oberkommandos der Wehrmacht_, Munich, 1958

Irving, David (ed.), _Breach of Security. The German Secret Intelligence File on Events Leading to the Second World War_, with an introduction by Donald C. Watt, London, 1968

Jacobsen, Hans-Adolf, _Der zweite Weltkrieg. Grundzuege der Politik und Strategie in Dokumenten_, Frankfurt, 1965

Jacobsen, Hans-Adolf, _1939–1945. Der zweite Weltkrieg in Chronik und Dokumenten_, 5th ed., 1961

Jodl, General Alfred, his interrogation by the Soviet authorities, translated by Dr. Arenz, _Wehrwissenschaftliche Rundschau_, 1961, vol. 11

Jodl, General Alfred, "Das dienstliche Tagebuch des Chefs des Wehrmachtfuehrungsamtes in OKW," October 13, 1938 to January 30, 1940, ed. by Walter Hubatsch in _Die Welt als Geschichte_, 1952, pp. 274–287; 1953, pp. 58–72; February 1 to May 20, 1940, in Doc. 1809-PS, in Trial of Major War Criminals, (q.v.) vol. XXVIII, pp. 397–435

Klee, Karl (ed.), _Dokumente zum Unternehmen Seeloewe. Die geplante deutsche Landung in England, 1940_, Goettingen, 1959

Kloess, Erhard (ed.), _Von Versailles zum zweiten Weltkrieg. Vertraege zur Zeitgeschichte, 1918–1939_, Munich, 1965

Krausnick, Helmut, "Aus den Personalakten von Admiral Wilhelm Canaris," in *Vierteljahreshefte fuer Zeitgeschichte*, 1962, v. 10

Krausnick, Helmut, "Hitler und die Morde in Polen," *ibid.*, 1963, vol. 11, pp. 197–98

Martinsen, Anthony, *Hitler and His Admirals*, New York, 1949

Nazi Conspiracy and Aggression, 8 vols., 2 supplements, Washington, 1946–48

North, John, *North-West Europe, 1944–45*, in United Kingdom Military History (Popular Series), London, 1956

Peter, Karl Heinrich (ed.), *Spiegelbild einer Verschwoerung. Die Kaltenbrunner-Berichte an Bormann und Hitler ueber das Attentat von 20. Juli 1944. Geheime Dokumente aus dem ehemaligen Reichssicherheitshauptamt*, Stuttgart, 1961, based on Series T-84, Rolls, 19 and 20, in National Archives, Washington, D.C.

Picker, H. (ed.), *Hitler's Tischgespraeche im Fuehrerahauptquartier, 1941–1942*, Bonn, 1951

Piekenbrock, General Hans, his interrogation in Soviet captivity, edited by Julius Marder, in *Mitteilungsblatt der Arbeitsgemeinschaft ehemaliger Offiziere*, of questionable authenticity

Poliakov, Leo, and Josef Wulf, *Das Dritte Reich und seine Diener. Dokumente*, Berlin-Grunewald, 1956

Polish Ministry of Information. *The German Fifth Column in Poland*, London, 1941

Rogge, O. John, *The Official German Report*, New York, 1961, based on the interrogation of 66 Nazi officials in 1945–46, by a team of the U.S. Justice Department and the FBI

Rosenberg, Alfred, *Das Politische Tagebuch Alfred Rosenbergs, 1934–35 und 1939–40*, ed. by Hans Guenther Seraphim, in *Quellensammlung zur Kulturgeschichte*, Goettingen, 1956

Schnabel, R., *Missbrauchte Mikrofone. Deutsche Rundfunkpropaganda im zweiten Weltkrieg. Eine Dokumentation*, Vienna, 1967

Schramm, Percy Ernst (ed.), *Kriegstagebuch des Oberkommandos der Wehrmacht (Wehrmachtfuehrungsstab)*, 4 vols. in seven parts, Frankfurt, 1961–65

Trevor-Roper, H.R. *Hitler's Secret Conversations*, with an introductory essay, "The Mind of Adolf Hitler," translated by Norman Cameron and R.H. Stevens, London, 1953

Trevor-Roper, H.R., *Blitzkrieg to Defeat. Hitler's War Directives 1939–1945*, London, 1964

Trial of German Major War Criminals. Proceedings of the International Military Tribunal Sitting in Nuremberg, November 20, 1945 to October 1, 1946, 42 vols., Nuremberg, 1947–49

U.S. Department of the Navy, *Fuehrer-Directives and Other Top-Level Directives of the German Armed Forces, 1939–1945*, 2 vols., Washington, D.C., 1946

U.S. Department of the Navy, *Fuehrer Conferences on Matters Dealing with the German Navy*, 9 vols., Washington, D.C., 1947

U.S. Department of State, *Documents on German Foreign Policy, 1918–1945*, series C and D, Washington, D.C.

U.S. Department of State, *The Last Days of Peace, August 9–September 3, 1939*, Washington, D.C., 1957
U.S. Department of State, *The Spanish Government and the Axis: Official German Documents*, Washington, D.C., 1946
U.S. Department of State, *Foreign Relations of the United States, Diplomatic Papers*, published annually in several volumes
U.S. Department of State, "The Case of Tyler G. Kent," Press Release No. 405, September 2, 1944

Diaries, Memoirs, Personal Narratives

Ame, C., *Guerra segreta in Italia, 1939–1943*, Rome, 1954
Baillie-Stewart, Norman, *The Officer in the Tower*, London, 1967
Bazna, E., *Ich war Cicero*, adapted by Hans Nogly, Munich, 1962
Bentwich, Norman, *I Understand the Risks*, London, 1950
Best, Sigismund Payton, *The Venlo Incident*, London, 1950
Bleicher, Hugo, *Colonel Henry's Story*, ed. by E. Borchers and Ian Colvin, London, 1954
Borchers, Erich, *Monsieur Jean*, Hannover, 1951
Bryant, Arthur, *The Turn of the Tide 1939–1943. A Study Based on the Diaries and Autobiographical Notes of Field Marshal The Viscount Alanbrooke*, London, 1957
Bryant, Arthur, *Triumph in the West. A History of the War Years Based on the Diaries of Field Marshal The Viscount Alanbrooke*, London, 1959
Buckmaster, Maurice J., *Specially Employed*, London, 1952
Burt, Leonard, *Commander Burt of Scotland Yard*, London, 1959
Carré, Mathilde-Lily, *I Was the Cat*, London, 1960
Chapman, Eddie, *The Real Eddie Chapman Story*, London, 1960
Churchill, Winston S., *The Second World War*, 6 vols., London, 1949–1951
Ciano, Count Galeazzo, *The Ciano Diaries*, ed. by Malcolm Muggeridge, London, 1946
Ciano, Count Galeazzo, *Ciano's Diplomatic Papers*, ed. by Malcolm Muggeridge, translated by Stuart Hood, London, 1948
Ciano, Count Galeazzo, *Ciano's Hidden Diary 1937–1938*, ed. by Robert Major, London, 1953
Cooper, Alfred Duff, *Old Men Forget*, the Memoirs of Lord Norwich, London, 1953
Dahlerus, B., *Sista försöket; London-Berlin sommaren 1939*, Stockholm, 1945
Dalton, Hugh, *The Fateful Years. Memoirs 1931–1945*, London, 1957
Dasch, George J., *Eight Spies Against America*, New York, 1959
Dewawrin, André (Colonel Passy), *Souvenirs*, 3 vols., Monte Carlo and Paris, 1947, 1951
Dodd, Martha, *Through Embassy Eyes*, New York, 1939
Dodd, William, Jr., and Martha Dodd, *Ambassador Dodd's Diary, 1933–1938*, with an introduction by Charles A. Beard, New York, 1941
Doenitz, Karl, *Zehn Jahre und Zwanzig Tage*, Bonn, 1958
Domvile, Admiral Barry, *From Admiral to Cabin Boy*, London, 1946

Douerlein, Peter, *Inside North Pole*, London, 1953

Duchess of Windsor, *The Heart Has its Reason*, London, 1956

Duke of Windsor, *A King's Story*, London, 1954

Eppler, J.W., *Rommel ruft Kairo. Aus dem Tagebuch eines Spions*, Guetersloh, 1959

Garby-Czerniawski, Roman, *The Big Network*, London, 1962

Geyr von Schweppenburg, Colonel, *Erinnerungen eines Militaerattaches, London 1933–1937*, Stuttgart, 1949

Gimpel, Erich, *Spion fuer Deutschland*, Munich, 1956

Giskes, H.J., *Spione ueberspielen Spione*, Hamburg, 1949

Gisevius, H.B., *Bis zum bitteren Ende*, 2 vols., Zurich, 1946–47

Goebbels, Josef P., *The Goebbels Diaries, 1942–1943*, ed. by Louis P. Lochner, Washington, D.C., 1948

Goerlitz, W. (ed.), *The Memoirs of Field Marshal Keitel*, translated by David Irving, New York, 1966

Goertz, Hermann, "My Story," in *Irish Times*, August 25 to September 10, 1947

Hayes, Carlton J.H., *Mission to Spain*, New York, 1946

Halder, General Franz, *Kriegstagebuch*, 3 vols., ed. by Hans-Adolf Jacobsen in collaboration with Alfred Philippi, Stuttgart, 1962–63

Hedin, Sven, *Utan uppdrag i Berlin*, Stockholm, 1953

Herslow, C., *Moskva-Berlin-Warszawa*, Stockholm, 1946

Hoare, Sir Samuel, *The Fourth Seal*,

Hoare, Sir Samuel (Lord Templewood), *Ambassador on Special Mission*, London, 1946

Hossbach, Friedrich von, *Zwischen Wehrmacht und Hitler, 1934–1938*, Wolfenbuettel, 1949

Hunt, Sir David, *A Don at War*, London, 1966

Ickes, Harold L., *Secret Diaries*, 1953

Ismay, J.L., *Memoirs of General Lord Ismay*, London, 1960

James, C., *I Was Monty's Double*, London, 1954

Kersten, Feliks, *Memoirs*, London, 1956

King, Cecil, *With Malice Toward None*, London, 1970

Knatchbull-Hugessen, Sir Hughe, *Diplomat in Peace and War*, London, 1949

Koller, Karl, *Der letzte Monat*, Mannheim, 1949

Krivitsky, Walter G., *In Stalin's Secret Service*, New York, 1940

Leahy, William D., *I Was There*, New York, 1950

Leonhard, Jakob, *Als Gestapo-Agent im Dienste der schweizerischen Gegenspionage*, Zurich, 1945

Lincoln, I.T.T. (pseud. of Ignatius Trebitsch), *Revelations of an International Spy*, New York, 1916

Lindbergh, Charles A., *The Wartime Journals of Charles A. Lindbergh*, New York, 1970

Loeff, Wolfgang, *Spionage. Aus den Papieren eines Abwehr-Offiziers*, Stuttgart, 1950

Macmillan, Harold, *Winds of Change, 1914–1939*, London, 1966

Macmillan, Harold, *The Blast of War, 1939–1945*, London, 1968

Maskelyne, J., *Magic—Top Secret*, London, 1949
Maschwitz, Eric, *No Chip on My Shoulder*, London, 1957
Moyzisch, Ludwig C., *Operation Cicero*, London, 1950
Noske, Gustav, *Von Kiel bis Kapp*, Berlin, 1920
Murphy, Robert, *Diplomat Among Warriors*, London, 1964
Papen, Franz von, *Der Wahrheit eine Gasse*, Munich, 1952
Philby, H.A.R. (Kim), *My Silent War*, London, 1968
Raeder, Erich, *Mein Leben*, 2 vols., Tuebingen, 1957
Ropp, William de, "His Own Story," in *Daily Mail* (London), October 28, 29, 30, 31, 1957
Sansom, A.W., *I Spied Spies*, London, 1965
Sas, H.I., "Het begon in Mei 1940," in *De Spiegel*, Oct. 7, 1953, pp. 22–25; October 14, 1953, pp. 16–18, fragments
Schmidt, Paul Otto, *Statist auf diplomatischer Boehne, 1923–1945*, Bonn, 1949
Schultze-Holthus, N., *Fruehrot in Iran. Abenteur im deutschen Geheimdienst*, Esslingen, 1952
Serano Suñer, Ramon, *Zwischen Hendaye und Gibraltar*, Zurich, 1958
Sergueiev, Lily, *Seul face à l'Abwehr*, Paris, 1966
Silber, Jules Crawford, *The Invisible Weapon*, New York, 1926
Skorzeny, Otto, *Geheimkommando Skorzeny*, Hamburg, 1950
Speer, Albert, *Erinnerungen*, Berlin, 1969
Strong, Sir Kenneth, *Intelligence at the Top. The Recollections of an Intelligence Officer*, London, 1968
Sulzberger, Cyrus L., *A Long Row of Candles. Memoirs and Diaries, 1934–1954*, London, 1969
Warlimont, Walter, *Im Hauptquartier der deutschen Wehrmacht, 1939–1944*, Frankfurt, 1964
Wedemeyer, Albert C., *Wedemeyer Reports!* New York, 1958
Wheeler, Burton K., *Yankee from the West*, with Paul F. Healy, New York, 1962
Whitwell, John (pseud. of Leslie Arthur Nicholson), *British Agent*, London, 1967
Winterbotham, Frederick W., *Secret and Personal*, London, 1969
Zacharias, Ellis M., *Secret Missions*, New York, 1946

BOOKS AND ARTICLES

Abshagen, Karl Heinz, *Canaris, Patriot und Weltbuerger*, Stuttgart, 1949
Accoce, Pierre, and Pierre Quet, *La guerre a eté gagne en Suisse*, Paris, 1966
Alexandrov, Victor, *The Tukchachevsky Affair*, Englewood Cliffs, N.J., 1964
Altmann, L. "Zur Psychologie des Spions," in *Die Weltkriegsspionage*, q.v. under Lettow-Vorbeck
Amort, C., and I.M. Jedlicka, *On l'appelait A-54*, Paris, 1966
Assmann, Kurt, *The Invasion of Norway*, Annapolis, Md., 1952

Astley, Joan Bright, *The Inner Circle. A View of the War at the Top*, London, 1971

Aswell, Edward C., "The case of the Ten Nazi Spies: How they worked— How the FBI caught them," *Harper's*, 1942 (June) pp. 1–21.

Bamler, Rudolf, "Der deutsche militaerische Geheimdienst und die Durch- fuehrung des zweiten Weltkrieges," in *Der zweite Weltkrieg*, Berlin, 1959

Bardanne, J., *Le colonel Nicolai, espion de génie*, Paris, 1947

Bartz, Karl, *Die Tragoedie der deutschen Abwehr*, Salzburg, 1955

Bauer, F. "Das Recht auf Widerstand und General Oster," in *Freiheit und Recht*, 1963 (July)

Baum, Walter, "Marine, Nationalsozialismus und Widerstand," in *Viertel- jahreshefte fuer Zeitgeschichte*, v. 11 (1963), pp. 16–48

Bechhofer-Roberts, C.E., *The Trial of William Joyce*, in The Old Bailey Trial Series, London, 1951

Bell, L., *Sabotage*, London, 1957

Benoist-Mechin, J., *Geschichte der deutschen Militaermacht, 1918–1946*, 10 vols., Oldenburg, 1965

Bergh, H. von, *ABC der Spione*, Pfaffenhofen, 1965

Bergier, J., *Agents secrets contre armes secretes*, Paris, 1955

Berthold, Will, *Brandenburger Division*, translated by Alan Neame, Lon- don, 1961

Bismarck, B.V., "Der Militaerattache im Nachrichtendienst, in *Die Welt- kriegsspionage, q.v.*, pp. 104–110

Blackstock, Paul W., *The Strategy of Subversion. Manipulating the Politics of Other Nations*, Chicago, 1964

Blackstock, Paul W., *Agents of Deceit. Frauds, Forgeries and Political In- trigue Among Nations*, Chicago, 1966

Blake, J. W., *Northern Ireland at War*, London, 1956

Bloch-Morhange, Jacques, *Les fabricants de guerre*, Paris, 1950, includes Canaris

Boldt-Christmas, G.E.F., *Voro vi neutrala*, Stockholm, 1946

Bondy, Louis T., *Racketeers of Hatred*, London, 1948

Boveri, Margaret, *Der Verrat im 20. Jahrhundert*, 2 vols., Hamburg, 1956, 1957

Brown Book of the Hitler Terror, New York, 1935

Brown Network. The Activities of the Nazis in Foreign Countries, with an introduction by the Earl of Listowel, New York, 1936

Bryans, J.L., *Secret Communications*, London, 1951

Buchheit, G., *Ludwig Beck, ein preussischer General*, Muenchen, 1964

Buchheit, G., *Der deutsche Geheimdienst. Geschichte der militaerischen Abwehr*, Muenchen, 1966

Buchheit, G., *Die anonyme Macht. Aufgaben, Methoden, Erfahrungen der Geheimdienste*, Frankfurt, 1969

Bucklay, C., *Norway. The Commandos. Dieppe*, London, 1951

Bulloch, John, *M.I.5. The Origin and History of the British Counter- Espionage Service*, London, 1963

Bulloch, John, *Akin to Treason*, London, 1966

Bullock, Allan, *Hitler. A Study in Tyranny*, London, 1954
Busch, Tristan (pseud. of Arthur Schuetz), *Entlarvter Geheimdienst*, Zurich, 1946
Burdick, Charles B., *Germany's Military Strategy and Spain in World War II*, Syracuse, N.Y., 1968
Carell, Paul (pseud. of Paul Schmidt), *Invasion: They are Coming*, translated by E. Osers, London, 1963
Carlson, John Roy, *Under Cover. My Four Years in the Nazi Underworld of America*, New York, 1943
Carlson, John Roy, *The Plotters*, New York, 1946
Carsten, F.L., *The Reichswehr and Politics, 1918 to 1933*, Oxford, 1966
Castellan, G., *Le rearmement clandestin du Reich 1930–1935, vu par le 2e Bureau de l'Etat major français*, Paris, 1954
Chester, Lewis, with Stephen Fay and Hugo Young, *The Zinoviev Letter. A Political Intrigue*, London, 1967
Chesterton, A.K., *Oswald Mosley. Portrait of a Leader*, London, 1936
Cippico, Aldo, *Diopunisca Anna Tobruk. La guerra dei agento segreto*, Rome, 1947
Cole, J.A., *Lord Haw-Haw & William Joyce*, London, 1964
Collins, F.L., *The FBI in Peace and War*, New York, 1940
Colvin, Ian, "The Hendaye Tapestry," in *The National and English Review*, vol. 135 (1950), June
Colvin, Ian, *Chief of Intelligence*, London, 1951
Colvin, Ian, *The Unknown Courier*, London, 1953
Colvin, Ian, *Vansittart in Office*, London, 1965
Cookridge, E.H., *Secrets of the British Secret Service*, London, 1948
Cookridge, E.H., *Inside S.O.E.*, London, 1966
Cookridge, E.H., *The Third Man. The Full Story of Kim Philby*, London, 1968
Cooper, Alfred Duff, *Operation Heartbreak*, New York, 1951, a fictionalized account of "Operation Mincemeat," see Ewen Montagu below
Crankshaw, E., *The Gestapo*, London, 1953
Cross, Colin, *The Fascists in Britain*, London, 1961
Dahms, H.G., *Der spanische Buergerkrieg 1936–1939*, Tuebingen, 1962
Dallin, David J., *Soviet Espionage*, New Haven, 1962
Davis, Kenneth S., *The Hero. Charles A. Lindbergh and the American Dream*, Garden City, N.Y., 1959
Deacon, Richard, *A History of the British Secret Service*, London, 1969
Deakin, F.W., *The Brutal Friendship*, London, 1964
Deakin, F.W., and G.R. Storry, *The Case of Richard Sorge*, London, 1966
Deindorfer, Robert G., *The Spies. An Anthology*, New York, 1969
Delarue, Jacques, *Histoire de la Gestapo*, Paris, 1962
Detwiler, Donald S., *Hitler, Franco und Gibraltar*, Wiesbaden, 1962
Deuerlein, Ernst (ed.), *Der Hitler-Putsch*, Stuttgart, 1962
Deutsch, Harold C., *The Conspiracy Against Hitler in the Twilight War*, Oxford, 1968
Donnevert, R. (ed.), *Wehrmacht und Partei*, Leipzig, 1938. The Canaris article is on pp. 44–57.

Dulles, A.W., *Germany's Underground*, New York, 1947

Dulles, A.W. (ed.), *Great True Spy Stories*, London, 1968

Ecke, H. (ed.), *Spying Still Goes On. Four Spies Speak*, with a foreword by Richard W. Rowan, New York, 1935

Edgar, J.H., and R.J. Armin, *Spionage in Deutschland*, Preetz, 1962

Elliott, Lawrence, "Hitler's undercover invasion of the United States," in *Secrets and Spies*, q.v., pp. 154–163

Erasmus, J., *Der geheime Nachrichtendienst*, Goettingen, 1952

Eyermann, K.-H., *Luftspionage*, 2 vols., Berlin, 1963

Fernandez Artucio, H., *The Nazi Octopus in South America*, London, 1943

Firmin, Stanley, *They Came to Spy*, London, 1946

Fleming, Peter, *Invasion 1940*, London, 1957

Flicke, W.F. *Spionagegruppe Rote Kapelle*, Kreuzlingen, 1953, fiction based on facts

Flicke, W.F., *Agenten Funken nach Moskau*, Kreuzlingen, 1954, fictionalized account of the Red Orchestra with solid documentation

Ford, Carey, with Alistair McBain, *Cloak and Dagger*, New York, 1948

Ford, Carey, *Donovan of OSS*, Boston, 1970

Foot, Alexander, *Handbook for Spies*, New York, 1950

Fraenkel, H., and R. Manvell, *Himmler. Kleinbuerger und Massenmoerder*, Berlin, 1965

Franklin, Charles, *The Great Spies*, London, 1967

Freund, Ludwig, *Politische Waffen. Grundkonzeption der westlichen Verteidigungsstrategie*, Frankfurt, 1966

Friedlaender, Saul, *Hitler et les Etas-Unis, 1939–1941*, Geneva, 1963

Furtwangler, F.J., "Admiral Canaris," in *Maenner, die ich sah und kannte*, Hamburg, 1951

Gauche, G., *Le deuxìeme Bureau au travail, 1935–1940*, Paris, 1954

Gedye, G.E.R., *Betrayal in Central Europe*, New York, 1939

George, W.D., *Surreptitious Entry*, New York, 1948

Gerson, L.D., *Schreider und die Spione*, Muenchen, 1950

Gilbert, Martin, and Richard Gott, *The Appeasers*, Boston, 1963

Giovannetti, A., *Der Vatikan und der Krieg*, Cologne, 1961

Gisevius, H.B., *Adolf Hitler. Versuch einer Deutung*, Muenchen, 1963

Goerlitz, Walter, *Der deutsche Generalstab*, Frankfurt, 1950

Goerlitz, Walter, *Der zweite Weltkrieg*, Stuttgart, 1951

Goerlitz, Walter, *Die Waffen-SS*, Berlin-Grunewald, 1960

Goerlitz, Walter, *Adolf Hitler*, Goettingen, 1960

Goldenberg, H., *"Das Wissen vom Gegner,"* *Soldatentum* (Berlin), 1938, pp. 259–263

Goodspeed, D.J., *The Conspirators. A Study of the Coup d'Etat*, London, 1962

Gordon, Harold J., *The Reichswehr and the German Republic 1919–1926*, Princeton, N.J., 1959

Goudsmit, S.A., *Alsos*, New York, 1947

Graml, Hermann, *"Die deutsche Militaeropposition vom Sommer 1950 bis zum Fruehjahr 1943,"* in *Vollmacht des Gewissens*, q.v., pp. 411–474

Graml, Hermann, *"Der Fall Oster,"* *Vierteljahreshefte fuer Zeitgeschichte*, vol. 14 (1966), no. 1

Greiner, Helmuth, *Die oberste Wehrmachtfuehrung, 1939–1943*, Wiesbaden, 1951

Groenberg, E. (pseud. of B. Smeds), *Jag van Gestapos agent*, Stockholm, 1944

Grote, H.H. von, *Vorsicht! Feind hoert mit! Eine Geschichte des Weltkriegs- und Nachriegsspionage*, Berlin, 1930

Gumbel, Emil, with B. Jacob, H. Lange, P. von Schreinech, *Deutschlands geheime Ruestungen*, Berlin, 1928

Gumbel, Emil J., *Vom Fememord zur Reichskanzlei*, Heidelberg, 1961

Hadley, Harold, "Adventures of a Diplomat," [George H. Earle, III], in Philadelphia *Daily News*, January 28, 29, 30, 31, 1963

Haestrup, J., *Kontakt med England*, Copenhagen, 1954

Hagen, Walter (pseud. of Dr. Wilhelm Hoettl), *Die geheime Front. Organisationen, Personen und Aktionen des deutschen Geheimdienstes*, Wien/Linz, 1950

Hagen, Walter, *Unternehmen Bernhard. Ein historischer Tatsachenbericht ueber die groesste Geldfaelschungsaktion aller Zeiten*, Wels, 1955

Halder, Franz, *Hitler als Feldherr*, Muenchen, 1949

Hall, J.W., *Trial of William Joyce*, London, 1954

Hartmann, Sverre, "*Kappellöp on Norgo,*" *Dagbladet* (Oslo), December 12, 14, 16, 19, 22, 1955

Havas, Laslo, *Hitler's Plot to Kill the Big Three*, translated by Kathleen Szasz, New York, 1969

Hegner, H.S. (pseud. Harry Wilde), *Die Reichskanzlei, 1933–1945*, Frankfurt, 1959

Heinz, E., "Spionageabwehr," in *Jahrbuch des deutschen Heeres*, Leipzig, 1938, pp. 120–127

Herbert, A., *The Allied Armistice with Italy*, Northampton, Mass., 1950

Herfeldt, O., *Schwarze Kapelle. Das grosse Funkspiel Vatikan-Berlin. Canaris-Heydrich*, Muenchen, no year

Hesse, Fritz, *Das Spiel um Deutschland*, Muenchen, 1953

Hibbert, C., *The Battle of Arnhem*, London, 1962

Historia secreta da guerra, 12 vols., Lisbon, 1949–1955

Hobatsch, W., *Die deutsche Besetzung von Daenemark und Norwegen, 1940*, Goettingen, 1952

Hoehne, Heinz, *Der Order unter dem Totenkopf. Die Geschichte des SS*, Hamburg, 1967

Hofer, W., *Die Entfesselung des zweiten Weltkrieges*, Frankfurt, 1960

Hollingworth, C., *The Three Weeks' War in Poland*, London, 1940

Hoover, John Edgar, "How the Nazi spy invasion was smashed," in *American* Magazine, vol. 138 (1944), September, pp. 20–21ff.

Hoover, John Edgar, "Hitler's Spying Sirens," *American* Magazine, vol. 138 (1944), December, pp. 40–41ff.

Hoover, John Edgar, "The Spy Who Double-Crossed Hitler," in *American* Magazine, vol. 141 (1946), May, pp. 23ff.

Hoover, John Edgar, "Enemy's Masterpiece of Espionage," in *Secrets and Spies*, q.v.

Horst, Cornelius van der, *Die Bendlerstrasse. Entscheidungen und Kampfe, 1918–1933*, Hamburg, 1958

Howarth, D., *The Dawn of D-Day*, London, 1959

Hutton, C., *Official Secret*, London, 1960

Hyde, H. Montgomery, *The Quiet Canadian*, London, 1962

Ingersoll, R., *Top Secret*, New York, 1946

Ind, Allison, *A Short History of Espionage*, London, 1963

Irwin, Will, and Thomas M. Johnson, *What You Should Know about Spies and Saboteurs*, New York, 1943

Johnson, E., and G. Almstedt, *Warszawa!*, Stockholm, 1944

Jones, E. "The psychology of Quislingism," in *International Journal of Psychoanalysis*, vol. 22 (1941), no. 1, pp. 1–6

Jones, John Price, and Paul Merrick Hollister, *The German Secret Service in America*, Boston, 1918

Jong, Louis de, *Holland Fights the Nazis*, London, 1942

Jong, Louis de, *Civil Resistance in the Netherlands*, Amsterdam, 1950

Jong, Louis de, *The German Fifth Column in the Second World War*, London, 1956

Jong, Louis de, *Het Koninkrijk der Nederlanden in de Tweede Wereldorloog*, 3 vols., The Hague, 1969–1970

Jowitt, Lord, *Some Were Spies*, London, 1954

Joyce, William, *Twilight Over England*, Berlin, 1940

Kahn, David, *The Codebreakers. The Story of Secret Writing*, London, 1968

Kaledin, Victor K., *The Moscow-Berlin Secret Service*, London, 1940

Karsai, Elek, *A budai Sándor Palotaban toertént*, Budapest, 1964

Kempner, R.M.W., "The highest paid spy in history," *Saturday Evening Post*, January 28, 1950

Kempner, R.M.W., *SS im Kreuzverhoer*, Frankfurt, 1964

Kern, Erich, *Verrat an Deutschland. Spione und Saboteure gegen das eigene Vaterland*, Goettinger, 1963

Kiel, H., *Canaris zweischen den Fronten*, Bremerhaven, 1950

Kimche, Jon, *Spying for Peace. General Guisan and Swiss Neutrality*, New York, 1941

Klein, Alexander, *The Counterfeit Traitor*, London, 1958

Knight, Mary, "The Secret War of Censors vs. Spies," in *Secrets and Spies*, pp. 259–263

Koehler, H., *Inside the Gestapo*, New York, 1950

Koop, Theodore, *Weapon of Silence*, Chicago, 1946

Kordt, Erich, *Wahn und Wirklichkeit*, Stuttgart, 1947

Kordt, Erich, *Nicht aus den Akten*, Stuttgart, 1950

Kotze, H. von., *"Hitler's Sicherheitsdienst im Ausland,"* in *Polit. Meinung*, vol. 8 (1963), no. 86

Krausnick, Helmut, *"Vorgeschichte und Beginn des militaerischen Widerstandes gegen Hitler,"* in *Vollmacht des Gewissens*, 2 vols., Frankfurt, 1960, vol. 1, pp. 177–384

Krausnick, Helmut, and Hermann Graml, *"Der deutsche Widerstand und die Alliierten,"* ibid., pp. 475–521

Kremer, J.V., *Le livre noir de l'espionnage*, Paris, 1954

Kriegsheim, Hans, *Getarnt, getaeuscht und doch getreu. Die geheimnisvollen Brandenburger*, Berlin, 1958

Langer, William L., and S. Everett Gleason, *The World Crisis and American Foreign Policy. The Challenge to Isolation, 1937–1940*, New York, 1952

Langer, William L., and S. Everett Gleason, *The Undeclared War, 1940–1941*, London, 1953

Lampe, David, *The Last Ditch*, London, 1968

Landau, H., *All's Fair*, New York, 1934

Lasswell, Harold D., "Policy and the Intelligence Function," in *The Analysis of Political Behavior* (New York), 1947, pp. 120–131

Laurens, Anne, *The Lindemans Affair*, London, 1969

Leasor, James, and Sir Leslie Hollis, *War at the Top*, London, 1959

Lettow-Vorbeck, Paul von, *Die Weltkriegsspionage*, Berlin, 1931

Leverkuehn, Paul, *Der geheime Nachrichtendienst der deutschen Wehrmacht im Kriege*, Frankfurt, 1960

Liddell Hart, Sir Basil H., *The Other Side of the Hill. Germany's Generals*, London, 1951

Liddell Hart, Sir Basil H., *Memoirs*, 2 vols., London, 1965

Lisager, Peter, and Marguerite Higgins, *Overtime in Heaven*, Garden City, N.Y., 1964

Liston, Robert, *The Dangerous World of Spies and Spying*, New York, 1967

Lockhart, Bruce R.H., *Friends, Foes and Foreigners*, London, 1947

Lockhart, Bruce R.H., *Comes the Reckoning*, London, 1957

Lossberg, Bernhard von, *Im Wehrmachtfuehrungsstab*, Hamburg, 1950

Lovell, Stanley P., *Of Spies and Strategems*, Englewood Cliffs, N.J., 1963

Lowell, J.R. (pseud. of Jan & Robert Lowell), *The Irish Game*, Englewood Cliffs, N.J., 1967

Lowenthal, Max, *The Federal Bureau of Investigation*, New York, 1950

Lusar, Rudolf, *Die deutschen Waffen und Geheimwaffen des 2. Weltkrieges und ihre Weiterentwicklung*, Muenchen, 1964

Lysing, H., *Men Against Crime*, New York, 1938

MacLeod, Ian, *Neville Chamberlain*, London, 1961

McLachlan, Donald, *Room 39. A Study in Naval Intelligence*, London, 1968

McNally, G.J., with Frederick Sondern, Jr., "The great Nazi counterfeit plot," in *Secrets and Spies*, q.v., pp. 507–14

Martens, A., *The Silent War*, London, 1961

Marwede, Friedrich Carl, "*Die Wahrheit ueber Canaris*," in *Weser Kurier*, December 6, 7, 8, 1949

Masur, Norbert, *En Jude talar med Himmler*, Stockholm, 1945

Mau, H., "*Die 'zweite' Revolution*," in *Vierteljahreshefte fuer Zeitgeschichte*, vol. 1 (1953)

Maugham, W. Somerset, *Ashenden or the British Agent*, London, 1927

Meissner, Hans Otto, and Harry Wilde, *Die Machtergreifung. Ein Bericht ueber die Technik des nationalsozialistischen Staatsstreichs*, Stuttgart, 1958

Melnikov, Daniel E., and Ludmilla B. Chernaya, *Dwulikij Admiral*, Moscow, 1965

Mendelssohn, Peter de, *Die nuernberger Dokumente*, Hamburg, 1947

Mennevee, R., *L'espionnage international en temps de paix*, Paris, 1929

Merkel, H., *"Ein Admiral kaempft fuer Frieden und Menschlichkeit,"* in *Marine Rundschau*, 1965 (December), vol. 62, pp. 170–176

Merkes, M., *"Die deutsche Politik gegenueber dem spanischen Buerger-krieg, 1936–1939,"* in *Bonner Historische Forschungen*, 1961

Miksche, F., *Secret Forces*, London, 1950

Mikusch, D. von, *Wassmuss, der deutsche Lawrence*, Leipzig, 1937

Minney, R.J., *No. 10 Downing Street*, London, 1963

Mullaly, Frederic, *Fascism Inside Britain*, London, 1946

Muellern, G., *Det har inte statt i tidningarna*, Stockholm, 1942

Muellern, H., *"Sveriges järnmalm och de Krigförandes planer, 1939–1940,"* in *Aktuellt och historisk*, 1953, pp. 81–112

Montagu, Ewen, *The Man Who Never Was*, London, 1953

Mosley, Leonard, *On Borrowed Time*, London, 1969

Moylan, Sir J., *Scotland Yard*, London, 1953

Munthe, M., *Sweet is War*, London, 1954

Newman, Al, "Britain's pet spy," *Newsweek*, May 28, 1945

Nicolai, Walter, *Geheime Maechte*, Berlin, 1921

Nicolai, Walter, *Nachrichtendienst, Presse und Volksstimmung*, Berlin 1920

Norman, Albert, *Operation Overlord*, Harrisburg, Pa., 1952

Nowinski, M.M., "Behind Poland's defeat," *American Mercury*, v. 49 (1940), April, pp. 400–404

Observer (pseud. of Dr. Will Grosse), *"Geheimdienst, Fahneneid and Hakenkreuz. Ein kritischer Tatsachenbericht aus der Taetigkeit der militaerischen Abwehr,"* in *Echo der Wiche*, passim, 1950

O'Callaghan, S., *Jackboot in Ireland*, London, 1958

O'Neill, Robert J., *The German Army and the Nazi Party, 1933–1939*, London, 1966

Orb, H., *"Die deutsche Spionage,"* in *Dreizehn Jahre Machtrausch*, Olten, 1945

O'Reilly, John, "I was a spy in Ireland," in *Sunday Dispatch* (London), July–August, 1952

Ott, K.A., *Der Mensch vor dem Standgericht*, Hamburg, 1948

Pawle, Gerald, *The Secret War*, 1939–1945, London, 1957

Peaslee, A., and Sir Reginald Hall, *Three Wars with Germany*, New York, 1944

Paetel, Karl O., *"Die SS. Ein Beitrag zur Sociologie des Nationalsozialis-mus,"* *Vierteljahreshefte fuer Zeitgeschichte*, 1954, no. 1

Page Bruce, with David Leitch and Philip Knightly, *The Philby Conspiracy*, London, 1968

Pearson, John, *The Life of Ian Fleming*, London, 1966

Pendar, K., *Adventure in Diplomacy*, New York, 1945

Perles, Alfred, *Great True Spy Adventures*, London, 1956

Perrault, Gilles, *Le secret du Jour J*, Paris, 1964

Perrault, Gilles, *L'orchestra rouge*, Paris, 1967

Piekalkiewicz, Janusz, *Spione, Agenten, Soldaten*, Muenchen, 1969

Pinter, I., *"Der Spionagechef. Wilhelm Hoettl, Leiter des Nacrichtendienstes in Ungarn, 1944,"* in *Unbestrafte Kriegsverbrecher*, Budapest, 1961, pp. 124–159
Pinto, Oreste, *Spy-catcher*, London, 1953
Pinto, Oreste, *Friend or Foe?* London, 1957
Pirie, A., *Operation Bernhard*, London, 1961
Pitt, Roxane, *The Courage of Fear*, London, 1957
Poelchau, H., *Die letzten Stunden*, Berlin, 1949
Posse, A., *Åtskilligt kan nu sägas*, Stockholm, 1949
Praun, Albert, *Soldat in der Telegraphen und Nachrichtentruppe*, Wuerzburg, 1966
Prothero, M., *The History of the C.I.D.*, London, 1934
Pruck, E., *"Der Abwehrchef. Versuch einer Entmythologisierung,"* in *Notweg*, 1954, no. 7
Pruck, E., *"Abwehraussenstelle Norwegen,"* in *Marine Rundschau*, vol. 53, no. 4, pp. 107ff.
Rachlis, Eugene, *They Came to Kill*, London, 1962
Rauschning, Hermann, *Die Revolution des Nihilismus*, Zurich, 1937
Reile, Oscar, *Geheime Ostfront*, Muenchen/Wels, 1962
Reile, Oscar, *Geheime Westfront*, Muenchen/Wels, 1963
Reitlinger, Gerald, *The SS. Alibi of a Nation*, London, 1956
Ribbentrop, Joachim von, *Memoirs*, London, 1954
Ridder, H.K.J., *Der Fall William Joyce*, Tuebingen, 1952
Riess, Curt, *Total Espionage*, New York, 1939
Riess, Curt, *"Das Geheimnis des Admirals,"* in *Die Weltwoche*, June 22–September 31, 1951
Rintelen, Enno von, *Mussolini als Bundesgenosse*, Tuebingen/Stuttgart, 1951
Rintelen, Franz von, *The Dark Invader*, New York, 1931
Rivet, L. *L'enigme de service renseignements allemand sous le regime hitlerien*, Paris, 1947
Robertson, E.M., *Hitler's Pre-War Policy and Military Plans, 1933–1939*, New York, 1967
Robertson, Terence, *Dieppe. The Shame and the Glory*, London, 1963
Roeseler, J., *"Die deutschen Plaene fuer eine Landung in England und die Luftschlacht um England in der Literatur,"* in *Jahresbibliographie*
Ronge, Maximilian, *Kriegs und Industriespionage*, Zurich, 1930
Roskill, S.W., *The Secret Capture*, London, 1959
Ross, Colin, *Unser Amerika*, Berlin, 1933
Rothfels, Hans, *"Die deutsche Opposition gegen Hitler,"* in *Fischer Buecherei* (revised edition), Frankfurt, 1969
Rowan, Richard W., *Terror in Our Time. The Secret Service of Surprise Attack*, New York, 1941
Rowan, Richard W., *Spy Secrets*, New York, 1946
Rowan, Richard W., and Robert G. Deindorfer, *The Story of Secret Service*, London, 1969
Rudlin, W.A., *The Growth of Fascism Inside Great Britain*, London, 1935
Rutledge, Brett, *The Death of Lord Haw-Haw*, New York, 1940

Ryan, Cornelius, *The Longest Day*, London, 1954

Sayers, M., and A.E. Kahn, *Sabotage*, New York, 1942

Schmid, Peter, "Admiral Canaris," in *Die Weltwoche* (Zurich), March 1, 1946

Schnabel, Reimund, *Macht ohne Moral*, Frankfurt, 1957

Schramm, Percy Ernst, *Hitler als militaerischer Fuehrer*, Frankfurt, 1962

Schramm, Wilhelm Ritter von, *Verrat im zweiten Weltkrieg. Kampf und Doppelspiel europaeischer Geheimdienste*, Duesseldorf, 1967

Schreider, Josef, *Das war das Englandspiel*, Muenchen, 1950

Schwarzwalder, John, *We Caught Spies*, New York, 1946

Seabury, Paul, *The Wilhelmstrasse. A Study of German Diplomats under the Nazi Regime*, Berkeley, Cal., 1954

Secrets and Spies. Behind-the-Scenes Stories of World War II, Pleasantville, N.Y., 1964

Seid, Alfred, "*Der englische Geheimdienst,*" in *Schriften des Deutschen Instituts fuer Aussenpolitische Forschung*, Berlin, 1940, no. 23

Sendtner, Kurt, "*Die deutsche Militaeropposition im ersten Kriegsjahr,*" in *Vollmacht des Gewissens*, q.v., pp. 385–532

Seraphim, H.G., " '*Felix*' und '*Isabella*,' " in *Die Welt als Geschichte*, Stuttgart, 1955, vol. 15

Seth, R., *Anatomy of Spying*, London, 1961

Seth, R., *The Undaunted. The Story of Resistance in Western Europe*, London, 1958

Sherwood, Robert, *Roosevelt and Hopkins*, New York, 1948

Shirer, William, *Rise and Fall of the Third Reich*, London, 1960

Shirer, William, *A Berlin Diary*, New York, 1940

Singer, Kurt, *Three-Thousand Years of Espionage*, London, 1948

Singer, Kurt, *Spies and Traitors*, Englewood Cliffs, N.J., 1948

Skodvin, M. "German and British-French Plans for Operations in Scandinavia," in *The Norseman*, London, 1951, vol. IX

Snow, John Howland, *The Case of Tyler Kent*, New York/Chicago, 1946

Soltikov, Michael, *Die Katze*, Hamburg, 1956

Speier, Hans, and Dr. Ernst Kris, *German Radio Propaganda*, New York, 1942

Speidel, Hans, *Invasion 1944*, Hamburg, 1949

Stacey, C.P., *The Canadian Army*, Ottawa, 1946

Stade, A. "*9 April 1040—och huruledes de allierada 'missade bussen' til Norge,*" in *Vår försvar*, 1953, no. 4, pp. 36–44

Stephen, Enno, *Geheimauftrag Irland. Deutsche Agenten im irischen Untergroundkampf 1939–1945*, Hamburg, 1961

Stowe, Leland, *Conquest by Terror*, New York, 1952

Stroebinger, R., *A.84. Spion mit drei Gesichtern*, Muenchen, 1966

Strong, Sir Kenneth, *Men of Intelligence. A Study of the Roles and Decisions of Chiefs of Intelligence from World War I to the Present Day*, London, 1970

Stuart, Francis, "Frank Ryan in Germany," in *The Bell* (Dublin), 1950, November

Sweet-Escott, B., *Baker Street Irregular*, London, 1965
Terkelsen, T.M., *Frontline in Denmark*, London, 1944
Thomas, Hugh, *The Spanish Civil War*, London, 1961
Thompson, Laurence, *1940. The Year of Britain's Supreme Agony*, London, 1966
Thompson, R.W., *D-Day. Spearhead of Invasion, with an introduction by Sir Basil Liddell Hart*, London, 1968
Thomson, Sir Basil, *My Experiences at Scotland Yard*, London, 1923
Thomson, G.P., *Blue Pencil Admiral*, London, 1947
Thorwald, Juergen, *Die ungeklaerten Faelle*, Stuttgart, 1950
Thorwald, Juergen, *Der Fall Pastorius*, Stuttgart, 1953
Thorwald, Juergen, *"Die unsichtbare Front,"* Stern (Hamburg), 1953
Toland, John, *The Last 100 Days*, London, 1968
Tompkins, D.C., *Sabotage*, Berkeley, Cal., 1961
Tompkins, Peter, *A Spy in Rome*, New York, 1962
Tompkins, Peter, *Italy Betrayed*, New York, 1966
Trevor-Roper, H.R., *The Last Days of Hitler*, London, 1947
Trevor-Roper, H.R., *The Philby Affair. Espionage, Treason and Secret Services*, London, 1968
Tuchman, Barbara W., *The Zimmermann Telegram*, London, 1959
Turrou, Leon G., *Nazi Spies in America*, New York, 1938
Valtin, Jan (pseud. of Heinrich Krebs), *Out of the Night*, New York, 1941
Van t'Hof, S.P., *Investigations as to the Military Resistance in the Netherlands*, Amsterdam, 1950
Vogelsang, Thilo, *Kurt von Schleicher. Ein General als Politiker*, Goettingen, 1965
Vollmacht des Gewissens, 2 vols., Frankfurt, 1960
Walker, David E., *Lunch with a Stranger*, London, 1957
Wall, Carl B., "The hunt for a spy," *The American Legion Magazine*, 1945
Weisenborn, G., *Der lautlose Aufstand*, Hamburg, 1953
Weizsaecker, Ernst von, *Erinnerungen*, Muenchen, 1950
West, Rebecca, *The New Meaning of Treason*, London, 1965
Whalen, Richard J., *The Founding Father. The Story of Joseph P. Kennedy*, London, 1965
Wheatley, Ronald. *German Plans for the Invasion of England, 1939–1942*, Oxford, 1958
Wheeler-Bennett, John, *Nemesis of Power. The German Army in Politics*, London, 1964
White, J.B., *The Big Lie*, London, 1956
White, L., *The Long Balkan Nights*, New York, 1944
Whitehead, Don, *The FBI Story. A Report to the People*, London, 1957
Wiedemann, Fritz, *Der Mann der Feldherr werden wollte*, Kettnig/Velbert, 1964
Wighton, C., with Guenther Peis, *Hitler's Spies and Saboteurs*, London, 1958
Wighton, C., *Pin-striped Saboteurs*, London, 1959
Willoughby, C.A., *Shanghai Conspiracy*, New York, 1952

Wucher, A., *Seit 5 Uhr 45 wird zurueckgeschossen. Ein Dokumentarbericht ueber den Beginn des zweiten Weltkrieges*, Muenchen, 1959
Wulf, Josef, *Heinrich Himmler*, Berlin-Grunewald, 1967
Young, Gordon, *The Cat with Two Faces*, London, 1958
Zipfel, Friedrich, *Gestapo und Sicherheitsdienst*, Berlin-Grunewald, 1968

Index

Abshagen, Heinz, 433
Abwehr, xvii
Abwehr:
  abandons Irish project, 228
  agents
    among British counterspies, 195
    awarded Iron Cross, 260
    blackmail of, 225
    capture of, 12, 64, 66, 183, 455–456, 461
    compromised, 100, 246
    counterespionage, 100
    couriers, 21, 28
    in diplomatic outposts, 414
    double, 85
    escape English dragnet, 173, 212
    execution of, 176
    fate of, 266, 284–285
    Irish for Germany, 193, 224
    lavish treatment of, 157, 258
    male prostitutes, 415
    obscurity of, 143
    pay of, 33, 48, 265, 300, 503
    personality types, 286
    recruiting of, 22, 32, 33, 46, 56, 77, 132, 137–141, 154, 221, 238, 256
    training of, 239, 302
    in U.S., 15, 20, 234, 312, 321
    in wartime England, 281–289
  alliance with Italian secret service, 12
  anti-sabotage experts, 202
  archives, captured, 53
  Branch IIIF, xx
  backs Franco, 513
  borrows U.S. dollars from Italians, 308
  Canaris named chief, 4
  chiefs of, xx, 24
  "Code Book," 406

and collaboration with Foreign Ministry, 10
communications, 10, 149
communications
  during Norway invasion, 209
counterespionage group, 10
couriers, 32, 46, 293, 313, 316
covers U.S., 448
crushed in U.S., 457
cryptosystem, 198
deceived by British double agents, 271
demolition of, 640
DK-group, 143
efficiency of, 598
employs Falangists, 515
in England, 15, 284
enlarges operations in Britain, 284
Enigma machine, 523
expanded by Canaris, 11
extent of, 164, 513
fails to detect North Africa invasion, 560
front organizations, 152
funds, 17–18, 441
Group I, 10
Hamburg branch, 40
Hauskappelle, 102
headquarters, xix
infiltrated by MI.5, 519
information on Scapa Flow, 190
intelligence from Texaco, 409
internal discord, 60
interrogators, 145
invasion plans for England, 236, 238
invades Poland, 167
and I.R.A., 221
Iraqui personnel, 231
Irish project, 224

Abwehr (*continued*)
 in Istanbul, 571
 kidnapping of German emigrés, 294
 lack of funds in Latin America, 308
 learns U.S. intention to join war, 390–391
 mail drops, 137, 182, 251
 M-branch, 143
 MI.5 double-agents, 227
 moves American base to Mexico, 305
 and Norway invasion, 207
 opens teahouse in London, 253
 "Operation Lena," 237
 operations
  begin in England, 72
  compromised in U.S., 65
  diminish in England, 196
  in Norway, 206
  organization of, 136
 overlooks 104 U.S. ships, 557
 penetrates S.I.S. in The Hague, 112
 "penetration," 255
 plan to disable Panama Canal, 51–54
 prepares for war, 141
 "Project No. 14," 53
 propaganda, 10
 radio transmitters in U.S., 317, 318
 reconnaissance in Spain, 559
 rendezvous at sea, 216
 revived by Canaris, 9
 in Rhineland, 90
 rivalry with RSHA, 4
 Roosevelt-Pell letters, 421
 sabotage, 10, 282, 432
 Section IIIF, 102
 setback in U.S., 58
 sets spy trap, 127
 shake-up by Canaris, 66
 smashed in Istanbul, 580
 smashes anti-Nazi plot, 123
 smuggles oil from Mexico, 307
 soldiers in stolen uniforms, 196
 in Spain, 449
 specious reports, 334
 "special operation" in U.S., 293
 spies on RAF installations, 74–76
 spying within, 102
 spy-routes, 234
 in Stockholm, 526
 super-spy, 259
 supplies Luftwaffe with aviation secrets, 39
 tactical spies, 234
 transmission of information, 32
 troubles in Mexico, 309
 in U.S., 293–303
 use of wireless, 160
 wartime surveillance, 172

Abwehrabteilung, *see* Abwehr
Abwehr II, 220, 433
 Irish desk, 193
 sabotage and sedition, 193
Abwehr III (counterespionage), 309
Adams, Donald O.R., 134
Admiral Graf Spee, 498, 499
A.G. Hillermann, Ltd., 153
Air Fleet II, 191
Alba, Duke of, 514
Aldrich, Bob, 302
Aldridge, Winthrop, 336
Allen, Charles B., 480
Allied war plans, 599
Almásay, László de, 540
Aluminum Co., of America, 433
Ambrosio, Vittorio, 584
Amé, Cesare, 584
America First Committee, 394
American:
 businessmen dealing with Germany on eve of war, 399
 diplomatic spies, 424
American Legion, 454
American Legion (U.S. Army transport ship), 500
American Office of Naval Intelligence, xviii
American Ordnance Association, 495, 499
Anderson, Sir John, 589
Angot, Pierre, 202
Anti-Nazi plot, 123
Anti-Semitic organizations, 130
Anti-Semitism, 338, 341, 453
Antwerp, capture of by Germans, 214
Armstrong, George, 283
Asmann, Max, 229
Astor, Dr. Richard, 435
Astor, Lady, 77
Atlantic Monthly, The, 487
Auenrode, Majon von, 513
Azevado, Gonzales de, 506

Badoglio, Pietro 582
Baillie-Stewart, Norman, 72
Baldwin, Stanley, 94
Balluseck, Hanna von, 142
Bamler, Rudolf, 9
Barber Asphalt Co., 412
Barclay's Bank (London), 11
Barth, Fritiof von, 525
Barth, Theodore H., 38
Bartlett, Captain, 82
Barton, Raymond O., 630
Barzini, Luigi Jr., 341
Bastian, Rear Admiral, 3
Bath Iron Works, 22

Battle of Britain, 268
Battle of France, 196, 345, 602
Bausch & Lomb, 437
Baxter, Angus, 131
Bazna, Elyesa, 415
Beach, William H., 414
Becker, Siegfried, 469
Beck, Ludwig, 88, 89
Bedford, 12th Duke of, 77
Behn, Colonel, 403
Beigbeder y Atienza, Juan, 514
Bell Telephone System, 586
Bennecke, Major, 205
Bensmann, Nikolaus, 333, 404, 495, 504,
    586
  coded mail, 407
  establishes transatlantic telephone link,
    408
Bentivegni, Colonel, 309
Benton, Kenneth, 279, 516
Berg, Jack, 281–282, 287
Bergmann, Julius, 431
Berle, Adolf A. Jr., 352, 356
Bernadotte, Count Folke, 536
Bertil, Prince, 550
Best, Payton Sigismund, 104
  establishes contact with ani-Nazi un-
    derground, 123
  kidnapped, 127
Bevins, John, 176, 614
Bibra, Herbert von, 611
Biddle, Anthony Drexel, 417
Birchall, Frederick T., 25
Bird Man of Morro Castle, 505
Bishcoff, Johannes, 136, 236, 495, 500,
    504
Bischoff & Company, 136
Bismarck, Prince Otto von, 97
Black Luftwaffe, 16
Blackmail, 225, 323
Blakeney, R.G.D., 77
Blancke, W. Wendell, 485
Blaum, Wolfgang, 52, 65–66, 435
Bleicher, Hugo, 618
Blitzkrieg, 167
Block, Fritz, 139
Blomberg, Werner von, xviii, 88, 96
  against Rhineland invasion, 89
Blunt, Frederick, 195
Bocholtz, Countess, 101
Boeckel, Jules, 158, 237, 244
Boehmler, Lucy, 428
Boetticher, Friedrich von, 40, 332, 484,
    476–481
Bohemia:
  occupation of, by Germany, 157
Bonin, Udo von, 27, 35, 143, 392
Borah, William, 200

Borchardt-Battuta, Paul Theodore, 428
Borchers, Heinrich Franz J., 485
Borchers, Johannes, 488
Bottrall, F.J. Ronald, 537
Boyle, Archibald R., 80, 176
Braak, Jan Villen Ter, 266, 283
Bradley, Omar N., 619
Brandy, R.L., 137
Brasser, Major, 162, 179, 212
Bredow, Ferdinand von, xviii
Bremen (steamship), 32, 41
Brewster Aeronautical Co., 445
Bristol Aircraft Co., 82
Britain/British
  Abwehr operations diminish, 196
  censorship, 314
  currency blockade, 308
  declares war on Germany, 121
  failure in Norway, 212
  interns aliens, 172
  "invasion" of, by I.R.A., 220
  use of radar, 161
Britain, Battle of, 268
British Intelligence, *see* S.I.S., *also* Es-
    pionage, British
British Secret Intelligence Service, xviii,
    103
British Union of Fascists, 130, 159
Brockhof, Alfred E., 328
Broglie, Jacqueline de, 630, 636
Brooke, Sir Alan Francis, 642
Bruggmann, Dr. Charles, 346, 348
Brunner, Peter Ferdinand, 153
Brussels, capture of by Germans, 214
Budyenny, Nikolai Putiloff, 616
Buelow, Bernhard von, 97
Bullitt, William C., 338, 387, 417, 587
Bulloch, John, 186
Burghardt, Joachim, 40, 135
Busch, Georg, 437
Buss, K.C., 80
Butler, Nicholas Murray, 336
Byers, Mortimer W., 458

Calero, José, 309
Calvo, Luis, 516
Carbe, Albert, 560
Carstenn, Wilhelm, 562
Casablanca Conference, 566
Campbell, Sir Ronald Ian, 589
Canaris, Wilhelm Franz, xviii, xx, 3,
    434, 458, 479, 607, 608
  and compromise of Abwehr, 60
  Abwehr agents arrested in U.S., 461
  appointed chief of Abwehr, 4
  expands Abwehr, 11
  and Abwehr internal security, 102
  takes over Abwehr, 9

Canaris, Wilhelm Franz (*continued*)
  on Abwehr in U.S., 297
  accomplishments in U.S., 303–304
  assigned Operation Felix, 558
  circumvents Hitler's orders to assas-
    sinate generals, 434
  commands invasion of Gibraltar, 237
  complains to Keitel, 485
  confrontation with von Roenne, 615
  doubts about Nazi regime, 169
  in early days of war, 203
  early life, 5
  escapes from Italian jail, 6
  expands bases abroad, 512
  fear of Gestapo, 102
  fired, 609
  and Franco-Russian pact, 88
  and Goertz downfall, 100
  and Hitler, 87
  and Hitler
    on English spy ban, 76
  leads intelligence team to Gibraltar,
    558
  on massacre of Poles, 170
  memorandum on U.S. arrests, 461–463
  moves American base to Mexico, 305
  in Navy, 7
  and Norway invasion, 207
  Norwegian venture, 205
  opens operations in England, 73
  orders shake-up of Abwehr, 66
  orders tactical agents into England,
    236
  at outbreak of war, 164
  given instructions for Polish invasion,
    165
  after Polish invasion, 168
  prepares Abwehr for war, 141
  prepares for invasion of England, 230
  relations with Japanese secret service,
    564
  succeeded by Walter Schellenberg, 553
  surprised by war on U.S., 505
  told to avoid antagonizing U.S., 293
  Himmler turns against, 612
  in Weimar plot, 5, 7
  in Wilhelmshaven, 27
Cárdenas, Lázaro, 351
Carillo, Alejandro, 354
Caroli, Goesta, 257
  captured by MI.5, 261
  double-crosses Operation Double-Cross,
    264
  fate of, 266
Carol II (of Rumania), 202
Carranza, Venustiano, 306
Carré, Mathilde, 248, 618
Castija, Count Alexandre de, 632

Cavaillez, Jean Marie, 507
Central Intelligence Agency, 330
Chamberlain, Neville, 146
  "Twilight War," 200
  warns Hitler on Poland, 171
Chambers-Hunter, W.E.A., 131
Chapman, Eddie, 287
Chappell, Private, 241
Chemical warfare, 498
Chernov, Mikhail Alexandrovich, 301
Ciano, Count Galeazzo, 195, 211
Chicago Tribune, 483
Chidson, M.R., 109
Chief of Staff (Watson), 483
Childs, Marquis W., 368
Christian Front, 395
Churchill-Roosevelt letters, 338–339, 344
Churchill, Winston, 235, 614
  on fall of Norway, 212
  meets Roosevelt in Casablanca, 566
  proposes mining Norwegian waters, 203
  receives news of Mussolini's downfall,
    589
  supervises deception of Luftwaffe dur-
    ing Blitz, 270
  taunts Hitler for delaying invasion, 596
Clausen, Fritz, 249
Clissman, Howard, 193
Coastal Defenses of Great Britain, The,
  235
Coburg, Duke of, 93
Codd, L.A., 495
Code-breaking, 197
Coded mail, 407
Codes/code-breaking, 339, *see also* Cryp-
  tography
Colban, Eric Andreas, 204
Colepough, William Curtis, 447
Combatti, Calogero, 137
Condo, Duchess Montabelli di, 252
Continental Trading Company, 105
Controlled agents, 516
Cooke, W.E. Hinchley, 61, 75
Coope, William Edwin, 82
Corcoran, William, 522
Cornelius, S.E., 544
Coughlin, Father Charles E., 395
Counterespionage, 453, 546
  Abwehr agents, 100, 195
  British, 61
  MI.5, 177
  use of captured agents, 175
  U.S., 310
Courier(s):
  delay of, 316
  German, in U.S., 32
  service, via commercial steamship, 313
  ships, 137

Cowgill, Felix Henry, 197
Craig, Malin, 62
Cripps, Sir Stafford, 548
Crisis, Professor de, 127
Crusader Oil Co., 352
Cryptanalysts, 197
Cryptography, 11, 197
  Abwehr, 198
  code-breaking, 339
Cryptologists, 473
Cuddahy, John, 336
Currency blockage, 308
Curtiss Aircraft, 29
Czechoslovakia:
  signs pact with Soviet Union, 87

Daily Mail, 534
Dalton, Hugh Reginald, 105
  commits suicide, 108
Dalton, Joseph N., 30
Daly, Mrs., 225
d'Andrea, Carmine, 494
Danielsen, Christian F., 22
Danish Nazi Party, 249
Dansey, Claude, 103, 121
Dasch, Georg, 433
Dassel, Felix, 619
Davissen, Dr., 422
Davis, William Rhodes, 234, 351–365, 387
  alliance with Hertslet, 373
  authorized by Goering to negotiate with F.D.R., 362
  contributes to Democratic Party, 366
  death of, 388
  in German campaign to influence U.S. elections, 383
  misrepresents U.S. policy to Germans, 358–362
  plans to defeat F.D.R., 369
  supplies oil to Italy during sanctions, 359
Dearborn, R.J., 408, 411
Debowski, Wilhelm Georg, *see* Sebold
Degrelle, Leon, 201
Delmar, S. Anthony, 306
Denham, Henry Mangles, 212, 525, 526, 528
Denning, Norman, 525
Denniston, Alastair, 197
Denny, George Jr., 395
Deutsche Bank, the, 11
Deuxième Bureau (of France), xviii, 123
  sabotage specialists, 202
Dieckhoff, Hans Heinrich, 322, 349, 376, 611
Dierks, Hans, 237, 244, 255
Diesel Research Co., 325

Dies, Martin, 454
Dies Committee, 295
Diggins, Charles, 137
Dimrock, Marshal E., 370
Dobler, Herbert, 414, 455
Dodge, H.W., 408
Doenitz, Grand Admiral:
  on Canaris, 145
  memoirs, 189
  on Scapa Flow, 189–190
Dohnanyi, Hans von, 458
Dold, Conradin Otto, 456
Domvile, Sir Barry, 77
Donay, Peter Franz Erich, 312
Donovan, William J., 310, 349
Dougle agents, 289–290
Douglas Radio Company, 319
Downe, Viscountess, 77
Draeger, Friedhelm, 485
Druecke, Theodore, 238, 243, 245
  executed, 247
Duffied, Eugene S., 481
Dugan, Joseph P., 473
Dulles, Allen W., 345, 346
Duquesne, Frederick Joubert, 46, 297, 324, 436–437, 456
Dutch military intelligence:
  in anti-Nazi plot, 125

Eady, Sir Wilfred Griffin, 589
Earle, George Howard III, 334, 572–580
Eberling, Rudolf, 328
Eden, Anthony, 94, 235, 589
Edgewood Arsenal, 498
Edmonds, J.E., 454
Edward VIII:
  attitude to Germany, 92
  on Rhineland invasion, 98
  von Hoesch on, 97
Eichenlaub, Richard, 313
Eilers, Carl Heinrich, 313
Eimer & Amend, 498
Eisenhower, Dwight, 585, 600, 621
Eisenlohr, Professor, 48
Eitel, Karl, 32, 314
Elgin, Henry W.T., 62
Ellis, Lionel Frederic, 598
Ellsen, Carl Christian Albrektsson, 524
Ellsworth, J.C., 464
Emig, Marianne, 74
Emmett, Christopher T., Jr., 380
Emmett, Pauline (Mrs. Granville), 335, 563
"Emmett Reports," 335
Emonotti, Dr., 544
England:
  inaction of, during Rhineland invasion, 95

England (*continued*)
  opposes Jewish migration, 108
Enigma machine, 284, 523
Entwistle, Frederick I., 39
Erikson, May, 248, 251–255
Erickson, Eric Siegfried, 522
Espionage:
  agents
    blackmail of, 225
    pay of, 33
    recruiting of, 22, 23
    treachery of, 122
  Allied invasion plans, 605
  American diplomatic spies, 424
  British
    in Denmark, 114
    destruction of "Z" organization, 130
    double-cross operations, 176
    in Germany, 110
    S.I.S., 103
    in The Hague, 109
  couriers, delay of, 316
  cover organizations, 22
  double agents, 85
  expenditures for, 17
  German(s)
    in England, 71–76, 77, 78, 100, 130, 232
    fate of fallen spies, 284–285
    given intelligence by British, 271
    in France, 141
    importance of during London Blitz, 270
    "Operation Lena," 237
    spy population in England, 134
    tap transatlantic telephone, 587
    targets and maps of England, 139
    in Panama Canal Zone, 51–54, 66
    in Poland, 141
    in South Wales, 131
    in Soviet Union, 301
    in U.S., 17–20, 24, 27, 29, 34, 38, 39, 46, 302, 457, 461
  Gestapo spies, 21
  Hungarians for Germans in England, 233
  Irish, for Germany, 132
  secret inks, 314–315
  urological intelligence, 330
  weather reports, importance of, 327
  women in, 136, 248
Essen, Count von, 537
Europa (steamship), 21, 32
Eurotank (Davis refinery in Hamburg), 353
Expanded Metal Co., 151

Fahrney, Merry, 467, 468, 487
Fairchild Aviation Corp., 18

Falangists:
  work for Abwehr, 515
Falkenhausen, Nikolaus von, 519
Falkenhorst, Nikolaus von, 207
FBI, 61, 66, 316, 465, 507, 562, 653
  in counterespionage, 453
FBI Story, The, 445
Fehse, Paul, 455
Feldman, Adolf von, 103 ,112
Fellowes, Daisy, 631, 633, 639
Fetzer, Dr. Friedrich, 354, 401
Fidrmuc, Paul, 519–520
Fischer, Alice, 527
Fish, Hamilton, 380
Fitch, T.C., 63
Flandin, 94
Fleming, Ian, 525
Flynn, Edward J., 385
Foote, Alexander, 345
Ford, Edsel, 404
Ford, Henry, 336, 404
Foreign Ministry (German):
  collaboration with Abwehr, 10
Forrestal, James V., 409
France:
  surrenders, 230, 399
  signs mutual assistance treaty with Russia, 87
  Battle of, 196, 345, 602
Franco, Francisco, 401, 448
François-Poncet, André, 90
Franco-Russian pact, 88
Frankenberg, Lieutenant von, 165
Franklin, Charles, 259
Franz, Captain, 144
  infiltrates S.I.S., 124
Fremery, Augustus de, 105
Freytag-Loringhoven, Colonel von, 446
Friede, Karl, 542
Fritsch, Hans von, xviii
Fritsch, Werner von, 88, 169
  against Rhineland invasion, 89
Fritz, 282, 287, *see also* Chapman, Eddie
Froehlich, Rene Charles, 428
Fuchs, Professor, 48
Fuetterer, Cuno Heribert, 211
Fuller, J.F.C., 77
Fyans, Captain, 78

Gaertner, Dieter, 225
Gagen, Inspector, 173
Gagern, Baron von, 7
Gamelin, Maurice, 91
Garcia, José Carlos, 599
Gardner, Nadya, 450
Gartenfeld, Lieutenant, 223, 260
Gassner, Dr. Otto, 323
Gayr, Baron, 90, 95
Geddes, Ross Campbell, 589

Gempp, Fritz, 16
George V, 92
George VI, 235, 524
German(s)/Germany:
    acquires Saar, 87
    attempt to influence U.S. election, 382
    breach of Munich pact, 158
    buys oil from America, 353
    captures Antwerp and Brussels, 214
    captures Norway, 210
    destroy Scapa Flow, 187
    fakes Polish provocation, 164–165
    Foreign Ministry official papers, 379
    intercept Roosevelt-Churchill phone
        call, 590
    invades Norway, 207
    invades Poland, 166
    invades Rhineland, 88
    launches Blitzkrieg, 167
    mission in U.S. becomes center for
        espionage, 378
    misuse of Abwehr intelligence, 422
    money in U.S. elections, 368
    money to defeat F.D.R., 371–372
    occupation of Bohemia and Moravia,
        157
    offensive in West, 214
    plans for invasion of Low Countries,
        213
    plans invasion of England, 230
    plans Rumania invasion, 211
    plans to defeat F.D.R., 374
    promotes U.S. isolationism, 379
    propaganda, 211
    reoccupies Narvik, 296
    repudiates Versailles Treaty, 87
    sabotage in England, 194
    signs treaty with Poles, 87
    spies become controlled British agents,
        287
    tries to influence U.S. elections, 366–
        367
German-American Bund, 319, 428, 435,
    454, 502
German Labor Front, 152
German intelligence, *see* Abwehr, *also*
    Espionage, German
Geroe, Emery, 524
Gestapo, 21
    makes spy arrests, 102, 128
    blackmail, 323
    plot to kidnap Willie Muenzenberg,
        294
    Polish massacre, 170
Gibraltar, invasion of, 237
Gienanth, Ulrich von, 476
Gill, Major, 197, 284
Gilmour, William Weir, 131
Gimpel, Erich, 447, 507

Giraud, Henri Honoré, 434
Giskes, Hermann J., 116, 122, 638, 641
Glaser, Erich, 59
Glen Martin bomber, 74, 297
Goddard, Robert H., 34–35
Godfrey, John, 176, 525
Goebbels, Joseph Paul, 21, 332, 561
Goering, Hermann, 53, 73, 356, 358, 400,
    544
    authorizes Davis to negotiate with
        F.D.R., 362
    leads reconnaissance over England, 270
    plans to defeat F.D.R., 369
    in session with Texaco president, 402
Goerlitz, Walter, 98, 207
Goertz, Hermann, 73–76, 222
    arrested, 75
    fails in Ireland, 224
    mission collapses, 100
    tribulations of, in Ireland, 223
Goldschmidt, Gabriela von, 532
Goody, Lance Corporal, 241
Grand, Laurence, 201
Granville, Christine, 248
Granville, Edgar, 633
Graziani, Marshal, 541
Great Spies, The (Franklin), 259
Greaves-Lord, Justice, 75
Greene, Graham, 518
Greifenfels, Stransky von, 202
Griebl, Ignatz Theodor, 20, 32, 65
Griffin, William, 388
Grogan, Stanley, 30
Grohse, Paul, 312
Groscurth, Helmuth, 10, 170
Groskopf, Hans Jochin, 39, 48, 276
Gross, Dr. Herbert, 300
Grossmann, Dr. Paul, 530
Goss, Gisbert, 52
Grote, Frank, 312, 455
Grunen, Stephan von, 282
Gubbins, Sir Collin, 201, 317
Gudenberg, Werner Georg, 19, 23, 29, 65
Guellich, Gustav, 33
Guffey, Joseph F., 367, 368
Gustaf V (of Sweden), 524
Gutmann, Ingeborg Waltraut, 52
Guttierez, Fernando, 309
Gyssling, Georg, 489

Haber, Oscar, 475
Haegele, Anton, 299
Haeupel, Fraülein, 514
Halder, Franz, 170, 234, 303, 602
Haller, Kurt, 193, 221
Hambourg, R.A., 495
Hamburger, Dr. Wilhelm, 580
Ham Common, 285, 516, 622, 638
Hammond, John Hays, 38, 336

Hansen, Hans, 256, 258–266, 595, 618, 621
  awarded Iron Cross, 260
  captured by MI.5, 261
  joins MI.5 Double-Cross, 260
  fate of, 266
Hansen, Georg, 613, 640
"Hans the Red Judas," 295
Hamilton, G.C. Hans, 151
Hanfstengel, Putzi, 79, 85
Harmer, Christopher, 618
Harnisch, Hans Rudolf Leo, 610
Harriman, W. Averill, 589
Harris, Thomas, 286, 622, 623
Hart, Herbert L.A., 195
Harwood, Henry, 498
Haslinger, Kaspar, 137
Hausberger, Walter von, 431, 436–439
Hausmann, Ulrich, 31
Haworth, Sir Lionel, 77
Hayes, Carlton, 425
Hayes, Stephen, 224
Hehenthal, William D., 425
Heidemann, Major, 235
Heimann, Reinhard von, 544, 545
Heine, Carl Edmond, 301
Held, Stephen Carroll, 224
Hendricks, Jan, 105, 128
Henlein, Konrad, 15
Henning, Honorious, 137
Herslow, Carl, 523
Hertslet, Dr. Joachim A., 306, 354
  enters U.S., 372
  taken over by Abwehr, 362
Herzner, Albrecht, 166
Heskith, Roger, 615, 621
Hesse, Fritz, 96
Hess, Rudolf, 81, 285, 563
Heusinger, Adolph, 166
Hewel, Walter, 583
Hewins, Ralph, 534
Higati, Lieutenant Colonel, 446
Hilgarth, Commander, 560
Hilgert, 306
Hillgarth, Alan, 525
Himmler, Heinrich, 4, 170, 427, 522, 536, 561, 588
  turns against Canaris, 612
Hirzel, Walter, 506
Hitler, Adolf, 582
  announces constitution of Luftwaffe, 83
  anti-Semitism of, 453
  assassination plot, 123
  and Baron de Ropp, 78
  bans spies in U.S., 431
  and Canaris, 87
  calls for extermination of Poles, 170
  on eve of Normandy invasion, 597
  decides to take Gibraltar, 558

  declares war on U.S., 505
  disinterest in Norway, 205
  drives to Dunkirk, 229
  on F.D.R., 331–332
  intends to arrest Italian government, 583
  invades Italy, 590
  launches Blitzkrieg, 167
  learns of Franco-Russian pact, 88
  and Norway failure, 208
  orders invasion of England, 230
  wants to keep U.S. neutral, 293
  warned by Chamberlain on Poles, 171
  objects to espionage in U.S., 305
  orders invasion of Rhineland, 88
  repudiates Versailles Treaty, 87
  signs treaty with Poles, 87
  scorns Abwehr reports, 409
  smear tactics against F.D.R., 349–350
  violates Dutch and Belgian neutrality, 201
  invades Rhineland, 76, 94
  on espionage, 14
  bans espionage against England, 72, 76, 130
  lifts espionage ban against England, 67, 131
Hoesch, Leopold von, 91–93
  on Edward VIII, 92, 97
  friendly with Prince of Wales, 92
Hoettl, Wilhelm, 418
Hoffmann, Gustav, 110
Hofmann, Johanna, 33, 56, 65
Hohlhaus, Alfred, 646
Holland, George W., 409
Holland, John, 201
Hollard, Michel, 317
Homlok, Sándor, 232
Hooper, John William, 105, 116, 122
Hooper, Stanford C., 478
Hoover, J. Edgar, 61, 310, 315, 372, 451, 455, 653
Hopkins, Harry, 334, 589
Hotel Taft, 43
Hoven, Dr. Jupp, 193
Hoyt, Charles W., 57
Hoyt, Ira F., 63
Hull, Cordell, 336, 338, 474, 574
Hungary/Hungarian(s):
  mission in England used by Abwehr, 232
  spy on British for Germans, 233
Hyde, H. Montgomery, 450

Ickes, Harold L., 331, 367, 395
Information, transmission of, 32
Ingalls, Laura, 476
International Russian Fascist Party, 443
Inverforth, Lord, 383

I.R.A. (Irish Republican Army), 193
  and Abwehr, 221
  "invades" Britain, 220
  in New York, 440
Ireland Aircraft Corp., 18
Irish:
  agents for Abwehr, 193
  in Abwehr II, 193
  revolutionaries go to Germany, 222
  saboteurs, 131
  underground in U.S., 440
Iron Cross:
  awarded to Abwehr agent, 260
Iron Duke (target ship), 183
Ismay, Pug, 176, 614

Jackson, Gardner, 358
Jacob, Berthold, 294
Jacob, Dr. Josef, 318
Jaenichen, Herbert, 46
Jagow, Dietrich von, 419
Jahnke, Felix, 313, 319, 465
Jahnke, Kurt, 562–566
Jahnke, Walter, 306
Jakobs, Josef, 284
James, William, 95
Janke, Willy, 169
Japanese intelligence, 473
Jebb, Ralph Gladwyn, 77
Jenkins, S.T., 316
Jews:
  smuggled to Palestine, 108
J.M. Winchester & Co., 504
Jodl, Alfred, 88, 484, 583, 597, 603
Johnson, Florence E., 74
Jones, Charles A., 351
Jones, Walter A., 367, 386
Jordana, Count, 425
Jordan, Jennie Wallace, 60
Jost, Walter, xviii, xix
Jowitt, Sir William, 248, 340
Joyce, William, 130, 341
Juhlin-Dannfelt, C.H., 528
Jung, Werner, 231

Kaercher, William Gustav, 319
Kahle, Horst, 190
Kahn, David, 472
Kaltenbrunner, Hans, 626
Kano, Viscount, 265
Kapp, Carl, 489
Kapp, Elizabeth, 572
Kappe, Walter, 435
Kasche, Siegfried, 585
Kaulbars, Baron Roland, 512
Kaulen, Friedrich Wilhelm, 140
Kautschke, Fritz, 560
Keitel, Wilhelm, xviii, 165, 170, 511
Kelen, Emery, 294

Kell, Sir Vernon, 72, 134, 186, 192, 194
Kelly, Joseph, 132, 133
Kempf, Hermann, 204
Kendrick, Thomas J., 133
Kennedy, Harold M., 459
Kennedy, Joseph P., 336, 471
Kennedy, Thomas, 351
Kent, Duke of, 84
Kent, Tyler Gatewood, 338, 341–345
Keppler, Wilhelm, 403
Kesselring, Albert, 83
Kettering, Charles F., 38
Keynes, Lord, 589
Khan, Noor Inayat, 248
Kieboom, Charles Albert van den, 238, 240, 241
Kierks, Hilmar G.J. (Hans), 135
Killinger, Manfred von, 490
Kintner, Robert, 371
Kirschenlohr, Captain, 144
Kischler, Dr. Hans, 540
Klausen, Olaf, 281–282, 287
Klein, Josef August, 319
Kleist-Schmenzin, Ewald von, 122
Kleyenstueber, Ludwig, 643
Kliemann, Emil, 620
Klop, Dirk, 125–126
Knatchbull-Hugessen, Sir Hughe, 415
Knoop, Theodore von, 486
Knox, Dillwyn, 197, 284
Knox, Frank, 419
Koedel, Marie, 497, 501
Koedel, Simon E., 297, 493–502, 586
Koehler, Walter, 457, 485, 645, 646, 649–653, 655–656
Kolmar, Hermann B., 234
Kolpe, Fritz, 347
Koutrik, Folkert Arie Van, 112, 115, 122
Kraemer, Karl-Heinz, 178, 237, 539–543, 546–555, 643
Kraus, Alfred Ignatz Maria, 630, 632, 634, 635
Kraus, Paul, 21, 24
Kreuger, Thorsten, 530
Kriegsorganisationen, 512
Krivitsky, Walter Gregorievitch:
  defects to U.S., 294
  harassed by Germans, 296
Krock, Arthur, 351
Krueger, Otto, 118
Kuechler, Georg von, 596
Kuhrig, Ernst Robert, 52
Kunze, Gerhard, 442, 502
Kutschke, Master Sergeant, 165

La Follette, Philip Fox, 390–395
Lahousen, Erwin von, xx, 15, 165, 168, 193, 220, 245, 293, 440
  in charge of Abwehr II, 433

Lahousen, Erwin von (*continued*)
   plans sabotage operations in U.S., 435
Lahr, Eugen, 489
Lamont, Thomas W., 336
Lampe & Schierenbeck, 136
Lange, Richard, 110
Lang, Hermann, 44, 297, 325, 456
Langton-Jones, Ronald, 384
Latchmere House, 285
Laurence, William L., 647
League of Nations, 94
Leahy, William D., 349
Leclerc, Jacques, 630
Lehmitz, Ernst Frederick, 505–506
Leigh, Russell, 262, 264, 271
Leissner, Wilhelm, 513, 514, 558, 599
Leith-Ross, Sir Frederick William, 589
LeMaire, Jennie, 414
Lemmens, Jan, 126
Lena Team, 243, 257, 283
   fate of, 266
Lerner, Max, 393
Leverkuehn, Dr. Paul, 572
Lewis, John L., 351–352, 354–355,
   357–365, 386
   alliance with Hertslet, 373
   breaks with F.D.R., 370
   in Davis plan to "buy" election, 371
   on national radio, 387
   supports Burton Wheeler, 384
Ley, Dr. Robert, 427
Liddell, Guy, 61, 195, 516
Liebknecht, Karl, 7, 298
Likus, Rudolf, 85
Lindbergh, Charles A., 336, 420, 478
Lindbert, Kurt, 51
Lippmann, Walter, 375
Lips, Wolfgang, 135
Liss, Ulrich, 235
Littel, Norman M., 370
Lodge, Henry Cabot, 336
Loerzer, Bruno, 81
London Blitz, 269
Longest Day, The, 625
Lonkowski, William, 17, 23, 28, 30, 65
Lossberg, Bernhard von, 96, 207
Louisa, Crown Princess (of Sweden), 537
Ludwig, Kurt Frederick, 427, 429, 430,
   452, 455, 486
Luftreise (magazine), 19
Luftwaffe:
   aerial reconnaissance, 282
   clandestine operations, 79
   exchanges info with RAF, 83
Luftwaffe, Black, 16
Lund, Roscher, 522
Luning, Heinz August, 505
Lurtz, Siegfried, 465, 485, 486
Luxemburg, Rosa, 7, 298

McCarthy, Sam, 217
   aborts sea rendezvous, 217
MacCaw, Colonel, 78
MacDonald, Ramsay, 78
McGee, Arthur, 319

Mackensen, Hans von, 339, 582
Maher, Dale W., 463
Mallett, Victor, 534
Malzahn, Freda von, 298
Manly, Chesly, 480, 482
Manstein, Erich von, 165
Marcks, Erich, xviii
Maringliano, Don Francesco, 340
Marshall, George C., 596
Martin, Eduardo Penja, 441
Martinez, Campos, 512, 611
Martin, John Miller, 589
Martini, Wolfgang, 161
Marwede, Major, 221
Maskelyne, Jasper, 288
Massigli, René, 543
Masson, Roger, 345
Masterman, John Cecil, 175, 195, 269
Matzhold, Asta, 575
Matzhold, Louis A., 333–335, 575–580
Maud, Mrs., 286
Maurer, Emil, 57
Mayer, Pauline, 428
Meerheimb, Lieutenant von, 435
Meier, Carl Heinrich, 238
   captured, 241
Mellon, Andrew W., 336
Menzel, Hermann, 51, 143, 190, 461
Metzger, Gerhard Joachim, 390, 394
Mexico:
   seizes property of oil companies, 351
Meydel, Baron, 305
Meyer-Dietring, Wilhelm, 627
Meyer, Dr. W. Ernst, 476, 488
"Microdot," 315
Microphotography, 33
MI.8 (Signals Intelligence Service), 197
MI.5 (British counterespionage), 61, 72,
   158, 173, 177, 181, 495
   arrests Tyler Kent, 342
   art of deception, 288
   captures Hansen and Caroli, 261
   captures Nikolaus Ritter, 178
   controlled agents, 287, 516
   deceived by Owens's triple-cross, 218
   detention center, 285
   double agents, 227, 289–290
   double agent "Snow," 213
   Double-Cross Committee, 271
   double-crossed by Caroli, 264
   and German sabotage, 194
   infiltrates Abwehr, 274–279
   internal crisis, 192

leadership crisis, 194
massive deception of Germany, 289
misleads Abwehr on eve of Blitz, 268
monitors Abwehr traffic, 284
new leaders, 195
operation Double-Cross, 214
penetrators, 181
recruits Hans Hansen as double agent, 260, 261–262
reports to Abwehr via Owens, 269
security crisis, 183
use of captured agents, 175
Milch, Erhard, 79, 82
Miller, Eugen de, 619
MI.6, *see* S.I.S.
Mitchell, Paddy, 227
Molnar, Adrienne, 572, 575, 578
Molzahn, Rev. Kurt E., 444, 488, 502
Montgomery, Sir Bernard, 615
Mooney, James, 404
Moore, William L., 408
Moravia:
occupation of, by Germany, 157
Morris, Leland, 425
Morrison, Herbert, 634, 635, 637, 639
Mortelli, George, 317
Mosley, Sir Oswald, 130
Mountbatten, Lord Louis, 537
Moyzisch, Ludwig C., 571, 604, 612
Mueller, Ernst, 57, 281
Mueller, Heinrich, 535, 553, 562
Mueller, Karl Victor, 428
Mueller, Vincent, 643
Muenzenberg, Willie, 294
Muggeridge, Malcolm, 518
Mundt, Karl E., 380
Munich pact:
breach of, by Germany, 158
Murphy, Frank, 454
Mussert, Anton 201
Mussolini, Benito, 582
Myner, Alexander, 159

Nagylásony, Dr. Gyoergy Barcza de, 232
Nasser, Gamal Abdel, 540
National Archives, U.S., 379
National Socialist League, 130
Naval Intelligence, American, xviii
Nazi(s)/Nazism
bureaucracy, 561
organizations in Britain, 159
plot against, 123
in pre-war Britain, 131
propaganda in U.S., 20
spies, 21
sympathizers in U.S., 353
Neurath, Baron von, 91
Newman-Hall, Fox, 137
New York Daily News, 483

New York Enquirer, 388
New York Herald Tribune, 411
New York Times, The, 298, 381, 493, 503
Nicholson, Leslie Arthur, 518
Nicolai, Walter, 56
Niebuhr, Dietrich, 498
Nikolaus, Major Georg, 306
Nipken, 465
Nissen, Christian, 226
Norden bombsight, 38–39, 45–47, 297, 326, 459
Norden, Carl T., 38
Norman, Sven, 523
Norte, Dr. Heinrich, 306
North Africa, invasion of, 561
North German Lloyd, 11
Norway:
captured by Germany, 210
repulses Germans, 208
Noske, Gustav, 7

Obéd, Henry, 226
Obermueller, A.D., 77, 80
O'Donovan, Jim, 222
Oechsner, Mrs. Frederick C., 423
Ohnesorge, Wilhelm, 587, 588
Oliver, Major, 285
Olmsted, C.H., 412
Onodera, General, 544
Operation Double-Cross, 214, 263, 271, 519, 618
double-crossed by Caroli, 264
Operation Felix, 558
Operation Lena, 237
Operation Overlord, 604, 621
Operation Pastorius, 433
Operation Sea Lion, 267, 596
Operation Tramp, 326–329
Oppenheim, Waldemar Baron von, 532– 537, 599
Orschoot, Willem van, 106, 125
Orgell, Guenther, 488
Osborne, D'Arcy Godolphin, 416
Osten, Ulrich von der, 427, 435, 448, 449–450
death of, 452
Othmer, Waldemar, 495, 502–504
Ott, Eugene, viii, 568
Owens, Arthur George, 137, 151
Owens, Johnny, 173, 212, 225, 262
arrested, 174
compromises himself, 217
data collected, 180
deceives both sides, 182
deceives MI.5, 218
as double agent, 177, 213
double crosses the British, 178
introduces MI.5 agent to Abwehr, 271– 272

Owens, Johnny (*continued*)
  last message, 279
  plans rendezvous at sea, 215
  reports via MI.5 during Blitz, 269
  role in London Blitz, 268, 269
  in triple-cross, 218
Owens Battery Equipment Co., 152
Oxenstierna, Captain J.G., 549, 550

Pagel, Hans Helmuth, 428
Panama Canal, 51–54
Papen, Franz von, 307
Parry, Vice Admiral R. St. P., 77
Pasha, Masri, 540
Pastorius, Daniel, 433
Patton, George S. Jr., 49
Patzig, Konrad, 4–5, 72
Payne, Morris B., 494
Pearson, Lady, 77
Peel, Colonel, 152, 173
Pell, Herbert, 416
  Minister to Hungary, 417
  papers stolen, 421
"Penetration," 255
Perrault, Giles, 284
Petersen, Dr. Carlheinz, 220
Petrie, Sir David, 195
Peyton, Bernard R., 423
Pfaus, Oskar Karl, 22, 439
Pflugk-Hartung, Georg von, 7
Pheiffer, Erich, 24, 27, 33, 135, 332
  demoted, 65, 66
Philby, Harold Adrian Russell (Kim),
      103, 195, 449, 502, 517, 519, 546,
      560
Piekenbrock, Hans, xx, 10, 27, 56, 293,
      435, 505, 511, 527, 558, 598
Pieper, Konrad, 153
Pilsudske, Marshall Joseph, 87
Planck, Erwin, xviii
Podesta, Luigi, 372
Poetsch, Waldemar, 114
Poland:
  invasion of, 166
  massacre in, 170
Pons, Sjord, 239, 240, 241
Porsche, Dr. Ferdinand, 301
Post, Marjorie, 336
Potocki, Count Jerzy, 387
Pound, Dudley, 212
Powell, G.B., 77
Pownall, General, 95
Praetorius, Karl, 135, 238, 256
Preetz, Willy, 227
Price, M.H., 464
Price, Ward, 575
Prien, Günther, 183
  ordered to attack Scapa Flow, 186

Prittwitz, F.W. von, 453
"Project No. 14," 53
Propaganda, 349–350
  German, 20, 211
Prostitutes, male:
  as Abwehr agents, 415
Protze, Traugott Andreas Richard, 100
  goes to The Hague, 111
  made head of Section IIIF, 102
Pruck, Major E., 205

Quisling, Vidkun, 201, 205, 281

Radar:
  use of, by English, 161
Radio, shortwave, 318
Raeder, Erich, xviii, 204, 229, 353
  appoints Canaris chief of Abwehr, 4
  prepares to invade England, 230
Ramirez, Pedro P., 610
Ramsay, Archibald H.M., 341
Raouf, Abdel, 540
Rauter, Wilhelm von, 506
Rawlings, N.L., 412
Ream, Marion, 443
Recke, Johann, 560
Reconnaissance, aerial, 235, 270, 282
Red Army Intelligence Service, 517
Rees, Maria Margareta van, 104
Reichenau, Major General von, 81
Reichssicherheitshauptamt (RSHA), 4
Reichswehr, 16, 94
Reile, Oscar, 90, 203, 618, 625
Reinhardt, Dr. Walther, 132
  expelled from England, 133
Reiss, Ignace, 295
Rekowski, Karl Berthold Franz, 306, 440,
      441–442
Renthe-Fink, Herr von, 249
Reuper, Karl Alfred, 312, 464, 465
Reydt, Guenther, 158, 172
Reynolds, Robert R., 336, 496
Rhineland:
  Abwehr operation in, 90
  invasion of, 94
Ribbentrop, Joachim von, 59–60, 610
Richter, Karl Richard, 284
Rickman, Alexander, 524
Rieber, Torkild, 400
  defies British embargo, 401
  difficulties with Germans, 405
  downfall, 410
  smuggles oil to Franco, 401
  unaware his representative in Ger-
      many is Abwehr agent, 405
  violates Neutrality Law, 401
Riess, Curt, 185
Rietz, Constanz Edouard du, 528

Rintelen, Enno von, 584
Ritgen, Dr. von, 564
Ritter, Karl, 347, 435, 546
Ritter, Nikolaus, 40, 135, 212, 237, 325, 415, 460
  captured by MI.5, 178
  organizes the collection of information in U.S., 41–47
  plans rendezvous at sea with Owens, 215
  transferred, 279
  Treff with Owens in Lisbon, 272
Roatta, Mario, 12, 416
Roberts, John W., 30
Robertson, Colonel Thomas A., 176, 271, 519, 617
Robertson, Joan, 263
Rockefeller, John D. Jr., 336
Rodgers, W.S.S., 411
Roeder, Everett Minster, 40, 46, 297, 325, 456
Roenne, Alexis von, 552, 600, 601–603, 616, 627
Roessler, Rudolf, 345
Rohleder, Rudolf, 527
Rohleder, Joachim, xx, 111
Rohwel, Guenther, 161
Rolls Royce, 152
Rolph, W.N., 213
  unmasked as German spy, 218
Rommel, Erwin, 460, 557, 584, 624
Roosevelt, Franklin D., 454, 470
  asked to intervene in British blockade, 356
  health of, 331
  intelligence reports on, 330–337
  meets Churchill in Casablanca, 566
  pledges "no war," 386
  rebuffs Davis plan, 370
Roosevelt-Churchill letters, 338–339, 344
Ropp, Baron William de, 77, 81
  as double agent, 85
  meets Duke of Kent, 84
  meets Hitler, 78
Roschmann, Hans, 559
Rosenberg, Alfred, 77, 84
  secret papers of, 79
Rosendahl, Charles E., 506
Rosenmann, Samuel I., 386
Royal Oak (battleship), 183
RSHA (*Reichssicherheitshauptamt*), 4
Rudloff, Hans-Jochen, 558
Ruedt, Baron von, 306
Ruege, 306
Rumrich, Guenther Gustav, 33, 57–67, 453
  arrested, 64

passport theft, 62–63
Rundstedt, Field Marshal von, 597, 624
Ryan, Cornelius, 625
Ryan, Frank, 225

Saar:
  reunited to Germany, 87
Sabotage/saboteurs, 131, 201, 282, 433, 435, 437–439, 445, 523
  in Polish invasion, 166
  in U.S., 432
Sabri, Hussein Sulficar, 540
Sadat, Anwar, 540
Salisbury, William, 192
Salman, Mohamed, 231
Salman, Ahmed, 231
Salmon, David A., 472
Sandel, Hermann, 135, 302, 321, 325, 460, 595
Sanjurjo, José, 448
Sansom, A.W., 542
Sansom, Odette, 248
Saturday Evening Post (magazine), 185, 295
Sauerma, Count Friedrich, 298, 299, 330
Scapa Flow, 186
  Admiral Doenitz on, 189–190
  destruction of, 183
  destroyed by Germans, 187
  mystery of, 188
Schacht, Dr. Hjalmar, 353
Schackow, Hans Heinrich, 52
Schaefer, Hans, 552
Scheffer, Paul, 300
Schellenberg, Walter, 127, 185, 536, 553, 561, 562, 587, 609, 613, 654
  incompetence of, 641
  invents intelligence, 567
Schickedanz, Arno, 78
Schierenbeck, Wilhelm, 136, 552
Schirach, Baldur von, 393
Schlabrendorff, Ferdinand von, 122
Schleebruegge, Friedrich Karl von, 307
Schlosser, Frederick Edward, 428
Schlueter, Karl, 21, 27, 33, 55, 61
Schmid, Josef, 82, 544
Schmidt, Captain, 144, 229
Schmiedehaus, Walter, 475
Schnitzler, Dr. Georg von, 487
Schnuch, Dr. Hubert, 298, 299
Scholz, Dr. Herbert, 455, 467, 487
Schramm, Professor Percy Ernst, 602
Schreiber, Hasso, 208
Schroeder, Erich, 566
Schroeter, Friedrich, 313
Schroetter, Karl Hermann, 428
Schuetz, Theodor, 55
Schwaben (freighter), 11

Scotland Yard, 173, 212
  Criminal Investigation Division, 72
Scott-Ford, Duncan Alexander Croall, 502
Scottish Fascist Democratic Party, 131
Sea Lion Operation, 283
Sebold, William G., 322–329, 457–462, 463
  betrays Germany, 459
Secret inks, 314–315, 450
Secret Intelligence Service (British), 80
Sergueiev, Lily, 286, 619–621
Sherwood, Robert E., 385
Shipley, Ruth B., 356–357
Short Brothers, 152
Shortwave radio:
  transmission from U.S., 317
Sicherheitsdienst, 561, 604, 612
Siefken, Louis, 452
Siemens Cipher Machine, 528
Signals Intelligence Service (MI.8), 197
Silber, Jules, 72
Simon, Walter, 227
Sinclair, Hugh, 80, 103
S.I.S. (British Secret Intelligence Service), 103, 196, 410
  agents, recruiting of, 152
  combats illegal Jewish immigration, 108
  compromised in Denmark, 114
  compromised in Holland, 110
  infiltrated by Abwehr, 124
  infiltrated by Kim Philby, 195
  internal discord, 116
  Otto Krueger compromised, 118
  penetrated by Abwehr in The Hague, 112
  sabotage/saboteurs, 201, 202
  smashed in Europe, 118–119, 121
  split, 104
Skorzeny, Otto, 641
Skrodzki, Helena O.C., 101
Smirnoff, Nicholas E., 341
Smith, John Frederick, 75, 541
Smith, Truman, 477
"Snow File," 158
Sohn, Heinrich, 44
Soltmann, Major, 235
Sorau, Heinrich, 324
Sorge, Dr. Richard, 564
Sosnovsky-Naletz, Juri de, xix, 101
Soviet Union:
  signs mutual assistance treaty with France, 87
  signs pact with Czechoslovakia, 87
Sperrle, Hugo, 16
Sperry, Elmer, 38
Spy/Spies:
  allegiances of, 175

Americans for Germany, 467
capture of, 12
diplomatic, 424
fate of, 284–285
German, in America, 15
hoax, 188
as controlled British agents, 287
in England, 15
motivations of, 140
pay of, 152
scare, 185
Sea Lion, 283
in Sweden, 521
tactical, 234
treachery of, 212, *see also* Espionage
Spy-ships, 214
Staatszeitung (newspaper), 41
Starziczny, Johannes, 318
Stein, Lilly, 297, 325
Stephan, Hans, 90
Stephenson, William, 310, 410, 450, 523
Stephens, "Tin-Eye," 285
Stevens, Richard Henry, 109
  establishes contact with anti-Nazi underground, 123
  kidnapped, 127
  plots to compromise Giskes, 122
Stieber, Wilhelm, 252
Stimson, Henry L., 285, 441, 483
Stockhousen, Lieutenant von, 225
Stohrer, Eberhard von, 514, 610
Stoltz, Colonel, 435
Strachey, Oliver, 197
Strempel, Heribert von, 352, 374, 388, 468
Stuart, Francis, 222
Stuart, Iseult, 223
Suarez, Eduardo, 354
Sulzberger, Cyrus L., 575
Suñer, Ramon Serrano, 425
Suzuki, Kijuro, 566
Swanson, Edward B., 409
Sweeney, Bob, 275
Szabo, Ilonka, 416, 418, 419
Szenes, Hannah, 248

Taft Hotel, 43
Tannhaeuser, Dr. Tegeliss, 440
Tapken, Joachim, 71
Teheran Conference, 604
Telefunken Company, 10, 318
Tester, Dr. A.A., 131
Texas Company, 400
  business with Germans, 401
Third Reich:
  spies of, 5
Thoma, Ritter von, 540
Thompson, Bernard, 296

Thomsen, Dr. Hans, 371, 373–374, 377–388, 431, 469–471, 529
  claims credit for anti-F.D.R. campaign, 379
Thomson, Sir Basil, 72
Thorne, Francis Andrew, 71
Thorwald, Juergen, 188
Times, The (of London), 449, 517
Tobin, Dan, 371
Tojo, Hideki, 564
Toledano, Vincente Lombardo, 354
Tollervey, Private, 241
Tower, Cyril F., 549
Travaglio, Johannes, 127
Trevor-Roper, Hugh, 196, 284
Tributh, Herbert, 225
Tripartite Pact, 563
Truman, Harry S., 349
Tschirra, Hans, 138
Tubbs, L. Clifford, 64
Turrou, Leon G., 64, 66

Udet, Ernst, 39
Ujlak, Lóránd Utassy de, 232
Ujszászy István de, 211, 232
Un-American Activities Committee, 295, 454
Utassy, Major Lorand, 232
  joins operation "XX," 233
Utermark, Albert, 527

Valenti, Heinz, 149–151
Vallecilla, Roberto Lanas, 506
Vansittart, Sir Robert, 91
Velasco, Don Angel Alcazar de, 515, 516
Versailles Treaty:
  violated by Germany, 87, 90
Vetterlein (telephone engineer), 587
Victor Emmanuel III, 582
Viereck, George Sylvester:
  campaign to influence U.S. elections, 380
Viljoen, Dr., 315
Vivian, Valentine, 103, 109
Vonsiatsky, Anastase Andreyevich, 443
Voss, Otto Herman, 19, 23, 28, 65
Vrinten, Adrianus J.J., 105, 109

Waag, Erika, 5
Waelti, Werner Heinrich, 238, 247
Wagner, Hans, 527
Wahlert, Paul von, 526
Waldberg, Jose Rudolf, 238, 240, 241
Waley, Sir David, 589
Walischewsky, Adolf, 456
Wallenberg, Jacob, 532
Wallenberg, Mark, 532, 534
Wallace, Henry A., 346, 348–349

Walsh, David A., 480
War Diary of German High Command, 538, 583, 585
Warlimont, Walter, 237, 624
Washington Times-Herald, 483
Wassner, Captain, 90, 95
Watson, Edwin M., 364
Watson, James E., 336
Watson, Mark Skinner, 483
Weather reports:
  importance of, 327
Weber-Drohl, Ernst, 221
  becomes double-agent, 222
Weber, Richard Ernst, 318, 319
Wedel, Colonel von, 167
Wedell, Alexander, W., 425
Wedemeyer, Albert C., 479
Weeks, Edward, 487
Wehring, Alfred, 185
Wehrle, Erna Frieda, 354
Weimar Republic, 7
Weisz, Commander, 202
Weizsaecker, Baron von, 461
Welles, Sumner, 366
Wellner, Lieutenant Commander, 190
Welsh Nationalist Party, 177, 179
Welsh saboteurs, 131
Wendt, Erika, 527
Wenger, Leon, 202
Wenninger, Major General, 82, 83, 90
Wenzlau, Heinrich, 539, 545
Wesemann, Dr. Hans, 294, 296
Wester, Karl, 542
Westrick, Gerhard Alois, 399, 403, 410
  persona non grata in U.S., 411
Weygand, Maxim, 434
Whalen, Richard, 337
Wheeler, Burton K., 334, 371, 478, 481
  gives secret information to newspaper, 482
  supported by John L. Lewis, 384
Wheeler-Hill, Axel, 22, 320, 456, 465
White, Dick, 176, 195
White, William Allen, 380
Whitehead, Don, 445
Wichmann, Herbert, 135, 236, 237, 260, 392, 460
Widar (spy-ship), 214
Wiedemann, Fritz, 488
Wigram, Ralph, 91, 98
Wiley, Samuel H., 363
Wilkinson, Ellen, 634
Williams, Gwyllem, 179, 226
  as double-agent, 227
Williams, Alford J. Jr., 479, 483
Willkie, Wendell L., 381
Willumeit, Otto, 444, 488
Wilson, Henry Warren, 383

Wilson, Holt, 194
Windels, Carl, 488
Winterbotham, Frederick William, 80
  meets Hitler, 81
Wireless:
  use of, by Abwehr, 160
Wirtz, Dr., 302
Witte, Vera de, 243, 245, 248
Witthoeft-Emden, Robert, 373, 474
Wittke, Lothar, 306
Witzke, Kapitaenleutnant, 179
Woehler, Alfred Johann, 475
Woermann, Ernst, 435
Wohltat, Dr. Helmuth, 358
Wolkoff, Anna, 340–343
Women in espionage, 136, 248

Wood, Don José Brugada, 516
Wood, Robert E., 336
Woods, Sam E., 363
World War II:
  beginning, 200
  sabotage, 201
Wozniak, Fedior, 443
Wright Aeronautical Corp., 19

Young, Kenneth Gilmour, 195

Zacharias, Ellis M., 31
Zapp, Professor, 315
Zimmermann, Arthur, 305
Zionists:
  smuggle Jews to Palestine, 108